# Lecture Notes in Computer Science    **11246**

*Commenced Publication in 1973*
Founding and Former Series Editors:
Gerhard Goos, Juris Hartmanis, and Jan van Leeuwen

More information about this series at http://www.springer.com/series/7407

Tiziana Margaria · Bernhard Steffen (Eds.)

# Leveraging Applications of Formal Methods, Verification and Validation

## Distributed Systems

8th International Symposium, ISoLA 2018
Limassol, Cyprus, November 5–9, 2018
Proceedings, Part III

 Springer

*Editors*
Tiziana Margaria
University of Limerick
Limerick, Ireland

Bernhard Steffen
TU Dortmund
Dortmund, Germany

ISSN 0302-9743 ISSN 1611-3349 (electronic)
Lecture Notes in Computer Science
ISBN 978-3-030-03423-8 ISBN 978-3-030-03424-5 (eBook)
https://doi.org/10.1007/978-3-030-03424-5

Library of Congress Control Number: 2018960391

LNCS Sublibrary: SL1 – Theoretical Computer Science and General Issues

This Springer imprint is published by the registered company Springer Nature Switzerland AG
The registered company address is: Gewerbestrasse 11, 6330 Cham, Switzerland

# Preface

Welcome to ISoLA 2018, the *8th International Symposium on Leveraging Applications of Formal Methods, Verification and Validation*, that was held in Limassol (Cyprus) during November 5–9, 2018, endorsed by EASST, the European Association of Software Science and Technology.

This year's event followed the tradition of its symposia forerunners held 2004 and 2006 in Cyprus, 2008 in Chalkidiki, 2010 and 2012 in Crete, 2014 and 2016 in Corfu, and the series of ISoLA Workshops in Greenbelt (USA) in 2005, Poitiers (France) in 2007, Potsdam (Germany) in 2009, in Vienna (Austria) in 2011, and 2013 in Palo Alto (USA).

As in the previous editions, ISoLA 2018 provided a forum for developers, users, and researchers to discuss issues related to the **adoption and use of rigorous tools and methods** for the specification, analysis, verification, certification, construction, test, and maintenance of systems from the point of view of their different application domains. Thus, since 2004 the ISoLA series of events has served the purpose of bridging the gap between designers and developers of rigorous tools on one hand, and users in engineering and in other disciplines on the other hand. It fosters and exploits synergetic relationships among scientists, engineers, software developers, decision makers, and other critical thinkers in companies and organizations. By providing a specific, dialogue-oriented venue for the discussion of common problems, requirements, algorithms, methodologies, and practices, ISoLA aims in particular at supporting researchers in their quest to improve the usefulness, reliability, flexibility, and efficiency of tools for building systems, and users in their search for adequate solutions to their problems.

The program of the symposium consisted of a collection of *special tracks* devoted to the following hot and emerging topics:

- A Broader View on Verification: From Static to Runtime and Back
  (Organizers: Wolfgang Ahrendt, Marieke Huisman, Giles Reger, Kristin Yvonne Rozier)
- Evaluating Tools for Software Verification
  (Organizers: Markus Schordan, Dirk Beyer, Stephen F. Siegel)
- Towards a Unified View of Modeling and Programming
  (Organizers: Manfred Broy, Klaus Havelund, Rahul Kumar, Bernhard Steffen)
- RV-TheToP: Runtime Verification from Theory to Industry Practice
  (Organizers: Ezio Bartocci and Ylies Falcone)
- Rigorous Engineering of Collective Adaptive Systems
  (Organizers: Rocco De Nicola, Stefan Jähnichen, Martin Wirsing)
- Reliable Smart Contracts: State of the Art, Applications, Challenges, and Future Directions
  (Organizers: Gerardo Schneider, Martin Leucker, César Sánchez)

- Formal Methods in Industrial Practice—Bridging the Gap
  (Organizers: Michael Felderer, Dilian Gurov, Marieke Huisman, Björn Lisper, Rupert Schlick)
- X-by-Construction
  (Organizers: Maurice H. ter Beek, Loek Cleophas, Ina Schaefer, and Bruce W. Watson)
- Statistical Model Checking
  (Organizers: Axel Legay and Kim Larsen)
- Verification and Validation of Distributed Systems
  (Organizer: Cristina Seceleanu)
- Cyber-Physical Systems Engineering
  (Organizers: J Paul Gibson, Marc Pantel, Peter Gorm Larsen, Jim Woodcock, John Fitzgerald)

The following events were also held:

- RERS: Challenge on Rigorous Examination of Reactive Systems (Bernhard Steffen)
- Doctoral Symposium and Poster Session (Anna-Lena Lamprecht)
- Industrial Day (Axel Hessenkämper, Falk Howar, Andreas Rausch)

Co-located with the ISoLA Symposium were:

- RV 2018: 18th International Conference on Runtime Verification (Saddek Bensalem, Christian Colombo, and Martin Leucker)
- STRESS 2018: 5th International School on Tool-based Rigorous Engineering of Software Systems (John Hatcliff, Tiziana Margaria, Robby, Bernhard Steffen)

Owing to the growth of ISoLA 2018, the proceedings of this edition are published in four volumes of LNCS: Part 1: Modeling, Part 2: Verification, Part 3: Distributed Systems, and Part 4: Industrial Practice. In addition to the contributions of the main conference, the proceedings also include contributions of the four embedded events and tutorial papers for STRESS.

We thank the track organizers, the members of the Program Committee and their referees for their effort in selecting the papers to be presented, the local Organization Chair, Petros Stratis, the EasyConferences team for their continuous precious support during the week as well as during the entire two-year period preceding the events, and Springer for being, as usual, a very reliable partner in the proceedings production. Finally, we are grateful to Kyriakos Georgiades for his continuous support for the website and the program, and to Markus Frohme and Julia Rehder for their help with the online conference service (EquinOCS).

Special thanks are due to the following organization for their endorsement: EASST (European Association of Software Science and Technology) and Lero – The Irish Software Research Centre, and our own institutions: TU Dortmund and the University of Limerick.

November 2018

Tiziana Margaria
Bernhard Steffen

# Organization

## Symposium Chair

Bernhard Steffen     TU Dortmund, Germany

## Program Chair

Tiziana Margaria     University of Limerick, Ireland

## Program Committee

| | |
|---|---|
| Wolfgang Ahrendt | Chalmers University of Technology, Sweden |
| Jesper Andersen | Deon Digital AG |
| Ezio Bartocci | TU Wien, Austria |
| Dirk Beyer | LMU Munich, Germany |
| Manfred Broy | Technische Universität München |
| Loek Cleophas | TU Eindhoven, The Netherlands |
| Rocco De Nicola | IMT School for Advanced Studies, Italy |
| Boris Düdder | University of Copenhagen, Denmark |
| Ylies Falcone | University of Grenoble, France |
| Michael Felderer | University of Innsbruck, Austria |
| John Fitzgerald | Newcastle University, UK |
| Paul Gibson | Telecom Sud Paris, France |
| Kim Guldstrand Larsen | Aalborg University, Denmark |
| Dilian Gurov | KTH Royal Institute of Technology, Sweden |
| John Hatcliff | Kansas State University, USA |
| Klaus Havelund | Jet Propulsion Laboratory, USA |
| Fritz Henglein | University of Copenhagen, Denmark |
| Axel Hessenkämper | Hottinger Baldwin Messtechnik GmbH |
| Falk Howar | Dortmund University of Technology and Fraunhofer ISST, Germany |
| Marieke Huisman | University of Twente, The Netherlands |
| Michael Huth | Imperial College London, UK |
| Stefan Jaehnichen | TU Berlin, Germany |
| Rahul Kumar | Microsoft Research |
| Anna-Lena Lamprecht | Utrecht University, The Netherlands |
| Peter Gorm Larsen | Aarhus University, Denmark |
| Axel Legay | Inria, France |
| Martin Leucker | University of Lübeck, Germany |

| | |
|---|---|
| Björn Lisper | Mälardalen University, Sweden |
| Leif-Nissen Lundæk | XAIN AG |
| Tiziana Margaria | Lero, Ireland |
| Marc Pantel | Université de Toulouse, France |
| Andreas Rausch | TU Clausthal, Germany |
| Giles Reger | University of Manchester, UK |
| Robby | Kansas State University, USA |
| Kristin Yvonne Rozier | Iowa State University, USA |
| Ina Schaefer | TU Braunschweig, Germany |
| Rupert Schlick | AIT Austrian Institute of Technology, Austria |
| Gerardo Schneider | University of Gothenburg, Sweden |
| Markus Schordan | Lawrence Livermore National Laboratory, USA |
| Cristina Seceleanu | Mälardalen University, Sweden |
| Stephen F. Siegel | University of Delaware, USA |
| César Sánchez | IMDEA Software Institute, Spain |
| Bruce W. Watson | Stellenbosch University, South Africa |
| Martin Wirsing | LMU München, Germany |
| James Woodcock | University of York, UK |
| Maurice ter Beek | ISTI-CNR, Italy |
| Jaco van de Pol | University of Twente, The Netherlands |

## Additional Reviewers

Yehia Abd Alrahman
Dhaminda Abeywickrama
Lenz Belzner
Saddek Bensalem
Egon Boerger
Marius Bozga
Tomas Bures
Rance Cleaveland
Giovanna Di Marzo Serugendo
Matthew Dwyer
Benedikt Eberhardinger
Rim El Ballouli
Thomas Gabor
Stephen Gilmore
Emma Hart
Arnd Hartmanns
Rolf Hennicker
Petr Hnetynka
Reiner Hähnle
Patrik Jansson
Einar Broch Johnsen

Neil Jones
Sebastiaan Joosten
Gabor Karsai
Alexander Knapp
Timothy Lethbridge
Chunhua Liao
Alberto Lluch-Lafuente
Alessandro Maggi
Dominique Méry
Birger Møller-Pedersen
Stefan Naujokat
Ayoub Nouri
Liam O'Connor
Doron Peled
Thomy Phan
Jeremy Pitt
Hella Ponsar
Andre Reichstaller
Jeff Sanders
Sean Sedwards
Christoph Seidl

# Contents – Part III

## Verification and Validation of Distributed Systems

## Cyber-Physical Systems Engineering

# Rigorous Engineering of Collective Adaptive Systems

# Rigorous Engineering of Collective Adaptive Systems Introduction to the 2nd Track Edition

Rocco De Nicola[1], Stefan Jähnichen[2], and Martin Wirsing[3(✉)]

[1] IMT School for Advanced Studies Lucca, Lucca, Italy
rocco.denicola@imtlucca.it
[2] TU Berlin and FZI Forschungszentrum Informatik, Berlin, Germany
stefan.jaehnichen@tu-berlin.de
[3] Ludwig-Maximilians-Universität München, Munich, Germany
wirsing@lmu.de

**Abstract.** A collective adaptive system consists of collaborating entities that are able to adapt at runtime to dynamically changing, open-ended environments and to new requirements. Rigorous engineering requires appropriate methods and tools that help guarantee that a collective adaptive system lives up to its intended purpose. This note gives an introduction to the track 'Rigorous Engineering of Collective Adaptive Systems.' It shortly presents the panel discussion on 'The Meaning of Adaptation: Mastering the Unforeseen?' and 18 scientific contributions, structured into six thematic sessions: Formal Modelling of Collective Adaptive Systems, Engineering Collective Adaptive Systems, Security and Analysis of Collective Adaptive Systems, Machine Learning and Evolutionary Computing for Collective Adaptive Systems, and Software Support for Programming and Modeling Collective Adaptive Systems.

**Keywords:** Adaptive system · Software engineering
Formal method · Rigorous method

A collective adaptive system, often also called ensemble, consists of collaborating entities that are able to adapt at runtime to dynamically changing, open-ended environments and to new requirements [1,2]. Often the entities of such a system have their own individual properties and objectives; interactions with other entities or with humans may lead to the emergence of unexpected phenomena. Examples of collective adaptive systems are smart cities, smart traffic, voluntary peer-to-peer clouds, robot swarms as well as socio-technical systems and the internet of things.

Rigorous engineering of collective adaptive systems requires appropriate methods and tools that help guarantee that a collective adaptive system lives up to its intended purpose. This includes theories for designing and analysing collective adaptive systems, techniques for programming and operating such systems, rigorous methods for devising adaptation mechanisms, validation and

© Springer Nature Switzerland AG 2018
T. Margaria and B. Steffen (Eds.): ISoLA 2018, LNCS 11246, pp. 3–12, 2018.
https://doi.org/10.1007/978-3-030-03424-5_1

verification techniques as well as approaches for ensuring security, trust and performance.

The track 'Rigorous Engineering of Collective Adaptive Systems' was initially inspired by the EU-funded research projects ASCENS [3], QUANTICOL [4] and the coordination action FOCAS[1]; it is a follow-up of two other successful tracks [5,6] on this research topic at ISOLA 2014 [7] and ISOLA 2016 [7].

The present edition attracted 18 research papers; each of them was refereed by at least two reviewers. A main event was the panel discussion entitled 'The Meaning of Adaptation: Mastering the Unforeseen?'. The papers of the track are partitioned into six thematic sessions: Formal Modelling of Collective Adaptive Systems, Engineering Collective Adaptive Systems, Security and Analysis of Collective Adaptive Systems, Machine Learning and Evolutionary Computing for Collective Adaptive Systems, and Software Support for Programming and Modeling Collective Adaptive Systems.

In the following the papers and the panel session are shortly introduced in the order of their presentations.

*Formal Modelling of Collective Adaptive Systems.* In this session process algebraic, logical and model-based methods are used for formally modelling dynamically reconfigurable architectures, ensemble requirements, and distributed ledgers.

The paper 'DReAM: Dynamic reconfigurable architecture modeling' [9] by Alessandro Maggi, Joseph Sifakis, and Rocco De Nicola introduces the DReAM framework for modeling dynamic reconfigurable architectures. A system is understood as a dynamically changing set of typed components and a system architecture is characterised by a set of coordination constraints. The DReAM language is based on the Propositional Interaction Logic [10] of the BIP framework [11] and extends it with operations for data exchange between components and by coordination terms for regulating interactions and reconfigurations among a set of components. Static architectures are modeled by Interaction Logic formulas. The main ingredient for modeling dynamic architectures is the new notion of 'motif' which is defined by a DReAM coordination term (cf. also the last paper of the track [42]). The DReAM framework is implemented as a Java API together with an execution engine.

Also the second paper 'Dynamic logic for ensembles' [12] by Rolf Hennicker and Martin Wirsing studies systems that are formed by a dynamically changing set of components. For such so-called ensembles the authors propose a dynamic logic for specifying the global behaviour of a system by desired and forbidden interaction scenarios. Bisimulation for ensembles is defined and it is shown that the Hennessy-Milner property holds, i.e. that ensemble bisimulation coincides with the logical equivalence induced by the proposed dynamic logic. A local notion of ensemble realisation as well as a notion of correctness are defined so that local bisimulation equivalence of process type expressions implies global bisimulation equivalence of the corresponding ensembles.

---

[1]  http://www.focas.eu.

In collective adaptive systems many parties interact and often need to keep track of complex interactions. Distributed ledger technologies such as Blockchains provide an electronic public transaction record of integrity without central ownership. Ledger technologies could be viewed as an underlying mechanism to administer and record the manifold adaptations of a technical system and thus provide trust and confidence to its users. In the paper 'Modelling the transition to distributed ledgers' [13] Jan Sürmeli, Stefan Jähnichen, and Jeff Sanders propose a formal model of distributed ledgers written in the specification language Z [14]. They present a reference model for transactions and a Z specification of centralised ledgers in an account-based setting. The model of distributed ledgers is a refinement of the transaction model and focuses on the structural aspects of ledgers.

*Engineering Collective Adaptive Systems.* This session discusses different aspects of engineering collective adaptive systems ranging from health applications to requirements engineering and hardware architectures.

For many diseases such as some arterial ones, physical exercise is recognized to be important to improve health conditions of patients. However, some exercises can be tiresome and cause pain to patients who may be tempted to avoid them in absence of a supervisor. In the paper 'A collective adaptive socio-technical system for remote- and self-supervised exercise in the treatment of intermittent claudication' [15] Jeremy Pitt, Kristina Milanovic, Alexander Coupland, Tim Allan, Alun Davies, Tristan Lane, Anna Maria Malagoni, Ankur Thapar, and Joseph Shalhoub propose to develop and deploy a healthcare application which provides patient exercise programmes that are both centrally organised and remotely supervised by a health practitioner, and self– organised and self–supervised by the patients themselves. The paper discusses appropriate engineering techniques for such health care applications; in particular, it addresses Value-Sensitive Design [16], the IDEAS framework [17] and formal methods including the event calculus [18], interaction design, the design of electronic social capital, and the system's 'shared reality'.

The second paper 'Engineering collectives of self-driving vehicles: the SOTA approach' [19] by Dhaminda Abeywickrama, Marco Mamei, and Franco Zambonelli introduces SOTA, a goal-oriented requirements engineering method for describing the overall domain and the requirements for an adaptive system. The paper illustrates the SOTA approach by the example of a fleet of self-driving vehicles and focuses on modeling and analysing functional and non-functional requirements of self-adaptation, as well as on analysing which information must be made available to a system to support its self-adaptive behavior.

The paper 'Synthesizing capabilities for collective adaptive systems from self-descriptive hardware devices – bridging the reality gap' [20] by Constantin Wanninger, Christian Eymüller, Alwin Hoffmann, Oliver Kosak, and Wolfgang Reif addresses the gap between simulated hardware and real hardware implementations. It proposes a novel architecture for realising collective adaptive systems on hardware devices for real world scenarios. The key idea is to equip hardware devices with self-descriptions and to use these self-descriptions for finding appropriate devices for the required user tasks. The feasibility of the approach is demonstrated by a case study of a sensor-based flight of a quadcopter.

*Panel: The Meaning of Adaptation: Mastering the Unforeseen?* The panel discussion was a main event of the track. As adaptation is the key technology for autonomous behaviour, there was a challenging panel discussion at the previous track on how unforeseen behaviour could be managed [21]. Adaptation has many facets and can be tackled by various so-called self–technologies. During this year's panel, Stefan Jähnichen as moderator and the panelists Lenz Belzner, Tomáš Bureš, Alexander Knapp, Jeremy Pitt, and Franco Zambonelli discussed with the audience what they consider to be the most important technologies to help systems to adapt [22]. 'Do you consider adaptivity to be a realistic and desirable property of technical systems?', 'what is the new challenge in software engineering for the design and implementation of adaptive systems? ', 'why should artificial intelligence open new horizons to implement adaptivity? ', 'can we expect machines to adapt by evolution?' as well as 'is there a mathematical characterisation of adaptation?' were some of the questions that were considered.

*Testing and Safety of Collective Adaptive Systems.* This session addresses testing methods and fault handling techniques for self-organising adaptive and autonomic systems.

Finding adequate software tests is an integral part of making adaptive systems controllable and trustworthy. The paper 'Mutation-based test suite evolution for self-organizing systems' [23] by André Reichstaller, Thomas Gabor, and Alexander Knapp studies test design for self–organising systems with a mutation-based test goal. Test execution in self-organising systems not only triggers an observable output but may also initiate a reconfiguration influencing the results of subsequent test cases. Similarly to the adaptation space [25], reconfiguration is controlled by a 'Corridor of Correct Behavior.' The paper investigates the suitability of various kinds of evolutionary algorithms for optimization and suggests two domain–specific extensions of the classical evolutionary approach for constructing test suites: 'phased extension' reducing the number of goal evaluations needed for optimization and 'penguin extension' increasing the overall fitness. The approach is evaluated using the case study of an adaptive, self-organising production cell.

The paper 'Adapting quality assurance to adaptive systems: the scenario coevolution paradigm' [24] by Thomas Gabor, Marie Kiermeier, Andreas Sedlmeier, Bernhard Kempter, Cornel Klein, Horst Sauer, Reiner Schmid, and Jan Wieg-hardt takes a more abstract view and presents a formal framework for adaptation and testing of adaptive systems using scenarios; it also discusses how such a framework can be used for increasing the trustworthiness of complex adaptive systems. In particular, the work extends the system model and the notion of adaptation space of [25] of the ASCENS project [26] by abstract definitions of self–adaptation and scenarios. A main contribution is also the concept of scenario coevolution for making quality assurance self–adaptive to match the capabilitiess of the self–adaptive system–under–test

Autonomous systems are subject to faults caused by the interaction with the environment. Often such systems are only partially observable, i.e. faults cannot be directly detected by the system and not all actions of the system can be observed. The third paper in this session tackles the problem of automatically detecting and handling faults that occur in autonomic systems. In 'Designing systems with detection and reconfiguration capabilities: a formal approach' [27], Iulia Dragomir, Simon Iosti, Marius Bozga, and Saddek Bensalem propose a systematic process for constructing a 'Fault Detection, Isolation and Recovery (FDIR) component' for a concurrent timed system with partial observability. The approach proceeds in two steps: the construction of a diagnoser for each diagnosable fault and the construction of a controller for each recovery strategy. An exact definition of the notion of diagnosability in the FDIR context for timed systems is given as well as an algorithm for automatically synthesizing runtime monitors for fault detection and recovery strategies for controller synthesis. The approach is currently under implementation in the BIP [11] framework.

*Security and Analysis of Collective Adaptive Systems.* The session consists of three papers proposing novel dynamic security rules, novel theoretically proven model reduction techniques, and a framework for evaluating the performance of self-organisation mechanisms.

Current concepts for security in static systems cannot easily cope with the high degree of dynamicity of collective adaptive systems. The paper 'Dynamic security specification through autonomic component ensembles' [28] by Rima Al Ali, Tomáš Bureš, Petr Hnetynka, Filip Krijt, František Plášil, and Jiří Vinárek presents an approach for dynamic access control of collective adaptive systems. Autonomic component ensembles [29] are enhanced by autonomically composable and context–dependent dynamic security rules to so-called security ensembles. The rules describe permitted interactions in the system and follow the system during its evolution. For the specification of the rules, an internal Scala-based DSL has been developed whereas for end-user usage, an external, end-user friendly DSL is given.

For analysing the interactions between the agents of a collective adaptive system it is often necessary to transform the system into an equivalent simpler and more tractable one. Prominent examples for such transfomations are the Markov Chain model reduction techniques based on lumpability (see e.g. [30]). In network analysis, centrality measures [31] such as Google's PageRank help to identify the most important nodes of a network by assigning an importance measure to each node. In the paper 'Differential equivalence yields network centrality' [32] Stefano Tognazzi, Mirco Tribastone, Max Tschaikowski, and Andrea Vandin investigate the relationship between centrality measures and backward differential equivalence, a generalisation of lumpability to general dynamical systems. They prove that any two backward differential equivalent nodes enjoy identical centrality measures. They also demonstrate the usefulness of this result and show that the corresponding reduction algorithm achieves substantial reductions of real-world networks from biochemistry, social sciences and computer engineering.

Reconfiguring a self-organising system can improve the quality of its computations but may also be a costly activity. The third paper 'Measuring and evaluating the performance of self-organization mechanisms within collective adaptive systems' [33] by Benedikt Eberhardinger, Hella Ponsar, Dominik Klumpp, and Wolfgang Reif proposes a framework enabling performance evaluation at design time in order to select the best-fitting self-organisation mechanism. The framework comprises a performance metric for distributed self-organisation mechanisms and a simulation concept for measuring performance. Centralised and localised self-organisation mechanisms are evaluated for a smart energy management system and a self-organising production cell.

*Machine Learning and Evolutionary Computing for Collective Adaptive Systems.* This session addresses the use of subsymbolic AI techniques for different collective adaptation scenarios: community energy systems, (simple) market situations, and on-demand services.

Modern energy systems comprise several local community energy systems which produce, consume, and sell energy. The paper 'Engineering sustainable and adaptive systems in dynamic and unpredictable environments' [34] by Rui P. Cardoso, Rosaldo J. F. Rossetti, Emma Hart, David Burth Kurka, and Jeremy Pitt models community energy systems as electronic institutions where each community is an agent, energy is treated as a common resource, and selling and consuming energy is governed by an operating policy. The key contributions of this work are two optimisation methods for automatically finding appropriate policies for this system model. The optimisation methods are based on genetic programming and reinforcement learning. Simulations with these algorithms show that the evolved policies clearly outperform the initially human-designed policy and enable the energy system to remain sustainable over time.

The paper 'The sharer's dilemma in collective adaptive systems of self–interested agents' [35] by Lenz Belzner, Kyrill Schmid, Thomy Phan, Thomas Gabor, and Martin Wirsing studies utility sharing of self-interested agents. Sharing utility with others may incentivise individuals to consider choices that are locally suboptimal but increase the global reward. A variant of distributed cross entropy optimisation is used to realise utility sharing in self-interested collective adaptive systems. The empirical results of two different market situations show that utility sharing increases the individual and the global reward. However, there is a dilemma: if there are defecting non-sharing agents in the group then sharing agents may be exploited by defecting agents and defecting agents gather more individual utility than the sharing ones. On the other hand, if too many agents defect their individual returns are smaller than the returns they would have got by sharing.

The paper 'Coordination model with reinforcement learning for ensuring reliable on-demand services in collective adaptive systems' [36] by Houssem Ben Mahfoudh, Giovanna Di Marzo Serugendo, Anthony Boulmier, and Nabil Abdennadher studies decentralised services which are built and composed on-demand and arise from the interaction of multiple sensors and devices. The bio-inspired SAPERE coordination model [37] is extended by reinforcement learning techniques in order to enhance quality of service. First results show that reinforcement learning helps to find more meaningful service compositions and to improve the correctness of the composition of services provided by diverse agents.

*Software Support for Programming and Modeling Collective Adaptive Systems.* The last session of the track presents software support for attribute-based interaction, dynamic reconfiguration of architectures, and simulating urban transportation systems.

In 'Data-driven modelling and simulation of urban transportation systems using Carma' [38] Natalia Zon and Stephen Gilmore present a collective adaptive systems model of an urban transportation system. The model is written in the stochastic process algebra language Carma [39] which supports the specification and analysis of collective adaptive systems. The results of the simulations of the Carma model are compared with real data collected from the city bus system in the city of Edinburgh. It is demonstrated that the simulation data are in good agreement with those observed in the real data.

The paper 'GoAt: Attribute-based interaction in Google Go' [40] by Yehia Abd Alrahman, Rocco De Nicola, and Giulio Garbi presents the first distributed implementation of the AbC calculus for attribute-based communication [41]. It defines an API, called GoAt, of AbC in the language Go. The API is parametric w.r.t. the distributed infrastructure. The main contribution is the implementation of three infrastructures with cluster, ring, and tree architectures. The paper also reports on an Eclipse plugin for GoAt programming in a high-level syntax. By using graph colouring as case study the performance of the three infrastructures is evaluated with the result that the cluster diverges with increasing graph size while the ring and the tree infrastructures still have acceptable performance.

The final paper of this track addresses again the dynamic reconfiguration of architectures. In 'Four exercises in programming dynamic reconfigurable systems: methodology and solution in DR-BIP' [42] Rim El Ballouli, Saddek Bensalem, Marius Bozga, and Joseph Sifakis present Dynamic Reconfigurable BIP (DR–BIP) as an extension of the BIP component framework [11] for programming reconfigurable systems encompassing various aspects of dynamism. As in the first paper of the track [9], the main concept for modeling dynamic architectures is the notion of motif. A system is composed of several architecture motifs, each motif consisting of a set of component instances and coordination rules. The main concepts of DR-BIP are illustrated by four case studies from the areas of fault-tolerant, mobile and autonomous systems.

**Acknowledgements.** As organisers of the track we would like to thank all authors and panelists for their valuable contributions, all reviewers for their careful evaluations and constructive comments, and all participants of the track for lively discussions. Our thanks go to Rolf Hennicker and Mirco Tribastone for carefully reading and commenting a draft of this paper. We are also gratuful to the ISOLA chairs Tiziana Margaria and Bernhard Steffen for giving us the opportunity to organise this track and to them and Springer–Verlag for providing us with the very helpful equinocs conference system.

# References

1. Hölzl, M., Rauschmayer, A., Wirsing, M.: Engineering of software-intensive systems: state of the art and research challenges. In: Wirsing, M., Banâtre, J.-P., Hölzl, M., Rauschmayer, A. (eds.) Software-Intensive Systems and New Computing Paradigms. LNCS, vol. 5380, pp. 1–44. Springer, Heidelberg (2008). https://doi.org/10.1007/978-3-540-89437-7_1
2. Kernbach, S., Schmickl, T., Timmis, J.: Collective adaptive systems: challenges beyond evolvability. CoRR abs/1108.5643 (2011)
3. Wirsing, M., Hölzl, M., Koch, N., Mayer, P. (eds.): Software Engineering for Collective Autonomic Systems. LNCS, vol. 8998. Springer, Cham (2015). https://doi.org/10.1007/978-3-319-16310-9
4. Bortolussi, L., et al.: A quantitative approach to the design and analysis of collective adaptive systems. In: 1st FoCAS Workshop on Fundamentals of Collective Systems, Taormina, Sicily, Italy, September 2013
5. Wirsing, M., De Nicola, R., Hölzl, M.M.: Rigorous engineering of autonomic ensembles - track introduction. In: [7], pp. 96–98 (2014)
6. Jähnichen, S., Wirsing, M.: Rigorous engineering of collective adaptive systems - Track introduction. In: [8], pp. 535–538 (2016)
7. Margaria, T., Steffen, B. (eds.): ISoLA 2014. LNCS, vol. 8803. Springer, Heidelberg (2014). https://doi.org/10.1007/978-3-662-45231-8
8. Margaria, T., Steffen, B. (eds.): ISoLA 2016. LNCS, vol. 9953. Springer, Cham (2016). https://doi.org/10.1007/978-3-319-47169-3
9. De Nicola, R., Maggi, A., Sifakis, J.: DReAM: Dynamic reconfigurable architecture modeling. In: Margaria, T., Steffen, B. (eds.) ISoLA 2018. LNCS, vol. 11246, pp. 13–31. Springer, Cham (2018)
10. Bliudze, S., Sifakis, J.: The algebra of connectors - structuring interaction in BIP. IEEE Trans. Comput. **57**(10), 1315–1330 (2008)
11. Basu, A., Bensalem, S., Bozga, M., Bourgos, P., Sifakis, J.: Rigorous system design: the BIP approach. In: Kotásek, Z., Bouda, J., Černá, I., Sekanina, L., Vojnar, T., Antoš, D. (eds.) MEMICS 2011. LNCS, vol. 7119, pp. 1–19. Springer, Heidelberg (2012). https://doi.org/10.1007/978-3-642-25929-6_1
12. Hennicker, R., Wirsing, M.: Dynamic logic for ensembles. In: Margaria, T., Steffen, B. (eds.) ISoLA 2018. LNCS, vol. 11246, pp. 32–47. Springer, Cham (2018)
13. Sürmeli, J., Jähnichen, S., Sanders, J.W.: Modelling the transition to distributed ledgers. In: Margaria, T., Steffen, B. (eds.) ISoLA 2018. LNCS, vol. 11246, pp. 48–62. Springer, Cham (2018)
14. Spivey, M.: The Z Notation - A Reference Manual. International Series in Computer Science. Prentice Hall, Upper Saddle River (1989)
15. Pitt, J., et al.: A collective adaptive socio-technical system for remote-and self-supervised exercise in the treatment of intermittent claudication. In: Margaria, T., Steffen, B. (eds.) ISoLA 2018. LNCS, vol. 11246, pp. 63–78. Springer, Cham (2018)
16. Friedman, B., Kahn Jr., P.H., Borning, A.: Value sensitive design and information systems. In: The Handbook of Information and Computer Ethics, pp. 69–101. Wiley (2008)
17. Mummah, S.A., Robinson, T.N., King, A.C., Gardner, C.D., Sutton, S.: IDEAS (Integrate, Design, Assess, and Share): a framework and toolkit of strategies for the development of more effective digital interventions to change health behavior. J. Med. Internet Res. **18**(12), e317 (2016). https://www.ncbi.nlm.nih.gov/pmc/articles/PMC5203679/

18. Kowalski, R., Sergot, M.: A logic-based calculus of events. New Gener. Comput. **4**, 67–95 (1986)
19. Abeywickrama, D.B., Mamei, M., Zambonelli, F.: Engineering collectives of self-driving vehicles: the SOTA approach. In: Margaria, T., Steffen, B. (eds.) ISoLA 2018. LNCS, vol. 11246, pp. 79–93. Springer, Cham (2018)
20. Wanninger, C., Eymüller, C., Hoffmann, A., Kosak, O., Reif, W.: Synthesizing capabilities for collective adaptive systems from self-descriptive hardware devices - bridging the reality gap. In: Margaria, T., Steffen, B. (eds.) ISoLA 2018. LNCS, vol. 11246, pp. 94–108. Springer, Cham (2018)
21. Jähnichen, S., Wirsing, M.: Adaptation to the unforeseen: do we master our autonomous systems? questions to the panel - panel introduction. In: [8]
22. Jähnichen, S., De Nicola, R., Wirsing, M.: The meaning of adaptation: mastering the unforeseen? In: Margaria, T., Steffen, B. (eds.) ISoLA 2018. LNCS, vol. 11246, pp. 109–117. Springer, Cham (2018)
23. Reichstaller, A., Gabor, T., Knapp, A.: Mutation-based test suite evolution for self-organizing systems. In: Margaria, T., Steffen, B. (eds.) ISoLA 2018. LNCS, vol. 11246, pp. 118–136. Springer, Cham (2018)
24. Gabor, T., et al.: Adapting quality assurance to adaptive systems: the scenario coevolution paradigm. In: Margaria, T., Steffen, B. (eds.) ISoLA 2018. LNCS, vol. 11246, pp. 137–154. Springer, Cham (2018)
25. Hölzl, M., Wirsing, M.: Towards a system model for ensembles. In: Agha, G., Danvy, O., Meseguer, J. (eds.) Formal Modeling: Actors, Open Systems, Biological Systems. LNCS, vol. 7000, pp. 241–261. Springer, Heidelberg (2011). https://doi.org/10.1007/978-3-642-24933-4_12
26. Wirsing, M., Hölzl, M., Tribastone, M., Zambonelli, F.: ASCENS: engineering autonomic service-component ensembles. In: Beckert, B., Damiani, F., de Boer, F.S., Bonsangue, M.M. (eds.) FMCO 2011. LNCS, vol. 7542, pp. 1–24. Springer, Heidelberg (2013). https://doi.org/10.1007/978-3-642-35887-6_1
27. Dragomir, I., Iosti, S., Bozga, M., Bensalem, S.: Designing systems with detection and reconfiguration capabilities: a formal approach. In: Margaria, T., Steffen, B. (eds.) ISoLA 2018. LNCS, vol. 11246, pp. 155–171. Springer, Cham (2018)
28. Al Ali, R., Bures, T., Hnetynka, P., Krijt, F., Plasil, F., Vinarek, J.: Dynamic security specification through autonomic component ensembles. In: Margaria, T., Steffen, B. (eds.) ISoLA 2018. LNCS, vol. 11246, pp. 172–185. Springer, Cham (2018)
29. Bures, T., Plasil, F., Kit, M., Tuma, P., Hoch, N.: Software abstractions for component interaction in the internet of things. IEEE Comput. **49**(12), 50–59 (2016)
30. Tschaikowski, M., Tribastone, M.: Exact fluid lumpability for Markovian process algebra. In: Koutny, M., Ulidowski, I. (eds.) CONCUR 2012. LNCS, vol. 7454, pp. 380–394. Springer, Heidelberg (2012). https://doi.org/10.1007/978-3-642-32940-1_27
31. Newman, M.: Networks: An Introduction. Oxford University Press Inc., New York (2010)
32. Tognazzi, S., Tribastone, M., Tschaikowski, M., Vandin, A.: Differential equivalence yields network centrality. In: Margaria, T., Steffen, B. (eds.) ISoLA 2018. LNCS, vol. 11246, pp. 186–201. Springer, Cham (2018)
33. Eberhardinger, B., Ponsar, H., Klumpp, D., Reif, W.: Measuring and evaluating the performance of self-organization mechanisms within collective adaptive systems. In: Margaria, T., Steffen, B. (eds.) ISoLA 2018. LNCS, vol. 11246, pp. 202–220. Springer, Cham (2018)

34. Cardoso, R.P., Rossetti, R.J.F., Hart, E., Kurka, D.B., Pitt, J.: Engineering sustainable and adaptive systems in dynamic and unpredictable environments. In: Margaria, T., Steffen, B. (eds.) ISoLA 2018. LNCS, vol. 11246, pp. 221–240. Springer, Cham (2018)

35. Belzner, L., Schmid, K., Phan, T., Gabor, T., Wirsing, M.: The sharer's dilemma in collective adaptive systems of self-interested agents. In: Margaria, T., Steffen, B. (eds.) ISoLA 2018. LNCS, vol. 11246, pp. 241–256. Springer, Cham (2018)

36. Mahfoudh, H.B., Di Marzo Serugendo, G., Boulmier, A., Abdennadher, N.: Coordination model with reinforcement learning for ensuring reliable on-demand services in collective adaptive systems. In: Margaria, T., Steffen, B. (eds.) ISoLA 2018. LNCS, vol. 11246, pp. 257–273. Springer, Cham (2018)

37. Zambonelli, F., et al.: Self-aware pervasive service ecosystems. In: The European Future Technologies Conference and Exhibition 2011, Procedia Computer Science, vol. 7, pp. 197–199 (2011)

38. Zon, N., Gilmore, S.: Data-driven modelling and simulation of urban transportation systems using CARMA. In: Margaria, T., Steffen, B. (eds.) ISoLA 2018. LNCS, vol. 11246, pp. 274–287. Springer, Cham (2018)

39. Bortolussi, L., et al.: CARMA: Collective adaptive resource-sharing Markovian agents. In: QAPL 2015. EPTCS, vol. 194, pp. 16–31 (2015)

40. Alrahman, Y.A., De Nicola, R., Garbi, G.: GoAt: attribute-based interaction in Google Go. In: Margaria, T., Steffen, B. (eds.) ISoLA 2018. LNCS, vol. 11246, pp. 288–303. Springer, Cham (2018)

41. Abd Alrahman, Y., De Nicola, R., Loreti, M.: On the power of attribute-based communication. In: Albert, E., Lanese, I. (eds.) FORTE 2016. LNCS, vol. 9688, pp. 1–18. Springer, Cham (2016). https://doi.org/10.1007/978-3-319-39570-8_1

42. El Ballouli, R., Bensalem, S., Bozga, M., Sifakis, J.: Four exercises in programming dynamic reconfigurable systems: methodology and solution in DR-BIP. In: Margaria, T., Steffen, B. (eds.) ISoLA 2018. LNCS, vol. 11246, pp. 304–320. Springer, Cham (2018)

# DReAM: Dynamic Reconfigurable Architecture Modeling

Rocco De Nicola[1(✉)], Alessandro Maggi[1(✉)], and Joseph Sifakis[2(✉)]

[1] IMT School for Advanced Studies Lucca, Lucca, Italy
{rocco.denicola,alessandro.maggi}@imtlucca.it
[2] Université Grenoble Alpes, Grenoble, France
Joseph.Sifakis@univ-genoble-alpes.fr

**Abstract.** Modern systems evolve in unpredictable environments and have to continuously adapt their behavior to changing conditions. The "DReAM" (Dynamic Reconfigurable Architecture Modeling) framework, has been designed for modeling reconfigurable dynamic systems. It provides a rule-based language, inspired from Interaction Logic, expressive and easy to use, and encompassing all aspects of dynamicity including parametric multi-modal coordination with creation/deletion of components as well as mobility. Additionally, it allows the description of both endogenous/modular and exogenous/centralized coordination styles and sound transformations from one style to the other. The DReAM framework is implemented in the form of a Java API bundled with an execution engine. It allows to develop runnable systems combining the expressiveness of the rule-based notation together with the flexibility of this widespread programming language.

## 1 Introduction

The ever increasing complexity of modern software systems has changed the perspective of software designers who now have to consider new classes of systems, consisting of a large number of interacting components and featuring complex interaction mechanisms. These systems are usually distributed, heterogeneous, decentralised and interdependent, and are operating in an unpredictable environments. They need to continuously adapt to changing internal or external conditions in order to efficiently use of resources and to provide adequate functionality when the external environment changes dynamically. Dynamism, indeed, plays a crucial role in these modern systems and it can be captured as the interplay of changes relative to the three features below:

1. the parametric description of interactions between instances of components for a given system configuration;
2. the reconfiguration involving creation/deletion of components and management of their interaction according to a given architectural style;
3. the migration of components between predefined architectural styles.

© Springer Nature Switzerland AG 2018
T. Margaria and B. Steffen (Eds.): ISoLA 2018, LNCS 11246, pp. 13–31, 2018.
https://doi.org/10.1007/978-3-030-03424-5_2

Architecture modeling languages should be equipped with concepts and mechanisms which are expressive and easy to use relatively to each of these features.

The first feature implies the ability of describing the coordination of systems that are parametric with respect to the numbers of instances of types of components; examples of such systems are Producer-Consumer systems with $m$ producers and $n$ consumers or Ring systems consisting of $n$ identical interconnected components.

The second feature is related to the ability of reconfiguring systems by adding or deleting components and managing their interactions taking into account the dynamically changing conditions. In the case of a reconfigurable ring this would require having the possibility of removing a component which self-detects a failure and of adding it back after recovery. Added components are subject to specific interaction rules according to their type and their position in the system.

The third aspect is related to the vision of "fluid architectures" [1] or "fluid software" [2] and builds on the concept that applications and objects live in an environment (we call it a *motif*) corresponding to an architectural style that is characterized by specific coordination and reconfiguration rules. Dynamicity of systems is modelled by allowing applications and objects to migrate among motifs and such dynamic migration allows a disciplined, easy-to-implement, management of dynamically changing coordination rules. For instance, self-organizing systems may adopt different coordination motifs to adapt their behavior and guarantee global properties.

The different approaches to architectural modeling and the new trends and needs are reviewed in detailed surveys such as [3–7]. Here, we consider two criteria for the classification of existing approaches: *exogenous vs. endogenous* and *declarative vs. imperative* modeling.

*Exogenous modeling* considers that components are architecture-agnostic and respect a strict separation between a component behavior and its coordination. This approach is adopted by Architecture Description Languages (ADL) [5]. It has the advantage of providing a global view of the coordination mechanisms and their properties. *Endogenous modeling* requires adding explicit coordination primitives in the code describing components' behavior. Components are composed through their interfaces, which expose their coordination capabilities. An advantage of endogenous coordination is that it does not require programmers to explicitly build a global coordination model. However, validating a coordination mechanism and studying its properties becomes much harder without such a model.

*Conjunctive modeling* uses logics to express coordination constraints between components. It allows in particular modular description as one can associate with each component its coordination constraints. The global system coordination can be obtained in that case as the conjunction of individual constraints of its constituent components. *Disjunctive modeling* consists in explicitly specifying system coordination as the union of the executable coordination mechanisms such as semaphores, function call and connectors. Merits and limitations of the two approaches are well understood. Conjunctive modeling allows abstraction and modular description but it involves the risk of inconsistency in case there is no architecture satisfying the specification.

This paper introduces the DReAM framework for modeling Dynamic Reconfigurable Architectures. DReAM uses a logic-based modeling language that encompasses the four styles mentioned above as well as the three mentioned features. A system consists of instances of types of components organized in a collection of motifs. Component instances can migrate between motifs depending on global system conditions. Thus, a given type of component can be subject to different rules when it is in a "ring" motif or in a "pipeline" one. Using motifs allows natural description of self-organizing systems (see Fig. 1).

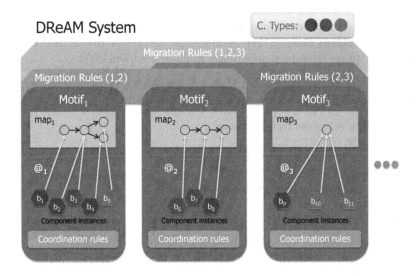

**Fig. 1.** Overview of a DReAM system

Coordination rules in a motif involve an interaction part and an associated operation. The former is modeled as a formula of the first order Interaction Logic [8] used to specify parametric interactions between instances of types of components. The latter specifies transfer of data between the components involved in the interaction. In this way, we can characterize parametric coordination between classes of components. The rules allow both conjunctive and disjunctive specification styles. We study to what extent a mathematical correspondence can be established between the two styles. In particular, we will see that conjunctive specifications can be translated into equivalent disjunctive global specifications while the converse is not true in general.

To enhance expressiveness of the different kinds of dynamism, each motif is equipped with a map, which is a graph defining the topology of the interactions in this motif. To parametrize coordination rules for the nodes of the map, an address function @ is provided defining the position $@(c)$ in the map of any component instance $c$ associated with the motif. Maps are also very useful to express mobility of components, in which case the connectivity relation of the map represents possible moves of components. Finally the language allows the modification of maps by adding or removing nodes and edges, as well as the dynamic creation and deletion of component instances.

## 2   Static Architectures - The **PIL** Coordination Language

We introduce the Propositional Interaction Logic (PIL) [8] used to model interactions between a given set of components. A system model is the composition of interacting components which are labelled transition systems, where the labels are port names and the states are control locations. Components are completely coordination-agnostic, as there is no additional characterization to ports and control locations beyond their names (e.g. we do not distinguish between input/output ports or synchronous/asynchronous components).

**Definition 1 (Component).** *Let $\mathcal{P}$ and $\mathcal{S}$ respectively be the domain of ports and control locations. A component is a transition system $B = (S, P, T)$ with*

- *$S \subseteq \mathcal{S}$: finite set of control locations;*
- *$P \subseteq \mathcal{P}$: finite set of ports;*
- *$T \subseteq S \times P \cup \{idle\} \times S$: finite set of transitions. Transitions $(s, p, s')$ are also denoted by $s \xrightarrow{p} s'$; $p \in P$ is the port offered for interaction, and each transition is labelled by a different port.*

*A component has a special port idle $\notin P$ that is associated to implicit loop transitions $\{s \xrightarrow{idle} s\}_{s \in S}$. This choice is made to simplify the theoretical development of our framework. Furthermore it is assumed that the sets of ports and control locations of different components are disjoint.*

A system definition is characterized by a set of components $B_i = (S_i, P_i, T_i)$ for $i \in [1, n]$. The *configuration* $\Gamma$ of a system is the set of the current control locations of each constituent component:

$$\Gamma = \{s_i \in S_i\}_{i \in [1..n]} \tag{1}$$

Given the set of ports $\mathcal{P}$, an interaction $a$ is any finite subset of $\mathcal{P}$ such that no two ports belong to the same component. The set of all interactions is isomorphic to $I(\mathcal{P}) = 2^{\mathcal{P}}$.

Given a set of components $B_1 \ldots B_n$ and the set of interactions $\gamma$, we can define a system $\gamma(B_1, \ldots, B_n)$ using the following operational semantics rule:

$$\frac{a \in \gamma \qquad \forall p \in a : s_i \xrightarrow{p} s_i'}{\{s_i\}_{[1..n]} \xrightarrow{a} \{s_i'\}_{[1..n]}} \tag{2}$$

where $s_i$ is the current control location of component $B_i$, and $a$ is an interaction containing exactly one port for each component $B_i$[1].

## 2.1   Propositional Interaction Logic (PIL)

Let $\mathcal{P}$ and $\mathcal{S}$ be respectively the domains of ports and control locations. The formulas of Propositional Interaction Logic $\mathsf{PIL}(\mathcal{P}, \mathcal{S})$ are defined by the syntax:

$$(\text{PIL formula}) \quad \Psi :: = p \in \mathcal{P} \mid \pi \mid \neg\Psi \mid \Psi_1 \wedge \Psi_2 \tag{3}$$

where $\pi : 2^{\Gamma} \mapsto \{\mathbf{true}, \mathbf{false}\}$ is a *state predicate*. We use logical connectives $\vee$ and $\Rightarrow$ with the usual meaning.

The models of the logic are interactions on $\mathcal{P}$ for a configuration $\Gamma$. The semantics is defined by the following satisfaction relation $\models_\Gamma$:

$$
\begin{array}{llll}
a \models_\Gamma \mathbf{true} & \text{for any } a & a \models_\Gamma \Psi_1 \wedge \Psi_2 & \text{if } a \models_\Gamma \Psi_1 \text{ and } a \models_\Gamma \Psi_2 \\
a \models_\Gamma p & \text{if } p \in a & a \models_\Gamma \neg\Psi & \text{if } a \not\models_\Gamma \Psi \\
a \models_\Gamma \pi & \text{if } \pi(\Gamma) = \mathbf{true} &
\end{array}
\tag{4}
$$

A monomial $\bigwedge_{p \in I} p \wedge \bigwedge_{p \in J} \neg p, I \cap J = \emptyset$ denotes a set of interactions $a$ s.t.:

1. the positive terms correspond to required ports for the interaction to occur;
2. the negative terms correspond to inhibited ports or to ports to which the interaction is "closed";
3. the non-occurring terms are optional ports.

Note that *idle* ports of components can appear in PIL formulas. Given a component with ports $P$ and idle port *idle*, the formula $idle \equiv \bigwedge_{p \in P} \neg p$, while $\neg idle \equiv \bigvee_{p \in P} p$.

As we can describe sets of interactions using PIL formulas, we can redefine rule (2) as follows, where $\Psi$ is a PIL formula.

$$\frac{a \models_\Gamma \Psi \qquad \forall p \in a : s_i \xrightarrow{p} s_i'}{\{s_i\}_{[1..n]} \xrightarrow{a} \{s_i'\}_{[1..n]}} \tag{5}$$

## 2.2   Disjunctive vs. Conjunctive Specification Style

It is shown in [8] how a function $\beta$ can be defined $\beta : I(P) \rightarrow PIL(P, S)$ associating with an interaction $a$ its characteristic PIL formula $\beta(a)$. For example, if $P = \{p, q, r, s, t\}$ then for the interaction $\{p, q\}$, $\beta(\{p, q\}) = p \wedge q \wedge \neg r \wedge \neg s \wedge \neg t$[2]. For the set of interactions $\gamma$ caused by the broadcast of $p$ to ports $q$ and $r$,

---

[1] Components $B_j$ not "actively" involved in the interaction will participate with their *idle* port s.t. $s_j' = s_j$.

[2] For the sake of conciseness, from now on we will omit the conjunction operator on monomials.

$\beta(\gamma) = p\neg s\neg t$. For the set of interactions $\gamma$ consisting of the singleton interactions $p$ and $q$, $\beta(\gamma) = (p\neg q \vee \neg pq) \wedge \neg r \neg s \neg t$. Finally $\beta(\{idle\}) = \neg p \neg q \neg r \neg s \neg t$ as $idle$ is the only port not belonging to $P$.

Note that the definition of the function $\beta$ requires knowledge of $P$. This function can be naturally extended to sets of interactions $\gamma$: for $\gamma = \{a_1, \ldots, a_n\}$, $\beta(\gamma) = \beta(a_1) \vee \ldots \vee \beta(a_n)$.

A set of interactions is specified in *disjunctive style* if it is described by a PIL formula which is a disjunction of monomials. A dual style of specification is the *conjunctive style* where the interactions of a system are the conjunction of PIL formulas. A methodology for writing conjunctive specifications proposed in [8] considers that each term of the conjunction is a formula of the form $p \Rightarrow \Psi_p$, where the implication is interpreted as a causality relation: for $p$ to be true, it is necessary that the formula $\Psi_p$ holds and this defines interaction patterns from other components in which the port $p$ needs to be involved.

For example, the interaction involving strong synchronization between $p_1$, $p_2$ and $p_3$ is defined by the formula $f_1 = (p_1 \Rightarrow p_2) \wedge (p_2 \Rightarrow p_3) \wedge (p_3 \Rightarrow p_1)$. Broadcast from a sending port $t$ towards receiving ports $r_1, r_2$ is defined by the formula $f_2 = (\textbf{true} \Rightarrow t) \wedge (r_1 \Rightarrow t) \wedge (r_2 \Rightarrow t)$. The non-empty solutions are the interactions $t$, $tr_1$, $tr_2$ and $tr_1 r_2$.

Note that by applying this methodology we can associate to a component with set of ports $P$ a constraint $\bigwedge_{p \in P} (p \Rightarrow \Psi_p)$ that characterizes the set of interactions where some port of the component may be involved. So if a system consists of components $C_1, \ldots, C_n$ with sets of ports $P_1, \ldots, P_n$ respectively, then the PIL formula $\bigwedge_{i \in [1,n]} \bigwedge_{p \in P_i} (p \Rightarrow \Psi_p)$ expresses a global interaction constraint. Such a constraint can be put in disjunctive form whose monomials characterize global interactions. Notice that the disjunctive form obtained in that manner contains the monomial $\bigwedge_{p \in P} \neg p$, where $P = \bigcup_{i \in [1..n]} P_i$, which is satisfied by the interaction where every component performs the *idle* action. This trivial remark says that in the PIL framework it is possible to express for each component separately its interaction constraints and compose them conjunctively to get global disjunctive constraints.

It is also possible to put in conjunctive style a disjunctive formula $\Psi$ specifying the interactions of a system with set of ports $P$. To translate $\Psi$ into a form $\bigwedge_{p \in P} (p \Rightarrow \Psi_p)$ we just need to choose $\Psi_p = \Psi[p = \textbf{true}]$ obtained from $\Psi$ by substituting $\textbf{true}$ to $p$. Given the inherent property of supporting the *idle* interaction, the translated conjunctive formula will be equivalent to $\Psi$ only if the latter allows global idling. Consider broadcasting from port $p$ to ports $q$ and $r$ (Fig. 2). The possible interactions are $p, pq, pr, pqr$ and $\emptyset$ (i.e. idling). The disjunctive style formula is: $\neg p \neg q \neg r \vee p \neg q \neg r \vee pq \neg r \vee p \neg qr \vee pqr = \neg q \neg r \vee p$. The equivalent conjunctive formula is: $(q \Rightarrow p) \wedge (r \Rightarrow p)$ that simply expresses the causal dependency of ports $q$ and $r$ from $p$.

The example below illustrates the application of the two description styles.

*Example 1 (Master-Slaves).* Let us consider a simple system consisting of three components: *master*, *slave*$_1$ and *slave*$_2$. The *master* performs two sequential requests to *slave*$_1$ and *slave*$_2$, and then performs some computation with them.

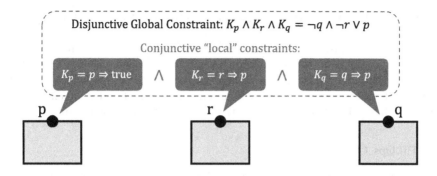

**Fig. 2.** Broadcast example: disjunctive vs conjunctive specification

Figure 3 shows the representation of such components.

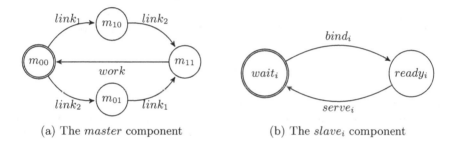

(a) The *master* component          (b) The *slave$_i$* component

**Fig. 3.** *master* and *slave$_i$* components

The set of allowed interactions $\gamma$ for the set of components $\{master, slave_1, slave_2\}$ can be represented via the following PIL formula using the disjunctive style:

$$\Psi_{disj} = (link_1 \wedge bind_1 \wedge idle_{s_2}) \vee (link_2 \wedge bind_2 \wedge idle_{s_1}) \vee (work \wedge serve_1 \wedge serve_2)$$

where $idle_{s_i} \equiv \neg bind_i \wedge \neg serve_i$ is the *idle* port of *slave$_i$*. Alternatively, the same interaction patterns can be modeled using the conjunctive style:

$$\Psi_{conj} = (link_1 \Rightarrow bind_1) \wedge (link_2 \Rightarrow bind_2) \wedge (bind_1 \Rightarrow link_1) \wedge (bind_2 \Rightarrow link_2) \wedge$$
$$(work \Rightarrow serve_1 \wedge serve_2) \wedge (serve_1 \Rightarrow work) \wedge (serve_2 \Rightarrow work)$$

The two formulas differ in the admissibility of the "no-interaction" interaction; the conjunctive formula $\Psi_{conj}$ allows all components to avoid interaction by performing a transition over their *idle* ports. To allow it, the formula $idle_m \wedge idle_{s_1} \wedge idle_{s_2}$ must be added to the chain of disjunctions in $\Psi_{disj}$.

# 3   Static Architectures with Transfer of Values: PILOps

We expand the PIL framework to allow data exchange between components. In order to do so, the definition of component will be extended with local variables and the coordination constraints will be expressed with PILOps, which expands PIL to a notation that is inspired by guarded commands. Finally, we extend the definitions for disjunctive and conjunctive styles and study their connections.

## 3.1   PILOps Components

**Definition 2 (PILOps Component).** *Let $S$ be the set of all component control locations, $\mathcal{X}$ the set of all local variables, and $\mathcal{P}$ the set of all ports. A component is a transition system $B := (S, X, P, T)$, where $S$, $P$ and $T$ are as in Definition 1 and $X \subseteq \mathcal{X}$ is a finite set local variables. As for ports and control locations, it is assumed that sets of local variables for different PILOps components are disjoint.*

A system is a set of coordinated components $B_i = (S_i, X_i, P_i, T_i)$ for $i = [1, n]$. The *configuration* $\Gamma$ of a system is described by the control locations of its components, and also the *valuation function* $\sigma : \mathcal{X} \mapsto \mathsf{V}$ mapping local variables to values:

$$\Gamma = \left( \{ s_i \in S_i \}_{i=[1..n]}, \sigma \right) \tag{6}$$

Interactions are still sets of ports belonging to different components. Using a term of PILOps to compose components, the system configuration $\Gamma$ evolves to a new configuration $\Gamma'$ by performing an interaction $a$, represented by $\Gamma \xrightarrow{a} \Gamma'$.

## 3.2   Propositional Interaction Logic with Operations (PILOps)

Let $\mathcal{P}$, $\mathcal{X}$ and $\mathcal{S}$ respectively be the domains of ports, local variables and control locations. The terms of PILOps$(\mathcal{P}, \mathcal{X}, \mathcal{S})$ are defined by the following syntax:

$$\begin{aligned}
\text{(PILOps term)} \quad & \Phi ::= \Psi \to \Delta \mid \Phi_1 \;\&\; \Phi_2 \mid \Phi_1 \parallel \Phi_2 \\
\text{(PIL formula)} \quad & \Psi ::= p \in \mathcal{P} \mid \pi \mid \neg\Psi \mid \Psi_1 \wedge \Psi_2 \\
\text{(set of ops.)} \quad & \Delta ::= \emptyset \mid \{\delta\} \mid \Delta_1 \cup \Delta_2
\end{aligned} \tag{7}$$

- operators $\&$ and $\parallel$ are *associative* and *commutative*, and $\&$ has higher precedence than $\parallel$;
- $\pi : 2^\Gamma \mapsto \{\mathbf{true}, \mathbf{false}\}$ is a state predicate;
- $\delta : 2^\sigma \mapsto 2^\sigma$ is an operation that transforms the valuation function $\sigma$.

The models of the logic are still interactions $a$ on $\mathcal{P}$, where the satisfaction relation is defined by the set of rules (4) for PIL with the following extension:

$$\begin{aligned}
a \models_\Gamma \Psi \to \Delta \quad & \text{if } a \models_\Gamma \Psi \\
a \models_\Gamma \Phi_1 \;\&\; \Phi_2 \quad & \text{if } a \models_\Gamma \Phi_1 \text{ and } a \models_\Gamma \Phi_2 \\
a \models_\Gamma \Phi_1 \parallel \Phi_2 \quad & \text{if } a \models_\Gamma \Phi_1 \text{ or } a \models_\Gamma \Phi_2
\end{aligned} \tag{8}$$

In other words, the operators & and $\parallel$ for PILOps terms are equivalent to the logical $\wedge$ and $\vee$ from the interaction semantics perspective.

Operations in $\Delta$ are treated differently: operations of rules combined with "&" are either performed all together if the associated PIL formulas hold for $a, \Gamma$ or not at all if at least one formula does not, while for rules combined with the "$\parallel$" operator a maximal union of operations satisfying the PIL formulas will be executed. We indicate the set of operations to be performed for $\Phi$ under $a, \Gamma$ as $[\![\Phi]\!]_{a,\Gamma}$, which is defined according to the following rules:

$$[\![\Psi \to \Delta]\!]_{a,\Gamma} = \begin{cases} \Delta & \text{if } a \models_\Gamma \Psi \\ \emptyset & \text{otherwise} \end{cases}$$

$$[\![\Phi_1 \ \& \ \Phi_2]\!]_{a,\Gamma} = \begin{cases} [\![\Phi_1]\!]_{a,\Gamma} \cup [\![\Phi_2]\!]_{a,\Gamma} & \text{if } a \models_\Gamma \Phi_1 \text{ and } a \models_\Gamma \Phi_2 \\ \emptyset & \text{otherwise} \end{cases}$$

$$[\![\Phi_1 \parallel \Phi_2]\!]_{a,\Gamma} = [\![\Phi_1]\!]_{a,\Gamma} \cup [\![\Phi_2]\!]_{a,\Gamma} \tag{9}$$

Two PILOps terms $\Phi_1, \Phi_2$ are *equivalent* if, for any interaction $a$ and configuration $\Gamma$, $[\![\Phi_1]\!]_{a,\Gamma} = [\![\Phi_2]\!]_{a,\Gamma}$.

**Axioms for PILOps.** The following axioms hold for PILOps terms:

& is associative, commutative and idempotent $\tag{10}$

$\Psi_1 \to \Delta_1 \ \& \ \Psi_2 \to \Delta_2 = \Psi_1 \wedge \Psi_2 \to \Delta_1 \cup \Delta_2$ $\tag{11}$

$\Phi \ \& \ \textbf{true} \to \emptyset = \Phi$ $\tag{12}$

$\parallel$ is associative, commutative and idempotent $\tag{13}$

$\Psi_1 \to \Delta \parallel \Psi_2 \to \Delta = \Psi_1 \vee \Psi_2 \to \Delta$ $\tag{14}$

$\Psi \to \Delta_1 \parallel \Psi \to \Delta_2 = \Psi \to \Delta_1 \cup \Delta_2$ $\tag{15}$

$\textbf{false} \to \Delta \parallel \Phi = \Phi$ $\tag{16}$

Absorption: $\Phi_1 \parallel \Phi_2 = \Phi_1 \parallel \Phi_2 \parallel \Phi_1 \ \& \ \Phi_2$ $\tag{17}$

Distributivity: $\Phi \ \& \ (\Phi_1 \parallel \Phi_2) = \Phi \ \& \ \Phi_1 \parallel \Phi \ \& \ \Phi_2$ $\tag{18}$

Normal disjunctive form (DNF): $\tag{19}$

$\Psi_1 \to \Delta_1 \parallel \Psi_2 \to \Delta_2 = \Psi_1 \wedge \neg\Psi_2 \to \Delta_1 \parallel \Psi_2 \wedge \neg\Psi_1 \to \Delta_2 \parallel \Psi_1 \wedge \Psi_2 \to \Delta_1 \cup \Delta_2$

Note that PILOps strictly contains PIL as a formula $\Psi$ can be represented by $\Phi \to \emptyset$. The operator & is the extension of conjunction with neutral element $\textbf{true} \to \emptyset$ and $\parallel$ is the extension of the disjunction with an absorption (17) and distributivity axiom (18). The DNF is obtained by application of the axioms. Note some important differences with PIL: the usual absorption axioms for disjunction and conjunction are replaced by a single absorption axiom (17) and there is no conjunctive normal form.

**Operations.** Operations $\delta$ in PILOps are assignments on local variables of components involved in an interaction of the form $x := f$, where $x \in \mathcal{X}$ is the local variable subject to the assignment and $f : V^k \mapsto V$, is a function on local variables $y_1, \ldots, y_k$ ($y_i \in \mathcal{X}$) on which the assigned value depends.

We can define the semantics of the application of the assignment $x := f$ to the valuation function $\sigma$ as:

$$(x := f)(\sigma) = \sigma\left[x \mapsto f\left(\sigma(y_1), \ldots, \sigma(y_k)\right)\right] \tag{20}$$

A set of assignment operations $\Delta$ is performed using a *snapshot semantics*. When $\Delta$ contains multiple assignments on the same local variable, the results are *non-deterministic*.

A PILOps term $\Phi$ is a coordination mechanism that, applied to a set of components $B_1 \ldots B_n$, gives a system defined by the following rule:

$$\frac{a \models_\Gamma \Phi \quad \forall p \in a : s_i \xrightarrow{p} s_i' \quad \sigma' \in \llbracket \Phi \rrbracket_{a,\Gamma}(\sigma)}{\left(\{s_i\}_{[1..n]}, \sigma\right) \xrightarrow{a} \left(\{s_i'\}_{[1..n]}, \sigma'\right)} \tag{21}$$

where $\llbracket \Phi \rrbracket_{a,\Gamma}(\sigma)$ is the set of valuation functions obtained by applying the operations $\delta \in \llbracket \Phi \rrbracket_{a,\Gamma}$ to $\sigma$ in every possible order (using a *snapshot semantics*).

## 3.3  Disjunctive vs. Conjunctive Specification Style in PILOps

We define disjunctive and conjunctive style specification in PILOps. We associate with $p \Rightarrow \Psi_p$ an operation $\Delta_p$ to be performed when an interaction involving $p$ is executed according to this rule. We call the PILOps term describing this behavior the *conjunctive term* $[p, \Psi_p, \Delta_p] = (\neg p \to \emptyset \parallel p \wedge \Psi_p \to \Delta_p)$. $\Delta_p$ may be executed when $p$ is involved in some interaction; otherwise, no operation is executed. The conjunction of terms of this form gives a disjunctive style formula. Consider for instance, the conjunction of two terms:

$$[p, \Psi_p, \Delta_p] \& [q, \Psi_q, \Delta_q] = (\neg p \to \emptyset \parallel p \wedge \Psi_p \to \Delta_p) \& (\neg q \to \emptyset \parallel q \wedge \Psi_q \to \Delta_q)$$
$$= \neg p \wedge \neg q \to \emptyset \parallel p \wedge \neg q \wedge \Psi_p \to \Delta_p \parallel q \wedge \neg p \wedge \Psi_q \to \Delta_q \parallel p \wedge q \wedge \Psi_p \wedge \Psi_q \to \Delta_p \cup \Delta_q$$

The disjunctive form obtained by application of the distributivity axiom (18) is a union of four terms corresponding to the canonical monomials on $p$ and $q$ and leading to the execution of no operation, either operation $\Delta_p$, $\Delta_q$ or both. It is easy to see that the conjunctive and disjunctive forms below are equivalent:

$$\underset{p \in P}{\&} (\neg p \to \emptyset \parallel p \wedge \Psi_p \to \Delta_p)$$

$$\underset{I \cup J = P}{\parallel} \left( \bigwedge_{i \in I} p_i \wedge \Psi_{p_i} \bigwedge_{j \in J} \neg p_j \to \bigcup_{i \in I} \Delta_{p_i} \right) \quad \text{where} \quad \bigcup_{p_i \in \emptyset} \Delta_{p_i} = \emptyset.$$

The converse does not hold. Given a disjunctive specification it is not always possible to get an equivalent conjunctive one. If we have a term of the form

$\|_{k \in K} \Psi \to \Delta_k$ over a set of ports $P$, it can be put in canonical form and will be the union of canonical terms of the form $\bigwedge_{i \in I} p_i \bigwedge_{j \in J} \neg p_j \to \Delta_{IJ}$. It is easy to see that for this form to be obtained as a conjunction of causal terms a sufficient condition is that for each port $p_i$ there exists an operation $\Delta_{p_i}$ such that $\Delta_{IJ} = \bigcup_{i \in I} \Delta_{p_i}$. That is, the operation associated with a port participating to an interaction is the same. This condition also determines the limits of the conjunctive and compositional approach.

*Example 2 (Master-Slaves).* Let us expand Example 1 by attaching data transfer between the *master* component and the two *slave*$_1$ and *slave*$_2$ components. We assume that the *master* has a *buffer* local variable taking the value obtained by adding the values stored in local variables *mem*$_1$ and *mem*$_2$ of the two respective slaves when they all synchronize through the ports *work*, *serve*$_1$, *serve*$_2$.

The set of allowed interactions $\gamma$ does not change, but using PILOps we can characterize the desired behaviour using the disjunctive style as follows:

$$\Phi_{disj} = link_1 \wedge bind_1 \wedge idle_2 \to \emptyset \parallel link_2 \wedge bind_2 \wedge idle_1 \to \emptyset \parallel$$
$$work \wedge serve_1 \wedge serve_2 \to buffer := mem_1 + mem_2$$

The conjunctive style version equivalent to $\Phi_{disj}$ (except for its allowance of the idling of all components) is the following:

$$\Phi_{conj} = [link_1, bind_1, \emptyset] \& [link_2, bind_2, \emptyset] \& [bind_1, link_1, \emptyset] \& [bind_2, link_2, \emptyset] \&$$
$$[work, serve_1 \wedge serve_2, buffer := mem_1 + mem_2] \&$$
$$[serve_1, work, \emptyset] \& [serve_2, work, \emptyset]$$

## 4   The DReAM Framework

In this Section we present the DReAM framework, allowing dynamism and reconfiguration which extends the static framework in the following manner. Components are instances of types of components and their number can dynamically change. Coordination between components in a motif, but also between the motifs constituting a system, is expressed by the DReAM coordination language, a first order extension of PILOps. In motifs coordination is parametrized by the notion of map which is an abstract relation used as a reference to model topology of the underlying architecture as well as component mobility.

### 4.1   Component Types and Component Instances

DReAM systems are constituted by *instances of component types*. Component types in DReAM correspond to PILOps components (see Definition 2), while component instances are obtained from a component type by renaming its control locations, ports and local variables with a unique *identifier*.

To highlight the relationships between component types and their defining sets we use a "dot notation":

- $b.S$ refers to the set of control locations $S$ of component type $b$ (same for ports and variables);
- $b.s$ refers to the control location $s \in b.S$ (same for ports and variables).

**Definition 3 (Component instance).** *Let $\mathcal{C}$ be the domain of instance identifiers $\mathcal{C}$ and $B = \langle b_1, \ldots, b_n \rangle$ be a tuple of component types where each element is $b_i = (S_i, X_i, P_i, T_i)$.*

*A set of component instances of type $b_i$ is represented by $b_i.C = \{b_i.c : c \in C\}$, for $1 \leq i \leq n$ and $C \subseteq \mathcal{C}$, and is obtained by renaming the set of control locations, ports and local variables of the component type $b_i$ with $c$, that is $b_i.c = (c.S_i, c.X_i, c.P_i, c.T_i)$. Without loss of genericity, we assume that instance identifiers uniquely represent a component instance regardless of its type.*

*The state of a component instance $b.c$ is therefore defined as the pair $\langle c.s, c.\sigma \rangle$, where $c.\sigma$ is the* valuation function *of the variables $c.X^3$. We use the same notation to denote ports, states and variables belonging to a given component instance (e.g. $c.p \in c.P$) and assume that ports of different component instances are still disjoint sets, i.e. $c.P \cap c'.P = \emptyset$ for $c \neq c'$.*

Transitions for component instances $c.T$ are obtained from the respective component type transitions $T$ via port name substitution, i.e. via the rule:

$$\frac{(s, p, s') \in T}{c.s \xrightarrow{c.p} c.s'} \tag{22}$$

### 4.2   The DReAM Coordination Language

The DReAM coordination language is essentially a first-order extension of PILOps where quantification over sets of components is introduced.

Given the domain of ports $\mathcal{P}$, the DReAM coordination language is defined by the syntax:

$$
\begin{aligned}
\text{(DReAM term)} \quad & \rho ::= \Phi \mid D\{\Phi\} \mid \rho_1 \,\&\, \rho_2 \mid \rho_1 \parallel \rho_2 \\
\text{(declaration)} \quad & D ::= \forall c : m.b \mid \exists c : m.b \mid D_1, D_2 \\
\text{(PILOps term)} \quad & \Phi ::= \Psi \to \Delta \mid \Phi_1 \,\&\, \Phi_2 \mid \Phi_1 \parallel \Phi_2 \\
\text{(PIL formula)} \quad & \Psi ::= c.p \in \mathcal{P} \mid \pi \mid \neg\Psi \mid \Psi_1 \wedge \Psi_2 \\
\text{(set of ops.)} \quad & \Delta ::= \emptyset \mid \{\delta\} \mid \Delta_1 \cup \Delta_2
\end{aligned}
\tag{23}
$$

- *Declarations* define the context of the term by declaring quantified ($\forall|\exists$) component variables ($c$) associated to instances of a given type ($b$) belonging to a motif $m$;
- Operators $\&$ and $\parallel$ are the same as the ones introduced in (7) for PILOps;
- $\pi : 2^\Gamma \mapsto \{\textbf{true}, \textbf{false}\}$ is a state predicate on the system configuration $\Gamma$;
- $\delta : 2^\Gamma \mapsto 2^\Gamma$ is an *operation* that transforms the system configuration $\Gamma$.

---

[3] Notice that when writing e.g. $c.s$ we are omitting the explicit reference to the component type $b$ and using a shorter notation compared to the complete one, e.g. $b.c.s$.

A DReAM coordination term is *well formed* if its PIL formulas and associated operations contain only component variables that are defined in its declarations. From now on, we will only consider well formed terms.

Given a system configuration, a coordination term can be translated to an equivalent PILOps term by performing a *declaration expansion* step, by expanding the quantifiers and replacing component variables with actual components.

**Declaration Expansion for Coordination Terms.** Given that DReAM systems host finite numbers of component instances, first-order logic quantifiers can be eliminated by enumerating every component instance of the type specified in the declaration. We thus define the *declaration expansion* $\langle \rho \rangle_\Gamma$ of $\rho$ under configuration $\Gamma$ via the following rules:

$$\langle \Phi \rangle_\Gamma = \Phi \qquad\qquad \langle \forall c : m.b\{\Phi\} \rangle_\Gamma = \underset{c^* \in m.b.C}{\&} \Phi[c^*/c]$$

$$\langle \rho_1 \,\&\, \rho_2 \rangle_\Gamma = \langle \rho_1 \rangle_\Gamma \,\&\, \langle \rho_2 \rangle_\Gamma \qquad \langle \exists c : m.b\{\Phi\} \rangle_\Gamma = \underset{c^* \in m.b.C}{\parallel} \Phi[c^*/c] \qquad (24)$$

$$\langle \rho_1 \parallel \rho_2 \rangle_\Gamma = \langle \rho_1 \rangle_\Gamma \parallel \langle \rho_2 \rangle_\Gamma \qquad \langle D_1, D_2\{\Phi\} \rangle_\Gamma = \langle D_1\{\langle D_2\{\Phi\}\rangle_\Gamma\}\rangle_\Gamma$$

where $m.b.C$ is the set of component instances of type $b$ in motif $m$, and $[c^*/c]$ is the substitution of the symbol $c$ with the actual identifier $c^*$ in the associated term.

By applying (24), any term can be transformed into a PILOps term, whose semantics is defined in Sect. 3.2:

### 4.3 Motif Modeling

A motif characterizes an independent dynamic architecture involving a set of component instances $C$ subject to specific *coordination terms* parameterized by a specific data structure called *map*.

**Definition 4 (Motif).** *Let $\mathcal{C}$ be the domain of component instance identifiers. A motif is a tuple $m := \langle C, \rho, Map_0, @_0 \rangle$, where $C \subseteq \mathcal{C}$ is the set of component instances assigned to the motif, $\rho$ is the coordination term regulating interactions and reconfigurations among them, and $Map_0, @_0$ are the initial configurations of the map associated to the motif and of the addressing function.*

*We assume that each component instance is associated with exactly one motif, i.e. $m_1.C \cap m_2.C = \emptyset$.*

A *Map* is a set of locations and a connectivity relation between them. It is the structure over which computation is distributed and defines a system of coordinates for components. It can represent a physical structure e.g. geographic map or some conceptual structure, e.g., cellular structure of a memory. In DReAM a map is specified as a graph $Map = (N, E)$, where:

- $N$ is a set of nodes or locations (possibly infinite);
- $E$ is a set of edges subset of $N \times N$ that defines the connectivity relation between nodes.

The relation $E$ defines a concept of neighborhood for components.

Component instances $C$ in a motif and its map are related through the (partial) *address function* $@ : C \to N$ binding each component in $C$ to a node $n \in N$ of the map.

Maps can be used to model a physical environment where components are moving. If the map is an array $N = \{(i,j)|i,j \in \mathsf{Integers}\} \times \{f,o\}$, the pairs $(i,j)$ represent coordinates and the symbols $f$ and $o$ stand respectively for free and obstacle. We can model the movement of $b$ such that $@(b) = ((i,j), f)$ to a position $(i+a, j+b)$ provided that there is a path from $(i,j)$ to $(i+a, j+b)$ consisting of free cells.

The *configuration* $\Gamma_m$ of motif $m$ is represented by the tuple

$$\Gamma_m = \langle m.C.s, m.C.\sigma, m.Map, m.@ \rangle \tag{25}$$

$$\equiv \langle \{c.s\}_{c \in m.C}, \{c.\sigma\}_{c \in m.C}, m.Map, m.@ \rangle \tag{26}$$

By modifying the configuration of a motif we can model:

- *Component dynamism*: The set of component instances $C$ may change by creating/deleting or migrating components;
- *Map dynamism*: The set of nodes or/and the connectivity relation of a map may change. This is the case in particular when an autonomous component e.g. a robot, explores an unknown environment and builds a model of it;
- *Mobility dynamism*: The address function $@$ changes to express mobility of components.

Different types of dynamism can be obtained as the combination of these three basic types.

**Reconfiguration Operations.** Reconfiguration operations realize component, map and mobility dynamism by allowing transformations of a motif configuration at runtime.

Component dynamism can be realized using the following statements:

- *create* $(b, n)$: creates an instance of type $b$ at node $n$ of the relevant map;
- *delete* $(c)$: deletes instance $c$.

Map dynamism can be realized using the following statements:

- *add* $(n)$: adds node $n$ to the relevant map;
- *remove* $(n)$: removes node $n$ from the relevant map, along with incident edges and components mapped to it;
- *add* $(n_1, n_2)$: adds edge $(n_1, n_2)$ to the relevant map;
- *remove* $(n_1, n_2)$: removes edge $(n_1, n_2)$ from the relevant map.

Mobility dynamism can be realized using the following statement:

- *move* $(c, n)$: changes the position of $c$ to node $n$ in the relevant map.

**Operational Semantics of Motifs.** Terms $\rho$ of the coordination language are used to compose component instances in a motif. The latter can evolve from a configuration $\Gamma_m$ to another $\Gamma_m''$ by performing a transition labelled with the interaction $a$ and characterized by the application of the set of operations $[\![\langle\rho\rangle_{\Gamma_m}]\!]_{a,\Gamma_m}$ iff $a \models \langle\rho\rangle_{\Gamma_m}$. Formally this is encoded by the following inference rule:

$$\frac{a \models_{\Gamma_m} \langle\rho\rangle_{\Gamma_m} \qquad \Gamma_m \xrightarrow{a} \Gamma_m' \qquad \Gamma_m'' \in [\![\langle\rho\rangle_{\Gamma_m}]\!]_{a,\Gamma_m}(\Gamma_m')}{\Gamma_m \xrightarrow{a} \Gamma_m''} \qquad (27)$$

- $\Gamma_m \xrightarrow{a} \Gamma_m'$ expresses the capability of the motif to evolve to a new configuration through interaction $a$ according to the simple PIL semantics of (5). By expanding the motif configuration we have indeed:

$$\frac{\forall c.p \in a : c.s \xrightarrow{c.p} c.s' \quad \text{with } c \in m.C}{\langle m.C.s, m.C.\sigma, m.Map, m.@\rangle \xrightarrow{a} \langle m.C.s', m.C.\sigma, m.Map, m.@\rangle} \qquad (28)$$

- $[\![\langle\rho\rangle_{\Gamma_m}]\!]_{a,\Gamma_m}(\Gamma_m')$ is the set of motif configurations obtained by applying the operations $\delta \in [\![\langle\rho\rangle_{\Gamma_m}]\!]_{a,\Gamma_m}$ in every possible order (evaluated using a snapshot semantics).

### 4.4   System-Level Operational Semantics

**Definition 5 (DReAM system).** *Let $B$ be a tuple of component types and $M$ a set of motifs. A DReAM system is a tuple $\langle B, M, \mu, \Gamma_0\rangle$ where $\mu$ is a migration term and $\Gamma_0$ is the initial configuration of the system.*

The migration term $\mu$ is a coordination term where the operations $\delta$ are of the form $migrate(c, m, n)$, which move a component instance $c$ to node $n$ in the map of motif $m$.

The global configuration of a DReAM system is simply the union of the configurations of the set of motifs $M$ that constitute it:

$$\Gamma = \bigsqcup_{m \in M} \Gamma_m = \left\langle \bigcup_m m.C.s, \bigcup_m m.C.\sigma, \bigcup_m m.Map, \bigcup_m m.@ \right\rangle \qquad (29)$$

where we overloaded the semantics of the union operator to combine different maps in a bigger one characterized by the union of the sets of nodes, edges and memory locations.

The system-level semantics is described by the following inference rule:

$$\frac{\Gamma_m \xrightarrow{a_m} \Gamma_m' \text{ for } m \in M \qquad a \models_{\Gamma'} \langle\mu\rangle_{\Gamma'} \qquad \Gamma'' \in [\![\langle\mu\rangle_{\Gamma'}]\!]_{a,\Gamma'}(\Gamma')}{\Gamma \xrightarrow{a} \Gamma''} \qquad (30)$$

- $\Gamma' = \bigsqcup_{m \in M} \Gamma'_m$;
- $a_m \subseteq a$ is a subset of the global interaction $a$ containing only ports of component instances belonging to motif $m$.

By performing interaction $a$ each motif first evolves on its own according to its coordination term, and then the whole system changes configuration according to the migration term $\mu$.

The DReAM coordination language and its semantics have been implemented in Java. The implementation involves two parts: a Java execution engine with an associated API and a domain-specific language (DSL) with an IDE for system modeling in DReAM. Details about the implementation as well as examples of systems modeled in DReAM are provided in the long version of this paper [9].

## 5   Related Work

DReAM allows both conjunctive and disjunctive style modeling of dynamic reconfigurable systems. It inherits the expressiveness of the coordination mechanisms of BIP [8] as it directly encompasses multiparty interaction and extends previous work on modeling parametric architectures [10] in many respects. In DReAM interactions involve not only transfer of values but also encompass reconfiguration and self-organization by relying on the notions of maps and motifs.

When the disjunctive style is adopted, DReAM can be considered as an exogenous coordination language, e.g., an ADL. A comparison with the many ADL's is beyond the scope of the paper. Nonetheless, to the best of our knowledge DReAM surpasses existing exogenous coordination frameworks in that it offers a well-thought and methodologically complete set of primitives and concepts.

When conjunctive style is adopted, DReAM can be used as an endogenous coordination language comparable to process calculi to the extent they rely on a single associative parallel composition operator. In DReAM this operator is logical conjunction. It is easy to show that for existing process calculi parallel composition is a specialization of conjunction in Interaction Logic. For CCS [11] the causal rules are of the form $p \Rightarrow \bar{p}$, where $p$ and $\bar{p}$ are input and output port names corresponding to port symbol $p$. For CSP [12], the causal rules implementing the interface parallel operator parameterized by the channel $a$ are of the form $a_i \Rightarrow \bigwedge_{a_j \in A} a_j$, where $A$ is the set of ports communicating through $a$.

Also other richer calculi, such as $\pi$-calculus [13], that offer the possibility of modeling dynamic infrastructure via channel passing can be modeled in DReAM with its reconfiguration operations. Formalisms with richer communication models, such as AbC [14], offering multicasting communications by selecting groups of partners according to predicates over their attributes, can also be rendered in DReAM. Attribute based interaction can be simulated by our interaction mechanism involving guards on the exchanged values and atomic transfer of values.

DReAM was designed with autonomy in mind. As such it has some similarities with languages for autonomous systems in particular robotic systems such as Buzz [15,16]. Nonetheless, our framework is more general as it does not adopt assumptions about timed synchronous cyclic behavior of components.

The relationships between our approach and graph based architectural description languages such as ADR [17] and HDR [18] will be the subject of future work.

Finally, DReAM shares the same conceptual framework with DR-BIP [19]. The latter is an extension of BIP with component dynamism and reconfiguration. As such it adopts an exogenous and imperative approach based on the use of connectors. A detailed comparison between DReAM and DR-BIP will be the object of a forthcoming publication.

# 6  Discussion

We have proposed a framework for the description of dynamic reconfigurable systems supporting their incremental construction according to a hierarchy of structuring concepts going from components to sets of motifs forming a system. Such a hierarchy guarantees enhanced expressiveness and incremental modifiability thanks to the following features:

**Incremental modifiability of models at all levels:** The interaction rules associated with a component in a motif can be modified and composed independently. Components can be defined independently of the maps and their context of use in a motif. Self-organization can be modeled by combining motifs, i.e., system modes for which particular interaction rules hold.

**Expressiveness:** This is inherited from BIP as the possibility to directly specify any kind of static coordination without modifying the involved components or adding extra coordinating components. Regarding dynamic coordination, the proposed language directly encompasses the identified levels of dynamicity by supporting component types and the expressive power of first order logic. Nonetheless, explicit handling of quantifiers is limited to declarations that link component names to coordinates.

**Flexible Semantics:** The language relies on an operational semantics that admits a variety of implementations between two extreme cases. One consists in precomputing a global interaction constraint applied to an unstructured set of component instances and choosing the enabled interactions and the corresponding operations for a given configuration. The other consists in computing separately interactions for motifs or groups and combining them.

The results about the relationship between conjunctive and disjunctive styles show that while they are both equally expressive for interactions without data transfer, the disjunctive style is more expressive when interactions involve data transfer. We plan to further investigate this relationship to characterize more precisely this limitation that seems to be inherent to modular specification. All results are too recent and many open avenues need to be explored. The language and its tools should be evaluated against real-life mobile applications such as autonomous transport systems, swarm robotics or telecommunication systems.

# References

1. Garlan, D.: Software architecture: a travelogue. In: Proceedings of the on Future of Software Engineering, pp. 29–39. ACM (2014)
2. Taivalsaari, A., Mikkonen, T., Systä, K.: Liquid software manifesto: the era of multiple device ownership and its implications for software architecture. In: Proceedings of the 38th Computer Software and Applications Conference, pp. 338–343. IEEE (2014)
3. Bradbury, J.S.: Organizing definitions and formalisms for dynamic software architectures. Technical report, vol. 477 (2004)
4. Oreizy, P., et al.: Issues in modeling and analyzing dynamic software architectures. In: Proceedings of the International Workshop on the Role of Software Architecture in Testing and Analysis, pp. 54–57 (1998)
5. Malavolta, I., Lago, P., Muccini, H., Pelliccione, P., Tang, A.: What industry needs from architectural languages: a survey. IEEE Trans. Softw. Eng. **39**(6), 869–891 (2013)
6. Butting, A., Heim, R., Kautz, O., Ringert, J.O., Rumpe, B., Wortmann, A.: A classification of dynamic reconfiguration in component and connector architecture description languages. In: Pre-proceedings of the 4th International Workshop on Interplay of Model-Driven and Component-Based Software Engineering, p. 13 (2017)
7. Medvidovic, N., Dashofy, E.M., Taylor, R.N.: Moving architectural description from under the technology lamppost. Inf. Softw. Technol. **49**(1), 12–31 (2007)
8. Bliudze, S., Sifakis, J.: The algebra of connectors - structuring interaction in BIP. IEEE Trans. Comput. **57**(10), 1315–1330 (2008)
9. De Nicola, R., Maggi, A., Sifakis, J.: Dream: Dynamic reconfigurable architecture modeling, arXiv preprint: http://arxiv.org/abs/1805.03724 (2018)
10. Bozga, M., Jaber, M., Maris, N., Sifakis, J.: Modeling dynamic architectures using Dy-BIP. In: Gschwind, T., De Paoli, F., Gruhn, V., Book, M. (eds.) SC 2012. LNCS, vol. 7306, pp. 1–16. Springer, Heidelberg (2012). https://doi.org/10.1007/978-3-642-30564-1_1
11. Milner, R.: A Calculus of Communicating Systems. Springer, Heidelberg (1980). https://doi.org/10.1007/3-540-10235-3
12. Brookes, S.D., Hoare, C.A., Roscoe, A.W.: A theory of communicating sequential processes. J. ACM **31**(3), 560–599 (1984)
13. Milner, R., Parrow, J., Walker, D.: A calculus of mobile processes, I. Inf. Comput. **100**(1), 1–40 (1992)
14. Alrahman, Y.A., De Nicola, R., Loreti, M.: On the power of attribute-based communication. In: Proceedings of the Formal Techniques for Distributed Objects, Components, and Systems - FORTE 2016–36th IFIP WG 6.1 Inernational Conference, pp. 1–18 (2016)
15. Pinciroli, C., Lee-Brown, A., Beltrame, G.: Buzz: An extensible programming language for self-organizing heterogeneous robot swarms, arXiv preprint arXiv:1507.05946 (2015)
16. Pinciroli, C., Beltrame, G.: Buzz: an extensible programming language for heterogeneous swarm robotics. In: 2016 IEEE/RSJ International Conference on Intelligent Robots and Systems (IROS), pp. 3794–3800. IEEE (2016)
17. Bruni, R., Lafuente, A.L., Montanari, U., Tuosto, E.: Style based reconfigurations of software architectures. Universita di Pisa, Technical report TR-07-17 (2007)

18. Bruni, R., Lluch-Lafuente, A., Montanari, U.: Hierarchical design rewriting with Maude. Electron. Notes Theor. Comput. Sci. **238**(3), 45–62 (2009)
19. El Ballouli, R., Bensalem, S., Bozga, M., Sifakis, J.: Four exercises in programming dynamic reconfigurable systems: methodology and solution in DR-BIP. In: Margaria, T., Steffen, B. (eds.) ISoLA 2018. LNCS, vol. 11246, pp. 304–320. Springer, Cham (2018)

# Dynamic Logic for Ensembles

Rolf Hennicker$^{(\boxtimes)}$ and Martin Wirsing

Ludwig-Maximilians-Universität München, Munich, Germany
hennicker@ifi.lmu.de

**Abstract.** An ensemble consists of collaborating entities that are able to adapt at runtime. In this work we consider a particular class of ensembles: an ensemble is formed by a dynamically changing set of entities which interact through message exchange. The members of an ensemble are instances of certain process types. They can be dynamically created to join an ensemble on demand. We propose a dynamic logic to describe the evolution of ensembles from a global perspective. Using the power of dynamic logic with diamond and box modalities over regular expressions of actions (involving message exchange and process creation) we can specify desired and forbidden interaction scenarios. Thus our approach is suitable to write formal requirements specifications for ensemble behaviours. An ensemble realisation takes a local view by giving a constructive specification for each single process type in terms of a process algebraic expression. Correctness of an ensemble realisation is defined semantically: its generated ensemble transition system must be a model of the requirements specification. We consider bisimulation of ensemble transition systems and show that our approach enjoys the Hennessy-Milner property. Moreover, we show that local bisimulation equivalence of process type expressions implies global bisimulation equivalence of the generated ensembles.

**Keywords:** Ensemble · Distributed system · Dynamic logic
Interaction scenario · Bisimulation · Hennessy-Milner theorem

## 1 Introduction

Collective adaptive systems, so-called ensembles, consist of collaborating entities that are able to adapt at runtime. Often the participants of ensembles have their own individual properties and objectives; interactions with other participants may lead to unexpected reactions. Formal methods can help to ensure the quality of ensemble systems and provide tools for modelling and analysing ensembles.

The ASCENS project has developed a systematic process for engineering ensembles [14,15]. Abstract programming and modeling is performed in the language SCEL [4], which is a generic, high-level language for programming autonomic systems. SCEL systems are built from components and can be dynamically extended by creating new components. Communication in SCEL is asynchronous by accessing knowledge repositories. Another ASCENS instance is

© Springer Nature Switzerland AG 2018
T. Margaria and B. Steffen (Eds.): ISoLA 2018, LNCS 11246, pp. 32–47, 2018.
https://doi.org/10.1007/978-3-030-03424-5_3

the DEECo framework [2]; it comprises an explicit programming construct for ensembles such that components can dynamically change their membership in an ensemble. Interaction of ensemble members is implicit and performed via knowledge exchange triggered by the DEECo infrastructure. Explicit message passing between ensemble members is proposed by the HELENA approach [8,12] where an ensemble is constituted by a collection of roles played by components of an underlying component system. The dynamic evolution of an ensemble in HELENA is generated from the role behaviours defined for each role type of an ensemble structure.

The above mentioned approaches provide constructive descriptions of ensemble-based systems. In this paper we add an abstract level on top by studying property-oriented specifications - similarly to "classical" top down development methodologies where only later concrete realisations are constructed which must be correct w.r.t. a given requirements specification. We consider a particular class of realisations: an ensemble realisation consists of a set of concurrent computing entities which collaborate in peer-to-peer manner through synchronous message exchange. The members of an ensemble are instances of certain process types. During ensemble evolution new ensemble participants for certain process types can be dynamically created to join an ensemble.

Specifications are written in a dynamic logic style [5] and describe collaborations which are typical for a certain ensemble. Our logic is tailored to specify complex interaction behaviours from a global perspective. The logic uses diamond and box modalities equipped with regular expressions of actions, like sequential composition and iteration. Atomic actions are either interactions (when an ensemble participant sends a message to another ensemble member) or the creation of a new instance for a certain process type. Additionally we introduce quantification over process instances. Using the power of dynamic logic, with all boolean connectives around, we can thus specify desired and forbidden interaction scenarios. Hence, our approach is suitable to write formal requirements specifications for global, complex interaction behaviours.

Semantic structures of our logic are ensemble transition systems. The semantics of an ensemble specification is given by the class of its models, i.e. by all ensemble transition systems which satisfy the axioms of the specification. This allows us to define a refinement relation between ensemble specifications by model class inclusion. We define a bisimulation relation between ensemble transition systems and show that the validity of ensemble sentences is preserved by ensemble bisimulation. Hence the semantics of an ensemble specification is closed under bisimulation equivalence. Moreover, for image-finite ensemble transition systems the validity of the same sentences implies bisimulation; thus the Hennessy-Milner property holds.

In the last part of this work, we study ensemble realisations and a formal correctness notion. An ensemble realisation takes a local view and specifies a behaviour for each single process type in terms of a process algebraic expression. All instances of the type must respect the prescribed behaviour. The realisation is correct, if the ensemble transition system generated from it satisfies the (logical) sentences of the requirements specification. Then two (bisimulation) equivalent ensemble realisations implement the same requirements specifications. Finally, we show that local bisimulation equivalence of process type expressions implies global bisimulation equivalence of the generated ensembles.

A specification format similar to ensemble realisations has been studied in [7]. There the focus was on open ensembles and their composition. Here we consider closed ensembles but, in contrast to [7], we study a logic for ensemble specifications and a correctness notion. This approach is considered as a first step towards a semantic-based development methodology for ensemble-based systems which later should also include open ensembles and compositionality results, like correctness preserving compositions of ensemble realisations. Moreover, our approach should provide a basis for specifying distributed systems of interacting components and therefore should still be extended to allow for asynchronous communication, like asynchronous multiparty session types [10]. In contrast to our approach, the framework of multiparty session types is strongly influenced by the $\pi$-calculus. It is not aimed at a logic but at process algebraic descriptions of global interaction protocols from which realisations (in the form of sets of local types) can be extracted by projection. An approach to specifying multiparty sessions carrying a logical flavour is given by the global types in [3]. Such global types use also compound actions, like sequential composition and iteration, and, moreover, are able to specify unconstrained composition of parallel activities. But they rely on a fixed number of participants and do not support modalities and negation.

The paper is organised as follows: In Sect. 2 we define syntax and semantics of ensemble specifications and show the invariance of sentences under ensemble bisimulation and the Hennessy-Milner property. Then, in Sect. 3 we study correct ensemble realisations. Some concluding remarks are given in Sect. 4.

## 2    Ensemble Specifications and Bisimulation Invariance

An ensemble specification describes behavioural properties of a system of collaborating entities. It takes a global view of an ensemble focusing on the desired (and not desired) interactions between the participants of an ensemble and on the creation of new ensemble members by demand. Syntactically, an ensemble specification is built over an ensemble signature which defines a set of process types. A process type does not yet fix a particular behaviour. It only determines a number of input and output message types which model the interaction capabilities provided by each instance of a process type. Message and process types are defined mutually recursive as follows:

1. A *message type* $mt$ is of the form $mtnm(pt\,p)$ where $mtnm$ is a (unique) message type name and $p$ is a formal parameter of some process type $pt$.
2. A *process type* $pt = (ptnm, mts_{in}, mts_{out})$ has a (unique) process type name $ptnm$ and sets $mts_{in}$ and $mts_{out}$ of input message types and output messages types respectively supported by $pt$. We write $\mathtt{mts}_{in}[pt]$ for $mts_{in}$, $\mathtt{mts}_{out}[pt]$ for $mts_{out}$, and $\mathtt{mts}[pt]$ for $mts_{in} \cup mts_{out}$.

An *ensemble signature* $\Sigma$ is a set of process types such that for each $pt' \in \Sigma$ and $mtnm(pt\,p) \in \mathtt{mts}[pt']$ we have $pt \in \Sigma$. We write $\mathtt{mts}[\Sigma]$ for the set of all message types used in process types of $\Sigma$. In this paper we consider only closed systems. Therefore we assume that any message type occurring as an input in $\mathtt{mts}_{in}[pt]$ for some $pt \in \Sigma$ occurs also as an output in $\mathtt{mts}_{out}[pt']$ for some $pt' \in \Sigma$, and conversely. Thus, for technical simplicity, we do not consider here open ensembles as in [7] and ensemble composition.

*Example 1.* Throughout this paper we consider a (simplified version of a) file transfer ensemble which runs on a peer-2-peer network supporting the distributed storage of files that can be retrieved upon request. Several peers work together to request and transfer a file: One peer plays the role of a **Requester** of the file, other peers act as **Routers** and the peer storing the requested file adopts the role of a **Provider**. Each kind of role is modelled by a process type whose instances can be created and run on the peer components. The idea of the collaboration is that a requester issues a request for the address of an appropriate provider (message type **reqAddr(Requester req)**). This address request is forwarded by routers through the network until a provider is found. Then the provider address is sent from the last active router to the requester (**sndAddr(Provider prov)**). Finally, the requester asks the provider for the file (**reqFile(Requester req)**) which is then sent to the requester (**sndFile(Provider prov)**). It may also happen that no appropriate provider is found. In this case a router sends a notification to the requester (**notFound(Router rout)**). The ensemble signature of the file transfer ensemble is graphically presented in Fig. 1. The directions of the message type arrows indicate for which process types a message type is input or output or both. Note that for **Router** the message type **reqAddr(Requester req)** is input *and* output since routers may forward address requests to other routers.[1]                                                           □

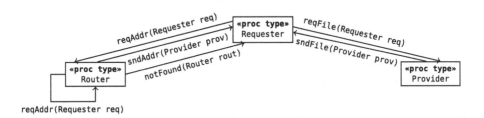

**Fig. 1.** Ensemble signature for the file transfer ensemble

To specify collaborations we use atomic actions and composed actions formed by sequential composition (;), union (+) and iteration (*) borrowed

---

[1] In this paper we do not model the peer components on which the processes run and we do not include parameters for transmitting data, like files. For that purpose we would need the general approach of the HELENA framework first introduced in [8].

from dynamic logic [5]. We assume given a countably infinite set $PVar$ of process instance variables. Three kinds of atomic actions are distinguished where $p, q, r \in PVar$:

(a) a create action $q := p.\mathbf{create}(pt)$ describes when a process $p$ creates a process $q$ of process type $pt$, (b) a communication action $(p \rightarrow q).mtnm(r)$ describes when a process $p$ sends a message to process $q$ transmitting the identity of process $r$, and (c) variable assignment $p := q$ assigns the identity of process $q$ to $p$. In this paper we assume synchronous, binary communication. This means that case (b) describes the simultaneous sending and receiving of the message. The set $Act(\Sigma)$ of $\Sigma$-actions $\alpha$ is defined by the grammar $\alpha ::= a \mid \alpha; \alpha \mid \alpha + \alpha \mid \alpha^*$ where $a$ is an atomic action. The sets $FV(\alpha)$ of free variables and $BV(\alpha)$ of bound variables of an action $\alpha$ are defined as expected where binding of a variable $q$ to process type $pt$ can only happen via a create action $q := p.\mathbf{create}(pt)$.

Besides the usual propositional logic constructs ensemble formulas can compare the identity of processes, they can be a modal formula with (composed) action $\alpha$ or they can be existentially quantified. For any ensemble signature $\Sigma$, the set $Fm(\Sigma)$ of $\Sigma$-formulas is defined by the following grammar

$$\varphi ::= \mathbf{tt} \mid p = q \mid \neg\varphi \mid \varphi \vee \varphi \mid \langle \alpha \rangle \varphi \mid \exists p{:}pt.\varphi$$

where $\alpha \in Act(\Sigma)$ and $p, q \in PVar$. The set $FV(\varphi)$ of free variables of a $\Sigma$-formula $\varphi$ is defined as expected where binding of variables can happen by: $FV(\langle\alpha\rangle\varphi) = FV(\alpha) \cup (FV(\varphi) \setminus BV(\alpha))$ and $FV(\exists p{:}pt.\varphi) = FV(\varphi) \setminus \{p\}$.

A $\Sigma$-sentence is a $\Sigma$-formula $\varphi$ without free variables, i.e. $FV(\varphi) = \emptyset$. The set of $\Sigma$-sentences is denoted by $Sen(\Sigma)$. An *initialisation sentence* is a $\Sigma$-sentence $\varphi$, which does not contain a modality $\langle\alpha\rangle$. The set of initialisation sentences is denoted by $ISen(\Sigma)$. We use the usual abbreviations $\mathbf{ff} = \neg\mathbf{tt}, p \neq q = \neg(p = q), \varphi \wedge \psi = \neg(\neg\varphi \vee \neg\psi), [\alpha]\varphi = \neg\langle\alpha\rangle\neg\varphi, \forall p{:}pt.\varphi = \neg\exists p{:}pt.\neg\varphi$.

For the semantic interpretation we use ensemble transition systems. In the following we assume given, for each ensemble signature $\Sigma$, a set $PId(\Sigma) = \bigcup_{pt\in\Sigma} PId(\Sigma)_{pt}$ being the disjoint union of countably infinite sets $PId(\Sigma)_{pt}$ of process instance identifiers of type $pt \in \Sigma$. An *ensemble state* over $\Sigma$ is a pair $\sigma = (pinsts, c)$ where $pinsts = \bigcup_{pt\in\Sigma} (pinsts_{pt})$ is the disjoint union of finite sets $pinsts_{pt} \subseteq PId(\Sigma)_{pt}$ of currently existing process instances of type $pt$ (similarly to a heap in object-oriented systems) and $c$ is a global control state. The set of ensemble states over $\Sigma$ is denoted by $States(\Sigma)$. If $\sigma = (pinsts, c)$ we write $\mathtt{pinsts}[\sigma]$ for $pinsts$, $\mathtt{pinsts}[\sigma]_{pt}$ for $pinsts_{pt}$ and $\mathtt{ctrl}[\sigma]$ for $c$.

Two kinds of labels are used on transitions which interpret the syntactic actions (a) and (b) from above by using process instance identifiers for process instance variables. A create label $j = i.\mathbf{create}(pt)$ expresses that process instance $i$ creates a process instance $j$ of type $pt \in \Sigma$. A label $(i \rightarrow j).mtnm(k)$ expresses a message exchange where process instance $i$ is the sender, $j$ is the receiver and $k$ is the actual parameter of a message with name $mtnm$. The set of $\Sigma$-labels is denoted by $Lab(\Sigma)$.

Ensemble transition systems constrain the use of labels on transitions by appropriate conditions. For instance, in case (a), when an instance $i$ initiates process creation it must belong to the currently existing instances of the ensemble, the new instance $j$ cannot belong to the ensemble state before creation and the instances in the next ensemble state are just the instances before enriched by $j$ such that $j$ has the desired type $pt$.

**Definition 1 (Ensemble transition system).** *Let $\Sigma$ be an ensemble signature. An* ensemble transition system *over $\Sigma$ (shortly $\Sigma$-ETS) is a tuple $T = (S, S_0, Lab(\Sigma), \rightarrow)$ such that*

- *$S \subseteq States(\Sigma)$ is a set of ensemble states,*
- *$S_0 \subseteq S$ is the set of initial ensemble states, and*
- *$\rightarrow\, \subseteq States(\Sigma) \times Lab(\Sigma) \times States(\Sigma)$ is a transition relation such that for all $(\sigma, l, \sigma') \in\, \rightarrow$ (briefly denoted by $\sigma \xrightarrow{l} \sigma'$) the following well-formedness conditions are satisfied:*
  *(a) if $l$ is of the form $j = i.\mathbf{create}(pt)$ then*
    $pinsts[\sigma'] = pinsts[\sigma] \cup \{j\}, i \in pinsts[\sigma], j \notin pinsts[\sigma]$ *and*
    $j \in pinsts[\sigma']_{pt}$.
  *(b) if $l$ is of the form $(i \rightarrow j).\mathbf{mtnm}(k)$ then*
    $pinsts[\sigma'] = pinsts[\sigma]$ *and there exist a message type $mt \in mts[\Sigma]$ of the form $mtnm(pt\,p)$ and process types $pt', pt'' \in \Sigma$ such that*
    - $mt \in mts_{out}[pt'] \cap mts_{in}[pt''], i \in pinsts[\sigma]_{pt'}, j \in pinsts[\sigma]_{pt''}$, *and*
      $k \in pinsts[\sigma]_{pt}$.

*The class of all ensemble transition systems over $\Sigma$ is denoted by $Trans(\Sigma)$.*

At next we define a satisfaction relation between ensemble transition systems and ensemble formulas. For this purpose, we have to consider environments which map process instance variables to process instance identifiers. Let $\Sigma$ be an ensemble signature. An *environment* is a function $e : PVar \rightarrow PId(\Sigma)$. The set of all environments over $\Sigma$ is denoted by $Env(\Sigma)$. Given an environment $e \in Env(\Sigma)$, a variable $p \in PVar$ and a process instance identifier $i \in PId(\Sigma)$, we can update the environment $e$ at $p$ and write $e[p \mapsto i]$ for the environment with $e[p \mapsto i](p) = i$ and $e[p \mapsto i](q) = e(q)$ for $q \neq p$.

To define the satisfaction relation for formulas of the form $\langle \alpha \rangle \varphi$ with $\alpha \in Act(\Sigma)$ we lift the semantic transition relation $\rightarrow$ of an ETS $T$ to environments and use as labels (composed) actions in $Act(\Sigma)$ containing process instance variables rather than process instance identifiers. Each ensemble transition system $T = (S, S_0, Lab(\Sigma), \rightarrow)$ gives rise to a transition relation

$$\twoheadrightarrow\, \subseteq (States(\Sigma) \times Env(\Sigma)) \times Act(\Sigma) \times (States(\Sigma) \times Env(\Sigma))$$

which is constructed according to the rules in Fig. 2.

The first two rules, (create) and (comm), have transitions of $T$ (denoted by $\rightarrow$) in their premises. The other rules deal with composed actions and have transitions of the form $\twoheadrightarrow$ in their premises. Then, for any state $\sigma$ of $T$ and environment $e \in Env(\Sigma)$ the satisfaction of ensemble formulas in $Fm(\Sigma)$ is inductively defined by

| (create) | $\sigma \xrightarrow{j=e(p).\mathbf{create}(pt)} \sigma'$ |
| | $(\sigma, e) \xrightarrow{q:=p.\mathbf{create}(pt)} (\sigma', e[q \mapsto j])$ |

| (comm) | $\sigma \xrightarrow{(e(p) \to e(q)).mtnm(e(r))} \sigma'$ |
| | $(\sigma, e) \xrightarrow{(p \to q).mtnm(r)} (\sigma', e)$ |

| (assignment) | $(\sigma, e) \xrightarrow{p:=q} (\sigma, e[p \mapsto e(q)])$ |
| | for all $(\sigma, e) \in States(\Sigma) \times Env(\Sigma)$ |

| (seq. composition) | $\dfrac{(\sigma, e) \xrightarrow{\alpha} (\hat{\sigma}, \hat{e}), (\hat{\sigma}, \hat{e}) \xrightarrow{\beta} (\sigma', e')}{(\sigma, e) \xrightarrow{\alpha;\beta} (\sigma', e')}$ |

| (union left) | $\dfrac{(\sigma, e) \xrightarrow{\alpha} (\sigma', e')}{(\sigma, e) \xrightarrow{\alpha+\beta} (\sigma', e')}$ |

| (union right) | $\dfrac{(\sigma, e) \xrightarrow{\beta} (\sigma', e')}{(\sigma, e) \xrightarrow{\alpha+\beta} (\sigma', e')}$ |

| (iteration refl.) | $(\sigma, e) \xrightarrow{\alpha^*} (\sigma, e)$ for all $(\sigma, e) \in States(\Sigma) \times Env(\Sigma)$ |

| (iteration trans.) | $\dfrac{(\sigma, e) \xrightarrow{\alpha^*} (\hat{\sigma}, \hat{e}), (\hat{\sigma}, \hat{e}) \xrightarrow{\alpha} (\sigma', e')}{(\sigma, e) \xrightarrow{\alpha^*} (\sigma', e')}$ |

where $p, q, r \in PVar$ and $j \in PId$.

**Fig. 2.** Lifting from semantic labels to syntactic actions and environments

- $T, \sigma, e \models \mathbf{tt}$,
- $T, \sigma, e \models p = q$ if $e(p) = e(q)$,
- $T, \sigma, e \models \neg\varphi$ if not $T, \sigma, e \models \varphi$,
- $T, \sigma, e \models \varphi \vee \psi$ if $T, \sigma, e \models \varphi$ or $T, \sigma, e \models \psi$,
- $T, \sigma, e \models \langle \alpha \rangle \varphi$ if there exists $(\sigma', e') \in States(\Sigma) \times Env(\Sigma)$ such that $(\sigma, e) \xrightarrow{\alpha} (\sigma', e')$ and $T, \sigma', e' \models \varphi$,
- $T, \sigma, e \models \exists p{:}pt.\varphi$ if there exists $i \in \mathbf{pinsts}[\sigma]_{pt}$ such that $T, \sigma, e[p \mapsto i] \models \varphi$.

If $\varphi \in Sen(\Sigma)$ is a $\Sigma$-sentence the environment is irrelevant and we can write $T, \sigma \models \varphi$. $T$ *satisfies* a $\Sigma$-sentence $\varphi$, denoted by $T \models \varphi$, if $T, \sigma \models \varphi$ for all initial states $\sigma \in S_0$.

**Definition 2 (Ensemble specification and refinement).** *An* ensemble specification *is a triple* $EnsSpec = (\Sigma, \Phi, \phi_0)$ *where* $\Sigma$ *is an ensemble signature,*

$\Phi \subseteq \text{Sen}(\Sigma)$ *is a set of $\Sigma$-sentences, called* axioms *of EnsSpec, and $\phi_0 \in \text{ISen}(\Sigma)$ is an* initialisation axiom. *A model of EnsSpec is a $\Sigma$-ETS which satisfies $\Phi$ and $\phi_0$. The semantics of EnsSpec is given by its model class, i.e. by the class*

$$Mod(EnsSpec) = \{T \in Trans(\Sigma) \mid T \models \varphi \text{ for all } \varphi \in \Phi \cup \{\phi_0\}\}.$$

*An ensemble specification $EnsSpec' = (\Sigma, \Phi', \phi_0')$ is a* refinement *of EnsSpec if $\emptyset \neq Mod(EnsSpec') \subseteq Mod(EnsSpec)$.*

*Example 2.* For the file transfer ensemble introduced in Example 1 we formulate an ensemble specification which requires (a) that there is exactly one initial state with one process instance of type `Requester` and no processes instances for the other types and (b) that a particular primary scenario and an alternative scenario should be feasible in any realisation of a file transfer ensemble. The initialisation axiom $\phi_0$ is

$$(\exists \text{req:Requester}.\forall \text{req':Requester}.\text{req}' = \text{req}) \wedge$$
$$\neg \exists \text{rout:Router}.\mathbf{tt} \wedge \neg \exists \text{prov:Provider}.\mathbf{tt}$$

In a primary scenario a requester starts the collaboration by creating a router process (on its connected peer) and asks the router for the address of a provider. Routers forward the request by creating a next router until a router is found who knows where the file is located. This router creates a provider process and sends the address of the provider to the requester. Finally, the requester asks the provider for the file and the provider sends the file to the requester. This scenario is specified as follows:

Let $\alpha =$
    `rout:=req.create(Router);(req→rout).reqAddr(req);`
    `(rout':=rout.create(Router);(rout→rout').reqAddr(req);rout:=rout')*`
Let $\beta =$
    `prov:=rout.create(Provider);(rout→req).sndAddr(prov);`
    `(req→prov).reqFile(req);(prov→req).sndFile(prov)`
The primary scenario is then specified by the sentence

$$\varphi_1 = \forall \text{req:Requester}.\langle \alpha; \beta \rangle \mathbf{tt}$$

which is the first axiom of our ensemble specification. It allows iterations of arbitrary (but finite) length for forwarding the request to newly created router processes until a provider is found.

Let $\gamma = $ `(rout→req).notFound(rout)` and $\varphi_2 = \forall \text{req:Requester}.[\alpha]\langle \beta + \gamma \rangle \mathbf{tt}$. The sentence $\varphi_2$ is the second axiom of our specification. It says that at any time during a routing phase a successful delivery of the file is possible or a requester is informed by the current router that no provider is found. Let us still note that by relaxing the initialisation axiom we could allow the existence of several requesters and then the semantics of the specification would allow the concurrent execution of several file transfer ensembles at the same time.    □

As an equivalence relation for ETSs we use ensemble bisimulation. In contrast to the usual bisimulation relation between processes, special care must be taken about the treatment of process instances. Similarly to [7], we abstract from the particular names of process instances by using, for related ensemble states $\sigma_1 = (pinsts_1, c_1)$ and $\sigma_2 = (pinsts_2, c_2)$, a bijective mapping between $pinsts_1$ and $pinsts_2$. More precisely, we consider process type preserving bijections $\kappa :$ $\mathrm{pinsts}[\sigma_1] \to \mathrm{pinsts}[\sigma_2]$ with $\kappa(\mathrm{pinsts}[\sigma_1]_{pt}) = \mathrm{pinsts}[\sigma_1]_{pt}$ for all $pt \in \Sigma$. Therefore, our bisimulation relation is ternary and relates ensemble states in accordance with a bijection between their process instances.

**Definition 3 (Ensemble bisimulation).** *Let $\Sigma$ be an ensemble signature and $T_1 = (S_1, S_{1,0}, Lab(\Sigma), \to_1)$ and $T_2 = (S_2, S_{2,0}, Lab(\Sigma), \to_2)$ be two ETSs over $\Sigma$. Let $\Delta = \{(\sigma_1, \sigma_2, \kappa) \mid \sigma_1 \in S_1, \sigma_2 \in S_2, \kappa : pinsts[\sigma_1] \to pinsts[\sigma_2]$ is bijective and process type preserving$\}$. A bisimulation relation between $T_1$ and $T_2$ is a relation $R \subseteq \Delta$, such that for all $(\sigma_1, \sigma_2, \kappa) \in R$ the following holds:*

*(1.1)* If $\sigma_1 \xrightarrow{j_1 = i_1.\mathbf{create}(pt)}_1 \sigma_1'$ then there exist $\sigma_2'$ and
$\sigma_2 \xrightarrow{j_2 = \kappa(i_1).\mathbf{create}(pt)}_2 \sigma_2'$ such that $(\sigma_1', \sigma_2', \kappa') \in R$ with $\kappa' = \kappa[j_1 \mapsto j_2]$.

*(1.2)* If $\sigma_1 \xrightarrow{(i_1 \to j_1).mtnm(k_1)}_1 \sigma_1'$ then there exist $\sigma_2'$ and
$\sigma_2 \xrightarrow{(\kappa(i_1) \to \kappa(j_1)).mtnm(\kappa(k_1))}_2 \sigma_2'$ such that $(\sigma_1', \sigma_2', \kappa) \in R$.

*(2.1)* If $\sigma_2 \xrightarrow{j_2 = i_2.\mathbf{create}(pt)}_2 \sigma_2'$ then there exist $\sigma_1'$ and
$\sigma_1 \xrightarrow{j_1 = \kappa^{-1}(i_2).\mathbf{create}(pt)}_1 \sigma_1'$ such that $(\sigma_1', \sigma_2', \kappa') \in R$ with $\kappa' = \kappa[j_1 \mapsto j_2]$.

*(2.2)* If $\sigma_2 \xrightarrow{(i_2 \to j_2).mtnm(k_2)}_2 \sigma_2'$ then there exist $\sigma_1'$ and
$\sigma_1 \xrightarrow{(\kappa^{-1}(i_2) \to \kappa^{-1}(j_2)).mtnm(\kappa^{-1}(k_2))}_1 \sigma_1'$ such that $(\sigma_1', \sigma_2', \kappa) \in R$.

*$T_1$ and $T_2$ are bisimulation equivalent, denoted by $T_1 \sim_e T_2$, if there exists a bisimulation relation $R \subseteq \Delta$ between $T_1$ and $T_2$ such that for all $\sigma_1 \in S_{1,0}$ there exists $\sigma_2 \in S_{2,0}$ and $\kappa_0$ such that $(\sigma_1, \sigma_2, \kappa_0) \in R$ and, conversely, for all $\sigma_2 \in S_{2,0}$ there exists $\sigma_1 \in S_{1,0}$ and $\kappa_0$ such that $(\sigma_1, \sigma_2, \kappa_0) \in R$.*

The following theorem shows that satisfaction of sentences is invariant under ensemble bisimulation. The proof relies on the fact that any bisimulation relation between two ETSs $T_1$ and $T_2$ can be lifted from semantic labels to syntactic labels, i.e. actions in $Act(\Sigma)$. If in addition, the two ETSs are image-finite[2] then also the converse holds. Thus the modal logic for ensembles satisfies the Hennessy-Milner property.

**Theorem 1 (Invariance theorem).** *Let $T_1$ and $T_2$ be two $\Sigma$-ETSs.*

*(1)* If $T_1 \sim_e T_2$ then for any ensemble sentence $\varphi \in Sen(\Sigma)$, $T_1 \models \varphi$ iff $T_2 \models \varphi$.

---

[2] This means that in any state there are at most finitely many outgoing transitions labelled with the same action. In particular, this means for any create action (see Definition 1(a)), the instance $j$ should be chosen from a finite set of new instances.

*(2) If $T_1$ and $T_2$ are image-finite then the converse of (1) holds, i.e. if for any ensemble sentence $\varphi \in \mathrm{Sen}(\Sigma)$, $T_1 \models \varphi$ iff $T_2 \models \varphi$ holds, then $T_1 \sim_e T_2$.*

As a consequence of (1), the model class *Mod(EnsSpec)* of an ensemble specification *EnsSpec* is closed under bisimulation equivalence.

## 3   Ensemble Realisations

In this section we propose a method to realise an ensemble specification in a constructive way following the ideas of the specification method in [7]. An ensemble realisation defines, for each process type *pt* of an ensemble signature $\Sigma$, a behaviour which must be respected by all instances of *pt* participating in an ensemble. Behaviours are described by process type expressions which are built from the process constructs and actions defined by the following grammar[3]

$$P :: = \mathbf{nil} \mid a.P \mid P_1 + P_2 \mid pt$$
$$a :: = X := \mathbf{create}(pt) \mid ?mtnm(ptX) \mid !Y.mtnm(X)$$

where *pt* ranges over the process types in $\Sigma$, $X$ and $Y$ are process instance variables and *mtnm* ranges over the names of message types in $\mathtt{mts}[\Sigma]$. The set of process type expressions over $\Sigma$ is denoted by *PExp($\Sigma$)*. **nil** denotes the null process, $aP$ action prefix, $P_1 + P_2$ nondeterministic choice and *pt* process type invocation. In contrast to atomic ensemble actions in *Act($\Sigma$)*, process type expressions contain receive and send actions seen from the perspective of a single process. A receive action $?mtnm(ptX)$ expresses that the current process is enabled to receive a message with an actual value of type *pt* which will be stored in the local variable $X$ of the process. A send action $!Y.mtnm(X)$ expresses that the current process is enabled to send a message to the process instance, denoted by (local) variable $Y$, carrying the current value of variable $X$ as actual parameter. A create action $X := \mathbf{create}(pt)$ expresses that the current process instance is enabled to create an instance of type *pt* which will be stored in the local variable $X$ of the current process. Create actions and receive actions open a local scope for variable $X$. We assume that the names of those variables are different from the predefined variable **self** which can always be used as an actual parameter to transmit the identity of a process instance for possible callbacks.

**Definition 4 (Ensemble realisation).** *An ensemble realisation is a triple EnsReal = $(\Sigma, Reals, pinsts_0)$ where $\Sigma$ is an ensemble signature, $Reals = \{pt = P_{pt} \mid pt \in \Sigma\}$ is a set of process type realisations with $P_{pt}$ a process type expression over $\Sigma$, and $pinsts_0$ is a non-empty set of process instance identifiers which exist in the initial state of ensemble execution.*

The semantics of an ensemble realisation is given in terms of an ensemble transition system. In this case the global control state $c$ of an ensemble state

---

[3] A more expressive syntax dealing with data and guards can be found in [12].

$\sigma = (pinsts, c)$ has a particular form: it is a function $c : pinsts \rightarrow LStates(\Sigma)$ assigning to each currently existing process instance $i \in pinsts$ a local state. A *local state* is a pair $l = (v, P)$ where $v$ is valuation of the local variables of a process instance $i$ and $P$ is a process expression recording the current computation state of $i$. We write $\mathtt{val}[l]$ for $v$ and $\mathtt{proc}[l]$ for $P$. The set of all local states over $\Sigma$ is denoted by $LStates(\Sigma)$. A *local variable valuation* is a partial function $v : PVar \rightarrow PId(\Sigma)$. The definition domain of $v$ contains the currently available local variables of a process instance. The set of all local variable valuations is denoted by $Val(\Sigma)$. Given a valuation $v$, a variable $X \in PVar$ and a process instance identifier $i \in PId(\Sigma)$, we can update $v$ at $X$ and write $v[X \mapsto i]$ for the valuation with $v[X \mapsto i](X) = i$ and $v[X \mapsto i](Y) = v(Y)$ for $Y \neq X$. The valuation with empty definition domain is denoted by $\emptyset$.

An ensemble realisation $EnsReal = (\Sigma, Reals, pinsts_0)$ determines the set of process instances when the ensemble starts its execution. This set determines also a starting control state of the ensemble: an *initial ensemble realisation state* of $EnsReal$ is the state $\sigma_0$ with $\mathtt{pinsts}[\sigma_0] = pinsts_0$ and, for all $pt \in \Sigma$ and $i \in \mathtt{pinsts}[\sigma_0]_{pt}$, $\mathtt{ctrl}[\sigma_0](i) = (\emptyset[\mathbf{self} \mapsto i], P_{pt})$ if $pt = P_{pt} \in Reals$.

In contrast to ensemble specifications (with loose semantics), an ensemble realisation determines a unique ensemble transition system. Structural operational semantics (SOS) rules define the allowed transitions. We pursue an incremental approach, similar to the Fork Calculus in [6], by splitting the semantics into two different layers. The first layer describes how a process type expression evolves according to the given constructs for process type expressions. The second layer builds on the first one by defining the evolution of ensemble realisation states.

*Evolution of process type expressions:* The first level formalises the progress of a single process expression. Figure 3 defines the SOS rules inductively over the structure of process type expressions. The rule for process type invocation relies on a given process type realisation, which is given in an ensemble realisation. We use the symbol $\hookrightarrow$ for transitions on the process type expression level.

| | |
|---|---|
| (action prefix) | $a.P \overset{a}{\hookrightarrow} P$ |
| (choice-left) | $\dfrac{P_1 \overset{a}{\hookrightarrow} P_1'}{P_1 + P_2 \overset{a}{\hookrightarrow} P_1'}$ |
| (choice-right) | $\dfrac{P_2 \overset{a}{\hookrightarrow} P_2'}{P_1 + P_2 \overset{a}{\hookrightarrow} P_2'}$ |
| (process type invocation) | $\dfrac{pt = P_{pt} \in Reals, \ P_{pt} \overset{a}{\hookrightarrow} P'}{pt \overset{a}{\hookrightarrow} P'}$ |

**Fig. 3.** SOS rules for process type expressions

*Evolution of Ensembles:* On the next level we consider ensemble realisation states and their transitions denoted by $\rightarrow$ in Fig. 4.

(create)
$$\dfrac{P_i \xrightarrow{X:=\textbf{create}(pt)} P_i'}{\sigma \xrightarrow{\textit{fresh}(\sigma,pt)=i.\textbf{create}(pt)} \sigma'}$$

whenever $i \in \text{pinsts}[\sigma], \text{proc}[\text{ctrl}[\sigma](i)] = P_i$,
$\text{pinsts}[\sigma'] = \text{pinsts}[\sigma] \cup \{\textit{fresh}(\sigma,pt)\}$, and
$\text{ctrl}[\sigma'] = \text{ctrl}[\sigma][i \mapsto (\text{val}[\text{ctrl}[\sigma](i)][X \mapsto \textit{fresh}(\sigma,pt)], P_i')]$
$$[\textit{fresh}(\sigma,pt) \mapsto (\emptyset[\textbf{self} \mapsto \textit{fresh}(\sigma,pt)], P_{pt})]$$
where $pt = P_{pt} \in \textit{Reals}$.

(comm)
$$\dfrac{P_i \xrightarrow{!Y.mtnm(Z)} P_i', \; P_j \xrightarrow{?mtnm(ptX)} P_j'}{\sigma \xrightarrow{(i \rightarrow j).mtnm(k)} \sigma'}$$

whenever there exist $pt', pt'' \in \Sigma$ such that
$mtnm(ptX) \in \text{mts}_{out}[pt'] \cap \text{mts}_{in}[pt''], i \in \text{pinsts}[\sigma]_{pt'}$,
$j \in \text{pinsts}[\sigma]_{pt''}, \text{val}[\text{ctrl}[\sigma](i)](Y) = j$,
$k \in \text{pinsts}[\sigma]_{pt}, \text{val}[\text{ctrl}[\sigma](i)](Z) = k$,
$\text{proc}[\text{ctrl}[\sigma](i)] = P_i, \text{proc}[\text{ctrl}[\sigma](j)] = P_j$,
$\text{pinsts}[\sigma'] = \text{pinsts}[\sigma]$, and
$\text{ctrl}[\sigma'] = \text{ctrl}[\sigma][i \mapsto (\text{val}[\text{ctrl}[\sigma](i)], P_i')]$
$$[j \mapsto (\text{val}[\text{ctrl}[\sigma](j)][X \mapsto k], P_j')].$$

**Fig. 4.** Semantics of ensemble realisations

The transitions in Fig. 4 are derived as follows: create actions $X := \textbf{create}(pt)$ on the process type level cause the creation of a new process instance in a given ensemble state $\sigma = (pinsts, c)$. We use the notation $fresh(\sigma, pt)$ to refer to the choice of a unique element in $PId_{pt}$ which does not belong to $pinsts_{pt}$. Since $PId_{pt}$ is countably infinite and $pinsts_{pt}$ is finite this is always possible. Let us now consider communication inside an ensemble by message exchange. In the semantics presented here we use synchronous, binary communication - rule (comm) - where message output and message input are performed simultaneously when process instances are able to communicate. If several process instances are able to communicate the choice is non-deterministic. If desired, it would be straightforward to adapt our formalism to asynchronous communication by introducing message buffers as done in [9]. Also broadcast communication could be easily defined by adjusting the rules appropriately.

**Definition 5 (Semantics of an ensemble realisation).** *The semantics of an ensemble realisation* $EnsReal = (\Sigma, Reals, pinsts_0)$ *is the ensemble transition* *system* $[\![EnsReal]\!] = (S, S_0, Lab(\Sigma), \rightarrow)$ *where* $S_0 = \{\sigma_0\}$ *consists of the initial ensemble realisation state of EnsReal and* $S$, $\rightarrow$ *are generated from* $S_0$ *by applying the rules in Figs. 3 and 4.*

Note that the rules in Fig. 4 guarantee the constraints for an ensemble transition system and preserve the condition for ensemble realisation states. In rule (create) the local variable $X$ of $i$ is introduced (or updated) by assigning the new process instance identifier to $X$. Similarly, in rule (comm) the local variable $X$ of $j$ is introduced (or updated) by assigning the actual parameter $k$ to $X$.

Two ensemble realisations $EnsReal_1$ and $EnsReal_2$ with the same signature $\Sigma$ are *equivalent* if $[\![EnsReal_1]\!] \sim_e [\![EnsReal_1]\!]$.

Our semantic notions lead to an obvious correctness definition for ensemble specifications and their realisations:

**Definition 6 (Correct ensemble realisation).** *Let* $EnsSpec = (\Sigma, \Phi, pinsts_0)$ *be an ensemble specification and* $EnsReal = (\Sigma, Reals, pinsts_0)$ *be an ensemble realisation over the same signature* $\Sigma$. *EnsReal is a correct realisation of EnsSpec if* $[\![EnsReal]\!] \in Mod(EnsSpec)$.

*Example 3.* We provide a realisation of the file transfer ensemble which satisfies the specification in Example 2. For each of the three process types a behaviour is defined in Fig. 5. Initially there exists exactly one process instance of type `Requester` and no instances for the other process types.[4]                    □

```
procBehaviour Requester =
   router := create(Router) .
   !router.reqAddr(self) .
   ( ?sndAddr(Provider prov) .
     !prov.reqFile(self) .
     ?sndFile(Provider pr) .
     nil)
   +
   ( ?notFound(Router ro) .
     nil)

procBehaviour Provider =
   ?reqFile(Requester req) .
   !req.sndFile(self) .
   nil
```

```
procBehaviour Router =
   ?reqAddr(Requester req) .
   ( router := create(Router) .
     !router.reqAddr(req) .
     nil)
   +
   ( prov := create(Provider) .
     !req.sndAddr(prov) .
     nil)
   +
   ( !req.notFound(self) .
     nil)
```

**Fig. 5.** Realisation of the file transfer ensemble

As an immediate consequence of Theorem 1(1) we obtain:

**Theorem 2 (Equivalent correct ensemble realisations).** *Let EnsSpec be an ensemble specification and* $EnsReal_1$ *and* $EnsReal_2$ *be two equivalent ensemble realisations. Then* $EnsReal_1$ *is a correct realisation of EnsSpec if and only if* $EnsReal_2$ *is a correct realisation of EnsSpec.*

---

[4] A formal proof that the realisation is correct must be done by semantic reasoning. Other verification techniques are an objective of future research.

It remains the question how to prove that two ensemble realisations are equivalent? The idea is to verify that for each process type $pt \in \Sigma$ the local process type expressions used for the behaviour definition of $pt$ in the two ensemble realisations are bisimulation equivalent in the usual sense of process algebra where bisimulation is defined as follows: a *bisimulation relation* for process type expressions over $\Sigma$ is a relation $R_p \subseteq PExp(\Sigma) \times PExp(\Sigma)$, such that for all $(P_1, P_2) \in R_p$ the following holds:

(1) If $P_1 \overset{a}{\hookrightarrow} P_1'$ then there exist $P_2'$ and $P_2 \overset{a}{\hookrightarrow} P_2'$ such that $(P_1', P_2') \in R_p$.
(2) If $P_2 \overset{a}{\hookrightarrow} P_2'$ then there exist $P_1'$ and $P_1 \overset{a}{\hookrightarrow} P_1'$ such that $(P_1', P_2') \in R_p$.

Two process type expressions $P_1, P_2 \in PExp(\Sigma)$ are *bisimulation equivalent*, denoted by $P_1 \sim_p P_2$, if there exists a bisimulation $R_p$ with $(P_1, P_2) \in R_p$.

Finally we show that local bisimulation equivalence of process type behaviours defined in ensemble realisations $EnsReal_1$ and $EnsReal_2$ implies global bisimulation equivalence of their generated ensemble transition systems.

**Theorem 3 (Proving equivalence of ensemble realisations).** *Let $EnsReal_1 = (\Sigma, Reals_1, pinsts_{1,0})$ and $EnsReal_2 = (\Sigma, Reals_2, pinsts_{2,0})$ be two ensemble realisations with $Reals_1 = \{pt = P_{1,pt} \mid pt \in \Sigma\}$ and $Reals_2 = \{pt = P_{2,pt} \mid pt \in \Sigma\}$ resp. If $P_{1,pt} \sim_p P_{2,pt}$ for all $pt \in \Sigma$ and if there exists a process type preserving bijection $\kappa : pinsts_{1,0} \rightarrow pinsts_{2,0}$, then $[\![EnsReal_1]\!] \sim_e [\![EnsReal_2]\!]$.*

*Proof.* Let $[\![EnsReal_k]\!] = (S_k, S_{k,0}, Lab(\Sigma), \rightarrow_k)$ be the ETSs of $EnsReal_k, k = 1, 2$. Then the following relation $B$ is an ensemble bisimulation. $B$ is defined by $(\sigma_1, \sigma_2, \kappa) \in B$ if the following three conditions hold:

(1) $\sigma_1 \in S_1, \sigma_2 \in S_2$,
(2) $\kappa : \texttt{pinsts}[\sigma_1] \rightarrow \texttt{pinsts}[\sigma_2]$ *is bijective and process type preserving*,
(3) for all $i \in pinsts[\sigma_1]$ and all $(v_1, P_1), (v_2, P_2)$ with $\texttt{ctrl}[\sigma_1](i) = (v_1, P_1)$ and $\texttt{ctrl}[\sigma_2](i) = (v_2, P_2)$ we have
   – $P_1 \sim_p P_2$,
   – the domains of $v_1$ and $v_2$ coincide, and
   – $\kappa(v_1(X)) = v_2(X)$ for all $X$ in the domain of $v_1$.

□

## 4   Conclusion

We have presented a first step towards the formal development of ensemble-based systems. Abstract requirements specifications are based on a novel logic which uses ideas from dynamic logic and allows us to express collaborations from the global perspective. The logic should be useful for any kind of distributed systems where cooperation is a central requirement. It is also useful to specify allowed and forbidden scenarios which underlie use case driven approaches to software development. Our logic differs from temporal logics (as used e.g. in [9] for the verification of HELENA models) since it focuses on interactions and scenarios. Of course, more case studies are still needed to validate the power of our logic. For the concrete construction of ensembles we consider ensemble realisations. They define a process algebraic expression for each process type used in an ensemble specification. Ensemble realisations and can be directly implemented using, for instance, the implementation framework of HELENA [13].

Our approach focuses on ensembles as first-class artifacts following a clear separation between syntax and semantics. In particular, we have shown that the sentences of our logic are invariant under ensemble bisimulation. Moreover we have provided a criterion for proving equivalence of ensemble realisations. There are many aspects for future research: extending the approach to components which can play different active roles as in HELENA (and thus being adaptive by changing roles [11]), studying open ensembles and their composition along the lines of [7], investigating more proof methods and developing tools.

Another direction concerns the support of asynchronous, multi-cast messages. A particular powerful approach is attribute-based communication which determines communication partners dynamically by evaluating predicates over component attributes; see [1]. Such communication can be seen as a volatile ensemble. Our approach, however, considers ensembles of longer durations and more complex collaborations performed by an ensemble to pursue a particular goal. Currently an ensemble specification describes the behaviour of one kind of ensemble but we are interested to take up the ideas for more flexible formations of ensembles and to build a logical framework which supports the dynamic creation of ensembles and their cooperation.

**Acknowledgement.** We are grateful to the reviewers of this paper for their useful hints and remarks.

# References

1. Abd Alrahman, Y., De Nicola, R., Loreti, M.: On the power of attribute-based communication. In: Albert, E., Lanese, I. (eds.) FORTE 2016. LNCS, vol. 9688, pp. 1–18. Springer, Cham (2016). https://doi.org/10.1007/978-3-319-39570-8_1
2. Bures, T., Gerostathopoulos, I., Hnetynka, P., Keznikl, J., Kit, M., Plasil, F.: DEECO: an ensemble-based component system. In: Proceedings of the 16th ACM SIGSOFT Symposium on Component Based Software Engineering (CBSE 2013), pp. 81–90. ACM (2013)
3. Castagna, G., Dezani-Ciancaglini, M., Padovani, L.: On global types and multi-party sessions. Log. Methods Comput. Sci. 8(1), 1–45 (2012)
4. De Nicola, R., Loreti, M., Pugliese, R., Tiezzi, F.: A formal approach to autonomic systems programming: the SCEL language. ACM Trans. Auton. Adapt. Syst. (TAAS) 9(2), 1–29 (2014)
5. Harel, D., Kozen, D., Tiuryn, J. (eds.): Dynamic Logic. MIT Press, Cambridge (2000)
6. Havelund, K., Larsen, K.G.: The fork calculus. In: Lingas, A., Karlsson, R., Carlsson, S. (eds.) ICALP 1993. LNCS, vol. 700, pp. 544–557. Springer, Heidelberg (1993). https://doi.org/10.1007/3-540-56939-1_101

7. Hennicker, R.: A calculus for open ensembles and their composition. In: Margaria, T., Steffen, B. (eds.) ISoLA 2016. LNCS, vol. 9952, pp. 570–588. Springer, Cham (2016). https://doi.org/10.1007/978-3-319-47166-2_40

8. Hennicker, R., Klarl, A.: Foundations for ensemble modeling – the HELENA approach. In: Iida, S., Meseguer, J., Ogata, K. (eds.) Specification, Algebra, and Software. LNCS, vol. 8373, pp. 359–381. Springer, Heidelberg (2014). https://doi.org/10.1007/978-3-642-54624-2_18

9. Hennicker, R., Klarl, A., Wirsing, M.: Model-checking HELENA ensembles with Spin. In: Martí-Oliet, N., Ölveczky, P.C., Talcott, C. (eds.) Logic, Rewriting, and Concurrency. LNCS, vol. 9200, pp. 331–360. Springer, Cham (2015). https://doi.org/10.1007/978-3-319-23165-5_16

10. Honda, K., Yoshida, N., Carbone, M.: Multiparty asynchronous session types. In: Proceedings of the 35th Annual ACM SIGPLAN-SIGACT Symposium on Principles of Programming Languages (POPL 2008), pp. 273–284. ACM (2008)

11. Klarl, A.: Engineering self-adaptive systems with the role-based architecture of HELENA. In: Proceedings of the 24th IEEE International Conference on Enabling Technologies: Infrastructure for Collaborative Enterprises, WETICE 2015, pp. 3–8. IEEE Computer Society (2015)

12. Klarl, A.: HELENA: Handling massively distributed systems with ELaborate ENsemble Architectures. Ph.D. thesis, LMU Munich, Germany (2016)

13. Klarl, A., Cichella, L., Hennicker, R.: From HELENA ensemble specifications to executable code. In: Lanese, I., Madelaine, E. (eds.) FACS 2014. LNCS, vol. 8997, pp. 183–190. Springer, Cham (2015). https://doi.org/10.1007/978-3-319-15317-9_11

14. Wirsing, M., Hölzl, M., Koch, N., Mayer, P. (eds.): Software Engineering for Collective Autonomic Systems. LNCS, vol. 8998. Springer, Cham (2015). https://doi.org/10.1007/978-3-319-16310-9

15. Wirsing, M., Hölzl, M., Tribastone, M., Zambonelli, F.: ASCENS: engineering autonomic service-component ensembles. In: Beckert, B., Damiani, F., de Boer, F.S., Bonsangue, M.M. (eds.) FMCO 2011. LNCS, vol. 7542, pp. 1–24. Springer, Heidelberg (2013). https://doi.org/10.1007/978-3-642-35887-6_1

# Modelling the Transition to Distributed Ledgers

Jan Sürmeli[1,2]([✉]), Stefan Jähnichen[1,2], and Jeff W. Sanders[3]

[1] Technische Universität Berlin, Berlin, Germany
{jan.suermeli,stefan.jaehnichen}@tu-berlin.de
[2] FZI Forschungszentrum Informatik am Karlsruher
Institut für Technologie, Karlsruhe, Germany
{jan.suermeli,stefan.jaehnichen}@fzi.de
[3] African Institute for Mathematical Sciences, Muizenberg, South Africa
jsanders@aims.ac.za

**Abstract.** The emergence of Distributed Ledger Technologies and Cryptocurrencies impacts on how transactions of various assets between parties in highly dynamical settings – such as the Internet of Things or Smart Cities – are modelled and implemented in several ways. We study this transition from centralized accounts with explicit owners towards distributed ledgers with challenge-based transaction access control. We capture the transition in a series of linked formal specifications in $Z$, enabling the comparison between the two settings. In particular, we provide a reference model and then refine it for the respective settings.

**Keywords:** Distributed ledger · Blockchain · Z · Formal specification

## 1 Introduction

The interconnected participants of the Internet of Things – such as humans, institutions, personal devices, sensors, containers or vehicles – autonomously exchange values, material goods, services, privileges and data in order to reach individual or common goals. These transactions of assets are recorded in ledgers, and new transactions are authorised based on existing records. In highly dynamic settings, such as in Smart Cities, participants may join and leave, and thus the topology of the underlying network is subject to change. Moreover, participants cooperate on a case by case basis instead of long-lasting partnerships, forming ensembles of components [5,17]. As a result, there is a general lack of trust between the participants, and the synchronisation of local ledgers is thus realised by a combination of double-entry bookkeeping and settlement through centralised trusted instances (cf. Fig. 1a).

Distributed Ledger Technologies [2,9–12,14–16,18] aim at reducing these synchronisation efforts: A distributed ledger is maintained by a peer-to-peer network based on a consensus protocol and cryptographic security measures tailored to the given use case. Generally, the goal is to allow the participants to prove the

© Springer Nature Switzerland AG 2018
T. Margaria and B. Steffen (Eds.): ISoLA 2018, LNCS 11246, pp. 48–62, 2018.
https://doi.org/10.1007/978-3-030-03424-5_4

validity of a transaction without requiring centralised trusted parties. The role of the distributed ledger varies based on the use case: In some cases, such as cryptocurrencies, the ledger stores the full transaction, and the participants of the transaction merely hold pointers and associated cryptographic keys in a wallet. In other cases, particularly for transferring more complex assets, the distributed ledger holds merely hashes of entries of local ledgers, where the actual transaction data is stored.

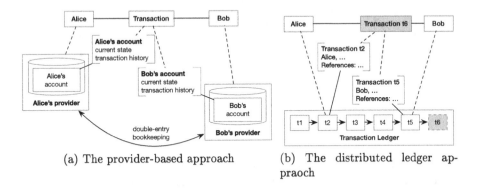

(a) The provider-based approach

(b) The distributed ledger approach

**Fig. 1.** Different approaches to transaction management

While local ledgers and centralised trusted parties rely on accounts to control access to assets, distributed ledgers identify participants differently (c.f. Fig. 1b): In its most basic form, a challenge – a function in a predefined programming language – is specified in order to guard an asset: Whoever can provide a solution for the challenge gains access. Usually, this solution contains cryptographic methods such as hashing a public key or checking a digital signature. Smart contracts or chain code further generalise this concept.

Hence, developing systems based on distributed ledgers varies from more traditional implementations. Moreover, given a system design for both approaches, it is a non-trivial task to define – let alone decide – their equivalence. This is further impeded by a plethora of implementations for distributed ledgers, varying in scope, features and maturity.

Our contribution is to construct a link between the two approaches by a series of specifications in the $Z$ notation [1, 13]: We start with a reference specification (Sect. 3) that captures the common concepts and serves as a 'greatest common divisor' of the two approaches. Then, we refine the specification for the provider-based and distributed setting in Sects. 4 and 5, respectively. The main focus of our work is the $Z$-specification of distributed ledgers in Sect. 5.

The scope for our specification is explained by using an example in Sect. 2. We present first insights in Sect. 6, discuss related work in Sect. 7, and conclude in Sect. 8.

## 2   Scope

In this section, we describe the scope of our series of specifications in Sects. 3, 4 and 5 by means of an example, culminating in the lifecycle of a transaction as visualised in Fig. 2.

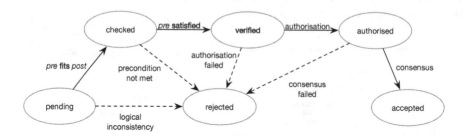

**Fig. 2.** The life cycle of a transaction

A transaction describes the usage or transfer of assets (e.g. material goods, services, privileges, data) by participants (e.g. persons, institutions, cars, devices) of a process. For example, consider an auction process [7, Chap. 9] auction where Alice offers a product that other participants can bid on. This process contains at least two transactions: A transaction bid where a bidder puts a bid on the item, and a transaction payment, where the auction winner pays for the item and gains an owner certificate.

As determined by the process and its context, in order to be consistent, a transaction $t$ requires a set ${}^\bullet t$ of *preconditions* to be fulfilled. Similarly, a transaction yields a set $t^\bullet$ of *postconditions*. A precondition or postcondition could require or indicate access to a specific asset, membership in a group, or compliance to law. Whether the preconditions fit to the postconditions depends on the underlying business logics.

Continuing our example, we first regard the transaction payment which will occur after the auction winner Bob has been chosen: Bob transfers funds to Alice. Presumably, there is a precondition solvency $\in {}^\bullet$payment stating that Bob has access to the funds to be transferred, and a postcondition transferred $\in$ payment${}^\bullet$ stating that Bob and Alice have lost and gained access to these funds, respectively. Now, consider the earlier transaction bid, describing Bob's bid on an item offered by Alice. Here, both solvency $\in {}^\bullet$bid and solvency $\notin {}^\bullet$bid are generally feasible, and the choice depends on the exact use case. However, bidding could require to be registered to the auction platform, so we could have a precondition registered $\in {}^\bullet$bid stating that Bob is registered to the platform.

The preconditions of a transaction are generally evaluated on the global state of a system. In a concurrent system, the preconditions likely only refer to the local states of parts of the system. For instance, the precondition solvency could be evaluated on some *account* of Bob at a specific bank – the state of other banks or other accounts at the same bank do not influence the precondition.

Following current developments in cryptocurrencies, solvency could instead be evaluated on a *ledger* holding the *transaction history* of all transactions regarding a given cryptocurrency. The precondition registered could be authorised by checking user credentials, or based on the postconditions of a previously occurred transaction register found in a ledger.

Apart from the preconditions of a transaction, the execution of a transaction may require *authorisation* by network participants: Usually, access to assets is restricted in certain ways. Sticking to the example process auction, the transactions bid and payment must at least be authorised by Bob, and there could be further restrictions: For instance, buying the item could require a license or minimum age. If Bob transfers the funds from a bank account, he likely has to provide credentials to prove that he owns the account in question. If Bob instead transfers the funds in a ledger-based cryptocurrency, the authorization process will probably look different: Instead of providing credentials, Bob will instead solve a cryptographic *challenge* in order to authorise the transaction, for instance by digitally signing a message or providing a zero-knowledge proof [8].

In a concurrent system, it could occur that a precondition of a transaction is no longer satisfied after the transaction has been authorised in parallel. For instance, Bob could buy more items than he could pay for on different platforms at the same time, or could end his registration with the platform at the time of the bidding. Thus, *consensus* between all relevant participants is not instant, and thus an authorised transaction could become invalid and a roll back could be required, possibly even invalidating further transactions. For instance, if payment requires that a bid has been placed before, an invalidated bid may also invalidate a subsequent payment. More so, if Bob would sell the owner certificate gained by payment, the invalidation of the bid could issue a chain of transactions to be invalidated.

We can summarise the life cycle of a transaction (cf. Fig. 2) by the states *pending*, where some network participant has communicated the transaction to the network, *checked* when the logic between preconditions and postconditions has been confirmed, *verified* when the preconditions have been verified on the respective local states, *authorised* after the required participants have given their agreement, and *accepted* when consensus is reached in the network is reached that it will not be invalidated. Before it is *accepted*, the transaction can become *rejected*. Whether a rejected transaction is kept on the network is up to the implementation and can depend on the last non-rejected state of the transaction.

The state of a transaction varies based on the observer, that is, it is differently perceived by different network participants. Hence, the current state of a transaction is effectively a function from the network participants into the set of states of a transaction, called a *marking*. Consensus then means that the state of the transaction is the same for every network participant. We note that rejection of already accepted transactions could be required in certain use cases. However, this can be implemented by further transactions describing the roll back.

# 3   A Reference Specification

We introduce a reference specification explaining the common concepts, from which we will derive further refined specifications. For readers familiar with distributed systems, the contents of this section may seem unsurprising and not interesting on its own. However, we note that the intuition behind it is to serve as a greatest common divisor of the two approaches compared in this paper.

## 3.1   Preliminaries

We formalise our specification in the $Z$-notation [1, 13]. The notation is based on set theory and first order logics. In addition, every object $a$ in $Z$ has exactly one type $\mathsf{T}$ (usually, a given set, a powerset of a type, a partial function over types, or a cartesian product of types), denoted by $a : \mathsf{T}$. In the interest of space, we omit a detailed description of the notation and recall specific notions only when necessary.

Throughout our specification, we use the following given sets as non further described types:

$$[\mathsf{NAME}, \mathsf{CONDITION}, \mathsf{DATA}]$$

Intuitively, $\mathsf{NAME}$ consists of unique names for network participants, $\mathsf{CONDITION}$ captures logical conditions over non-further specified domains, and $\mathsf{DATA}$ describes arbitrary, non-further described data objects.

## 3.2   Networks and Participants

Our specification will start from networks of participants, will specify transactions and their possible states as observed by participants.

A *network* consists of a set of *participants*, on our level of abstractions, only a set of names, denoted by *participants* : $\mathbb{P}\,\mathsf{NAME}$. The set may change over time, specifying joining and leaving participants, i.e. we may have *participants'* $\neq$ *participants*.

```
┌─ Network ─────────────────────────────────
│  participants : ℙ NAME
│
└────────────────────────────────────────────
```

Operations for joining and leaving can be mimicked by the appropriate set operations, and are omitted in interest of space.

## 3.3   Transactions and Their States

A *transaction* describes the transfer of assets between partners, requiring a set of preconditions to be fulfilled and promising a set of postconditions. A transaction is given by its set of *partners*, its set *pre* of *preconditions*, its set *post* of *postconditions*, and a data field *data*. As we do not want to restrict the type of preconditions and postconditions at this point, we introduce the given sort CONDITION.[1] We specify that each partner must also be a network participant.

```
┌─ Transaction ─────────────────────────────────────
│ Network
│ partners : ℙ NAME
│ post, pre : ℙ CONDITION
│ data : DATA
├───────────────────────────────────────────────────
│ partners ⊆ participants
```

We further require immutability of sets of partners, preconditions and postconditions. In the schema *TransactionImmutability*, $\Delta$*Transaction* is the conjunction of schema transaction and the variant of *Transaction* where each object $a$ in *Transaction* is replaced by $a'$, modeling a state change from $a$ to $a'$.

```
┌─ TransactionImmutability ─────────────────────────
│ ΔTransaction
├───────────────────────────────────────────────────
│ partners' = partners
│ pre' = pre
│ post' = post
```

In a distributed system, the state of a transaction is not a property of the transaction, but differs based on the observing participant. We first define possible transaction states and transitions between this states: A *transaction state* can be either *pending, checked, verified, authorised, accepted* or *rejected*, denoted by the free type declaration TSTATE ::= *pnd* | *chk* | *ver* | *aut* | *acc* | *rej*. The state transitions must follow the binary relation $\leadsto$: TSTATE $\leftrightarrow$ TSTATE, which we define as in Fig. 2. In the following schema, $(\leadsto_1 \cup \leadsto_2)^*$ denotes the reflexive, transitive closure of $\leadsto_1 \cup \leadsto_2$.

```
┌─ TransactionStates ───────────────────────────────
│ TSTATE ::= pnd | chk | ver | aut | acc | rej
│ ⇝ : TSTATE ↔ TSTATE
├───────────────────────────────────────────────────
│ ⇝ = (⇝₁ ∪ ⇝₂)*
│ ⇝₁ = {(pnd, chk), (chk, ver), (ver, aut), (aut, acc)}
│ ⇝₂ = (TSTATE \ {acc}) × {rej}
```

A *marking* describes the state of a given transaction as observed by the respective network participants. We specify this by a partial function *marking* : NAME $\nrightarrow$ TSTATE from the set of names to the set of transaction states, where the domain dom *marking* of *marking* is a subset of the network participants. Intuitively, *participants* \ dom *marking* is the set of network participants not knowing the transaction, and thus not holding a state for it.

---

[1] We remark that the preconditions and postconditions of a transaction are not to be confused with the preconditions and postconditions of a $Z$ schema. Identifying the set *pre* with *pre_Transaction* would require to know the preconditions at specification.

```
┌─ Marking ──────────────────────────────────────────────────
│ Transaction
│ TransactionStates
│ marking : NAME ⇸ TSTATE
├────────────────────────────────────────────────────────────
│ dom marking ⊆ participants
```

We require that once a transaction is known to a participant, it stays known unless the participant leaves the network. We require that each participant starts the lifecycle of the transaction with *pending*, and follows the state order relation.

```
┌─ Step ─────────────────────────────────────────────────────
│ ΔMarking
├────────────────────────────────────────────────────────────
│ dom marking ∩ participants' ⊆ dom marking'
│ ∀ p : dom marking • marking(p) ↝ marking'(p)
```

So far, the preconditions and postconditions of a transaction are not related. The intuition is that transactions containing arbitrary combinations of preconditions and postconditions may be submitted to the network. Other participants will then check whether the postconditions of a transaction are backed by its preconditions. We specify this by defining a check criterion – a set of pairs of sets of preconditions and postconditions – and require it to be fulfilled for every step from *pnd* to *chk*. We note that the set *checked* may be infinite, and thus may in practice rather be implemented by a predicate.

```
┌─ CheckTransaction ─────────────────────────────────────────
│ Step
│ criterion : ℙ CONDITION ↔ ℙ CONDITION
│ p : dom marking
├────────────────────────────────────────────────────────────
│ (pre, post) ∈ criterion
│ marking(p) = pnd
│ marking'(p) = chk
```

## 4    Refinement 1: Account-Based Setting

We refine the reference specification from Sect. 3 for a provider-based system. In a provider-based system, some network participants are *providers* which manage the accounts.

```
┌─ AccNetwork ───────────────────────────────────────────────
│ Network
│ providers : ℙ NAME
├────────────────────────────────────────────────────────────
│ providers ⊆ participants
```

An account is managed by a provider, and owned by a set of network participants. We specify states of accounts merely by a given set ACCOUNT_STATE:

```
__ Account _____
  AccNetwork
  provider : providers
  owners : ℙ participants
  state : ACCOUNT_STATE
```

In this setting, a transaction is based on a set of accounts, whose state is modified by the transaction. The preconditions thus require certain account states, and the postconditions promise certain account states.

```
__ AccTransaction _____
  Account
  Transaction
  accounts : ℙ Account
  _____
  accounts' = accounts
  ∀ φ : pre ∪ post • φ : ℙ₁ (Accounts ⇸ ACCOUNT_STATE)
  ∀ φ : pre ∪ post ∀ f ∈ φ • dom f ⊆ accounts
  ∀ a : accounts • a.owners ∩ partners ≠ ∅
```

We note that the outcome of a transaction is 'deterministic' if each $\varphi \in post$ is singleton.

We require that the accounts in a transaction are immutable.

```
__ AccTransitionImmutability _____
  ΔAccTransaction
  _____
  accounts' = accounts
```

Now, we refine the schema *Marking*:

```
__ AccMarking _____
  AccNetwork
  AccTransaction
  Marking
```

A transaction in a provider-based system will only be verified if the preconditions are fulfilled.

```
__ AccVerifying _____
  ΔAccMarking
  _____
  ∀ a : accounts • provider(a) ∈ dom marking' ∧ marking'(provider(a)) = ver
    ⇒ ∀ φ : pre • ∃ f ∈ φ • a ∈ dom f ⇒ f(a) = a.state
```

A provider will only accept if the providers of all accounts relevant to the transaction have at least authorised the transaction. It is assumed that after all providers have accepted the transaction, the postconditions hold.

─── *AccAccept* ─────────────────────────────────────────

$\Delta AccMarking$

─────────────────────────────────────────────────────────

$\forall\, a : accounts \bullet provider(a) \in \text{dom } marking' \land marking'(provider(a)) = acc$
$\Rightarrow \forall\, b : accounts \bullet provider(b) \in \text{dom } marking \land marking(b) \in \{aut, acc\}$

$(\forall\, a : accounts \bullet provider(a) \in \text{dom } marking' \land marking'(provider(a)) = acc)$
$\Rightarrow \forall \varphi \in post \bullet \exists f \in \varphi \bullet \forall b \in \text{dom } f \bullet f(b) = b.state'$

─────────────────────────────────────────────────────────

## 5    Refinement 2: Distributed Ledgers

In this section, we refine our reference specification in three steps: We first model transactions with their preconditions and postconditions in Sect. 5.1. We then turn to specifying distributed ledgers containing such transactions in Sect. 5.2. Finally, we discuss classes of distributed ledgers in Sect. 5.3.

### 5.1    Modelling Transactions

In a distributed ledger, each precondition of a transaction points to a postcondition of a another transaction[2]. Hence, we require a scheme for uniquely referencing postconditions. As the system is distributed, the address of a postcondition is (at least partially) determined during insertion into the ledger. In our specification, the address of a postcondition consists of two parts:

1. *A local postcondition index i:* Each postcondition of a transaction has an index, which is unique inside the transaction. However, we can have several different transactions with the same postcondition indices. For instance, the postconditions could be numbered. We note that the index can be chosen when the transaction is created, and without knowledge of other transactions.
2. *A global transaction address a:* Each transaction is assigned a unique address upon insertion into the distributed ledger. For instance, one could use a timestamp of the insertion time, or a hash of the transaction itself. We note that the transaction address is not necessarily known at the time of transaction creation, but is determined during the insertion into the ledger.

Together, $a$ and $i$ form a globally unique identifier $(a, i)$ for the postcondition with index $i$ of the transaction with address $a$.

    As postconditions determine usage or consumption rights for assets, we need a control mechanism to determine who may use a postcondition as a precondition. To this end, each postcondition is guarded by a data predicate called a *challenge*. Every input data evaluating the challenge to true is called a *solution*. Whoever can provide a solution for the challenge of a postcondition $\varphi$ may use $\varphi$ for one

─────────────────────────

[2] Technically, we can imagine preconditions referencing postconditions which are not stored in the distributed ledger. We assume such 'external' preconditions to be stored in the data part of the transaction.

of their preconditions. In existing implementations, verifying a given solution is less complex than finding one. In fact, guessing a solution is often assumed to be intractable.

Summarising, we specify each postcondition by a pair $(i \mapsto d)$ of an index $i \in$ INDEX and some data $d \in$ DATA describing the postcondition. We specify uniqueness for indices by specifying the set *post* of postconditions of a transaction as a binary partial function *post* : INDEX $\nrightarrow$ DATA instead of a set of pairs[3]. Each postcondition $(i \mapsto d)$ is guarded by a challenge *challenge*$(i)$, that is, a function DATA $\rightarrow \mathbb{B}$.

Accordingly, each precondition is pair $(a, i)$ of a transaction address $a$, and a postcondition index $i$. Moreover, for each precondition $(a, i)$, the transaction holds data *proposal*$(a, i)$ as a proposed solution for the challenge guarding the respective postcondition, that is, the postcondition with index $i$ of transaction with address $a$. We stress that *proposal*$(a, i)$ is not necessarily a solution.

In addition to these refined notions of preconditions and postconditions, a transaction in a distributed ledger offers a set of *promises*: Every pair $(i, s)$ of a postcondition index $i$ and a solution $s$ of *post*$(i)$ is a promise. We note that introducing this set is simplifying the formal model; however, the set of promises is not to be implemented.

---
*DistributedLedgerTransaction* _____

*Transaction*
*prc* : ADDRESS $\leftrightarrow$ INDEX
*proposal* : (ADDRESS $\times$ INDEX) $\nrightarrow$ DATA
*post* : INDEX $\nrightarrow$ DATA
*challenge* : INDEX $\nrightarrow$ (DATA $\rightarrow \mathbb{B}$)
*promises* : INDEX $\leftrightarrow$ DATA

dom *prc* = dom *proposal*
dom *post* = dom *challenge*
*promises* = $\{(i, s) : $ INDEX $\times$ DATA $\mid i \in$ dom *post* $\wedge$ *challenge*$(i)(s) = $ true$\}$

---

We note that the solution set of a challenge could be empty, that is, we could have $c(q) = $ false for all $q : $ DATA. In this case, the postcondition can never be used as a precondition, and so its index does not occur in the set of promises. This edge case is used in some implementations such as Bitcoin to store arbitrary data inside postconditions.

## 5.2    Modelling the Distributed Ledger

A distributed ledger is a collection of transactions. As explained earlier, each of these transactions is given a unique address when inserted. Hence, we specify the contents of a distributed ledger as a partial function $tx$ from the set of possible addresses into the set of transactions.

---
[3] This is well-defined because every $n$-ary partial function $f : A_1 \times \cdots \times A_n \nrightarrow A$ can be conceived as the set of all tuples $(a_1, \ldots, a_n, f(a))$ with $a_i \in A_i$ for each $1 \leq i \leq n$.

In order to reason about the relationship between preconditions and post-conditions of different transactions, we specify the sets of promises and requirements inside a ledger: A promise $(a, i, s)$ means that the transaction $tx(a)$ has a postcondition index $i$ guarded by some challenge with solution $s$. A requirement $(a, i, q)$ means that there exist a transaction $t$ and a precondition in $t.pre$ pointing to postcondition index $i$ of transaction $tx(a)$, and proposal $q$.

---

*DistributedLedger*

*DistributedLedgerTransaction*
$tx$ : ADDRESS $\nrightarrow$ *DistributedLedgerTransaction*
*requirements* : $\mathbb{P}$ (ADDRESS × INDEX × DATA)
*promises* : $\mathbb{P}$ (ADDRESS × INDEX × DATA)

---

*requirements* $= \bigcup_{a \in \text{dom } tx} tx(a).proposal$
*promises* $= \bigcup_{a \in \text{dom } tx} \{a\} \times tx(a).promises$

---

We visualise an example instance of the schema *DistributedLedger* in Fig. 3. Transactions are displayed as rectangles, transaction addresses are written in circles. Preconditions $((a, i) \mapsto q)$ are drawn in rounded rectangles with inscription $a \rangle i \rangle q$. Similarly, postconditions $(i \mapsto c)$ are drawn as rounded rectangles with inscription $i \rangle c$. The dashed arrows visualise the respective precondition-postcondition dependencies. For instance, precondition $(1, 3)$ with proposal $q_{2,1}$ of transaction $tx(2)$ refers to postcondition with index 3 of transaction $tx(1)$ guarded by challenge $c_{1,2}$.

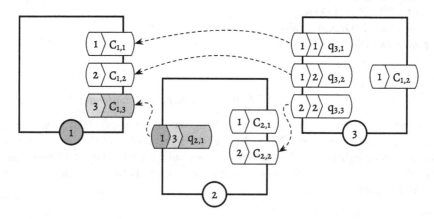

**Fig. 3.** Three transactions $tx(1)$, $tx(2)$ and $tx(3)$ in a distributed ledger. Preconditions and postconditions are displayed on the left and right, respectively.

## 5.3   Properties of Distributed Ledgers

Based on the notions of requirements and promises, we can define a simple notion of consistency. Intuitively, we require that every requirement is backed by a promise, formalised by a subset relation.

```
__ ConsistentDistributedLedger _____
  DistributedLedger
 _____
  requirements ⊆ promises
```

Revisiting Fig. 3, we observe: If the ledger is consistent, $q_{2,1}$ is a solution of $c_{1,3}$.

So far, our specification does not enforce any kind of order on the transactions inside a ledger. For practical applications, however, it is often desired that preconditions do not 'point into the future'. Thus, it is sensible to define an occurrence order for the transactions. As we have a distributed setting, this order is rather a partial order (causality) than a total order (temporal order). However, we leave the exact specification open, and merely specify a relationship $\leq$ between the addresses.

```
__ OrderedDistributedLedger _____
  DistributedLedger
  ≤ : dom tx ↔ dom tx
 _____
  ∀ a, a' : dom tx • (∃(a, i) ∈ tx(a').pre) ⇒ a ≤ a'
```

In practice, $\leq$ is well-founded, that is, we have no infinite descending chains. We note that this requires to have transactions with empty sets of preconditions[4].

Every order $\leq$ on the transaction addresses in ledger of Fig. 3 satisfies $tx(1) \leq tx(2) \leq tx(3)$, as the precondition of $tx(2)$ points to postconditions of $tx(1)$ and the preconditions of $tx(3)$ points to postconditions of $tx(1)$ and $tx(2)$.

In some use cases, some or all postconditions may only be used once, that, is, one forbids 'double spending' of postconditions. In the most simple case, each postcondition may be used only once:

```
__ NoDoubleSpending _____
  DistributedLedger
 _____
  ∀ a₁, a₂ ∈ dom tx
     • tx(a₁).pre ∩ tx(a₂).pre ≠ ∅ ⇒ a₁ = a₂
```

The ledger in Fig. 3 is an instance of *NoDoubleSpending*. In contrast to that, the ledger in Fig. 4 violates schema *NoDoubleSpending*, because the postcondition $(1 \mapsto c_{1,1})$ of $tx(1)$ is a precondition of both $tx(2)$ and $tx(3)$.

In a more elaborate case, one may assume a specific upper bound for each postcondition. Inside the transaction, one could specify a function *cap* as a partial function INDEX $\nrightarrow \{1, 2, 3, \ldots \}$). Inside the ledger, one could have a partial function ADDRESS $\times$ INDEX $\nrightarrow \{1, 2, 3, \ldots \}$. This function could also be determined by capacities given in the transactions themselves. A capacity of 0 can always be specified by using an insolvable challenge.

---

[4] In Blockchain-jargon, these transactions are part of the 'genesis block'.

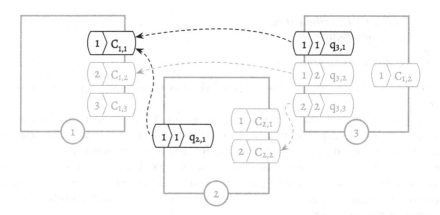

**Fig. 4.** An instance of *DistributedLedger* but not of *NoDoubleSpending*.

## 6   First Insights

Our formalisation of distributed ledgers focuses on the structural aspects of verifying and authorising a transaction in a distributed ledger. Our specification lacks steps in distributed ledgers, that is, the description of how network participants update their state of a transaction. Assuming some form of replication of the distributed ledger on participants, we can already draw first conclusions.

Verification and authorisation in distributed ledgers do not rely on the availability of specific account providers: Every network participant who has access to the distributed ledger can check its consistency (cf. Schema *ConsistentDistributedLedger*), that is, whether each requirement is backed by a promise. While consistency can be checked by only 'going backwards' in the history, preventing double spending (cf. Schema *NoDoubleSpending*) requires to go forward as well.

Distributed ledgers provide a higher level of transparency, as the history of a transaction is traceable for all network participants. Depending on the use case, this could be both an advantage and a disadvantage. The guarding mechanism of challenges enables a potential for privacy as the usage of a postcondition is not linked to an individual. However, it might result in potential for fraud, assuming that it is easier to guess a solution than faking identity towards a trusted party.

If the distributed ledger is replicated over the whole network, then every network participant must store much more data than in an account-based approach, where trusted parties store the accounts and transaction histories of the account owners.

## 7   Related Work

Our contribution focuses on providing a general view on the approach, and comparing it to the approach of a provider-based system. In order to provide a general view, we abstract from specific implementations, such as Bitcoin or

Ethereum [18]. Other work on distributed ledger technologies and their properties exist, as surveyed e.g. by [4,15]. So far, the focus has mostly been on the protocols in use and their respective guarantees.

In [6], the authors introduce the notion of the Transaction Graph in order to provide formal semantics for Blockchains. The approach is based on partial orders of transactions that consume and produce states, similar to our notion of preconditions and postconditions. We extend this work by providing a base of comparison to provider-based systems with intermediary providers. In addition, our specification explicitly captures the authorisation process based on challenges, which is omitted in [6]. In lieu, the authors of- [6] describe concrete refinements of their model for Bitcoin, Ethereum and Hyperledger [2], which we leave for future work.

Another related contribution can be found in [3]. There, the authors aim at modeling Bitcoin transactions, capturing Bitcoin-specific mechanisms, such as certain types of output scripts and multi-signature verifications. Our approach is more general, and is also capable to model other distributed ledgers, however, we leave a bigger gap between model and implementation.

## 8    Conclusion and Future Work

In this paper, we study the transition from provider-based systems to distributed ledgers by starting from a general specification, and refining this for the approaches, accordingly. While the commonalities of the two approaches are captured by the reference specification, its differences need to be studied in more depth. We see this as first direction for future work.

Our specification does not capture dynamic aspects such as chain code/smart contracts other than the programmatic protection of postconditions by challenges. This could be done by refining the *data* attribute of a transaction.

One could also further refine our specification for more concrete blockchain implementations, such as Bitcoin or Ethereum. This would serve as an evaluation of the approach, and would in addition allow to compare the specified implementations.

## References

1. Abrial, J., Schuman, S.A., Meyer, B.: Specification language. In: McKeag, R.M., Macnaughlen, A.M. (eds.) On the Construction of Programs, pp. 343–410. Cambridge University Press, Cambridge (1980)
2. Androulaki, E., et al.: Hyperledger fabric: a distributed operating system for permissioned blockchains. In: Proceedings of the Thirteenth EuroSys Conference, EuroSys 2018, pp. 30:1–30:15. ACM, New York (2018). https://doi.org/10.1145/3190508.3190538, http://doi.acm.org/10.1145/3190508.3190538
3. Atzei, N., Bartoletti, M., Lande, S., Zunino, R.: A formal model of Bitcoin transactions. IACR Cryptology ePrint Archive 2017, 1124 (2017). http://eprint.iacr.org/2017/1124

4. Bonneau, J., Miller, A., Clark, J., Narayanan, A., Kroll, J.A., Felten, E.W.: SoK: research perspectives and challenges for Bitcoin and cryptocurrencies. In: IEEE Symposium on Security and Privacy, pp. 104–121. IEEE Computer Society (2015)

5. Bures, T., Plasil, F., Kit, M., Tuma, P., Hoch, N.: Software abstractions for component interaction in the Internet of Things. Computer 49(12), 50–59 (2016). https://doi.org/10.1109/MC.2016.377

6. Cachin, C., Caro, A.D., Moreno-Sanchez, P., Tackmann, B., Vukolic, M.: The transaction graph for modeling blockchain semantics. IACR Cryptology ePrint Archive 2017, 1070 (2017). http://eprint.iacr.org/2017/1070

7. Easley, D.A., Kleinberg, J.M.: Networks, Crowds, and Markets - Reasoning About a Highly Connected World. Cambridge University Press, Cambridge (2010). http://www.cambridge.org/gb/knowledge/isbn/item2705443/?site_locale=en_GB

8. Goldwasser, S., Micali, S., Rackoff, C.: The knowledge complexity of interactive proof systems. SIAM J. Comput. 18(1), 186–208 (1989)

9. Lindman, J., Tuunainen, V.K., Rossi, M.: Opportunities and risks of blockchain technologies-a research agenda. In: Proceedings of the 50th Hawaii International Conference on System Sciences (2017)

10. Mainelli, M., Smith, M.: Sharing ledgers for sharing economies: an exploration of mutual distributed ledgers (aka blockchain technology). J. Financ. Perspect. 3(3), 38–58 (2015)

11. Marc, P.: Blockchain technology: principles and applications. In: Xavier Olleros, F., Zhegu, M. (eds.) Handbook of Research on Digital Transformations. Edward Elgar, Cheltenham (2016)

12. Nakamoto, S.: Bitcoin: a peer-to-peer electronic cash system (2008). http://bitcoin.org/bitcoin.pdf

13. Spivey, J.M.: The Z Notation - A Reference Manual. Prentice Hall International Series in Computer Science. Prentice Hall, Englewood Cliffs (1989)

14. Swanson, T.: Consensus-as-a-service: a brief report on the emergence of permissioned, distributed ledger systems (2015)

15. Tschorsch, F., Scheuermann, B.: Bitcoin and beyond: a technical survey ondecentralized digital currencies. IEEE Commun. Surv. Tutor. 18(3), 2084–2123 (2016). https://doi.org/10.1109/COMST.2016.2535718

16. Walport, M.: Distributed ledger technology: beyond block chain (2016)

17. Wirsing, M., Hölzl, M., Koch, N., Mayer, P. (eds.): Software Engineering for Collective Autonomic Systems - The ASCENS Approach. LNCS, vol. 8998. Springer, Cham (2015). https://doi.org/10.1007/978-3-319-16310-9

18. Wood, G.: Ethereum: a secure decentralised generalised transaction ledger (2018). https://ethereum.github.io/yellowpaper/paper.pdf

# A Collective Adaptive Socio-Technical System for Remote- and Self-supervised Exercise in the Treatment of Intermittent Claudication

Jeremy Pitt[1]([✉]), Kristina Milanovic[1], Alexander Coupland[2], Tim Allan[3], Alun Davies[2], Tristan Lane[2], Anna Maria Malagoni[2], Ankur Thapar[2], and Joseph Shalhoub[2]

[1] Department of Electrical and Electronic Engineering,
Imperial College London, London, UK
{j.pitt,kristina.milanovic08}@imperial.ac.uk
[2] Department of Surgery and Cancer, Imperial College London, London, UK
{alexander.coupland,alun.davies,tristan.lane,annamaria.malagoni,
ankur.thapar,joseph.shalhoub}@imperial.ac.uk
[3] NHS Digital/Royal College of Art, London, UK
timothy.allan@network.rca.ac.uk

**Abstract.** Vascular surgeons have recognised that the condition of many patients presenting with intermittent claudication and peripheral arterial disease is better treated by physical exercise rather than endovascular or surgical intervention. Such exercise causes pain, though, before and until the health improvements are realised. Therefore, patients experiencing pain tend to stop doing that which causes it, unless they are supervised performing the necessary exercise programmes. However, supervised exercise is an extremely costly and time-consuming use of medical resources.

To overcome this series of problems, we propose to develop and deploy a healthcare application which provides patient exercise programmes that are *both* centrally organised and remotely supervised by a health practitioner, *and* self-organized and self-supervised by the patients themselves. This demands that two dimensions of adaptation should be addressed: adaptation prompted by the health practitioner as the patient group improves and meets programme targets; and adaptation prompted from within the patient group enabling them to manage their own community effectively and sustainably.

This position paper explores this application from the perspective of engineering a collective adaptive system for a mobile healthcare application, providing both remote- and self-supervised exercise. This requires, on the one hand, converging recent technological advances in sensors and mobile devices, audio and video connectivity, and social computing; with, on the other hand, innovative value-sensitive and user-centric design methodologies, together with formal methods for interaction and interface design and specification. The ultimate ambition is to create a 'win-win-win' situation in which the benefits of exercise as a treatment,

© Springer Nature Switzerland AG 2018
T. Margaria and B. Steffen (Eds.): ISoLA 2018, LNCS 11246, pp. 63–78, 2018.
https://doi.org/10.1007/978-3-030-03424-5_5

the reduced costs of supervision, and the pro-social incentives to perform the exercise are all derived from computer-supported self-organised collective action.

# 1  Introduction

Patients with narrowing or blockage of arteries in their legs may suffer from pain in their legs on walking, commonly in the calf. This is caused by an inadequate blood supply and is diagnosed as *intermittent claudication.*

Vascular surgeons have recognised that the condition of many patients presenting with intermittent claudication and peripheral arterial disease is better treated by exercise rather than endovascular or surgical intervention [7,8]. Moreover, there are long-lasting benefits of supervised exercise over and above revascularisation, which include development of a social network, additional cardiac training and motivational therapy [13]. The initial problem, though, is that this exercise causes pain, before and until the health improvements are realised; but patients experiencing pain tend to stop doing that which causes it – unless they are supervised performing the necessary exercise programmes. Given the scale of the problem, though, supervised exercise can be an extremely costly and time-consuming use of medical resources, assuming that patients even have access to a hospital-based programme.

However, recent years have seen three significant advances in ICT (information and communication technologies): firstly, the development of low-cost sensors integrated with mobile devices which can monitor activity and other health indicators; secondly, increased connectivity which enables virtual (remote) meetings with high quality audio and video; and thirdly, the widespread application of social computing, in which people use social networking and associated tools to develop 'digital communities' to address public action problems. Indeed, it has been argued that the value of communities is that they can resolve certain types of collective and public action situations which are resistant to purely market-based or policy-based solutions [17]. Such situations increasingly arise in the digital society, where the added-value of information, reciprocity or other pro-social behaviour is indeterminate, and/or the qualitative nature of traded services is subjective and cannot simply be measured by kilowatts, tons, etc.

We contend that the provision of supervised exercise programmes can be construed as just such a collective action situation. Consequently, this paper proposes to converge these developments to engineer a system to support exercise programmes for the treatment of intermittent claudication. However, extensive experience of rehabilitation and exercise programmes has revealed that it is fundamental that the engineering of any health-centred computer system should incorporate the direct social relationship between the health practitioner and the patient group at its core; but similarly the 'democratisation' of such socio-technical systems through self-organised collective choice arrangements (i.e. those affected by 'the rules' participate in the selection, modification and application of those rules) can be critical to community formation, its sustainability, and a successful achievement of intended goals.

Therefore, what is required is a *collective adaptive socio-technical system* [10], in which exercise programmes are organized, monitored and supervised through the joint collaboration of both health practitioners and the patients themselves, using a combination of both *remote*- and *self*-supervision. Two dimensions of adaptation need to be addressed: adaptation prompted by the health practitioner as the patient group improves and meets programme targets; and adaptation prompted from within the patient group to manage their own community.

Engineering such a collective adaptive socio-technical system also requires addressing a number of software engineering challenges, not least recognising that the system must meet 'supra-functional' requirements targeting social or qualitative values, like improving collective public health, community well-being or individual 'quality of life' measures. However, recent methodological advances like value-sensitive design [9] also need to be taken into consideration, in conjunction with innovative interface design to support self-governance, to visualise community 'well-being' and to incentivise pro-social behaviour [24].

However, the engineers of collective adaptive of socio-technical systems, especially those underlying the digital transformation, require methodological support for significantly more complex types of design, in particular designs that are sensitive to 'supra-functional' requirements' like (human) values, possess the capacity for continuous re-design and self-organisation, and encapsulate mechanisms for self-governance, knowledge aggregation and coordination that are attuned to context, e.g. the type and scale of problem being addressed, and the type and nature of the social relationships being digitised.

This *position paper* explores this issue from the perspective of designing and implementing a collective adaptive system for a healthcare application, providing remote- and self-supervised exercise for the treatment of diseases such as intermittent claudication, which can respond more effectively to physical exercise rather than surgical intervention. The paper presents an eclectic 'toolset' of possible techniques that might be used to engineer such systems. Following a (partial) envisionment of a proposed system in Sect. 2, Sect. 3 reviews two design methodologies and Sect. 4 considers (formal) specification of three necessary components of such a system: events and the effect of events; interface and interaction design; and the design of social capital, currency, and the system's 'shared reality'.

Our ultimate aim is to create a 'win-win-win' situation in which the benefits of exercise as a treatment, the diminished costs of supervision, and the incentives to follow given exercise programmes are all derived from self-organised collective action based on sound engineering of collective adaptive socio-technical systems. Remote supervision will also improve access to this treatment in areas where no such service is currently available, and improve availability of this treatment in resource-poor healthcare systems, but do have access to smartphones and a communications infrastructure. However, we also conclude that while there appears to be no 'silver bullet' approach to rigorous engineering of collective adaptive systems, this nevertheless presents opportunities for co-design and generativity.

## 2 (Partial) System Envisionment

Addressing peripheral arterial disease is a significant and unmet clinical and health economic need, but the treatment of intermittent claudication using supervised exercise remains largely under-utilised due to a lack of appropriate resources. In addition, we note that other medical conditions, such as diabetes and hypertension, can also be managed by a similar convergence of self-supervision and ICT, and interactive self-governance. Therefore, we propose an alternative approach based on a digital community for *self-organised, self-supervised exercise,* based on: firstly: information and communication technologies (ICT), including new healthcare sensors and devices; secondly, computing models based on self-organising socio-technical systems to provide communal support and collective action (cf. [25]); and thirdly, structures and procedures that reflect the different relationships in patient-patient self-organisation and the practitioner-patient self-organisation.

In a preliminary investigation, we have experimented with the design and envisionment of a mobile device-based app to support self-organised, self-supervised exercise *within* the patient group. Example interface mock-ups for tracks, groups and communications are illustrated in Fig. 1, illustrating the interface design of a putative app which applies some ideas from gamification with the intention to increase self-efficacy. This app is an exploration game in which to progress, the user must exercise in real life. The user has an avatar that has crashed on an unknown world and has been injured. In order to heal themselves and to stay alive they must explore the area and find items such as food or medicinal plants. To do so, the user tracks their walks through the app. Items are awarded at the end of the session depending on how far they've walked. The users can also connect through the app to find people to exercise with and, by tracking exercise in a group, they can pick up bonus items that are too 'heavy' to lift alone, providing both self-supervision, monitoring and mutual verification. If the users stick to the schedule they are rewarded, and incentivised – in appropriate ways (see below).

Such envisionment is useful for exploratory purposes. For example, when this lab-based envisionment was first demonstrated to healthcare professionals, there were two observations. The first was a recommendation for a 'first aid' facility, for example to have some first aid tips or an SOS button on the app that alerts emergency services. Secondly, system designers need to recognise that this approach to 'gamification' (based on an avatar landing on alien planet and needing to survive) may not be readily 'accessible' to the target demographic of patients who are suffering from intermittent claudication. The concept of an analogy or story on which the patient can put their exercise programme in context is potentially beneficial; but system designers have to ensure that gamification is appropriate to the user demographic.

Therefore the overall approach to envisionment needs system designers to work with healthcare professionals, especially when it comes to formulating an exercise plan that can be self-created, prescribed, monitored and adapted for a particular patient group by a qualified professional health practitioner. Participatory design and user-centred systems design are standard approaches, but for the design of gamification and self-organising socio-technical systems some other design methods need to be considered, as discussed in the next section.

(a)                     (b)                     (c)

**Fig. 1.** App interface mock-ups for self-organised, self-supervised exercise.

## 3   Design Methodologies

This section reviews two design methodologies pertinent to the design of self-organising healthcare application: one highlighting the role of user values in design, and the other emphasising the use of digital interventions which can support and encourage behavioural change. Both patient values and changing patient behaviour are, of course, crucial aspects of self-organised and self-supervised exercise.

### 3.1   Value-Sensitive Design (VSD)

In [9], it is suggested that VSD brings forward a "unique constellation of eight features", which included proactive influence on technological design from an early stage in the process; enlarging the scope of applications in which values arise as "supra-functional" requirements; the integration and iteration of conceptual, empirical and technical investigations; enlarging the scope of values beyond co-operation and participation to include justice, welfare, virtue, etc.; distinguishing between usability and values with ethical significance; consideration of different classes of stakeholder; being an interactional theory; and building from the psychological proposition that values are universal, if possibly culturally relative.

Healthcare seems to be a particularly promising test application to apply the methodology of VSD for digital communities. For example, we can start with a value of central interest – quality of life and patient care – and move from that value to its implications for app interface design and context of use (remote- and self-supervised exercise). We can next examine the roles of peer-to-peer self-help communities and centralised practitioner-patient group communities in a wider context, with multiple stakeholders and polycentric governance (multiple centres of decision-making). We can identify several direct and indirect stakeholders (e.g. patients, clinicians, health service providers, policy advisors, public health officials, and insurance providers), and from an understanding their co-dependence, we can start to identify and coordinate the values and benefits for each stakeholder group.

Critically, one of the most important values in healthcare applications is *privacy* and the confidential treatment of patient data. However, privacy by design [5] can be seen as an instance of value-sensitive design, and following these principles can help design systems with privacy as primary system requirement (explicitly meeting legal requirements, for example, with respect to GDPR (General Data Protection Regulation)).

## 3.2   The IDEAS Framework

The rise of mHealth technologies that need to serve both healthcare provider and patient to be efficacious, raises new questions about how best to innovate in the mHealth era. Traditionally, the healthcare sector has relied on linear models of innovation whereby development and commercialisation of a 'product' has followed basic science and applied research; this is commonly known as the 'lab-bench to bedside' model. This traditional approach is slow and potentially produces products that are sub-optimal from the patient perspective.

Modern approaches to bring innovative ideas from conception to market require an alternative approach; one that places patients (users) at the centre of the design process alongside lead clinicians. Ultimately promoting patient responsibility and encouraging them to take control of their own collective health outcomes [2], as well as producing products that the desired user group are likely to use.

The IDEAS Framework (Integrate, Design, Assess and Share), as illustrated in Fig. 2 has been proposed as a method for developing digital interventions that lead to effective behavioural change. This approach is grounded in behavioural theory; has an in-depth understanding of the target population, by asking "what

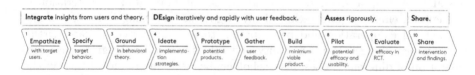

**Fig. 2.** The IDEAS design framework.

matters most" to them; products are rapidly and iteratively designed with multiple episodes of user feedback and are subjected to rigorous evaluation before generalised dissemination [14].

# 4 Formal Specification

Complementing these design methodologies, there are three further aspects that need to be considered in the design and specification of a healthcare application. These are the formal specification of self-adaptation; the visualisation of self-governance; and the construction of shared reality in socio-technical systems. Each of these aspects will be discussed in turn in this section.

Section 4.1 presents a possible formalism for specifying, reasoning about and implementing self-adaptation of the rules, which also includes normative aspects like permission, obligation and institutionalised power [11]. Section 4.2 addresses the issue of interface and affordance design based on the idea of interactive self-governance, and Sect. 4.3 picks up on the incentivisation of self-supervised exercise through the use of social capital.

## 4.1 Reasoning About Events

In many applications, especially those with it is often necessary to reason about actions, constraints on actions, and the effects of actions, which in turn are dependent on who performed the action – or rather, which person occupying a designated *role* performed the action, i.e. some actions have different adaptive effects depending on whether it was a patient or a practitioner who performed it. This section outlines a formalism for specifying and reasoning about actions which can be used at both design-time (e.g. for proving system properties) and at run-time as an executable specification (e.g. for determining the validity and computing the effects of actions).

**The Event Calculus (EC).** The Event Calculus (EC) [12] is a logic formalism for representing and reasoning about actions or events and their effects. The EC is based on a many-sorted first-order predicate calculus. For the version used here, the underlying model of time is linear, so we use non-negative integer time-points (although this is not an EC restriction). It is not assumed that time is discrete (the numbers need not correspond to a uniform duration) but we do impose a relative/partial ordering for events: for non-negative integers, $<$ is sufficient.

An *action description* in EC includes axioms that define: the action occurrences, with the use of happensAt predicates; the effects of actions, with the use of initiates and terminates predicates; and the values of the fluents, with the use of initially and holdsAt predicates. Table 1 summarises the main EC predicates. EC variables, that start with an upper-case letter, are assumed to be universally quantified unless otherwise indicated. Predicates, function symbols and constants start with a lower-case letter.

**Table 1.** Main predicates of the event calculus.

| Predicate | Meaning |
|---|---|
| $Act$ happensAt $T$ | Action $Act$ occurs at time $T$ |
| initially $F = V$ | The value of fluent $F$ is $V$ at time 0 |
| $F = V$ holdsAt $T$ | The value of fluent $F$ is $V$ at time $T$ |
| $Act$ initiates $F = V$ at $T$ | The occurrence of action $Act$ at time $T$ initiates a period of time for which the value of fluent $F$ is $V$ |
| $Act$ terminates $F = V$ at $T$ | The occurrence of action $Act$ at time $T$ terminates a period of time for which the value of fluent $F$ is $V$ |

Where $F$ is a *fluent*, which is a property that is allowed to have different values at different points in time, the term $F = V$ denotes that fluent $F$ has value $V$. Boolean fluents are a special case in which the possible values are *true* and *false*. Informally, $F = V$ holds at a particular time-point if $F = V$ has been *initiated* by an action at some earlier time-point, and not *terminated* by another action in the meantime.

Events initiate and terminate a period of time during which a fluent holds a value continuously. Events occur at specific times (when they *happen*). A set of events, each with a given time, is called a *narrative*.

The utility of the EC comes from being able to reason with narratives. Therefore, the final part of an EC specification is the domain-independent 'engine' which computes what fluents hold, i.e. have the value *true* in the case of boolean fluents, or what value a fluent takes, for each multi-valued fluent. This can be used to compute a 'state' of the specification in terms of the fluents representing institutional facts. This state changes over time as events happen, and includes the roles, (institutionalised) powers, permissions and obligations of agents, and the protocols selected to implement a community's operational-, collective- and constitutional-choice rules [16].

A particularly relevant concept to formalise is of *institutionalised power* [11], by which a designated agent occupying a distinguished role is empowered to perform specific actions of conventional significance, which result in "seeing to it that" *institutional facts* are true (facts which are true by agreement, or convention, in the context of the institution). Examples include an agent in the role of auctioneer in an auction house 'decision arena' banging a gavel and saying "sold", which sees to it that the auctioned lot is contracted to the highest bidder in return for payment of the bid price; or an agent in the role of priest in the context of a marriage ceremony 'decision arena' pronouncing two people "man and wife" sees to it that they are married (according to the religious institution; according to the state, the fact that they are married may only be true after another act of conventional significance, for example signing a register).

Institutionalised power is particularly important to specify because of the different roles and relations that obtain in remote- and self-supervised exercise: the institutionalised powers that exist between peers within the self-supervised patient group are rather different from the institutionalised powers that exist between the practitioner and her patients. Powers, permissions and obligations of agents can be uniformly represented in EC using the following boolean fluents:

$$\mathbf{pow}(Agent, Action) = \ldots$$
$$\mathbf{per}(Agent, Action) = \ldots$$
$$\mathbf{obl}(Agent, Action) = \ldots$$

We illustrate the formal specification of powers, permissions and obligations in the EC in the next subsection.

**Self-supervised Exercise.** This section presents an example specification for reasoning about events in the context of self-supervised exercise. We assume (for simplicity) that there are only two roles, *health_practitioner* and *patient*. A person occupying the health-practitioner role can assign a person who is a patient to a group, and appoint a member of that group to the role of being a supervisor for that group. Both actions are subject to certain conditions: the assignment to a group depends on the readiness of the patient for the exercise regime of the group; while the appointment to the supervisor role depends on the number of times the patient him/herself has been supervised exercising (recorded by an exercise count $ex\_ct$). These institutionalised powers can be specified as follows:

$\mathbf{pow}(HP, assign(HP, P, G, H)) = true$   holdsAt   $T$   $\leftarrow$

   $role\_of(HP, health\_practitioner, H) = true$   holdsAt   $T$   $\wedge$

   $role\_of(P, patient, H) = true$   holdsAt   $T$   $\wedge$

   $regime(G, H) = L1$   holdsAt   $T$   $\wedge$

   $readiness(P, H) = L2$   holdsAt   $T$   $\wedge$

   $L1 \leq L2$

$\mathbf{pow}(HP, appoint(HP, P, G, H)) = true$   holdsAt   $T$   $\leftarrow$

   $role\_of(HP, health\_practitioner, H) = true$   holdsAt   $T$   $\wedge$

   $members(G, H) = M$   holdsAt   $T$   $\wedge$

   $P \in M$   $\wedge$

   $threshold(G, H) = T$   holdsAt   $T$   $\wedge$

   $ex\_ct(P, G, H) = S$   holdsAt   $T$   $\wedge$

   $S \geq T$

When the health practitioner $HP$ performs either an empowered assignment or appointment action, then the results are as follows:

$$assign(HP, P, G, H) \text{ initiates } members(G, H) = [P \mid M] \text{ at } T \leftarrow$$
$$members(G, H) = M \text{ holdsAt } T \wedge$$
$$\mathbf{pow}(HP, assign(HP, P, G, H)) = true \text{ holdsAt } T$$
$$appoint(HP, P, G, H) \text{ initiates } role\_of(P, G, H) = supervisor \text{ at } T \leftarrow$$
$$\mathbf{pow}(HP, appoint(HP, P, G, H)) = true \text{ holdsAt } T$$

The power to supervise, and the effect of a *self-supervision* can then be specified as follows:

$$\mathbf{pow}(P1, supervise(P1, P2, G, H)) = true \text{ holdsAt } T \leftarrow$$
$$members(G, H) = M \text{ holdsAt } T \wedge$$
$$P1 \in M \wedge$$
$$P2 \in M \wedge$$
$$role\_of(P1, G, H) = supervisor \text{ holdsAt } T \wedge$$
$$supervise(P1, P2, G, H) \text{ initiates } ex_c t(P2, G, H) = S \text{ at } T \leftarrow$$
$$supervisions(P2, G, H) = S \text{ holdsAt } T \wedge$$
$$S1 = S + 1 \wedge$$
$$\mathbf{pow}(P1, supervise(P1, P2, G, H)) = true \text{ holdsAt } T$$

In other words, a patient $P1$ is empowered to supervise a patient $P2$ if s/he is appointed to the role within the group by an empowered health practitioner; and the effect of a supervision of $P2$ (reported by $P1$) is to increase $P2$'s exercise count (so that when it reaches or passes the group threshold, $P2$ can also be appointed to a supervisor role).

## 4.2 Interface and Interaction Design

In [3], we described a Serious Game called *Social mPower*, which investigated how smart meters could be used to encourage pro-social behaviour and collective action (as opposed to simply monitoring or managing electricity consumption). Based on this work and other exemplars [23], we have derived the following interface guidelines for implementing interactive self-governance in collective adaptive socio-technical systems:

- Interface cues and affordances for collective action, indicating that participants are engaged in a collective action situation – for example the use of avatars, and especially those which express emotions [26];
- Visualisation: appropriate presentation and representation of data, making what is conceptually significant perceptually prominent, in particular significant events, the status of rules, the progress of protocols and the structure of multiple organisations – for example, the status of norms and powers;

- Social networking: fast, convenient and cheap communication channels to support the propagation of messages in a seamless, unobtrusive way – emphasising contextually meaningful private communication between members of a local community known to each other, rather than global platforms that encourage the pursuit of 'followers', 'friends' or 'likes' from strangers;
- Feedback: inform individuals that their ('small', individual) pro-social action $X$ contributed to some ('large', collective) action $Y$ which achieved beneficial outcome $Z$ – for example the representation of the collective ambience or 'mood' according to monitored physical contributions of collective members;
- Incentives: typically in the form of social capital [19], awarded for absolute/collective rather than relative/individual endeavour and achievement.

These guidelines are offered in the same 'spirit' as Nielsen's ten usability heuristics for user interface design [15], i.e. these guidelines are currently closer to 'rules of thumb' than specific methodological steps. This iteration of the guidelines for the purposes of this position paper is at a much earlier stage of development than Nielsen's heuristics, and much more work is required to make them fully operational for the increased benefit of system developers. However, in relation to the (partial) envisionment of Sect. 2, it would be possible to apply the guidelines for future interface development.

For example, for the first guideline, various indicators of successful collective action could be used, for example, multiple ants carrying a leaf that each on their own could not. However, as suggested above, the use of avatars for personalisation, demonstrating status (e.g. through some indication of emotive state) and cor conveying a sense of belonging could be helpful.

For the second guideline, three of the most important aspects to visualise would be the 'health' status of the collective (i.e. group 'well being' rather than personal health of the group members), the extent of individual contributions, and progress towards the next 'readiness' level. One possible visualisation that captures all three could be inspired by the Forest app[1] Each member of the group is represented by a tree, and the tree grows (or withers) according to active contribution.

For the third guideline, many social media applications become unusable as the group becomes larger. It is therefore important for the health practitioner to maintain 'workable' group sizes. Furthermore, the app should support standard conversation types (or allow the user to customise such conversations). For example, if there is a regular meeting time and place, then there should be a screen for that week (or month's) meeting, offering a button for indicating intention to participate (or not), and showing who is/is not currently committed to participating. There should not be a need for sending notifications, if a member of the group is concerned with attendance then they can consult this screen.

For the fourth and fifth guidelines, these could possibly also be achieved through the appropriate visualisation, for example showing an animation of the

---

[1] https://www.forestapp.cc/en/. This app encourages people to stay concentrated on their jobs and away from their Smartphones by growing a forest through not interacting with their phone during designated times.

forest growing as an historical record, but also an option to see what the forest *would have* looked like without the individual's contribution. The aim would be to provide a better incentive to increased participation than 'naming and shaming'. However, the final guideline on incentives is related to a more general concern about *values*, in the form of social capital, as discussed in the next subsection.

### 4.3 Construction of Shared Reality

In remotely-supervised exercise, the health practitioner is in effect a centralised controller, and orchestration of collective action can follow a 'leader'. For the self-supervised exercise, the patient community must instead rely on *self-organisation* to achieve the necessary agreement on, or synchronisation of, collective action. However, self-organising approaches often require other incentives to participate, contribute, or select an action which maximises the collective, rather than individual, utility.

One possible type of incentive is social capital. Social capital has been defined as attributes of individuals that assist them with resolving collective action situations [18]. These attributes come in many forms, such as trustworthiness, social networks, and institutions. However, we find that while social capital is fine as a concept, as a term it is potentially misleading, as it suggests something that can be owned, traded or (even worse) 'spent'.

For example, in an experiment to examine self-organisation based on negotiation and social capital, we examined a consumer exchange arena in which social capital was represented in terms of 'favours' [19]. Whenever one consumer traded a good with another which resulted in a more favourable arrangement, it counted as a 'favour'; moreover, if the exchange benefitted both then it counted as *two* favours. Over time, the favour-based situation achieved a more optimal distribution of goods; however, the risk is that, in a less abstract formulation, the favours could become commodified as currency. Therefore, in *digital communities*, there is fundamental tension is between retaining the complexity-reducing short-cuts offered by transactional information, which could be realised through a community cryptocurrency, without losing the benefits of relational information that social capital brings with it.

In self-supervised exercise, the digital representation social capital in terms of concrete attributes or as the consequence of specific actions or event which can be recorded with the use of the Event Calculus. However, this runs the risks of commodifying the concept, with the concomitant loss of the actual 'value' or leverage that social capital has or can achieve (cf. [21]). In other words, it is more important not to focus so much on what social capital *is*, but on what social capital *does*; and what it does is to coordinate expectations [20] and provide a basis for community governance [4]. Therefore, any framework for *electronic* social capital which can be used to support successful collective action in self-organising systems will need not just to define, in computational form, the attributes that agents need to represent and reason with, but also the *processes* by which those same agents can coordinate their expectations and govern their communities.

This is the principal requirement of a framework for electronic social capital in a mobile healthcare application: it should define data structures for representing attributes of agents (i.e. in objective terms such as reputation and institutions, and subjective terms such as their social networks), and also define processes for updating, evaluating and visualising social capital. In fact, as an *axial currency*, careful consideration needs to be give to its design and deployment [22], beyond the engineering of the collective adaptive systems itself.

Therefore, social capital, which encompasses all concepts created by institutions (such as the norms and values mentioned previously), fits within the framework of Artificial Social Constructivism (ASC). This theory, based on the original premise from [1], expands on the idea that language shapes society. This idea has been highlighted previously in the medical field, specifically in online weight loss communities, where community language is used to indicate appropriate behaviour when members are interacting with one another [6]. ASC proposes that by allowing human users and digital agents to educate each other about norms of behaviour, a shared reality can be created where both the users and the agents uphold values they find important. This is particularly important in scenarios such as this, where the user needs to feel invested in the technology and in its assistance to reach a common goal, here being exercise despite pain, in order keep using it.

## 5   Summary and Conclusions

The accumulation of atherosclerotic disease in the lower limbs can result in narrowing or occlusion of arteries. The resultant reduction in blood supply to the musculature of the affected limb(s) can result in pain in the leg, distal to diseased site, that occurs on exertion. Pain is predictably relieved by rest. This predictable onset and offset of symptoms caused by a restricted blood supply is known as intermittent claudication. These symptoms are often the first clinical manifestation of peripheral arterial disease (PAD).

PAD prevalence increases with age and may be as high as 20% in populations aged over 75. The treatment of intermittent claudication includes the management of atherosclerotic risk factors, such as smoking, hypertension, diabetes and hypercholesterolaemia. In addition, the National Institute for Health and Care Excellence (NICE) recommends that patients diagnosed with intermittent claudication should be offered access to a supervised exercise programme. This consists of monitored exercise 2 h per week for at least 3 months.

Nationally, the provision of supervised exercise programmes is poor. In 2009 only 24% of vascular surgery departments had access to a supervised exercise programme; by 2016 only a modest improvement was observed, with 39% of departments having access. Such a lack of provision is disappointing given recent evidence that successfully run supervised exercise programmes can be as effective as invasive management for lower limb atherosclerosis6.

The chronic underfunding and lack of access to supervised exercise programmes makes adherence to NICE guidelines impossible for most NHS Trusts. Novel methods aimed at improving access to supervised exercise programmes are required. The design and development of a remotely supervised exercise programme delivered by a disease-specific mobile phone application would be a novel and cost-effective method for delivering exercise therapy. The app will allow accurate measurement of walking distances and regular remote supervision by clinical teams who will have the ability to interact with patients by sending messages via the app.

In this paper, we have proposed that the development of a disease-specific application to enable remotely supervised and self-regulated exercise and the creation of a resultant digital community will best serve the needs of healthcare professionals and patients alike. However, the proposed system has the characteristics a collective adaptive socio-technical system, and this requires:

- collectivity: we need to be polycentric, i.e. we have people and software involved in the decision-making, and the people are "empowered" in those decision-making processes in different ways, in particular the health practitioner to patient group is a centralised one, while within the patient group it is a decentralised (or peer-to-peer) one. Software in this case needs to be largely data collecting but privacy preserving, and providing analytics to support the decision-making processes and for the health economics, evaluation, etc.
- adaptivity: one of the important innovations being proposed here is the synthesis of remote and self-supervision with the extra insight of adaptation in *two* dimensions: adaptation initiated by the health practitioner as the capabilities/health of the patient group improves with exercise, and adaptation initiated within the patient group to incentive and visualise that progress.

However, as evidenced by the eclectic mix of design methodologies, formal specification languages and interaction design techniques presented in this position paper, there is no 'silver bullet' approach to rigorous engineering of a collective adaptive system in conjunction with the requirements of a mobile healthcare application. There is no need to despair, though, since the corollary is increased opportunities for co-design and most importantly, generativity (the ability for people to fashion new tools out of existing ones that were neither expected nor intended by the original tool's designers [27]).

# References

1. Berger, P., Luckmann, T.: The Social Construction of Reality. Penguin Books, London (1966)
2. Bhatti, Y., del Castillo, J., Olson, K., Darzi, A.: Putting Humans at the Center of Health Care Innovation. Harvard Business Review (2018)
3. Bourazeri, A., Pitt, J.: An agent-based serious game for decentralised community energy systems. In: Dam, H.K., Pitt, J., Xu, Y., Governatori, G., Ito, T. (eds.) PRIMA 2014. LNCS (LNAI), vol. 8861, pp. 246–253. Springer, Cham (2014). https://doi.org/10.1007/978-3-319-13191-7_20

4. Bowles, S., Gintis, H.: Social capital and community governance. Econ. J. **112**(483), F419–F436 (2002)
5. Cavoukian, A.: Privacy by design [leading edge]. IEEE Technol. Soc. Mag. **31**(4), 18–19 (2012)
6. Chancellor, S., Hu, A., De Choudhury, M.: Norms matter: contrasting social support around behavior change in online weight loss communities. In: Proceedings of the 36th ACM Conference on Human Factors in Computing Systems (CHI 2018) (Paper no. 666), pp. 1–14 (2018)
7. Cheetham, D., Burgess, L., Ellis, M., Williams, A., Greenhalgh, R., Davies, A.: Does supervised exercise offer adjuvant benefit over exercise advice alone for the treatment of intermittent claudication? A randomised trial. Eur. J. Vasc. Endovasc. Surg. **27**, 17–23 (2004)
8. Conte, M., et al.: Society for vascular surgery practice guidelines for atherosclerotic occlusive disease of the lower extremities: management of asymptomatic disease and claudication. J. Vasc. Surg. **61**(3), 2S–41S (2015)
9. Friedman, B., Kahn, P., Borning, A.: Value sensitive design and information systems. In: Himma, K., Tavani, H. (eds.) The Handbook of Information and Computer Ethics, pp. 69–101. Wiley, Hoboken (2008)
10. Hillston, J., Pitt, J., Wirsing, M., Zambonelli, F.: Collective adaptive systems: qualitative and quantitative modelling and analysis (dagstuhl seminar 14512). Dagstuhl Rep. **4**(12), 68–113 (2014). https://doi.org/10.4230/DagRep.4.12.68
11. Jones, A., Sergot, M.: A formal characterisation of institutionalised power. J. IGPL **4**(3), 427–443 (1996)
12. Kowalski, R., Sergot, M.: A logic-based calculus of events. New Gener. Comput. **4**, 67–95 (1986)
13. Mazari, F., et al.: Long-term outcomes of a randomized clinical trial of supervised exercise, percutaneous transluminal angioplasty or combined treatment for patients with intermittent claudication due to femoropopliteal disease. J. Vasc. Surg. **65**(4), 1239–1240 (2017)
14. Mummah, S., Robinson, T., King, A., Gardner, C., Sutton, S.: Ideas (integrate, design, assess, and share): a framework and toolkit of strategies for the development of more effective digital interventions to change health behavior. J. Med. Internet Res. **18**, e317 (2016)
15. Nielsen, J.: Usability Engineering. Academic Press, San Diego (1994)
16. Ostrom, E.: Governing the Commons: The Evolution of Institutions for Collective Action. Cambridge University Press, Cambridge (1990)
17. Ostrom, E.: Beyond markets and states: polycentric governance of complex economic systems. In: Grandin, K. (ed.) Les Prix Nobel. The Nobel Prizes 2009, pp. 408–444. Nobel Foundation (2010)
18. Ostrom, E., Ahn, T.: Foundations of Social Capital. An Elgar Reference Collection. Edward Elgar Publishing, Cheltenham (2003)
19. Petruzzi, P.E., Busquets, D., Pitt, J.: Experiments with social capital in multi-agent systems. In: Dam, H.K., Pitt, J., Xu, Y., Governatori, G., Ito, T. (eds.) PRIMA 2014. LNCS (LNAI), vol. 8861, pp. 18–33. Springer, Cham (2014). https://doi.org/10.1007/978-3-319-13191-7_2
20. Peyton Young, H.: Social norms. In: Durlauf, S., Blume, L. (eds.) The New Palgrave Dictionary of Economics, 2nd edn. Palgrave Macmillan, London (2008)
21. Pitt, J., Nowak, A.: The reinvention of social capital for socio-technical systems. IEEE Technol. Soc. Mag. **33**(1), 27–33 (2014)
22. Pitt, J., Clippinger, H., Sorensen, C.: Values, axial currencies and computational axiology. IEEE Technol. Soc. Mag. (2018, to appear)

23. Pitt, J., Diaconescu, A.: Structure and governance of communities for the digital society. In: Workshop on Self-Improving System Integration (2015)
24. Pitt, J., Diaconescu, A.: Interactive self-governance and value-sensitive design for self-organising socio-technical systems. In: FAS* Workshop Proceedings: SASO$^{ST}$ (2016)
25. Valetto, G., et al.: All together now: collective intelligence for computer-supported collective action. In: 2015 IEEE International Conference on Self-Adaptive and Self-Organizing Systems Workshops, SASO Workshops 2015, Cambridge, MA, USA, pp. 13–18, 21–25 September 2015
26. Vasalou, A., Joinson, A., Bänziger, T., Goldie, P., Pitt, J.: Avatars in social media: balancing accuracy, playfulness and embodied messages. Int. J. Hum. Comput. Stud. **66**, 801–811 (2008)
27. Zittrain, J.: The Future of the Internet – And How to Stop It. Yale University Press, New Haven (2008)

# Engineering Collectives of Self-driving Vehicles: The SOTA Approach

Dhaminda B. Abeywickrama[1], Marco Mamei[2], and Franco Zambonelli[2(✉)]

[1] Agents, Interaction and Complexity Group,
School of Electronics and Computer Science, University of Southampton,
Southampton, UK
dhaminda.abeywickrama@soton.ac.uk
[2] Dipartimento di Scienze e Metodi dell'Ingegneria,
University of Modena and Reggio Emilia, Via Amendola 2,
42122 Reggio Emilia, Italy
{marco.mamei,franco.zambonelli}@unimore.it

**Abstract.** Future cities will be populated by myriads of autonomous self-driving vehicles. Although individual vehicles have their own goals to pursue in autonomy, they may also be part of a collective of vehicles, as in the case of a fleet of vehicles of a car sharing company. Accordingly, they may also be required to act in a coordinated way towards the achievement of specific collective goals, or to meet specific city-level objectives. This raises the issue of properly engineering the behavior of such collective of vehicles, by properly capturing their collective requirements also in consideration of their individual goals, and understanding which knowledge about the state of the collective they must be provided with. In this context, this paper shows how the SOTA model can be a very effective tool to support the engineering of self-driving vehicle collectives. SOTA, by bringing together the lessons of goal-oriented requirements engineering, context-aware systems, and dynamical systems modeling, has indeed the potential for acting as a general reference model to help tackle some key issues in the design and development of complex collective systems immersed in dynamic environments, as collectives of self-driving vehicles are.

**Keywords:** Self-driving vehicles · Software engineering
Self-adaptation

## 1 Introduction

As we are entering the era of autonomous cars, many envision that future urban mobility will no longer be primarily supported by private vehicles, but rather by fleets of autonomous vehicles, either owned by private companies or by the municipality itself, and devoted to car or ride sharing [5,8], and to the delivery of merchandise [16]. Thus, properly organizing and managing such fleets will be of primary importance in future cities.

© Springer Nature Switzerland AG 2018
T. Margaria and B. Steffen (Eds.): ISoLA 2018, LNCS 11246, pp. 79–93, 2018.
https://doi.org/10.1007/978-3-030-03424-5_6

Such management will have to account the diverse and mostly unpredictable demands of individual citizens, commercial activities, and industries. Also, it will have to account for resource restrictions related to, e.g., availability of parking lots and availability of charging stations (we assume the vehicles are electric ones). In terms of objectives, the management will have to harmonize at the best with the needs of individual vehicles (that is, of the citizens that have rented a vehicle), the needs of the fleet (i.e., or of the company that owns the fleet) as a whole, and possibly the specific constraints imposed by the municipality (e.g., in terms of traffic or pollution).

Overall, then, the management of such fleets will resemble the management of collective adaptive systems that are called to operate in open-ended and unpredictable environments [4]. Accordingly, software infrastructures in charge of the fleet will have to become self-adaptive in their behavior [17], i.e., capable of dynamically adapting their behavior without human supervision. Thus, they can respond to changing situations and unexpected contingencies without suffering malfunctionings or degrading of quality of service.

In the past few years, several research works have been devoted to identify models [7,18], languages [6,14], and tools [2], to support the development of collective self-adaptive software systems. However, a key issue that is still open is the identification of general modeling frameworks to help tackling the many complex issues associated with the proper engineering of collective self-adaptive systems. These issues include: proper analysis and verification of functional and non-functional requirements of self-adaptation, and the analysis and identification of the knowledge requirements, i.e., of which information must be made available to a system to support its self-adaptive behavior.

To tackle this issue, we previously proposed [1] a sort of "black-box" approach to adaptation in which, abstracting from the actual mechanisms via which to achieve adaptation, we questioned about "what adaptation is for" from the viewpoint of system requirements and observable dynamic behavior of a system. The result of this process is SOTA ("State Of The Affairs"), a robust conceptual framework that, by grounding on the lessons of goal-oriented requirements engineering [12], dynamical systems modeling [20] and multidimensional context modeling [13], can provide effective conceptual support to self-adaptive software development.

In particular, the key idea in SOTA is to perceive a self-adaptive software system, like the one needed for the management of collectives of self-driving vehicles, as a sort of complex dynamic system immersed in a virtual $n$-dimensional phase space, each dimension being associated to either some internal software parameters or some external environmental parameters of interest for the execution of the system. The adaptive execution of the system can then be modeled in terms of movements in such space. Functional requirements (i.e., goals) are associated to areas of the phase space the system has to reach, non-functional requirements are associated to the trajectory the system should try to walk through, whereas self-adaptation is associated to the capability of the system to re-join proper trajectories when moved away from it. For example, a fleet of self-driving vehicles could have a functional requirement of arriving at destination on time, and a non-functional requirement of keeping the overall energy consumption below a certain threshold.

Indeed, in the area of complex software systems, it has been extensively argued that dynamical systems modeling can be a powerful tool to analyze the behavior of complex systems [23], and several studies exist in that direction (e.g., [19]). SOTA commits to the above perspective, but it adopts a totally different endeavour. In fact, it exploits dynamical systems as a means to model and engineer the behavioral and awareness requirements, rather than as a means to analyze the behavior of existing systems.

The exploitation of the SOTA model in the engineering of self-adaptive systems (possibly in conjunction with, and complementing, more traditional conceptual tools for goal-oriented requirements engineering [12, 15]), and in particular of collective systems of self-driving vehicles, brings several advantages:

- SOTA can be used as a tool to support the process of identifying which knowledge must be made available to the system and its components, and what degree of situation awareness they should reach to support adaptivity [22];
- SOTA can be used to early assess self-adaptation requirements via model-checking techniques [3], towards a better and more sound process of requirements engineering for self-adaptive systems.

The remainder of this paper is organized as follows. Section 2 provides an overview of the SOTA model. Section 3 shows how SOTA can be applied to a scenario of a collective of self-driving vehicles. Section 4 discusses how SOTA can be adopted to assess the knowledge or awareness requirements. Section 5 shows how the SOTA model can be an effective tool for the early assessment of requirements for self-adaptive systems via model checking. Finally, Sect. 6 concludes the paper.

## 2   SOTA Model

SOTA builds on existing approaches to goal-oriented requirements engineering [12, 15] and, for modeling the adaptation dimension, it integrates and extends recent approaches on multidimensional modeling of context, such as the "Hyperspace Analogue to Context" (HAC) approach [13]. In particular, such generalization and extensions are aimed at enriching goal-oriented and context modeling with elements of dynamical systems modeling [20], so as to account for the general needs of dynamic self-adaptive systems and components.

The term SOTA stems from "State Of The Affairs", which is a concept central in SOTA. The state of the affairs of a system is intended as any characteristics of the system itself and of the environment in which it lives and executes that may affect its behavior and that may be relevant with respect to its capabilities of achieving the objectives it was built for. In other words: (i) given a specific state of the affairs, i.e., the overall situation in which the system is; (ii) given that the state of the affairs can change due to both the internal activities of the system and the external dynamics of the environment; and (iii) a self-adaptive system must be able to trigger internal activities that enable it to achieve desirable state of the affairs (i.e., the goals or objectives it was built for) despite the external dynamics.

## 2.1  SOTA Space

SOTA assumes that the current "state of the affairs" $S(t)$ at time $t$, of a specific entity $e$ (let it be an individual component or an ensemble of components) can be described as a tuple of $n$ $s_i$ values, each representing a specific aspect of the current situation of the entity/ensemble and of its operational environment:

$$S(t) = \langle s_1, s_2, \ldots, s_n \rangle$$

As the entity executes, $S$ changes either due to the specific actions of $e$ or because of the dynamics of $e$'s environment. Thus, we can generally see this evolution of $S$ as a movement in a virtual $n$-dimensional space $\mathbf{S}$ (see Fig. 1):

$$\mathbf{S} = \mathbf{S}_1 \times \mathbf{S}_2 \times \ldots \times \mathbf{S}_n$$

Or, according to the standard terminology of dynamical systems modeling, we can consider $\mathbf{S}$ as the phase space of $e$ and its evolution that can be caused by internal actions or by external contingencies as a movement in such phase space.

To model such evolution of the system in terms of "transitions", $\theta(t, t+1)$ expresses a movement of $e$ in the $\mathbf{S}$, i.e.,

$$\theta(t, t+1) = \langle \delta s_1, \delta s_2, \ldots, \delta s_n \rangle, \delta s_1 = (s_1(t+1) - s_1(t))$$

A transition can be endogenous, i.e., induced by actions within the system itself, or exogenous, i.e., induced by external sources. The existence of exogenous transitions is particularly important to account for. In fact, the identification of such sources of transitions (i.e., the identification of which dimensions of the SOTA space can induce such transitions) enables identifying what can be the external factors requiring adaptation.

## 2.2  Goals and Utilities

The requirements of a complex software (and more generally ICT) system can be naturally expressed in terms of the general objectives it has to achieve, which in turn typically decomposes into specific goals [9], to be achieved by either individual entities of the system or ensembles of entities.

A *goal* by definition is the eventual achievement of a given state of the affairs. Therefore, in very general terms, a specific goal $G_i$ for the entity $e$ can be represented as a specific point, or more generally as a specific area, in the SOTA space. That is:

$$G_i = A_1 \times A_2 \times \ldots \times A_n, A_i \subseteq \mathbf{S}_i$$

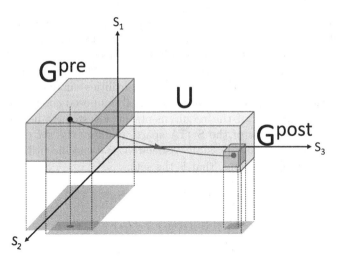

**Fig. 1.** The trajectory of an entity in the SOTA space, starting from a goal precondition and trying to reach the postcondition while moving in the area specified by the utility.

More specifically, a goal $G_i$ of an entity $e$ may not necessarily be always active. Rather, it could be the case that a goal of an entity will only get activated when specific conditions occur. In these cases, it is useful to characterize a goal in terms of a precondition $G_i^{pre}$ and a postcondition $G_i^{post}$, to express when the goal has to activate and what the achievement of the goal implies. Both $G_i^{pre}$ and $G_i^{post}$ represent two areas or points in the space $\mathbf{S}$. In simple terms, when an entity $e$ finds itself in $G_i^{pre}$ the goal gets activated and the entity should try to move in $\mathbf{S}$ so as to reach $G_i^{post}$, where the goal is to be considered achieved (see Fig. 1). Clearly, a goal with no precondition is like a goal whose precondition coincides with the whole space, and it is intended as a goal that is always active.

As goals represent the eventual state of the affairs that a system or component has to achieve, they can be considered functional requirements. However, in many cases, a system should try to reach its goals by adhering to specific constraints on how such a goal can be reached. By referring again to the geometric interpretation of the execution of an entity as movements in the space $\mathbf{S}$, one can say that sometimes an entity should try or be constrained to reach a goal by having its trajectory be confined within a specific area (see Fig. 1). We call these types of constraints on the execution path that a system/entity should try to respect as *utilities*, to reflect a nature that is similar to that of non-functional requirements.

As goals, a utility $U_i$ can be typically expressed as a subspace in $\mathbf{S}$, and can be either a general one for a system/entity (the system/entity must always respect the utility during its execution) or one specifically associated to a specific goal $G_i$ (the system/entity should respect the utility while trying to achieve the goal). For the latter case, the complete definition of a goal is:

$$G_i = \{G_i^{pre}, G_i^{post}, U_i\}$$

In some cases, it may also be helpful to express utilities as relations over the derivative of a dimension. That is to express not the area the trajectory should stay in but rather the *direction* to follow in the trajectory (e.g., try to minimize execution time, where execution time is one of the relevant dimensions of the state of affairs). It is also worth mentioning that utilities can derive from specific system requirements or can derive from externally imposed constraint.

A complete definition of the requirements of a system-to-be thus implies identifying the dimensions of the SOTA space, defining the set of goals (with pre- and postconditions, and possibly associated goal-specific utilities) and the global utilities for such systems, that is the sets:

$$\mathbf{S} = \mathbf{S}_1 \times \mathbf{S}_2 \times \ldots \times \mathbf{S}_n$$

$$\mathbf{G} = \{G_1, G_2, \ldots, G_m\}$$

$$\mathbf{U} = \{U_1, U_2, \ldots, U_p\}$$

Of course, during the identification of goals and utilities, it is already possible to associate goals and utilities locally to specific components of the system as well as globally, to the system as a whole. Thus, the above sets can be possibly further refined by partitioning them among local and global ones.

## 3  Engineering Collectives of Self-driving Vehicles

In this section, we exemplify how it is possible to address the problem of engineering collectives of self-driving vehicles (i.e., the management of a fleet of autonomous vehicles for car sharing services) using the SOTA approach. Such a scenario is characterized for being immersed in unpredictable and dynamic environment, which makes features of self-adaptation particularly important. Let us now conceptualize the problem in detail.

- A fleet $F$ has a set of vehicles. A vehicle $V_i$ has a set of planned rides, i.e., $R = \{R_1, R_2, \ldots, R_n\}$. Each planned ride is defined by a location $L_i$, a starting time $_iT_S^R$, and duration $_iD^R$. A route alternative can be provided from ride $R_i$ to $R_{i+1}$ as $_iR^D$.
- The departure time and arrival time of a vehicle are provided by $_iT_S^D$ and $_iT_E^D$, respectively.
- The battery state of charge or energy level of a vehicle $V_i$ at departure time is defined by $_iE_S^D$, while $_iE_E^D$ specifies battery level at arrival time.
- The goal of a vehicle $V_i$ is to arrive in time at the appointment, so that $_iT_E^D <= {_iT_S^D}$, and the battery level should never run out, so it is required that $_iE_E^D > 0$.
- The charging of a vehicle could occur during the appointment duration.
- A set of parking lots can be present where each one is defined by a name $PLname$. Similarly, a set of charging stations can be defined with each one having a name $CSname$. The available parking spaces and charging stations in location $L$ can be defined as $ParkSpotsNum$ and $ChargeSpotsNum$.

The overall transportation system can be conceptually modeled as SOTA entities ($e$) moving in the SOTA space ($\mathbf{S}$). These entities could be an individual entity (e.g., vehicle), or a group of entities (e.g., fleet of vehicles; infrastructure resources, such as parking lots, charging stations and roads). Both vehicles and the fleet can be modeled in terms of entities that have goals ($G_i$), which can be at the individual (single vehicle) or global level (a fleet). Similarly, utilities ($U_i$) can be identified, related to how such goals can be achieved, also at the individual or global level. In the SOTA space, the locations, departure or arrival times, and battery energy levels correspond to the dimensions of the SOTA space, while a goal or utility can be represented as a specific point or area of the phase space.

From the point of view of a *vehicle* ($V_i$), a key goal is to reach the destination within time and battery energy level. We can characterize this goal in terms of a precondition and a postcondition to express when the goal has to achieve and what the achievement of the goal implies. For example, the preconditions can be ($G_i^{pre}$) to check whether the list of planned rides is known; the parking lots are assigned; the charging stations are assigned; and the battery state of charge level is sufficient at trip start. The postcondition ($G_i^{post}$) can be the actual goal itself, such as reach the destination within the time allocated and within the battery state of charge level. In the same manner, utilities ($U_i$) can be identified at the individual vehicle level, as a general one or as one associated to a specific goal of the vehicle.

For example, Fig. 2 illustrates a portion of the case study. A vehicle $V_i$ starting at $L_0$ has the goal of completing planned ride $R_i$ and arrive at location $L_i$ (for simplicity of drawing we consider a one dimensional spatial extend – road – indicated by L). The figure illustrates a part of the SOTA space focusing on three dimensions: location, time and battery level. For readability, we represent both the 3D space and also 2D projections. The goal $G_i$ of vehicle $V_i$ is represented by the blue box: the vehicle has to be at location $L_i$ at $_iT_S^R$ time, with a battery level greater than 0. The utility $U_i$ (i.e., non-functional requirements) of $V_i$ is represented by the green box: the vehicle battery level should not become too low. The state of vehicle $V_i$ is a point in this space and its actions describe the red trajectory in the space: $V_i$ reach its goal on time consuming some battery, but remaining within the non-functional requirements/boundaries.

From the viewpoint of a *fleet* ($F$), we can associate goals and utilities to the system as a whole, i.e., globally. Maximizing the usage of vehicles is a key requirement for the fleet. In this regard, we can identify two goals ($G_i$) for the fleet $F$. They are: (i) distributing the vehicles of the fleet fairly in the city at midnight every day; and (ii) creating and assigning trips for the vehicles. The preconditions ($G_i^{pre}$) for the *distribute vehicles* goal are checking whether the time is midnight, and distribution of the vehicles in the city is imbalanced. The postcondition ($G_i^{post}$) is the actual redistribution of the vehicles in a fair and balanced manner. In the meantime, the precondition for the *create trips* goal can be to check whether the vehicles are available before assigning trips for them. The postconditions can be whether the rides list, parking lots and charging stations have been assigned for the vehicles.

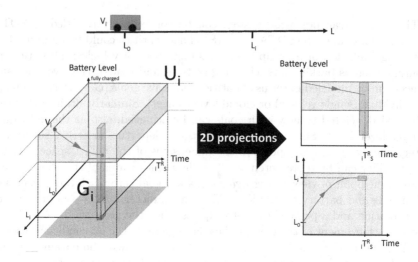

**Fig. 2.** SOTA space in the case study. The figure illustrates a portion of the case study. A vehicle $V_i$ starting at $L_0$ has the goal of completing planned ride $R_i$ and arrive at location $L_i$. The goal $G_i$ of vehicle $V_i$ is represented by the blue box. The utility $U_i$ of $V_i$ is represented by the green box. (Color figure online)

As for global utilities $(U)$, these can be a general one for the fleet or one specifically associated to a specific goal of the fleet. For example, there can be a utility for all the vehicles in the fleet to avoid roads with tolls or avoid localities that have disruptions. Some global utilities of the fleet which can be expressed as relations over the derivative of a dimension are: maximize usage of vehicles in the fleet, minimize journey time or cost, and minimize battery consumption.

As provided for a vehicle, we can identify the relevant dimensions (**S**) of the state of affairs for a fleet. They are: current locations of the vehicles in the fleet; availability of the vehicles; availability and capacity of the infrastructure resources; battery energy levels of the vehicles; current traffic information; and journey times and costs.

## 4   SOTA Space and Knowledge Requirements

The "state of the affairs" is a very general concept, and its dimensions include anything relevant to keep a system up and running (i.e., hardware, software, environmental features) [1]. Therefore, identifying what are the relevant dimensions around which to model the SOTA space is a necessary activity towards the building of a self-adaptive system. However, when discussing about self-adaptive systems, such identification also directly relates to identifying: (i) the knowledge (i.e., what dimensions) that must be made available to entities to enable self-adaptation; (ii) the type of sensors (i.e., physical or virtual) that must be available from components to gather the necessary knowledge.

## 4.1   Identification

For both of them, areas $A_i \subseteq \mathbf{S}_i$ can be expressed in terms of conditional expressions over the values in $\mathbf{S}_i$. In the case where one dimension $S_i$ is not relevant for either a specific goal or utility, then $A_i \equiv \mathbf{S}_i$.

Indeed, in many practical cases, goals and utilities involve only a limited fraction of the state space. That is, $G_i$ is expressed as a set of points or areas in an $m$-dimensional space (with $m < n$), projection of the original space. If we consider a base vector: $B =< b_1, b_2, \ldots b_n >, b_i \in \{0, 1\}$ such that $b_i = 0 \Leftrightarrow \forall G_i \in \mathbf{G} \wedge \forall U_i \in \mathbf{U} \longrightarrow A_i \equiv \mathbf{S}_i$, then goals and utilities can be expressed in the sub-dimensional space: $\mathbf{SS} = B \times \mathbf{S}$. The sub-dimensional space $SS$ is important because it defines what information is relevant for the system. That is, it drives the requirements for which knowledge has to be acquired, modeled, and made available to services.

In addition, one should also account for specific contingency situations of SOTA that may affect the capability of a system of achieving its goal in respect of the utilities, and that are not explicit in either $\mathbf{G}$ or $\mathbf{U}$. It may be necessary to identify these contingencies, identify when and how they could affect the capability of the system, and turn these explicitly either as utility functions or as "impossible areas", i.e., areas of the SOTA space in which the system, however self-adaptive, will no longer be able to achieve.

Let us examine some contingency situations with respect to a vehicle and a fleet. As mentioned in Sect. 3, a vehicle has a goal of reaching a destination within time and battery energy level. However, during mobility it could find that the assigned parking lot is no longer available, or its battery level is running out. At the same time, a fleet has a goal of creating trips for the vehicles, but a vehicle in the fleet could leave later than its scheduled time for an appointment, thus affecting the trips of the other vehicles in the fleet. Some of these contingency situations could affect the capability of the system, and can be shown in the SOTA space as impossible areas that are no longer achievable. For instance, a fleet has a goal of distributing the vehicles of the fleet in a balanced manner in the city at midnight every day. However, there could be a disruption in the road due to maintenance work in a particular area of the city, which is unavoidable. This will result in some vehicles not being distributed fairly.

So far, we assume that all dimensions in $\mathbf{S}$ are independent from each other; that is, a movement in $\mathbf{S}_i$ does not affect the positions in the other dimensions $\mathbf{S}_j$. Unfortunately, this is not always the case: the characteristics of the domain can induce additional constraints. For instance, in a vehicle, its driving style (e.g., speed) and battery state of charge level are interlinked, a change in speed implies a change in battery state of charge. Also, the list of planned rides of a vehicle could be affected by other dimensions, such as availability of the infrastructure resources (e.g., parking lots), and current traffic information. Similarly, in a fleet, the locations of the vehicles could be constrained by the availability of the infrastructure resources. Therefore, along with the identification of the goals and utility sets $\mathbf{G}$ and $\mathbf{U}$, it can be useful to identify constraints on the SOTA dimensions and on the "trajectories" that a system can follow on them.

## 4.2  Sensors and Virtualization

Each dimension of the SOTA space implies sensors. However, this is not an issue per se: a number of different sensors are available to measure the most diverse features. For example, an e-vehicle has a range of sensors to measure different SOTA context dimensions, such as: GPS (global positioning system) sensor, accelerometer sensors, ABS (anti-lock brake system) sensors, gyrometer sensors, steering angle sensors, sensors in the battery, and temperature and humidity sensors inside the vehicle.

Most of these sensors report the values in terms of numeric time series, whereas within the SOTA space, it will be better to consider movements as represented in values which are meaningful. The problem lies in providing services with an appropriate view of what's happening, i.e., leveraging the low-level perspective of the actual sensors into that of a "virtual sensor" which is capable of providing an appropriate view representation of the values in that dimension. In general, virtual sensors are useful for: (i) grouping a number of physical sensors for the sake of fault tolerance; (ii) converting sensor readings into relevant information; and (iii) grouping different physical sensors allowing multi-modal recognition capabilities. During the modeling of a system, the issue of identifying what types of virtual sensors are required to enable and facilitate adaptation is thus necessary to properly drive activities related to knowledge modeling and processing. The latter is required to turn physical sensors into virtual ones.

Another important aspect of the virtualization process is that it detaches the provisioning of the virtual information from that of the actual sensors. Let us consider some examples of virtual sensors in the case study for a vehicle: (i) battery state of charge: the charge level of the battery which can be determined using the current and voltage measurements from the battery's sensors. Similarly, battery state of health can be calculated to indicate the overall condition of the battery; (ii) a virtual sensor to measure dynamics of a vehicle: the angle of the steering from the steering angle sensor can be used to determine where the front wheels are pointed. This measurement when combined with measurements from the yaw, accelerometer and wheel speed sensors, it is possible to measure the dynamics of the vehicle which can be used by the stability control system of the vehicle; (iii) climate comfort sensor: the temperature and humidity sensors inside the vehicle can be used to calculate climate comfort level for the user, which can be *eco* or *maximal*.

An example of a virtual sensor for the fleet is calculating and determining whether current distribution of vehicles in a fleet is fair or imbalanced, depending on the individual locations of the vehicles which can be acquired through their individual GPS sensors and by the aggregation of all individual locations into a sort of aggregate indicator of imbalance in fleet distribution.

## 5  Model Checking SOTA Requirements

It is possible to adopt SOTA as an effective tool to perform an early, goal-level, *model checking analysis* [11] for self-adaptive systems. Our approach allows the developers of complex self-adaptive systems to validate the actual correctness of the self-adaptive requirements at an early stage in the software life-cycle.

SOTA supports a simple operational model [3] that makes it possible to adapt and apply existing model-checking techniques to goals and utilities, and thus assess and improve requirements identification. Our target event-based model for reasoning about goals and utilities is labeled transitions systems (LTSs), which provides a simple formalism for compositional reasoning in architectural context. This formalism is supported by a tool that provides a wide range of analysis and animation capabilities. Thus, our model checking approach is based on the formal verification, validation and simulation techniques provided by the Labeled Transition System Analyzer (LTSA) [11], and its process calculus Finite State Processes. The formalism that we use to model goals and utilities is Fluent Linear Temporal Logic (FLTL) assertions. The entities–a single *vehicle* and a *fleet*– represent the SOTA entities moving in the SOTA space. In operational terms, this can be expressed as multiple processes or LTSs, and the overall execution of the system modeled as a concurrent event-based one, in which the process transitions (of an exogenous or endogenous type) correspond to movements in the SOTA space.

As described in [3], the overall model checking process of SOTA requirements has four main stages: requirements modeling using i* framework [21], SOTA grammar and language, transform goals and utilities to asynchronous FLTL, and verification. We refer the reader to [3] on details of the operationalization of the SOTA model, and the application of the approach to simple e-mobility examples. This paper specifically focuses on the verification stage with case study exemplifications where model checking is applied to: (i) validate whether a set of required preconditions and postconditions forms a complete operationalization of a single goal (i.e., single goal operationalization); and (ii) check the satisfaction of global goals or utilities.

## 5.1  Validate Single Goal Operationalization

As mentioned in Sect. 2.2, a goal $G_i$ can be characterized by a precondition $G_i^{pre}$ and a postcondition $G_i^{post}$. Also, a goal $G_i$ can be associated to a utility $U_i$ that needs to be respected while trying to achieve $G_i$. In the SOTA model, these goals and utilities are expressed as a subspace in **S**. For validating single goal operationalization, we check whether a set of preconditions, postconditions and/or a goal-associated utility forms a complete operationalization (i.e., all the conditions in the set of preconditions, postconditions and/or a goal-based utility are satisfied) of a requirement [3]. This is to ensure that the operationalization of goals and utilities has been performed correctly by the engineer from the SOTA model.

To achieve this, the assertions created for a requirement (e.g., preconditions, postconditions) are composed with the event-based behavioral model, and then model checking can be performed using the LTSA. If the operationalization of the requirement is incomplete, for example, let us assume that a required precondition has been omitted inadvertently, then the LTSA model checker will generate a counterexample trace identifying the error. For example, as mentioned in Sect. 2, the reach destination goal of a vehicle $(V_i)$ has a precondition $(G_i^{pre})$ to check the battery state of charge is sufficient at trip start. Also, there can be a utility $(U_i)$ to ensure climate comfort level inside the vehicle is maintained while the vehicle reaches its destination. The postcondition of the goal $(G_i^{post})$ is the actual goal itself, which is to reach the destination within the battery state of charge level and on time. Now assume that the precondition for this goal has been omitted during the operationalizing process by the engineer inadvertently. This will result in violating of the assertion created for the goal. Thus, the model checker will generate a counterexample (error) trace annotated with the constraints which were violated, which can be used by the engineer to identify the error and correct the requirements model.

## 5.2 Validate Global Goal/Utility Satisfaction

In addition to checking single goal operationalization, we can perform model checking to check the satisfaction of global goals or global utilities by operational models that describe the behavior of multiple components. Such validation will ensure that the operationalization of the global goals and utilities from the SOTA model has been performed correctly by the engineer. For this, we check whether a set of goals or utilities forms a complete operationalization (i.e., all the goals or utilities are satisfied) of a global requirement. In SOTA terms, such validation means the checking the requirements of the set of goals $G$ or utilities $U$:

$$\mathbf{G} = \{G_1, G_2, \ldots, G_n\}, |\mathbf{G}| > 1$$

$$\mathbf{U} = \{U_1, U_2, \ldots, U_n^e\}, |\mathbf{U}| > 1$$

For example, in the case study, a global goal $(G)$ for the fleet is to maximize usage of vehicles. This global goal can be composed of two goals on distributing the vehicles of the fleet fairly in the city at midnight every day; and creating and assigning trips for the vehicles. In another example, the global utility to avoid roads with tolls for the fleet can be composed of the utilities of individual vehicles in the fleet. To validate these, the assertions created for the goals and utilities can be composed, and then model checking can be performed by the LTSA to check the overall satisfaction of the global goal or utility. If the operationalization is incomplete, for instance, a required goal or utility has been omitted by the engineer, the LTSA will produce an error trace which can be used by the engineer to locate the error and correct it.

In this manner, by performing validation of single and global goal operationalization, we identify any incompleteness of the SOTA goal-oriented requirements model. However, a typical problem that may occur in goal-oriented modeling is that an *inconsistency* or an *implicit requirement* [10] can result in a deadlock in the specification, as discussed next.

## 5.3   Detect Inconsistencies

An inconsistency in the specification could occur due to several reasons. These can be (i) if the postcondition of a goal does not imply its precondition then the system might be in a state where the postcondition $G_i^{post}$ is true but the precondition $G_i^{pre}$ is not true. So the goal needs to be satisfied but it is not, leading to an inconsistency; (ii) if the operational model is derived from conflicting goals. Therefore, it is important to detect inconsistencies in the SOTA operational model as deadlocks.

To illustrate an example of the first type, in the e-mobility case study, let us consider that the reach destination goal of a vehicle $V_i$ has a precondition $(G_i^{pre})$ to check whether a parking lot and a charging station have been assigned. There could be a situation where the precondition of the goal is not satisfied, i.e., charging station has not been assigned for the trip. This is although the vehicle is able to reach the destination within the time and energy levels (i.e., the postconditions $G_i^{post}$ are satisfied).

As for the inconsistencies that occur from conflicting goals, let us consider two entities $SC_1$ and $SC_2$ that are to be composed into an ensemble or group of entities $SCE$. First, assume that $SC_1$ and $SC_2$ have two shared goals $G_i$ and $G_j$, which share the same $n$-dimensional SOTA space $S$. The preconditions of the two goals overlap but the postconditions do not overlap. That is:

$$G_i^{pre} \cap G_j^{pre} \neq \emptyset \wedge G_i \cap G_j = \emptyset$$

Therefore, both these goals could be activated and pursued at the same time in two paths in the SOTA space $S$, and this should not be the case. Second, assume that $SC_1$ and $SC_2$ have two goals $G_i$ and $G_j$ and the goals' preconditions and postconditions both overlap. That is:

$$G_i^{pre} \cap G_j^{pre} \neq \emptyset \wedge G_i \cap G_j \neq \emptyset$$

Therefore, both these goals could be activated and pursued at the same time in the same direction of the SOTA space $S$. We can perform LTSA model checking to detect such inconsistencies that arise from conflicting goals as deadlocks in the specification. Next in order to describe the inconsistencies that can occur from conflicting goals, two examples from the e-mobility case study are provided.

For the first conflicting goals situation, assume that there are two vehicle entities ($V_1$ and $V_2$) of the fleet $F$, which have been composed into an ensemble. Let us consider that these two vehicles have been assigned to the same user for a trip that has two planned rides ($R_1$ and $R_2$). That is, vehicle $V_1$ has been assigned a ride $R_1$ to travel to the first appointment at location $L_1$, and afterwards vehicle $V_2$ has a ride $R_2$ to travel to the second appointment at location $L_2$. Here, both vehicles ($V_1$ and $V_2$) can have the same preconditions at the trip start, such as they are available at the time of trip creation. However, now assume that during mobility, if vehicle $V_1$ reaches an insufficient level of battery charge level, and it is not able to reach location $L_1$ in time, then the postconditions of both $V_1$ and $V_2$ entities do not match any more. That is, the goals of these entities will be conflicting. In such a situation, the system may be in a state where both operations could take place in two paths, thus leading to an inconsistency.

On the other hand, for the second conflicting goals situation, consider two vehicles $V_1$ and $V_2$ of a fleet $F$ that have been assigned to the user for the same trip. Here, both vehicles will have overlapping preconditions and postconditions as they require to reach the same destination within the time allocated. Here the system could be in a state where both operations taking place towards the same direction, which should not be the case. This is because there is no next state that will satisfy both the postconditions of the two goals. These inconsistencies in the SOTA operational model can be overcome, first through the explicit modeling of additional constraints to handle them, and then composing them with the event-based behavioral model and performing LTSA model checking.

## 6   Conclusions and Future Work

Future fleets of self-driving vehicles will be examples of collective adaptive systems that are required to act in a coordinated way towards the harmonized achievement of both individual and collective goals. This paper presented the SOTA approach for the engineering of such kind of systems, focusing in particular on proper analysis and modeling of functional and non-functional requirements of self-adaptation, and the analysis and identification of which information must be made available to a system to support its self-adaptive behavior.

Future work will exploit the results of the SOTA modeling as a guide towards the adaptive identification of the most suitable coordination patterns for a fleet of self-driving vehicles, depending on their current operating conditions.

## References

1. Abeywickrama, D.B., Bicocchi, N., Zambonelli, F.: SOTA: towards a general model for self-adaptive systems. In: Proceedings of the IEEE 21st International WETICE 2012 Conference, pp. 48–53, June 2012
2. Abeywickrama, D.B., Hoch, N., Zambonelli, F.: Engineering and implementing software architectural patterns based on feedback loops. Scalable Comput. Pract. Exp. 15(4), 291–308 (2014)
3. Abeywickrama, D.B., Zambonelli, F.: Model checking goal-oriented requirements for self-adaptive systems. In: Proceedings of the 19th IEEE International Conference and Workshops on Engineering of Computer-Based Systems, pp. 33–42, April 2012
4. Belzner, L., Hölzl, M.M., Koch, N., Wirsing, M.: Collective autonomic systems: towards engineering principles and their foundations. Trans. Found. Mastering Change 1, 180–200 (2016)
5. Bicocchi, N., Mamei, M., Sassi, A., Zambonelli, F.: On recommending opportunistic rides. IEEE Trans. Intell. Transp. Syst. 18(12), 3328–3338 (2017)
6. De Nicola, R., Loreti, M., Pugliese, R., Tiezzi, F.: A formal approach to autonomic systems programming: the SCEL language. TAAS 9(2), 7:1–7:29 (2014)

7. Giese, H., Vogel, T., Diaconescu, A., Götz, S., Kounev, S.: Architectural concepts for self-aware computing systems. In: Kounev, S., Kephart, J., Milenkoski, A., Zhu, X. (eds.) Self-Aware Computing Systems, pp. 109–147. Springer, Cham (2017). https://doi.org/10.1007/978-3-319-47474-8_5

8. Hoch, N., Bensler, H.-P., Abeywickrama, D., Bureš, T., Montanari, U.: The E-mobility case study. In: Wirsing, M., Hölzl, M., Koch, N., Mayer, P. (eds.) Software Engineering for Collective Autonomic Systems. LNCS, vol. 8998, pp. 513–533. Springer, Cham (2015). https://doi.org/10.1007/978-3-319-16310-9_17

9. Lapouchnian, A., Liaskos, S., Mylopoulos, J., Yu, Y.: Towards requirements-driven autonomic systems design. ACM SIGSOFT Softw. Eng. Notes **30**(4), 1–7 (2005)

10. Letier, E., Kramer, J., Magee, J., Uchitel, S.: Deriving event-based transition systems from goal-oriented requirements models. Autom. Softw. Eng. **15**(2), 175–206 (2008)

11. Magee, J., Kramer, J.: Concurrency: State Models and Java Programs, 2nd edn. Wiley, Chichester (2006)

12. Mylopoulos, J., Chung, L., Yu, E.S.K.: From object-oriented to goal-oriented requirements analysis. Commun. ACM **42**(1), 31–37 (1999)

13. Rasch, K., Li, F., Sehic, S., Ayani, R., Dustdar, S.: Context-driven personalized service discovery in pervasive environments. World Wide Web **14**(4), 295–319 (2011)

14. Salvaneschi, G., Ghezzi, C., Pradella, M.: Contexterlang: a language for distributed context-aware self-adaptive applications. Sci. Comput. Program. **102**(Suppl. C), 20–43 (2015). https://doi.org/10.1016/j.scico.2014.11.016

15. Souza, V.E.S.: Requirements-based Software System Adaptation. Ph.D. thesis, DISI University of Trento (2012)

16. Uhlemann, E.: Connected-vehicles applications are emerging [connected vehicles]. IEEE Veh. Technol. Mag. **11**(1), 25–96 (2016)

17. Weyns, D.: Software engineering of self-adaptive systems: an organised tour and future challenges. In: Taylor, R., Kang, K.C., Cha, S. (eds.) Handbook of Software Engineering. Springer (2017)

18. Weyns, D., Malek, S., Andersson, J.: Forms: unifying reference model for formal specification of distributed self-adaptive systems. ACM Trans. Auton. Adapt. Syst. **7**(1), 8 (2012)

19. Williams, R.A.: Lessons learned on development and application of agent-based models of complex dynamical systems. Simul. Model. Pract. Theory (2017). https://doi.org/10.1016/j.simpat.2017.11.001

20. Yam, Y.B.: Dynamics of Complex Systems. Perseus Books, New York (2002)

21. Yu, E.S.K.: Modelling strategic relationships for process reengineering. Ph.D. thesis, UMI Order No. GAXNN-02887 (Canadian dissertation) (1995)

22. Zambonelli, F., Bicocchi, N., Cabri, G., Leonardi, L., Puviani, M.: On self-adaptation, self-expression, and self-awareness in autonomic service component ensembles. In: 2011 Fifth IEEE Conference on Self-adaptive and Self-organizing Systems Workshops, pp. 108–113, October 2011. https://doi.org/10.1109/SASOW.2011.24

23. Zambonelli, F., Van Dyke Parunak, H.: Signs of a revolution in computer science and software engineering. In: Petta, P., Tolksdorf, R., Zambonelli, F. (eds.) ESAW 2002. LNCS (LNAI), vol. 2577, pp. 13–28. Springer, Heidelberg (2003). https://doi.org/10.1007/3-540-39173-8_2

# Synthesizing Capabilities for Collective Adaptive Systems from Self-descriptive Hardware Devices Bridging the Reality Gap

Constantin Wanninger, Christian Eymüller(✉), Alwin Hoffmann(✉),
Oliver Kosak(✉), and Wolfgang Reif(✉)

Institute for Software and Systems Engineering,
University of Augsburg, Augsburg, Germany
{wanninger,eymueller,hoffmann,kosak,reif}@isse.de

**Abstract.** In the field of collective adaptive systems (CASs) robotic applications are mostly executed in a simulated environment with simulated hardware and abstract capabilities due to their complexity. These simulated systems usually cannot be applied in reality without major modifications. We propose an approach to bridge the gap between abstract capabilities and the execution of concrete capabilities on real hardware through a semantic description of the hardware itself, its drivers, interfaces and capabilities, enabling the realization of CAS in the real world. With a plug and play mechanism for hardware modules and the semantic description it is now possible to develop a CAS without committing to a concrete set of hardware and, moreover, the set of hardware to the requirements of the system.

## 1 Introduction

Collective systems exist in almost all areas of nature [6] (e.g., flocks of birds, herds of animals) and technology [20] (e.g., computer networks, robot teams). All of these systems have the common characteristic that groups of individual agents provide more functionality than each individual. Besides collective approaches, adaptive approaches can be added to manage even more complex problems. An example for a collective system is a group of ants carrying one big leaf on a narrow surface. If there are gaps on the forest floor, adaptive systems are needed to react to the environmental influences, like building a bridge out of other ants [28]. Such compound systems are called collective adaptive system (CAS) [21]. Mobile robots are typically used for the illustration of CASs on real hardware (e.g., [12,14,18]). These systems mostly use robots that are heavily customized for accomplishing specific tasks. For example, Unmanned Aerial Systems (UAS) equipped with gas sensors are used to find chemical clouds [23] or for the detection of forest-fires infrared cameras are mounted to UAS [10]. One problem of such systems is that they are very inflexible and must be redesigned

© Springer Nature Switzerland AG 2018
T. Margaria and B. Steffen (Eds.): ISoLA 2018, LNCS 11246, pp. 94–108, 2018.
https://doi.org/10.1007/978-3-030-03424-5_7

in case of changing requirements or new use cases. In this case hardware specific code, mostly written in C or C++, must be altered or rewritten.

This paper proposes an approach for the reconfiguration of robot hardware at runtime without the need to alter or rewrite hardware specific code. Therefore a plug and play mechanism with semantic self-descriptions of the hardware modules is used. These self-descriptions include static information about the hardware (e.g., weight of a hardware module) in form of *properties*. In addition, executable *capabilities* (e.g., "measure temperature") of a hardware module are deposited in the self-description of each hardware module. Capabilities can be either provided by a single hardware element (e.g., a quadcopter has the capability "fly") or by a combination of multiple hardware elements through combining their self-descriptions (e.g., a quadcopter with a GPS sensor has the capability "fly to position"). This information about hardware modules allows the development of CASs without committing to a specific set of hardware. The goal is to create a system in which each hardware module supplies interfaces to capabilities, which can be executed by agents within a CAS, rather than creating an agent with a fixed set of capabilities. In order to realize such a system, an adapter for devices (i.e., sensors and actuators) is created to enrich the hardware with semantic annotations and a common interface to provide capabilities for the usage in CASs. We call these systems "Self-Descriptive Devices" (SDDs).

In sum, this paper contains the following contributions for facilitating the use of hardware devices within CASs:

(1) Storage and usage of distributed properties;
(2) Methods for the automatic provision of capabilities for agents;
(3) Determination of appropriate hardware for capabilities;
(4) Task fulfillment through combined capabilities;

As a running example various hardware modules (i.e., quadcopter that can be equipped with multiple modular sensor modules) are used to demonstrate the advantages of the developed technique. Each SDD, no matter if it is a quadcopter or a sensor module, provides a self-description. In case of a quadcopter, it has properties like "maximum payload" and "weight" and capabilities like "fly to position". Furthermore these simple capabilities of multiple SDDs can be composed to more complex capabilities of the whole system. For example capabilities like "sensor-based flight" can be created out of the capability "fly to position" of the quadcopter and the capability "measure sensor value" of a mounted sensor module.

This paper is structured as follows: Sect. 2 describes which objectives the paper pursues. In Sects. 3 and 4 the structure and realization of SDDs in CASs is described. Afterwards the architecture and realization are evaluated in a case study (Sect. 5). Section 6 shows related research fields and Sect. 7 finally concludes the paper.

## 2   Objectives and Challenges

The objective of our approach is to establish an architecture for multi-agent applications in the field of collective adaptive systems with real modular hardware. In view of the variety of possible applications, a common denominator must be found. In many projects, e.g., [5,7,24,25] the term capability is used for interactions with (simulated) hardware. For example the project of Preece et al. [25] use the term to define if a camera can be mounted on an UAS with the semantic annotation "can mount" for every camera type. This interpretation of capability is only indirectly coupled with real hardware and serves as descriptive information to define the *properties* of the UAS. From our point of view, a property qualifies static information like, e.g., physical specifications (e.g., geometric models, weight, ...) or hardware specific limitations (e.g., sensor accuracy, motor speed, ...). The storage, distribution and usage of properties is a fundamental challenge in this paper and serves to give an appropriate answer to the hardware device, regarding the question:

(1)  "What am I?"

Projects like Knowrob [31] use the term capability to describe executable procedures. For example, the annotation "grab cup" can be executed and an industrial robot starts the appropriate procedure. This procedure in turn uses properties (e.g., pictures, geometric details and grasp pattern) to support the automated execution. This interpretation of capabilities with dependencies to properties is also used in this paper. For example, a UAS with the properties "payload" and a mounted sensor with the property "weight" has to determine if the capabilities "fly to position" or "fly direction" are feasible (e.g., weight is lower than the payload). This example illustrates the dependency between the capability "fly" and the property "weight". The capability "fly to position" can further use the "battery capacity" in combination with the "weight" and "power consumption" to estimate the "flight time". The challenge lies in linking the capabilities to executable processes with a common interface for the usage as well as providing a mechanism for the creation and usage of dependencies between properties and capabilities. These dependencies give an answer to the question:

(2)  "Am I capable of doing it?"

The description of hardware with properties and the access of its functionality with capabilities have to be established on real hardware. Every hardware element should provide its self-description i.e., its properties and capabilities. One objective is to offer capabilities over several hardware parts. For example, a quadcopter must be equipped with a distance sensor to offer the capability "sensor-based flight". To realize such configurable robots with self descriptive hardware elements in real world applications, various challenges must be overcome. For a common physical interface, the hardware elements must on the one hand be able to handle multiple physical interfaces in order to support a large set of components like sensors, actuators and combinations thereof. On the other hand the hardware elements must offer a common communication interface for the exchange of corresponding values between them. This communication interface should also be used for the exchange of capabilities and properties. For the programming of an agent, the capabilities and properties must be traceable to the corresponding hardware element and actual configuration of hardware elements (e.g., the quadcopter should use a mounted sensor for the capability "sensor-based flight"). This information answers the question:

(3) "With what should I do it?"

Projects like [15,17,29] combine the capabilities of multiple agents, e.g., several mobile robots pull a child, while one single robot can not apply the force to pull it. In this example the user task "carry child" can be divided into several agent tasks "carry subject" which the combination of agents has to solve. This task decomposition of user tasks into agent tasks with coordination mechanisms between agents is not in the scope of this paper. However, we want to establish a mechanism to enable the agent to solve the task with a combination of capabilities. The agent task should express the requirements in an abstract manner (e.g., sensor based flight to position). The information, which sensors and actuators (e.g., position sensor, quadcopter) are needed and the procedure how they interact (e.g., fly to position combines a position sensor with the flight capability of a quadcopter) is one challenge, which is focused on in this paper. The definition of abstract requirements for the instantiation of capabilities with distributed properties finally leads to the question:

(4) "What am I supposed to do?"

For simulated environments as well as real hardware.

## 3   Concept

This paper provides an architecture for the realization of multi-agent applications in the field of collective adaptive systems with real, modular hardware, as shown in Fig. 1. To give an overview over the proposed system, we start with the user of the multi-agent system, who is able to define so called *User Tasks*. These are tasks that can only be handled by a set of agents, for example "fly triangle formation to position 1 m over ground for 15 min". Such tasks are decomposed into multiple *Agent Tasks* that can be assigned to a single agent of the multi-agent system, e.g., "sensor-based flight to position 1 m over ground for 15 min". For the decomposition of the user tasks, a distributed multi-agent reasoning system is used in our overall architecture, presented in Kosak et al. [22]. After the agent task has been assigned to an agent the advantages of our proposed system come into play. The following paragraphs address the questions from the previous section with an analog equation.

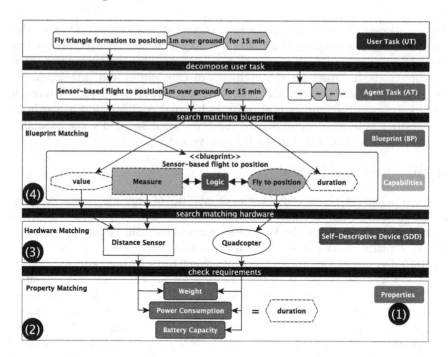

**Fig. 1.** Structure of the entire system from a given task of the user over the decomposition into capabilities to the selection of the required hardware.

With the requirements defined in the agent task, the agent searches for a blueprint in a set of predefined blueprints that can cover these requirements (*Blueprint Matching* (4)). *Blueprints* are a schematic representation of composed capabilities and depict how capabilities may be interconnected to more complex capabilities. For example, a task "sensor-based flight to position 1 m over ground" can be composed of the basic capabilities "fly to position" and "measure". With the help of the appropriate blueprints, the decomposition of a task into single basic capabilities is realized.

After the decomposition of a task into individual capabilities, the agent is capable of searching for hardware that possesses these capabilities and can fulfill the given task. This step is called *Hardware Matching* (3). In our example, we have a quadcopter that has a capability "fly to position" and a distance sensor that has a capability "measure distance to ground". From the information of the hardware's capabilities, the agent can determine with which hardware configuration it can fulfill the task.

Before execution of the task, a final check is made to ensure the agent is able to fulfill the task with the given hardware. For this check we use *Property Matching* (2), which guarantees that the constraints of each hardware module are met, for example if the task has the constraint that the sensor-based flight must last at least 15 min. Consequently, the system must check whether the desired flight duration can be achieved by the given set of hardware. For this check several properties (i.e., "weight", "power consumption" and "battery capacity") of each attached hardware module are used.

After the concept of the entire system has been presented, the distribution of the concept to the individual hardware modules is described. Every agent in our CAS is composed of one Logic Device (LD) and a set of Self-Descriptive Devices (SDDs) as shown in Fig. 2. An SDD is a device which consists of the actual hardware, for example a distance sensor, and a Self-Description Adapter (SDA), which is responsible for the self-description of the hardware component. The SDA includes the communication interface, the semantic datasheet for self-description of the hardware with its capabilities and properties (1) and a driver to interact with the specific hardware for using its capabilities. Thus, SDDs provide the information used for the hardware and property matching of the system.

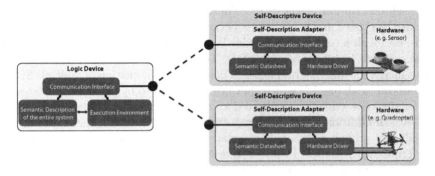

**Fig. 2.** Schematic structure of the system for our running example. This system is comprised of a quadcopter-SDD, a sensor-SDD and an Logic Device (LD).

An LD is a device which maintains a runtime environment for the execution of capabilities of multiple SDDs and provides an interface to the agent and thus represents an independent subsystem. LDs have a set of predefined blueprints that can be used to find a suitable hardware set and to utilize this blueprint with the real capabilities of the selected hardware for the execution of the agent task. Both LD and SDD communicate with each other over connections using wired or wireless interfaces. The communication interface is used on the one hand to transmit the semantic datasheets and on the other hand to query sensor values and set commands for actuators. One of the main components of an LD is the semantic description of the whole subsystem. This means all self-descriptions of each SDD are sent to the LD, where they are joined to form a complete knowledge base. For the execution of capabilities, we also need an execution environment, that can interact with mobile robots, actuators and sensors. For example, one agent of a CAS (e.g., mobile robot) consists of one LD and several sensor and actuator SDDs. In the quadcopter example, we use a single board computer attached to the quadcopter which runs an LD. This SDD has a connection to a quadcopter SDD and some sensor SDDs.

# 4    Implementation

The following section details the implementation of the four main concepts involved in the realization of SDD and LD: (Sect. 4.1) Distributed knowledge, (Sect. 4.2) Hardware and Property Matching, (Sect. 4.3) Blueprints and (Sect. 4.4) Deployment and Execution of Capabilities.

## 4.1    Distributed Knowledge

In order to create a common knowledge base of all SDDs connected to one LD, the distributed information of each SDD must be collected and processed. The information on properties and capabilities of each SDD is stored in form of a "Resource Description Framework" (RDF) ontology (e.g., the Semantic Sensor Network Ontology [3] for sensor data), where only the instances are specified in the self-description of the SDD. The abstract form of the ontology, which contains the classes and associations between them, is exclusively stored on the LD. To establish a common knowledge base, the abstract ontology is completed by the concrete instances of each SDD. To this end, the framework Jena [2] is used to merge the different ontologies. Therefore, a combination of multiple SDDs communicate with one LD which they are connected to by physical interfaces to transfer the knowledge. This collected knowledge is then available for the agent of a CAS. In addition to the merging of semantic data sheets, there is even the possibility of adding additional information to the ontology itself by inserting RDF-Triples with "Simple Protocol And RDF Query Language" (SPARQL) [26] INSERT statements. This extensibility is crucial due to the incredible variety of sensors and actuators (e.g., a new type of sensor is used). With such INSERT statements the user is able to add classes as well as instances to the ontology as needed.

## 4.2    Hardware and Property Matching

The created knowledge base can be used to find the required hardware to fulfill a given task. Therefore SPARQL queries are used to search for SDDs with specific capabilities or properties. By using SPARQL filter functions, the system is not only able to search for hardware devices which have a certain capability, but the search can be restricted even more precisely with help of the associated properties of a capability. For example if a task needs the capability "measure", it can be specified which value should be measured or with what accuracy the value is measured. These constraints of capabilities can be added by the user of a task by adding SPARQL filter functions to the task definition. After the search for and filtering of capabilities, the agent is able to use the found hardware for the execution of the task. If multiple SDD possibilities are found, the agent is even able to choose which hardware is most suitable for the task. If no suitable set of SDDs is found, the user is informed that no matching hardware devices were found for the execution of the given task.

If a set of SDDs is found, which is able to fulfill the given task, the property matching is executed. Therefore constraints of capabilities and constraints given by the user or agent tasks are considered. Constraints of capabilities may be for example that the capability "fly to position" can only be executed with a take-off weight of 1 kg. Task constraints may be for example that the sensor-based flight must last at least 15 min. This constraint check is realized through SPARQL queries. For the constraints of the take-off weight, the sum of the weight of all SDDs is queried and checked if its under 1 kg. The second example is more complex. For the calculation of the flight time, a function can be created that depends on "weight", "power consumption" and "battery capacity" of the entire system. Once all constraints are satisfied the execution starts, otherwise the user gets notified.

## 4.3 Blueprints

Between the abstract formulation of a requirement of a task (e.g., "sensor-based flight to position") and the decomposition into individual capabilities, a lack of information exists. This lack is eliminated by using blueprints to describe how to compose individual capabilities to more complex capabilities.

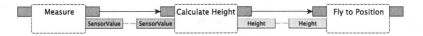

**Fig. 3.** Extract of the blueprint "sensor-based flight to position" with the capabilities "measure" and "fly to Position" and a logic component "calculate height"

Figure 3 shows an example of a blueprint for the composed capability "sensor-based flight to position". A blueprint consists of multiple semantic components (dashed boxes) which describe actions that can be executed. These actions can be capabilities or logical components, like calculation components (e.g., "calculate height") which in turn have control flow ports (boxes without description) as well as a data flow ports (boxes with names) and can be used to interconnect the semantic components. Control flow ports are used to set the order of execution while data flow ports serve to transfer data between multiple semantic components. In our example, the capability "measure" is used to influence the "height" parameter of the capability "fly to position". Each data flow port has a semantic description, which means it knows its content, its data type and its unit. For example, the capability "measure" in a blueprint, can be represented by a semantic component with a data flow port "sensor value" which measures distance values in meters.

Through this semantic description, the logical components are able to adjust their logic. To give an example, it makes a difference if a distance sensor or a temperature sensor (value must be mapped) is connected to the semantic component "calculate height". In both situations, the sensor value must be converted into a height in meters. As described in Sect. 3, the placeholder of the blueprint is filled with concrete capabilities if capable SDDs are found in the hardware matching. After all capability placeholders of the blueprint are filled, the composed capability can be executed.

### 4.4    Deployment and Execution of Capabilities

Agents use blueprints to define which capabilities they need to execute their task. The blueprints must decide at runtime, which concrete hardware they use, thus a mechanism is necessary to load interfaces to enable the execution of capabilities. For this reason, a loading mechanism for hardware specific interfaces was created, that is capable of using semantically annotated code fragments. These fragments are Linked Open Data [34] compliant, stored in HTML sites and are linked to the appropriate self-description of the individual SDDs.

Figure 4 shows the deployment of a system with a quadcopter SDD, a sensor SDD and an LD. As described in Sect. 4.1 the LD includes the knowledge base consisting of the abstract ontology and the self-description of each SDD. The self-descriptions are sent to the LD when the SDD is added to the system. If the execution of a capability is required, a SPARQL query is used to get a URI for the code fragments of the SDD driver. Subsequently these code fragments are downloaded from the web or a snapshot, which is directly stored in an SDD, compiled at runtime and integrated into the Robotics API [30], which is responsible for the control of the sensors and actuators. Afterwards these fragments can be executed. All code fragments contain interfaces for the execution of capabilities within an SDD. For example, a sensor SDD has a function `getSensorValue()` or a quadcopter SDD has a function `flyToPosition(Position)`.

Because of the modularity, the system is able to exchange real SDDs for simulated SDDs and vice versa. So it makes no difference if it works on real or simulated hardware. Thereby the system is even capable of executing capabilities on a combination of simulated and real hardware devices.

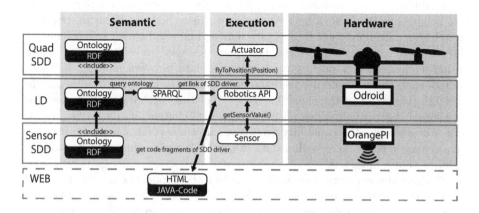

**Fig. 4.** Deployment of the running example with two SDDs and one LD

## 5 Proof of Concept

To show the feasibility of our approach and to implement a CAS in reality, several SDD prototypes were developed. These SDD prototypes consist of the actual hardware module (e.g., a sensor) and a single-board computer, which is responsible for the control of the hardware, the self-description of the hardware component and provides a wireless communication interface for the communication with the LD. These two components are encapsulated in a 3D printed case with a plug connection to enable the combination of several SDDs with an LD to an overall system (see Fig. 5).

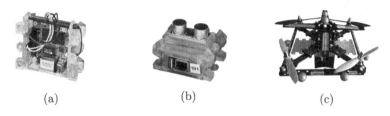

(a)                        (b)                        (c)

**Fig. 5.** Hardware prototype of an SDD adapter (a) for sensors and actuators. The used hardware is an Orange PI Zero with Wireless LAN in a custom 3D printed case with magnetic connectors. Prototype of a distance sensor SDD with an SR04 distance sensor (b). Prototype of a quadcopter SDD (c) with magnetic connectors for two SDD prototypes

The running example "sensor-based flight of a quadcopter" is used to determine whether our approach answers the questions mentioned in Sect. 2. By merging the distributed self-descriptions of each SDD to an overall knowledge base we can answer the question *"What am I?"*. By using constraints in form of SPARQL queries and filters, the agent is able to define constraints for the execution of tasks. With these constraints the system is able to answer the question *"Am I capable of doing it?"*. It has been shown that the system is even capable of selecting hardware or giving suggestions to the user which hardware should be used for the execution of a task. For example, if there are requirements like "measure temperature" the system will select a temperature sensor SDD or otherwise will inform the agent that no matching sensor SDD was found. This answers the question *"With what should I do it?"*. The Question *"What am I supposed to do?"* is answered by blueprints, which are used for the decomposition of tasks into a set of capabilities. After all questions have been resolved and a suitable hardware configuration has been found, the task can be executed.

With the developed system it is possible to use values of a sensor SDD to influence the behaviour of actuators like a quadcopter SDD. Figure 6a shows the flight of a quadcopter that adjusts its height according to the measured distance to the ground with a distance sensor SDD, with the blueprint shown in Fig. 3. As a test setup a quadcopter SDD equipped with an LD and a distance sensor SDD flew along a specified route with obstacles. For the navigation of the route,

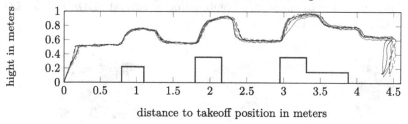

(a) time lapse recording of a quadcopter equipped with an ultra sonic distance sensor (SR-04) and obstacles on the ground for the sensor-based flight

(b) analysis of the sensor based flight (multiple runs) with obstacles within a indoor tracking system to get an accurate position of the quadcopter

**Fig. 6.** Case study: sensor-based distance flight

an indoor tracking system was used, which also recorded the exact position of the quadcopter, as shown in Fig. 6b. To validate the suggestion of SDDs, the capability "sensor-based flight" can be executed with distance sensor SDDs as well as with temperature sensor SDDs. The sensor-based temperature flight is comparable to a kind of thermometer. If the measured temperature increases or decreases the distance of the quadcopter to the ground matches the change.

By merging the self-descriptions of each SDD of an agent, it is possible to generate an added value for the overall system. Because the total weights, power consumptions and power reserves are known for each SDD, it is possible to calculate the average flight time of a quadcopter. Through the plug and play mechanism of the SDDs, it is possible to calculate the flight time dynamically depending on the current configuration of the system.

Figure 7 shows the comparison between the calculated flight time and the actually measured flight time with different takeoff weights of a quadcopter. From this data a function was derived, which predicts the flight time depending on the weight of the combined system with additional LDs. Hence, it is possible to evaluate the constraints whether a capability can be performed for a given duration as required in the example from Fig. 1.

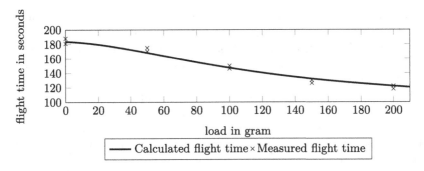

**Fig. 7.** Comparison between calculated and measured flight time with multiple runs with different weights

# 6   Related Work

The following section will investigate related work in relevant research fields emphasizing potentials as well as limitations in the context of Self-Descriptive Device (SDD). The presented architecture for SDDs addresses two areas: self awareness and modular hardware.

Due to many different protocols and storage possibilities for sensor data, common ontologies such as the Semantic Sensor Network Ontology [3] have been utilized. The advantage of the semantic storage in ontologies is primarily the usage of semantic reasoners (e.g., queries as described in Subsect. 4.2). In the field of geographic research, where many sensors are used to validate weather models, this ontology is used to convert stored binary data into semantically annotated data (e.g., [4,8,11,33]). The approach of Dibley et al. [13] goes one step further with a hardware adapter where this conversion takes place. In contrast to the architecture presented in this paper only sensors are semantically annotated and a transfer to capabilities is not in the focus of these approaches.

The project *Cubelets* [16] focuses the influence of measurements on corresponding actuators. Every sensor or actuator in this project is separated into one modular hardware element with a common physical interface. The communication is instead very primitive. Every sensor provides a value between 0 and 255 which is in turn used by the actuators. With this mechanism, primarily intended for educational purposes, reactive robots or systems can be built, however predefined processes (e.g., drive to position) are not possible. The idea of combined capabilities, derived from several hardware elements is focused on in the projects [9,29], in which homogeneous hardware is combined to gain locomotive capabilities. Heterogeneous aspects like e.g., combining a sensor with an actuator are not considered in these projects.

The robot operating system (ROS) [27] is a middleware for robots which allows publish-subscribe as well as service oriented communication mechanisms. In ROS, sensors and actuators can be integrated and tested within a simulation environment as well as on real hardware. The project *H-ROS* [1] aims to simplify the connection between hardware elements with a common interface for communication in an ID-based plug and play manner. Each module must be plugged into a backbone, which is connected with a so called cognition. Within the cognition, the offered services of other connected H-ROS modules can be used in programs. Semantic annotations with dependencies on capabilities, as described in Sect. 3 are not in the focus of this project.

The project *Knowrob* [31] defines executable capabilities based on sensor information performed by (industrial) robots. Abstract capabilities (e.g., grab cup), geometric information (e.g., sensor position) as well as knowledge derived from observations of humans are stored within a common knowledge base built upon Semantic Web techniques. The abstract capabilities use this knowledge to subdivide themselves into executable robot motions. This subdivision is similar to the decomposition of capabilities. Modular self-descriptive devices as well as combined capabilities described in Subsect. 4.3 are not in the scope of this project.

To the best of our knowledge the combination of self description in a system of modular hardware with a capability interface for agents within a CAS is novel.

# 7   Conclusions

In this paper we have proposed an architecture for the realization of collective adaptive systems (CASs) on hardware devices for real world scenarios. With this architecture, we are able to fulfill tasks by analyzing the given requirements. Through the self-description and the plug and play mechanism of each Self-Descriptive Device (SDD), we are capable to compile a detailed description of the composed total system. Using this detailed description of properties and capabilities of each hardware component, it is possible to compose capabilities in a semantically correct way according to blueprints. The agent can use the blueprint on the one hand to execute the capabilities if they can be instantiated with the current set of hardware and on the other hand get a suggestion if the actual hardware can not handle it. If a system can handle a defined task it can execute this task in a simulated environment as well as on real hardware or even in a mixed reality. With an increasing amount of data the system can give further useful information about the system, like for example the rough estimation of the flight time mentioned in Sect. 5. This consistent and expandable architecture is in our point of view an important basis for the creation of CASs with real hardware in the real world.

Future research will focus on the autonomous reconfiguration of agents through the automatic exchange of SDDs with recommender techniques. Associated with this, predictive maintenance of SDDs will be examined. So the SDD can give information about its condition and if it is defective, it can be replaced autonomously e.g., to facilitate long term measurements with quadcopters and replaceable intelligent batteries. A first approach for the resource allocation on agent level is presented in Hanke et al. [19]. Nevertheless, future work will focus on the parallel execution of blueprints allocated to the same resources based on a previous work [32].

# References

1. Hardware ROS (2018). https://www.h-ros.com/
2. JENA Framework (2018). https://jena.apache.org/
3. Semantic Sensor Network Ontology (2018). https://www.w3.org/TR/vocab-ssn/
4. Barnaghi, P., Wang, W., Dong, L., Wang, C.: A linked-data model for semantic sensor streams. In: 2013 IEEE International Conference on Green Computing and Communications and IEEE Internet of Things and IEEE Cyber, Physical and Social Computing, pp. 468–475 (2013)
5. Barreiro, J., Boyce, M., Do, M., Frank, J., et al.: EUROPA: a platform for AI planning, scheduling, constraint programming, and optimization. In: 4th International Competition on Knowledge Engineering for Planning and Scheduling (ICKEPS) (2012)
6. Bonabeau, E., Dorigo, M., Theraulaz, G.: Swarm Intelligence: From Natural to Artificial Systems, 1st edn. Oxford University Press, Oxford (1999)
7. Braubach, L., Pokahr, A., Lamersdorf, W.: Extending the capability concept for flexible BDI agent modularization. In: Bordini, R.H., Dastani, M.M., Dix, J., El Fallah Seghrouchni, A. (eds.) ProMAS 2005. LNCS (LNAI), vol. 3862, pp. 139–155. Springer, Heidelberg (2006). https://doi.org/10.1007/11678823_9
8. Bröring, A., Maué, P., Janowicz, K., Nüst, D., Malewski, C.: Semantically-enabled sensor plug & play for the sensor web. Sensors 11(8), 7568–7605 (2011)
9. Cao, Y., Leng, Y., Sun, J., Zhang, Y., Ge, W.: 360botG2 - an improved unit of mobile self-assembling modular robotic system aiming at exploration in real world. In: 41st Annual Conference of the IEEE Industrial Electronics Society, IECON 2015, pp. 001716–001722. IEEE (2015)
10. Casbeer, D.W., Kingston, D.B., Beard, R.W., McLain, T.W.: Cooperative forest fire surveillance using a team of small unmanned air vehicles. Int. J. Syst. Sci. 37(6), 351–360 (2006)
11. Compton, M., Henson, C., Lefort, L., Neuhaus, H., Sheth, A.: A survey of the semantic specification of sensors. In: Proceedings of the 2nd International Conference on Semantic Sensor Networks, vol. 522, pp. 17–32. CEUR-WS.org (2009)
12. Daniel, K., Dusza, B., Lewandowski, A., Wietfelds, C.: AirShield: a system-of-systems MUAV remote sensing architecture for disaster response. In: Proceedings of 3rd Annual IEEE Systems Conference (SysCon) (2009)
13. Dibley, M., Li, H., Rezgui, Y., Miles, J.: An integrated framework utilising software agent reasoning and ontology models for sensor based building monitoring. J. Civ. Eng. Manag. 21(3), 356–375 (2015)
14. Dorigo, M., et al.: Swarmanoid: a novel concept for the study of heterogeneous robotic swarms. In: IEEE Conference on Robotics, Automation and Mechatronics (RAM), vol. 20, no. 4, pp. 60–71 (2013)
15. Dorigo, M., et al.: The SWARM-BOTS project. In: Şahin, E., Spears, W.M. (eds.) SR 2004. LNCS, vol. 3342, pp. 31–44. Springer, Heidelberg (2005). https://doi.org/10.1007/978-3-540-30552-1_4
16. Gross, M.D., Veitch, C.: Beyond top down: designing with cubelets. Tecnologias, Sociedade e Conhecimento 1(1), 150–164 (2013)
17. Gross, R.: Self-assembling robots. KI 22(4), 61–63 (2008)
18. Gross, R., Dorigo, M.: Towards group transport by swarms of robots. Int. J. Bio-Inspired Comput. 1(1–2), 1–13 (2009)
19. Hanke, J., Kosak, O., Schiendorfer, A., Reif, W.: Self-organized resource allocation for reconfigurable robot ensembles. In: 2018 IEEE 12th International Conference on Self-Adaptive and Self-Organizing Systems, September 2018

20. Kernbach, S.: Structural Self-organization in Multi-agents and Multi-robotic Systems. Logos Verlag Berlin GmbH, Berlin (2008)
21. Kernbach, S., Schmickl, T., Timmis, J.: Collective adaptive systems: challenges beyond evolvability. arXiv preprint arXiv:1108.5643 (2011)
22. Kosak, O.: Facilitating planning by using self-organization. In: 2017 IEEE 2nd International Workshops on Foundations and Applications of Self* Systems (FAS*W), pp. 371–374, September 2017
23. Kovacina, M.A., Palmer, D., Yang, G., Vaidyanathan, R.: Multi-agent control algorithms for chemical cloud detection and mapping using unmanned air vehicles. In: IEEE/RSJ International Conference on Intelligent Robots and Systems, vol. 3, pp. 2782–2788 (2002)
24. Morgan, D., Subramanian, G.P., Chung, S.J., Hadaegh, F.Y.: Swarm assignment and trajectory optimization using variable-swarm, distributed auction assignment and sequential convex programming. Int. J. Robot. Res. **35**(10), 1261–1285 (2016)
25. Preece, A., et al.: Matching sensors to missions using a knowledge-based approach. In: Proceedings of SPIE: Defense Transformation and Net-Centric Systems, vol. 6981, p. 698109–1 (2008)
26. Prud, E., Seaborne, A., et al.: SPARQL query language for RDF (2006)
27. Quigley, M., et al.: ROS: an open-source Robot Operating System. In: ICRA Workshop on Open Source Software, Kobe, vol. 3, p. 5 (2009)
28. Reid, C.R., Lutz, M.J., Powell, S., Kao, A.B., Couzin, I.D., Garnier, S.: Army ants dynamically adjust living bridges in response to a cost–benefit trade-off. Proc. Natl. Acad. Sci. **112**(49), 15113–15118 (2015)
29. Romanishin, J.W., Gilpin, K., Rus, D.: M-blocks: momentum-driven, magnetic modular robots. In: 2013 IEEE/RSJ International Conference on Intelligent Robots and Systems, pp. 4288–4295, November 2013
30. Schierl, A.: Object-oriented modeling and coordination of mobile robots. Doctoral thesis, Universität Augsburg (2017)
31. Tenorth, M., Beetz, M.: KNOWROB - knowledge processing for autonomous personal robots. In: 2009 IEEE/RSJ International Conference on Intelligent Robots and Systems, pp. 4261–4266 (2009)
32. Vistein, M., Angerer, A., Hoffmann, A., Schierl, A., Reif, W.: Flexible and continuous execution of real-time critical robotic tasks. Int. J. Mechatron. Autom. **4**(1), 27–38 (2014)
33. Xue, L., Liu, Y., Zeng, P., Yu, H., Shi, Z.: An ontology based scheme for sensor description in context awareness system. In: 2015 IEEE International Conference on Information and Automation, pp. 817–820 (2015)
34. Yu, L.: Linked open data. In: Yu, L. (ed.) A Developers Guide to the Semantic Web, pp. 409–466. Springer, Heidelberg (2011). https://doi.org/10.1007/978-3-642-15970-1_11

# The Meaning of Adaptation: Mastering the Unforeseen?

Stefan Jähnichen[1], Rocco De Nicola[2], and Martin Wirsing[3]([⊠])

[1] Technische Universität Berlin and FZI Forschungszentrum Informatik Berlin, Berlin, Germany
stefan.jaehnichen@tu-berlin.de
[2] IMT School for Advanced Studies Lucca, Lucca, Italy
rocco.denicola@imtlucca.it
[3] Ludwig-Maximilians-Universität München, Munich, Germany
wirsing@lmu.de

**Abstract.** This short paper gives an introduction to a panel held as part of the track on 'Rigorous Engineering of Collective Adaptive Systems' at ISOLA 2018. The discussion was structured on the basis of twenty questions ranging from the evolution and universality of autonomous systems to correctness, reliability, and legal issues. 'Do you consider adaptivity to be a realistic and desirable property of technical systems?', 'what is the new challenge in software engineering for the design and implementation of adaptive systems?', 'why should artificial intelligence open new horizons to implement adaptivity?', 'can we expect machines to adapt by evolution?' as well as 'is there a mathematical characterisation of adaptation?' were some of the questions that were considered. For all questions, the paper also indicates related work.

**Keywords:** Adaptation · Autonomy · Software engineering
Artificial intelligence

The panel discussion on 'The Meaning of Adaptation: Mastering the Unforeseen?' was focused on the prospects and the state-of-the-art in engineering adaptive and autonomous systems. Stefan Jähnichen (TU Berlin) as moderator and the panelists Lenz Belzner (Maiborn Wolff), Tomáš Bureš (Charles University Prague), Alexander Knapp (University of Augsburg), Jeremy Pitt (Imperial College London), and Franco Zambonelli (University of Modena and Reggio Emilia) discussed this controversial topic based on a list of twenty questions presented in the following. The panel discussion was a follow-up of the panel at ISOLA 2016 [1] entitled 'Adaptation to the Unforeseen: Do we Master our Autonomous Systems' [2]. Some of the questions had been discussed on the previous panel but were still considered important and relevant to be discussed again.

More than 50 years ago, Zadeh wrote that 'it is very difficult – perhaps impossible – to find a way of characterising in concrete terms the large variety of ways in which adaptive behaviour can be realised' [3]. Also today there are

© Springer Nature Switzerland AG 2018
T. Margaria and B. Steffen (Eds.): ISoLA 2018, LNCS 11246, pp. 109–117, 2018.
https://doi.org/10.1007/978-3-030-03424-5_8

different definitions of the notion of adaptive system [4]. In a 'black-box view' it refers to systems with the property to adapt and react to changing environments (see e.g. [5,6]) or more generally, to all situations occurring during its life time, correctly and reliably. In a 'white-box view' an adaptive system 'is characterised by its ability to change its control rules through experience, [...] this means that understanding observed differences in behaviour can be approached only by looking at the internal changes in the mechanics of a system' [7] or similarly, that an adaptive program 'has a distinguished collection of control data that can be modified at run-time. [8]' These definitions address different aspects of the notion of adaptation. This led to the first question for the panel.

Q1: What is your notion of adaptivity? Can you explain the term or even give a definition?

A collective adaptive system, often also called ensemble, consists of collaborating entities that are able to adapt at runtime to dynamically changing, open-ended environments and to new requirements [9,10]. Examples are robot swarms and socio-technical systems such as smart city or smart health care applications. In such a system we can distinguish the behaviour of the individual entities and the behaviour of the whole system.

Q2: In a collective adaptive system do you see a difference between the adaptivity of the elements and of the system as a whole?

Without much doubt, the term 'adaptive' identifies one of the most challenging topics we currently explore. The question comes up whether such a behaviour is feasible, implementable, or even desirable.

Q3: Do you consider adaptivity to be a realistic and desirable property of technical systems?
Q4: Can you give some examples of applications for which adaptivity is not just desired but essential?
Q5: Is there a formal/mathematical characterisation of adaptivity? If not, can you envisage such a characterisation?

A formal or mathematical characterisation is probably considered a useful tool. However, the effort to build such a model and make it known and usable is definitely hard work (see e.g. [11]). The main question might be whether or not it is worthwhile to develop such a model and what it could be used for. Main implementation techniques are control loops, optimisation, learning and statistical techniques [12–14] as well as methods for restructuring and reconfiguration (e.g. in this volume [15–18]). For collective adaptive systems such techniques need to be extended to consider many entities [13,14]; in addition, the different forms of interaction have to be taken into account (see in this volume [19]).

Q6: For you, what are the basic techniques for implementing an adaptive system? And which techniques are needed when many components are involved that can dynamically change the interaction strategy?

Adaptivity is not just a new term as many of our systems show adaptive behaviour based on long researched and implemented control theory [20]. However, it seems that nowadays the notion of adaptivity has reached a new level based on technologies from Artificial Intelligence (AI).

Q7: What is the relationship of adaptivity to control theory and how AI may open new horizons for the implementation of adaptivity?

The successes of IBM Watson in the Jeopardy quizz show [21] and of artificial neural networks in the Go competition [22] made AI and in particular machine learning the new buzzwords in order to solve problems. On a more technical level, AI methods are also used for engineering collective adaptive systems (see e.g. in this volume [23–25]). However, in many aspects, AI just relies on progresses in statistics and is heavily related to the notion of probability which immediately raises questions of reliability and even more importantly of trustworthiness and security (see e.g. [26–29]). AI is also considered to be a huge step forward towards human intelligence taken up by machines [30, 31]. Humans have the ability to adapt to many different and even unforeseen states, but can we expect our systems to show a similar behaviour?

Q8: How do you think AI can be used to implement adaptivity? Is achieving a behaviour with a high probability sufficient to guarantee trustworthiness and security of our systems?

Q9: The term machine learning is provocative as it suggests that machines can learn similar to human beings. What is your view on machine learning and how does it distinguish from human learning?

Q10: What are the most appropriate formalisms in machine learning for engineering collective adaptive systems?

Current software engineering approaches might not be sufficient as unforeseen functionalities may be needed in order to react correctly in all circumstances; issues such as self-adaptation, awareness and evolution have to be taken into account [14]. As also addressed in the contributions of this track, the well-known software engineering processes—be they agile or waterfall—have to be adapted [32–34]; adequate requirements [35], specification [36–38], design [39–41], analysis [43,44], verification [42], testing [45], and security techniques [46] will have to be considered (for a comprehensive approach see [47]).

Q11: What are the new challenges in software engineering for the design and implementation of adaptive systems? In addition, what do 'adaptive software engineering', 'adaptive testing' and 'adaptive verification' mean to you?

Q12: Can specific modelling techniques, programming concepts and verification methods help building adaptive systems? If yes, how?

Q13: How can so-called non-functional properties like security and performance be handled?

Our computers are commonly considered as being the most flexible and, in this sense, the most adaptive systems mankind has ever invented and, observing how computers penetrate all our life and take control in almost all applications, we have to acknowledge at least the ubiquity and universal applicability of computing equipment. Obviously, the underlying reason for being adaptive and universal originates from the very simple basic mechanism to manipulate binary numbers and the ongoing minimization technologies for electronic circuits. However, more importantly, for offering adaptiveness, we need programmability of such machines relying on human intelligence and creativity, and on human abilities to master complexity by exploiting mathematics and computer science technologies.

Q14: Humans seem to adapt by evolution. Can we expect machines to adapt by evolution, too? What could be the meaning of evolution in a technical context?

In today's technologies the term 'autonomous' plays a major role. It denotes a system which performs its task without human intervention like e.g. automatic lawn mowers, smart home equipments, driverless train systems, or autonomous cars [48]. The most challenging question which comes up when following the life cycle of the term autonomy is the potential to construct a system which behaves and operates similarly to or even better than a human being. The current technology has not got so far (see e.g. [49]), and personally, we doubt it will ever do. However, we think it is needed to discuss how far the boundary towards such behaviours could be pushed and whether autonomic operations at least in a certain context can be offered with highest safety guarantees and thrustworthiness.

Q15: Do you envision a universal autonomous system? Will robots ever be able to substitute human interaction?

Q16: What are the means to establish trust in autonomous systems?

It is difficult to imagine that a human being can build a system that adapts to all and above all to all unforeseen situations – since the term 'unforeseen' describes circumstances that man has not foreseen. If we restrict ourselves to some foreseen unforeseen behaviours which we might be able to handle [11,50], we have to consider a problem of completeness. Did we cover the whole set of behaviours or did we omit some? This, of course, raises questions of complexity, as the number of such situations might be close to infinity and thus, not foreseeable at all. In order to handle such complexity, we have to restrict the adaptability of our systems to a certain context in which we are able to capture all different behaviours, or which at least enables us to classify and cluster such situations. Smart home environments [51] which rely on a small number of sensors and autonomous trains [52] may be examples of such contexts.

Q17: Can you imagine other contexts in which autonomous behaviour could play a dominant role?

However, autonomous systems are on their way and will definitely make it into our daily life. Autonomous cars are already seen on our streets and the first severe accidents prove that they are not as safe as we had hoped. Thus, scientists call again for more maths and formalisms in their development, but obviously proving the correctness of an autonomous system is much harder than in the standard, non-autonomous case. [53]. It is not just a matter of logic and logical proofs but it has to incorporate statistical evidence, too, and, last but not least, it has to integrate the physical properties of such systems, like acceleration, loss of weight or the compression of gas under pressure. In our view, in order to capture autonomicity in a safe and reliable way, in the near future there will be a convergence of modeling and development techniques based on logical, statistical, and numerical methods which also involve the explicit treatment of physical properties of a system (cf. [27,29]). But there are already strong signs that this is taking place. Methods such as statistical model checking or probabilistic model checking are mixing some of the aspects mentioned above (see e.g. [42,54,55]).

Q18: Do you expect autonomous systems to be more vulnerable against malicious attacks? If yes, how do you propose to handle security issues?

Besides the mentioned technical properties, another, often neglected aspect are public laws and regulations systems have to conform with [56]. Adaptation will probably make it more difficult to handle such non-functional requirements and request strict (and probably new) methods to prove conformance. For example, engineers are currently arguing that the most severe obstacles to drive autonomously on our streets are not technical but of legal nature, and concern warranty and guilt (see e.g. [57]).

Q19: How would you propose to cover legal and warranty issues in the development and dissemination phases of (collective) adaptive systems?

Coming back to the initial discussion, many novel applications such as autonomous systems, smart city infrastructures, or smart health applications do exhibit some degree of adaptation.

Q20: Which systems do you consider being the cutting edge application to introduce adaptability as an outstanding and highly requested feature?

The term adaptation refers to the property of systems to adapt and react correctly and reliably to all situations occurring during their life time. To ensure reliability, safety and security of adaptive systems novel rigorous engineering techniques are needed where AI approaches as well as mathematical and foundational methods do play a prominent role. Governments should address the risks and the unintended consequences of using adaptive systems by introducing laws and regulations about liability, privacy and cybersecurity and by developing specific strategies for handling the risks for the environment and for the possible losses of jobs.

**Acknowledgements.** As organisers of the panel we would like to thank the panelists for the stimulating panel discussion and the ISOLA chairs Tiziana Margaria and Bernhard Steffen for giving us the opportunity to organise this panel. Our thanks go to Mirco Tribastone for carefully reading and commenting a draft of the paper.

# References

1. Margaria, T., Steffen, B. (eds.): ISoLA 2016, Part I. LNCS, vol. 9952. Springer, Cham (2016). https://doi.org/10.1007/978-3-319-47166-2
2. Jähnichen, S., Wirsing, M.: Adaptation to the unforeseen: do we master our autonomous systems? Questions to the panel – panel introduction. In: [1], pp. 639–641 (2016)
3. Zadeh, L.A.: On the definition of adaptivity. Proc. IEEE **51**(3), 469–470 (1963)
4. Bruni, R., et al.: Reconciling white-box and black-box perspectives on behavioral self-adaptation. In: [47], pp. 163–184 (2015)
5. Hölzl, M., Wirsing, M.: Towards a system model for ensembles. In: Agha, G., Danvy, O., Meseguer, J. (eds.) Formal Modeling: Actors, Open Systems, Biological Systems. LNCS, vol. 7000, pp. 241–261. Springer, Heidelberg (2011). https://doi.org/10.1007/978-3-642-24933-4_12
6. Abeywickrama, D.B., Bicocchi, N., Zambonelli, F.: SOTA: towards a general model for self-adaptive systems. In: Reddy, S., Drira, K. (eds.) WETICE 2012, pp. 48–53. IEEE Computer Society Press (2012)
7. Anderson, S., Bredeche, N., Eiben, A.E., van Steen, M.: Adaptive Collective Systems – Herding black sheep. BookSprints for ICT Research (2013)
8. Bruni, R., Corradini, A., Gadducci, F., Lluch Lafuente, A., Vandin, A.: A conceptual framework for adaptation. In: de Lara, J., Zisman, A. (eds.) FASE 2012. LNCS, vol. 7212, pp. 240–254. Springer, Heidelberg (2012). https://doi.org/10.1007/978-3-642-28872-2_17
9. Hölzl, M., Rauschmayer, A., Wirsing, M.: Engineering of software-intensive systems: state of the art and research challenges. In: Wirsing, M., Banâtre, J.-P., Hölzl, M., Rauschmayer, A. (eds.) Software-Intensive Systems and New Computing Paradigms. LNCS, vol. 5380, pp. 1–44. Springer, Heidelberg (2008). https://doi.org/10.1007/978-3-540-89437-7_1
10. Kernbach, S., Schmickl, T., Timmis, J.: Collective adaptive systems: challenges beyond evolvability. CoRR abs/1108.5643 (2011)
11. Wirsing, M., Hölzl, M., Tribastone, M., Zambonelli, F.: ASCENS: engineering autonomic service-component ensembles. In: Beckert, B., Damiani, F., de Boer, F.S., Bonsangue, M.M. (eds.) FMCO 2011. LNCS, vol. 7542, pp. 1–24. Springer, Heidelberg (2013). https://doi.org/10.1007/978-3-642-35887-6_1
12. de Lemos, R., et al.: Software engineering for self-adaptive systems: a second research roadmap. In: de Lemos, R., Giese, H., Müller, H.A., Shaw, M. (eds.) Software Engineering for Self-Adaptive Systems II. LNCS, vol. 7475, pp. 1–32. Springer, Heidelberg (2013). https://doi.org/10.1007/978-3-642-35813-5_1
13. Hillston, J., Pitt, J., Wirsing, M., Zambonelli, F.: Collective adaptive systems: qualitative and quantitative modelling and analysis (Dagstuhl seminar 14512). In: Dagstuhl Reports 4, Schloss Dagstuhl Leibniz-Zentrum für Informatik (2015)
14. Belzner, L., Hölzl, M., Koch, N., Wirsing, M.: Collective autonomic systems: towards engineering principles and their foundations. In: Steffen, B. (ed.) Transactions on Foundations for Mastering Change I. LNCS, vol. 9960, pp. 180–200. Springer, Cham (2016). https://doi.org/10.1007/978-3-319-46508-1_10

15. Maggi, A., Sifakis, J., De Nicola, R.: DReAM: dynamic reconfigurable architecture modeling. In: Gruschka, N. (ed.) NordSec 2018. LNCS, vol. 11252, pp. 13–31. Springer, Cham (2018)
16. El Ballouli, R., Bensalem, S., Bozga, M., Sifakis, J.: Four exercises in programming dynamic reconfigurable systems: methodology and solution in DR-BIP. In: Gruschka, N. (ed.) NordSec 2018. LNCS, vol. 11252, pp. 304–320. Springer, Cham (2018)
17. Dragomir, I., Iosti, S., Bozga, M., Bensalem, S.: Designing systems with detection and reconfiguration capabilities: a formal approach. In: Gruschka, N. (ed.) NordSec 2018. LNCS, vol. 11252, pp. 155–171. Springer, Cham (2018)
18. Eberhardinger, B., Ponsar, H., Klumpp, D., Reif, W.: Measuring and evaluating the performance of self-organization mechanisms within collective adaptive systems. In: Gruschka, N. (ed.) NordSec 2018. LNCS, vol. 11252, pp. 202–220. Springer, Cham (2018)
19. Abd Alrahman, Y., De Nicola, R., Garbi, G.: GoAt: attribute-based interaction in Google Go. In: Gruschka, N. (ed.) NordSec 2018. LNCS, vol. 11252, pp. 288–303. Springer, Cham (2018)
20. Kilian, C.: Modern Control Technology. Thompson Delmar Learning (2005)
21. Kelly III, J., Hamm, S.: Smart Machines: IBM's Watson and the Era of Cognitive Computing. Columbia University Press, New York City (2013)
22. Silver, D., et al.: Mastering the game of Go with deep neural networks and tree search. Nature **529**, 484–489 (2016)
23. Cardoso, R.P., Rossetti, R.J.F., Hart, E., Burth Kurka, D., Pitt, J.: Engineering sustainable and adaptive systems in dynamic and unpredictable environments. In: Gruschka, N. (ed.) NordSec 2018. LNCS, vol. 11252, pp. 221–240. Springer, Cham (2018)
24. Belzner, L., Schmid, K., Phan, T., Gabor, T., Wirsing, M.: The Sharer's dilemma in collective adaptive systems of self-interested agents. In: Gruschka, N. (ed.) NordSec 2018. LNCS, vol. 11252, pp. 241–256. Springer, Cham (2018)
25. Ben Mahfoudh, H., Di Marzo Serugendo, G., Boulmier, A., Abdennadher, N.: Coordination model with reinforcement learning for ensuring reliable on-demand services in collective adaptive systems. In: Gruschka, N. (ed.) NordSec 2018. LNCS, vol. 11252, pp. 257–273. Springer, Cham (2018)
26. Nguyen, A., Yosinski, J., Clune, J.: Deep neural networks are easily fooled: high confidence predictions for unrecognizable images. In: IEEE Conference on Computer Vision and Pattern Recognition (CVPR 2015), 10 p. (2015)
27. Amodei, D., Olah, C., Steinhardt, J., Christiano, P., Schulman, J., Mané, D.: Concrete problems in AI safety. CoRR abs/1606.06565 (2016)
28. Di Marzo Serugendo, G.: Engineering adaptivity, universal autonomous systems, ethics and compliance issues. In: [1], pp. 714–719 (2016)
29. Vassev, E.: Safe artificial intelligence and formal methods. In: [1], pp. 704–713 (2016)
30. Kurzweil, R.: The Singularity is Near. Penguin Group, New York (2005)
31. Bostrom, N.: Superintelligence: Paths, Dangers, Strategies. Oxford University Press, Oxford (2014)
32. Inverardi, P., Mori, M.: A software lifecycle process to support consistent evolutions. In: de Lemos, R., Giese, H., Müller, H.A., Shaw, M. (eds.) Software Engineering for Self-Adaptive Systems II. LNCS, vol. 7475, pp. 239–264. Springer, Heidelberg (2013). https://doi.org/10.1007/978-3-642-35813-5_10

33. Hölzl, M., Koch, N., Puviani, M., Wirsing, M., Zambonelli, F.: The ensemble development life cycle and best practises for collective autonomic systems. In: [47], pp. 325–354 (2015)
34. Gabor, T., et al.: Adapting quality assurance to adaptive systems: the scenario coevolution paradigm. In: Gruschka, N. (ed.) NordSec 2018. LNCS, vol. 11252, pp. 137–154. Springer, Cham (2018)
35. Abeywickrama, D.B., Mamei, M., Zambonelli, F.: Engineering collectives of self-driving vehicles: the SOTA approach. In: Gruschka, N. (ed.) NordSec 2018. LNCS, vol. 11252, pp. 79–93. Springer, Cham (2018)
36. Pitt, J., Schaumeier, J., Artikis, A.: Axiomatization of socio-economic principles for self-organizing institutions. ACM Trans. Auton. Adapt. Syst. $\mathbf{7}$(4), 1–39 (2012)
37. Hennicker, R., Wirsing, M.: Dynamic logic for ensembles. In: Gruschka, N. (ed.) NordSec 2018. LNCS, vol. 11252, pp. 32–47. Springer, Cham (2018)
38. Sürmeli, J., Jähnichen, S., Sanders, J.W.: Modelling the transition to distributed ledgers. In: Gruschka, N. (ed.) NordSec 2018. LNCS, vol. 11252, pp. 48–62. Springer, Cham (2018)
39. IBM Corporation: An architectural blueprint for autonomic computing. Technical report, IBM (2005)
40. Pitt, J., et al.: A collective adaptive socio-technical system for remote- and self-supervised exercise in the treatment of intermittent claudication. In: Gruschka, N. (ed.) NordSec 2018. LNCS, vol. 11252, pp. 63–78. Springer, Cham (2018)
41. Wanninger, C., Eymüller, C., Hoffmann, A, Kosak, O., Reif, W.: Synthesizing capabilities for collective adaptive systems from self-descriptive hardware devices – bridging the reality gap. In: Gruschka, N. (ed.) NordSec 2018. LNCS, vol. 11252, pp. 94–108. Springer, Cham (2018)
42. Combaz, J., Bensalem, S., Tiezzi, F., Margheri, A., Pugliese, R., Kofroň, J.: Correctness of service components and service component ensembles. In: [47], pp. 107–159 (2015)
43. Tognazzi, S., Tribastone, M., Tschaikowski, M., Vandin, A.: Differential equivalence yields network centrality. In: Gruschka, N. (ed.) NordSec 2018. LNCS, vol. 11252, pp. 186–201. Springer, Cham (2018)
44. Zon, N., Gilmore, S.: Data-driven modelling and simulation of urban transportation systems using Carma. In: Gruschka, N. (ed.) NordSec 2018. LNCS, vol. 11252, pp. 274–287. Springer, Cham (2018)
45. Reichstaller, A., Gabor, T., Knapp, A.: Mutation-based test suite evolution for self-organizing systems. In: Gruschka, N. (ed.) NordSec 2018. LNCS, vol. 11252, pp. 118–136. Springer, Cham (2018)
46. Al Ali, R., Bureš, T., Hnetynka, P., Krijt, F., Plášil, F., Vinárek, J.: Dynamic security specification through autonomic component ensembles. In: Gruschka, N. (ed.) NordSec 2018. LNCS, vol. 11252, pp. 172–185. Springer, Cham (2018)
47. Wirsing, M., Hölzl, M., Koch, N., Mayer, P. (eds.): Software Engineering for Collective Autonomic Systems: Results of the ASCENS Project. LNCS, vol. 8998. Springer, Cham (2015). https://doi.org/10.1007/978-3-319-16310-9
48. Gartner: Top 10 Strategic Technology Trends for 2017. Gartner, Inc. (2016)
49. Mitchell, T., et al.: Never-ending learning. Commun. ACM $\mathbf{61}$(5), 103–115 (2018)
50. Güdemann, M., Nafz, F., Ortmeier, F., Seebach, H., Reif, W.: A specification and construction paradigm for organic computing systems. In: Proceedings of the 2nd International Conference on Self-Adaptive and Self-Organizing Systems, pp. 233–242. IEEE (2008)

51. Badica, C., Brezovan, M., Bădică, A.: An overview of smart home environments: architectures, technologies and applications. CEUR Workshop Proceedings, vol. 1036, pp. 78–85 (2013)
52. International Association of Public Transport: World report on metro automation. UITP, July 2016
53. Koopman, P., Wagner, M.: Challenges in autonomous vehicle testing and validation. In: 2016 SAE World Congress (2016)
54. Kwiatkowska, M.: Model checking and strategy synthesis for stochastic games: from theory to practice. In: ICALP 2016, Schloss Dagstuhl - Leibniz-Zentrum für Informatik 2016. LIPIcs, vol. 55, pp. 4:1–4:18 (2016)
55. Huang, X., Kwiatkowska, M., Wang, S., Wu, M.: Safety verification of deep neural networks. In: Majumdar, R., Kunčak, V. (eds.) CAV 2017, Part I. LNCS, vol. 10426, pp. 3–29. Springer, Cham (2017). https://doi.org/10.1007/978-3-319-63387-9_1
56. Taeihagh, A., Min Lim, H.S.: Governing autonomous vehicles: emerging responses for safety, liability, privacy, cybersecurity, and industry risks. Transp. Rev., 26 (2018). https://doi.org/10.1080/01441647.2018.1494640
57. Brodsky, J.S.: Autonomous vehicle regulation: how an uncertain legal landscape may hit the brakes on self-driving cars. Berkeley Tech. L. J. **31**, 851–879 (2016)

# Mutation-Based Test Suite Evolution for Self-Organizing Systems

André Reichstaller[1]([✉]), Thomas Gabor[2], and Alexander Knapp[1]

[1] Institute for Software and Systems Engineering, University of Augsburg,
Augsburg, Germany
{reichstaller,knapp}@isse.de
[2] Institute for Informatics, LMU Munich, Munich, Germany
thomas.gabor@ifi.lmu.de

**Abstract.** We consider test design as an optimization problem. The challenge is to find a set of test cases, the so-called test suite, that optimizes two quantifiable requirements: First, the effort needed for test execution should be minimal; a given test budget usually sets a maximum for the size of the test suite. Second, the test suite should maximize the score of a given test goal estimating its error detection capability, e.g., by the use of coverage or risk metrics. This paper studies test design for testing self-organizing systems with a mutation-based test goal. Equipped with a reconfiguration mechanism, this kind of a distributed system adapts its internal structure and thus its behavior to changing environmental conditions at run time. Test execution at a time step $t$ consequently not only triggers an observable output at $t + 1$, but might also bring about a reconfiguration of the system under test influencing the result of subsequently executed test cases. Formalizing the evolving sequential decision problem of test case executions by dependency graphs, in which we try to find optimal sets of paths for the mutation-based goal, we investigate the suitability of various kinds of evolutionary algorithms for optimization. All of the considered algorithms are evaluated using a concrete case study of an adaptive, self-organizing production cell.

## 1 Testing Self-Organizing Systems

"Testing is the process of executing a program with the intent of finding errors" [21]. Since exhaustively executing a program with all imaginable inputs $I$ is in practice not feasible, it is up to the tester to choose a subset $I' \subset I$ which is expected to find most of the errors. This challenge, generally referenced as *test design*, can be seen as a problem of optimization: Given a goal function $\Gamma : 2^I \to \mathbb{R}$ that quantifies the expectation of detected errors for all possible subsets of inputs, we strive to find the optimal $I' \subset I$ with $|I'| = k$, where $k$ denotes the maximum number of permitted executions, that fulfills the constraints in time and cost. Since general solutions for this subset selection problem are computationally expensive – exhaustive search would need $\binom{|I|}{k}$ goal evaluations

© Springer Nature Switzerland AG 2018
T. Margaria and B. Steffen (Eds.): ISoLA 2018, LNCS 11246, pp. 118–136, 2018.
https://doi.org/10.1007/978-3-030-03424-5_9

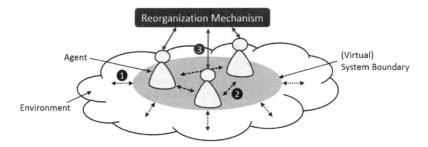

**Fig. 1.** Fundamental setup of self-organizing systems: Distributed software agents (often embedded in physical machines) continually interact with their environment (denoted by arrow type ❶). The joint system behavior is strongly influenced by inter-agent communication (❷) through message passing. If an agent detects an environmental fault hindering the current system approach, it triggers a reorganization mechanism (❸) which computes and distributes a new valid configuration.

– it is common to solve specific instances with heuristic approaches that build on domain-specific knowledge.

*Self-organizing* (SO) systems [8] are distributed systems with the particular characteristic that they are able to adapt their internal structure at run time to changing environmental conditions; see Fig. 1 for the fundamental setup. This kind of self-adaptation builds on an internal system state which is spread over the physically distributed agent components and, when necessary, is modified by a so-called *reorganization mechanism* computing and distributing an adapted agent component configuration in a central or again distributed manner by message passing. Reorganizations are triggered by monitoring the current configuration and the environment. In the *Restore Invariant Approach* (RIA) [17] a "corridor of correct behavior" (CCB) is used which is described by invariants and where imminent leaving of the corridor results in a reorganization.

Though affecting the actual run-time behavior, the internal states and configuration of an SO system usually are not accessible from outside the system boundaries; changes to the system configuration rather are the indirect result of reorganization triggerings than the direct product of a reaction to an input. For testing an SO system and, in particular, solving the resulting optimization problem, the limited influence of the tester on the system configuration hence raises implications on the test goal and the test strategy:

1. *Test goal*: The expectation of detected errors for a set of test inputs is strongly associated with the (expected) system reaction on them. The current system state shall consequently have the same influence on $\Gamma$ as on the reaction. Given the internal state space $S_{\text{sys}}$ we get the new signature $\Gamma_{\text{SO}} : 2^{I \times S_{\text{sys}}} \to \mathbb{R}$.

2. *Strategy*: An input $i \in I$ at time step $t$ influences future system states by possibly triggering previously unforeseen reconfigurations. Test execution at $t$ thus influences the score, as we call the evaluation of $\Gamma$ for particular inputs, of

---

**Algorithm 1.** Mutation-based test suite evaluation

---

**Require:** $p \equiv$ reference version of the program under test
  $O \equiv$ set of mutation operators
  $S \equiv$ mutation score function

1  **function** killed($\pi$)                          ▷ $\pi$: test case input sequence of length $|\pi|$
2    $K_\pi \leftarrow \emptyset$                         ▷ map of killed mutants, indexed by mutants
3    **for all** $o \in O$ **do**
4      $m \leftarrow$ mutated version of $p$ by application of $o$
5      reset system state
6      **for** $t \leftarrow 1..|\pi|$ **do**                    ▷ iterate through time steps
7        $\textit{eff} \leftarrow p.execute(\pi(t))$
8        $\textit{eff}_m \leftarrow m.execute(\pi(t))$
9        **if** $\textit{eff} \neq \textit{eff}_m$ **then**
10          $K_\pi[m] = (\textit{eff}, \textit{eff}_m)$                      ▷ mutant killed
11          **break**                          ▷ continue with next mutation operator
12    **return** $K_\pi$                                 ▷ return killed mutants
13  **function** $\Gamma_M(TS)$                   ▷ $TS$: test suite of test input sequences
14    $K \leftarrow \emptyset$                   ▷ map of killed mutants, indexed by test input sequences
15    **for** $\pi \in TS$ **do**                      ▷ iterate through test input sequences
16      $K[\pi] \leftarrow$ killed($\pi$)
17    **return** $S(K)$                              ▷ return mutation score

---

the following inputs. Test design evolves from an ad hoc towards a sequential decision problem: optimization needs to take into account dynamic interactions between the tester and the system under test (SuT). In consequence, our test goal $\Gamma_{SO}$ needs to consider input sequences $\pi : T \to I$ over time steps $T = [1..|T|]$ starting from an initial system state $\sigma_0 \in S_{sys}$ instead of sets of pairs of inputs and system states: $\Gamma_{SO} : 2^{I^T} \to \mathbb{R}$.

For the first implication we previously investigated a mutation-based test goal for SO systems [23]. Following the classic mutation testing technique [9], it determines how many of the mutants that simulate the effect of communication errors during reorganization a test suite reveals. Here, we consider a slightly modified goal not only taking into account the number, but also the effect of revealed mutants on the CCB, which leads to a *weighted* mutation score (Sect. 2). For solving the resulting optimization problem for the second implication, we study the eligibility of meta-heuristic search approaches, or, more concretely, of custom variants of classical evolutionary algorithms. We present a novel evolutionary mutation as well as a recombination operator that are particularly suitable for solving sequential optimization problems (Sect. 3), but may also be useful for various applications beyond test design. An evaluation of the proposed approaches by means of a concrete case, testing a self-organizing, adaptive production cell, shows promising results (Sect. 4). Encouraged by those results and considering related approaches and challenges (Sect. 5), we are planning several combinations and extensions of the presented approaches in the future (Sect. 6).

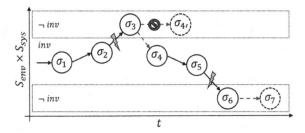

**Fig. 2.** Corridor of correct behavior

## 2  A Mutation-Based Test Goal

The mutation testing approach [9] supplies a direct operationalization for the principal goal of finding faults (as effects of errors) through detecting failures: A reference version of the program under test $p$ and a set of *mutation operators O* that mimic particular, common errors are assumed given. Modified versions of $p$ are generated by applying the operators from $O$. These so-called *mutants* of $p$ simulate the effect of introduced errors and thus potentially comprise faults. Each of the mutants is executed with each of the test cases from a test suite recording those mutants that show an effect deviating from the effect of $p$; such a mutant is said to be *killed* by the test case. Finally, for evaluating the test suite, a *mutation score function S* is applied to the record of killed mutants.

Algorithm 1 outlines this mutation-based test suite evaluation $\Gamma_{\mathrm{M}}(TS)$ for a test suite $TS$ of sequences of test cases from the inputs $I$ each of length at most $|T|$. In particular, it considers the case that the execution of one test case in a sequence influences the outcome of the next. We denote the execution of program $q$ with a test case $tc \in I$ on the current system state of $S_{\mathrm{sys}}$ by $q.execute(tc)$ returning the observable effect of the resulting state. $\Gamma_{\mathrm{M}}(TS)$ first records the mutation results for each $\pi \in TS$ and then applies the score function $S$ to the computed map of killed mutants. For a test case sequence $\pi$, killed($\pi$) executes the program $p$ and each mutant resulting from $O$ from a freshly reset system state with $\pi$ comparing the effects until either the sequence is completed or the mutant has been detected.

While a classical mutation score function would simply return the overall number of killed mutants, we suggest a more fine-grained categorization of observed effect deviations leading to a *weighted* mutation score. This categorization builds on a basic SO architectural concept: the *corridor of correct behavior* (CCB), for which the remainder of this section suggests appropriate assignments of $O$ and $S$ for testing SO systems.

### 2.1  The Corridor of Correct Behavior

Our mutation-based testing approach for SO systems assumes that the behavioral specification of the system under test is, or can be, formalized by the *Restore*

*Invariant Approach* (RIA) [17]. Initially introduced as a generic formalism for the specification and the implementation of Organic Computing systems, the RIA and the underlying CCB also proved useful in enabling systematic and automatic tests for SO systems [11]. The CCB guides reorganization in the RIA with logical predicates describing wanted properties of internal and external states. The conjunction of those predicates yields an invariant for the system's specified run-time behavior. Instead of continuously trying to optimize a quantifiable goal, reorganization is only performed if the invariant is broken, i.e., the CCB is left. The reorganization mechanism is assumed to restore the invariant through reorganization then, such that the system can continue to work as expected.

The invariant (see Fig. 2) considers both, the environmental state space $S_{env}$ as well as the internal state space $S_{sys}$. As soon as changing environmental conditions violate the invariant, reorganization is triggered by a monitoring mechanism. There are two cases in which the invariant remains broken after reorganization: There might be no possibility for "healing", i.e., re-establishing the invariant by reorganization at all. Since we can say that this is caused by higher force (the system cannot directly control $S_{env}$), this case is not as relevant for testing. The other case, however, is relevant as it indicates the existence of errors: if there was a possibility for re-establishing the invariant, but the reorganization mechanism did not do that. By testing we strive to reveal this latter case.

The CCB allows us to concentrate the test effort on the reorganization mechanism, as this ensures that the system behavior complies with its specification at run time: A test case $tc$ now amounts to choosing an environmental state, i.e., $S_{env}$ becomes the test input space $I$. Testing the program $p$ of the reorganization mechanism by executing $tc$ in the current system state, i.e., implementing $p.execute(tc)$, then involves three steps:

1. Establish the particular environmental state $tc$ which, in combination with the current system state violates the invariant.
2. Observe the system's reaction and its effect on the overall state.
3. Evaluate and, where appropriate, classify the effect against the corridor.

## 2.2   Mutation Operators

Successful reorganization requires correct state perception by the agents, correct computation of internal state adaptations by the reorganization mechanism, and correct realization of the delivered adaptation tasks by the agents. Since all of these critical routines are interconnected through message passing between the agents and the reorganization mechanism, a common cause for system failures are errors in communication. In [23] we elaborated the following exemplary mutation operators which are able to mimic those typical reorganization errors:

- *Lost Reconfiguration Message (LRM)*: As soon as an agent finds that a predicate of the invariant is violated it should normally send a *reconfiguration message* to trigger the reconfiguration mechanism. This mutation operator suppresses such messages, such that there might be no reconfiguration in spite of an incorrect system configuration.

- *Needless Reconfiguration Message (NRM)*: The inverse of an LRM: A particular agent signals the violation of a predicate, although there actually is none. Consequently, unnecessary reconfiguration steps might be triggered.
- *False Reconfiguration (FR)*: This operator mimics the loss of a message that was sent by the reconfiguration mechanism to trigger adaption. In consequence, one agent will (maybe erroneously) retain its previous internal state – this could result again in an incorrect system configuration.

For SO systems, we thus choose the set $O$ of mutation operators to consist of *LRM, NRM, FR* instantiated to each agent.

## 2.3  A Weighted Mutation Score

Considering Algorithm 1, the final score for $TS$ is determined by a function $S$ which assesses deviations in the observed effects when testing $p$ and when testing the generated mutants. In its classic form, the score simply counts the number of mutants killed by $TS$:

$$S_c(K) = |M(K)| \text{ with } M(K) = \{m \mid \exists \pi \in TS \,.\, K[\pi][m] \neq \emptyset\} \,. \tag{1}$$

Besides this classic mutation score we suggest an extension for testing with the CCB, which additionally takes the severity of killed mutants into account. This might be seen as rewarding the test suite for revealing preferably serious failures. The idea behind such a risk markup is that the more serious failures revealed by systematic testing, the lower the probability that such serious failures occur in real operation (cf. [22]).

Considering the CCB we build the severity levels on a classification of possible test results (as we call the effect observed after executing a program with a test case): If test execution results in reorganization, i.e., the reorganization mechanism transferred a state outside the corridor to the inside again, we assign the result to the class *reorg*. Otherwise, we assign it to $\neg reorg$. Function $C$ : $Eff \rightarrow \{reorg, \neg reorg\}$ determines the class of an effect in *Eff*. Comparing the effects *eff* and $eff_m$ as they are gained in Algorithms 1 and 1 of Algorithm 1, we quantify the severity levels of the four possible permutations with a severity function $Sev : Eff \times Eff \rightarrow \mathbb{R}$:

$$Sev(eff, eff_m) = \begin{cases} 1 & \text{if } C(eff) = C(eff_m) \\ 2 & \text{if } C(eff) = reorg \wedge C(eff_m) = \neg reorg \\ 3 & \text{if } C(eff) = \neg reorg \wedge C(eff_m) = reorg \end{cases} \tag{2}$$

The first case is obviously the most harmless one. If a test case triggers reorganization in both program versions (or in neither), we can argue that no real failure was detected. However, as the mutant has been killed (cf. Algorithm 1 in Algorithm 1), we still assign a slight severity score. The remaining cases indicate that the killed mutant simulated a real failure. In the second case, no valid state was established even though this would be possible. Such a failure would require human intervention in real operation. The third case, where a valid state was established even though this should be impossible, implies even higher costs in real operation, as it mostly results in a contradiction between software and hardware. The quantified severity levels are the basis for the weighted mutation score

$$S_{\mathrm{w}}(K) = \sum\nolimits_{m \in M(K)} Agg(\{Sev(K[\pi][m]) \mid \pi \in TS\}) , \qquad (3)$$

where $Agg$ aggregates the multiset of severities observed when a single mutant was killed by more than one test case occurring $TS$. The operator $Agg$ can be instantiated, e.g., with $\sum$ or max. We suggest to use $\sum$ if the errors simulated by the mutation operator are assumed to be *transient*, which means that the error does not always trigger a failure if covered. For the others, the *persistent* errors, we suggest to use max.

## 3   Evolutionary Test Strategies

Given a mutation-based test goal $\Gamma_{\mathrm{M}}$ as it is implemented in Algorithm 1 and instantiated with mutation operators $O$ and mutation score function $S$, just as described in the previous section, the challenge is now to find a test suite $TS$ that optimizes this goal in terms of the obtained score. We further demand that $|TS|$ conforms with a predefined maximum number of investable time steps $k$ such that if each test sequence of $TS$ has a length of (at most) $|T|$, $k = |TS| \cdot |T|$. In case of a self-organizing SuT the search for such a test suite has to face the following two challenges:

1. The effects of test cases in terms of killed mutants are dependent on the full history of previously executed test cases in a test sequence due to reconfigurations as adaptations to these previous environmental influences; in particular, executing a test case influences the future scores. The search space for the optimal test suite is thus given by a *dependency graph* with the initial system state as root, effects and their killed mutants as nodes, and the test cases as edges; see Fig. 3 for a small example.
2. Each evaluation of a test suite $TS$ is at the cost of $k \cdot |O|$ program executions at worst. The only factor that we can influence for practicability is thus the number of evaluations that has to be kept to a minimum.

These challenges give rise to a general optimization problem: find a number of paths through a graph in the most efficient way, such that their collected nodes optimize a given goal. For the aggregation by $\sum$, when disregarding that test suites are sets, a single best path could just be repeated, and optimization would be reduced to the well-established problem of finding a single path with maximum score [20]. The aggregation operator max, however, directly considers sets of nodes for evaluation and is sensitive to duplicates; greedy approaches iteratively choosing the single best rated path are doomed to fail. We now report on some experiments with different evolutionary algorithms for mastering this problem. Utilizing the new technique of *phased evolution* (cf. Sect. 3.2) we manage to cut the number of needed goal evaluations; endowing the evolutionary

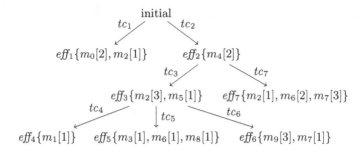

**Fig. 3.** Exemplary dependency graph with seven test cases $tc_1, \ldots, tc_7$ annotated by the set of killed mutants respectively. The numbers in squared brackets denote the severity of killed mutants. The best test suite of size $|TS| = 2$ for max-aggregation comprises of the two sequences $\pi_4 = \langle tc_2, tc_3, tc_6 \rangle$ and $\pi_5 = \langle tc_2, tc_7 \rangle$ scoring 14. For $\sum$-aggregation, however, the best test suite with $|TS| = 2$ is $\{\pi_3, \pi_5\}$ with $\pi_3 = \langle tc_2, tc_3, tc_5 \rangle$ with a score of 19.

mutation and recombination operators with domain specific semantics derived from a similarity function between test cases, we leverage the classical evolutionary algorithm to cope with the data structure of test sequences in *penguin evolution* (cf. Sect. 3.3).

## 3.1   Evolutionary Algorithms

Evolutionary algorithms are a wide-spread probabilistic optimization technique [12]. As they do not require a gradient on the solution space to be computable, they are often used in the automatic generation of test cases for software [20, 26]. In more recent years, the research community considered the issue of *whole test suite generation*, in which the aim of applying an evolutionary algorithm is not to find the most important test cases but instead to find the ideal combination of test cases that make up a concise but approximately complete test suite for a given software [13].

We first discuss the basis of an evolutionary process for whole test suite generation, which we will augment in the following sections. Any evolutionary algorithm works on a set of solution candidates, also called *individuals*. In our case, a single individual $TS$ represents a whole test suite. The set of currently considered individuals is also called a *population* $P$ and thus forms a subset of the domain of all possible test suites. As is usual for evolutionary algorithms, we set a fixed limit $|P| = m$ on the population size. Furthermore, we employ a fixed limit of execution time (measured in evaluations or generations as we discuss later) instead of a quality threshold as would be possible as well. However, especially for our later experiments we are most interested in the comparison of the quality of various approaches within a given time frame, as for software testing the requirement is more likely formulated to produce the best test suite within the available time rather than to produce a test suite as fast as possible.

---

**Algorithm 2.** Evolutionary Algorithm for Test Suite Generation

---

**Require:** $n \equiv$ maximum amount of generations

$\qquad m \equiv$ maximum amount of individuals in the population

$\qquad r_{\text{recomb}}, r_{\text{mut}}, r_{\text{hyper}} \equiv$ rates of evolutionary operators

$\qquad evaluate \equiv$ fitness/objective function

$\qquad rnd \equiv$ random number generator on codomain $[0, 1]$

$\qquad generate \equiv$ genetic operator that randomly generates a test suite

$\qquad mutate \equiv$ genetic operator that randomly applies small changes to a test suite

$\qquad combine \equiv$ function that combines two test sequences to produce a new one

$\qquad select\_parent \equiv$ randomized function returning a mating candidate in a population

1  $P \leftarrow \emptyset$

2  **for** $j = 0, \ldots, m - 1$ **do**                                      ▷ Random Initialization

3  $\quad P \leftarrow P \cup \{generate()\}$

4  **for** $i = 0, \ldots, n - 1$ **do**

5  $\quad$ **for all** $TS \in P$ **do**                                      ▷ Recombination

6  $\quad\quad$ **if** $rnd() < r_{\text{recomb}}$ **then**

7  $\quad\quad\quad mate \leftarrow select\_parent(P)$

8  $\quad\quad\quad child \leftarrow (\textbf{null})^{|TS|}$

9  $\quad\quad\quad$ **for** $k = 0, \ldots, |TS| - 1$ **do**

10 $\quad\quad\quad\quad child[k] \leftarrow TS[k]$ **or** $mate[k]$ **or** $combine(TS[k], mate[k])$

11 $\quad\quad\quad P \leftarrow P \cup \{child\}$

12 $\quad$ **for all** $TS \in P$ **do**                                      ▷ Mutation

13 $\quad\quad$ **if** $rnd() < r_{\text{mut}}$ **then**

14 $\quad\quad\quad P \leftarrow P \cup \{mutate(TS)\}$

15 $\quad$ **for all** $TS \in P$ **do**                                      ▷ Hypermutation

16 $\quad\quad$ **if** $rnd() < r_{\text{hyper}}$ **then**

17 $\quad\quad\quad P \leftarrow P \cup \{generate()\}$

18 $\quad$ **while** $|P| > m$ **do**                                      ▷ Selection

19 $\quad\quad P \leftarrow P \setminus \{\arg\min_{TS \in P} evaluate(TS)\}$

20 **return** $\arg\max_{TS \in P} evaluate(TS)$                                      ▷ Result

---

Algorithm 2 shows the typical structure of such an evolutionary algorithm. It starts with a random initialization and repeats its other operations for a fixed amount of times $n$. Each of these repetitions is also called a *generation*. We will discuss the various operators in greater detail now.

*Random Initialization.* This step generates the initial population by generating random test suites. Note that *generate* is not a mathematical function as it returns a newly generated object each time it is called. We use the term *genetic operator* for common evolutionary operations that use random effects.

*Recombination.* We chose a variant of recombination that grants the chance to recombine to each individual (irregardless of its fitness), but chooses its respective mate with respect to higher fitness. Effectively, we found this to be a good compromise between allowing exploration (using all individuals for recombination) and exploitation (favoring the better ones). The former is guaranteed by applying a fixed chance $r_{\text{recomb}}$ for the choice of any individual for recombination. The randomized function *select_mate* performs the latter by iterating over the population, returning the $n$th-fittest individual with probability $2^{-n}$. We then first create an empty test suite (i.e., containing no test sequences but already of required size $|TS|$) in the variable *child*. We then iterate over the number of test suites that is used for all our suites and complete the child by performing one random choice of three operations with equal probability (as denoted by the **or** operator): (a) we reuse the test sequence of the first (randomly chosen) parent, or (b) we use the test sequence of the second (chosen according to fitness) parent, or (c) we call a special function *combine* that builds a new test sequence out of the test sequences stemming from both parents. We show in Sect. 3.3 how to effectively implement such a function. Leaving out option (c) entirely would result in a more standard evolutionary algorithm that still manages to produce effective (but not as good) test suites (see Sect. 4.2). The recombination can then be considered as a standard uniform crossover at the whole suite level.

Even though recombination is a common step integral to almost all evolutionary algorithms, we did not present it as a black-box genetic operator but put a bit of its implementation into the description in Algorithm 2 to accurately describe how our implementation of *select_mate* fits in. The function *combine* thus does not accurately represent the whole genetic operation "recombination" the way *mutate* and *generate* do.

*Mutation.* Each individual is subject to mutation with a chance of $r_{mut}$. When chosen, the *mutate* operator generates a new individual through small random changes to the original. It is not obvious how a *small* change can be accurately quantified or guaranteed in the domain of test suites. It is, however, important that mutation operates on a small scale as it is our main exploratory operator and large mutations may (systematically) jump over some solutions. We tackle this problem in Sect. 3.3. An alternative to caring about the "smallness" of the changes is to just pick a random test sequence of the suite and re-generate it through random walk within the dependency graph starting at a randomly chosen point in the test sequence, which results in a rather big change with each mutation. We compare these approaches in Sect. 4.2. Note that in contrast to some evolutionary algorithms (and biological evolution), we only add mutated individuals to the population instead of having them replace their original counterparts.

*Hypermutation.* During the hypermutation step, we simply generate new individuals at random disregarding the previous course of evolution, and add them to the population. For this purpose, we use the same *generate* operator as in the random initialization step. Adding these new individuals increases exploratory behavior and thus helps prevent getting stuck in local optima. In parallel to the other operators (and their respective application rates), we base the amount of generated individuals on the population size $|P|$ and the given parameter $r_{hyper}$. In fact, the phases extension discussed in Sect. 3.2 turns the evolutionary algorithm into a dynamic optimization problem, for which the use of hypermutation has been highly suggested [16].

*Selection.* In the selection step we simply choose the $m$ best individuals to keep for the next generation. For the description in Algorithm 2 we choose a notation that does not need to introduce list slicing, although the implementation uses a computationally more efficient functional equivalent to the algorithm presented here.

*Result.* Finally, we return the best individual found in the last population of the last generation. This is also the best individual found overall, as all of our operations in the steps within each generation only add new individuals but never overwrite their parents. The fitness function *evaluate* in our case applies $\Gamma_M$ to the $TS$. As long as we do not change its semantics this means that we always keep the best individuals around. This feature is called *elitism* within the field of evolutionary algorithms. While the search process is (even without elitism) expected to strive for better individuals anyway, elitism ensures that it is monotone, as we will see in Sect. 4.2.

## 3.2   Phases Extension

Having discussed the basic functionality of our evolutionary algorithm for test suite generation, we now introduce the first of two extensions to it. This extension considers improving the performance of the search. We show in Sect. 4.2 that it manages to produce comparable results with roughly half the goal evaluations.

Generally speaking, we can observe that there is a noticeable relation between the fitness of a test suite $TS$ and the fitness of a single test sequence $\pi \in TS$, i.e., the fitness of the suite $\{\pi\}$. As discussed, the best test suite of $x$ test sequences (with maximum length $|T|$) will usually not consist of the $x$ best rated test sequences, as these will likely overlap in killed mutants and thus have poor overall coverage. However, it seems intuitive to start with one of the best rated test sequences and then build a suite around it. We could thus split the test suite generation problem into various sub-problems of iteratively finding test sequences given certain constraints (from previously found test sequences). But evolutionary algorithms provide us with a much more elegant approach, which we call *phase-based evolution*: we adjust the objective of the evolutionary process and the data structure of its individuals during the progression of evolutionary search. We start our evolutionary process with individuals that contain test suites $TS \in P$ of size $|TS| = 1$, i.e., all test suites only contain a single test sequence. We run this evolutionary search for the best single test sequence for a while: if we eventually want to search for a test suite $TS$ of size $|TS| = x$ after $n$ generations, we run this reduced search problem for roughly $\frac{n}{x}$ generations. Then we augment all individuals to represent a test suite with two test sequences by adding a randomly generated test sequence to each individual. We proceed to expand the problem domain of the search every $\frac{n}{x}$ generations until generation $n$, having actually employed the original fitness function for a size $x$ test suite only for the last $\frac{1}{n}$ generations. This approach works well in case the time of each of these evolutionary phases does run long enough to find reasonable results but not long enough to fully converge. The evolutionary search thus hits a point where it has a rough idea about the best single test sequence but still has multiple open options. At this point, it proceeds to search for a larger test suite, with limited option for the first spot of a test suite. Using the phases extension, we can cut the total amount of goal evaluations roughly in half, since the average test suite is only $\frac{x+1}{2}$ test sequences in size throughout the course of evolution.

### 3.3  Penguin Extensions

The second extension targets two points: (1) "merging" two test sequences into one within the *combine* function and (2) applying meaningfully small changes in the search domain of test suites within the *mutate* operator. The main problem of both is the handling of test case dependencies: Two test sequences $\pi_1$ and $\pi_2$ cannot simply be combined by attaching the tail of $\pi_2$ to the head of $\pi_1$ (as in the traditional one-point crossover operation [12]), since the configurations in the second half of $\pi_2$ might not conform to those of the first half of $\pi_1$. We utilize a method we call *penguin recombination* instead. Its name is inspired by an imaginary instance of our evolutionary algorithm being used to compute the evolution of animals, where dependencies in combination and mutation can be observed as well. If we consider two test sequences as different species such as a parrot and a fish, we notice that they cannot meaningfully recombine through crossover; but, inspired by nature, we can at least evolve the parrot to another bird that is most similar to the fish, resulting in perhaps a penguin. For applying this metaphor to the test sequences considered, we utilized a notion of similarity which we introduced in [23].

*Similarity Between Test Sequences.* We showed that faults that result from errors which are emulated by the mutation operators mentioned in Sect. 2.2 have no influence on one another, as they are distributed over different entities that are only connected through message passing. This basically means that a fault in the source code of one agent does not affect the path passed through control flow of another. We showed that we are in this case able to determine which of all the possibly generated faults $F$ (as result of applying mutation operators) a test case would generally cover [23]. We can thus represent a test case by a *label vector*, a binary vector $v$ of length $|F|$, with $v_i = 1$ if the fault $F_i$ is covered and $v_i = 0$ otherwise. Such a vector can be viewed as indicator for the path taken through the distributed control flow in an SO system in response to the input of an executed test case. Building on this insight we proposed a dissimilarity metric comparing two test cases based on their label vectors $v_1$ and $v_2$:

$$Dist(v_1, v_2) = |\{l \in \{1, \ldots, n\} \mid v_1[l] \neq v_2[l]\}| . \tag{4}$$

The more dissimilar two test cases are w.r.t. (4) the more fruitful it might be to execute them both instead of only one of them. Writing $tc.v$ for the label vector of test case $tc$, we extended this metric for assessing the representativeness or similarity of whole test sequences $\pi_1$ and $\pi_2$, i.e., paths through the dependency graph by

$$Rep(\pi_1, \pi_2) = \sum_{tc_2 \in \pi_2} \min_{tc_1 \in \pi_1} Dist(tc_1.v, tc_2.v) . \tag{5}$$

*Penguin Recombination.* Using this path distance, two test sequences $\pi_1$ and $\pi_2$ can be combined as follows: we cut a part of the beginning of $\pi_1$ at a random length, resulting in the incomplete test sequence $\pi_1^A$ so that $\pi_1^A; \pi_1^B = \pi_1$ for some $\pi_1^B$. There now exist multiple paths that may follow, of which $\pi_1^B$ is one possibility. Of all the possibilities $\pi_1^B, \pi_1^{B'}, \ldots$ within the current configuration at $\pi_1^A$, we compute their similarity to $\pi_2^B$, which is the second part of $\pi_2$ after cutting off $\pi_2$ at the same length as $\pi_1$. We choose the most similar completion $\pi_1^{B*} \sim \pi_2^B$ to produce a new test sequence $\pi_3 = \pi_1^A; \pi_1^{B*}$. This test sequence has a similar setup as $\pi_1$ but after a certain point tries to mimic as many features of $\pi_2$ as possible, i.e., become as much of a fish as a parrot can.

*Penguin Mutation.* The mutation operator is implemented analogously, almost as a recombination of a test sequence $\pi$ with itself. We cut off $\pi$ at some random point, resulting in $\pi^A; \pi^B = \pi$. Furthermore, we cut off the first test case of $\pi^B$, resulting in $\pi_{\text{orig}}^B; \pi^C = \pi^B$. We then add one test case at random to $\pi^A$, which we name $\pi_{\text{rand}}^B$, and make sure that $\pi_{\text{rand}}^B \neq \pi_{\text{orig}}^B$. From that point on, we complete $\pi^A; \pi_{\text{rand}}^B$ by generating the test sequence $\pi^{C*} \sim \pi^C$. We return the mutated test sequence $\pi' = \pi^A; \pi_{\text{rand}}^B; \pi^{C*}$ with only a single test case changed and afterwards trying to mimic the original $\pi$ as closely as still possible. We argue that this is the minimal (and still general) mutation one can implement for the domain of test sequences.

# 4    Evaluation

We evaluated the presented approaches by means of a concrete case study of a self-organizing, adaptive production cell. After describing the case considered in Sect. 4.1 we will provide the results in Sect. 4.2.

## 4.1    Case Study: An Adaptive Production Cell

We consider evolving a test suite for a self-organizing, adaptive production cell. As depicted in Fig. 4, the considered setup comprises four robots (R1, R2, R3, R4) and three mobile carts (C1, C2, C3). The robots are equipped with tools and corresponding capabilities such as Drill, Insert, Tighten, and Polish. The carts are able to carry workpieces along given routes. Each of the robots can be associated with a particular role which lets it apply a sequence of capabilities on present workpieces. The self-organizing production cell's behavior at a point in time $t$ is thus determined by the overall role allocation and cart routes in $t$. A corridor of correct behavior (cf. Sect. 2.1) monitors the satisfiability of tasks in the presence of environmental faults, such as a broken driller for a specific robot. Triggered by violations an SO mechanism calculates and distributes a new valid configuration at run-time.

Testing the SO mechanism in the described setup means to simulate environmental faults by use of test drivers in order to subsequently evaluate the established, new configuration of the cell. While the inputs of a single test case

(a) The resource flow starts to the left where $R_1$ drills a hole into incoming workpieces. Workpieces are successively transported by $C_1$, $C_2$, and $C_3$. The robots apply their tools. Once $R_4$ is done, the workpieces leave the system.

(b) After $R_4$ loses its polish tool, the resource flow is reconfigured: $R_3$ is taking over the previous role of $R_4$.

**Fig. 4.** A schematic overview of the self-organizing robot cell case study. The task is to apply the drill, insert, tighten, and polish capabilities to all incoming workpieces. Each robot's available tools are shown to its right with D, I, T, and P; the currently allocated ones are underlined. (a) shows an exemplary configuration of the robot cell. As depicted in (b), faults result in tool losses that self-organization can cope with by reconfiguring the resource flow.

are defined by a fixed number of environmental faults (55 in our case), a test sequence starting at a fixed role allocation with no activated faults, sequentially activates the faults defined by the comprised test cases. The result of a test case depends on the current role allocation, which can be viewed as an internal system state, and this current role allocation is established by the preceding test cases. The dependency graph of test cases hence is connected by role allocations before and after the test case execution. For our experiments, we generated the test suite to minimize by use of the S# framework [10] resulting in a graph with 7524 test cases as nodes and 8 884 634 edges in between them.

## 4.2 Results

For evaluation we applied our approach to the mentioned dependency graph. We tested a standard evolutionary algorithm evolving a test suite as well as both of our extensions individually and their combination. We also ran baseline experiments using random search. We used a population of size $m = 50$ evolving for $n = 1000$ generations. We produced test suites of (eventual) size $x = 10$ from our test data comprising test sequences of length up to $|T| = 10$, i.e., $k = 100$. We chose $r_{recomb} = 0.3$ and $r_{mut} = r_{hyper} = 0.1$ for the hyperparameters providing a lot of random exploration to the algorithm favoring generality of our results over sample efficiency. The total computation time of all evolutionary processes included in the test was 1.6 h on a machine with an Intel Core i7 processor at 2.9 GHz and 16 GB of memory. The results are shown in Figs. 5(a) and (b). It can be clearly seen that the phases extension eventually achieves very similar results to both non-phase-based variants, but with considerable savings in computational resources. Furthermore, it is also evident that both penguin variants outperform their non-penguin counterparts. Again, this validates our approach and shows that the additional knowledge given to the algorithm in form of the similarity function pays off with better end results.

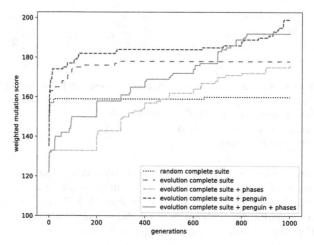

(a) Performance evaluation of evolutionary test generations strategies compared to a random baseline. The penguin recombination and mutation manages to produce better results than the naïve approach. Interestingly, for both cases, about the same quality of results can be reached using the phased evolutionary algorithm with significantly less computational effort, see Fig. 5b.

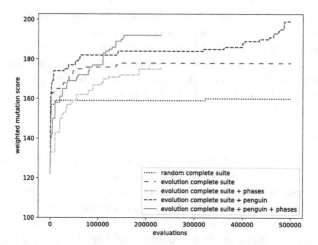

(b) The same experiment as in Fig. 5a plotted against the number of test sequence evaluations performed. It can be seen that the phase-based extension uses only about half the evaluations compared to the standard approach, reaching about the same performance earlier in the case of the penguin variant.

**Fig. 5.** Performance evaluation results

# 5   Related Work

Extensive use of adaptivity, such as self-organization, necessitates research on adequate methods of engineering them reliably [8,28]. Finding adequately powerful software tests is an integral part of making adaptive systems controllable and trustworthy [1,3,6], even though some new methods regarding, e.g., runtime testing [4,7,14], need to be developed. The concept of simultaneously using machine learning methods to generate the adaptivity of the SuT as well as the power of the test suite has been sketched for neural networks as *adversarial learning* [2,19].

We considered test suites for self-organizing systems, and the application of evolutionary algorithms for their generation w.r.t. a mutation-based test goal. While it seems quite common to use fault-based techniques for evaluating the quality of test suites [5,24,29], the huge majority of approaches, including the cited ones, applies other test goals for actual generation or the minimization process. This might be due to the high costs for goal evaluation, which we were able to reduce by the phases extension. The mutation operators and the case study were taken from our previous work, where we considered the test suite reduction problem for SO systems [23]. Also the severity-based mutant weighting was inspired by our previous work in which we approached the task of risk-based interoperability testing using reinforcement learning [22].

Here, we made use of search-based testing techniques [20] for generating test suites which are adequate w.r.t. a mutation-based test goal. Within the field of evolutionary algorithms, test case generation has been researched for some time [20,26] with whole suite generation sparking interest more recently [13]. Using evolutionary algorithms for dynamically changing problems has been envisioned from their very beginning [12,27]. Some approaches have already introduced dynamics into originally non-dynamic problems in order to improve the quality of the search result [15,25]. These also use measurements related to the similarity between individuals in their evaluation, which may then change over time as the population changes. Similarity has been incorporated into the recombination process e.g. in [18], though on a different level than in our approach, viz. at the level of mate selection mirroring biological evolution.

# 6   Conclusion

We suggested two domain specific extensions of a classical evolutionary approach on constructing test suites of given length w.r.t. a mutation-based test goal for testing self-organizing systems. The first, the *phased* extension, reduced the number of goal evaluations needed for optimization, the second, the *penguin* extension, was shown to increase the overall fitness attained. Both aspects are highly relevant for test suite construction. Though our evaluation just considered a single concrete case, testing a self-organizing production cell, we expect to be able to generalize our findings in future. Applications to be considered include code-level test sequence and test suite generation. With respect to the presented mutation-based test goal the future plan is to combine the severity-based weighting scheme of mutants suggested here with the concept of *higher-order mutants* for self-organizing systems that we investigated previously [23]. Also here we envision several cut points with practice-oriented applications, such as test suite minimization and construction for distributed systems, waiting for being explored.

**Acknowledgment.** This research is partly funded by the research project *Testing self-organizing, adaptive Systems (TeSOS)* of the German Research Foundation. We thank the anonymous reviewers for their helpful comments.

# References

1. Amodei, D., Olah, C., Steinhardt, J., Christiano, P., Schulman, J., Mané, D.: Concrete problems in AI safety (2016). https://arxiv.org/pdf/1606.06565
2. Arjovsky, M., Bottou, L.: Towards principled methods for training generative adversarial networks (2017). https://arxiv.org/pdf/1701.04862
3. Belzner, L., Beck, M.T., Gabor, T., Roelle, H., Sauer, H.: Software engineering for distributed autonomous real-time systems. In: Proceedings of the 2nd International Workshop on Software Engineering for Smart Cyber-Physical Systems, pp. 54–57. ACM (2016)
4. Belzner, L., Gabor, T.: Bayesian verification under model uncertainty. In: Proceedings of the 3rd International Workshop on Software Engineering for Smart Cyber-Physical Systems, pp. 10–13. IEEE (2017)
5. Black, J., Melachrinoudis, E., Kaeli, D.: Bi-criteria models for all-uses test suite reduction. In: Proceedings of the 26th International Conference on Software Engineering, pp. 106–115. IEEE (2004)
6. Bures, T., Weyns, D., Klein, M., Haber, R.E.: 1st International Workshop on Software Engineering for Smart Cyber-Physical Systems (SEsCPS 2015). In: Proceedings of the 37th International Conference on Software Engineering, vol. 2, pp. 1009–1010. IEEE (2015)
7. Calinescu, R., Ghezzi, C., Kwiatkowska, M., Mirandola, R.: Self-adaptive software needs quantitative verification at runtime. Comm. ACM **55**(9), 69–77 (2012)
8. de Lemos, R., et al.: Software engineering for self-adaptive systems: a second research roadmap. In: de Lemos, R., Giese, H., Müller, H.A., Shaw, M. (eds.) Software Engineering for Self-Adaptive Systems II. LNCS, vol. 7475, pp. 1–32. Springer, Heidelberg (2013). https://doi.org/10.1007/978-3-642-35813-5_1
9. DeMillo, R.A., Lipton, R.J., Sayward, F.G.: Hints on test data selection: help for the practicing programmer. Computer **11**(4), 34–41 (1978)
10. Eberhardinger, B., Seebach, H., Klumpp, D., Reif, W.: Test case selection strategy for self-organization mechanisms. In: Spillner, A., Winter, M., Pietschker, A. (eds.) Test, Analyse und Verifikation von Software – Gestern, Heute, Morgen, pp. 139–157. dpunkt (2017)
11. Eberhardinger, B., Seebach, H., Knapp, A., Reif, W.: Towards testing self-organizing, adaptive systems. In: Merayo, M.G., de Oca, E.M. (eds.) ICTSS 2014. LNCS, vol. 8763, pp. 180–185. Springer, Heidelberg (2014). https://doi.org/10.1007/978-3-662-44857-1_13

12. Eiben, A.E., Smith, J.E.: Introduction to Evolutionary Computing. Natural Computing Series, vol. 53. Springer, Heidelberg (2003). https://doi.org/10.1007/978-3-662-05094-1
13. Fraser, G., Arcuri, A.: Evosuite: automatic test suite generation for object-oriented software. In: Proceedings of the 19th ACM SIGSOFT Symposium and 13th European Conference on Foundations of Software Engineering, pp. 416–419. ACM (2011)
14. Fredericks, E.M., Ramirez, A.J., Cheng, B.H.C.: Towards run-time testing of dynamic adaptive systems. In: Proceedings of the 8th International Symposium on Software Engineering for Adaptive and Self-Managing Systems, pp. 169–174 (2013)
15. Gabor, T., Belzner, L., Linnhoff-Popien, C.: Inheritance-based diversity measures for explicit convergence control in evolutionary algorithms. In: Proceedings of the Genetic and Evolutionary Computation Conference (2018)
16. Grefenstette, J.J.: Genetic algorithms for changing environments. In: Proceedings of the Parallel Problem Solving from Nature, vol. 2, pp. 139–146. Elsevier (1992)
17. Güdemann, M., Nafz, F., Ortmeier, F., Seebach, H., Reif, W.: A specification and construction paradigm for organic computing systems. In: Proceedings of the 2nd International Conference on Self-adaptive and Self-organizing Systems, pp. 233–242. IEEE (2008)
18. Ishibuchi, H., Shibata, Y.: A similarity-based mating scheme for evolutionary multiobjective optimization. In: Cantú-Paz, E. (ed.) GECCO 2003, Part I. LNCS, vol. 2723, pp. 1065–1076. Springer, Heidelberg (2003). https://doi.org/10.1007/3-540-45105-6_116
19. Lowd, D., Meek, C.: Adversarial learning. In: Proceedings of the 11th ACM SIGKDD International Conference on Knowledge Discovery in Data Mining, pp. 641–647. ACM (2005)
20. McMinn, P.: Search-based software test data generation: a survey. Softw. Test. Verif. Reliab. 14(2), 105–156 (2004)
21. Myers, G.J., Sandler, C., Badgett, T.: The Art of Software Testing. Wiley, Hoboken (2011)
22. Reichstaller, A., Eberhardinger, B., Knapp, A., Reif, W., Gehlen, M.: Risk-based interoperability testing using reinforcement learning. In: Wotawa, F., Nica, M., Kushik, N. (eds.) ICTSS 2016. LNCS, vol. 9976, pp. 52–69. Springer, Cham (2016). https://doi.org/10.1007/978-3-319-47443-4_4
23. Reichstaller, A., Eberhardinger, B., Ponsar, H., Knapp, A., Reif, W.: Test suite reduction for self-organizing systems: a mutation-based approach. In: Proceedings of the 13th International Workshop on Automation of Software Test (2018)
24. Rothermel, G., Harrold, M.J., Von Ronne, J., Hong, C.: Empirical studies of test-suite reduction. Softw. Test. Verif. Reliab. 12(4), 219–249 (2002)
25. Ursem, R.K.: Diversity-guided evolutionary algorithms. In: Guervós, J.J.M., Adamidis, P., Beyer, H.-G., Schwefel, H.-P., Fernández-Villacañas, J.-L. (eds.) PPSN 2002. LNCS, vol. 2439, pp. 462–471. Springer, Heidelberg (2002). https://doi.org/10.1007/3-540-45712-7_45
26. Wappler, S., Lammermann, F.: Using evolutionary algorithms for the unit testing of object-oriented software. In: Proceedings of the Annual Conference on Genetic and Evolutionary Computation, pp. 1053–1060. ACM (2005)
27. Weicker, K.: Evolutionary Algorithms and Dynamic Optimization Problems. Der Andere Verlag, Berlin (2003)

28. Wirsing, M., Hölzl, M., Koch, N., Mayer, P. (eds.): Software Engineering for Collective Autonomic Systems: The ASCENS Approach. LNCS, vol. 8998. Springer, Cham (2015). https://doi.org/10.1007/978-3-319-16310-9
29. Zhang, L., Marinov, D., Zhang, L., Khurshid, S.: An empirical study of JUnit testsuite reduction. In: Proceedings of the 22nd International Symposium on Software Reliability Engineering, pp. 170–179. IEEE (2011)

# Adapting Quality Assurance to Adaptive Systems: The Scenario Coevolution Paradigm

Thomas Gabor[1]([✉]), Marie Kiermeier[1], Andreas Sedlmeier[1],
Bernhard Kempter[2], Cornel Klein[2], Horst Sauer[2], Reiner Schmid[2],
and Jan Wieghardt[2]

[1] LMU Munich, Munich, Germany
{thomas.gabor,marie.kiermeier,andreas.sedlmeier}@ifi.lmu.de
[2] Siemens AG, Munich, Germany
{bernhard.kempter,cornel.klein,horst.sauer,reiner.schmid,
jan.wieghardt}@siemens.com

**Abstract.** From formal and practical analysis, we identify new challenges that self-adaptive systems pose to the process of quality assurance. When tackling these, the effort spent on various tasks in the process of software engineering is naturally re-distributed. We claim that all steps related to testing need to become self-adaptive to match the capabilities of the self-adaptive system-under-test. Otherwise, the adaptive system's behavior might elude traditional variants of quality assurance. We thus propose the paradigm of scenario coevolution, which describes a pool of test cases and other constraints on system behavior that evolves in parallel to the (in part autonomous) development of behavior in the system-under-test. Scenario coevolution offers a simple structure for the organization of adaptive testing that allows for both human-controlled and autonomous intervention, supporting software engineering for adaptive systems on a procedural as well as technical level.

**Keywords:** Self-adaptive system · Software engineering
Quality assurance · Software evolution

## 1 Introduction

Until recently, the discipline of software engineering has mainly tackled the process through which humans develop software systems. In the last few years, current break-throughs in the fields of artificial intelligence and machine learning have enabled new possibilities that have previously been considered infeasible or just too complex to tap into with "manual" coding: Complex image recognition, natural language processing, or decision making as it is used in complex games are prime examples. The resulting applications are pushing towards a broad audience of users. However, as of now, they are mostly focused on non-critical areas of use, at least when implemented without further human supervision.

© Springer Nature Switzerland AG 2018
T. Margaria and B. Steffen (Eds.): ISoLA 2018, LNCS 11246, pp. 137–154, 2018.
https://doi.org/10.1007/978-3-030-03424-5_10

Software artifacts generated via machine learning are hard to analyze, causing a lack of trustworthiness for many important application areas.

We claim that in order to reinstate levels of trustworthiness comparable to well-known classical approaches, we need not essentially reproduce the principles of classical software test but need to develop a new approach towards software testing. We suggest to develop a system and its test suite in a competitive setting where each sub-system tries to outwit the other. We call this approach *scenario coevolution* and attempt to show the necessity of such an approach. We hope that trust in that dynamic (or similar ones) can help to build a new process for quality assurance, even for hardly predictable systems.

Following a top-down approach to the issue, we start in Sect. 2 by introducing a formal framework for the description of systems. We augment it to also include the process of software and system development. Section 3 provides a short overview on related work. From literature review and practical experience, we introduce four core concepts for the engineering of adaptive systems in Sect. 4. In order to integrate these with our formal framework, Sect. 5 contains an introduction of our notion of scenarios and their application to an incremental software testing process. In Sect. 6 we discuss which effect scenario coevolution has on a selection of practical software engineering tasks and how it helps implement the core concepts. Finally, Sect. 7 provides a short conclusion.

## 2 Formal Framework

In this section we introduce a formal framework as a basis for our analysis. We first build upon the framework described in [1] to define adaptive systems and then proceed to reason about the influence of their inherent structure on software architecture.

### 2.1 Describing Adaptive Systems

We roughly adopt the formal definitions of our vocabulary related to the description of systems from [1]: We describe a system as an arbitrary relation over a set of variables.

**Definition 1** (System [1]). Let $I$ be a (finite or infinite) set, and let $\mathcal{V} = (V_i)_{i \in I}$ be a family of sets. A *system* of type $\mathcal{V}$ is a relation $S$ of type $\mathcal{V}$.

Given a System $S$, an element $s \in S$ is called the state of the system. For practical purposes, we usually want to discern various parts of a system's state space. For this reason, parts of the system relation of type $\mathcal{V}$ given by an index set $J \subseteq I$, i.e., $(V_j)_{j \in J}$, may be considered *inputs* and other parts given by a different index set may be considered *outputs* [1]. Formally, this makes no difference to the system. Semantically, we usually compute the output parts of the system using the input parts.

We introduce two more designated sub-spaces of the system relation: *situation* and *behavior*. These notions correspond roughly to the intended meaning of inputs and outputs mentioned before. The situation is the part of the system state space that fully encapsulates all information the system has about its state. This may include parts that the system does have full control over (which we would consider counter-intuitive when using the notion of "input"). The behavior encapsulates the parts of the system that can only be computed by applying the system relation. Likewise, this does *not* imply that the system has full control over the values. Furthermore, a system may have an *internal state*, which is parts of the state space that are neither included in the situation nor in the behavior. When we are not interested in the internal space, we can regard a system as a mapping from situations to behavior, written $S = X \overset{Z}{\rightsquigarrow} Y$ for situations $X$ and behaviors $Y$, where $Z$ is the internal state of the system $S$. Using these notions, we can more aptly define some properties on systems.

Further following the line of thought presented in [1], we want to build systems out of other systems. At the core of software engineering, there is the principle of re-use of components, which we want to mirror in our formalism.

**Definition 2** (Composition). Let $S_1$ and $S_2$ be systems of types $\mathcal{V}_1 = (V_{1,i})_{i \in I_1}$ and $\mathcal{V}_2 = (V_{2,i})_{i \in I_2}$, respectively. Let $\mathcal{R}(\mathcal{V})$ be the domain of all relations over $\mathcal{V}$. A *combination operator* $\otimes$ is a function such that $S_1 \otimes S_2 \in \mathcal{R}(\mathcal{V})$ for some family of sets $\mathcal{V}$ with $V_{1,1}, ..., V_{1,m}, V_{2,1}, ..., V_{2,n} \in \mathcal{V}$.[1] The application of a combination operator is called *composition*. The arguments to a combination operator are called *components*.

Composition is not only important to model software architecture within our formalism, but it also defines the formal framework for interaction: Two systems interact when they are combined using a combination operator $\otimes$ that ensures that the behavior of (at least) one system is recognized within the situation of (at least) another system.

**Definition 3** (Interaction). Let $S = S_1 \otimes S_2$ be a composition of type $\mathcal{V}$ of systems $S_1$ and $S_2$ of type $\mathcal{V}_1$ and $\mathcal{V}_2$, respectively, using a combination operator $\otimes$. If there exist a $V_1 \in \mathcal{V}_1$ and a $V_2 \in \mathcal{V}_2$ and a relation $R \in V_1 \times V_2$ so that for all states $s \in S$, $(proj(s, V_1), proj(s, V_2)) \in R$, then the components $S_1$ and $S_2$ interact with respect to $R$.

We can model an open system $S$ as a combination $S = C \otimes E$ of a core system $C$ and its environment $E$, both being modeled as systems again.

Hiding some of the complexity described in [1], we assume we have a logic $\mathfrak{L}$ in which we can express a system goal $\gamma$. We can always decide if $\gamma$ holds for a given system, in which case we write $S \models \gamma$ for $\gamma(S) = \top$. Based on [1], we can use this concept to define an adaptation domain:

**Definition 4** (Adaptation Domain [1]). Let $S$ be a system. Let $\mathcal{E}$ be a set of environments that can be combined with $S$ using a combination operator $\otimes$. Let

---

[1] In [1], there is a more strict definition on how the combination operator needs to handle the designated inputs and outputs of its given systems. Here, we opt for a more general definition.

$\Gamma$ be a set of goals. An *adaptation domain* $\mathcal{A}$ is a set $\mathcal{A} \subseteq \mathcal{E} \times \Gamma$. $S$ can adapt to $\mathcal{A}$, written $S \Vdash \mathcal{A}$ iff for all $(E, \gamma) \in \mathcal{A}$ it holds that $S \otimes E \models \gamma$.

**Definition 5** (Adaptation Space [1]). Let $\mathcal{E}$ be a set of environments that can be combined with $S$ using a combination operator $\otimes$. Let $\Gamma$ be set of goals. An *adaptation space* $\mathfrak{A}$ is a set $\mathfrak{A} \subseteq \mathfrak{P}(\mathcal{E}, \Gamma)$.

We can now use the notion of an adaptation space to define a preorder on the adaptivity of any two systems.

**Definition 6** (Adaptation [1]). Given two systems $S$ and $S'$, $S'$ is at least as adaptive as $S$, written $S \sqsubseteq S'$ iff for all adaptation spaces $\mathcal{A} \in \mathfrak{A}$ it holds that $S \Vdash \mathcal{A} \implies S' \Vdash \mathcal{A}$.

Both Definitions 4 and 5 can be augmented to include soft constraints or optimization goals. This means that in addition to checking against boolean goal satisfaction, we can also assign each system $S$ interacting with an environment $E$ a *fitness* $\phi(S \otimes E) \in F$, where $F$ is the type of fitness values. We assume that there exists a preorder $\preceq$ on $F$, which we can use to compare two fitness values. We can then generalize Definitions 4 and 5 to respect these optimization goals.

**Definition 7** (Adaptation Domain for Optimization). Let $S$ be a system. Let $\mathcal{E}$ be a set of environments that can be combined with $S$ using a combination operator $\otimes$. Let $\Gamma$ be a set of Boolean goals. Let $F$ be a set of fitness values and $\preceq$ be a preorder on $F$. Let $\Phi$ be a a set of fitness functions with codomain $F$. An *adaptation domain* $\mathcal{A}$ is a set $\mathcal{A} \subseteq \mathcal{E} \times \Gamma \times \Phi$. $S$ can adapt to $\mathcal{A}$, written $S \Vdash \mathcal{A}$ iff for all $(E, \gamma, \phi) \in \mathcal{A}$ it holds that $S \otimes E \models \gamma$.

Note that in Definition 7 we only augmented the data structure for adaptation domains but did not actually alter the condition to check for the fulfillment of an adaptation domain. This means that for an adaptation domain $\mathcal{A}$, a system needs to fulfill all goals in $\mathcal{A}$ but is not actually tested on the fitness defined by $\phi$. We could define a fitness threshold $f$ we require a system $S$ to surpass in order to adapt to $\mathcal{A}$ in the formalism. But such a check, written $f \preceq \phi(S \otimes E)$, could already be included in the Boolean goals if we use a logic that is expressive enough.

Instead, we want to use the fitness function as soft constraints: We expect the system to perform as well as possible on this metric, but we do not (always) require a minimum level of performance. However, we can use fitness to define a fitness preorder on systems:

**Definition 8** (Optimization). Given two systems $S$ and $S'$ as well as an adaptation space $\mathcal{A}$, $S'$ is at least as optimal as $S$, written $S \preceq_{\mathcal{A}} S'$, iff for all $(E, \gamma, \phi) \in \mathcal{A}$ it holds that $\phi(S \otimes E) \preceq \phi(S' \otimes E)$.

**Definition 9** (Adaptation with Optimization). Given two systems $S$ and $S'$, $S'$ is at least as adaptive as $S$ with respect to optimization, written $S \sqsubseteq^* S'$ iff for all adaptation domains $\mathcal{A} \in \mathfrak{A}$ it holds that $S \Vdash \mathcal{A} \implies S' \Vdash \mathcal{A}$ and $S \preceq_{\mathcal{A}} S'$.

Note that so far our notions of adaptivity and optimization are purely exten-
sional, which originates from the black box perspective on adaptation assumed
in [1].

## 2.2   Constructing Adaptive Systems

We now shift the focus of our analysis a bit away from the question "When is
a system adaptive?" towards the question "How is a system adaptive?". This
refers to both questions of software architecture (i.e., which components should
we use to make an adaptive system?) and questions of software engineering (i.e.,
which development processes should we use to develop an adaptive system?).
We will see that with the increasing usage of methods of artificial intelligence,
design-time engineering and run-time adaptation increasingly overlap [2].

**Definition 10** (Adaptation Sequence). A series of $|I|$ systems $\mathcal{S} = (S_i)_{i \in I}$ with
index set $I$ with a preorder $\leq$ on the elements of $I$ is called an *adaptation
sequence* iff for all $i, j \in I$ it holds that $i \leq j \implies S_i \sqsubseteq^* S_j$

Note that we used adaptation with optimization in Definition 10 so that a
sequence of systems $(S_i)_{i \in I}$ that each fulfill the same hard constraints ($\gamma$ within a
singleton adaptation space $\mathfrak{A} = \{\{(E, \gamma, \phi)\}\}$) can form an adaptation sequence
iff for all $i, j \in I$ it holds that $i \leq j \implies \phi(S_i \otimes E) \preceq \phi(S_j \otimes F)$. This is the
purest formulation of an optimization process within our formal framework.[2]

Such an adaptation sequence can be generated by continuously improving a
starting system $S_0$ and adding each improvement to the sequence. Such a task
can both be performed by a team of human developers or standard optimization
algorithms as they are used in artificial intelligence. Only in the latter case, we
want to consider that improvement happening within our system boundaries.
Unlike the previously performed black-box analysis of systems, the presence of
an optimization algorithm within the system itself does have implications for the
system's internal structure. We will thus switch to a more "grey box" analysis
in the spirit of [3].

**Definition 11** (Self-Adaptation). A system $S_0$ is called *self-adaptive* iff the
sequence $(S_i)_{i \in \mathbb{N}, i < n}$ for some $n \in \mathbb{N}$ with $S_i = S_0 \otimes S_{i-1}$ for $0 < i < n$ and some
combination operator $\otimes$ is an adaptation sequence.

Note that we could define the property of self-adaptation more generally by
again constructing an index set on the sequence $(S_i)$ instead of using $\mathbb{N}$, but
chose not to do so to not further clutter the notation. For most practical purposes, the adaptation is going to happen in discrete time steps anyway. It is also
important to be reminded that despite its notation, the combination operator $\otimes$

---

[2] Strictly speaking, an optimization *process* would further assume there exists an optimization relation $o$ from systems to systems so that for all $i, j \in I$ it holds that
$i \leq j \implies o(S_i, S_j)$. But for simplicity, we consider the sequence of outputs of the
optimization process a sufficient representation of the whole process.

does not need to be symmetric and likely will not be in this case, because when constructing $S_0 \otimes S_{i-1}$ we usually want to pass the previous instance $S_{i-1}$ to the general optimization algorithm encoded in $S_0$.[3] Furthermore, it is important to note that the constant sequence $(S)_{i \in \mathbb{N}}$ is an adaptation sequence according to our previous definition and thus every system is self-adaptive with respect to a combination operator $X \otimes Y =_{\mathrm{def}} X$. However, we can construct non-trivial adaptation sequence using partial orders $\sqsubset$ and $\prec$ instead of $\sqsubseteq$ and $\preceq$. As these can easily be constructed, we do not further discuss their definitions in this paper. In [1] a corresponding definition was already introduced for $\sqsubset$.

The formulation of the adaptation sequence used to prove self-adaptivity naturally implies some kind of temporal structure. So basing said structure around $\mathbb{N}$ implies a very simple, linear and discrete model of time. More complex temporal evolution of systems is also already touched upon in [1]. As noted, there may be several ways to define such a temporal structure on systems. We refer to related and future work for a more intricate discussion on this matter.

So, non-trivial self-adaptation does imply some structure for any self-adaptive system $S$ of type $\mathcal{V} = (V_i)_{i \in I}$: Mainly, there needs to be a subset of the type $\mathcal{V}' \subseteq \mathcal{V}$ that is used to encode the whole relation behind $S$ so that the already improved instances can sufficiently be passed on to the general adaptation mechanism.

For a general adaptation mechanism (as we previously assumed to be part of a system) to be able to improve a system's adaptivity, it needs to be able to access some representation of its goals and its fitness function. This provides a grey-box view of the system. We remember that we assumed we could split a system $S$ into situation $X$, internal state $Z$ and behavior $Y$, written $S = X \overset{Z}{\rightsquigarrow} Y$. If $S$ is self-adaptive, it can form a non-trivial adaptation sequence by improving on its goals or its fitness. In the former case, we can now assume that there exists some relation $G \subseteq X \cup Z$ so that $S \models \gamma \iff G \models \gamma$ for a fixed $\gamma$ in a singleton-space adaptation sequence. In the latter case, we can assume that there exists some relation $F \subseteq X \cup Z$ so that $\phi(S) = \phi(F)$ for a fixed $\phi$ in a singleton-space adaptation sequence.

Obviously, when we want to construct larger self-adaptive systems using self-adaptive components, the combination operator needs to be able to combine said sub-systems $G$ and/or $F$ as well. In the case where the components' goals and fitnesses match completely, the combination operator can just use the same sub-system twice. However, including the global goals or fitnesses within each local component of a system does not align with common principles in software architecture (such as encapsulation) and does not seem to be practical for large or open systems (where no process may ensure such a unification). Thus, constructing a component-based self-adaptive system requires a combination operator that can handle potentially conflicting goals and fitnesses. We again define such a system for a singleton adaptation space $\mathfrak{A} = \{\{(E, \gamma, \phi)\}\}$ and leave the generalization to all adaptation spaces out of the scope of this paper.

---

[3] Constructing a sequence $S_i := S_{i-1} \otimes S_{i-1}$ might be viable formulation as well, but is not further explored in this work.

**Definition 12** (Multi-Agent System). Given a system $S = S_1 \otimes ... \otimes S_n$ that adapts to $\mathcal{A} = \{(E, \gamma, \phi)\}$. Iff for each $1 \leq i \leq n$ with $i, n \in \mathbb{N}, n > 1$ there is an adaptation domain $\mathcal{A}_i = \{(E_i, \gamma_i, \phi_i)\}$ so that (1) $E_i = E \otimes S_1 \otimes ... \otimes S_{i-1} \otimes S_{i+1} \otimes ... \otimes S_n$ and (2) $\gamma_i \neq \gamma$ or $\phi_i \neq \phi$ and (3) $S_i$ adapts to $\mathcal{A}_i$, then $S$ is a *multi-agent system* with agents $S_1, ..., S_n$.

For practical purposes, we usually want to use the notion of multi-agent systems in a transitive way, i.e., we can call a system a multi-agent system as soon as any part of it is a multi-agent system according to Definition 12. Formally, $S$ is a multi-agent system if there are systems components $S', R$ so that $S = S' \otimes R$ and $S'$ is a multi-agent system. We argue that this transitivity is not only justified but a crucial point for systems development of adaptive systems: Agents tend to utilize their environment to fulfill their own goals and can thus "leak" their goals into other system components. Not that Condition (2) of Definition 12 ensures that not every system constructed by composition is regarded a multi-agent system; it is necessary to feature agents with (at least slightly) differing adaptation properties.

For the remainder of this paper, we will apply Definition 12 "backwards": Whenever we look at a self-adaptive system $S$, whose goals or fitnesses can be split into several sub-goals or sub-fitnesses we can regard $S$ as a multi-agent system. Using this knowledge, we can apply design patterns from multi-agent systems to all self-adaptive systems without loss of generality. Furthermore, we need to be aware that especially if we do not explicitly design multi-agent coordination between different sub-goals, such a coordination will be done implicitly. Essentially, there is no way around generalizing software engineering approaches for self-adaptive systems to potentially adversarial components.

## 3    Related Work

Many researchers and practitioners in recent years have already been concerned about the changes necessary to allow for solid and reliable software engineering processes for (self-)adaptive systems. Central challenges were collected in [4], where issues of quality assurance are already mentioned but the focus is more on bringing about complex adaptive behavior in the first place. The later research roadmap of [5] puts a strong focus on interaction patterns of already adaptive systems (both between each other and with human developers) and already dedicates a section to verification and validation issues, being close in mind to the perspective of this work. We fall in line with the roadmap further specified in [6–8].

While this work largely builds upon [1], there have been other approaches to formalize the notion of adaptivity: [9] discusses high-level architectural patterns that form multiple inter-connected adaptation loops. In [10] such feedback loops are based on the MAPE-K model [11]. While these approaches largely focus on the formal construction of adaptive systems, there have also been approaches that assume a (more human-centric or at least tool-centric) software engineering perspective [12–15]. We want to discuss two of those on greater detail:

In the results of the *ASCENS* (Autonomous Service Component ENSembles) project [2], the interplay between human developers and autonomous adaptation has been formalized in a life-cycle model featuring separate states for each the development progress of each respective feedback cycle. Classical software development tasks and self-adaptation (as well as self-monitoring and self-awareness) are regarded as equally powerful contributing mechanisms for the production of software. Both can be employed in junction to steer the development process. In addition, ASCENS built upon a (in parts) similar formal notion of adaptivity [3,16] and sketched a connection between adaptivity in complex distributed systems and multi-goal multi-agent learning [17].

*ADELFE* (Atelier de Développement de Logiciels à Fonctionnalité Emergente) is a toolkit designed to augment current development processes to account for complex adaptive systems [18,19]. For this purpose, ADELFE is based on the Rational Unified Process (RUP) [20] and comes with tools for various tasks of software design. From a more scientific point of view, ADELFE is also based on the theory of adaptive multi-agent systems. For ADELFE, multi-agent systems are used to derive a set of stereotypes for components, which ease modeling for according types of systems. It thus imposes stronger restrictions on system design than our approach intends to.

Besides the field of software engineering, the field of artificial intelligence research is currently (re-)discovering a lot of the same issues the discipline of engineering for complex adaptive systems faced: The highly complex and opaque nature of machine learning algorithms and the resulting data structures often forces black-box testing and makes possible guarantees weak. When online learning is employed, the algorithm's behavior is subject to great variance and testing usually needs to work online as well. The seminal paper [21] provides a good overview of the issues. When applying artificial intelligence to a large variety of products, rigorous engineering for this kind of software seems to be one of the major necessities lacking at the moment.

## 4    Core Concepts of Future Software Engineering

Literature makes it clear that one of the main issues of the development of self-adapting systems lies with *trustworthiness*. Established models for checking systems (i.e., verification and validation) do not really fit the notion of a constantly changing system. However, these established models represent all the reason we have at the moment to trust the systems we developed. Allowing the system more degrees of freedom thus hinders the developers' ability to estimate the degree of maturity of the system they design, which poses a severe difficulty for the engineering progress, when the desired premises or the expected effects of classical engineering tasks on the system-under-development are hard to formulate.

To aid us control the development/adaptation progress of the system, we define a set of *principles*, which are basically patterns for process models. They describe the changes to be made in the engineering process for complex, adaptive systems in relation to more classical models for software and systems engineering.

**Concept 1** (System and Test Parallelism). The system and its test suite should develop in parallel from the start with controlled moments of interchange of information. Eventually, the test system is to be deployed alongside the main system so that even during runtime, on-going online tests are possible [22]. This argument has been made for more classical systems as well and thus classical software test is, too, no longer restricted to a specific phase of software development. However, in the case of self-learning systems, it is important to focus on the evolution of test cases: The capabilities of the system might not grow as experienced test designers expect them to compared to systems entirely realized by human engineering effort. Thus, it is important to conceive and formalize how tests in various phases relate to each other.

**Concept 2** (System vs. Test Antagonism). Any adaptive systems must be subject to an equally adaptive test. Overfitting is a known issue for many machine learning techniques. In software development for complex adaptive systems, it can happen on a larger scale: Any limited test suite (we expect our applications to be too complex to run a complete, exhaustive test) might induce certain unwanted biases. Ideally, once we know about the cases our system has a hard time with, we can train it specifically for these situations. For the so-hardened system the search mechanism that gave us the hard test cases needs to come up with even harder ones to still beat the system-under-test. Employing autonomous adaptation at this stage is expected to make that arms race more immediate and faster than it is usually achieved with human developers and testers alone.

**Concept 3** (Automated Realization). Since the realization of tasks concerning adaptive components usually means the application of a standard machine learning process, a lot of the development effort regarding certain tasks tends to shift to an earlier phase in the process model. The most developer time when applying machine learning techniques, e.g., tends to be spent on gathering information about the problem to solve and the right setup of parameters to use; the training of the learning agent then usually follows one of a few standard procedures and can run rather automatically. However, preparing and testing the component's adaptive abilities might take a lot of effort, which might occur in the design and test phase instead of the deployment phase of the system life-cycle.

**Concept 4** (Artifact Abstraction). To provide room for and exploit the system's ability to self-adapt, many artifacts produced by the engineering process tend to become more general in nature, i.e., they tend to feature more open parameters or degrees of freedom in their description. In effect, in the place of single artifacts in a classical development process, we tend to find families of artifacts or processes generating artifacts when developing a complex adaptive system. As we assume that the previously only static artifact is still included in the set of artifacts available in its place now, we call this shift "generalization" of artifacts. Following this change, many of the activities performed during development shift their targets from concrete implementations to more general artifact, i.e., when building a test suite no longer yields a series of runnable test cases but instead produces a test case generator. When this principle is broadly applied, the development activities shift towards "meta development". The developers are concerned with setting up a process able to find good solutions autonomously instead of finding the good solutions directly.

## 5  Scenarios

We now want to include the issue of testing adaptive systems in our formal framework. We recognize that any development process for systems following the principles described in Sect. 2 produces two central types of artifacts: The first one is a system $S = X \overset{Z}{\leadsto} Y$ with a specific desired behavior $Y$ so that it manages to adapt to a given adaptation space. The second is a set of situations, test cases, constraints, and checked properties that this system's behavior has been validated against. We call artifacts of the second type by the group name of *scenarios*.

**Definition 13** (Scenario). Let $S = X \overset{Z}{\leadsto} Y$ be a system and $\mathcal{A} = \{(E, \gamma, \phi)\}$ a singleton adaptation domain. A tuple $c = (X, Y, g, f), g \in \{\top, \bot\}, f \in \mathrm{cod}(\phi)$ with $g = \top \iff S \otimes E \models \gamma$ and $f = \phi(S \otimes E)$ is called *scenario*.[4]

Semantically, scenarios represent the experience gained about the system's behavior during development, including both successful ($S \models \gamma$) and unsuccessful ($S \not\models \gamma$) test runs. As stated above, since we expect to operate in test spaces we cannot cover exhaustively, the knowledge about the areas we did cover is an important asset and likewise result of the systems engineering process.

Effectively, as we construct and evolve a system $S$ we want to construct and augment a set of scenarios $C = \{c_1, ..., c_n\}$ alongside with it. $C$ is also called a *scenario suite* and can be seen as a toolbox to test $S$'s adaptation abilities with respect to a fixed adaptation domain $\mathcal{A}$.

While formally abiding to Definition 13, scenarios can be encoded in various ways in practical software development, such as:

*Sets of data points of expected or observed behavior.* Given a system $S' = X' \leadsto Y'$ whose behavior is desirable (for example a trained predecessor of our system or a watchdog component), we can create scenarios $(X', Y', g', f')$ with $g' = \top \iff S' \otimes E_i \models \gamma_i$ and $f' = \phi_i(S' \otimes E_i)$ for an arbitrary amount of elements $(E_i, \gamma_i, \phi_i)$ of an adaptation domain $\mathcal{A} = \{(E_1, \gamma_1, \phi_1), ..., (E_n, \gamma_n, \phi_n)\}$.

*Test cases the system mastered.* In some cases, adaptive systems may produce innovative behavior before we actively seek it out. In this cases, it is helpful to formalize the produced results once they have been found so that we can ensure that the system's gained abilities are not lost during further development

---

[4] If we are only interested in the system's performance and not *how* it was achieved, we can redefine a scenario to leave out $Y$.

or adaptation. Formally, this case matches the case for "observed behavior" described above. However, here the test case $(X, Y, g, f)$ already existed as a scenario, so we just need to update $g$ and $f$ (with the new and better values) and possibly $Y$ (if we want to fix the observed behavior).

*Logical formulae and constraints.* Commonly, constraints can be directly expressed in the adaptation domain. Suppose we build a system against an adaptation domain $\mathcal{A} = \{(E_1, \gamma_1, \phi_1), ..., (E_n, \gamma_n, \phi_n)\}$. We can impose a hard constraint $\zeta$ on the system in this domain by constructing a constrained adaptation domain $\mathcal{A}' = \{(E_1, \gamma_1 \wedge \zeta, \phi_1), ..., (E_n, \gamma_n \wedge \zeta, \phi_n)\}$ given that the logic of $\gamma_1, ..., \gamma_n, \zeta$ meaningfully supports an operation like the logical "and" $\wedge$. Likewise a soft constraint $\psi$ can be imposed via $\mathcal{A}' = \{(E_1, \gamma_1, \max(\phi_1, \psi), ), ..., (E_n, \gamma_n, \max(\phi_n, \psi))\}$ given the definition of the operator max that trivially follows from using the relation $\preceq$ on fitness values. Scenarios $(X', Y', g', f')$ can then be generated against the new adaptation domain $\mathcal{A}$ by taking pre-existing scenarios $(X, Y, g, f)$ and setting $X' = X, Y' = Y, g = \top, f = \psi((X \rightsquigarrow Y) \otimes E)$.

*Requirements and use case descriptions (including the system's degree of fulfilling them).* If properly formalized, a requirement or use case description contains all the information necessary to construct an adaptation domain and can thus be treated as the logical formulae in the paragraph above. However, use cases are in practical development more prone to be incomplete views on the adaptation domain. We thus may want to stress the point that we do not need to update all elements of an adaptation domain when applying a constraint, i.e., when including a use case. We can also just add the additional hard constraint $\zeta$ or soft constraint $\psi$ to some elements of $\mathcal{A}$.

*Predictive models of system properties.* For the most general case, assume that we have a prediction function $p$ so that $p(X) \approx Y$, i.e., the function can roughly return the behavior $S = X \rightsquigarrow Y$ will or should show given $X$. We can thus construct the predicted system $S' = X \rightsquigarrow p(X)$ and construct a scenario $(X, p(X), g, f)$ with $g = \top \iff S' \otimes E \models \gamma$ and $f = \phi(S' \otimes E)$.

All of these types of artifacts will be subsumed under the notion of scenarios. We can use them to further train and improve the system and to estimate its likely behavior as well as to perform tests (and ultimately verification and validation activities).

*Scenario coevolution* describes the process of developing a set of scenarios to test a system during the system-under-tests's development. Consequently, it needs to be designed and controlled as carefully as the evolution of system behavior [23, 24].

**Definition 14** (Scenario Hardening). Let $c_1 = (X_1, Y_1, g_1, f_1)$ and $c_2 = (X_2, Y_2, g_1, f_2)$ be scenarios for a system $S$ and an adaptation domain $\mathcal{A}$. Scenario $c_2$ is *at least as hard* as $c_1$, written $c_1 \leq c_2$, iff $g_1 = \top \implies g_2 = \top$ and $f_1 \leq f_2$.

**Definition 15** (Scenario Suite Order). Let $C = \{c_1, ..., c_m\}$ and $C' = \{c'_1, ...,$ $c'_n\}$ be sets of scenarios, also called scenarios suites. Scenario suite $C'$ is *at least as hard* as $C$, written $C \sqsubseteq C'$, iff for all scenarios $c \in C$ there exists a scenario $c' \in C'$ so that $c \leq c'$.

**Definition 16** (Scenario Sequence). Let $\mathcal{S} = (S_i)_{i \in I}, I = \{1, ..., n\}$ be an adaptation sequence for a singleton adaptation space $\mathfrak{A} = \{\mathcal{A}\}$. A series of sets $\mathcal{C} = (C_i)_{i \in I}$ is called a scenario sequence iff for all $i \in I, i < n$ it holds that $C_i$ is a scenario suite for $S_i$ and $\mathcal{A}$ and $C_i \sqsubseteq C_{i+1}$.

We expect each phase of development to further alter the set of scenarios just as it does alter the system behavior. The scenarios produced and used at a certain phase in development must match the current state of progress. Valid scenarios from previous phases should be kept and checked against the further specialized system. When we do not delete any scenarios entirely, the continued addition of scenarios will ideally narrow down allowed system behavior to the desired possibilities. Eventually, we expect all activities of system test to be expressible as the generation or evaluation of scenarios. New scenarios may simply be thought up by system developers or be generated automatically.

Finding the right scenarios to generate is another optimization problem to be solved during the development of any complex adaptive system. Scenario evolution represents a cross-cutting concern for all phases of system development. Treating scenarios as first-class citizen among the artifacts produced by system development thus yields changes in tasks throughout the whole process model.

# 6    Applications of Scenario Coevolution

Having both introduced a formal framework for adaptation and the testing of adaptive systems using scenarios, we show in this section how these frameworks can be applied to aid the trustworthiness of complex adaptive systems for practical use.

## 6.1    Criticality Focus

It is very important to start the scenario evolution process alongside the system evolution, so that at each stage there exists a set of scenarios available to test the system's functionality and degree of progress (see Concept 1). This approach mimics the concept of agile development where between each sprint there exists a fully functional (however incomplete) version of the system. The concept of scenario evolution integrates seamlessly with agile process models.

In the early phases of development, the common artifacts of requirements engineering, i.e., formalized requirements, serve as the basis for the scenario evolution process. As long as the adaptation space $\mathfrak{A}$ remains constant (and with it the system goals), system development should form an adaptation sequence. Consequently, scenario evolution should then form a scenario sequence for that adaptation sequence. This means (according to Definition 16), the scenario suite is augmented with newly generated scenarios (for new system goals or just more specialized subgoals) or with scenarios with increased requirements on fitness.[5] Ideally, the scenario evolution process should lead the learning components on the right path towards the desired solution. The ability to re-assign fitness priorities allows for an arms race between adaptive system and scenario suite (see Concept 2).

*Augmenting Requirements.* Beyond requirements engineering, it is necessary to include knowledge that will be generated during training and learning by the adaptive components. Mainly, recognized scenarios that work well with early version of the adaptive system should be used as checks and tests when the system becomes more complex. This approach imitates the optimization technique of importance sampling on a systems engineering level. There are two central issues that need to be answered in this early phase of the development process:

- Behavior Observation: How can system behavior be generated in a realistic manner? Are the formal specifications powerful enough? Can we employ human-labeled experience?
- Behavior Assessment: How can the quality of observed behavior be adequately assessed? Can we define a model for the users' intent? Can we employ human-labeled review?

*Breaking Down Requirements.* A central task of successful requirements engineering is to split up the use cases in atomic units that ideally describe singular features. In the dynamic world, we want to leave more room for adaptive system behavior. Thus, the requirements we formulate tend to be more general in notion. It is thus even more important to split them up in meaningful ways in order to derive new sets of scenarios. The following design axes (without any claim to completeness) may be found useful to break down requirements of adaptive systems:

- Scope and Locality: Can the goal be applied/checked locally or does it involve multiple components? Which components fall into the scope of the goal? Is emergent system behavior desirable or considered harmful?
- Decomposition and Smoothness: Can internal (possibly more specific) requirements be developed? Can the overall goal be composed from a clear set of subgoals? Can the goal function be smoothened, for example by providing intermediate goals? Can subgoal decomposition change dynamically via adaptation or is it structurally static?
- Uncertainty and Interaction: Are all goals given with full certainty? Is it possible to reason about the relative importance of goal fulfillment for specific goals a priori? Which dynamic goals have an interface with human users or other systems?

---

[5] Note that every change in $\mathfrak{A}$ starts new sequences.

## 6.2  Adaptation Cooldown

We call the problem domain available to us during system design the *off-site domain*. It contains all scenarios we think the system might end up in and may thus even contain contradicting scenarios, for example. In all but the rarest cases, the situations one single instance of our system will face in its operating time will be just a fraction the size of the covered areas of the off-site domain. Nonetheless, it is also common for the system's real-world experience to include scenarios not occurring in the off-site domain at all; this mainly happens when we were wrong about some detail in the real world. Thus, the implementation of an adaptation technique faces a problem not unlike the *exploration/exploitation dilemma* [25], but on a larger scale: We need to decide, if we opt for a system fully adapted to the exact off-site domain or if we opt for a less specialized system that leaves more room for later adaptation at the customer's site. The point at which we stop adaptation happening on off-site scenarios is called the off-site adaptation border and is a key artifact of the development process for adaptive systems.

In many cases, we may want the system we build to be able to evolve beyond the exact use cases we knew about during design time. The system thus needs to have components capable of *run-time* or *online adaptation*. In the wording of this work, we also talk about *on-site adaptation* stressing that in this case we focus on adaptation processes that take place at the customer's location in a comparatively specific domain instead of the broader setting in a system development lab. Usually, we expect the training and optimization performed on-site (if any) to be not as drastic as training done during development. (Otherwise, we would probably have not specified our problem domain in an appropriate way.) As the system becomes more efficient in its behavior, we want to gradually reduce the amount of change we allow. In the long run, adaptation should usually work at a level that prohibits sudden, unexpected changes but still manages to handle any changes in the environment within a certain margin. The recognized need for more drastic change should usually trigger human supervision first.

**Definition 17** (Adaptation Space Sequence). Let $S$ be a system. A series of $|I|$ adaptation spaces $\mathbb{A} = (\mathfrak{A}_i)_{i \in I}$ with index set $I$ with a preorder $\leq$ on the elements of $I$ is called an *adaptation domain sequence* iff for all $i, j \in I, i \leq j$ it holds that: $S$ adapts to $\mathfrak{A}_j$ implies that $S$ adapts to $\mathfrak{A}_i$.

System development constructs an adaptation space sequence (c.f. Concept 4), i.e., a sequence of increasingly specific adaptation domains. Each of those can be used to run an adaptation sequence (c.f. Definition 10) and a scenario sequence (c.f. Definition 16, Concept 2) to test it.

For the gradual reduction of the allowed amount of adaptation for the system we use the metaphor of a "cool-down" process: The adaptation performed on-site should allow for less change than off-site adaptation. And the adaptation allowed during run-time should be less than what we allowed during deployment. This ensures that decisions that have once been deemed right by the developers are hard to change later by accident or by the autonomous adaptation process.

### 6.3   Eternal Deployment

For high trustworthiness, development of the test cases used for the final system test should be as decoupled from the on-going scenario evolution as possible, i.e., the data used in both processes should overlap as little as possible. Of course, following this guideline completely results in the duplication of a lot of processes and artifacts. Still, it is important to accurately keep track of the influences on the respective sets of scenarios. A clear definition of the off-site adaptation border provides a starting point for when to branch off a scenario evolution process that is independent of possible scenario-specific adaptations on the system-under-test's side. Running multiple independent system tests (cf. ensemble methods [26,27]) is advisable as well. However, the space of available independently generated data is usually very limited.

For the deployment phase, it is thus of key importance to carry over as much information as possible about the genesis of the system we deploy into the run-time, where it can be used to look up the traces of observed decisions. The reason to do this now is that we usually expect the responsibility for the system to change at this point: Whereas previously, any system behavior was overseen by the developers who could potentially backtrack any phenomenon to all previous steps in the system development process, now we expect on-site maintenance to be able to handle any potential problem with the system in the real world, requiring more intricate preparation for maintenance tasks (c.f. Concept 3). We thus need to endow these new people with the ability to properly understand what the system does and why.

Our approach follows the vision of *eternal system design* [28], which is a fundamental change in the way to treat deployment: We no longer ship a single artifact as the result of a complex development process, but we ship an image of the process itself (cf. Concept 4). As a natural consequence, we can only ever add to an eternal system but hardly remove changes and any trace of them entirely. Using an adequate combination operator, this meta-design pattern is already implemented in the way we construct adaptation sequences (c.f. Definition 10): For example, given a system $S_i$ we could construct $S_{i+1} = X \overset{Z}{\rightsquigarrow} Y$ in a way so that $S_i$ is included in $S_{i+1}$'s internal state $Z$.

As of now, however, the design of eternal systems still raises many unanswered questions in system design. We thus resort to the notion of scenarios only as a sufficient system description to provide explanatory power at run-time and recommend to apply standard "destructive updates" to all other system artifacts.

## 7   Conclusion

We have introduced a new formal model for adaptation and test processes using our notion of scenarios. We connected this model to concrete challenges and arising concepts in software engineering to show that our approach of scenario coevolution is fit to tackle (a first few) of the problems when doing quality assurance for complex adaptive systems.

As already noted throughout the text, a few challenges still persist. Perhaps most importantly, we require an adequate data structure both for the coding of systems and for the encoding of test suites and need to prove the practical feasibility of an optimization process governing the software development life-cycle. For performance reasons, we expect that some restrictions on the general formal framework will be necessary. In this work, we also deliberately left out the issue of meta-processes: The software development life-cycle can itself be regarded as system according to Definition 1. While this may complicate things at first, we also see potential in not only developing a process of establishing quality and trustworthiness but also a generator for such processes (akin to Concept 4).

Systems with a high degree of adaptivity and, among those, systems employing techniques of artificial intelligence and machine learning will become ubiquitous. If we want to trust them as we trust engineered systems today, the methods of quality assurance need to rise to the challenge: Quality assurance needs to adapt to adaptive systems!

# References

1. Hölzl, M., Wirsing, M.: Towards a system model for ensembles. In: Agha, G., Danvy, O., Meseguer, J. (eds.) Formal Modeling: Actors, Open Systems, Biological Systems. LNCS, vol. 7000, pp. 241–261. Springer, Heidelberg (2011). https://doi.org/10.1007/978-3-642-24933-4_12
2. Wirsing, M., Hölzl, M., Koch, N., Mayer, P. (eds.): Software Engineering for Collective Autonomic Systems. LNCS, vol. 8998. Springer, Cham (2015). https://doi.org/10.1007/978-3-319-16310-9
3. Bruni, R., Corradini, A., Gadducci, F., Lluch Lafuente, A., Vandin, A.: A conceptual framework for adaptation. In: de Lara, J., Zisman, A. (eds.) FASE 2012. LNCS, vol. 7212, pp. 240–254. Springer, Heidelberg (2012). https://doi.org/10.1007/978-3-642-28872-2_17
4. Salehie, M., Tahvildari, L.: Self-adaptive software: landscape and research challenges. ACM Trans. Auton. Adapt. Syst. (TAAS) (2009)
5. de Lemos, R., et al.: Software engineering for self-adaptive systems: a second research roadmap. In: de Lemos, R., Giese, H., Müller, H.A., Shaw, M. (eds.) Software Engineering for Self-Adaptive Systems II. LNCS, vol. 7475, pp. 1–32. Springer, Heidelberg (2013). https://doi.org/10.1007/978-3-642-35813-5_1
6. Bures, T., et al.: Software engineering for smart cyber-physical systems–Towards a research agenda: Report on the first international workshop on software engineering for smart CPS. ACM SIGSOFT Softw. Eng. Notes 40(6), 28–32 (2015)
7. Belzner, L., Beck, M.T., Gabor, T., Roelle, H., Sauer, H.: Software engineering for distributed autonomous real-time systems. In: Proceedings of the 2nd International Workshop on Software Engineering for Smart Cyber-Physical Systems, pp. 54–57. ACM (2016)
8. Bures, T., et al.: Software engineering for smart cyber-physical systems: challenges and promising solutions. ACM SIGSOFT Softw. Eng. Notes 42(2), 19–24 (2017)
9. Oreizy, P., et al.: An architecture-based approach to self-adaptive software. IEEE Intell. Syst. Their Appl. 14(3), 54–62 (1999)

10. Arcaini, P., Riccobene, E., Scandurra, P.: Modeling and analyzing MAPE-K feedback loops for self-adaptation. In: Proceedings of the 10th International Symposium on Software Engineering for Adaptive and Self-Managing Systems. IEEE Press (2015)
11. Kephart, J.O., Chess, D.M.: The vision of autonomic computing. Computer **36**(1), 41–50 (2003)
12. Elkhodary, A., Esfahani, N., Malek, S.: FUSION: a framework for engineering self-tuning self-adaptive software systems. In: Proceedings of the 18th ACM SIGSOFT International Symposium on Foundations of Software Engineering. ACM (2010)
13. Andersson, J., et al.: Software engineering processes for self-adaptive systems. In: de Lemos, R., Giese, H., Müller, H.A., Shaw, M. (eds.) Software Engineering for Self-Adaptive Systems II. LNCS, vol. 7475, pp. 51–75. Springer, Heidelberg (2013). https://doi.org/10.1007/978-3-642-35813-5_3
14. Gabor, T., Belzner, L., Kiermeier, M., Beck, M.T., Neitz, A.: A simulation-based architecture for smart cyber-physical systems. In: 2016 IEEE International Conference on Autonomic Computing (ICAC), pp. 374–379. IEEE (2016)
15. Weyns, D.: Software engineering of self-adaptive systems: an organised tour and future challenges (2017)
16. Nicola, R.D., Loreti, M., Pugliese, R., Tiezzi, F.: A formal approach to autonomic systems programming: the SCEL language. ACM Trans. Auton. Adapt. Syst. (TAAS) **9**(2), 7 (2014)
17. Hölzl, M., Gabor, T.: Reasoning and learning for awareness and adaptation. In: Wirsing, M., Hölzl, M., Koch, N., Mayer, P. (eds.) Software Engineering for Collective Autonomic Systems. LNCS, vol. 8998, pp. 249–290. Springer, Cham (2015). https://doi.org/10.1007/978-3-319-16310-9_7
18. Bernon, C., Camps, V., Gleizes, M.-P., Picard, G.: Tools for self-organizing applications engineering. In: Di Marzo Serugendo, G., Karageorgos, A., Rana, O.F., Zambonelli, F. (eds.) ESOA 2003. LNCS (LNAI), vol. 2977, pp. 283–298. Springer, Heidelberg (2004). https://doi.org/10.1007/978-3-540-24701-2_19
19. Bernon, C., Camps, V., Gleizes, M.P., Picard, G.: Engineering adaptive multi-agent systems: the ADELFE methodology. In: Agent-Oriented Methodologies, pp. 172–202. IGI Global (2005)
20. Kruchten, P.: The Rational Unified Process: An Introduction. Addison-Wesley Professional, Boston (2004)
21. Amodei, D., Olah, C., Steinhardt, J., Christiano, P., Schulman, J., Mané, D.: Concrete problems in AI safety. arXiv preprint arXiv:1606.06565 (2016)
22. Calinescu, R., Ghezzi, C., Kwiatkowska, M., Mirandola, R.: Self-adaptive software needs quantitative verification at runtime. Commun. ACM **55**(9), 69–77 (2012)
23. Arcuri, A., Yao, X.: Coevolving programs and unit tests from their specification. In: Proceedings of the 22nd IEEE/ACM International Conference on Automated Software Engineering, pp. 397–400. ACM (2007)
24. Fraser, G., Arcuri, A.: Whole test suite generation. IEEE Trans. Softw. Eng. **39**(2), 276–291 (2013)
25. Črepinšek, M., Liu, S.H., Mernik, M.: Exploration and exploitation in evolutionary algorithms: a survey. ACM Comput. Surv. (CSUR) **45**(3), 35 (2013)
26. Dietterich, T.G.: Ensemble methods in machine learning. Mult. Classif. Syst. **2000**, 1–15 (1857)

27. Hart, E., Sim, K.: On constructing ensembles for combinatorial optimisation. Evol. Comput., 1–21 (2017)
28. Nierstrasz, O., Denker, M., Gîrba, T., Lienhard, A., Röthlisberger, D.: Change-enabled software systems. In: Wirsing, M., Banâtre, J.-P., Hölzl, M., Rauschmayer, A. (eds.) Software-Intensive Systems. LNCS, vol. 5380, pp. 64–79. Springer, Heidelberg (2008). https://doi.org/10.1007/978-3-540-89437-7_3

# Designing Systems with Detection and Reconfiguration Capabilities: A Formal Approach

Iulia Dragomir[(✉)], Simon Iosti, Marius Bozga, and Saddek Bensalem

Univ. Grenoble Alpes, CNRS, Grenoble INP,
VERIMAG, 38000 Grenoble, France
`iulia.dragomir@univ-grenoble-alpes.fr`

**Abstract.** The design of functionally correct autonomous systems which operate in an unknown environment and that satisfy reliability, availability, maintainability, and safety (RAMS) requirements is a challenge. In this paper we focus on the detection and reconfiguration features these systems must provide. Indeed, evolving in an unknown environment can invalidate the assumptions made during the design phase. In particular, different hardware components might fail and provide erroneous inputs to the system, which will pass in a degraded mode where the expected RAMS do not hold anymore. Such faults need to be detected as early as possible and reconfiguration strategies must be applied to bring the system back into a nominal mode where the RAMS are satisfied. We propose an automated design process based on formal methods to develop Fault Detection, Isolation and Recovery (FDIR) components targeting partially observable timed systems. We describe how to automatically synthesize runtime monitors, design reconfiguration strategies, and obtain full-fledged FDIR components. We illustrate the approach on a case study inspired from autonomous robotics applications.

## 1 Introduction

Mission- and safety-critical systems must satisfy a plethora of important Reliability, Availability, Maintainability and Safety (RAMS) properties, which is a hard problem to establish at design time. The reason is two-fold: (i) the built systems are very complex and verification techniques do not always scale on real-life applications, and (ii) such systems often work in unknown environments that may not satisfy at execution time the assumptions made at design time. This is the case of autonomous systems that execute in an environment subject to faults and failures. For instance, a hardware component might overheat, which leads the entire system in a degraded mode and where the above mentioned requirements do not hold anymore.

This work has been supported by the HORIZON 2020 PROGRAMME Strategic Research Cluster (SRC) (awards #730080 and #730086).
Grenoble INP—Institute of Engineering Univ. Grenoble Alpes.

© Springer Nature Switzerland AG 2018
T. Margaria and B. Steffen (Eds.): ISoLA 2018, LNCS 11246, pp. 155–171, 2018.
https://doi.org/10.1007/978-3-030-03424-5_11

A desired functionality of safety-critical systems in general, and autonomous systems in particular, is to detect and handle systematically and dynamically the faults that have occurred. The handling of such faults could be either simple by giving control of the system to a human user or complex by applying predefined strategies for recovery. Autonomous systems usually fall in the latter case, where they should implement without any external intervention complex recovery strategies that aim to bring the system back into a safe state where RAMS hold again. This involved functionality is implemented by *Fault Detection, Isolation and Recovery* (FDIR) *components*, which extend such systems with adaptive and collaborative features. On one hand, the adaptive aspect is inherent to the definition of FDIR components that steer the system operation depending on environment and specific operating conditions. On the other hand, the collaborative aspect arises as various subsystems and FDIR are generally interacting together for achieving a common goal. At system level, such subsystems are components while the goals are maintaining individual RAMS properties. At mission level, goals can be more involved and concern high-level objectives.

An FDIR component runs in parallel with the system, and (i) detects faults as early as possible with respect to their occurrence and (ii) executes a predefined recovery strategy with respect to the detected fault. The extended system can contain one or multiple FDIR components, which can have a monolithic or hierarchical architecture, can be centralized or distributed, or any combination. The process of designing/implementing FDIR components is *ad-hoc*, based on one's full understanding of the system under design, the component to be produced and the system's (possibly textual) specification. This implies considering a large number of faults and failures, their interactions and effects on the system, which raises correctness and completeness questions.

We answer such problems by proposing a methodology based on formal methods to build FDIR components. The aim is to automatically derive correct FDIR components from the design of the system under study with faults, the RAMS requirements it must satisfy and the recovery strategies to be applied in case of faults. We describe how to automatically synthesize runtime monitors for fault detection, design the recovery strategies for controller synthesis and obtain full-fledged FDIR components. Moreover, we tackle the above problems in the context of timed systems and partial observability, where faults cannot be directly detected by the system and not all of the system's actions can be observed. We illustrate the approach and its feasibility on an excerpt of an industrial autonomous robotics application.

*Paper Structure.* We formalize timed systems with partial observability (for the FDIR context) in Sect. 2. In Sect. 3 we describe the methodology for designing FDIR components as a subprocess of the general system design. The algorithms for diagnoser synthesis and controller implementation for our definition of timed systems are given and illustrated in Sects. 4 and 5, respectively. We discuss the work related to the methodology as well as the diagnoser and controller synthesis problems in Sect. 6 before concluding.

## 2   Timed Systems

We consider a system modeled as a network of timed automata (TA) [2]. Before formally defining timed automata, we introduce some notations.

Let $X$ be a finite set of variables called *clocks*. A *clock valuation* is a mapping $v : X \to \mathbb{R}_+$. We write $\mathbf{0}$ for the valuation of all clocks of $X$ to 0. Given $\delta \in \mathbb{R}_+$, $(v + \delta)(x) = v(x) + \delta$. For $r \subseteq X$, $v[r]$ is the reset of clocks in $r$, i.e., the valuation defined by $v[r](x) = v(x)$ if $x \notin r$ and $v[r](x) = 0$ otherwise. Let $\Phi(X)$ be the set of convex constraints on $X$ given by the grammar $\varphi ::= true \,|\, x < c \,|\, x \le c \,|\, x = c \,|\, x > c \,|\, x \ge c \,|\, \varphi \wedge \varphi$, with $c \in \mathbb{Q}_+$. Given a constraint $g \in \Phi(X)$ and a valuation $v$, we write $v \models g$ if $g$ is satisfied by the valuation $v$.

**Definition 1 (Timed automaton).** *A timed automaton (TA) A is a tuple $(L, l_0, X, Inv, \Sigma, E)$ where $L$ is a finite set of locations, $l_0 \in L$ is the initial location, $X$ is a finite set of clocks, $Inv : L \to \Phi(X)$ is a function associating to each location some clock constraint, $\Sigma = \Sigma_o^c \oplus \Sigma_o^u \oplus \Sigma_u^s \oplus \Sigma_u^f$ is a finite set of actions separated into observable/unobservable (denoted with subscript) and controllable/uncontrollable (denoted with superscript) as explained below, and $E \subseteq L \times \Phi(X) \times \Sigma \times 2^X \times L$ is the transition relation.*

A timed automaton is a finite automaton enriched with a set of real-valued clocks that allow to measure time delays. In this computational model, time passes at the same rate for all clocks, i.e., $\dot{x} = 1$. Time elapse is restricted in each location with a clock constraint. A transition, usually denoted by $l \xrightarrow[r]{[g]\,a} l'$, moves from a location $l$ to a location $l'$ by executing an action $a \in \Sigma$. The transition is enabled and can be fired only when the current valuation of clocks satisfies the guard $g \in \Phi(X)$. Besides the executed action, a transition can also perform resets on the specified set $r \subseteq X$ of clocks.

With respect to the definition given in [2], the main difference is the *partial observability condition*. It is modeled by the two types of actions a TA can define: observable actions $\Sigma_o$ and unobservable actions $\Sigma_u$. The observable actions are further refined into controllable ones $\Sigma_o^c$ and uncontrollable ones $\Sigma_o^u$. The controllable observable actions act as "actuators" for the FDIR component, while uncontrollable observable actions act as "sensors" for fault detection. The unobservable actions are also refined into regular ones (also called silent) $\Sigma_u^s$ and faulty ones $\Sigma_u^f$. Silent actions correspond to internal computations often denoted by $\tau$. Fault actions are those that model the different types of faults of a component. Please note that all the above sets are disjoint. By taking $\Sigma_o^c = \emptyset$, $\Sigma_u^s = \{\tau\}$ and $\Sigma_u^f = \emptyset$, we obtain the usual definition of TA with silent actions. The definition from [18,29] is obtained for $\Sigma_o^c = \emptyset$, $\Sigma_u^s = \{\tau\}$ and $\Sigma_u^f = \{f\}$.

The semantics of a timed automaton is a Timed Transition System (TTS). A state of the TA is a pair $(l, v) \in L \times \mathbb{R}_+^X$ that consists of a discrete location $l \in L$ and the current valuation of all clocks $v$. The initial state is the pair $(l_0, \mathbf{0})$. From a state $(l, v)$ such that $v \models Inv(l)$, the TA can progress either by a discrete transition (i.e., an action) or by letting time elapse. The transition relation $\rightarrow$ of the corresponding TTS is generated by the following rules:

1. For $a \in \Sigma$, $(l, \mathrm{v}) \xrightarrow{a} (l', \mathrm{v}')$ if $l \xrightarrow[r]{[g]\ a} l'$ such that $\mathrm{v} \models g$, $\mathrm{v}' = \mathrm{v}[r]$, and $\mathrm{v}' \models Inv(l')$.

2. For $\delta \in \mathbb{R}_+$, $(l, \mathrm{v}) \xrightarrow{\delta} (l, \mathrm{v}')$ if $\mathrm{v}' = \mathrm{v} + \delta$, $\mathrm{v} \models Inv(l)$ and $\mathrm{v}' \models Inv(l)$.

A *run* $\rho$ of $A$ from a state $(q_0, \mathrm{v}_0)$ is a possibly infinite sequence $\rho = (q_0, \mathrm{v}_0) \xrightarrow{\delta_0} (q_0, \mathrm{v}_0 + \delta_0) \xrightarrow{a_1} (q_1, \mathrm{v}_1) \ldots \xrightarrow{a_n} (q_n, \mathrm{v}_n) \xrightarrow{\delta_n} \ldots$ where $\forall i$, $q_i \in L$, $a_i \in \Sigma$, $\delta_i \in \mathbb{R}_+$, $\mathrm{v}_i : X \rightarrow \mathbb{R}_+$, $\mathrm{v}_{i+1} = \mathrm{v}_i + \delta_i$ or $\mathrm{v}_{i+1} = \mathrm{v}_i[r_i]$ depending on the incoming transition and $q_i \xrightarrow[r_i]{[g_i]\ a_{i+1}} q_{i+1}$ $(\in E)$. The set of executions of $A$ from a state $s$ is denoted by $Runs_A(s)$. The set of runs of $A$ is $Runs_A = Runs_A((l_0, \mathbf{0}))$. We say that a run is $f$-*faulty*, denoted $faulty(\rho, f)$, if $\exists i$ such that $a_i = f$. For a run $\rho$, let $time(\rho) = \sum_i \delta_i$, the sum of all delays in $\rho$. If $\rho$ is an infinite run, then $time(\rho)$ is the limit of the sum (possibly $\infty$). We say that $\rho$ is *non-Zeno* if $time(\rho) = \infty$ and *Zeno* otherwise.

The *trace* of a run $\rho$ with respect to a set of observable actions $\Sigma'_o$, denoted $trace_{\Sigma'_o}(\rho)$, is the sequence $\delta_0 a_1 \delta_1 a_2 \ldots a_n \delta_n \ldots$ made only of time elapse and observable actions, i.e., $\forall i$, $a_i \in \Sigma'_o$ and $\delta_i \in \mathbb{R}_+$. If $\Sigma'_o = \Sigma_o$ (all the observables of a system), we obtain the usual trace definition.

A system is given by the parallel composition of the different timed automata it models. This means that the automata execute in parallel and synchronize on the common observable actions. We assume that the sets of clocks, silent actions and fault actions are mutually disjoint. This condition can be easily satisfied by renaming the common clocks or actions.

**Definition 2 (Parallel composition).** *Let $A_i = (L_i, l_0^i, X_i, Inv_i, \Sigma^i, E_i)$, $i \in \{1, 2\}$, be two TA such that $X_1 \cap X_2 = \emptyset$, $(\Sigma_u^s)^1 \cap (\Sigma_u^s)^2 = \emptyset$ and $(\Sigma_u^f)^1 \cap (\Sigma_u^f)^2 = \emptyset$. Their parallel composition denoted $A_1 \parallel A_2$ is the TA $(L, l_0, X, Inv, \Sigma, E)$ where*

- $L = L_1 \times L_2$,
- $l_0 = (l_0^1, l_0^2)$,
- $X = X_1 \cup X_2$,
- $Inv : L \rightarrow \Phi(X)$, $Inv(l_1, l_2) = Inv(l_1) \wedge Inv(l_2)$,
- $\Sigma = \Sigma_o^c \oplus \Sigma_o^u \oplus \Sigma_u^s \oplus \Sigma_u^f$ *with* $\Sigma_i^j = (\Sigma_i^j)^1 \cup (\Sigma_i^j)^2$, $(i, j) \in \{(o, c), (o, u), (u, s), (u, f)\}$,
- $E \subseteq L \times \Phi(X) \times \Sigma \times 2^X \times L$ *is the set of transitions given by*
  - $(l_1, l_2) \xrightarrow[r_1 \cup r_2]{[g_1 \wedge g_2]\ a} (l'_1, l'_2)$ *if* $a \in \Sigma^1 \cap \Sigma^2$, $l_1 \xrightarrow[r_1]{[g_1]\ a} l'_1$ *and* $l_2 \xrightarrow[r_2]{[g_2]\ a} l'_2$,
  - $(l_1, l_2) \xrightarrow[r_1]{[g_1]\ a} (l'_1, l_2)$ *if* $a \in \Sigma^1 \setminus \Sigma^2$ *and* $l_1 \xrightarrow[r_1]{[g_1]\ a} l'_1$, *and*
  - $(l_1, l_2) \xrightarrow[r_2]{[g_2]\ a} (l_1, l'_2)$ *if* $a \in \Sigma^2 \setminus \Sigma^1$ *and* $l_2 \xrightarrow[r_2]{[g_2]\ a} l'_2$.

*Running Example.* Figure 1 presents a fragment of an autonomous system case study[1] that will be used as the running example throughout this paper. This

---

[1] The case study presented here is inspired from an autonomous robotics system. The original system contains more components, behavior and requirements.

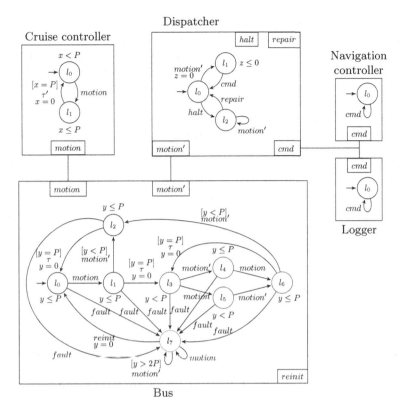

**Fig. 1.** An example of an autonomous cruise controller system with faults during communication. (Color figure online)

system aims to transfer and dispatch motion commands from an automated cruise controller to the actual navigation system and a logger.

The system is modeled as a network of five communicating timed automata as follows. The *cruise controller* sends in every $[0, P)$ time interval the *motion* command to be executed.[2] This request travels through a *bus* to a *dispatcher*. The *dispatcher* sends the request to the *navigation controller* which is responsible for its mechanical execution. Additionally the request is stored in a *logger* for debugging purposes, possibly through replay.

The *bus* models a 2 element memory and has the following behavior. Once it receives a *motion* request and it is not busy, it can delay the request transfer up to $P$. In that case it waits for the next period of the *cruise controller* and "restarts" its behavior. This behavior describes the nominal mode of the bus and is depicted by the states in black in Fig. 1 (from $l_0$ to $l_2$). However, the bus

---

[2] For simplicity we abstract here the actual motion commands (possibly represented as multiple parameters of the *motion*, *motion'*, and *cmd* actions, respectively), and their mechanical execution.

could be busy and the *motion* request is delayed for transfer at $P$ or in the next period $[0, P)$. We then consider the bus to pass in a degraded mode depicted by the states in blue (from $l_3$ to $l_6$). During the transfer another request can be received. If both are handled before $P$, the bus has recovered and goes back to the nominal mode. Otherwise it stays in the degraded mode. While transferring the request, the bus can experience some hardware issues and fails denoted by the *fault* action in the automaton. In this case the bus goes into the fail mode depicted by the $l_7$ red state, and in which the received requests are either delayed after $2P$, lost or multiplied.

The *dispatcher* assumes the nominal behavior of the *bus*: it receives requests steadily, within the $[0, 2P)$ period. If this requirement is not satisfied (due to a faulty behavior of the *bus*), the *dispatcher* must stop transferring requests (action *halt*). This means that the received motion commands are ignored until the network is reinitialized (action *reinit*) and the dispatcher is aware of it (action *repair*). The above description corresponds to the FDIR specification.

# 3    A Formal Approach for Designing FDIR Components

The design of FDIR components is a sub-process of the general system design, as illustrated in Fig. 2. The methodology we propose includes several manual activities related to the design of the system that allow obtaining the inputs needed for the automated synthesis of FDIR components. These activities are suggested for system engineering by different standards, such as EECS standards [21] for space applications.

The main input of the methodology is the safety requirements. The first activity consists of building a system design from requirements and system description (i.e., what the system should do), which we call *requirements analysis*. The obtained design is usually made of two parts: the *nominal model* and the *fault model*. The nominal model defines the system architecture and its behavior in a "correct" environment (i.e., an environment that behaves accordingly to the assumptions). In this case, the nominal behavior should satisfy by default the (safety) requirements it is derived from. The fault model complements the nominal one by describing which faults components can manifest and what is the expected behavior after a fault occurrence. Usually the two models are obtained separately, since the fault model requires additional study of the fault specifications (e.g., of the hardware platform). Then, the two models are assembled into the *extended model* by merging techniques, which is used for FDIR design. For the sake of simplicity, we consider in the following that the output of the requirements analysis activity is the extended model.

*Example.* Figure 1 depicts the extended model of the case study, as the *bus* component models both nominal and faulty behavior. The nominal behavior consists of forwarding the *motion* request in the $[0, 2P)$ period – the nominal and degraded modes. The faulty behavior delays, loses or multiplies the *motion* requests after a *fault* – the fail mode.

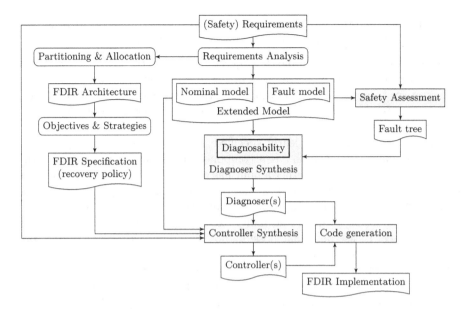

**Fig. 2.** Proposed formal approach for automated FDIR components design.

The second activity is the *Partitioning & Allocation*. Its aim is to associate the system requirements to the elements that must satisfy them, such as components, (sub-)systems or mission phases. As a result, the FDIR architecture is designed in relation to the system architecture and both nominal and fault-related requirements. The FDIR architecture can be centralized/distributed, monolithic/hierarchical or any combination. Please note that depending on the FDIR architecture, the automated design of FDIR component can become an undecidable problem, e.g., the decentralized partial observability control problem [30].

*Example.* For the case study in Fig. 1, the requirement to satisfy is that *motion'* command is issued within one period in the best case and within two periods in the worst case. This deadline can be missed only in the case of a fault, when the *bus* becomes unresponsive and all messages are delayed after $2P$, and the *dispatcher* should not transfer any request. In consequence, the requirement is associated with the *bus* and *dispatcher* components. The FDIR component architecture we consider is a centralized flat one consisting of one diagnoser and one controller connected to the *bus* and *dispatcher* components.

The third and last activity is the *Objectives & Strategies*. From the FDIR architecture and the system requirements, an FDIR specification describing the recovery policy is derived. The recovery policy is defined at system level by *objectives* and at component level by *strategies*. Objectives are related to the system requirements for the fault model, i.e., required behavior in the presence of failures. Strategies usually contain the functional steps to be performed given the fault and the objective to achieve. The aim of a strategy is to bring the system back in a *good* (safe) state after faults, where the RAMS hold.

*Example.* In the running example the objective is to stop the *dispatcher* until the *bus* is reinitialized and the correctness of the *motion'* requests can be assumed. The strategy to apply is the following: *halt* the dispatcher immediately after a fault is detected, *reinit* the *bus* and inform the *dispatcher* about the *bus* status (action *repair*).

Once all the inputs are clearly specified, the first automated step is *diagnoser(s) synthesis*. A *diagnoser* is a component that runs in parallel with the system and gives verdicts whether a fault has occurred or not yet. A diagnoser is synthesized for each fault (type) that can be detected. A fault $f$ can be detected if the system satisfies the *diagnosability* condition: given a set of observable actions, there are no nominal and faulty executions (labeled with $f$) that have the same trace. Please note that possibly not all faults need to satisfy this condition, just as diagnosers do not have to be synthesized for all faults. Indeed, only a subset of the fault actions set could be relevant with respect to the safety requirements to ensure. These faults can be identified through *model-based safety assessment* techniques [14], such as building the *fault tree* (i.e., Boolean combinations of faults). Additionally, statistical model-checking could be applied to identify those faults most likely to happen. Describing how to perform safety assessment is outside the scope of this paper.

The second automated step is the *controller synthesis* which can be performed if the system's faults are diagnosable and the diagnosers have been synthesized. When a diagnoser detects a fault, an alarm is raised which triggers a controller. The controller is a component running in parallel with the system and implementing the recovery strategies specified for the fault (type). Its aim is to bring the system back to states/modes where the safety requirements hold. This step synthesizes a controller from the specified recovery strategies and with respect to the system and diagnoser(s) behaviors, thus ensuring the FDIR objectives.

Finally, the diagnosers and controllers are assembled into the FDIR component from which code is generated (in C++ for example). The generated code can be deployed and run online with the actual system implementation.

This approach is general enough to be applied for both untimed and timed systems, only the synthesis algorithms need to be adapted to the corresponding case. In the following we describe the algorithms for diagnoser and controller synthesis for timed systems with partial observability as formalized in Sect. 2, and we illustrate them on the example from Fig. 1. These algorithms and the approach are currently under implementation in the BIP framework [5].

## 4   Formal Detection and Synthesis

A fault $f$ can be detected by a diagnoser if the system is $f$-$\Sigma_o'$-*diagnosable*. Intuitively, a system is $f$-$\Sigma_o'$-diagnosable if there are no executions having the same trace with respect to a set of observables $\Sigma_o'$ where one is labelled with the fault and the other not. With the notation from Sect. 2, the diagnosability condition is formalized as follows.

**Definition 3 ($f$-$\Sigma'_o$-diagnosability).** *Let $S$ be a system represented as a TA, $f \in \Sigma^f_u$ and $\Sigma'_o \subseteq \Sigma^u_o$. $S$ is $f$-$\Sigma'_o$-diagnosable if $\forall \rho \in Runs_S$ such that $faulty(\rho, f)$, $\nexists \rho' \in Runs_S$ such that $\neg faulty(\rho', q)$ and $trace_{\Sigma'_o}(\rho) = trace_{\Sigma'_o}(\rho')$.*

Please note in the definition above the *minimality condition* on the observables for fault detection: the set of observables is at most the set of uncontrollable observables of the system, i.e, $\Sigma'_o \subseteq \Sigma^u_o$. Additionally, the controllable observables should not be considered for the fault detection as those are actions commanded by the controller. If they would be taken into consideration for diagnosability, a circular behavioral dependency between the diagnoser and the controller could be created at runtime.

The algorithm for checking $f$-$\Sigma'_o$-diagnosability consists of the following steps:

1. Compute a copy $A$ of $S$ such that uncontrollable actions not in $\Sigma'_o$ become silent actions and controllable actions and the corresponding transitions are removed from the TA: $A = (L^A, l^A_0, X^A, Inv^A, (\Sigma^u_o)^A \oplus (\Sigma^s_u)^A \oplus (\Sigma^f_u)^A, E^A)$ with $(\Sigma^u_o)^A = \Sigma'_o$, $(\Sigma^s_u)^A = (\Sigma^u_o \setminus \Sigma'_o) \oplus \Sigma^s_u$ and $E^A = E \setminus \{l \xrightarrow[r]{[g]\ a} l'| a \in \Sigma^c_o\}$.

2. Compute a copy $B$ of $A$ such that $f$ is removed from the set of faults, clocks, silent and fault actions are renamed with respect to $A$, and all transitions labeled with $f$ are removed from $E$. Formally, $B = (L^B, l^B_0, X^B, Inv^B, (\Sigma^u_o)^B \oplus (\Sigma^s_u)^B \oplus (\Sigma^f_u)^B, E^B)$ with $X^B$ unique w.r.t. $A$, $(\Sigma^u_o)^B = \Sigma'_o$, $(\Sigma^s_u)^B = (\Sigma^u_o \setminus \Sigma'_o) \oplus \Sigma^s_u$ unique w.r.t. to $A$, $(\Sigma^f_u)^B = \Sigma^f_u \setminus \{f\}$ unique w.r.t. $A$, and $E^B = E^A \setminus \{l \xrightarrow[r]{[g]\ f} l'\}$.

3. Compute $A \parallel B$ and check that $\forall \rho \in Runs_{A\parallel B}$ such that $faulty(\rho, f)$, $\rho$ is Zeno.

This algorithm is performed independently for every fault that might occur in the system (possibly only the relevant ones obtained through *safety assessment*).

Intuitively, the algorithm synchronizes two copies of the model from which the transitions labeled with controllable actions are removed. The copy $A$ is the behavior with faults projected on the set of observables $\Sigma'_o$. The copy $B$ is similar except the transitions labeled with the fault under study $f$ are removed. The synchronization of $A$ and $B$ gives two types of executions: Zeno and non-Zeno. If a common execution labeled with $f$ is non-Zeno, it means that the distinction of which execution was actually performed – with $f$ from $A$ or without $f$ from $B$ – cannot be made by the diagnoser. In contrast, if all runs $\rho$ labeled with $f$ are Zeno, the diagnoser is able to make the distinction after $time(\rho)$.

The definition and algorithm for checking diagnosability are similar to the ones in [18,29] for timed systems. The difference comes from the splitting of observable actions into controllable and uncontrollable, and the removal of controllable actions such that diagnosability does not depend on actions enforced

by a controller as explained above. As these changes are linear in the number of
actions considered, it follows from [29] that it runs in PSPACE.

The running example from Fig. 1 has the following actions based on the
components ports: $\Sigma_o^c = \{reinit, halt, repair\}$, $\Sigma_o^u = \{motion, motion', cmd\}$,
$\Sigma_u^s = \{\tau, \tau'\}$ and $\Sigma_u^f = \{fault\}$. By taking $\Sigma_o' = \{motion'\}$, the system is $fault$-
$\Sigma_o'$-diagnosable. In the construction above, all runs $\rho$ labeled with $fault$ will
reach the location $(l_7, l_5)$ or $(l_7, l_6)$ of the composition and $time(\rho) = 2P$. Therefore, such executions are Zeno and the system is diagnosable. The action $motion'$
gives in fact the minimal set of sensors for detecting a fault. Any extended subset,
e.g., monitoring also $motion$, preserves the diagnosability condition.

If a fault action satisfies the diagnosability condition, a diagnoser can be
synthesized for its detection. Intuitively, a diagnoser monitors the observables
on which diagnosability has been checked and raises an alarm when the states
the system is in are marked as error. The diagnoser can be viewed, in general, as
the TA obtained through determinization of the system under study and with
respect to the specified observables $\Sigma_o'$ and $\Sigma_o^c$. Determinization of TA is an
undecidable problem [2,31], except for some classes [4,13,25,28]. In consequence,
an algorithm for on-the-fly determinization of a copy of the system with marked
faulty locations is generated. This algorithm is inspired from [18,29], and the
differences are discussed below.

As mentioned, the diagnosis algorithm works on a copy of the system with
marked faulty locations. Each location is associated with two bits: 0 if no fault
has occurred and 1 otherwise. The transition relation is also duplicated: transitions labeled with an observable or silent action keep the bit of the source
location, while transitions labeled with a fault change the bit to 1.[3] This modification is needed since the faults of the system are unobservable, and therefore
the detection is based on the system state. We call this copy the *diagnosis model*
and it is formalized as follows.

**Definition 4 (Diagnosis model).** *The diagnosis model $S'$ for $f$-$\Sigma_o'$-*
*diagnosable $S$ is the TA $(L', (l_0, 0), X, Inv', \Sigma_o^c \oplus \Sigma_o' \oplus \{\tau\}, E')$ where $L' =*
*$L \times \{0, 1\}$, $Inv'(l, n) = Inv(l)$ and $E'$ is given by the relation:*

- $(l, n) \xrightarrow[r]{[g]\ a} (l', n)$ *for $n \in \{0, 1\}$ if $l \xrightarrow[r]{[g]\ a} l'$ and $a \in \Sigma_o^c \oplus \Sigma_o'$*

- $(l, n) \xrightarrow[r]{[g]\ \tau} (l', n)$ *for $n \in \{0, 1\}$ if $l \xrightarrow[r]{[g]\ a} l'$ and $a \in (\Sigma_u^u \setminus \Sigma_o') \oplus \Sigma_u^s \oplus (\Sigma_u^f \setminus \{f\})$*

- $(l, n) \xrightarrow[r]{[g]\ \tau} (l', 1)$ *for $n \in \{0, 1\}$ if $l \xrightarrow[r]{[g]\ f} l'$*

The algorithm implemented by the diagnoser is given in Algorithm 1. We
denote by $W$ the set of current states for monitoring. Initially, this set consists
of all states of the diagnosis model $DM$ reachable in 0 time by firing only $\tau$
actions (i.e., former unobservable and observable actions on which the detection
does not depend). Additionally, a Boolean variable $b$ modeling whether a fault
has been raised is set to false.

---

[3] Please note that for simplicity of the diagnoser algorithm, all silent and fault actions
   are renamed as $\tau$ in Definition 4.

---

**Algorithm 1.** Timed diagnoser implementation loop.

---

**Input:** Diagnosis model $DM = (L \times \{0,1\}, (l_0, 0), X, \Sigma_o \cup \{\tau\}, E)$,
        timeout $\in \mathbb{R}_+$, $x \notin X$ clock

1   $W \longleftarrow \{s \in L \times \mathbb{R}_+^X \mid \rho = (l_0, 0, \mathbf{0}) \xrightarrow{\tau *} s \wedge time(\rho) = 0\}$

2 **while** *true* **do**

3      $b \longleftarrow false$

4      **while** *true* **do**

5          **if** $\forall s \in W.\ s = (l, 1, v)$ *and* $\neg b$ **then**

6              raise alarm

7              $b \longleftarrow true$

8          **end**

9          $x \longleftarrow 0$

10         await $(action\ a)$ or $(x = \mathsf{timeout})$

11         **if** $a$ *is* restart **then**

12             $W \longleftarrow \{(l, 0, v) \mid \forall s \in W.\rho = s \xrightarrow{(\delta/\tau)*} (l, n, v) \wedge time(\rho) = x\}$

13             break

14         **else**

15             **if** *action a* **then**

16                 $W \longleftarrow \{s'' \mid \forall s \in W.\ \rho = s \xrightarrow{(\delta/\tau)*} s' \xrightarrow{a} s'' \wedge time(\rho) = x\}$

17             **else**

18                 $W \longleftarrow \{s' \mid \forall s \in W.\ \rho = s \xrightarrow{(\delta/\tau)*} s' \wedge time(\rho) = \mathsf{timeout}\}$

19             **end**

20         **end**

21      **end**

22 **end**

---

The diagnoser main implementation loop is given next. The current states are checked for being faulty, i.e., the bit 1 is set in the diagnosis model for all of them. If it is the case and no alarm has been raised so far ($b$ is false), the latter is triggered. In both cases, the diagnoser keeps monitoring the system: (i) a clock $x$ is set to 0 and (ii) an action $a$ or the lapse of time to timeout is observed. For an observation $a$, $x$ will contain the time elapse since the last match. In the case of a matched $a$, the diagnoser computes the next states of the system as follows: first it fires all internal actions $\tau$ such that the entire execution time takes $x$ time units; then it fires the event $a$ and updates the set of reached states. If the event $a$ is the specific action restart of the controller, the bit is additionally set to 0 for all computed states. If no event is observed in a timeout period, the set of reachable states is again updated by firing all internals during the predefined timeout period.

*Example.* For the case study in Fig. 1, the diagnoser has a timeout value of $2P$. Indeed at moment $2P$, the only state reachable is $(l_7, 1, 2P)$, at which the alarm action is raised. We give in Fig. 3 a symbolic representation as TA for this diagnoser.

The difference between Algorithm 1 and the algorithm from [18,29] is mainly related to the FDIR setting and the controller component. While in [18,29] a valid diagnoser consistently outputs alarm once a fault is detected, our algorithm allows for a restart of the monitoring. This is due to the implementation of a controller which handles faulty behavior and brings the system into safe states. To ensure that the fault detection happens from states coherent with the actual system states after a restart, the diagnoser monitors also the controllable observable actions defined for the controller. Finally, for a more detailed discussion about the implementation of diagnosers, the reader is referred to [29].

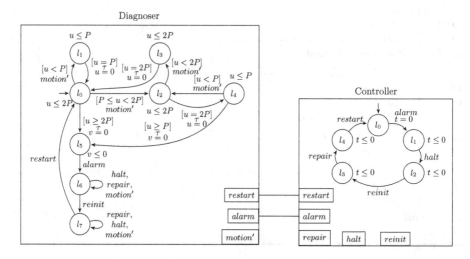

**Fig. 3.** Components of the synthesized FDIR component.

## 5    Implementing Reconfiguration Strategies

Once a fault is detected, a controller takes charge to bring the system back into safe states. This controller, if one exists, can be automatically synthesized just as the diagnoser. The construction of the controller is based on the system under study including diagnosers, FDIR specification (recovery strategies), and requirement(s) describing the safe state after a fault.

There are several works in the literature tackling controller synthesis algorithms from logical specifications (e.g. untimed automata built from LTL formulas [24]). The (safety) requirement is expressed in some logic and the algorithm works only on the system under study. This problem is known to be a hard one, and even undecidable in some cases [20,22]. In the FDIR context, we make use of the recovery strategies contained in the FDIR specification which define the functional steps to apply in case of a fault. An incomplete controller is manually built from these strategies, and refined and validated on the system.

We consider the incomplete controller to be modeled as a TA. This automaton is structurally refined by using the appropriate *alarm* and *restart* of the diagnoser, and adding a transition labeled with *restart* as last step of the modeled recovery strategy. This transformation is needed to be able to inform the corresponding diagnoser that the detected fault has been handled and to uphold the reactive aspect of these systems.

*Example.* On the running example, the recovery strategy describes that once the fault is detected, the *dispatcher* must stop transferring requests until the *bus* is reinitialized and it is aware of it. The functional sequence derived from this specification is *halt* followed by *reinit* and *repair*. This sequence is triggered by *alarm* from the diagnoser and informs its execution by action *restart*. The execution of the controller is enforced by invariants which deactivate time elapse. The corresponding TA is given in Fig. 3.

The validity of a controller is checked with respect to the set of safe states to be reached modeled by the safety requirement. This can be achieved through model-checking the system including the FDIR component with respect to the safety requirement. As this is a reachability problem of the safe states, the validation effort of a controller is in PSPACE.

*Example.* In our example, the safety requirement is that the *bus* has been reinitialized and the *dispatcher* is aware of it. The safe states projection on the two components consists of $(l_0, l_0)$. With respect to this requirement the controller proposed in Fig. 3 is valid.

Once the controller has been validated, code (e.g., in C++) can be generated. This code can be obtained independently for the diagnoser(s), controller(s) or the full-fledged FDIR component. Under the assumption of code generation correctness, the FDIR implementation can be deployed on the platform together with the actual system and its online expected behavior is met.

## 6   Related Work

How to build correct FDIR components from complete system specifications is a recent topic of interest in the literature [10,32]. FDIR components are usually obtained through *ad-hoc* processes and need extensive testing to ensure their correctness for mission and safety-critical applications. In this paper we propose the use of formal methods to tackle this issue and obtain correct-by-construction FDIR implementations.

Our approach is similar to the one in [10]. The main differences cover the domain of application and code generation feature. This paper considers real-time systems represented as timed automata, while in [10] systems are untimed and represented as symbolic transition systems. Therefore, the algorithms applied for synthesis are different. The focus of [10] is on the safety assessment [9] with timed failure propagation models, which are modeled by the user. In our approach, safety assessment is not mandatory as diagnosability can be checked for all fault types and diagnosers can be synthesized for all of them. However, safety assessment can be performed with respect to the given safety requirements based on automatically generated fault trees. The artifacts give information about the subset of faults that need to be detected and the minimal subset of sensors needed. Additionally, risk analysis can be performed along safety assessment using statistical model-checking (available in the BIP framework). The recovery strategies from [10] are modeled in a flavor of Linear Temporal Logic (LTL) [26], while we consider them specified as timed automata which is arguably more intuitive and expressive for modeling. Finally, our approach allows to generate code for the FDIR implementation, which is not considered in [10].

The two synthesis problems considered here – diagnoser and controller synthesis – have however been studied independently of the FDIR context. For example, [27] describes the diagnosability problem for one and multiple faults, and introduces the notion of fault type for untimed systems. [19] describes a framework for diagnoser synthesis in the untimed case and from LTL specifications. In [6,7], runtime verification for 3-value Timed LTL is used for fault detection.

In the context of timed diagnoser synthesis, the most related works to ours are the ones from [11,16,18,29]. As described in Sect. 4, the main differences consist of the representation of a system to accommodate FDIR components and the adaptation of the algorithms to this representation. More specifically, in our framework a system defines both controllable and uncontrollable observables, and diagnosability is checked on a subset of uncontrollable observables. The controllable actions are however monitored by the diagnoser, in order to ensure the correct restart of the detection once the recovery strategy is successfully applied. This feature of the diagnoser allows enforcing FDIR capabilities on reactive systems, different to [29] where a diagnoser is considered valid if it does not change the verdict after a detected fault.

The controller synthesis problem is studied in several works that use a more general formalism than ours. The usual approach is a game-based one: the problem is seen as a game between the environment (playing uncontrollable actions) and the controller [17]. In the untimed case, the general problem with specifications given as LTL formulas is well understood and decidable, but usually not tractable, even though some work has been done towards applicability of the algorithms [24]. An approach that is closer to ours in the untimed case, building a controller by adding transitions to an incomplete one under safety and liveness requirements, is considered in [3].

The timed case is much more involved, and the decidability of the problem heavily relies on parameters such as partial observability, access to (un)limited resources, and type of specifications [12,15,20]. For example, in [23] a controller is synthesized from a template by parameter instantiation, while [8,22] use Timed Computational Tree Logic [1] specifications.

## 7   Conclusion

In this paper we present an approach based on formal methods for the correct-by-construction design of FDIR components. This approach performs several manual steps for obtaining the inputs required: the system under study consisting of both the nominal and the faulty behavior, the recovery strategies and requirements to satisfy modeled as automata. The approach proceeds by synthesizing an FDIR component in two steps: (i) a diagnoser is generated for each diagnosable fault and (ii) a controller is produced for each recovery strategy by completion of its incomplete representation as automaton. The FDIR component is validated by model-checking techniques and code (e.g., in C++) is generated as FDIR implementation. This implementation can be deployed with the system for the online detection and enforcement of safety requirements.

The proposed approach can be applied for both untimed and timed systems. We define the notion of diagnosability in the FDIR context for timed systems and we propose algorithms for the automated generation of full-fledged timed FDIR components. We illustrate the approach and the algorithms on an autonomous system case study with faults during communication.

The approach presented here is currently under implementation in the BIP framework and validation in two real-life case studies from our industrial partners. As future work we are interested in validating and comparing the synthesized FDIR implementation with respect to developer written ones, as means to quantify this approach with respect to standard FDIR coding ones. In order to optimize the synthesized FDIR implementations, we are interested to study model-based safety assessment with statistical model-checking techniques and in the context of stochastic faults.

On a more general note, we are interested in devising a pattern-based language for modeling recovery strategies, and a synthesis or learning algorithm for building the controller. This language could be extended and used for specifying data-/state-based safety requirements as inputs, besides the event-based ones considered in this paper. This would require the introduction of a dynamic observer as a filter for the FDIR component, to transform the data-/state-based property into an event-based one. Ideally, the previously mentioned algorithm will perform this step automatically. Finally, we are interested in considering more complex FDIR architectures as targets (e.g., distributed ones) and adapt the algorithms to such cases.

# References

1. Alur, R., Courcoubetis, C., Dill, D.: Model-checking in dense real-time. Inf. Comput. **104**(1), 2–34 (1993)
2. Alur, R., Dill, D.L.: A theory of timed automata. Theor. Comput. Sci. **126**(2), 183–235 (1994)
3. Alur, R., Tripakis, S.: Automatic synthesis of distributed protocols. SIGACT News **48**(1), 55–90 (2017)
4. Baier, C., Bertrand, N., Bouyer, P., Brihaye, T.: When are timed automata determinizable? In: Albers, S., Marchetti-Spaccamela, A., Matias, Y., Nikoletseas, S., Thomas, W. (eds.) ICALP 2009. LNCS, vol. 5556, pp. 43–54. Springer, Heidelberg (2009). https://doi.org/10.1007/978-3-642-02930-1_4
5. Basu, A., Bozga, M., Sifakis, J.: Modeling heterogeneous real-time components in BIP. In: SEFM 2006, pp. 3–12 (2006)

6. Bauer, A., Leucker, M., Schallhart, C.: Model-based runtime analysis of distributed reactive systems. In: ASWEC 2006, pp. 243–252 (2006)
7. Bauer, A., Leucker, M., Schallhart, C.: Monitoring of real-time properties. In: Arun-Kumar, S., Garg, N. (eds.) FSTTCS 2006. LNCS, vol. 4337, pp. 260–272. Springer, Heidelberg (2006). https://doi.org/10.1007/11944836_25
8. Behrmann, G., Larsen, K.G., Rasmussen, J.I.: Beyond liveness: efficient parameter synthesis for time bounded liveness. In: Pettersson, P., Yi, W. (eds.) FORMATS 2005. LNCS, vol. 3829, pp. 81–94. Springer, Heidelberg (2005). https://doi.org/10.1007/11603009_7
9. Bittner, B., et al.: The xSAP safety analysis platform. In: Chechik, M., Raskin, J.-F. (eds.) TACAS 2016. LNCS, vol. 9636, pp. 533–539. Springer, Heidelberg (2016). https://doi.org/10.1007/978-3-662-49674-9_31
10. Bittner, B., et al.: An integrated process for FDIR design in aerospace. In: IMBSA 2014, pp. 82–95 (2014)
11. Bouyer, P., Chevalier, F., D'Souza, D.: Fault diagnosis using timed automata. In: FOSSACS 2005, pp. 219–233 (2005)
12. Bouyer, P., D'Souza, D., Madhusudan, P., Petit, A.: Timed control with partial observability. In: Hunt, W.A., Somenzi, F. (eds.) CAV 2003. LNCS, vol. 2725, pp. 180–192. Springer, Heidelberg (2003). https://doi.org/10.1007/978-3-540-45069-6_18
13. Bouyer, P., Jaziri, S., Markey, N.: On the determinization of timed systems. In: Abate, A., Geeraerts, G. (eds.) FORMATS 2017. LNCS, vol. 10419, pp. 25–41. Springer, Cham (2017). https://doi.org/10.1007/978-3-319-65765-3_2
14. Bozzano, M., Villafiorita, A.: Design and Safety Assessment of Critical Systems, 1st edn. Auerbach Publications, Boston (2010)
15. Cassez, F.: Efficient on-the-fly algorithms for partially observable timed games. In: Raskin, J.-F., Thiagarajan, P.S. (eds.) FORMATS 2007. LNCS, vol. 4763, pp. 5–24. Springer, Heidelberg (2007). https://doi.org/10.1007/978-3-540-75454-1_3
16. Cassez, F.: A note on fault diagnosis algorithms. In: IEEE CDC 2009, pp. 6941–6946 (2009)
17. Cassez, F., David, A., Fleury, E., Larsen, K.G., Lime, D.: Efficient on-the-fly algorithms for the analysis of timed games. In: Abadi, M., de Alfaro, L. (eds.) CONCUR 2005. LNCS, vol. 3653, pp. 66–80. Springer, Heidelberg (2005). https://doi.org/10.1007/11539452_9
18. Cassez, F., Tripakis, S.: Fault diagnosis of timed systems. In: Communicating Embedded Systems - Software and Design, October 2009
19. Cimatti, A., Pecheur, C., Cavada, R.: Formal verification of diagnosability via symbolic model checking. In: IJCAI 2003, pp. 363–369 (2003)
20. D'souza, D., Madhusudan, P.: Timed control synthesis for external specifications. In: Alt, H., Ferreira, A. (eds.) STACS 2002. LNCS, vol. 2285, pp. 571–582. Springer, Heidelberg (2002). https://doi.org/10.1007/3-540-45841-7_47
21. European Cooperation for Space Standardization: Website. http://www.ecss.nl/
22. Faella, M., La Torre, S., Murano, A.: Dense real-time games. In: LICS 2002, pp. 167–176 (2002)
23. Finkbeiner, B., Peter, H.-J.: Template-based controller synthesis for timed systems. In: Flanagan, C., König, B. (eds.) TACAS 2012. LNCS, vol. 7214, pp. 392–406. Springer, Heidelberg (2012). https://doi.org/10.1007/978-3-642-28756-5_27
24. Kupferman, O., Piterman, N., Vardi, M.Y.: Safraless compositional synthesis. In: Ball, T., Jones, R.B. (eds.) CAV 2006. LNCS, vol. 4144, pp. 31–44. Springer, Heidelberg (2006). https://doi.org/10.1007/11817963_6

25. Lorber, F., Rosenmann, A., Nickovic, D., Aichernig, B.K.: Bounded determinization of timed automata with silent transitions. Real Time Syst. **53**(3), 291–326 (2017)
26. Pnueli, A.: The temporal logic of programs. In: SFCS 1977, pp. 46–57 (1977)
27. Sampath, M., Sengupta, R., Lafortune, S., Sinnamohideen, K., Teneketzis, D.: Failure diagnosis using discrete-event models. IEEE Trans. Control. Syst. Technol. **4**(2), 105–124 (1996)
28. Suman, P.V., Pandya, P.K.: Determinization and expressiveness of integer reset timed automata with silent transitions. In: Dediu, A.H., Ionescu, A.M., Martín-Vide, C. (eds.) LATA 2009. LNCS, vol. 5457, pp. 728–739. Springer, Heidelberg (2009). https://doi.org/10.1007/978-3-642-00982-2_62
29. Tripakis, S.: Fault diagnosis for timed automata. In: Damm, W., Olderog, E.-R. (eds.) FTRTFT 2002. LNCS, vol. 2469, pp. 205–221. Springer, Heidelberg (2002). https://doi.org/10.1007/3-540-45739-9_14
30. Tripakis, S.: Undecidable problems of decentralized observation and control on regular languages. Inf. Process. Lett. **90**(1), 21–28 (2004)
31. Tripakis, S.: Folk theorems on the determinization and minimization of timed automata. Inf. Process. Lett. **99**(6), 222–226 (2006)
32. Wander, A., Forstner, R.: Innovative fault detection, isolation and recovery strategies on-board spacecraft: state of the art and research challenges. Deutscher Luft- und Raumfahrtkongress (2012)

# Dynamic Security Specification Through Autonomic Component Ensembles

Rima Al Ali, Tomas Bures, Petr Hnetynka$^{(\boxtimes)}$, Filip Krijt,
Frantisek Plasil, and Jiri Vinarek

Faculty of Mathematics and Physics, Charles University,
Malostranske namesti 25, Prague, Czech Republic
{alali, bures, hnetynka, krijt, plasil,
vinarek}@d3s.mff.cuni.cz

**Abstract.** One of the key properties of autonomic component systems is their dynamicity and context-dependence of their behavior. In contrast to systems with a static architecture, their components interact and collaborate in an ad-hoc fashion depending on their internal state and location, the state of other components and their locations, timing and history of events/state of external (uncontrolled) environment. This high degree of dynamicity collides with traditional approaches to security, which typically rely on static hierarchies of roles and a static assignment of roles. To address this problem, we formulate security rules which are autonomically composable and context-dependent; in their evolution, they follow the dynamicity and context-dependence of the autonomic components. Based on our previous work with autonomic component ensembles, we show how ensembles can be exploited to define security rules to control interactions in a system of autonomic components.

**Keywords:** Smart systems · Autonomic components · Component coalitions
Component ensembles · Architecture description language

## 1 Introduction

A trend common to all modern systems that can be seen as systems of cooperating autonomic components is the high-degree of interconnectedness and dynamically evolving and changing structure and behavior. This is common for various domains including smart buildings, smart traffic, smart production, etc. All these systems significantly increase their value by aggregating and exploiting data from different sources and typically also of different governance. Furthermore, they are open and dynamic in the sense that they admit integration with other systems, which further increases their value. Connected with adaptivity, as the property that allows them to continuously monitor their state and context, these systems often also dynamically reconfigure themselves and establish ad-hoc cooperation with other systems so as to address the situation at hand. Examples of this are numerous spanning cases like rescue robots that dynamically form cooperation groups to perform rescue operations, UAVs or UUVs performing collective navigation survey of a designated area, and vehicles cooperating in parking and other maneuvers. In the domain of smart buildings (which is the case we

© Springer Nature Switzerland AG 2018
T. Margaria and B. Steffen (Eds.): ISoLA 2018, LNCS 11246, pp. 172–185, 2018.
https://doi.org/10.1007/978-3-030-03424-5_12

borrow from our projects), this can be sensors and various smart devices which cooperate towards the goal of reducing energy consumption via smart HVAC (heating, ventilation and air-conditioning) and towards the goal of ensuring physical security by monitoring the movement and responsibilities of persons and controlling the physical access by means of smart door locks.

A common challenge in these systems is the security (both digital and physical). Obviously, the ability to cooperate across system and governance boundaries is one part of the problem. The other part of the problem is the dynamicity that stems from the adaptation of a system to its current context. As part of this adaptation, the cooperating components (robots, cars, devices, suppliers, etc.) as well as the security requirements may change. A rather common example of a context-dependent security requirement is the one of emergency exit doors which in normal operation are supposed to stay closed, but should be opened in case of an emergency. More complex examples include allowing data exchange among components only if the components are part of the same process (e.g., robots sharing information about a victim whom they are trying to rescue, or cars sharing driving intent in case they are involved in an overtaking maneuver).

The presence of dynamicity (in peers and security requirements themselves) significantly complicates the challenge of ensuring security. While the current state of the art has a number of approaches to cope with security in static systems (e.g., role-based access control, rule set-based access control, graph-based access control), they cannot easily cope with a high-degree of dynamicity. Even approaches that have been developed to take context into account (e.g., context-based access control, attribute-based access control), do not easily count with dynamicity and context involving a coordinated action of multiple components and the potential uncertainty that comes as the results of adaptive and complex systems.

In this paper, we formulate an approach to autonomically composable and context-dependent security rules that follow the dynamicity and context-dependence of the autonomic components a system is composed of. We base our work on our previous work on autonomic component ensembles [3]. We define a new type of security ensembles that describe permitted interactions in the system and follow the system during its evolution. We complement this with an approach to match ensembles to the current state of the system so as to resolve the binding of dynamic security rules to current situations and to generate the set of actions permitted at a given moment given the components in the system and their context. In this course, we allow also modeling components that are not controlled by the system (e.g., humans and 3rd party components) where the state of a component is not directly observable, but instead has to be derived.

The paper is structured as follows. In Sect. 2, the running example is described. Section 3 presents our approach to dynamic security specification through autonomic component ensembles while in Sect. 4 we describe a user-oriented external DSL for ensemble and security specifications. In Sect. 5, related work is discussed and Sect. 6 concludes the paper.

## 2 Running Example

In the rest of the paper, as a particular example on which we illustrate our approach, we use the following real-life scenario with dynamically evolving physical security constraints. Let us imagine a software development company in which developers work in parallel on several projects. Each of these projects is for a different customer and each of them is assigned to a different team of developers. To ensure the protection of customers' intellectual property, the development teams are distinct and, additionally, security constraints dictate that developers from different teams must not communicate with each other and they are not allowed to stay in the same room (working rooms or lunch rooms). To address these constraints, the developers are guided (via their mobile phones or smart-watches or a similar device) as to in which rooms in the company building they can stay.

In order to make the code examples in the following sections easily readable, we limit the scenario as follows. The company building contains a set of Rooms separated by Doors. The Rooms are of three different types – Lunchrooms (marked L1–L3), Corridors (C1–C3) and Working rooms (W1–W3). Each of the Lunchrooms and Working rooms has a capacity depicting the number of persons allowed in that room (each Working room and Lunchroom has in our scenario capacity of 2 while Corridors have infinite capacity). There are two development teams A and B – each of the developers belongs to one of them. A developer is always in one of the following two modes – WantingToEat and Working; when in the Working mode, he/she should be in a Working room and similarly for the WantingToEat mode and a Lunchroom.

The situation is depicted in Fig. 1 (figures in this section are actual screenshots from a simulator of the scenario we have developed to illustrate the approach). The shape distinguishes the team affinity of the developer (a circle or square); the color distinguishes the mode (blue for the Working state while orange for the WantingToEat one). The developer's label (in the circle or square) shows an ID of the developer (A1, A2, ..., B1, B2, ...) and an assigned room (it is possible that no room is assigned).

The goal of the system is to control which room a developer is permitted to enter while ensuring the security and space constraints. Namely, the rules are as follows:

1. Developers from different teams must not meet in Working rooms or Lunchrooms.
2. The number of developers assigned to a room must not exceed its capacity.
3. Utility of the Lunchrooms and Working rooms is maximized, i.e., the number of developers in the WantingToEat mode assigned to Lunchrooms and the number of developers in the Working mode assigned to Working rooms is maximized (with respect to the first rule).

The behavior of the developers has the following phases:

1. Each Developer may change his/her current mode. The probability of switching to the other mode increases with time spent in the current mode.
2. The system assigns rooms to Developers while maximizing its Utility (i.e., efficiency of the rooms' utilization).
3. The assigned room is communicated to the particular Developers.
4. The developer tries to move to the assigned room.

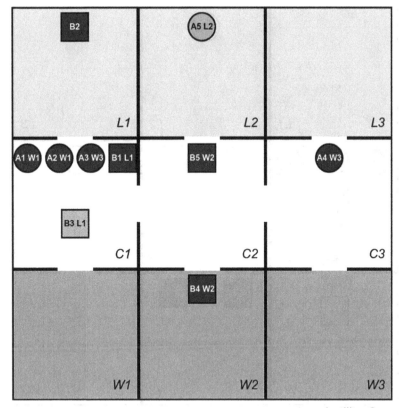

step: 4 utility: 8

**Fig. 1.** Scenario map picturing rooms and developers

5. To move to an adjacent room, the Developer passes through a Door, which opens only for a Developer with the assigned room.
6. Simultaneously, the Door can reject passing if the Developer would end up in a Lunchroom or Working room with a Developer from a different team. While this may be seen as redundant, it is necessary due to the dynamicity of the system and due to the inability of the system to directly enforce behavior of the developers (who are humans and thus beyond direct control of the system; the system can only ask them to do something – e.g., to have a lunch in a given room – but it has no means to force them). For example, there may arise a situation depicted on Fig. 2 – the A1 developer moves to the W1 room while the B1 developer changed his/her mode and obtained a new room assignment (the L1 room), however for some reason he/she still remains in W1 and thus A1 cannot enter W1.

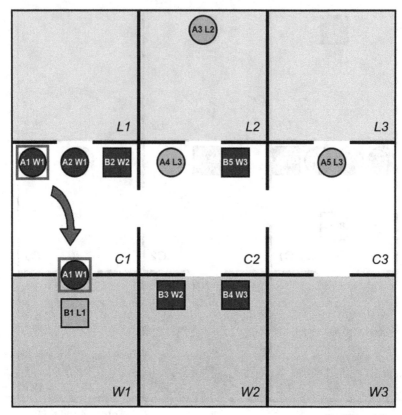

step: 2 utility: 10

**Fig. 2.** Entry for the developer A1 to room W1 is rejected due to the presence of the developer B1

## 3  Ensembles for Security

To describe and reason about security in dynamic systems, such as the one presented in the running example, we extend our approach to autonomic component ensembles [3, 4]. The principal idea behind autonomic component ensembles is to represent system entities (e.g., persons, devices, robots, machines, rooms, doors, etc.) as components and cooperation and coalitions among the entities as ensembles. In our model, an ensemble is specified as a type, which is instantiated (potentially multiple times) for cooperation in given situations. Being context-dependent, an instance of an ensemble is typically localized temporally and spatially.

From the semantics perspective, a *component* represents an autonomous (potentially mobile) entity, which has its own state (we use term *knowledge*). A component performs periodic activity in which it senses the environment (updating its knowledge), performs computation and actuation.

An *ensemble* is a group of components formed to perform joint goal or coordinate some activity. Members of an ensemble are established dynamically at runtime. An ensemble is determined by its *membership condition* – a predicate over components' types and knowledge. Ensembles can be hierarchically decomposed into further sub-ensembles. The semantics is that members of a sub-ensemble must be members of the parent ensemble too. This way, a top-level ensemble defines the goal of the system as a whole. A component can be a member of multiple ensembles at the same time, which naturally reflects the fact that a component may be part of a number of functionally orthogonal cooperations.

To give an example from the robot coordination domain, an ensemble is for instance a group of three robots that collectively transport an item. The ensemble condition selects from the available robots with the right type of a gripper three robots that are the closest to the item to be transported. Once formed, the ensemble is then responsible for computation of coordinated movement, such that robots maintain a formation needed to transport the item.

In the case of using ensembles for modeling and controlling security, we follow the same idea. The difference however is that while in the example with the robots, we used the ensemble prescriptively to control the robot collaboration, in this paper, we use ensembles to describe existing types of situations and collaborations. Thus instead of specifying coordinated actions of components, we specify what data are allowed to be shared among particular components in an ensemble. Contrary to defining static hierarchies of permissions, the security rules carried by ensembles are dynamic because they are dynamically instantiated along with ensembles to reflect dynamic situations bound to temporal and spatial context.

Similarly to our previous work, we complement the specification with a framework that utilizes a CSP solver (Choco solver in particular) to resolve ensembles – that means to determine which ensemble instances to create and which components to assign to them.

### 3.1   Concepts and Semantics

To illustrate the semantics and to allow for rapid experiments with variations of the semantics, we developed a Scala internal DSL for specification and resolution of ensembles. The implementation can be found at http://github.com/d3scomp/tcoof-security. Though the DSL may not be first choice for specifications which are supposed to be provided by end-users (we sketch an alternative end-user oriented specification in Sect. 4), it has exact semantics based on Scala language.

In the Scala DSL, we model all components and ensembles as classes. In our scenario, the components are Rooms and Developers. The cooperation among components is modeled via ensembles. In our scenario, it is the Lunch group, which is a group of developers that share the same lunchroom.

The specification of the running example in our Scala DSL is shown in Fig. 3. Lines 4–9 define the various types of rooms. A Room is determined by its type, name and capacity. Lines 11–16 specify the Developer component. A Developer is determined by their name and the team to which they belong. Additionally, a developer has a mode, which distinguishes the intent of the developer. In our example, we model only

```
1.    class SecurityScenario extends Model ... {
2.
3.       // Domain entities
4.       abstract class Room(name: String, capacity: Int)
5.           extends Component { ... }
6.       class WorkingPlace(name: String, capacity: Int)
7.           extends Room(name, capacity)
8.       class LunchRoom(name: String, capacity: Int) extends
                                              Room(name, capacity)
9.       class Corridor(name: String) extends Room(name, Int.MaxValue)
10.
11.      abstract class DeveloperMode
12.      object Working extends DeveloperMode
13.      object WantingToEat extends DeveloperMode
14.
15.      class Developer(name: string, team: String, mode: DeveloperMode)
16.          extends Component { ... }
17.
18.      // A group of co-workers from the same team that share a Lunch Room
19.      class LunchGroup(room: LunchRoom) extends Ensemble {
20.          ...
21.
22.          // developers in the group can only be those that are from the given team
23.          val developers = role(components.select[Developer]
24.              .filter(_.mode == WantingToEat)
25.
26.          membership {
27.              // all developers must be in WantingToEat state
28.              developers.allEqual(_.team) &&
29.
30.              // the number of developers in room must not exceed its capacity
31.              developers.cardinality <= room.capacity
32.          }
33.
34.          utility {
35.              developers.cardinality
36.          }
37.
38.          allow(developers, room, "enter")
39.      }
40.
41.      class System extends RootEnsemble {
42.          // Set of potential ensembles (one potential ensemble per team and room)
43.          val lunchGroups = ensembles(
44.              allLunchRooms.map(room => new LunchGroup(room, team)
45.          )
46.
47.          membership {
48.              // every developer can be assigned only to one group
49.              lunchGroups.map(_.developers).allDisjoint
50.          }
51.
52.          ...
53.      }
54. }
```

**Fig. 3.** Example of using TCOOF-ADL in partitioning agents to rooms

two modes: Working and WantingToEat. As components represent beyond-control-entities (components' behavior is not directly controlled by the system), the specification does not contain any functional code of components.

The main idea of the specification comes in the description of the LunchGroup ensemble. The ensemble gives permission to developer to enter a particular Lunch room while making sure that they can fit in the room and that members of two different teams cannot meet in the same lunchroom. At the same time, it also optimizes the allocation of lunchrooms to developers, such that the lunch rooms are utilized to the maximum extent.

The LunchGroup ensemble is given on lines 19–39. The ensemble is qualified by the lunchroom (the room is given as a parameter to the ensemble class). This means that there will be one potential instance of the ensemble per LunchRoom. An important aspect here is the potentiality. This means that the instance of the ensemble will be considered in constructing the ensembles, but it does not have to be constructed in the end (e.g., if there are not enough developers to occupy all lunchrooms).

The ensemble specifies which entities take part in it. In our case, one entity is the room which qualifies the ensemble, the other entities are the particular developers which are allowed to the particular room. The developers are specified via the role construct on lines 23–24. This says that the ensemble will have a role which comprises the developers that want to eat. Technically, we use the standard collection operators and lambda functions to filter components based on their mode. The components assigned this way form a domain for the role. Particular developers will be then selected from this domain such that all other conditions (e.g., constraints on capacity, exclusivity of teams, etc.) are met.

The conditions based on which the particular components are chosen in the roles are given in the "membership" section of the ensemble (lines 26–39). It states that all developers selected for the role "developers" should belong to the same team and that their number has to fit the room capacity.

Generally, it is possible to have multiple roles in the ensembles (e.g., if one wanted to distinguish between developers and testers) and to state relationships between the roles (e.g., set relationships like that components selected for one role should be also present in another role of the same ensemble instance).

The optimization of the selection is driven by the utility function (lines 34–36). In our example, we use a simple utility function that equals to the number of developers in an ensemble. As the whole system utility is computed as a sum of utilities over all ensemble instances, this leads to maximizing the number of developers which are assigned to a lunchroom and given access to it. Note, however, that if there are more developers than the overall capacity of the lunchrooms, there will remain some developers without access to any lunchroom. This naturally corresponds to a congestion situation where some developers will simply have to wait until others are finished with their lunch.

The relationship between ensemble instances is established by a root ensemble called System (lines 41–53). Here we exploit the hierarchical structure of ensembles and assume a single root ensemble, which is a singleton, in which all other ensembles are (transitively) nested. As a parent to the LunchGroup ensemble instance, the root ensemble specifies the potential instances of LunchGroup ensembles and specifies constraints over the ensembles. In our case, we create one potential LunchGroup ensemble instance per room (lines 43–45) and posit that the LunchGroups should be mutually disjoint in terms of developers they contain (lines 47–50).

The structure that has been specified via the DSL is then resolved by our framework that internally utilizes the CSP solver. The resolution creates the LunchGroup ensemble instances and assigns Developer components to them.

Finally, the security is specified via **allow** statements in ensembles (line 38). The **allow** statements are formed as triples: subject, object, permission. The subject and object refer to entities grouped by the ensemble. In our case, it gives access to developers that have been selected by the ensemble resolution as members of a particular LunchGroup to enter the corresponding lunchroom.

## 4   End-User DSL

In the previous section, we have presented the ensemble concepts, and the running example via our Scala-based TCOOF-ADL language. While an internal DSL hosted in a general-purpose programming language such as Scala certainly has its advantages – most prominently a fast prototyping loop as well as the power and the tooling of a mature language – it also has several notable drawbacks. Since there is no explicit new grammar and infrastructure, we are limited to modeling the newly introduced concepts by using the features of the host language; ideally, the mapping is fairly clean (e.g., components to classes), but in some cases this repurposing of the host language features to unintended use cases results in an API that is downright cumbersome to use. At the same time, since all code used in the internal DSL is a general Scala code, there are no additional compile-time checks that could be enforced and that could inform the end-user when they are using the ensemble concepts in ways they should not.

Being well aware of this impracticality of internal DSL for end-user usage, we have been also developing an external, end-user friendly DSL with explicit grammar in parallel to the more feature-prototyping focused TCOOF-ADL. This DSL, named the Ensemble Definition Language (EDL for short) [10], is being developed using the Eclipse language development tools, namely the Xtext[1] grammar definition language, as well as the Xtend[2] programming language. In this section, we show the extension of EDL for security, named EDL-S. The EDL-S is not intended to capture all the nuances of a large-scale system architecture; instead, it is positioned as a focused declarative specification of the types of ensembles that can exist in the system, the constraints they must satisfy, and how to decide which ensembles the system should form at runtime – mapping almost exactly to the part of the specification that must be written by the end-user to capture the security rules that should be enforced by the system.

Precisely describing all the first-class concepts in EDL-S is out of the scope of this paper; however, an illustration of EDL-S possibilities is shown in Fig. 4 describing a part of the running example. In particular, the focus is on the assignment of developers to lunchrooms, as discussed in Sect. 3. The specification starts with two entity definitions – essentially interfaces prescribing data properties – representing the two types of entities relevant to the assignment: the developers and the lunchrooms. Note that there is no notion of how the entities operate – whether backed by regular components, or components representing beyond-control entities is irrelevant for the assignment, providing nice low coupling with the rest of the system. The assignment rules

---

[1] http://www.eclipse.org/Xtext/.

[2] http://www.eclipse.org/xtend/.

themselves are represented by the ensemble specification starting on line 14. Line 15 declares that all lunchroom assignments must have a unique lunchroom (represented by the **id** construct). The specification then defines a single role on line 18 by the name **developers**, representing a list of developers assigned to this specific lunchroom, the choice of which is restricted by the where construct to only include developers currently interested in eating (since this particular EDL-S fragment concerns only lunchroom assignment) as an optimization for solving. The constraints constructs are then used to restrict the number of assigned developers by the capacity of the particular room (line 20), as well as to prohibit developers from different teams in a single room (line 21). The requirement for optimality in terms of maximal room usage is represented by the fitness construct, specifying that the benefit of an assignment is gauged by how many developers have been assigned to the room in question (line 22). Finally, the security is specified via **allow** statements (line 24), similarly as in the TCOOF-ADL code in Fig. 3.

```
 1. package SecurityScenario
 2.
 3. entity Developer
 4.    name: string
 5.    team: string
 6.    mode: [ working, wantingToEat ]
 7. end
 8.
 9. entity LunchRoom
10.      name : string
11.      capacity : int
12.    end
13.
14.    ensemble LunchGroup
15.      id room : LunchRoom
16.      membership
17.        roles
18.          developers [0..*] : Developer where it.mode == wantingToEat
19.        constraints
20.          constraint sum developers <= room.capacity
21.          constraint allEqual developers it.team
22.        fitness sum developers
23.      permissions:
24.        allow developers enter room
```

**Fig. 4.** Example of using EDL-S in partitioning agents to rooms

As can be seen from the example, the focused nature of the EDL-S provides a compact, highly legible declarative specification that is much better suited for the end-user than the internal DSL is, allowing us to naturally capture the ensemble concepts as first-class language entities. In addition to ease of use, the explicit grammar provides us with more possibilities compared to a hosted implementation – of course, this comes at the cost of more development effort, as any extra feature must first be implemented. Since the concepts' precise semantics are now captured directly, the language can be much more restrictive, allowing for more powerful compile-time checks and resulting guarantees as to what the user can write without getting a compilation error. At the same time, this restrictiveness enables smarter auto completion, again with more comfort potential for the end-user. Being language independent, the specification can theoretically be compiled into a multitude of languages and platforms, enabling interoperability – though we currently generate Java code and use JVM as the backend. The additional compilation step also enables us to reason about the specification itself and use code generation to support advanced features. Overall, having a focused DSL for specification of the assignment rules provides us with a lot of flexibility and comfort for the end-user, and a clean separation from the operational logic of the system, which can be handled by the TCOOF-ADL implementation.

## 5  Related Work

Commonly, there are two perspectives for dealing with dynamic security – at design-time by analyzing access rights and security policies, and at runtime by using security enforcement. In both perspectives, there are many aspects that can influence security management and thus there are a number of approaches dealing with it.

Regarding design-time, there are approaches based on UML. For example, authors in [8, 9] define UML profiles allowing for expressing security concerns in a designed system. While the profile in [9] targets general systems, the profile in [8] targets SOA and is built over UML extensions for SOA. Both the profiles primarily target secure transfer of objects in a system, nevertheless they do not cope with highly-dynamic systems. The work in [1] combines both design-time and run-time perspectives as it defines its UML profile for security concerns but also defines an aspect-based approach of applying security at runtime. As the previous profiles, the approach does not cope with highly-dynamic systems.

A very close related area is access control and access permission for shared resources. In [16], the authors propose a modeling approach OrBAC (Organization Based Access Control), which allows expressing user permission specifications in dynamically changing environment of a Virtual organization (dynamically shared resources of physical organizations). The approach deals with dynamicity of resources; however, by themselves, the permissions are static with fixed sets of roles, contexts, etc. A similar approach used in [11] for security management in networks where the access control permissions and data flows are described using Role-Based Access Control (RBAC) model. In comparison, our approach allows for modeling beyond-control entities (humans, etc.) in the same way as regular components are modeled and thus we can deal with the uncertainty that is an inherent part of autonomic systems.

To deal with security in autonomic systems, it is necessary to take into consideration the system context. In [13], a survey of current (2009-2015) context-aware middlewares, especially targeting IoT like systems, is presented. The context itself is typically managed by ontology-based models [20]. In general, security (and privacy) issues are targeted only by a minority (three out of eleven) of these middlewares and primarily, only basic security aspects like user identification and authorization have been dealt with. From the security point of view, the most advanced is FlexRFID [6], which uses Role-Based Access Control model (similarly as the approaches discussed above).

In [5], both the context and uncertainty are targeted by adaptive security policies. The approach depends on context-aware role-based access control, which provides dynamicity within given permissions after evaluating the current situation. The uncertainty here is related to security threats and resource access and it is captured by using stochastic models. However, the approach does not deal with communication and interplay among multiple entities.

In [21], a conceptual design that enables building of security mechanisms for mobile self-aware devices is presented. The proposed design contains three sybsystems: (i) meta-level for self-awareness, (ii) extended meta-level for security mechanisms, and (iii) base-level for resources. The meta-level subsystems are responsible for the realization of self-awareness and provide actual security rules for the base-level subsystem. In general, the whole structure is similar to a MAPE-K loop. The whole approach primarily targets only devices like mobile phones and their security aspects like access control and virus/malware detection.

The security management framework dynSMAUG is presented in [12]. The cornerstone of the framework is the concept of a situation, which is described in the form of "when *situation* and *conditions* then *security actions*". Situations are calculated based on processing of series of events in a system. The security policies (authorization decision, obligations,...) in actions are expressed via the XACMLv3 language [18]. The concept of situations has high expressivity and allows for capturing dynamic constraints like time, location, workflows, etc. However, the framework deployment architecture primarily considers sensors-actuators systems only and does not explicitly consider beyond-control entities.

Another approach is described in [14] and it proposes contextual contracts defining privacy and quality-of-context (QoC) agreements. For modeling heterogeneous QoC criteria, the approach relies on QoCIM meta-model [15]. The framework primarily targets privacy in IoT systems and thus considers only producer-consumer-like architectures (in fact in the same manner as the previous framework).

An approach for dynamic policy adaptation is presented in [19]. A policy is understood as a tuple of a label function (partitioning the business space into regions) and a ranking function (provide a quantitative value of the desirability of a state). Thus, the policies can be applied to almost any feature in a system (nevertheless the authors explicitly consider features like security and resource allocation). The approach is based on automated learning of actual policies while human users express the policies in terms of higher level goals. The approach is more on the conceptual side and, as the authors claim, it focuses more on the theoretical part of the problem.

To deal with the uncertainty in trust management, the paper [22] applies fuzzy logic for the definition and evaluation of trust. The actual trust policies are generated from the fuzzy logic based rules. Authors target federate trust management over service-oriented architecture, which considers building trustworthiness cross domains/organizations with adapting to context and requirements. Also, the authors claim that uncertainty cannot be treated as a probability and thus cannot be described by a probability model; however, the claim is not further detailed and explained in the paper.

Regarding the ensembles themselves, there exist several frameworks based on them. Helena [7], JRESP [17] and DEECo [3] are examples of such frameworks. Also, Ab$^a$CuS [2] can be considered here even though it is not strictly an ensemble-based framework however it is built on the same principles. None of these frameworks consider security aspects and/or has been used to deal with security issues.

# 6 Conclusion

In this paper, we have presented an approach to autonomically composable and context-dependent dynamic security rules. These rules follow the dynamicity and context-dependence of the autonomic components a system is composed of. The whole approach is based on autonomic component ensembles, which are groups of components dynamically formed to perform joint goals or coordinate some activity and thus they are an ideal concept to capture dynamic rules.

For specification of the rules, an internal Scala-based DSL has been developed (available at http://github.com/d3scomp/tcoof-security). This DSL primarily allows for fast and rapid prototyping however it might be hard to use for end-users without programming skills. Thus we have developed an end-user oriented external DSL which explicitly captures the concept of ensembles. The main downside of this DSL is its complex and time-consuming development.

The presented approach is not limited to our DSLs only but can be applied in any technology and/or framework that is based on the concept of ensembles.

As an ongoing work, we plan to further extend possibilities of TCOOF-ADL (and also of EDL) to capture more complex security rules. Also, we are applying the approach in projects in which we are participating.

**Acknowledgement.** The work was partially supported by TA ČR project TRUST 4.0 no. TF04000064 and partially supported by Charles University institutional funding SVV 260451.

# References

1. Almorsy, M., Grundy, J., Ibrahim, Amani S.: MDSE@R: model-driven security engineering at runtime. In: Xiang, Y., Lopez, J., Kuo, C.-C.J., Zhou, W. (eds.) CSS 2012. LNCS, vol. 7672, pp. 279–295. Springer, Heidelberg (2012). https://doi.org/10.1007/978-3-642-35362-8_22
2. Abd Alrahman, Y., De Nicola, R., Loreti, M.: Programming of CAS systems by relying on attribute-based communication. In: Margaria, T., Steffen, B. (eds.) ISoLA 2016. LNCS, vol. 9952, pp. 539–553. Springer, Cham (2016). https://doi.org/10.1007/978-3-319-47166-2_38
3. Bures, T., et al.: Software abstractions for component interaction in the internet of things. Computer **49**(12), 50–59 (2016)
4. Bures, T., et al.: Trait-based language for smart cyber-physical systems. Technical report D3S-TR-2017-01, Charles University (2017)
5. Chaisiri, S., Ko, R.K.L.: From reactionary to proactive security: context-aware security policy management and optimization under uncertainty. In: Proceedings of Trustcom/BigDataSE/ISPA 2016, Tianjin, China, pp. 535–543. IEEE (2016)
6. El Khaddar, M.A., et al.: A policy-based middleware for context-aware pervasive computing. Int. J. Pervasive Comput. Commun. **11**(1), 43–68 (2015)

7. Hennicker, R., Klarl, A.: Foundations for ensemble modeling – the HELENA approach. In: Iida, S., Meseguer, J., Ogata, K. (eds.) Specification, Algebra, and Software. LNCS, vol. 8373, pp. 359–381. Springer, Heidelberg (2014). https://doi.org/10.1007/978-3-642-54624-2_18

8. Hoisl, B., et al.: Modeling and enforcing secure object flows in process-driven SOAs: an integrated model-driven approach. Softw. Syst. Model. **13**(2), 513–548 (2014)

9. Jürjens, J.: UMLsec: extending UML for secure systems development. In: Jézéquel, J.-M., Hussmann, H., Cook, S. (eds.) UML 2002. LNCS, vol. 2460, pp. 412–425. Springer, Heidelberg (2002). https://doi.org/10.1007/3-540-45800-X_32

10. Krijt, F. et al.: Intelligent ensembles - a declarative group description language and java framework. In: Proceedings of SEAMS 2017, Buenos Aires, Argentina, pp. 116–122. IEEE (2017)

11. Laborde, R., Barrère, F., Benzekri, A.: A security management information model derivation framework: from goals to configurations. In: Dimitrakos, T., Martinelli, F., Ryan, P.Y.A., Schneider, S. (eds.) FAST 2005. LNCS, vol. 3866, pp. 217–234. Springer, Heidelberg (2006). https://doi.org/10.1007/11679219_16

12. Laborde, R. et al.: dynSMAUG: a dynamic security management framework driven by situations. In: Proceedings of CSNet 2017, Rio de Janeiro, Brazil, pp. 1–8. IEEE (2017)

13. Li, X., et al.: Context aware middleware architectures: survey and challenges. Sensors **15**(8), 20570–20607 (2015)

14. Machara, S. et al.: Trust-based context contract models for the internet of things. In: Proceedings of UIC/ATC 2013, Vietri sul Mere, Italy, pp. 557–562. IEEE (2013)

15. Marie, P., Desprats, T., Chabridon, S., Sibilla, M.: The QoCIM framework: concepts and tools for quality of context management. In: Brézillon, P., Gonzalez, A.J. (eds.) Context in Computing, pp. 155–172. Springer, New York (2014). https://doi.org/10.1007/978-1-4939-1887-4_11

16. Nasser, B., Laborde, R., Benzekri, A., Barrère, F., Kamel, M.: Access control model for inter-organizational grid virtual organizations. In: Meersman, R., Tari, Z., Herrero, P. (eds.) OTM 2005. LNCS, vol. 3762, pp. 537–551. Springer, Heidelberg (2005). https://doi.org/10.1007/11575863_73

17. Nicola, R.D. et al.: A formal approach to autonomic systems programming: the SCEL language. ACM Trans. Auton. Adapt. Syst. **9**(2), 7:1–7:29 (2014)

18. OASIS: eXtensible Access Control Markup Language (XACML) Version 3.0 (2013)

19. Pelaez, A. et al.: Dynamic adaptation of policies using machine learning. In: Proceedings of CCGrid, Cartagena, Colombia, pp. 501–510. IEEE (2016)

20. Mohsin Saleemi, M., Díaz Rodríguez, N., Lilius, J., Porres, I.: A framework for context-aware applications for smart spaces. In: Balandin, S., Koucheryavy, Y., Hu, H. (eds.) NEW2AN/ruSMART-2011. LNCS, vol. 6869, pp. 14–25. Springer, Heidelberg (2011). https://doi.org/10.1007/978-3-642-22875-9_2

21. Thanigaivelan, N.K., Nigussie, E., Virtanen, S., Isoaho, J.: Towards self-aware approach for mobile devices security. In: Rak, J., Bay, J., Kotenko, I., Popyack, L., Skormin, V., Szczypiorski, K. (eds.) MMM-ACNS 2017. LNCS, vol. 10446, pp. 171–182. Springer, Cham (2017). https://doi.org/10.1007/978-3-319-65127-9_14

22. Wu, Z., Weaver, A.C.: Application of fuzzy logic in federated trust management for pervasive computing. In: Proceedings of COMPSAC 2006, Chicago, USA, pp. 215–222. IEEE (2006)

# Differential Equivalence Yields Network Centrality

Stefano Tognazzi[1]([⊠]), Mirco Tribastone[1], Max Tschaikowski[1],
and Andrea Vandin[2]

[1] IMT School for Advanced Studies, Lucca, Italy
stefano.tognazzi@imtlucca.it
[2] DTU Compute Copenhagen, Lyngby, Denmark

**Abstract.** One of the most distinctive features of collective adaptive
systems (CAS) is the presence of many individuals which interact with
each other and with the environment, giving rise to a system-level
behaviour that cannot be analyzed by studying the single agents in isolation. The interaction structure among the individuals of CAS is often
captured by networks where nodes denote individuals and edges interactions. Understanding the interplay between the network topology and the
CAS dynamics calls for tools from network theory in order, for instance,
to identify the most important nodes of a network. Centrality measures
address this task by assigning an importance measure to each node, a
possible example being the famous PageRank algorithm of Google. In
this paper we investigate the relationship between centrality measures
and model reduction techniques, such as lumpability of Markov chains,
which seek to reduce a model into a smaller one that can be processed
more efficiently, while preserving information of interest. In particular,
we focus on the relation between network centrality and backward differential equivalence, a generalization of lumpability to general dynamical
systems. We show that any two backward differential equivalent nodes
enjoy identical centrality measures. By efficiently obtaining substantial
reductions of real-world networks from biochemistry, social sciences and
computer engineering, we demonstrate the applicability of the result.

**Keywords:** Networks · Centrality measures · Model reduction
Efficient algorithms

## 1 Introduction

More and more often we are facing systems consisting of a large number of entities, each with its own status, goals, and dynamics, which interact with each
other (and with the environment) giving rise to an *emergent behaviour*, i.e. the
system-level dynamics, that cannot be directly inferred by studying single individuals in isolation. Systems with such distinctive features are often referred to
as collective adaptive systems (CAS). Given the importance of the interactions

© Springer Nature Switzerland AG 2018
T. Margaria and B. Steffen (Eds.): ISoLA 2018, LNCS 11246, pp. 186–201, 2018.
https://doi.org/10.1007/978-3-030-03424-5_13

in CAS, one possible approach to their analysis consists in conveniently representing the interaction structure in the form of a network, enabling a plethora of analysis techniques widely used in network theory [32].

Examples of networks arise in many real-world applications, with possible examples being collaboration, gene regulation, trust, internet and social networks. Identifying important components and structural properties of networks is crucial, and it has enjoyed substantial interest during the last decades, combining such diverse fields as graph theory, algebra and dynamical systems. Celebrated insights include, but are not limited to, small world phenomena and the concept of scale-free networks. Among many established notions, we focus on centrality measures [32] and exact role assignment [40].

Centrality measures are a common tool to identify nodes with a high impact in a network. Instead, exact role assignment (also known as regular equivalence), has been used since the late seventies [26,40] to formalize the idea "that nodes who occupy the same social position relate in the same ways with other nodes who are themselves in the same positions" [40]. Using the lingo of computer science, regular equivalence corresponds to the classic notion of bisimulation [2,25] and can be therefore computed efficiently by the partition refinement algorithm of Paige and Tarjan [33], whose running time is linear in the numbers of edges and logarithmic in the number of nodes. Surprisingly, it was not before 2003 that this fact has been observed [26], allowing one to avoid the usage of the cubic time algorithm CATREGE from 1993 [26].

The partition refinement algorithm of Paige and Tarjan was also key in the development of efficient model reduction algorithms for quantitative models [20,36]. The main idea behind model reduction is to relate the original dynamical model in a formal way to a reduced dynamical model such that a solution of the reduced model allows one to draw formal conclusions about the solution of the original model. In [16,38], the original algorithm [33] has been extended to efficiently compute the coarsest lumpable partition [7] of a Markov chain. In a similar vein of research, [2] presented an extension to probabilistic bisimulation in the style of Larsen and Skou [25]. The original algorithm [33] has been recently extended to efficiently compute the coarsest differential equivalence [10–12], a model reduction technique for systems of ordinary differential equations (ODEs) that are a natural modeling language for biochemical models [8,17], dependable systems [6,19] and analytical performance models [5,24]. In particular, [9,13,14] introduced a partition refinement algorithm that efficiently computes the largest differential equivalence.

The present work relates centrality measures, model reduction techniques and efficient algorithms. More specifically, by applying differential equivalence to the linear dynamical system that is induced by the adjacency matrix of a graph, we observe that any two differential equivalent nodes enjoy the same eigenvector, Katz and PageRank centrality. The relevance of the result is demonstrated by efficiently computing substantial reductions (that yields coarse quotient partitions with large blocks) of published real-world networks, including protein interaction networks, scientific collaboration networks, routing networks, email networks and networks capturing YouTube.

**Paper Outline.** Section 2 reviews the background material, while Sect. 3 relates backward differential equivalence to centrality measures. Section 4, instead, features an extensive experimental evaluation on real-world networks. Section 5 concludes the paper.

## 2    Background

*Notation.* Let $\mathcal{V}$ be a finite index set and let $\mathbb{R}^{\mathcal{V}}$ denote the set of functions from $\mathcal{V}$ to $\mathbb{R}$. Elements of $\mathbb{R}^{\mathcal{V}}$ and $\mathbb{R}^{\mathcal{V} \times \mathcal{V}}$ are called vectors and matrices, respectively. The set of variables is denoted by $\{x_i \mid i \in \mathcal{V}\}$. A partition of $\mathcal{V}$ is denoted by $\mathcal{H}$, its blocks by $H$. Partition $\mathcal{H}'$ refines partition $\mathcal{H}$ if for every $H' \in \mathcal{H}'$ there exists some $H \in \mathcal{H}$ such that $H' \subseteq H$.

### 2.1    Centrality Measures

Given a directed graph $G = (\mathcal{V}, E)$, the adjacency matrix $A \in \mathbb{R}^{\mathcal{V} \times \mathcal{V}}$ is obtained by setting $A_{i,j} = 1$ if $(i,j) \in E$ and $A_{i,j} = 0$ if $(i,j) \notin E$. Note that we can cover undirected graphs by ensuring that $(i,j) \in E$ if and only if $(j,i) \in E$. Our discussion on centrality measures follows standard literature, see for instance [32].

*Eigenvector Centrality.* For each node $i \in \mathcal{V}$, the corresponding eigenvector centrality $x_i^*$ is defined as the average of eigenvector centralities of all nodes reachable from $i$, i.e., $x_i^* = \frac{1}{\lambda} \sum_{j \in \mathcal{V}} A_{i,j} x_j$, where $\frac{1}{\lambda}$ is some positive constant. More formally, one requires the following.

**Definition 1.** *The centrality measure of an adjacency matrix $A$ is well-defined if there exists a unique $\lambda^* > 0$ and a unique non-negative $x^* \in \mathbb{R}^{\mathcal{V}}$ such that $Ax^* = \lambda^* x^*$ and $\|x^*\| = 1$.*

The centrality eigenvector is often computed by the power iteration method, introduced next.

**Definition 2.** *Fix a graph $G = (\mathcal{V}, E)$ and let $A \in \mathbb{R}^{\mathcal{V} \times \mathcal{V}}$ denote the underlying adjacency matrix. Then, given some nonzero vector $x^0 \in \mathbb{R}^{\mathcal{V}}$, the power iteration sequence $(x^k)_k$ is given by $x^{k+1} = Ax^k / \|x^k\|$ for all $k \geq 0$.*

The power iteration method is known to converge under the following common assumption.

**(H)** Assume that $A$ has a unique largest eigenvalue $\lambda^*$ that has a unique non-negative eigenvector $x^*$ with $\|x^*\| = 1$.

Armed with **(H)**, the following can be proven if $x^0 = \mathbb{1}$, where $\mathbb{1}_i := 1$ for all $i \in \mathcal{V}$.

**Theorem 1.** *Under the assumption of (H), the centrality eigenvector is well-defined and the power iteration sequence $(x^k)_k$ converges, as $k \to \infty$, to the centrality eigenvector when $x_i^0 = \mathbb{1}$.*

*Proof.* Thanks to **(H)**, the power iteration method is known to converge to $x^*$ whenever $\langle x^*, x^0 \rangle \neq 0$, see [18]. Since $x^*$ is a non-negative eigenvector, we can pick $i^* \in H^*$ such that $x_{i^*}^* > 0$. With this, it holds that $\langle x^*, x^0 \rangle = \sum_i x_i^* \geq x_{i^*}^* > 0$ because $x^*$ is non-negative.

*Katz Centrality.* Eigenvector centrality may not be well-defined. Katz centrality addresses this problem by adding a predefined value $\beta > 0$ to each centrality. More formally, Katz centrality is given by $x_i^* = \alpha \sum_{j \in \mathcal{V}} A_{i,j} x_j + \beta$, where $\alpha > 0$ is some constant. Ultimately, this can be rewritten to $x^* = (I - \alpha A)^{-1} \mathbb{1}$, where $\beta$ can be set to 1 without loss of generality.

Similarly to eigenvector centrality, Katz centrality is not obtained by solving the linear system $x^* = (I - \alpha A)^{-1} \mathbb{1}$ directly. Instead, the following iterative computation is used.

**Theorem 2.** *Assume that $\|\alpha A\| < 1$. Moreover, set $x^0 := \mathbb{1}$ and $x^{k+1} := \alpha A x^k + \mathbb{1}$ for all $k \geq 0$. Then, $(x^k)_k$ converges to the Katz centrality as $k \to \infty$.*

*PageRank Centrality.* A potential disadvantage of Katz centrality and eigenvector centrality is that nodes with high centrality propagate their authority to their peers. PageRank centrality accounts for this fact by dividing the propagated centrality by the number of outgoing edges of a node. More formally, the PageRank centrality is given by $x_i^* = \alpha \sum_{j \in \mathcal{V}} A_{i,j} \frac{x_j}{d_j} + \beta$, where $d_j$ denotes the degree of node $j \in \mathcal{V}$. By removing nodes which have no outgoing edges, we may assume without loss of generality that $d_j \geq 1$ for all $j \in \mathcal{V}$. With this, it holds that $x^* = (I - \alpha D^{-1} A)^{-1} \mathbb{1}$, where $D$ is the degree matrix, i.e., $D_{i,j} = d_i$ if $i = j$ and $D_{i,j} = 0$ otherwise.

The following holds true.

**Theorem 3.** *Define $x^0 := \mathbb{1}$ and $x^{k+1} := \alpha D^{-1} A x^k + \mathbb{1}$ for all $k \geq 0$ and some $0 < \alpha < 1$. Then, $(x^k)_k$ converges to the Pagerank centrality as $k \to \infty$.*

It is known that $D^{-1} A$ defines a discrete-time Markov chain with $\|D^{-1} A\|_\infty = 1$. The coefficient $\alpha$ is commonly known as damping factor and is usually set to 0.85.

## 2.2    Backward Differential Equivalence

We next provide a brief introduction to backward differential equivalence (BDE), a model reduction technique for dynamical systems [9,14]. For the benefit of presentation we restrict ourselves to linear dynamical systems in discrete time, even though the actual theory is stated for nonlinear continuous time dynamical systems.

**Definition 3.** *Fix the discrete time system $x^{k+1} = Ax^k$ with initial condition $x(0)$ and a partition $\mathcal{H}$ of the index set $\mathcal{V}$.*

- *Let $\mathcal{U}_\mathcal{H} \subseteq \mathbb{R}^\mathcal{V}$ be the linear subspace of vectors that are uniform on $\mathcal{H}$, that is, $\mathcal{U}_\mathcal{H} = \{x \in \mathbb{R}^\mathcal{V} \mid x_i = x_j, H \in \mathcal{H}, i, j \in H\}$.*
- *A partition $\mathcal{H}$ is BDE if $\mathcal{U}_\mathcal{H}$ is an invariant space of $A$, i.e., if $A(\mathcal{U}_\mathcal{H}) \subseteq \mathcal{U}_\mathcal{H}$.*

*Example 1.* Let us consider the dynamical system $x^{k+1} = Ax^k$ given by

$$\begin{aligned}
x_1^{k+1} &= 0.5x_2^k + 0.5x_3^k \\
x_2^{k+1} &= 0.5x_2^k + 0.5x_1^k \\
x_3^{k+1} &= 0.5x_3^k + 0.5x_1^k
\end{aligned} \tag{1}$$

The matrix underlying the above dynamical system is given by $A = ((0.0, 0.5, 0.5), (0.5, 0.5, 0.0), (0.5, 0.0, 0.5))^T$, where $^T$ denotes the transpose of a vector. It is not hard to see that $\mathcal{H} = \{\{1\}, \{2, 3\}\}$ is a BDE of $x^{k+1} = Ax^k$. ◊

We next present BDE reduction in the context of linear dynamical systems.

**Definition 4.** *Assume that $\mathcal{H} = \{H_1, \ldots, H_m\}$ is a BDE partition of the dynamical system $x^{k+1} = Ax^k$.*

- *For any $H \in \mathcal{H}$, fix some representative $i_H \in H$ of $H$ and let $\hat{\mathcal{V}} = \{i_H \mid H \in \mathcal{H}\}$ denotes the set of representatives underlying $\mathcal{H}$.*
- *For any set $I \subseteq \mathcal{V}$, let $\mathbb{1}_I \in \mathbb{R}^\mathcal{V}$ be such that $\mathbb{1}_I(i) = 1$ if $i \in I$ and $\mathbb{1}_I(i) = 0$ otherwise.*
- *The reduced dynamical system $\hat{x}^{k+1} = \hat{A}\hat{x}^k$ with $\hat{x} \in \mathbb{R}^{\hat{\mathcal{V}}}$ arises from $A$ in two steps. First, eliminate the equations of non-representative variables. Afterwards, replace any $x_j$ by its representative, i.e., replace any $x_j$ with $\hat{x}_{i_H}$ when $j \in H$ and $H \in \mathcal{H}$. In matrix language, this corresponds to $\hat{A} = (\mathbb{1}_{\{i_{H_1}\}}, \ldots, \mathbb{1}_{\{i_{H_m}\}})^T \cdot A \cdot (\mathbb{1}_{H_1}, \ldots, \mathbb{1}_{H_m})$.*

*Example 2.* Let us reduce (1) in the case when $i_{H_1} = 1$ and $i_{H_2} = 2$. We first remove the equation of $x_3$ because $H_2 = \{2, 3\}$. Afterwards, we replace any $x_1$ with $\hat{x}_1$, any $x_2$ with $\hat{x}_2$ and any $x_3$ with $\hat{x}_2$. From this we obtain $\hat{x}_1^{k+1} = \hat{x}_2$ and $\hat{x}_2^{k+1} = 0.5\hat{x}_1 + 0.5\hat{x}_2$. It is not hard to see that this corresponds to $\hat{x}^{k+1} = \hat{A}\hat{x}^k$ when $\hat{A}$ is computed using the algebraic expression from Definition 4:

$$\hat{A} = \begin{pmatrix} 1 & 0 & 0 \\ 0 & 1 & 0 \end{pmatrix} \begin{pmatrix} 0.0 & 0.5 & 0.5 \\ 0.5 & 0.5 & 0.0 \\ 0.5 & 0.0 & 0.5 \end{pmatrix} \begin{pmatrix} 1 & 0 \\ 0 & 1 \\ 0 & 1 \end{pmatrix} = \begin{pmatrix} 0.0 & 1.0 \\ 0.5 & 0.5 \end{pmatrix}$$

◊

The relation between the original and the reduced dynamical system is as follows [12].

**Theorem 4.** *The following holds true.*

- *A partition $\mathcal{H}$ is a BDE of $x^{k+1} = Ax^k$ if and only if $x^0 \in \mathcal{U}_\mathcal{H}$ implies $x^k \in \mathcal{U}_\mathcal{H}$ for all $k \geq 0$.*
- *Let $\mathcal{H}$ be a BDE of $x^{k+1} = Ax^k$. Then, if $\hat{x}^0_{i_H} = x^0_{i_H}$ for all $H \in \mathcal{H}$ and $\hat{x}$ denotes the solution of the BDE reduction $\hat{x}^{k+1} = \hat{A}\hat{x}^k$ subject to $\hat{x}^0$, it holds that $\hat{x}^k_{i_H} = x^k_{i_H}$ for all $k \geq 0$ and $H \in \mathcal{H}$.*

Theorem 4 ensures that the original dynamical solution can be obtained by solving the reduced dynamical system whenever the initial condition $x^0$ is uniform on $\mathcal{H}$, i.e., when $x^0 \in \mathcal{U}_\mathcal{H}$.

*Proof.* See [9,37, Theorem 3].

*Example 3.* If $x^0 = (0.2, 0.4, 0.4)$, then the solution of (1) satisfies $x^k_2 = x^k_3$ for all $k \geq 0$. Moreover, if $\hat{x}^0_1 = 0.2$, $\hat{x}^0_2 = 0.4$, $\hat{x}^{k+1}_1 = \hat{x}^k_2$ and $\hat{x}^{k+1}_2 = 0.5\hat{x}^k_1 + 0.5\hat{x}^k_2$, it holds that $\hat{x}^k_1 = x^k_1$ and $\hat{x}^k_2 = x^k_2 = x^k_3$ for all $k \geq 0$. ◇

The following result ensures that there exists a unique coarsest BDE partition $\mathcal{H}$ that yields the best possible reduction.

**Proposition 1.** *For a given dynamical system $x^{k+1} = Ax^k$, there exists a coarsest BDE partition $\mathcal{H}$. That is, for any BDE partition $\mathcal{H}'$ of $x^{k+1} = Ax^k$, it holds that $\mathcal{H}'$ refines $\mathcal{H}$.*

*Proof.* See [9, Theorem 3].

The coarsest BDE partition can be computed efficiently [9,14] as stated next.

**Theorem 5.** *There exists a partition refinement algorithm that needs $\mathcal{O}(|A| \cdot \log(|\mathcal{V}|))$ steps to compute the coarsest BDE partition of $x^{k+1} = Ax^k$, where $A \in \mathbb{R}^{\mathcal{V} \times \mathcal{V}}$ and $|A|$ denotes the number of non-zero entries in $A$.*

*Proof.* See [9, Theorem 3].

*Remark 1.* The section discusses BDE in the context of linear dynamical systems. We wish to point out, however, that [12] captures nonlinear dynamical systems of the form $x^{k+1} = F(x^k)$. In particular, the partition refinement algorithm from [14] generalizes to the case when $F$ is given in terms of multi-variate polynomials and enjoys a polynomial time and space complexity in the number of monomials present in $F$.

## 2.3 Stochastic Lumpability

We next provide an account on lumpability of Markov chains [7] and relate it to BDE.

**Definition 5.** *Given a set of nodes $\mathcal{V}$, we define the following.*

- *A transition matrix $P \in \mathbb{R}^{\mathcal{V} \times \mathcal{V}}$ satisfies $p_{i,j} \geq 0$ and $\sum_k p_{i,k} = 1$ for all $i, j \in \mathcal{V}$.*
- *For an initial probability distribution $\pi^0$ on $\mathcal{V}$, the transient probabilities of the discrete time Markov chain (DTMC) induced by $P$ are given by $(\pi^{k+1})^T = (\pi^k)^T P$.*
- *A partition $\mathcal{H}$ is an exactly lumpable partition of $P$ when, for all $k > 0$, $\pi^k \in \mathcal{U}_{\mathcal{H}}$ for all initial probability distributions $\pi^0 \in \mathcal{U}_{\mathcal{H}}$ and $t \geq 0$.*

The entry $p_{i,j}$ corresponds to the transition probability from state $i$ into state $j$. The original matrix from Example 2 is an example of a transition matrix.

The next result is well-known in the area of Markov chains [7].

**Theorem 6.** *A partition $\mathcal{H}$ is an exactly lumpable partition of a transition matrix $P$ if and only if, for any $H, H' \in \mathcal{H}$ and $i, j \in H$ it holds that $\sum_{k \in H'} P_{k,i} = \sum_{k \in H'} P_{k,j}$.*

Theorem 6 states essentially that $\mathcal{H}$ is an exactly lumpable partition whenever the cumulative transition probabilities from block $H'$ into any two nodes of block $H$ coincide.

Similarly to BDE, it is possible to define a reduced transition matrix $\hat{P}$ which underlies an exactly lumpable partition $\mathcal{H}$ of $P$.

**Theorem 7.** *For an exactly lumpable partition $\mathcal{H}$ of $P$, set $\hat{P}_{i_H, i_{H'}} := \sum_{k \in H} P_{k, i_{H'}}$ for all $H, H' \in \mathcal{H}$. Then, $\hat{P}$ defines a lumped DTMC with states $\{i_H \mid H \in \mathcal{H}\}$ whose transient probabilities $\hat{\pi}$ satisfy $\hat{\pi}^k_{i_H} = \pi^k_{i_H}$ for all $H \in \mathcal{H}$ and $k \geq 0$ if the initial probability distribution obeys $\pi^0 \in \mathcal{U}_{\mathcal{H}}$.*

It can be proven that BDE coincides with exact lumpability on the domain of DTMCs.

**Theorem 8.** *Let $P$ be a transition matrix and $\mathcal{H}$ a partition of $\mathcal{V}$. Then, $\mathcal{H}$ is an exactly lumpable partition of $P$ if and only if $\mathcal{H}$ is a BDE of $P^T$.*

*Proof.* In [12] it has been shown that this is true for continuous time Markov chains (CTMCs). Any CTMC can be turned into a DTMC (and vice versa) while preserving many important properties, including lumpability [7]. This shows the statement.

*Remark 2.* The transpose in Theorem 8 is due to the fact that probabilities are commonly denoted as row vectors instead of column vectors. Because of this, the dynamical system of $\pi$ is given by $(\pi^{k+1})^T = (\pi^k)^T P$, while that of $x$ is given by $x^{k+1} = A x^k$.

There are established algorithms for the efficient computation of the coarsest exactly lumpable partition of a Markov chain [16,38]. In fact, the partition refinement algorithm from [9,14] can be seen as an extension of [16,38] to general dynamical systems. While the specialized algorithm [16,22] has been reported to outperform the more general algorithm [9], the complexity bounds of both algorithms coincide for Markov chains [9].

## 2.4   Exact Role Assignment

We start by giving the definition of exact role assignment [26,40].

**Definition 6.** *Given a symmetric adjacency matrix $A \in \{0,1\}^{\mathcal{V} \times \mathcal{V}}$ and $i \in \mathcal{V}$, let $N^+(i)$ denote the out-neighbors of $i$, that is $N^+(i) := \{j \in \mathcal{V} \mid (i,j) \in A\}$. A surjective mapping $r : \mathcal{V} \to \hat{\mathcal{V}}$ with $\hat{\mathcal{V}} \subseteq \mathcal{V}$ is an exact role assignment if, for all $i, j \in \mathcal{V}$, $r(i) = r(j)$ implies $r(N^+(i)) = r(N^+(j))$.*

The following result allows one to express exact role assignment as a bisimulation.

**Theorem 9.** *Given a symmetric adjacency matrix $A \in \{0,1\}^{\mathcal{V} \times \mathcal{V}}$ and a partition $\mathcal{H}$ of $\mathcal{V}$, set $r(i) = i_H$ when $i \in H$ for $H \in \mathcal{H}$.*

- *$r$ is an exact role assignment if and only if for all $H, H' \in \mathcal{H}$ and $i, j \in H$, it holds that $\sum_{k \in H'} A_{i,k} = \sum_{k \in H'} A_{j,k}$.*
- *It holds that $\sum_{k \in H'} A_{i,k} = \sum_{k \in H'} A_{j,k}$ if and only if $\sum_{k \in H'} A_{k,i} = \sum_{k \in H'} A_{k,j}$ is valid.*

*Remark 3.* The sum criterion of the exact role assignment resembles the exact lumpability from Theorem 6 because $P = A^T$, see Theorem 8 and Remark 2. Note, however, that $A$ is not a stochastic matrix, as required by exact lumpability.

## 3   Centrality and Model Reduction

Clustering techniques such as minimal cut [1], normalized cut [35] or $k$-means [39] clustering have been studied substantially in the past. In [30] normalized cut has been related to the eigenvector corresponding to the second largest eigenvalue of the transition matrix $P$ of the normalized Laplace matrix.

The following results shows that BDE is a natural generalization of exact role assignment (and exact lumpability, as has been already observed in [12]).

**Theorem 10.** *Let $A \in \mathbb{R}^{\mathcal{V} \times \mathcal{V}}$ (in particular, $A$ may have negative entries) and $\mathcal{H}$ a partition of $\mathcal{V}$.*

- (i) *$\mathcal{H}$ is a BDE of $x^{k+1} = Ax^k$ if and only if, for all $H, H' \in \mathcal{H}$ and $i, j \in H$, it holds that $\sum_{k \in H'} A_{i,k} = \sum_{k \in H'} A_{j,k}$.*
- (ii) *In the case when $A$ is an adjacency matrix of an undirected graph, $\mathcal{H}$ is a BDE of $x^{k+1} = Ax^k$ if and only if, for all $H, H' \in \mathcal{H}$ and $i, j \in H$, it holds that $\sum_{k \in H'} A_{i,k} = \sum_{k \in H'} A_{j,k}$ and $\sum_{k \in H'} A_{k,i} = \sum_{k \in H'} A_{k,j}$.*
- (iii) *In the case when $A$ is an adjacency matrix of an undirected graph, $\mathcal{H}$ is a BDE of $x^{k+1} = Ax^k$ if and only if $\mathcal{H}$ is an exact role assignment.*

*Proof.* Since $\mathcal{H}$ is a BDE of $A$, it holds that $A \cdot \mathbb{1}_{H'} \in \mathcal{U}_{\mathcal{H}}$ which in turn implies $\mathbb{1}_{\{i\}} \cdot A \cdot \mathbb{1}_{H'} = \mathbb{1}_{\{j\}} \cdot A \cdot \mathbb{1}_{H'}$. This yields the first claim. The second claim follows trivially thanks to $A = A^T$. The third claim is a direct consequence of Theorem 9

Additionally to the graph theoretical characterization of BDE from Theorem 10, we next show that any two nodes of a BDE block enjoy identical Katz, pagerank and eigenvector centrality.

**Definition 7.** *Fix a non-negative matrix $A$ and assume that the diagonal of the degree matrix $D$, given by $d_{ii} = \sum_{j \neq i} A_{i,j}$, is positive.*

- *Let $\mathcal{H}$ be a BDE of $x^{k+1} = Ax^k$ and let $\hat{A}$ denote the corresponding BDE reduction. Then, the reduced power iteration sequence $(\hat{x}^k)_k$ is given by $\hat{x}^0 := \hat{\mathbb{1}}$ and $\hat{x}^{k+1} = \hat{A}\hat{x}^k$ for all $k \geq 0$, where $\hat{\mathbb{1}}_{i_H} = 1$ for all $H \in \mathcal{H}$.*
- *Let $\mathcal{H}$ be a BDE of $x^{k+1} = Ax^k$ and let $\hat{A}$ denote the corresponding BDE reduction. Then, for any $0 < \alpha < \|A\|$, the reduced Katz sequence is given by $\hat{x}^0 := \hat{\mathbb{1}}$ and $\hat{x}^{k+1} := \alpha\hat{A}\hat{x}^k + \hat{\mathbb{1}}$ for all $k \geq 0$.*
- *Let $\mathcal{H}$ be a BDE of $x^{k+1} = D^{-1}Ax^k$ and let $\hat{A}$ denote the corresponding BDE reduction. Then, for any $0 < \alpha < 1$, the reduced Pagerank sequence is given by $\hat{x}^0 := \hat{\mathbb{1}}$ and $\hat{x}^{k+1} := \alpha\hat{A}\hat{x}^k + \hat{\mathbb{1}}$ for all $k \geq 0$.*

Similarly to the case of ODE systems, the original sequences can be obtained from the reduced ones.

**Theorem 11.** *Fix a non-negative matrix $A$, assume that the diagonal of the degree matrix $D$ is positive and let $\mathcal{H}$ be a BDE of $x^{k+1} = Ax^k$.*

(i) *$\mathcal{H}$ is also a BDE of $x^{k+1} = D^{-1}Ax^k$, where $D$ denotes the degree matrix of $A$.*

(ii) *For any centrality measure from Definition 7, $x^* \in \mathcal{U}_{\mathcal{H}}$ and the corresponding reduced sequence $(\hat{x}^k)_k$ converges to $\hat{x}^* \in \mathbb{R}^{\hat{\mathcal{V}}}$, where $\hat{x}^*_{i_H} = x^*_{i_H}$ for all $H \in \mathcal{H}$ (in the case of eigenvector centrality, we additionally require **(H)**).*

*Proof.* Note that Theorem 10 implies $\sum_{k \in H'} A_{i,k} = \sum_{k \in H'} A_{j,k}$ for all $H, H' \in \mathcal{H}$ and $i, j \in H$. This yields $d_i = \sum_{H' \in \mathcal{H}} \sum_{k \in H'} A_{i,k} = \sum_{H' \in \mathcal{H}} \sum_{k \in H'} A_{j,k} = d_j$. With this, we infer that $\mathcal{H}$ is a BDE of $x^{k+1} = D^{-1}Ax^k$. In the following we prove the statements concerning reduced sequences. Eigenvector centrality: The fact that $\mathcal{H}$ is a BDE of $x^{k+1} = Ax^k$ ensures that $A(\mathcal{U}_{\mathcal{H}}) \subseteq \mathcal{U}_{\mathcal{H}}$. Hence, the power iteration sequence remains in $\mathcal{U}_{\mathcal{H}}$ and the statement follows from Theorem 1. Katz centrality: Similarly to eigenvector centrality, we know that $A(\mathcal{U}_{\mathcal{H}}) \subseteq \mathcal{U}_{\mathcal{H}}$. Since $\mathbb{1} \in \mathcal{U}_{\mathcal{H}}$, we obtain $x^{k+1} = \alpha Ax^k + \mathbb{1} \in \mathcal{U}_{\mathcal{H}}$ whenever $x^k \in \mathcal{U}_{\mathcal{H}}$ and Theorem 2 yields the claim. Pagerank centrality: Since $\mathcal{H}$ is a BDE of $x^{k+1} = D^{-1}Ax^k$, we conclude that $D^{-1}A(\mathcal{U}_{\mathcal{H}}) \subseteq \mathcal{U}_{\mathcal{H}}$. Arguing as in the case of Katz centrality and invoking Theorem 3 instead of Theorem 2, we obtain the claim.

Theorem 11 states that members of the same group have the same centrality measure regardless whether Katz, pagerank or eigenvector centrality is used. The computation of the centrality measures via the reduced sequence is outlined in Algorithm 1. Note also that (i) implies that the coarsest BDE $\mathcal{H}$ of $A$ is the coarsest (ordinarily) lumpable partition of the transition matrix $D^{-1}A$, see [7].

**Require:** Non-negative matrix $A$, numerical threshold $\delta > 0$.
   **procedure** COMPUTECENTRALITYVIAREDSEQUENCE($A$)
      $\eta \leftarrow \infty$
      $\hat{x}^{\text{old}} \leftarrow \hat{\mathbb{1}}$
      $\hat{A} \leftarrow ComputeCoarsestReduction(A)$                               ▷ See Theorem 5
      **while** $\eta \geq \delta$ **do**
         $\hat{x} \leftarrow ComputeNextSequenceElement(\hat{A}, \hat{x}^{\text{old}})$
         $\eta \leftarrow \|\hat{x} - \hat{x}^{\text{old}}\|$
         $\hat{x}^{\text{old}} \leftarrow \hat{x}$
      **end while**
      $x^* \leftarrow Expand(\hat{x})$                        ▷ $x_i^* := \hat{x}_{i_H}^*$ for all $H \in \mathcal{H}, i \in H$
      **return** $x^*$
   **end procedure**

**Fig. 1.** Centrality computation via reduced sequence.

Hence, it is in principle possible to apply the specialized partition refinement algorithms for Markov chains [16,22,38] instead of the one for general dynamical systems [9]. We wish to stress, however, that the proof of this fact requires the notion of BDE and Theorem 11.

Theorem 11 yields the following.

**Corollary 1.** *Exact role assignment yields Katz, pagerank and eigenvector centrality.*

As pointed out earlier, eigenvectors of adjacency matrices are crucial for clustering. The eigenvectors of the BDE reduction $\hat{A}$ will provide only a proper subset of all eigenvectors in general. In particular, it is not clear how to check whether the subset contains the $k$ largest eigenvector without considering the original matrix.

We wish to stress the following.

*Remark 4.* While it is known that exact role assignment preserves certain algebraic properties such as eigenvalues [26], we are not aware of any result that would establish that exact role assignment preserves Katz, pagerank and eigenvector centrality.

## 4 Experimental Results

In this section we present the results of our experimental evaluation on some real world case studies [15,29]. We measure the performance of our approach in terms of model reduction ratio.

*Implementation and Environment.* The input is the adjacency matrix $A$ of a graph $G = (\mathcal{V}, E)$. In Theorem 5 an efficient algorithm is presented to compute the coarsest BDE, such algorithm is implemented in the tool ERODE (Evaluation and Reduction of ODEs) [13]. The experimental evaluation hereby presented has been performed using a Matlab prototype linked to ERODE which was used to compute the reduced models. We present results on *directed* and *undirected* graphs. All the experiments ran on a machine with an Intel Xeon E7-4830v4, with a 64-bits architecture at 2 GHz, 14 cores, 112 CPUs and 500 GB of RAM.

*The Instances.* In order to provide some real-world case studies we ran our proposed reduction technique on some networks obtained from the SNAP (Stanford Large Network Dataset Collection) and the Florida Sparse Matrix collection repositories.

We first present the *undirected graphs* instances:

- *GD06-Theory*: this is a hierarchical network with 3 levels, proposed in a graph design contest as an "artificially symmetric" one. The main node is connected to 9 children nodes, each of which is connected to 9 children nodes. With this design there are exactly 3 classes if we partition with respect to the centrality measures, because all of the grandchildren will have the same score (the lowest). Intuitively, this shows that a natural interpretation of the blocks is obtained from our proposed methodology. We remark that, although it is hard to find real-world examples which are *exactly* symmetric like this particular instance, Table 2 shows that we achieve good reductions on real-world networks.
- *Yeast protein interaction network*: this network was developed by Barabasi et al. [21] in order to study the interaction between proteins in yeast.
- *Collaboration networks*: we have four different collaboration networks that belong in this category. In our results we present a collaboration network in the field of general relativity research from Arxiv [28], the Erdős collaboration network [4] and two different co-authorship networks from Citeseer. It has been shown in [3,34] that this type of collaboration networks obtained from real-world problems tend to have an hierarchical structure; this confirms that we obtain good reductions with our notion of reduction on hierarchical networks.
- *Autonomous Systems*: these networks are obtained from routing networks, these networks reduce well and include one autonomous system from the SNAP repository which contains 733 different daily snapshots of the same graph [27]. In Table 2 we present only one of those instances as they have a similar rate of reduction to one another. This is expected as this graph is a stable network (i.e., there is no drastic change in the network from one day to another). This same concept applies to the Oregon routing network instance.
- *Enron email network*: this is a classic benchmark of a network obtained by tracking the email interactions between the members of the Enron Corporation [23].
- *YouTube*: this is a network of interactions between YouTube channels [31].

The aforementioned case studies are the subset of the datasets on which our technique proved to be the most efficient on in terms of reduction. We present the results with respect to the reduction ratio. The reduction ratio is defined as the ratio of the size of the reduced model and the size of the original model. The

**Table 1.** Case studies results

| Undirected Graphs | | | |
|---|---|---|---|
| *Instance* | Original size | Reduced size | Reduction ratio |
| GD06-Theory | 102 | 3 | 2.94% |
| Yeast protein interaction network | 1871 | 1091 | 58.31% |
| Collaborations in General Relativity | 5243 | 3394 | 64.73% |
| Erdős collaboration network | 5535 | 1902 | 34.36% |
| Autonomous system (SNAP) | 6475 | 3691 | 57.00% |
| Oregon routing network | 10671 | 5484 | 51.39% |
| Autonomous system (Florida) | 22964 | 11935 | 51.97% |
| Enron email network | 36693 | 20418 | 55.65% |
| Dictionary | 39328 | 26994 | 68.64% |
| Caida routers | 192245 | 150463 | 78.27% |
| Citeseer coauthorship network | 227321 | 155593 | 68.45% |
| Citeseer copaper network | 434103 | 150316 | 34.63% |
| YouTube | 1134891 | 684011 | 60.27% |

results are presented in Table 2. Each row represents an instance from the list presented in the last paragraph. We show its original size, its reduced size and the reduction ratio.

We obtain considerable reductions for networks of different sizes. We wish to stress again that the reduction is *exact*, meaning that two nodes are in the same block if and only if they exactly have the same eigenvector centrality score. This is the reason behind the fact that the best reduction is obtained from the instance *GD-06*: as explained earlier, this instance was built artificially and its property of having a symmetric defined three-level hierarchical structure induces a partition which is composed by three blocks, one per level. In real world networks it is rare that two or more nodes share exactly the same centrality score because of the fact that real world networks do not have a particularly symmetrical hierarchical structure due to the inhomogeneous nature of interactions between peers. Despite of this, we are able to produce good reductions, particularly in networks that arise from academic collaborations. The intuitive reason is that these types of collaboration tend to have a more regular and symmetric hierarchical structure; therefore the chances of two nodes having exactly the same eigenvector centrality scores are higher.

**Table 2.** Case studies results

Directed Graphs

| Instance | Original size | Reduced size | Reduction ratio |
|---|---|---|---|
| Glossary | 73 | 41 | 56.16% |
| Graph Design '96 | 112 | 6 | 5.36% |
| PhDs in computer science | 1883 | 225 | 11.95% |
| Kohonen citation network | 4471 | 766 | 17.13% |
| EPA web pages | 4733 | 598 | 12.63% |
| Gnutella p2p network | 6302 | 2208 | 35.04% |
| Wikipedia who-votes-on-whom | 8299 | 4216 | 50.80% |
| EVA corporate inter-relationships | 8498 | 215 | 2.53% |
| California web search | 9665 | 1817 | 18.80% |
| Stanford CS web | 9915 | 3657 | 36.88% |
| Gnutella p2p network (I) | 10880 | 4340 | 39.89% |
| Gnutella p2p network (II) | 26519 | 6741 | 25.42% |
| Enron email traffic | 69245 | 7437 | 10.74% |
| Epinions trust network | 75889 | 41055 | 54.10% |
| Slashdot social network | 82169 | 57561 | 70.05% |
| Stanford web graph | 281905 | 129335 | 45.88% |
| CNR web crawl | 325558 | 85419 | 26.24% |
| Notre Dame web graph | 325730 | 49952 | 15.34% |
| Berkely.edu + stanford.edu web | 685252 | 292492 | 42.68% |
| Flickr web crawl | 820879 | 370145 | 45.09% |
| .eu domain web crawl | 862665 | 341687 | 39.60% |
| Google web graph | 916429 | 354624 | 38.70% |
| .in domain web crawl | 1382909 | 333283 | 24.10% |
| Wikipedia pages | 1634990 | 1116472 | 68.29% |

Similarly, we provide a set of *directed graphs* case studies:

- *Academic instances*: *PhD in Computer Science* and *Kohonen citation network* arise from academic real-world examples. The first instance describes a network where an edge from node $i$ to node $j$ means that $i$ is a PhD student of $j$ while the latter describes a network of citations.
- *Web infrastructures*: different instances of web infrastructure are presented. *EPA web pages, Gnutella p2p network, Stanford Computer Science, Stanford web graph, CNR web, Notre Dame web, Berkley and Stanford domains, European domain web, Google web, Indian domain web, Flickr web* and *Wikipedia* all fall in this category. The main underlying theme of all these instances is that are generated from world wide web problems. Nodes represent web pages while directed edges from one node to another are hyperlinks. Some instances

appear more than once in Table 2 (for example, Gnutella p2p network appears multiple times), as we present the results on the same network infrastructure on different days. Differently from the undirected instances, these directed instances are not stable and they present differences in size and structure on different days.

- *Enron*: differently from the instance provided in its undirected version, here we link together two nodes with the meaning of $i$ has sent a mail to $j$.
- *Social Networks*: we present some benchmarks on trust networks and social networks. Such instances are the following: *Wikipedia who-votes-on-whom*, *Epinions trust network* and *Slashdot social network*. The first is a network in which an edge has a source node $i$ and a target node $j$ if $i$ voted for $j$. The *Epinions trust network* describes the relationship between users of epinions.com. This social network is a general consumer review website where members can decide whether to *trust* the reviews of other members. The trust relationships form the web of trust which is then combined with review ratings to determine which reviews are shown to a user. Last, slashdot.org is a technology-related news website that features user-submitted and editor-evaluated news. In 2002 Slashdot introduced the Slashdot Zoo which allowed users to tag each other as friend or foes. The presented instance captures those relationships obtained in February 2009.

## 5 Conclusions and Future Work

In this paper we have related network centrality to differential equivalence, a model reduction technique that generalizes stochastic lumpability. We have shown that differential equivalence coincides with the exact role assignment on undirected graphs and that differential equivalent nodes have the same Katz, pagerank and eigenvector centrality. The relevance of the result was demonstrated by efficiently computing substantial reductions of published real-world networks, including protein interaction networks, scientific collaboration networks, routing networks, email networks and networks capturing YouTube.

Future work will focus on the development of approximate notions of differential equivalence and the study of already established notions of $\varepsilon$-lumpability and near-lumpability of Markov chains. Thanks to the theory established in this paper, this will naturally lead to approximate exact role assignments. The need for an approximate version of exact role assignments is motivated by the fact that nodes on the "periphery" of a network are often distinguished by differential equivalence while featuring almost identical centrality measures.

## References

1. Arora, S., Rao, S., Vazirani, U.V.: Expander flows, geometric embeddings and graph partitioning. J. ACM **56**(2), 5:1–5:37 (2009)
2. Baier, C., Engelen, B., Majster-Cederbaum, M.E.: Deciding bisimilarity and similarity for probabilistic processes. J. Comput. Syst. Sci. **60**(1), 187–231 (2000)

3. Barabasi, A.-L., Dezso, Z., Regan, E., Yook, S.-H., Oltvai, Z.: Scale-free and hierarchical structures in complex networks, vol. 661, no. 1 (2003)
4. Batagelj, V., Mrvar, A.: Pajek datasets, June 2006. http://vlado.fmf.uni-lj.si/pub/networks/data/
5. Bobbio, A., Gribaudo, M., Telek, M.: Analysis of large scale interacting systems by mean field method. In: QEST, pp. 215–224 (2008)
6. Bortolussi, L., Gast, N.: Mean field approximation of uncertain stochastic models. In: DSN, pp. 287–298 (2016)
7. Buchholz, P.: Exact and ordinary lumpability in finite Markov chains. J. Appl. Probab. **31**, 59–74 (1994)
8. Cardelli, L., Csikász-Nagy, A., Dalchau, N., Tribastone, M., Tschaikowski, M.: Noise Reduction in complex biological switches. Sci. Rep. (2016)
9. Cardelli, L., Tribastone, M., Tschaikowski, M., Vandin, A.: Efficient syntax-driven lumping of differential equations. In: Chechik, M., Raskin, J.-F. (eds.) TACAS 2016. LNCS, vol. 9636, pp. 93–111. Springer, Heidelberg (2016). https://doi.org/10.1007/978-3-662-49674-9_6
10. Cardelli, L., Tribastone, M., Tschaikowski, M., Vandin, A.: Forward and backward bisimulations for chemical reaction networks. In: CONCUR, pp. 226–239 (2015)
11. Cardelli, L., Tribastone, M., Tschaikowski, M., Vandin, A.: Comparing chemical reaction networks: a categorical and algorithmic perspective. In: LICS, pp. 485–494 (2016)
12. Cardelli, L., Tribastone, M., Tschaikowski, M., Vandin, A.: Symbolic computation of differential equivalences. In: 43rd ACM SIGPLAN-SIGACT Symposium on Principles of Programming Languages (POPL) (2016)
13. Cardelli, L., Tribastone, M., Tschaikowski, M., Vandin, A.: ERODE: a tool for the evaluation and reduction of ordinary differential equations. In: Legay, A., Margaria, T. (eds.) TACAS 2017. LNCS, vol. 10206, pp. 310–328. Springer, Heidelberg (2017). https://doi.org/10.1007/978-3-662-54580-5_19
14. Cardelli, L., Tribastone, M., Tschaikowski, M., Vandin, A.: Maximal aggregation of polynomial dynamical systems. PNAS **114**(38), 10029–10034 (2017)
15. Davis, T.A., Yifan, H.: The university of florida sparse matrix collection. ACM Trans. Math. Softw. **38**(1), 1:1–1:25 (2011)
16. Derisavi, S., Hermanns, H., Sanders, W.H.: Optimal state-space lumping in Markov chains. Inf. Process. Lett. **87**(6), 309–315 (2003)
17. Feret, J., Danos, V., Krivine, J., Harmer, R., Fontana, W.: Internal coarse-graining of molecular systems. PNAS **106**(16), 6453–6458 (2009)
18. Golub, G.H., Van Loan, C.F.: Matrix Computations, 3rd edn. Johns Hopkins University Press, Baltimore (1996)
19. Iacobelli, G., Tribastone, M.: Lumpability of fluid models with heterogeneous agent types. In: DSN, pp. 1–11 (2013)
20. Iacobelli, G., Tribastone, M., Vandin, A.: Differential bisimulation for a Markovian process algebra. In: Italiano, G.F., Pighizzini, G., Sannella, D.T. (eds.) MFCS 2015. LNCS, vol. 9234, pp. 293–306. Springer, Heidelberg (2015). https://doi.org/10.1007/978-3-662-48057-1_23
21. Jeong, H., Mason, S.P., Barabasi, A.-L., Oltvai, Z.N.: Lethality and centrality in protein networks. Nature **411**(6833), 41–42 (2001)
22. Katoen, J.-P., Zapreev, I.S., Hahn, E.M., Hermanns, H., Jansen, D.N.: The ins and outs of the probabilistic model checker MRMC. Perform. Eval. **68**(2), 90–104 (2011)

23. Klimt, B., Yang, Y.: The enron corpus: a new dataset for email classification research. In: Boulicaut, J.-F., Esposito, F., Giannotti, F., Pedreschi, D. (eds.) ECML 2004. LNCS (LNAI), vol. 3201, pp. 217–226. Springer, Heidelberg (2004). https://doi.org/10.1007/978-3-540-30115-8_22

24. Kowal, M., Tschaikowski, M., Tribastone, M., Schaefer, I.: Scaling size and parameter spaces in variability-aware software performance models (T). In: ASE, pp. 407–417 (2015)

25. Larsen, K.G., Skou, A.: Bisimulation through probabilistic testing. In: POPL, pp. 344–352 (1989)

26. Lerner, J.: Role assignments. In: Brandes, U., Erlebach, T. (eds.) Network Analysis: Methodological Foundations. LNCS, vol. 3418, pp. 216–252. Springer, Heidelberg (2005). https://doi.org/10.1007/978-3-540-31955-9_9

27. Leskovec, J., Kleinberg, J., Faloutsos, C.: Graphs over time: densification laws, shrinking diameters and possible explanations. In: KDD 2005, pp. 177–187 (2005)

28. Leskovec, J., Kleinberg, J., Faloutsos, C.: Graph evolution: densification and shrinking diameters. ACM Trans. Knowl. Discov. Data 1(1), 2 (2007)

29. Leskovec, J., Krevl, A.: SNAP datasets: Stanford large network dataset collection, June 2014. http://snap.stanford.edu/data

30. Meila, M., Shi, J.: Learning segmentation by random walks. In: NIPS 2000, Denver, pp. 873–879 (2000)

31. Mislove, A., Marcon, M., Gummadi, K.P., Druschel, P., Bhattacharjee, B.: Measurement and analysis of online social networks. In: Proceedings of the 5th ACM/Usenix Internet Measurement Conference (IMC 2007), San Diego, October 2007

32. Newman, M.: Networks: An Introduction. Oxford University Press Inc., New York (2010)

33. Paige, R., Tarjan, R.E.: Three partition refinement algorithms. SIAM J. Comput. 16(6), 973–989 (1987)

34. Ravasz, E., Barabási, A.-L.: Hierarchical organization in complex networks. Phys. Rev. E 67, 026112 (2003)

35. Shi, J., Malik, J.: Normalized cuts and image segmentation. IEEE Trans. Pattern Anal. Mach. Intell. 22(8), 888–905 (2000)

36. Tschaikowski, M., Tribastone, M.: Exact fluid lumpability for markovian process algebra. In: CONCUR, pp. 380–394 (2012)

37. Tschaikowski, M., Tribastone, M.: Approximate reduction of heterogenous nonlinear models with differential hulls. IEEE TAC 61(4), 1099–1104 (2016)

38. Valmari, A., Franceschinis, G.: Simple $O(m \log n)$ time Markov chain lumping. In: Esparza, J., Majumdar, R. (eds.) TACAS 2010. LNCS, vol. 6015, pp. 38–52. Springer, Heidelberg (2010). https://doi.org/10.1007/978-3-642-12002-2_4

39. Vinnikov, A., Shalev-Shwartz, S.: K-means recovers ICA filters when independent components are sparse. In: ICML 2014, Beijing, 21–26 June 2014, pp. 712–720 (2014)

40. Wasserman, S., Faust, K.: Social Network Analysis: Methods and Applications, vol. 8. Cambridge University Press, Cambridge (1994)

# Measuring and Evaluating the Performance of Self-Organization Mechanisms Within Collective Adaptive Systems

Benedikt Eberhardinger[(✉)], Hella Ponsar, Dominik Klumpp, and Wolfgang Reif

Institute for Software and Systems Engineering, University of Augsburg, Augsburg, Germany
{eberhardinger,ponsar,reif}@isse.de,
dominik.raphael.klumpp@student.uni-augsburg.de

**Abstract.** By restructuring and reconfiguring itself at run-time, a collective adaptive system (CAS) is able to fulfill its requirements under uncertain, ever-changing environmental conditions. Indeed, this process of self-organization (SO) is of utmost importance for the ability of the CAS to perform. However, it is hard to design high-performing SO mechanisms, because the environmental conditions are partially unpredictable at design time. Thus, a crucial aid for the development of SO mechanisms is a tool set enabling performance evaluations at design time in order to select the best-fitting mechanism and parametrize it. We present a metric for measuring the performance of an SO mechanism as well as a framework that enables evaluation of this metric. The proposed metric is evaluated for different kinds of SO mechanisms in two case studies: a smart energy management system and a self-organizing production cell.

## 1 Performance of Self-Organization Mechanisms

The performance of software denotes its capabilities in its execution. These capabilities might be determined either by a theoretical analysis or by an experimental evaluation. In general, two measures are of interest: the solution quality and the time taken to achieve the solution [11]. Whereas theoretical analysis are based on abstraction, theorems, and proofs in order to find an asymptotic bound on the dominant operation under a worst-case or average-case mode, experimental evaluation relies on execution, logging, and measuring according to a set of metrics. The knowledge gained from the performance analysis, theoretical as well as experimental, is used for engineering efficient and effective software. The gain for the engineers highly depends on the quality of the analysis.. However, achieving a high quality for the analysis is a challenging task [11]. Theoretical as well as experimental analysis are foremost challenged when the system under evaluation is indeterministic, highly parallel, interactive, or highly dependent on

© Springer Nature Switzerland AG 2018
T. Margaria and B. Steffen (Eds.): ISoLA 2018, LNCS 11246, pp. 202–220, 2018.
https://doi.org/10.1007/978-3-030-03424-5_14

unforeseeable run-time conditions. All these aspects are characteristics of collective adaptive systems (CAS) [4]. A CAS uses its abilities to reconfigure and restructure itself at run-time in order to cope with an ever-changing environment. Self-organization (SO) mechanisms are used to fulfill this reconfiguration and restructuring task. An important aspect, that is exploited by most of the SO mechanisms (cf. [1]), is that mostly that process can be carried out locally, i.e., in a small part of the overall system. This makes the SO mechanisms scalable and effective which has a great impact on the overall system performance. However, it is far from obvious how to design and implement the best performing SO mechanism for a certain system, because SO mechanisms have to operate under ever-changing environmental conditions that are partially unpredictable at design time. This demands a powerful performance analysis to support this task. In our approach, we face the challenge by focusing on an experimental analysis, following van Dyke Parunak and Brueckner [15], who argue that there is a need of experimental evaluation of SO mechanisms, because the concepts of theoretical analysis are stretched to their limits given that the majority of SO systems are formally undecidable.

This paper contains the following contributions for measuring and evaluating the performance of SO mechanisms within CAS: (1) A *performance metric* for distributed SO mechanisms; (2) a *simulation concept* for measuring performance; (3) a *framework for performance evaluation* incorporating these two concepts; (4) an *intensive evaluation* of different mechanisms within different systems.

The rest of the paper is structured as follows: We introduce our two case studies in Sect. 2. The performance metrics of SO mechanisms are derived in Sect. 3. Section 4 describes our evaluation framework that is used to evaluate the metrics. Within the framework we evaluate the two cases studies according to the introduced metrics in Sect. 5. Section 6 places the contribution of this paper into the related work and Sect. 7 finally concludes the paper.

## 2   Case Studies

We use two different case studies with different SO mechanisms throughout this paper as well as in our evaluation. First, a self-organizing production cell and second, a self-organizing smart grid. Both are categorized as CAS, according to [4]. Our first case study represents the class of systems with *discrete* SO mechanisms and the second case study the class of *continuous* SO mechanisms. Discrete SO mechanisms are working on a discrete input space, e.g., a tool that breaks and forces a reconfiguration, and continuous SO mechanisms are working on a continuous input space, e.g., a quality rating index where the system's configuration depends on.

### 2.1   Self-Organizing Production Cell

Future production scenarios demand for much more flexibility [12] than today's shop floor design to cope with the trend towards small series production, individualized products and the reuse of production stations for different tasks. These future CAS will integrate SO mechanisms to resolve the tasks of decentralized decision making, to optimize the systems structure, and to autonomously react to component failures at runtime increasing the system's robustness. We envision self-organizing production cells, where the production stations are modern robots equipped with toolboxes and the ability to change their tools whenever necessary (self-awareness). They are connected via mobile carts that are able to carry workpieces and to reach robots in any order. Thus, the production cell is able to fulfill any task which corresponds to tools (capabilities) available in the cell. This is possible due to the SO mechanisms that reconfigures the carts and robots in a way that the tools are applied to the workpieces in the correct order.

## 2.2 Self-Organizing Virtual Power Plants in Smart Grids

The wide-spread installation of weather-dependent power plants as well as the bunch of new consumer types like electric vehicles put a lot of strain on power grids. To save expenses, gain more flexibility, and deal with uncertainties, future *autonomous* power management systems have to take advantage of the full potential of dispatchable prosumers[1] by incorporating them into the scheduling scheme. Further, aleatoric uncertainties have to be anticipated when creating schedules and compensated for locally to prevent their propagation through the system. To meet the challenges of future power management systems, Steghöfer et al. [18] presented the concept of Autonomous Virtual Power Plants (AVPPs) which represent self-organizing groups of two or more power plants of various types that form a CAS. The organizational structure represents a *partitioning*, i.e., every power plant is a member of exactly one AVPP, which is established and maintained by a (partitioning-based) SO algorithm. AVPPs autonomously adapt their structure to changing internal or environmental conditions, they are able to live up to the responsibility of maintaining an organizational structure enabling the system to hold the balance between energy supply and demand. In particular, if an AVPP repeatedly cannot satisfy its assigned fraction of the overall demand or compensate for its local uncertainties, it triggers a reconfiguration of the partitioning. To cope with the vast number of dispatchable power plants, the concept of AVPPs proposes a scalable, hierarchical structure in which AVPPs act as intermediaries. This system decomposition reduces the number of dispatchable power plants each AVPP controls resulting in shorter scheduling times for each AVPP and the overall system.

## 3    Performance Metric for Distributed SO Mechanisms

In our previous work [6], we evaluated in-depth performance metrics given by the literature regarding their ability to cope with SO algorithms and mechanisms. For this purpose, we implemented the six most promising metrics and applied them to an SO mechanism. The results was, that none of the investigated metrics

---

[1] We use the term "prosumer" to refer to producers as well as consumers.

were fully capable to judge the performance of an SO mechanism. Thus, we derived a set of requirements that metrics have to fulfill [6]:

**Req. 1:** The **locality** of SO mechanisms has to be taken into account and the aspects of *time* and *solution quality* have to be evaluated within the subsystems (changing over run-time) that are differently affected by the SO mechanisms, e.g., one subsystem can be reconfigured while another one keeps on working. Furthermore, it is important to be able to assess the performance of the entire system based on the performance of the subsystems.

**Req. 2:** Since SO mechanisms have control over the system's structure, their performance strongly influences those of the entire system. So the overhead of a reconfiguration can be worthwhile if it sufficiently improves the behavior of the controlled system. Consequently, a metric has to take the **benefit of the reconfiguration** into account.

**Req. 3:** The interpretation of a value provided by a metric strongly depends on the current state of the system. In self-organizing systems, the possible values for the solution quality can change over time. For instance, a solution quality of 0.7 would be optimal if possible values were defined by the interval $[0, 0.7]$ but quite bad if they stem from the interval $[0, 200]$; the same applies to the parameter *time*. Consequently, there is a need for **dynamic boundaries for the evaluation**—a result from the ever-changing environment of SO mechanisms.

We used these requirements in order to form a metric that is able to cope with decentralized SO mechanisms, is defined locally, respects the benefit of a reconfiguration, and handles dynamic boundaries. The performance of a system is composed of two parts: time performance and quality performance. Thus the performance $p$ of a system $sys$ is defined by the following metric:

$$p(sys) = w_t \cdot tp(sys) + w_q \cdot qp(sys), \tag{1}$$

where $w_t + w_q = 1$ has to be fulfilled. The factors $w_t$ and $w_q$ enable to weight the importance of the time quality $tp(sys)$ and the quality performance $qp(sys)$. The codomain of the metric is $[0, 1]$, where a greater value means a better performance of SO mechanism. The system $sys$ consists of agents (resp. components) $a \in sys$ which are controlled by the SO mechanism that is analyzed in $r \in R$ evaluation runs.

### 3.1   Time Performance of SO Mechanisms

Evaluating the time performance $tp(sys)$ requires a clear definition of what the time performance of an SO mechanism is. For classical analysis of time performance the answer is: the duration from execution to the appearance of the output. [11] Applying that approach to SO mechanisms is not sufficient, since we have to deal with two aspects (1) SO algorithms are mostly anytime algorithms that are terminated after a certain time and (2) the performance is also depicted by the time to a next reconfiguration. This is due to the fact, that the time performance of the controlled system is effected by the SO mechanism as it might be slowed down or stopped, that effect needs to be respected, too. Consequently, we are not directly interested in the time to a solution we are interested in its time impact, i.e., the time used for SO compared to the time where the system runs without disturbances. Due to the characteristics of SO mechanisms there is no single point where the time could be measured, because SO mechanisms solve problems in a distributed fashion. Thus, the calculation is for instance achieved by building a coalition of components that are capable to solve the problem without the rest of the system. This is the case in the production cell case study where a group of robots is able to find a new configuration if a capability, e.g., a drill, is broken. The measurement is consequently no central affair. The time of reconfiguration, i.e, the time involved in finding a new system configuration, needs to be measured for each agent $a \in sys$ as follows:

$$tp(a,r) = 1 - \frac{\sum_{s \in r} \text{reconfigurationTime}(r, a, s)}{\text{duration}(r)}, \tag{2}$$

where the time performance is measured by calculating the ratio of the time needed for reconfiguration for a single agent $a$ in a run $r$ consisting of $s$ steps, given by reconfigurationTime$(r, a, s)$ in unit of time, to the duration of the run $r$ where the measurement has taken place, supplied by duration$(r)$ in the same unit of time. This is different in two ways from evaluating classical mechanisms or algorithms, like in [11]: the measurement is a time ratio and is measured locally. The metric value of Eq. (2) is prorated with the resulting values of all agents $a \in sys$ in order to gain the time performance of the system by computing the average of all values:

$$tp(r, sys) = avg_a^{sys} tp(a, r) \tag{3}$$

The concrete average function influences the result and has to be chosen with care. The same average function is applied to compute the time performance of the system $tp(sys)$ by prorating the results of all evaluation runs $r \in R$ as follows:

$$tp(sys) = avg_r^R tp(r, sys) \tag{4}$$

The codomain of $tp(sys)$ as well as $tp(r, sys)$ and $tp(a, r)$ is $[0, 1]$, and a value close to 1 indicates a better achieved time performance.

## 3.2 Quality Performance of SO Mechanisms

The quality performance $qp(sys)$ determines how good the particular solutions of an SO mechanism have been. However, judging the quality of a solution is highly dependent on the particular SO mechanism as well as the system and its environment. This is due to the fact that the quality is measured according to the influence of the SO mechanism on the controlled system. The SO mechanism in the production cell case study controls which robot and which cart has to carry out which task. It consequently influences the ability of the system to produce workpieces and effects the overall output resp. throughput. The quality of the SO mechanism is determined by the throughput, the number of processing actions, that the system is able to apply within an evaluation run. This value can be measured locally for each robot, that is processing a workpiece, and then aggregated for the entire system. The SO mechanism in the energy grid case study clusters resp. anti-clusters the power plants into virtual power plants. The optimality of this decision could be measured by the mix value of the virtual power plants. The solution quality is evaluated by measuring the domain-dependent quality function $\text{quality}(r, a)$ for an evaluation run $r$ of each agent $a \in sys$. As the measured value is dependent upon the context it is normalized by the value which is the best possible one:

$$qp(r, a) = \frac{\text{quality}(r, a)}{\text{quality}_{\max}(r, a)} \tag{5}$$

To prorate $qp(r, a)$ for all $a \in sys$ the average is built according to

$$qp(r, sys) = avg_a^{sys} qp(r, a) \tag{6}$$

The codomain of $qp(r, a)$ as well as $qp(r, sys)$ is $[0, 1]$, and a value close to 1 indicates a better achieved quality, since 1 would imply that the maximum performance has been reached. In order to form the proration for $qp(sys)$ different average functions might be appropriate, as described for the time performance before. Thus, $qp(sys)$ is defined as follows:

$$qp(sys) = avg_r^R qp(r, sys) \tag{7}$$

## 4  Performance Evaluation Framework

In order to measure and evaluate the performance of an SO mechanism it is of utmost importance to establish a test bed where the performance of the mechanism can be analyzed in a systematic, comprehensible, and representative fashion. For the implementation of an according framework we rely on the requirements derived in [6] that encompass the following two main concerns:

**Req. 4:** The framework's components should support the generation of evaluation runs, the simulation itself, and the application of performance metrics.

**Req. 5:** In order to achieve significant results, the evaluation must comprise **simulation runs** that induce an environmental behavior reflecting likely conditions under which the SO mechanisms have to operate.

We base our evaluation framework shown in Fig. 1 on the previously developed testing approaches [5,7], that have originally been used for functional testing. Basically, it consists of an **Evaluation Suite Generator**, an **Execution**, and a **Monitoring and Evaluation** component. The model-based approach is used in all fragments, which is enabled by having executable as well as changeable models. The overall evaluation framework consists of a static and a dynamic part. The static part is used for enabling automated execution as well as automated evaluation. The dynamic part is used for generating evaluation suites.

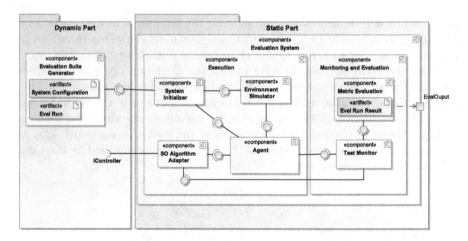

**Fig. 1.** The *UML* component diagram shows the essential components of the evaluation framework, consisting of two main components.

Based on a description of the System Configuration the Evaluation Suite Generator derives different possible System Configurations for evaluation. The Evaluation System is afterwards started by initializing the static part that uses Agents to set up the environment of the SO mechanism that is plugged into the evaluation framework. The Evaluation Runs are generated and executed in the same step (we follow an online testing approach for the evaluation of the performance that enables arbitrary length of evaluation runs). Each action of the SO mechanism is monitored and evaluated due to the implemented performance metrics. The overall evaluation is mainly driven by environmental changes, i.e., changes in the controlled environment of the investigated SO mechanism. In the production cell scenario such a change might be a faulty robot or drill that causes the SO mechanism to reconfigure the production cell. For the energy grid scenario a change can be a fluctuation in the production of a power plant due to a changing weather condition of the solar plant leading to a change in the fulfillment degree of the previously calculated schedule that in turn causes the SO mechanism to reconfigure the AVPP.

### 4.1   Generating Unbiased Evaluation Runs

In order to supply significant results (fulfilling *Req. 5*), the evaluation runs need to be comprehensible and representative. To illustrate this challenge, let's consider the following example in the production cell scenario: There is only one robot actively using a drill; if the environmental change is to damage the drill, that causes a reconfiguration. However, if the time performance is computed based on the time passed since the last reconfiguration, the environmental action has a direct influence on the performance result of the investigated SO mechanisms. The correlation is unintended, since the evaluation should not influence the outcome, the system under evaluation should be the only influence factor. But, it is not possible to completely diminish this influence factor within a simulation. To get the best results there are two solutions: (1) to evaluate the system with every combination of environmental conditions or (2) to select the most representative combination of environmental conditions which represent the reality best. Due to the complexity of the environment it is not possible to follow option (1).

There is a necessity to select a representative combination of environmental conditions, i.e., take samples for all possible combination. The result from that sample is a set of evaluation runs. For these evaluation runs we compute a metric, based on Eq. (1). If this metric value is equal to the metric value for option (1) it is called *unbiased*. An unbiased metric value with a low number of samples is called *efficient* [14]. Sampling could be performed in different manners with different effects. There is the possibility to select random samples from the abstract environment states. Random sampling implies that each possible environmental change has the same probability of being chosen at any stage during the sampling process to become part of the evaluation run. However, that does not fully reflect the reality of the environment that is modeled and from which the states are sampled. This is the case for the production cell as well as the energy grid scenario: The failure rates of the production tools, on the one site, and the weather conditions for the power plants, on the other side, are nonuniform in their occurrences if real world processes are observed. There are probability distributions that describe the failure rates, that are well investigated in the field of reliability engineering [13], namely mean-time-to-failure rates as well as mean-time-to-repair rates.

## 4.2   Modeling the Environment for Evaluating the Performance of SO Mechanisms

Our approach uses a model representation of the environment, where we abstract from concrete states to classes of states. We use a Markov chain model describing how likely it is that a sequence of states occurs or that a state occurs after a particular state, similar to our previous approach [5] where we formed so called environmental profiles. That means there are not just the weather conditions *rainy*, *sunny*, and *cloudy*, but there is also the information whether it is possible to have *rainy* weather after *sunny* weather and how probable it is. The models are distinguished by the class of SO mechanism. For an SO mechanism with a discrete input space, we apply failure models, from the reliability theory, used for a fault injection approach (cf. [7]). The faults are injected into the controlled environment of the SO mechanism. For an SO mechanisms with a continuous input space, we apply the approach of environmental profiles. The first delivers samples as a set of faults (also an empty set is possible) that should be injected and the latter delivers a set of environmental changes. The resulting evaluation runs are used as representative combinations of environmental conditions which represent the reality best and address *Req. 5*.

### 4.3 Integrating the Evaluation Sequence Selection in the Evaluation Framework

In the evaluation framework (cf. Fig. 1) these models are used to feed the Environment Simulator by generating Eval Runs in the Evaluation Suite Generator. The approach is building upon a model-based testing approach, as described in [5,7], allowing for describing the different parts of the SO mechanism and its environment in order to generate evaluation sequences. The modeling language used at hands is S# [8], an executable modeling language, that is equipped with the ability to execute the model. The execution has direct influence on the Agents controlled by the mechanism under evaluation. This online evaluation run generating process allows for endless execution runs. To select the number of all evaluation steps in all runs to be executed, we use the following formula that allows selection of the length by defining the acceptable estimation error $\Delta\mu$ [14]:

$$n \geq z^2 \frac{\sigma^2}{(\Delta\mu)^2}, \tag{8}$$

where $n$ is the number of all evaluation steps in all runs, $z$ is the standard normal distribution (SND) value (taken from an SND table) of the expected distribution, and $\sigma^2$ is the to be estimated standard deviation (SD) by taking $n$ evaluation runs. For our evaluation the acceptable estimation error might be $\pm 1\%$ with an confidence interval of 95%. The confidence interval states the probability that the expected metric value $p(sys)$ is within a given symmetric interval of $[p(sys)-b; p(sys)+b]$ where $b$ is called the confidence border. The actual selection of the value $b := z\sigma_{p(sys)} \equiv z\frac{\sigma}{\sqrt{n}}$ is defined by the expected SD and $z$ as the corresponding value of the SND that is expected. Indeed, the number $n$ is the actual number we would like to know and it could be determined by Eq. (8) given the confidence interval and the acceptable estimation error. However, the value $\sigma^2$ is unknown, since it is the also unknown SD to be estimated by the evaluation runs. Thus, we have to use a rather gross estimate of $\sigma^2$. In order to play it safe, $\sigma^2$ should be set to 0.25, leading to a rather to big estimate for the value $n$, since this the maximum value to be selected [14]. So we select $\sigma^2 = 0.25$ and have the following equation to be solved having given $z = 1.96$ by taking the value form the SND table and the confidence interval of 0.95: $n \geq z^2 \frac{\sigma^2}{(\Delta\mu)^2} = 1.96^2 \frac{0.25}{0.01^2} = 9604$.

## 5 Evaluation

We used two different self-organizing systems for evaluating the accomplishments of our metric as described in Sect. 3 and the evaluation framework specified in Sect. 4. Within this evaluation we answer the following research questions:

**RQ 1:** Is it possible to determine differences in the SO mechanisms' performance during the assessment of the performance of the entire CAS?

**RQ 2:** SO mechanisms have great impact on the overall performance of the controlled system. Is it possible to quantify this impact reasonably for SO mechanisms?

**RQ 3:** SO systems are faced with an ever-changing environment; their performance depends on the current run time setting of the system. Are these dynamic performance boundaries reflected in the performance evaluation in a way to provide a comprehensive analysis?

**RQ 4:** The simulation environment might influence the outcome. Is the evaluation framework able to establish conditions for continuous and discrete SO mechanisms that are able to produce comparable results in different settings?

These research questions are derived from a set of requirements for metrics and performance evaluation of SO mechanisms, that we developed in [6]. We selected the case studies as they represent the two different input spaces of SO mechanisms, described in Sect. 2. Thus, we are able to demonstrate the two different possible instance of the evaluation framework. In order to investigate the metric in depth for each case study we used several different SO mechanisms.

### 5.1   Local and Central Reconfiguration in an SO Production Cell

In the production cell case study, we compare a central SO mechanism working with global knowledge with a coalition-formation mechanism with local knowledge only. The centralized mechanism always stops the entire system when a configuration deficiency is detected. It removes the current configuration entirely, computes a new configuration and distributes it. The localized mechanism on the other hand forms a coalition of agents, starting with the agent that detected the problem. It recruits more and more neighbouring agents, until the agents in the coalition are able to solve the problem at hand among themselves. Only the configurations of those agents within the coalition that must necessarily change their roles is updated. Both mechanisms employ the same algorithm to find a solution within their set of available agents. They differ in the selection of those agents as well as in the method of distribution for the computed solution.

**Evaluation Setting.** We evaluate both mechanisms within three different setups of the production cell case study: firstly, a setup with few agents (6 robots, 4 carts), and high redundancy with regards to available capabilities (each robot has ≈66.7% of the existing capabilities), we refer to this setup as *FA/HR* below; secondly, a setup with more agents (10 robots, 4 carts), and low redundancy (40%), referred to as *MA/LR*; and lastly one with more agents (10 robots, 4 carts), and high redundancy (70%), *MA/HR*. Each model is simulated with both algorithms in several simulation runs. Within each run, environment faults are activated and deactivated randomly according to their respective MTTF and MTTR. For greater comparability, we simulate the systems with the same random seeds, i.e, expose both algorithms to the same environmental conditions.

The numbers of the evaluation are shown in Table 1. As the shown data is aggregated over 100 runs with 1000 steps each, the shown number are showing the average value. As outlined in Sect. 4, the concrete choose of the average function is up to the test engineer. One way of choosing is to get more insights in the data. The data is, for this purpose, first tested on normal distribution. The Shapiro-Wilk test, performed on the data, showed p-value $< 0.05$ which is indicating a nonparametric data set for the measurements. For nonparametric data, it is hard to select a good fitting average functions. For the given data set the arithmetic mean was evaluated as well as the median. The arithmetic mean is selected in the case when additions of the values is meaning full, while the median is more focused on clustering the data in two equal sized data heaps. That makes the arithmetic more prone to outliers compared to the mean value. Thus, the expectation would be, that the values differ, as we have no normal distribution. However, both values are almost equal for all the data. Leading to the assumption that the data is tightly clustered, which is the case. The data as we process it in the metrics is well suited by addition as an average function. Thus, the following data plots the arithmetic average value as the chosen average function. Indeed, it is of further interest to investigate the dispersion of the data. This gives more insights on the state of the data given. A measures for the dispersion is the range of data given. However, for the arithmetic mean the standard deviation (SD) is the average of choice. Indeed, the SD is prone to a normal distribution. However, the data is tightly clustered around the mean, thus, we opt for the SD in the statistics, delivering the best insight on the dispersion of the given data set. For the further results the different results of the different configurations and the different settings have being tested according to the independence of the results. Due to the fact that no distribution is assumed at the given data set the Mann-Whitney-Wilcoxon test has been performed to show the independency. The Mann-Whitney-Wilcoxon test resulted in a p-value $< 0.05$. Thus, the following discussion of the value is grounded on the given independency.

### Discussion of the Evaluation Results

*RQ 1:* The results of our evaluation as shown in Table 1 clearly indicate that the centralized mechanism yields greater quality, i.e., allows for greater throughput. This is surprising, as one would expect the locality of the coalition-formation mechanism to yield better results, since it allows some parts of the system to be reconfigured while other parts keep working. However, this effect was not pronounced enough in our case study to overcome the negative aspects: the coalition has only a subset of the centralized mechanism's knowledge, and it will always prefer a localized solution, leading to little division of labor. On the other hand, we can see that the coalition-formation mechanism has better time performance, i.e., the relation between working time and reconfiguration time for individual agents is better. This shows the benefit of not involving every agent in every reconfiguration. The coalition-formation is much more efficient in this respect, for the smallest model almost twice as efficient as the centralized mechanism. As a result, agents can perform more production steps between two subsequent reconfigurations. In reality the effect on performance would be even more pronounced because physically stopping production costs more time than

**Table 1.** Evaluation results for the two SO mechanisms "Centralized", and "Coalition-Formation" with different production cell setups. All values are averages over evaluation runs with 100 steps each; values in parenthesis denote SDs.

| Mechanism | Centralized | | | Coalition-Formation | | |
|---|---|---|---|---|---|---|
| Model | FA/HR | MA/LR | MA/HR | FA/HR | MA/LR | MA/HR |
| $tp(sys)$ | 0.9728 | 0.8579 | 0.8596 | 0.9963 | 1.0000 | 1.0000 |
| | $(3e-3)$ | $(4e-4)$ | $(1e-2)$ | $(6e-4)$ | $(3e-5)$ | $(2e-6)$ |
| $qp(sys)$ | 0.5909 | 0.9432 | 0.7022 | 0.4987 | 0.7560 | 0.5779 |
| | (0.03) | (0.06) | (0.04) | (0.03) | (0.04) | (0.04) |
| $p(sys)$ $w_t = 0.5, w_q = 0.5$ | 0.7819 | 0.9005 | 0.7809 | 0.7475 | 0.8780 | 0.7889 |
| $p(sys)$ $w_t = 0.1, w_q = 0.9$ | 0.6291 | 0.9347 | 0.7180 | 0.5484 | 0.7804 | 0.6200 |
| $p(sys)$ $w_t = 0.9, w_q = 0.1$ | 0.9347 | 0.8664 | 0.8439 | 0.9466 | 0.9756 | 0.9577 |
| #Modified Roles per Reconf. | 7.85 | 16.67 | 13.73 | 8.41 | 11.74 | 10.71 |
| | (2.65) | (6.67) | (5.06) | (3.83) | (11.17) | (7.51) |
| #Reconf. / #Involved Agents per Reconf. | 0.45 | 0.52 | 0.46 | 0.88 | 0.74 | 0.76 |
| | (0.12) | (0.13) | (0.12) | (0.16) | (0.19) | (0.20) |
| #Steps between Agent Reconf. | 6.87 | 1.99 | 3.10 | 12.84 | 3.83 | 6.04 |
| | (6.91) | (2.41) | (3.41) | (21.53) | (5.10) | (9.49) |

it does in our simulation. Similarly, changing role allocations would correspond to physical tool changes, also requiring great amounts of time. For larger models, the coalition mechanism outperforms the centralized mechanism in this respect as well. We measured the time performance locally for each agent, compute a performance for the complete evaluation run and approximate results for the entire system through a series of runs. The quality is measured similar as the number of processing steps applied by agents within a run, this information is gathered locally for each agent and then aggregated. Hence, to answer *RQ 1*, two different mechanisms are comparable despite their different views on the overall system (local and central). The metrics deliver a clear indication of the advantages of the different mechanisms.

*RQ 2:* The solution quality can be weighted higher or lower in order to consider the SO mechanism's influence on the system performance. This enables us to control the influence of the quality parameter with the time parameter. The quality is best measured in the MA/LR setting, that indicates, that the quality is depended from the actual setting as well. Nevertheless, it is still possible to quantify a recent difference between the quality of the centralized and the coalition setting. That undermines an effect, that is assumed for decentralized mechanisms: it is often stuck to local optima. This effect is reasonably quantified here.

*RQ 3:* Our metric can also account for the dynamic performance boundaries of SO (*RQ 3*). Remember that the quality ratings equal the system's actual productivity, measured by production actions, e.g., drill, compared to the maximal possible productivity. For the maximal possible quality as referenced in Eq. (6), we executed a system run for each setup without any environment faults. For the FA/HR setting of 484 production actions was achieved, 336 production actions for the MA/LR setting, and 343 production actions for the MA/HR setting. One step can encompass at most one production action, hence this value abstracts from the concrete time required. Thus, a larger system with low redundancies is prone to be less productive due to long transits. Here, the same initial system configuration is used for calculating the maximum quality as well as for starting the evaluation. That initial configuration encompasses, amongst other things, the initial role allocation (i.e., which robot and which cart is applying which capability) of the system. However, when the system encounters a faulty environment, the maximal throughput in ideal conditions may in many cases be unreachable even with the best SO mechanism, which explains the relatively low scores for both algorithms.

Further, high time performance ratings can be achieved by both algorithms: even though a faulty environment leads to more time spent on reconfigurations, it influences the total simulation time in the same manner, thus limiting its influence on the quotient. By assigning a lower weight to the quality ratings, we can account for this imbalance to some extent. Similarly, there exists a certain disconnect between the time required for processing steps in our simulations and in reality, the former being much lower. This disconnect does not exist for reconfiguration times, and therefore it affects the time performance as defined in Eq. (2). However, it does so equally for both compared mechanisms.

Hence, while the absolute values in the simulation differ from the realization in a real hardware application scenario the metric has to be taken with a grain of salt for the quantitative comparison, the relation between the two mechanisms remains still the same and thus still allows for a fair qualitative comparison. In order to give a more complete picture, we also included the number of discrete steps the system makes between two reconfigurations involving the same agent, on average.

*RQ 4:* Lastly, we consider the evaluation system's influence on our results in *RQ 4*. The SD for time performance and quality in our evaluation results is low, less than 0.01 for time performance, and less than 0.06 for the quality rating. We can thus assume the results are unbiased. The high SDs for per-reconfiguration results (the last three rows) is expected: the amount of necessary reconfiguration changes and the frequency of reconfigurations depend on the respectively occurring environment faults, whose frequency and impact vary greatly.

## 5.2    Self-Organized Creation of Virtual Power Plants in Smart Grids

For the evaluation within the self-organized creation of virtual power plants in a smart grid we used an SO mechanism called *PSOPP* [2] (*P*article *S*warm *O*ptimizer for the *P*artitioning *P*roblem). The PSOPP is a particle swarm optimizer that partitions a set of agents representing a (sub)system into pairwise disjoint and non-empty groups. These groups constitute the (sub)system's configurational structure. Feasible organizational structures can be described by so-called partitioning constraints that restrict the number and the size of these groups. PSOPP is an anytime algorithm and a metaheuristic that optimizes the groups' composition with respect to an objective function. In our evaluation, PSOPP is used to optimize the groups' composition in each so-called separate AVPPs of a hierarchically structured system.

**Evaluation Setting.** We executed 100 generated evaluation runs, each comprising 300 evaluation steps leading to a size of the evaluation run that is bigger than the smallest useable size calculated using Eq. (8). In order to investigate two different SO mechanisms we instantiated the PSOPP algorithm with two different settings: (1) In the setting *PSOPP HP*, PSOPP established partitionings according to an homogeneous partitioning objective function defined in [2]. (2) In the setting *PSOPP k-means*, PSOPP established heterogeneous partitionings according to the well-known k- means objective function. All evaluation runs have been performed in a distributed cluster of 12 computers with an Intel Core-i5 CPU and 4GB RAM for about a week. We performed each setting on a predefined system structure consisting of 1, 2, and 5 separate subsystems and 1000 controlled power plants within the system that are clustered to AVPPs by the SO mechanism. Each subsystem has one instance of the investigated SO mechanism (PSOPP HP or PSOPP k-means).

The results of our evaluation are summarized in Table 2. Having a closer look at Table 2 the performance metric $p(sys)$ (cf. Eq. (1)) is shown for all instances with three different configurations according to their weights, a balanced weighting, a favor for quality, and a favor for time. As we computed the data from 100 different evaluation runs by using the arithmetic mean value with the according SD. The selection of the average function here followed the same approach as described in the setting of the production cell. The investigated data are also not normal distributed, but tightly clustered, making the mean value a good fit for describing the data. The normal distribution was tested and the p-value resulted in <0.05. Further, the independency between the values to compare was test by the Mann-Whitney-Wilcoxon test with a resulting p-value < 0.05. Overall we have observed very slight variants of the performance over the runs and observed no big outliers.

### Discussion of the Evaluation Results

*RQ 1:* A first observation is that the decrease of agents involved in the reconfiguration has a rather low impact on the $tp(sys)$ value in both types of SO

**Table 2.** Evaluation results for the two settings "PSOPP HP" and "PSOPP k-means" with different numbers of AVPPs. All values are averages over evaluation runs with 300 steps; values in parenthesis denote SD.

| Setting | PSOPP HP | | | PSOPP k-means | | |
|---|---|---|---|---|---|---|
| #Separate Subsystems | 1 | 2 | 5 | 1 | 2 | 5 |
| $tp(sys)$ | 0.87 | 0.86 | 0.90 | 0.02 | 0.02 | 0.02 |
| | (0.11) | (0.27) | (0.02) | (0.002) | (0.004) | (0.007) |
| $qp(sys)$ | 0.96 | 0.96 | 0.96 | 0.99 | 0.99 | 0.99 |
| | (0.02) | (0.01) | (0.01) | (0.01) | (0.01) | (0.01) |
| $p(sys)$ $w_t = 0.5, w_q = 0.5$ | 0.92 | 0.91 | 0.94 | 0.51 | 0.51 | 0.51 |
| | (0.07) | (0.15) | (0.02) | (0.03) | (0.05) | (0.09) |
| $p(sys)$ $w_t = 0.1, w_q = 0.9$ | 0.95 | 0.95 | 0.95 | 0.89 | 0.89 | 0.89 |
| | (0.04) | (0.05) | (0.01) | (0.03) | (0.06) | (0.10) |
| $p(sys)$ $w_t = 0.9, w_q = 0.1$ | 0.88 | 0.87 | 0.91 | 0.12 | 0.12 | 0.12 |
| | (0.04) | (0.19) | (0.02) | (0.02) | (0.03) | (0.06) |
| #Reorganized Separate Subsystems | 1.05 | 2.88 | 11.01 | 141.57 | 244.11 | 501.36 |
| | (0.32) | (0.88) | (1.98) | (17.93) | (43.11) | (113.11) |
| #Reconfigured Agents per Reconf. | 1000.00 | 696.78 | 252.47 | 1000.00 | 734.74 | 499.51 |
| | (0.00) | (400.14) | (288.34) | (0.00) | (335.52) | (284.18) |

mechanisms. That effect is also shown in the number of reorganizations performed in the different setting compared with the involved number of agents in a reorganizations. The more separate subsystems the less agents are on average involved in a reorganization, but also the more reorganizations are necessary for keeping up the goals of the SO mechanism. This seems to be an effect of the decentralized knowledge that is lower than the central knowledge and thus leads to a higher need for reconfigurations. This effect is reflected in the metric, by having almost the same value despite a changing subsystem size. These local effects are handled in the metric. Same for $qp(sys)$, all values have been gathered locally. The value for the quality function for PSOPP HP setting is stating how similar the AVPPs are in their composition. Thus, the goal it the minimization of the SD of the average state values of the power plants in each AVPPs. For the k-means setting the similarity of the average state is the measure of quality for each AVPP. For $qp(sys)$, in the HP and the k-means setting, a similar effects are shown as for the time performance: the increasing number of separate subsystems has no impact on the quality of the system. Measuring the performance locally is consequently able to judge over the global system without neglecting the structure of the system and the SO mechanisms.

*RQ 2:* Having $p(sys)$ for the two different SO mechanism in the scenario we can clearly observe that the homogeneous partitioning is in favor. That reflects the fact that homogeneous partitioning is more robust than k-means, as described by Anders et al. [2]. However, the robustness has a slight price in quality, that is overall more optimal with k-means (see the $qp(sys)$ values). Nevertheless, that comes with a high price of a very poor $tp(sys)$ result. To achieve a better rating for PSOPP k-means a possible allocation of the weights is $w_t = 0.03$, $w_q = 0.97$. However, it is not recommended to choose such a strong favor for one part of $p(sys)$ since it ignores one of the two important performance factors. Thus, to answer *RQ 2* the benefit can be considered and even more the influence can be steered individually.

*RQ 3:* The answer to *RQ 3* is shown in the fact that we observed fluctuations throughout the evaluation runs within the maximum. That is different from the production cell case study, where the maximum for the quality performance was computed for a run not for a step. In this case study the maximum value is dynamically calculated at each step for a single subsystem. Since the value is depended from the current state of the controlled power plants in a subsystem. That is highly necessary to normalize the different achievements in the different system steps.

*RQ 4:* *RQ 4* questions whether the results are adequate regarding the conditions under which they were measured. This question is hard to answer with the resulting data, since we have no gold standard to compare with. However, our argumentation of Eq. (6) indicates that we have an accuracy of at least 0.95 for the measurements. The inaccuracy of 0.05 is within the variation of the $p(sys)$ value according to the SD and consequently negligible. Thus, we have established an adequate evaluation framework.

# 6    Related Work

In [6], we provided an overview on performance metrics for SO mechanisms and evaluated their abilities. We identified several metrics for adaptation (resp. self-adaptation) algorithms in the literature. And only very few that are focused on SO as we described it in [6]. As is the case with classical algorithms, the metrics can be clustered into *time-oriented metrics* and *solution-quality-oriented metrics*. The research survey of Villegas et al. [20] as well as the criteria for the evaluation of self-* systems of Kaddoum et al. [9] are *time-oriented metrics* that reflect the relationship between time for adaptation and working time. The performance metrics of Becker et al. [3], Tarnu and Tiemann [19], Reinecke et al. [17], and Kantert et al. [10] address the *solution quality* of the algorithm.

*Time-Oriented Metrics:* The metrics *WAT* [9], *A* [20], and *U* [20] rely on the ratio between working time and adaptivity time resp. the mean time to fail and the mean time to recover. All three focus on the impact of the adaptation on the working system and reflect the stability as well as the robustness of the configurations established by the SO mechanism. Unfortunately, the locality of

SO mechanisms is neglected by the three metrics. Thus, a reconfiguration in a small part of the system is rated as an adaptation period of the entire system as is for a reconfiguration within a huge part of the system. In our approach we address this issue by measuring locally. Considering only the time-oriented metrics, it is possible that an SO mechanism, that causes the system to work inefficiently is rated very good in terms of time if it generates a robust structure. Such a metric is not sufficient to rate the performance of an SO mechanism with all its responsibilities. Therefore, we combined time-oriented metrics with solution-quality-oriented metrics to rate the overall performance of an SO mechanism.

*Solution-Quality-Oriented Metrics:* To rate the performance of an SO mechanism, the optimality of its solution plays a crucial role. The metrics proposed in [3, 19] are quite similar in how they measure the normalized fitness of the SO mechanism over time. Challenges that arise during the evaluation of SO mechanisms with the metrics defined in [3, 19] are mainly caused by the locality of the SO mechanisms. This is a major difference to the adaptation algorithm considered in [3] as well as in [19] who regard a central approach of only one adaptation algorithm within the entire system. In case of multiple subsystems, as is the case with our energy grid scenario, the metrics could be applied to the separate subsystems, but it is not obvious how to calculate the performance for the overall system. The *Ad* metric [17] intends to smooth the development of the fitness value. Alas, the metric shows some bad side effects, as elaborated in [6]. Thus, it is hard to use the value for performance evaluation. Quantifying how robust an achieved solution of an SO mechanism is is the focus of [10]. That is measured by how fast the mechanisms are able to recover from disturbances and attacks from outside.

This metric is describing the quality performance by the time for regaining a target output of the system. This approach is, in contrast to our approach, focused on robustness against external attacks. A similar approach was made by Pitt et al. [16], focusing on the aspects of procedural justice as a values for participation, transparency and balancing in an CAS. Compared to the here presented approach [16] is focused on openness and transparency, we are a more generic approach. Indeed, one possibility is to include the metrics of [16] as the quality measure (Eq. (7)) in our approach.

## 7    Conclusion

We provide a tool set for measuring and evaluating the performance of SO mechanisms. This tool set is able to support the engineering process of developing suitable SO mechanisms for collective adaptive systems (CAS). As we have shown in our evaluation (Sect. 5), different kinds of SO mechanisms for different kinds of systems can be easily compared and rated, enabling to choose and optimize a suitable solution. One important contribution, that is extending the state of the art, is that our metric is able to fully exploit the local behavior of distributed SO mechanisms for time performance as well as quality performance. Reflecting ever-changing environmental conditions was important for the evaluation framework to select the most representative evaluation runs as well as for rating the achieved solution of the SO mechanism.

There are still some limitations to our approach. The metrics have the advantage of aggregating the performance of the SO mechanisms, but that aggregation is sometimes hiding information about the cause of the resulting performance. Furthermore, the quality performance must be defined by the user of the metric, we are not able to offer a gold standard for SO mechanisms here. Consequently, the results have to be judged by a skilled SO engineer and need some qualified input. Nevertheless, the framework and the development metrics have proven as a valuable tool for assessing the performance of SO mechanisms within CAS.

**Acknowledgment.** This research is sponsored by the research project *Testing self-organizing, adaptive Systems (TeSOS)* of the *German Research Foundation*.

# References

1. Anders, G., Seebach, H., Nafz, F., Steghöfer, J.P., Reif, W.: Decentralized reconfiguration for self-organizing resource-flow systems based on local knowledge. In: Proceedings of the 8th IEEE International Conference and Workshops on Engineering of Autonomic and Autonomous Systems (EASe 2011), pp. 20–31. IEEE (2011)
2. Anders, G., Siefert, F., Reif, W.: A particle swarm optimizer for solving the set partitioning problem in the presence of partitioning constraints. In: Proceedings of the 7th International Conference on Agents & AI (ICAART) (2015)
3. Becker, M., Luckey, M., Becker, S.: Performance analysis of self-adaptive systems for requirements validation at design-time. In: 9th ACM SIGSOFT International Conference on Quality of Software Architectures (QoSA 2013). ACM (2013)
4. Belzner, L., Hölzl, M., Koch, N., Wirsing, M.: Collective autonomic systems: towards engineering principles and their foundations. In: Steffen, B. (ed.) Transactions on Foundations for Mastering Change I. LNCS, vol. 9960, pp. 180–200. Springer, Cham (2016). https://doi.org/10.1007/978-3-319-46508-1_10
5. Eberhardinger, B., Anders, G., Seebach, H., Siefert, F., Knapp, A., Reif, W.: An approach for isolated testing of self-organization algorithms. In: de Lemos, R., Garlan, D., Ghezzi, C., Giese, H. (eds.) Software Engineering for Self-Adaptive Systems III. Assurances. LNCS, vol. 9640, pp. 188–222. Springer, Cham (2017). https://doi.org/10.1007/978-3-319-74183-3_7
6. Eberhardinger, B., Anders, G., Seebach, H., Siefert, F., Reif, W.: A research overview and evaluation of performance metrics for self-organization algorithms. In: Proceedings of the 9th International Conference on Self-Adaptive and Self-Organizing Systems Workshops, pp. 122–127. IEEE (2015)
7. Eberhardinger, B., Habermaier, A., Seebach, H., Reif, W.: Back-to-back testing of self-organization mechanisms. In: Wotawa, F., Nica, M., Kushik, N. (eds.) ICTSS 2016. LNCS, vol. 9976, pp. 18–35. Springer, Cham (2016). https://doi.org/10.1007/978-3-319-47443-4_2
8. Habermaier, A., Eberhardinger, B., Seebach, H., Leupolz, J., Reif, W.: Runtime model-based safety analysis of self-organizing systems with S#. In: 2015 IEEE International Conference on Self-Adaptive and Self-Organizing Systems Workshops (SASOW), pp. 128–133. IEEE (2015)

9. Kaddoum, E., Raibulet, C., Georgé, J., Picard, G., Gleizes, M.P.: Criteria for the evaluation of self-* systems. In: Proceedings of the 2010 ICSE Workshop on Software Engineering for Adaptive and Self-Managing Systems, pp. 29–38 (2010)
10. Kantert, J., Tomforde, S., Müller-Schloer, C., Edenhofer, S., Sick, B.: Quantitative robustness - a generalised approach to compare the impact of disturbances in self-organising systems. In: Proceedings of the 9th International Conference on Agents and Artificial Intelligence, ICAART 2017, pp. 39–50 (2017)
11. McGeoch, C.: A Guide to Experimental Algorithmics. Cambridge University Press, Cambridge (2012)
12. Monostori, L.: Cyber-physical production systems: roots, expectations and R&D challenges. Procedia CIRP **17**, 9–13 (2014)
13. Musa, J.D.: A theory of software reliability and its application. IEEE Trans. Softw. Eng. **1**(3), 312–327 (1975)
14. Neyman, J.: Outline of a theory of statistical estimation based on the classical theory of probability. Phil. Trans. R. Soc. Lond. A **236**(767), 333–380 (1937)
15. Parunak, H.V.D., Brueckner, S.A.: Software engineering for self-organizing systems. In: Proceedings of the 12th International Workshops on Agent-Oriented Software Engineering (AOSE 2011), pp. 1–22 (2011)
16. Pitt, J., Busquets, D., Riveret, R.: Procedural justice and 'Fitness for Purpose' of self-organising electronic institutions. In: Boella, G., Elkind, E., Savarimuthu, B.T.R., Dignum, F., Purvis, M.K. (eds.) PRIMA 2013. LNCS (LNAI), vol. 8291, pp. 260–275. Springer, Heidelberg (2013). https://doi.org/10.1007/978-3-642-44927-7_18
17. Reinecke, P., Wolter, K., Van Moorsel, A.: Evaluating the adaptivity of computing systems. Perform. Eval. **67**(8), 676–693 (2010)
18. Steghöfer, J.P., Anders, G., Siefert, F., Reif, W.: A system of systems approach to the evolutionary transformation of power management systems. In: Proceedings of INFORMATIK - Workshops on Smart Grids. LNI. Köllen Verlag (2013)
19. Taranu, S., Tiemann, J.: On assessing self-adaptive systems. In: Proceedings of the 8th International Conference on Pervasive Computing and Communications Workshops, pp. 214–219. IEEE (2010)
20. Villegas, N.M., Müller, H.A., Tamura, G., Duchien, L., Casallas, R.: A framework for evaluating quality-driven self-adaptive software systems. In: Proceedings of the 6th International Symposium on Software Engineering for Adaptive and Self-Managing Systems, pp. 80–89. ACM (2011)

# Engineering Sustainable and Adaptive Systems in Dynamic and Unpredictable Environments

Rui P. Cardoso[1]([✉]), Rosaldo J. F. Rossetti[1], Emma Hart[2],
David Burth Kurka[3], and Jeremy Pitt[3]

[1] Department of Informatics, University of Porto, Rua Dr Roberto Frias, s/n,
4200-465 Porto, Portugal
{rui.peixoto,rossetti}@fe.up.pt
[2] School of Computing, Edinburgh Napier University, Edinburgh EH10 5DT, UK
e.hart@napier.ac.uk
[3] Department of Electrical and Electronic Engineering, Imperial College London,
London SW7 2BT, UK
{d.kurka,j.pitt}@imperial.ac.uk

**Abstract.** Electronic institutions are socially-inspired multi-agent systems, typically operating under a set of policies, which are required to determine system operation and to deal with violations and other non-compliant behaviour. They are often faced with a dynamic population of agents, social network, and environment and their policy should suit this context. However, there is usually a large space of possible system policies, but no tractable systematic method to find an appropriate policy given a joint state of the population, social network, and the environment. We have developed a model of an energy system which encompasses several inter-connected community energy systems. We propose two methods, an *offline* and an *online* procedure, which enable this system model to *approximately optimise* its performance through adaptation and evolution of its operating policy. The policies evolved by our procedures *clearly outperform* a baseline policy we have designed by hand. Both procedures return policies which are appropriate for a system, given some performance criterion, without a human designer's intervention. This could lay the foundations for the development of a new methodological paradigm for the engineering of collective adaptive systems based on the convergence of electronic institutions and evolutionary computing.

## 1 Introduction

Some agent systems are socially-inspired: they are governed by rules and policies (are "rule-based" or "norm-governed") and the agents form virtual societies, referred to as electronic institutions (EIs). These are typically open systems – with heterogeneous and autonomous agents – with no central control or decision-making, and may be characterised by a dynamically changing environment. They

© Springer Nature Switzerland AG 2018
T. Margaria and B. Steffen (Eds.): ISoLA 2018, LNCS 11246, pp. 221–240, 2018.
https://doi.org/10.1007/978-3-030-03424-5_15

should ideally have mechanisms for dealing with unpredictable changes, respond-ing adequately when the performance is deteriorating, enabling sustainability and durability. In order to determine their operation and to prevent undesir-able or non-compliant behaviour, a possible consequence of their openness to autonomous agents acting on behalf of third parties, these systems must have a policy in place. Examples of the EI paradigm include sensor networks, robotic swarms, and smart grids.

When this type of system is used to manage the access to a shared resource, the problem is referred to as common-pool resource (CPR) management. Ostrom [14] presents several design principles for enduring institutions in the context of CPR management, including the notion that policies should be *mutable* in order to suit the environment. Some authors have proposed mechanisms to opera-tionalise these principles and apply them to the design of EIs [18], while also drawing other concepts from political and economic science to enable the agents to both *self-govern* and *self-organise* the adaptation of policies in the face of potentially unpredictable changes in the environment, such as distributive jus-tice [18,19] and knowledge management [17]. Self-governing and self-organisation both imply the active participation of the actors within an EI in the decision-making process.

Other approaches for dealing with dynamic environments have been inspired by Biology. Methods have been proposed to adapt autonomic components using evolutionary computing (EC) techniques as a response to environmental changes, e.g. [4,5]. These components exhibit cognition, namely learning and decision-making abilities, leading to collective *self-awareness*. Evolutionary approaches have also been used in other contexts. For example, genetic programming (GP) has been widely used to provide approximate solutions to optimisation problems, e.g. [2], and to evolve and adapt rules of different sorts over multiple time scales in the face of a problem space whose structure changes dynamically, e.g. [9,20].

Integrated community energy systems (CESs) may be viewed as EIs for the management of a CPR. They integrate distributed energy resources, such as pho-tovoltaic cells and wind turbines, into local energy systems, meeting some or all of the local energy demands. The local energy systems are connected to a wider regional/national grid and local communities are not just passive consumers, but also active prosumers who generate and supply energy and may provide services to the larger system. This system has a dynamically changing environ-ment: it faces fluctuations in the availability of resources, load, and demand over time, caused by seasonality, geographic location, and shifts in weather patterns, amongst other factors. The literature on CESs is mostly devoted to optimisa-tion models for the planning and integration of these systems. In this project, we have modelled and simulated an energy system consisting of many inter-connected CESs and proposed methods for automatically constructing system policies.

Our top-level goal is to explore how adaptation through evolution of policies can assist the design of collective adaptive systems which remain sustainable over time when faced with a dynamically changing environment, since policy modification mechanisms are necessary in order to cope with potentially unpredictable environmental changes. In a norm-governed system, a single policy may not be appropriate for all situations. For example, an energy system could have the following modes of operation: decentralised (peer-to-peer) when demands are low, with all the energy being produced by the local communities; centralised when the system is overloaded, with communities trading exclusively with the regional/national grid; or a hybrid approach for normal levels of load and demand. Besides this, surprising events could occur which result in deterioration of the performance, rendering the current policy no longer fit. This is expected to be the case in energy systems with several distributed energy resources across multiple communities: weather can be unpredictable and unstable, affecting the production rate of intermittent renewable resource converters such as solar panels and wind turbines. Ideally, systems should be able to recover from performance losses after a reasonable number of time steps. In general, there could be a very large space of possible system policies. There is no systematic way of finding an appropriate policy given a joint state of the population of agents, their social network, and the environment [16]; it may not be tractable or possible to search the entire space of possible policies exhaustively.

Our research question is whether we can use GP to generate, adapt, and evolve policies under which systems operate in order to ensure that they remain sustainable over time. The specific problem we have addressed in this project is to automatically find operating policies which are approximately optimal for a given system according to some performance criterion – i.e., policies we would consider *appropriate*. This could assist designers in building systems for which it is hard to come up with a policy leading to good performance and which may be faced with a dynamic environment requiring constant modification and adaptation of policies. Even a human expert might lack not only the knowledge necessary to determine whether a given policy will result in good performance or to compare alternative policies, but also the creativity needed to design sufficiently good policies. The "ideal" policy for a given system may be counter-intuitive to a person, but an heuristic search over the space of possible policies, which is the base of what we propose in this work, is not sensitive to that.

In order to address the problem specified above, we have started by creating a model of an energy system in which several communities produce and consume energy and used it to run simulations to observe how different policies behave. We have used binary decision trees to represent policies. The key contributions of this work are two optimisation methods for automatically finding appropriate policies for this system model. The first one is an *offline* procedure which returns a policy that approximately optimises system performance using GP. The second method is an *online* procedure which evolves and adapts a population of policies over time by applying them to the system in turn and using performance history to increasingly improve the general quality of the policies in each new generation, drawing inspiration from reinforcement learning (RL) techniques. Results show that the policies resulting from these procedures clearly outperform a baseline policy which we have designed by hand.

The modelling approach we propose and the procedures we have implemented and tested for finding approximately optimal policies could provide the foundations for the development of a new methodological paradigm for the engineering of collective adaptive systems. The results are encouraging and provide insight into the effects of adaptation and innovation, through evolution of a set of policies, on the sustainability of a distributed system for CPR management, applied to the context of CESs. This work is also innovative in the sense that it brings together the paradigms of socially-inspired and biologically-inspired computing, as we have drawn notions from EIs when modelling a system in which energy is treated as a CPR and have used GP to evolve and adapt its policy.

This paper is structured as follows. In Sect. 2, we discuss relevant background to this work, focusing on EIs, EC and GP, and CESs. In Sect. 3, we provide a description of the steps we have followed and the methods we have implemented. In Sect. 4, we discuss experimental results. In Sect. 5, we present the main conclusions which have emerged from this work and reflect on directions for future research.

## 2    Background

In a position paper, Pitt and Hart [16] proposed the integration of the socially-inspired design patterns of EIs with the biologically-inspired techniques used in EC and GP to adapt and innovate the policy of a system as a response to dynamic and unpredictable changes in the environment. In this section, we review some key concepts which have enabled the implementation of this approach. In Sect. 2.1, we explore the notion of EIs. In Sect. 2.2, we review some work on EC and GP. In Sect. 2.3, we present concepts and issues related to CESs.

### 2.1    Electronic Institutions

Agent-based systems which are governed by rules and policies – for example, for managing collective resources – are referred to as electronic institutions (EIs). Agents form societies and often seek individual goals, as well as common objectives. In open systems, agents are heterogeneous and may not comply with the system policy. Self-organisation means that a certain system is able "to change its organisation without explicit command during its execution time" [6]. This concept has been applied to many fields, among which multi-agent systems (MASs) [22].

Ostrom [14] proposes a view of self-organising institutions for the management of CPRs, in which the rules of an institution govern the appropriation and provision of shared resources and should be mutable by other rules and *adaptable to suit the environment*. Ostrom also identifies eight design principles for the management of CPRs in *enduring* self-organising institutions after arguing that, unlike predicted by game theory, CPR management does not necessarily result in a "tragedy of the commons", in which a group of self-interested and rational agents eventually depletes a shared resource.

Pitt *et al.* [18] axiomatise these principles, expressing them in logical form. This formal specification is used to implement a test bed to show that they result in enduring EIs for the management of CPRs. They note that a strategy resulting in a sub-optimal distribution in the short term might prove better in the long term if the resource is not depleted. They analyse the problem of allocating endogenous resources with an implementation of the Linear Public Good (LPG) game [7]. They resort to a framework which enables the specification of a protocol stack which agents can use to alter the policies of a system at runtime [1]. The specification space is formally defined by a number of degrees of freedom, such as the allocation method (ration, queue, etc.). The rules are formalised using Event Calculus [12], which is an action- and event-oriented language. The experimental results show that the principles defined by Ostrom do entail enduring management of CPRs in self-organising EIs.

The principles, however, do not explicitly concern a notion of fairness and justice. Pitt *et al.* [15] build on this work by analysing the mechanisms influencing the fairness of the result of a resource allocation. Agents self-organise the allocation process by participating in a voting procedure. The authors note that an outcome which is unfair at a given time step could be part of a sequence of fair cumulative outcomes, a notion which is important for economies of scarcity. Rescher [19] presents the concept of distributive justice, identifying several ways of distributing resources based on legitimate claims. Pitt *et al.* draw inspiration from Rescher's work to study mechanisms which influence the fairness of a resource allocation procedure, with the LPG game being once again used as an example application. The results reveal robustness to purposeful violations. Among the assessment metrics used are the number of remaining agents in a cluster of the LPG game, the utility for the agents, and the fairness of the allocation method.

### 2.2 Evolutionary Computing and Genetic Programming

Evolutionary Computing (EC), in its broader sense, draws inspiration from biological evolution to solve problems, involving population-based stochastic search approaches [2]. Genetic Programming (GP) is based on Darwin's theory of evolution and the mechanisms it describes, namely natural selection, evolving solutions to problems according to the principle of "survival of the fittest". These approaches have been widely used to find approximate solutions to many optimisation problems, as well as classification problems. Since it has been used to evolve rules, which can be functions, heuristics, or other sorts of decisions, it seems appropriate to apply GP to the evolution and adaptation of the operating policy of a system.

Sim *et al.* [20] describe an innovative hyper-heuristic system. They propose a lifelong machine learning (LML) system called NELLI, which learns continuously over time using prior knowledge, applying it to a combinatorial optimisation problem. An Artificial Immune System (AIS) encompasses heuristics and problems interacting in a network, with problems viewed as pathogens and heuristics as antibodies. The key idea is that the problems "provide a minimal representative map of the problem space" and each heuristic solves a niche of problems. The system continuously generates new heuristics in response to a stream of incoming problems and it was applied to the 1D bin-packing problem. The results show that it is efficient and scalable, outperforming human-designed heuristics, and adapting efficiently to unseen problems.

Hart and Sim [9] describe NELLI-GP, the successor of NELLI. They address the Job Shop Scheduling Problem (JSSP), in which several operations are scheduled for execution in multiple machines. Heuristics are sequences of rules and they propose an ensemble of heuristics which are evolved using GP, with baseline dispatching rules as building blocks. The rules themselves are formulated as trees of operations, returning a real value which determines the priority of an operation. GP is used to evolve new heuristics to be included in the ensemble, as well as new rules to be part of the sequence of dispatching rules which make up a heuristic. The results show that using an ensemble is preferable over a single heuristic and that the system generalises well from the training set. The ensembles are reusable: after being fitted to a data set, they can be used with a different one (adaptation). Their system outperforms other scheduling rules and hyper-heuristic approaches for the JSSP.

### 2.3 Community Energy Systems

Integrated community energy systems (CESs) are "a modern development to reorganise local energy systems to integrate distributed energy resources and engage local communities" [11]. They ensure self-supply of energy and are also capable of supplying the larger energy system. Local communities are no longer considered passive consumers, but rather active prosumers who also produce energy. Following the motto "think globally, act locally", CESs can help tackle global energy and climate challenges. However, they face challenges; energy generation using intermittent renewable resources is *difficult to forecast*. Flexible generation can be achieved with conventional fuels.

Much of the literature on this subject is concerned about the planning and optimisation of integrated CESs. Huang *et al.* [10] review methodologies and software which address community energy planning (CEP). Linear (LP) and non-linear programming (NLP) are common techniques to obtain solutions to this optimisation problem, although many approximation algorithms, such as genetic algorithms (GAs), have also been developed [3].

### 2.4 Summary

In this section, we have reviewed some approaches which have been proposed so far to deal with unpredictable changes in dynamic environments. Among the references on EIs, there is a focus on the application of concepts from social, political, and economic science, such as self-organisation, self-governance, distributive justice, or knowledge management, to digital organisations as a mechanism for enabling their actors to collectively adapt and modify policies. The literature on EC includes studies of how different biologically-inspired techniques may be used to adapt autonomic components, such as agents, and their social network as a response to environmental changes. A relevant concept in this context is collective self-awareness, which is achieved when the agents are capable of learning from past experience and making decisions autonomously. We have also reviewed several applications of GP to a number of problems, e.g. optimisation. Rules of different sorts are represented as trees and are evolved using GP. The sources on CESs are mainly concerned with planning this sort of system and optimising energy consumption, making use of tools for modelling and simulation. The ultimate goal of our work has been to draw inspiration from the concepts discussed in the reviewed literature to propose a new methodological paradigm for the design of collective adaptive systems. In particular, we have explored methods for approximately optimising policies in an EI using GP.

## 3   Methodology

This section describes the methodological approach followed in this work for the modelling and simulation of an energy system which is capable of adapting its policy over time.

### 3.1   Model

The first step towards answering the research question we propose in this work, whether adaptation and innovation of the policy of a system through evolution are capable of leading to improved endurance and sustainability, has been to model an energy system encompassing several CESs. In this model, energy is treated as a CPR and communities are modelled as agents; they have energy demands and can generate energy from a number of renewable sources. Three sources of renewable energy have been considered, namely solar power, wind turbines, and hydropower converters.

Communities have neighbours and are part of an energy system. The energy system can also generate and feed energy to compensate for any lack of self-generated power. Communities are able to trade energy amongst themselves, using a simplified version of the Contract Net Protocol [21], and with the central system. At each time step, the energy system uses the current operating policy to determine the mode of operation of the system for that time step, as explained in detail in Sect. 3.2. Figure 1 summarises the domain model of the system.

At each time step, the utility of the energy allocation method is calculated for each community, taking into account the costs of importing energy, both from other communities and the central system, and storing energy produced in excess, as well as the revenues from exports. The cumulative satisfaction for community $i$ at time step $t$ is calculated with the most recent utility value, $u_t^i$, as follows:

$$s_t^i = (1 - w) \times s_{t-1}^i + w \times u_t^i, \text{ with } s_0^i = 0 \tag{1}$$

The $w$ parameter weights the importance of past satisfactions and the current utility when updating a community's satisfaction.

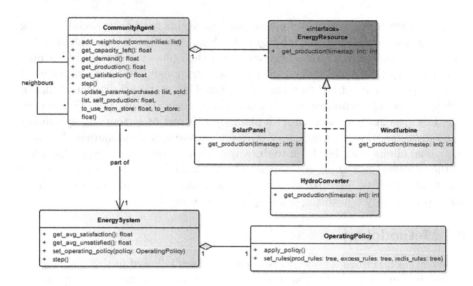

**Fig. 1.** Domain model of the energy system

## 3.2   Representation, Innovation, and Adaptation of Policies

Given the need to evolve and adapt the operating policy of the system, we represent it with decision trees. At each time step, the policy is applied in order to determine a *mode of operation*. In our model, the mode of operation has three degrees of freedom:

– What the communities should do with the energy they have produced at the current time step: either use it to satisfy their own demands (self-supply) or sell it all to the central system.
– In the case of self-supply, what the communities should do with any excess of energy: sell to the central system; store as much as capacity allows and sell the excess; trade it with neighbours and sell the excess; store, trade, and sell; or trade, store, and sell.
– If any demands have not been satisfied, the central system will ensure they are met by first reselling the energy which has been purchased from the communities and producing energy on demand (accounting for production costs) when necessary. The communities receive the energy according to several possible criteria: greatest demand, greatest production, lowest satisfaction, random, or ration.

For each degree of freedom, a decision tree selects one of the possible values with which it can be instantiated. There are therefore $2 \times 5 \times 5 = 50$ possible modes of operation at each time step. The inner nodes of the tree test the values of system-wide variables which are collected at each time step, returning a Boolean value (i.e., the decision trees are binary). Based on the literature about EIs, CPR management, and CESs, as well as on knowledge regarding the system model we have created, we have selected the following system variables to be collected and tested at each time step:

- Number of communities (fixed)
- Average satisfaction across all communities
- Total energy production at the communities
- Total self-supply of energy
- Average difference between self-supplied energy and demand
- Average difference between current assets (energy produced and stored) and demand
- Number of unsatisfied agents (negative satisfaction)
- Total energy stored
- Total demand
- Total difference between current assets (energy produced and stored) and demand
- Average capacity left
- Gini index of satisfaction inequality

As a first step, we devised a default policy whose performance could be compared to that of the operating policies which are evolved by the procedures discussed in this paper. Figure 2 shows the default decision tree for selecting what the communities should do with the energy they produce (the first degree of freedom), as an example of the type of decision trees which are evolved and manipulated by our procedures.

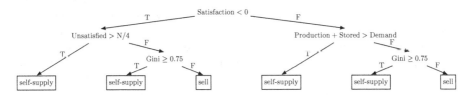

**Fig. 2.** Default decision tree encapsulating rules which determine what the communities should do with the energy they have produced at each time step.

We considered two approaches for approximately finding an optimal policy for the system. The first approach is GP optimisation and is detailed in Sect. 3.3. The second approach consists of adapting and evolving policies in runtime and is explained in Sect. 3.4.

### 3.3 Offline Procedure

In order to find an optimal operating policy *a priori*, we implemented a GP algorithm which evaluates alternatives by running the model with each of a population of policies for the number of time steps corresponding to a week

(168, since time steps represent hours). A performance metric is calculated as follows, where satisfaction and the proportion of unsatisfied agents are averaged out after a week has passed:

$$
\begin{aligned}
\text{performance} = {} & \alpha \times \text{average satisfaction} \\
& - \beta \times \text{average proportion of unsatisfied agents}
\end{aligned}
\tag{2}
$$

The $\alpha$ parameter determines how much the average satisfaction favours the performance measure and the $\beta$ parameter determines how much the average proportion of unsatisfied agents penalises it ($\alpha > 0$ and $\beta \geq 0$). An initial population of operating policies (each a tuple with three decision trees, one for each degree of freedom) is generated randomly using "ramped half and half" [13]. In GP optimisation, the set of function nodes is usually finite; in this case, the set of possible inner nodes for the decision trees is theoretically infinite, so we randomly initialise a large set of function nodes at the start of the procedure. At each iteration of the optimisation procedure, the operating policies are evaluated *in parallel* by running *instances of the same model* for 168 time steps (a week) and computing a performance value. The performance values are then used as fitness values to evolve a new generation using standard GP operations, namely reproduction, crossover, and mutation, which are described by Koza [13]. Reproduction randomly selects individuals to be copied to the following generation with a probability which should grow monotonically with respect to the fitness value (we have used Softmax probabilities). The crossover operation randomly selects pairs of individuals, again with a probability which is higher the higher their fitness, and crosses them element-wise, each element being a tree in the triple which makes up an operating policy. The mutation operation also selects individuals based on their fitness and creates new individuals by replacing parts of their trees with randomly generated subtrees; its goal is to introduce variability when searching for new solutions. The procedure keeps track of the best operating policy it has found so far and returns it after a certain number of generations have been evolved. This policy is the one which led to the greatest performance value after running the model, and therefore is approximately optimal. This procedure is described in pseudocode by Algorithm 1.

## 3.4   Online Procedure

Adapting and evolving policies in runtime poses further challenges. When searching the space of possible operating policies in order to optimise system performance, we do not have a way of assigning a fitness value to alternative policies in order to compare them *a priori*, as would be necessary to implement "hill climbing" or other local search methods. The performance of a policy must be measured by first running the model with it for a certain amount of time. The method we propose draws inspiration from both GP and RL. An initial population of operating policies is randomly generated using the "ramped half and half" method and a policy is selected when the model starts running. A decision is made periodically about which operating policy in the current population

**Algorithm 1.** Finding an optimal policy *a priori* using GP

---

Choose model *params* to generate instances of the same model
Choose parameters for the initial population: $max\_dt\_depth\_gen$, $n\_dt\_each$,
$max\_ot\_depth\_gen$, $n\_ot\_each$
Choose parameters for evolution: $max\_dt\_depth$, $copy\_perc$, $cross\_perc$, $mut\_perc$,
$elitist$
Choose number of iterations: $N$
$population \leftarrow$ generate_initial_population($max\_dt\_depth\_gen, n\_dt\_each,$
$max\_ot\_depth\_gen, n\_ot\_each$)
$max\_fit \leftarrow -\infty$
$best\_policy \leftarrow \emptyset$
**for** $Gen = 1$, $Gen \leq N$; $Gen \leftarrow Gen + 1$ **do**
    $fits \leftarrow \emptyset$
    **for** $policy \in population$ **do**
        $model \leftarrow$ Model($params$)
        $model$.set_policy($policy$)
        **for** $i = 0$, $i < WEEK\_DURATION$, $i \leftarrow i + 1$ **do**
            $model$.step()
        **end for**
        $fit = model$.get_average_fitness() (Eq. 2)
        **if** $fit > max\_fit$ **then**
            $max\_fit \leftarrow fit$
            $best\_policy \leftarrow policy$
        **end if**
        $fits \leftarrow fits \cup \{(policy, fit)\}$
    **end for**
    $population \leftarrow$ evolve_new_generation($population, fits, max\_dt\_depth, copy\_perc,$
    $cross\_perc, mut\_perc, elitist$)
**end for**
**return** $best\_policy$

---

should be tried. An operating policy is selected every 24 time steps (hours) based
on Softmax probabilities calculated from the current fitness values. After a policy $i$ has been put in use for 24 time steps, a *reward* is calculated based on the
observed performance:

$$r_i^t = \text{performance}^t \tag{3}$$

The observed system performance, performance$^t$, is calculated as in Eq. 2,
considering the average satisfaction and average proportion of unsatisfied agents
over the most recent 24 time steps. The fitness value of a policy $i$, fit$_i$, is initialised
to 0. After applying policy $i$ on the system for 24 time steps, its fitness value is
updated as follows:

$$\text{fit}_i \leftarrow \begin{cases} r_i^t & \text{if the policy had not yet been tried} \\ (1 - \Omega) \times \text{fit}_i + \Omega \times r_i^t & \text{otherwise} \end{cases} \tag{4}$$

$\Omega$ is the *learning rate*, weighting the importance of the most recent reward to the overall fitness of the operating policy. At each 336 time steps, two weeks' time, the fitness values are used to evolve a new generation of operating policies, using standard GP techniques as those described earlier. In order to promote variability among the members of the population, new random policies are added to each generation, besides those resulting from the reproduction, crossover, and mutation operations; this is the *hypermutation* step proposed by Grefenstette [8] and it is introduced here because the population size should be small[1]. When calculating Softmax probabilities for selecting policies to be tried on the system, we have found it beneficial to divide all fitness values by a *temperature* parameter, which is a positive value that is decremented over time, divided by 2 every 168 time steps (a week's time) until it reaches 1. This is intended to promote early exploration of many different policies and thereby to prevent premature convergence to good but sub-optimal policies. The population size is also decreased linearly over time. If an elitist strategy is employed, the best policies found so far are guaranteed to be passed on to the following generation, thus becoming increasingly likely to be selected as less and less exploration takes place. A high-level pseudocode description of this runtime procedure is given in Algorithm 2.

This approach does, in our view, address the problem of reconciling the following:

- We want to evolve and adapt the current set of policies, converging to an approximately optimal performance.
- We are unable to know how good a policy is until it has been tried on the system model.
- Policy selection and adaptation must be done in runtime; the system must not backtrack after trying a policy and policies must be tried sequentially.

The method we propose is intended to be a mechanism for enabling exploration of different policies, *ideally* converging to policies which maximise performance. Past history is taken into account when iteratively updating the fitness values of the operating policies which have been tried, drawing inspiration from RL techniques in the sense that we reward good policies and penalise bad policies after their performance on the system has been observed. The GP part of the procedure is the search method, intended to find a population of policies which approximately optimise system performance by taking the iterative updates to the fitness values into account.

---

[1] Testing policies every 24 time steps and evolving a new generation every two weeks' time means that a maximum of only 14 policies out of each generation can be tested. Fitness values are initialised to 0, which could be an overestimation. Large population sizes would cause many policies not to be tested, which could result in many bad policies being added to following generations. Hypermutation promotes variability in smaller populations.

**Algorithm 2.** Evolving a population of operating policies in runtime

---

Choose model *params*
Choose parameters for the initial population: $max\_dt\_depth\_gen$, $n\_dt\_each$, $max\_ot\_depth\_gen$, $n\_ot\_each$
Choose parameters for evolution: $max\_dt\_depth$, $copy\_perc$, $cross\_perc$, $mut\_perc$, $elitist$, $lr$, $initial\_temperature$, $gen\_threshold$
$model \leftarrow$ Model($params$)
$population \leftarrow$ generate_initial_population($max\_dt\_depth\_gen, n\_dt\_each$, $max\_ot\_depth\_gen$)
$current\_policy \leftarrow$ select_random_policy($population$)
$model$.set_policy($current\_policy$)
$temperature \leftarrow initial\_temperature$
$fits \leftarrow \emptyset$
$initial\_population\_size \leftarrow$ len($population$)
$population\_size \leftarrow initial\_population\_size$
$generation \leftarrow 1$
**while** not terminated **do**
    $model$.step()
    **if** $timestep$ mod $DAY\_DURATION = 0$ **then**
        $reward \leftarrow model$.get_last_avg_fitness()
        $fitness \leftarrow$ update_fitness($current\_policy, reward$) (Eq. 4)
        **if** $current\_policy$ not in $fits$ **then**
            $fits \leftarrow fits \cup \{(current\_policy, fitness)\}$
        **else**
            Update $fits$ with ($current\_policy, fitness$)
        **end if**
        $current\_policy \leftarrow$ select_random_policy($population, fits, temperature$)
        $model$.set_policy($current\_policy$)
    **end if**
    **if** $timestep$ mod $WEEK\_DURATION = 0 \land temperature > 1$ **then**
        $temperature \leftarrow$ max($temperature/2, 1$)
    **end if**
    **if** $timestep$ mod $(2 \times WEEK\_DURATION) = 0$ **then**
        **if** $generation > gen\_threshold \land population\_size > initial\_population\_size/2$ **then**
            $population\_size \leftarrow$ max($population\_size - initial\_population\_size/3$, $initial\_population\_size/2$)
        **end if**
        $population \leftarrow$ evolve_new_generation($population, fits, population\_size$, $max\_dt\_depth, copy\_perc, cross\_perc, mut\_perc, elitist$)
        $generation \leftarrow generation + 1$
    **end if**
**end while**

---

# 4    Experimental Results

In this section, we present and discuss the results of the experiments we have carried out with our system model and proposed methods.

## 4.1    Performance of the Offline Optimisation Procedure

Regarding the offline procedure for the optimisation of a single operating policy *a priori*, experiments have been carried out as an attempt to answer the following questions:

1. For the same model instance, to what extent is the quality of the evolved policy (in terms of the resulting system performance) robust with respect to the stochastic nature of the optimisation procedure?
2. For the same model instance, are the solutions obtained with different runs of the optimisation procedure similar in terms of their consequences, i.e., are the same modes of operations applied in the same context?

In order to answer these questions, the optimisation procedure described in Sect. 3.4 was run 30 times on the same model, each time returning an operating policy which approximately maximises the performance metric given by Eq. 2, with $\alpha = 1$ and $\beta = 5$. At each time step, each community's satisfaction was updated with $w = 0.5$ (refer to Eq. 1). The decision trees in the initial population had a maximum depth of 3, with a maximum permissible depth of 5 for new trees resulting from crossover. The initial population size is $18^2$ and, when evolving a new generation, 10% of the new population results from the reproduction operation, 40% from crossover, and 50% from mutation. This parameter setting is summarised in Table 1. The median maximum performance value after 30 executions of the procedure was 8.122. The sample standard deviation was $2.94 \times 10^{-2}$, which shows that there is little variation in the maximum performance value when running the procedure several times. This enables us to conclude that the procedure is indeed robust with respect to the stochastic nature of GP, as the performance of the solutions found is approximately the same for the same model when comparing different executions. The performance value obtained for the same model with our default policy was 3.519, showing how hard it is for a system designer to find an optimal policy and the usefulness of the optimisation procedure. The policy obtained using GP (approximate) optimisation results in a *clearly better performance* when compared to the default policy we designed.

In order to answer the second question, we then took each of the 30 operating policies obtained and compared the modes of operation selected at each time step. Recall that a mode of operation is given by instantiating the three degrees of freedom mentioned in Sect. 3.1. We then counted the number of unique modes of operation selected at each time step; the median value was 5. This means that, in

---

[2] While this would be a small population size for many GP problems, we have empirically determined it to be appropriate in this case.

**Table 1.** Parameters for the experiments with the offline optimisation procedure

| $\alpha$ | 1 |
|---|---|
| $\beta$ | 5 |
| $w$ | 0.5 |
| $max\_dt\_depth\_gen$ | 3 |
| $max\_dt\_depth$ | 5 |
| $initial\_pop\_size$ | 18 |
| $copy\_perc$ | 0.1 |
| $cross\_perc$ | 0.4 |
| $mut\_perc$ | 0.5 |
| $elitist$ | False, apply the reproduction operation (probabilistic copy of individuals) |

the case of our system model, there are several locally optimal policies, resulting in different sequences of modes of operation, yielding approximately the same system performance. There is, however, a certain degree of similarity between these sequences, given the median value of 5 out of a possible maximum of 30 unique modes of operation at each time step (given that there are 50 possible modes, as mentioned in Sect. 3.2). Table 2 summarises the results obtained after 30 runs of the offline optimisation procedure.

**Table 2.** Results after 30 runs of the offline optimisation procedure (baseline default policy for comparison)

| Median maximum performance | 8.122 |
|---|---|
| Sample standard deviation of the maximum performance | $2.94 \times 10^{-2}$ |
| Median number of unique modes of operation at each time step | 5 |
| Performance with the baseline default policy | 3.519 |

All solutions obtained from different runs have approximately the same performance value. However, the fact that these solutions are fairly diverse in terms of the sequences of modes of operation in which they result[3], as discussed above, indicates that they are, in fact, local optima and that there could be an even better solution which the procedure has failed to find. We began the discussion in this paper by claiming that it is hard to find an optimal policy given a certain environment. Indeed, since the mode of operation chosen at a given time step will affect future performance in the case of our system model, we would have

---

[3] This refers to functional diversity (a sequence of modes of operation is a consequence of applying one or more policies to the system over time), rather than structural diversity (the shape of the trees which make up a policy).

to consider all possible sequences of modes up until a certain time step, select one which maximises performance, and then come up with a set of rules which results in that sequence. This is a combinatorial problem which quickly becomes intractable as the final time step grows and this formulation is only applicable to cases where the final time step is bounded; in real-world cases, the system is continuously running and our online method for adaptation and evolution of the operating policy in runtime seems more useful.

## 4.2    Performance of the Online Optimisation Procedure

The offline optimisation procedure returns a single policy which has been evaluated on the system for 168 time steps (a week). The online procedure, on the other hand, tests several policies on the system over time for a number of time steps corresponding to many weeks, with one policy affecting the performance of subsequent policies. In this section, we try to compare the performance of the online procedure to that of the offline procedure by calculating an average weekly performance (last 168 time steps), but the reader should keep in mind that the performance metrics for both procedures are not exactly the same. Regarding the online optimisation procedure, experiments have been carried out as an attempt to answer the following questions:

1. Is the system able to improve its performance over time by evolving and adapting its policy?
2. For the same model instance, does the system usually converge to approximately the same performance as the one obtained by running the offline optimisation procedure?

In order to answer the questions above, we have executed the online procedure upon the same model instance 30 times. At each time step, average daily (last 24 time steps) and weekly (last 168 time steps) performance values have been calculated, with the goal to see how many times the weekly performance successfully converged to a value close to 8, which is the *approximately optimal value found by the offline procedure*. Again, $\alpha = 1$, $\beta = 5$, and $w = 0.5$. The maximum depth for the decision trees is the same as before. The initial population size is 12, the initial *temperature* is 320, $\Omega = 0.5$, and, when evolving a new generation, 20% of the new population is the result of copying individuals using an elitist strategy, 10% is the result of crossover, 10% is the result of mutation, and the remaining 60% are new policies generated randomly with the intention of introducing more variability and preventing early convergence to sub-optimal policies. This parameter setting is summarised in Table 3.

Figure 3 shows the weekly performance after 1800 time steps for each of the runs. The performance values tend to be close to the one reported in Sect. 4.1, which means that the online procedure does usually converge to the same performance as the one obtained with the offline procedure. These are good results, considering that the procedure is essentially testing several policies in runtime, *optimising by means of trial and error*. However, convergence is expected to

**Table 3.** Parameters for the experiments with the online optimisation procedure

| | |
|---|---|
| $\alpha$ | 1 |
| $\beta$ | 5 |
| $w$ | 0.5 |
| $max\_dt\_depth\_gen$ | 3 |
| $max\_dt\_depth$ | 5 |
| $initial\_pop\_size$ | 12 |
| $initial\_temperature$ | 320 |
| $\Omega$ | 0.8 |
| $copy\_perc$ | 0.2 |
| $cross\_perc$ | 0.1 |
| $mut\_perc$ | 0.1 |
| $elitist$ | True |

depend on how easy it is to find an optimal system policy in a particular problem domain. We argue that it is more important to converge to a population of good policies than it is to find an optimal policy, even though the method did converge to the hypothetically optimal performance (the one obtained with the offline optimisation procedure) in most of the tests which have been carried out.

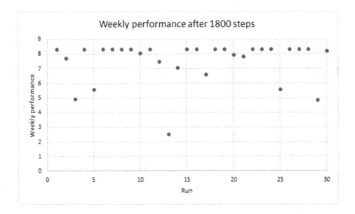

**Fig. 3.** Weekly performance after 1800 steps for each of the 30 runs of the online procedure

The graph of Fig. 4 shows how the daily and weekly performance values evolve over time for one of the runs, in which the performance converged to a value close to the performance obtained with the offline procedure. The graph shows that the procedure is able to improve system performance over time. With some initial instability caused by exploration of several different policies (due to a larger value of the temperature parameter), the weekly fitness increases over time, converging to a value close to 8. Online adaptation and evolution of system policies seems to have more practical advantages if we realistically assume that the system behaviour over time is not known, or hard to predict, *a priori* and that the system is running continuously, without a bounded final time step. These assumptions seem appropriate for real-world use cases of EIs.

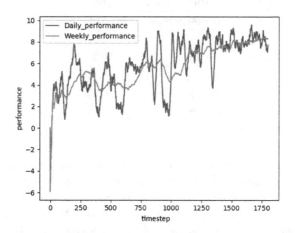

**Fig. 4.** Daily (last 24 time steps) and weekly (last 168 time steps) performance when adapting and evolving the operating policy in runtime.

## 5   Conclusions and Future Work

This paper describes in detail our research into how adaptation through evolution of policies can assist the design of collective adaptive systems which remain sustainable over time in the face of dynamic environments that may change unpredictably. The problem we have addressed has been to find operating policies which are approximately optimal for a system, given some performance criterion. We have modelled an energy system encompassing several integrated CESs where each community is an agent and energy is treated as a CPR. We have proposed mechanisms which enable this system model to optimise its performance over time through adaptation and evolution of its operating policy. The results show that these optimisation procedures are useful and could lead to a better understanding of mechanisms which enable a system to remain sustainable over time. The policies evolved by our procedures *clearly outperform* the policy we have initially designed ourselves.

The representation of system policies has been a key issue throughout the modelling of the system. Representing the policies with binary decision trees has enabled us to apply GP operations when generating and evolving them. This representation is also appropriate for *drawing explanations* about the output of our optimisation procedures. The trees can easily be translated into a sequence of potentially nested `if-then-else` rules, which may help human designers to gain insight about the system operation and what makes a good policy, enabling them to construct better policies themselves or to provide more useful "building blocks" for the procedures to find policies automatically.

The methods we have presented return policies which are appropriate for a system, given some performance criterion, without a human designer's intervention. The contributions of this work are highly significant, since our proposal, for which we presented a proof of concept, could lay the foundations for the development of a new methodological paradigm for the engineering of collective adaptive systems based on the convergence of electronic institutions and evolutionary computing. Our approach could be used to assist system designers, so far required to rely mostly on their own intuition, in *systematically* finding good policies, which could generally lead to better performance and provide support for adaptation mechanisms in the face of non-deterministic changes in dynamic environments. In future work, we would like to look into increasing the complexity of the energy system model which we have created in this project and to further study our optimisation procedures, applying them to other problem domains and exploring other heuristic approaches besides GP.

# References

1. Artikis, A.: Dynamic specification of open agent systems. J. Log. Comput. **22**(6), 1301–1334 (2012)
2. Bartz-Beielstein, T., Branke, J., Mehnen, J., Mersmann, O.: Evolutionary algorithms. Wiley Interdiscip. Rev. Data Min. Knowl. Discov. **4**, 178–195 (2014)
3. Bucking, S., Dermardiros, V.: Distributed evolutionary algorithm for co-optimization of building and district systems for early community energy masterplanning. Appl. Soft Comput. **63**(Suppl C), 14–22 (2018)
4. Capodieci, N., Hart, E., Cabri, G.: Designing self-aware adaptive systems: from autonomic computing to cognitive immune networks. In: Proceedings - IEEE 7th International Conference on Self-Adaptation and Self-Organizing Systems Workshops, SASOW 2013, pp. 59–64 (2014)
5. Capodieci, N., Hart, E., Cabri, G.: Artificial immunology for collective adaptive systems design and implementation. ACM Trans. Auton. Adapt. Syst. **11**(2), 1–25 (2016)
6. Di Marzo Serugendo, G., Gleizes, M.P., Karageorgos, A.: Self-organization in multi-agent systems. Knowl. Eng. Rev. **20**, 165–189 (2005)
7. Gächter, S.: Conditional cooperation: behavioral regularities from the lab and the field and their policy implications about the centre or contact. Economics and Psychology. A Promising New Cross-Disciplinary Field, April 2006 (2006-3), pp. 19–50 (2007)
8. Grefenstette, J.J.: Genetic algorithms for changing environments. In: PPSN, vol. 2, pp. 137–144 (1992)
9. Hart, E., Sim, K.: A hyper-heuristic ensemble method for static job-shop scheduling. Evol. Comput. **24**(4), 609–635 (2016)

10. Huang, Z., Yu, H., Peng, Z., Zhao, M.: Methods and tools for community energy planning: a review. Renew. Sustain. Energy Rev. **42**, 1335–1348 (2015)
11. Koirala, B.P., Koliou, E., Friege, J., Hakvoort, R.A., Herder, P.M.: Energetic communities for community energy: a review of key issues and trends shaping integrated community energy systems. Renew. Sustain. Energy Rev. **56**, 722–744 (2016)
12. Kowalski, R., Sergot, M.: A logic-based calculus of events. New Gener. Comput. **4**(1), 67–95 (1986)
13. Koza, J.R.: Genetic Programming: On the Programming of Computers by Means of Natural Selection. MIT Press, Cambridge (1992)
14. Ostrom, E.: Governing the commons: the evolution of institutions for collective action. South. Econ. J. **60**, 249–251 (2015)
15. Pitt, J., Busquets, D., Macbeth, S.: Distributive justice for self-organised common-pool resource management. ACM Trans. Auton. Adapt. Syst. **9**(3), 1–39 (2014)
16. Pitt, J., Hart, E.: For flux sake: the confluence of socially-and biologically-inspired computing for engineering change in open systems. In: Proceedings - 2017 IEEE 2nd International Workshops on Foundations and Applications of Self* Systems, FAS*W 2017, pp. 45–50 (2017)
17. Pitt, J., Ober, J., Diaconescu, A.: Knowledge management processes and design principles for self-governing socio-technical systems. In: Proceedings - 2017 IEEE 2nd International Workshops on Foundations and Applications of Self* Systems (FAS*W), pp. 97–102, Los Alamitos, CA, USA (2017)
18. Pitt, J., Schaumeier, J., Artikis, A.: Axiomatization of socio-economic principles for self-organizing institutions. ACM Trans. Auton. Adapt. Syst. **7**(4), 1–39 (2012)
19. Rescher, N.: Distributive Justice. G - Reference, Information and Interdisciplinary Subjects Series. University Press of America, New York (1982)
20. Sim, K., Hart, E., Paechter, B.: A lifelong learning hyper-heuristic method for bin packing. Evol. Comput. **23**(1), 37–67 (2015)
21. Smith, R.G.: The contract net protocol: high-level communication and control in a distributed problem solver. IEEE Trans. Comput. **29**(12), 1104–1113 (1980)
22. Ye, D., Zhang, M., Vasilakos, A.V.: A survey of self-organization mechanisms in multiagent systems. IEEE Trans. Syst. Man Cybern. Syst. **47**, 441–461 (2017)

# The Sharer's Dilemma in Collective Adaptive Systems of Self-interested Agents

Lenz Belzner[1]([⊠]), Kyrill Schmid[2], Thomy Phan[2], Thomas Gabor[2], and Martin Wirsing[2]

[1] MaibornWolff, Munich, Germany
belzner@ifi.imu.de
[2] LMU Munich, Munich, Germany

**Abstract.** In collective adaptive systems (CAS), adaptation can be implemented by optimization wrt. utility. Agents in a CAS may be self-interested, while their utilities may depend on other agents' choices. Independent optimization of agent utilities may yield poor individual and global reward due to locally interfering individual preferences. Joint optimization may scale poorly, and is impossible if agents cannot expose their preferences due to privacy or security issues.

In this paper, we study utility sharing for mitigating this issue. Sharing utility with others may incentivize individuals to consider choices that are locally suboptimal but increase global reward. We illustrate our approach with a utility sharing variant of distributed cross entropy optimization. Empirical results show that utility sharing increases expected individual and global payoff in comparison to optimization without utility sharing.

We also investigate the effect of greedy defectors in a CAS of sharing, self-interested agents. We observe that defection increases the mean expected individual payoff at the expense of sharing individuals' payoff. We empirically show that the choice between defection and sharing yields a fundamental dilemma for self-interested agents in a CAS.

## 1 Introduction

In collective adaptive systems (CAS), adaptation can be implemented by optimization wrt. utility, e.g. using multi-agent reinforcement learning or distributed statistical planning [1–5]. Agents in a CAS may be self-interested, while their utilities may depend on other agents' choices. This kind of situation arises frequently when agents are competing for scarce resources. Independent optimization of each agent's utility may yield poor individual and global payoff due to locally interfering individual preferences in the course of optimization [6,7]. Joint optimization may scale poorly, and is impossible if agents do not want to expose their preferences due to privacy or security issues [8].

A minimal example of such a situation is the coin game [9] (cf. Fig. 1. Here, a yellow and a blue agent compete for coins. The coins are also colored in yellow

© Springer Nature Switzerland AG 2018
T. Margaria and B. Steffen (Eds.): ISoLA 2018, LNCS 11246, pp. 241–256, 2018.
https://doi.org/10.1007/978-3-030-03424-5_16

or blue. Both agents can decide whether to pick up the coin or not. If both agents opt to pick up the coin, one of them receives it uniformly at random. If an agent picks up a coin of its own color, it receives a reward of 2. If it picks up a differently colored coin, it gets a reward of one. Each agent wants to maximize its individual reward. If agents act purely self-interested, then each agent tries to pick up each coin, resulting in suboptimal global reward. However, if rewards can be shared among agents, then agents will only pick up coins of their own color. They receive a share that is high enough to compensate for not picking up differently colored coins. This increases individual and global reward alike.

There are many examples for this kind of situation. For example, energy production in the smart grid can be modeled in terms of a CAS of self-interested agents. Each participant has to decide locally how much energy to produce. Each agent wants to maximize its individual payoff by selling energy to consumers in the grid. However, the price is depending on global production. Also, global overproduction is penalized. Routing of vehicles poses similar problems. Each vehicle wants to reach its destination in a minimal amount of time. However, roads are a constrained resource, and for a globally optimal solution, only a fraction of vehicles should opt for the shortest route. In both scenarios, the ability of agents to share payoff may increase individual and global reward alike.

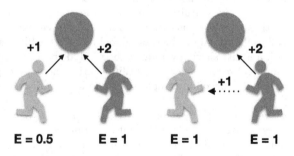

**Fig. 1.** Two agents competing for a coin: if agent 1 (yellow) on the left side happens to get the coin it will get a reward of +1 whereas agent 2 (blue) will get a reward of +2 for it. If there is a fifty-fifty chance for an agent to get the coin when both agents are trying to collect it, the expected values are 0.5 for agent 1 and 1 for agent 2 when both agents independently optimize their utility. In contrast, if there is the possibility to share reward then agents could learn to do the following: agent 1 (yellow) resists to collect the coin. That increases the blue agent's probability for getting a reward to 1. The blue agent transfers reward (e.g. 1) to the yellow agent. This leaves agents with expected values of 1 each and therefore defines a strong Pareto improvement compared to the former outcome. (Color figure online)

In this paper, we study distributed optimization with utility sharing for mitigating the issue of contrasting individual goals at the cost of expected individual and global reward. To illustrate our ideas, we propose a utility sharing variant of distributed cross entropy optimization. Empirical results show that utility sharing increases expected individual and global payoff in comparison to optimization without utility sharing.

We then investigate the effect of defectors participating in a CAS of sharing, self-interested agents. We observe that defection increases the mean expected individual payoff at the expense of sharing individuals' payoff. We empirically show that the choice between defection and sharing yields a fundamental dilemma for self-interested agents in a CAS.

The paper makes the following contributions.

- We motivate utility sharing as a means to mitigate conflicts and increase expected individual and global reward in CAS of self-interested agents.
- We propose distributed optimization with sharing (DOS) as an algorithm to realize utility sharing in self-interested CAS.
- We evaluate DOS empirically, showing that it increases individual and global reward in expectation.
- We investigate the effect of defecting, non-sharing individuals in a group of self-interested sharing agents. We show that the choice between defection and cooperation yields a fundamental dilemma for self-interested agents in collective adaptive systems.

The remainder of the paper is structured as follows. In Sect. 2 we discuss related work. We introduce DOS in Sect. 3. We discuss our empirical results and the Sharer's Dilemma in Sect. 4. We conclude in Sect. 5.

## 2   Related Work

In general, we see our work in the context of collective adaptive systems (CAS) [2,3] and multi-agent systems [10]. In particular, we are interested in CAS where agents are adaptive through optimization of actions of policies wrt. a given individual or global utility function. These settings can for example be modeled in terms of distributed constrained optimization problems [11], or as stochastic games [12].

Searching for optimal actions or learning policies can be done by open- or closed-loop planning, potentially enhanced with learned components such as search exploration policies or value functions [5,13–16]. Another approach for learning optimal policies in multi agent domains such as CAS is multi agent reinforcement learning (MARL) [1,17] and its modern variants based on deep learning for scaling up to more complex domains [4,18,19]. A recent example of planning-based deep MARL combines open-loop search and learned value functions in fully cooperative multi-agent domains [5].

In the case of self-interested agents, the Coco-Q algorithm was proposed [20]. Coco-Q has been evaluated for discrete two-player matrix games, and requires explicit knowledge of other agents' utilities. In some sense, our study of sharing in CAS extends the Coco-Q approach to continuous optimization with more than two agents. Also, we model the amount sharing as a free parameter to be learned in the course of optimization.

In the context of a research on emergent social effects in MARL [6,7,9,21], a recent report investigated the effects of inequity aversion and utility sharing in temporally extended dilemmas [22]. The authors state that "it remains to be seen whether emergent inequity-aversion can be obtained by evolving reinforcement learning agents" [22]. Our current work is a first step into this direction, and shows that the question of whether to share or not poses a dilemma in and for itself, at least in the case of stateless optimization (in contrast to learning policies).

## 3   Distributed Optimization with Sharing

We model decision making in a CAS as a stochastic game $(X, N, A, p, R)$ [12].

- $X$ is a finite set of states.
- $N = \{0, ..., n\}$ is a finite set of agents.
- $A = \times_{i \in N} A_i$ is a set of joint actions. $A_i$ is a finite set of actions for agent $i$.
- $p(x'|x, a)$ is a distribution modeling the probability that executing action $a \in A$ in state $x \in X$ yields state $x' \in X$.
- $R = \{r_i\}_{i \in N}, r_i : X \times A \to \mathbb{R}$ is a set of reward functions, one for each agent.

In the following, we assume $X = \{x\}$ consists of a single state, and $\forall a \in A :$ $p(x|x, a) = 1$. As $x$ is unique, we will not consider it in further notation.

We assume that $r_i$ is available to agent $i$ in terms of a generative model that may be queried for samples $a$, e.g. a simulation of the application domain. Each agent only has access to its own reward function, but does not know the reward functions of other agents.

The task of a self-interested agent $i$ is to find an action that maximizes its payoff. However, its payoff $r_i(a), a \in A$ in general depends on the choices of other agents. One way to deal with this dependency is to perform optimization jointly for all agents, that is $\max_{a \in A} : \sum_{i \in N} r_i(a)$. However, in a CAS with self-interested agents, each participant tries to maximize its individual reward. Also, in many situations participating agents would not want to expose their individual reward functions to others due to privacy or security issues [8]. In these situations, joint optimization wrt. global reward is not feasible. Note that optimization of self-interested individuals is non-stationary due to changes in others' choices as they optimize for themselves.

### 3.1   Reward Sharing

We define agents' utilities as $u_i$. We consider the two different cases we are interested in:

1. Individual, purely self-interested optimization
2. Self-interested optimization with the option to share individual rewards

**Pure Self-interest.** When optimizing independently and purely self-interested, $u_i(a) = r_i(a)$.

**Sharing.** Sharing agents choose a share $s_i \in \mathbb{R}, s_i \geq 0$ additionally to $a_i$. We denote the joint shares by $s = \times_{i \in N} s_i$. Given $n$ agents, a joint action $a \in A$ and a joint share $s \in \mathbb{R}^n, s_i \geq 0$ for all $i$, we define individual agents' utility $u_i$ for distributed optimization with sharing as follows.[1]

$$u_i(a, s) = r_i(a) - s_i + \frac{\sum_{j, j \neq i} s_j}{n - 1} \tag{1}$$

Shares are uniformly distributed among all other agents. There are no bilateral shares. Note that this sharing mechanism is an arbitrary choice.

For example, sharing yields the following utilities for two agents.

$$u_0(a, s) = r_0(a) - s_0 + s_1$$
$$u_1(a, s) = r_1(a) - s_1 + s_0$$

### 3.2 Distributed Optimization with Sharing

We now give a general formulation of distributed optimization with sharing (DOS). DOS is shown in Algorithm 1. Each agent maintains a policy $\pi_i(a_i)$, i.e. a distribution over actions and shares. It is initialized with an arbitrary prior distribution. A rational agent wants to optimize its policy such that the expectation of reward is maximized: $\max \mathbb{E}_a r_i(a)$, where $a \sim \times_{i \in N} \pi_i(a_i)$. Note that optimization of an individual's policy depends on the policies of all other agents. Also note that policy optimization of self-interested individuals is non-stationary due to changes in others' policies as they optimize for themselves.

After initialization, DOS performs the following steps for a predefined number of iterations.

1. Each agent samples a multiset of $n_{\text{sample}}$ actions from its policy and communicates it to other agents.
2. A list of joint actions is constructed from the communicated action lists of other agents.
3. The utility of each joint action is determined according to Eq. 1.
4. The policy is updated in a way that increases the likelihood of sampling high-utility actions and shares.

After $n_{\text{iter}}$ iterations, each agent samples an action and a share from its policy, executes the action, and shares reward accordingly. The resulting joint action yields the global result of DOS.

### 3.3 Cross-Entropy DOS

In general, DOS is parametric w.r.t. modeling and updating of policies $\pi_i$. As an example, we instantiate DOS with cross entropy optimization [23]. We label this instantiation CE-DOS.

---

[1] We can account for the change of signature of $u_i$ by extending the action space $A_i$ of each agent accordingly: $A_{s,i} = A_i \times \mathbb{R}, A_s = \times_{i \in N} A_{s,i}$.

**Algorithm 1.** Distributed Optimization with Sharing (DOS)

---

1: initialize $\pi_i$ for each agent $i$
2: **for** $n_{\text{iter}}$ iterations **do**
3:    **for** each agent $i$ **do**
4:        sample $n_{\text{sample}}$ actions and shares $a_i, s_i \sim \pi_i$
5:        broadcast sampled actions and shares
6:    **for** each agent $i$ **do**
7:        build joint actions $a = \times_{i \in N} a_i$ and shares $s = \times_{i \in N} s_i$
8:        clip $s_i$ such that $0 \leq s_i \leq r_i(a)$
9:        determine utility $u_i(a, s)$ according to Eq. 1
10:       update $\pi_i$ to increase the likelihood of high-utility samples
11: **for** each agent $i$ **do**
12:    execute $a_i$ and share $s_i(a)$ sampled from $\pi_i$

---

For CE-DOS, we model a policy $\pi$ as isotropic normal distribution $\mathcal{N}(\mu, \sigma)$. I.e., each parameter of an action is sampled from a normal distribution that is independent from other action parameter distributions. Note that it is also possible to model policies in terms of normal distribution with full covariance, but the simpler and computationally less expensive isotropic representation suffices for our illustrative concerns. As prior CE-DOS requires initial mean $\mu_0$ and standard deviation $\sigma_0$ for a policy (cf. Algorithm 2, line 1). I.e. initial actions before any optimization are sampled as follows.

$$a_i \sim \mathcal{N}(\mu_0, \sigma_0) \tag{2}$$

Updating a policy (cf. Algorithm 1, line 12–15) is done by recalculating mean and variance of the normal distribution. We want the update to increase the expected sample utility. For each of $n_{\text{iter}}$ iterations, we sample $n_{\text{sample}}$ actions and shares $a_i, s_i \sim \pi_i$ from each agent's policy, and build the corresponding joint actions $a = \times_{i \in N} a_i$ and shares $s = \times_{i \in N} s_i$.

Each agent evaluates sampled actions and shares according to its utility $u_i(a, s)$. From the set of evaluated samples of each agent, we drop a fraction $\psi \in (0, 1]$ of samples from the set wrt. their utilities. That is, we only keep high utility samples in the set. We then compute mean and variance of the action parameters in the reduced set, and use them to update the policy. A learning rate $\alpha \in (0, 1]$ determines the impact of the new mean and variance on the existing distribution parameters: E.g. let $\mu_t$ and $\sigma_t$ be the mean and standard deviation of a normal distribution modeling a policy at iteration $t$, then

$$\mu_{t+1} = (1 - \alpha)\mu_t + \alpha\mu_{\text{new}}$$
$$\sigma_{t+1} = (1 - \alpha)\sigma_t + \alpha\sigma_{\text{new}}$$

where $\mu_{\text{new}}$ and $\sigma_{\text{new}}$ are mean and standard deviation of the elite samples. We require a lower bound $\sigma_{\text{min}}$ on the standard deviation of policies in order to maintain a minimum amount of exploration.

The hyperparameters of CE-DOS are thus as follows.

- A stochastic game $(X, N, A, p, R)$
- Number of iterations $n_{\text{iter}}$
- Number of samples $n_{\text{sample}}$ from the policy at each iteration
- Prior mean $\mu_0$ and standard deviation $\sigma_0$ for policies
- Lower bound $\sigma_{\text{min}}$ on the policy standard deviations
- Fraction $\psi \in (0, 1]$ of elite samples to keep
- Learning rate $\alpha \in (0, 1]$

---

**Algorithm 2.** Cross Entropy DOS

1: Intitialize $\pi_i \leftarrow \mathcal{N}(\mu_0, \sigma_0)$ for each agent $i$
2: **for** $n_{\text{iter}}$ iterations **do**
3:     **for** each agent $i$ **do**
4:         sample $n_{\text{sample}}$ actions and shares $a_i, s_i \sim \pi_i$
5:         broadcast sampled actions and shares
6:     **for** each agent $i$ **do**
7:         build joint actions $a = \times_{i \in N} a_i$ and shares $s = \times_{i \in N} s_i$
8:         clip $s_i$ such that $0 \leq s_i \leq r_i(a)$
9:         determine utility $u_i(a, s)$ according to Eq. 1
10:       keep $\psi \cdot n_{\text{sample}}$ elite samples $a, s$ with highest utility
11:       compute $\mu_{\text{new}}$ and $\sigma_{\text{new}}$ from $a_i, s_i$ in the elite samples
12:       $\mu_{t+1} \leftarrow (1 - \alpha)\mu_t + \alpha\mu_{\text{new}}$
13:       $\sigma_{t+1} \leftarrow (1 - \alpha)\sigma_t + \alpha\sigma_{\text{new}}$
14:       $\sigma_{t+1} \leftarrow \max(\sigma_{t+1}, \sigma_{\text{min}})$
15:       $\pi_i \leftarrow \mathcal{N}(\mu_{t+1}, \sigma_{t+1})$
16: **for** each agent $i$ **do**
17:     $a_i, s_i \sim \pi_i$
18:     execute $a_i$ and share $s_i$

---

# 4 Experimental Results and the Sharer's Dilemma

We experimentally analyzed the effects of sharing in collective adaptive systems of self-interested agents.

## 4.1 Domains

We evaluated the effect of sharing utilities with CE-DOS in two synthetic domains. In these domains, a CAS of self-interested agents has to balance individual and global resource consumption (or production, respectively).

For example, the energy market in the smart grid can be modeled as a CAS of self-interested agents. Each participant has to decide locally how much energy to produce. Each agent wants to maximize its individual payoff by selling energy to consumers in the grid. Therefore, each agent would like to maximize its individual energy production. However, the selling price per unit is typically non-linearly depending on global production. For example, global overproduction is penalized.

There are a number of corresponding real world problems, for example energy production and consumption in the smart grid, traffic routing, passenger distribution to individual ride hailing participants, cargo distribution on transport as a service, routing of packets in networks, distribution of computational load to computers in a cluster, and many more.

We now define two market models (simple and logistic) as domains for evaluating the effects of sharing in CAS of self-interested agents.

**Simple Market.** We model individual and global production, and use their relation for calculating utilities in such a scenario. We set $A_i = \mathbb{R}^1$ as individual agents' action space, $a_i \in A_i$ models the production amount. The sum $\sum_{i \in N} a_i$ models the global production.

We define the reward of each agent as the relation of its own individual resource consumption to the global resource consumption. I.e. the reward correlates to an agents market share. We introduce a slope parameter $\xi$ to control the utility slope of individual and global consumption.

$$r_i(a) = \frac{a_i}{\left(\sum_{j \in N} a_j\right)^{\xi}} \tag{3}$$

In this setup, a rational agent would like to increase its own consumption until saturation. I.e. a monopoly is able to produce cheaper than two small producers, and therefore an inequal production amount unlocks more global reward. If all agents act rationally by maximizing their individual $a_i$, in general the corresponding equilibrium is not equal to the global optimum.

**Logistic Market.** We modeled another market scenario for investigating the effects of sharing in CAS of self-interested agents. As before, each agent has to choose the amount of energy to use for production of a particular good. I.e. $A_i \in [.1, 4]$, as in the simple market domain. Note that this is an arbitrary choice.

Each agent has a logistic production curve $p_i : A_i \to [0, 1]$ as a function of its invested energy. For example, this models different production machine properties. The logistic curve $p_i$ is given as follows.

$$p_i(a_i) = \frac{1}{1 + e^{-c(a_i - o)}} \tag{4}$$

Here, $c \in \mathbb{R}$ defines the steepness of the logistic function, and $o \in \mathbb{R}$ determines the offset on the x-axis.

Global production $prod$ is the sum of individual production $\sum_i p_i(a_i)$. A price function (i.e. an inverse logistic function) defines the price per produced unit, given global production $prod$.

$$price(prod) = 1 - \frac{1}{1 + e^{-c(prod - o)}} \tag{5}$$

The reward for an agent is defined as the product of its produced units and the global price.

$$r_i(a) = p_i(a_i) \cdot price(prod) \text{ where } prod = \sum_{j \in N} p_j(a_j) \tag{6}$$

Figure 2 shows an example of production and price functions in the logistic market domain.

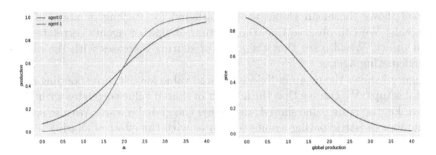

**Fig. 2.** Example production functions (left) and global price function (right) in the logistic market domain.

## 4.2   Setup

For our experiments, we used the following setup of CE-DOS.[2]

- We consider a stochastic game with $n$ agents, that is $N = \{1, ..., n\}$.
- We set $n = 10, n = 50$ and $n = 100$ in our experiments.
- Individual action spaces were set as $A_i = [.1, 4]$. We clipped actions when sampling them from the policy.
- We define the individual reward functions by Eq. 3 or Eq. 6, respectively.
- We set the number of iterations $n_{iter}$ for CE-DOS to 100.
- We draw $n_{sample} = 100$ samples from the policy per iteration for each agent.
- We set the prior mean $\mu_0 = 0$ and standard deviation $\sigma_0 = 1$.
- We set the fraction of elite samples $\psi = 0.25$.
- We set the learning rate $\alpha = 0.5$.
- We set the minimal policy standard deviation $\sigma_{min} = 0.2$.

We sampled domain parameters uniformly from the following intervals.

- We sampled the slope parameter $\xi$ from $[2, 4]$ in the simple market domain.
- We sampled logistic steepness $c$ and offset $o$ from $[1, 3]$ for all production and cost functions in our experiments with the logistic market domain.

---

[2] Code available online: https://github.com/lenzbelzner/sharers_dilemma.

We varied the number of sharing agents to measure the effect of defecting (i.e. non-sharing) agents that participate in the stochastic game together with sharing individuals.

Note that for the results we report here, we clipped the sharing values such that agents are only able to share up to their current reward, i.e. $s_i \leq r_i(a)$ for a given $a \in A$. In general, other setups with unbound sharing are possible as well.

## 4.3  Effect of Sharing on Global Reward

Figure 3 shows the mean global utility gathered for varying numbers of sharing agents. We can observe that the fraction of sharing agents correlates with global utility. We also see that the effect of sharing increases with the number of participating agents.

Figure 4 shows the mean individual shared value for the corresponding experimental setups. We can see that the amount of shared value correlates with global reward. I.e. the more value shared, the higher the global reward. We also see that the number of participating agents correlates with the effect of sharing.

## 4.4  Sharer's Dilemma

Figure 5 shows the Schelling diagrams for the corresponding experiments. A Schelling diagram compares the mean individual utility of sharers and defectors based on the global number of sharing agents [24]. We can see that agents that choose to defect gather more individual utility than the sharing ones.

The shape of the Schelling diagrams in Fig. 5 shows that sharing in collective adaptive systems with self-interested agents yields a dilemma in our experimental setups.

### Should an individual agent share or defect?

There is no rational answer to this question for an individual self-interested agent. If the agent chooses to share, it may be exploited by other agents that are defecting. However, if the agent chooses to defect, it may hurt its individual return by doing so in comparison to having chosen to share.

Note that the amount of sharing is a free parameter to be optimized by DOS. This means that all behavior we observe in our experiments is emergent. The combination of available resources, interdependency of agents' actions and the ability to share lets agents decide to share with others based on their intrinsic motivation.

Our results illustrate a potential reason for emergence of cooperation and inequity aversion in CAS of only self-interested agents. They also give an explanation to the existence of punishment of individuals that exploit societal cooperation at the cost of sharing individuals' and global reward.

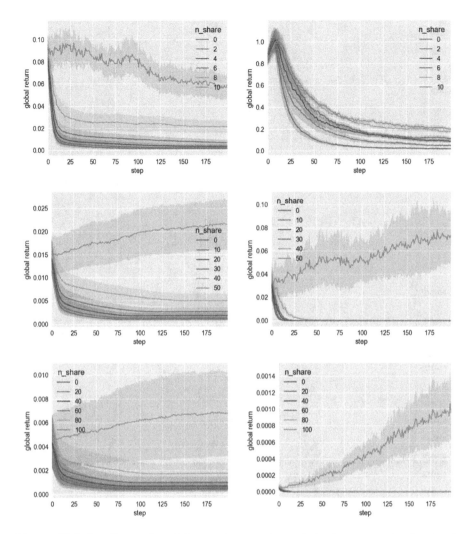

**Fig. 3.** Global utility gathered for varying numbers of sharing agents in the simple market (left column) and logistic market (right column) domains. 10 agents (top row), 50 agents (center row) and 100 agents (bottom row) in total. Solid line shows empirical mean of 10 experimental runs, shaded areas show .95 confidence intervals. Best viewed on screen in color. (Color figure online)

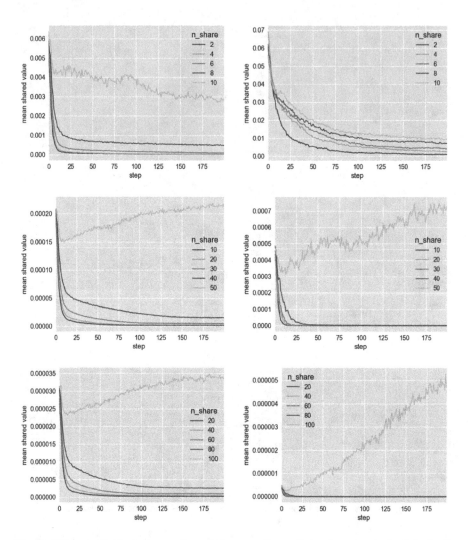

**Fig. 4.** Mean individual shares for varying numbers of sharing agents in the simple market (left column) and logistic market (right column) domains. 10 agents (top row), 50 agents (center row) and 100 agents (bottom row) in total. Solid line shows empirical mean of 10 experimental runs, shaded areas show .95 confidence intervals. Best viewed on screen in color. (Color figure online)

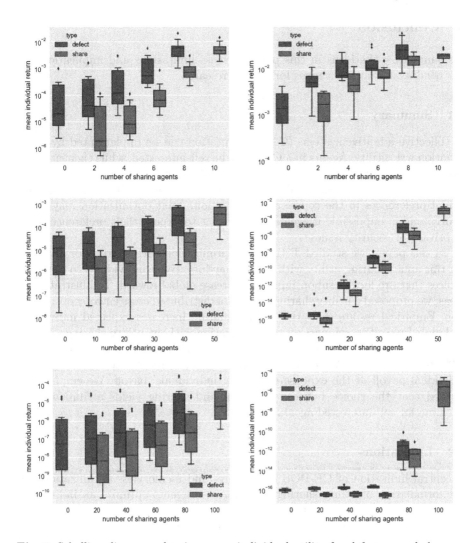

**Fig. 5.** Schelling diagrams showing mean individual utility for defectors and sharers, for varying numbers of sharing agents in the simple market (left column) and logistic market (right column) domains. Note the log scale on the y-axis. 10 agents (top row), 50 agents (center row) and 100 agents (bottom row) in total. 10 experimental runs. Best viewed on screen in color. (Color figure online)

# 5   Conclusion

We summarize the ideas in this paper, discuss limitations and implications of our results, and outline venues for further research.

## 5.1   Summary

In collective adaptive systems (CAS), adaptation can be implemented by optimization wrt. utility. Agents in a CAS may be self-interested, while their utilities may depend on other agents' choices. Independent optimization of each agent's utility may yield poor individual and global payoff due to locally interfering individual preferences in the course of optimization. Joint optimization may scale poorly, and is impossible if agents do not want to expose their preferences due to privacy or security issues.

In this paper, we studied distributed optimization with sharing for mitigating this issue. Sharing utility with others may incentivize individuals to consider choices that are locally suboptimal but increase global reward. To illustrate our ideas, we proposed a utility sharing variant of distributed cross entropy optimization. Empirical results show that utility sharing increases expected individual and global payoff in comparison to optimization without utility sharing.

We also investigated the effect of defectors participating in a CAS of sharing, self-interested agents. We observed that defection increases the mean expected individual payoff at the expense of sharing individuals' payoff. We empirically showed that the choice between defection and sharing yields a fundamental dilemma for self-interested agents in a CAS.

## 5.2   Limitations

A central limitation of CE-DOS is its state- and memoryless optimization. In our formulation of utility sharing self-interested agents optimize an individual action and share that maximizes their utility. However, our formulation does not account for learning decision policies based on a current state and other learning agents. In this case, the utility of each agent would also depend on concrete states, transition dynamics and potentially also on models agents learn about other participants [25,26].

As there is no temporal component to the optimization problems that we studied in this paper, it is also not possible to study the effect of gathering wealth in our current setup. We think that the dynamics of sharing in temporally extended decision problems may differ from the ones in stateless optimization. For example, corresponding observations have been made for game theoretic dilemmas, where optimal strategies change when repeating a game (in contrast to the optimal strategy when the game is only played once) [27]. Similar research has been conducted in the field of reinforcement learning, however not accounting for utility sharing so far [6].

We also want to point out that exposing shares eventually provides ground for attack for malicious agents [8]. Albeit indirectly, exposed shares carry information about individual utility landscapes, allowing attackers to potentially gather sensitive information about agents' internal motivations. Agents in critical application domains should consider this weakness when opting to share.

### 5.3 Future Work

In future work, we would like to transfer our approach to temporally extended domains and model sharing in CAS with multi-agent reinforcement learning. Hopefully, this would enable studying sharing and the Sharer's Dilemma in more complex domains.

We also think that there are many interesting options for realizing sharing besides equal distribution as formulated in Eq. 1. For example, our formulation does not allow for bilateral shares or formation of coalitions. Also, we would be interested to study the effect of wealth on emergent cooperation and defection. Another interesting line would be to investigate the effects of punishment in CAS of self-interested agents.

As an application domain, it would be interesting to exploit the duality of planning and verification. For example, agents utility could model individual goal satisfaction probability. Sharing could be used to increase individual and global goal satisfaction probability in CAS.

## References

1. Tan, M.: Multi-agent reinforcement learning: Independent vs. cooperative agents. In: Proceedings of the Tenth International Conference on Machine Learning, pp. 330–337 (1993)
2. Hillston, J., Pitt, J., Wirsing, M., Zambonelli, F.: Collective adaptive systems: qualitative and quantitative modelling and analysis (dagstuhl seminar 14512). In: Dagstuhl Reports, vol. 4. Schloss Dagstuhl-Leibniz-Zentrum fuer Informatik (2015)
3. Belzner, L., Hölzl, M., Koch, N., Wirsing, M.: Collective autonomic systems: towards engineering principles and their foundations. In: Steffen, B. (ed.) Transactions on Foundations for Mastering Change I. LNCS, vol. 9960, pp. 180–200. Springer, Cham (2016). https://doi.org/10.1007/978-3-319-46508-1_10
4. Foerster, J., Nardelli, N., Farquhar, G., Torr, P., Kohli, P., Whiteson, S., et al.: Stabilising experience replay for deep multi-agent reinforcement learning. arXiv preprint arXiv:1702.08887 (2017)
5. Phan, T., Belzner, L., Gabor, T., Schmid, K.: Leveraging statistical multi-agent online planning with emergent value function approximation. In: Proceedings of the 17th Conference on Autonomous Agents and Multi Agent Systems, International Foundation for Autonomous Agents and Multiagent Systems (2018)
6. Leibo, J.Z., Zambaldi, V., Lanctot, M., Marecki, J., Graepel, T.: Multi-agent reinforcement learning in sequential social dilemmas. In: Proceedings of the 16th Conference on Autonomous Agents and Multi Agent Systems, International Foundation for Autonomous Agents and Multiagent Systems, pp. 464–473 (2017)

7. Perolat, J., Leibo, J.Z., Zambaldi, V., Beattie, C., Tuyls, K., Graepel, T.: A multi-agent reinforcement learning model of common-pool resource appropriation. In: Advances in Neural Information Processing Systems, pp. 3646–3655 (2017)

8. Brundage, M., et al.: The malicious use of artificial intelligence: forecasting, prevention, and mitigation. arXiv preprint arXiv:1802.07228 (2018)

9. Lerer, A., Peysakhovich, A.: Maintaining cooperation in complex social dilemmas using deep reinforcement learning. arXiv preprint arXiv:1707.01068 (2017)

10. Van der Hoek, W., Wooldridge, M.: Multi-agent systems. Found. Artif. Intell. **3**, 887–928 (2008)

11. Fioretto, F., Pontelli, E., Yeoh, W.: Distributed constraint optimization problems and applications: a survey. arXiv preprint arXiv:1602.06347 (2016)

12. Shapley, L.S.: Stochastic games. Proc. Natl. Acad. Sci. **39**(10), 1095–1100 (1953)

13. Silver, D., et al.: Mastering the game of go with deep neural networks and tree search. Nature **529**(7587), 484–489 (2016)

14. Silver, D., et al.: Mastering chess and shogi by self-play with a general reinforcement learning algorithm. arXiv preprint arXiv:1712.01815 (2017)

15. Silver, D., et al.: Mastering the game of go without human knowledge. Nature **550**(7676), 354 (2017)

16. Anthony, T., Tian, Z., Barber, D.: Thinking fast and slow with deep learning and tree search. In: Advances in Neural Information Processing Systems, pp. 5366–5376 (2017)

17. Littman, M.L.: Markov games as a framework for multi-agent reinforcement learning. In: Machine Learning Proceedings, pp. 157–163. Elsevier (1994)

18. Foerster, J., Assael, I.A., de Freitas, N., Whiteson, S.: Learning to communicate with deep multi-agent reinforcement learning. In: Advances in Neural Information Processing Systems, pp. 2137–2145 (2016)

19. Tampuu, A., et al.: Multiagent cooperation and competition with deep reinforcement learning. PLoS ONE **12**(4), e0172395 (2017)

20. Sodomka, E., Hilliard, E., Littman, M., Greenwald, A.: Coco-Q: learning in stochastic games with side payments. In: International Conference on Machine Learning, pp. 1471–1479 (2013)

21. Peysakhovich, A., Lerer, A.: Prosocial learning agents solve generalized stag hunts better than selfish ones. arXiv preprint arXiv:1709.02865 (2017)

22. Hughes, E., et al.: Inequity aversion resolves intertemporal social dilemmas. arXiv preprint arXiv:1803.08884 (2018)

23. Kroese, D.P., Rubinstein, R.Y., Cohen, I., Porotsky, S., Taimre, T.: Cross-entropy method. In: Encyclopedia of Operations Research and Management Science, pp. 326–333. Springer, New York (2013)

24. Schelling, T.C.: Hockey helmets, concealed weapons, and daylight saving: a study of binary choices with externalities. J. Confl. Resolut. **17**(3), 381–428 (1973)

25. Foerster, J.N., Chen, R.Y., Al-Shedivat, M., Whiteson, S., Abbeel, P., Mordatch, I.: Learning with opponent-learning awareness. arXiv preprint arXiv:1709.04326 (2017)

26. Rabinowitz, N.C., Perbet, F., Song, H.F., Zhang, C., Eslami, S., Botvinick, M.: Machine theory of mind. arXiv preprint arXiv:1802.07740 (2018)

27. Sandholm, T.W., Crites, R.H.: Multiagent reinforcement learning in the iterated prisoner's dilemma. Biosystems **37**(1–2), 147–166 (1996)

# Coordination Model with Reinforcement Learning for Ensuring Reliable On-Demand Services in Collective Adaptive Systems

Houssem Ben Mahfoudh[1,2(✉)], Giovanna Di Marzo Serugendo[1(✉)],
Anthony Boulmier[1,2(✉)], and Nabil Abdennadher[2(✉)]

[1] University of Geneva, Route Drize 7, 1227 Geneva, Switzerland
{Houssem.Benmahfoudh,Giovanna.Dimarzo,Anthony.Boulmier}@unige.ch
[2] University of Applied Science of Western Switzerland,
Rue de la Prairie 4, 1202 Geneva, Switzerland
Nabil.abdennadher@hesge.ch
http://www.cui.unige.ch
http://lsds.hesge.ch

**Abstract.** Context-aware and pervasive systems are growing in the market segments. This is due to the expansion of Internet of things (IoT) devices. Current solutions rely on centralized services provided by servers gathering all requests and performing pre-defined computations involving pre-defined devices. Large-scale IoT scenarios, involving adaptation and unanticipated devices, call for alternative solutions. We propose here a new type of services, built and composed on-demand, arising from the interaction of multiple sensors and devices working together as a decentralized collective adaptive system. Our solution relies on a bio-inspired coordination model providing a communication platform among multi-agent systems working on behalf of these devices. Each device provides few simple services and data regarding its environment. On-demand services derive from the collective interactions among multiple sensors and devices. In this article, we investigate the design and implementation of such services and define a new approach that combines coordination model and reinforcement learning, in order to ensure reliable services and expected quality of services (QoS), namely convergence of composition, of coherent result and convergence of learning. We present an IoT scenario showing the feasibility of the approach and preliminary results.

**Keywords:** Reliable services · Coordination model
Collective adaptive system · Bio-inspired systems
On-demand services · Multi-agent learning · Reinforcement Learning

## 1 Introduction

The next generation of advanced infrastructures will be characterized by the presence of complex networks of pervasive systems, composed of thousands of

© Springer Nature Switzerland AG 2018
T. Margaria and B. Steffen (Eds.): ISoLA 2018, LNCS 11246, pp. 257–273, 2018.
https://doi.org/10.1007/978-3-030-03424-5_17

heterogeneous devices, sensors and actuators consuming and producing high-volumes of interdependent data. Sensors are becoming smarter, cheaper and smaller. They are equipped with increased memory and processing capabilities. In this context, services span wide pervasive systems, involving a very large number of multiple devices. The limited computing resources in sensor networks demand a light service implementation.

Fog and edge-computing solutions [27] already challenge centralized solutions by pushing some of the computation away from central servers and closer to the devices themselves. There is still a need to accommodate large-scale scenarios, to adapt to arriving or departing devices, and to ensure reliability and expected quality of services.

Our vision to meet these requirements consists in moving to a fully decentralized system, working as a collective adaptive system, with the three following characteristics: (1) dynamic services composed and provided on-demand; (2) such services result from the multiple interactions of the devices involved in the production of the services and working as a decentralized collective adaptive system; (3) use of reinforcement learning for ensuring reliability.

Coordination models [33] provide a natural solution for scaling up such scenarios. They are appealing for developing collective adaptive systems working in a decentralized manner, interacting with their local environment, since the shared tuple space on which they are based is a powerful paradigm to implement bio-inspired mechanisms (e.g. stigmergy) for collective interactions. Coordination infrastructures provide the basic mechanisms and the necessary middleware to implement and deploy collective adaptive systems. Therefore, our proposal is based on a bio-inspired coordination model that ensures communication and tasks' coordination among heterogeneous, accommodating adaptation to continuously changing devices. It implements some rules that autonomous entities (devices) employ to coordinate their behavior, usually following information gathered from their local environment.

Our previous work on self-composition of services [12,13,26], also based on a bio-inspired coordination model, exploits syntactic means only (i.e. shared keywords for input, output types) as a basis for building on-the-fly chains of services, out of web services, sensors' data geographically dispersed over a city. We didn't consider reliability of provided services in terms of results or convergence. In this paper, to tackle reliability, we extended the coordination model with reinforcement learning, specifically tackled IoT scenarios and addressed reliability and QoS. Section 2 discusses related works. Section 3 presents background information on the coordination model and reinforcement learning from which our work derives from. Section 4 presents our coordination model and its extension with reinforcement learning (RL). Section 5 then presents our approach to compose reliable services on-demand followed by a scenario with a practical use case in Sect. 6. Section 7 discusses implementation and deployment, as well as current results. Finally, we come to a conclusion and future work in Sect. 8.

## 2   Related Works

Orchestration [24] is an automated arrangement, coordination, and management of services. It relies on an orchestrator who sequentially invokes services by using the "invoke" and "reply" function in order to provide a combined response. It depends totally on the composition schema which means a low level of robustness and no-fault tolerance. Choreography [25] is an interaction between multiple services without passing by a central control. Every service executes its part of work according to other services. They use the "send" and "receive" function to communicate and to provide a composite service.

The static character of these traditional composition approaches has been recently challenged by so-called dynamic service composition approaches involving semantic relations [29], and/or Artificial Intelligence planning techniques [31]. Early works on dynamic building or composing services at run-time include spontaneous self-composition of services [21]. One of the main challenges of these approaches is their limited scalability and the strong requirements that they pose on the details of service description. Evolutionary approaches such as those based on Genetic Algorithms (GA) have also been proposed for service composition [7], motivated by the need of determining the services participating in a composition that satisfies certain Quality of Service (QoS) constraints [3]. In relation with non-functional properties, Cruz Torres et al. [10] propose to control composition of services aiming at maintaining a specified Quality of Service of the composition (end-to-end) despite any perturbances arising in the system. This approach uses ant colony optimization to disseminate and retrieve QoS in an overlay network of available services, which then serve as a basis for selecting services in a composition. McKinley [19] proposes parameters' adaptation by dynamic re-composition of software during its execution, such as switching behaviors and algorithms or adding new on-the-fly behavior. Supporting technologies include aspect-orientation, computational reflection (introspection), and component-based design.

Coordination models have proven useful for designing and implementing distributed systems. They are particularly appealing for developing self-organizing systems, since the shared tuple space on which they are based is a powerful paradigm to implement self-organizing mechanisms, particularly those requiring indirect communication (e.g. stigmergy). Previous coordination model are deployed on one node (device), such as Linda [14], an early coordination model initially designed for only one node, or distributed across several nodes such as TuCSoN [22] based on Linda, TOTA [17] and Proto [4]. These coordination are often inspired from nature. As said above, our previous work on self-composition of services [12,13] relies on a bio-inspired coordination model, but exploits syntactic means only to perform self-composition.

Multi-agent learning solutions are appealing since they help adapting to complex and dynamically changing environments. This is particularly true for concurrent multi-agent learning where a given problem or search space is subdivided into smaller problems and affected to different agents. Issues with concurrent learning relate to appropriate ways to dividing feedback among the agents, and the risk of agents invalidating each other's adaptation [23]. Recent work on constructivist learning approaches, inspired from cognitive sciences, attempt at removing pre-defined goals, avoiding objective functions [18]. Other approaches, such as the Self-Adaptive Context-Learning (SACL) Pattern [15] involve, or each entity (e.g. device), a set of dedicated agents collaborating to learning contexts and mapping the current state of agents perceptions to actions and effects.

To the best of our knowledge, no approach currently combines learning, coordination model, and self-composing (built on-demand) services.

## 3   Background Knowledge

### 3.1   Coordination Model

The concept of a coordination model [8] depicts the way a set of entities interact by means of a set of interactions. A coordination model consists of : the *entities* being coordinated, the *coordination rules*, to which entities are subjected during communication processes and the *coordination media*, that identifies conveyed *data* and its treatment. Our work derives from the SAPERE model [32], a coordination model for multi-agent pervasive systems inspired by chemical reactions [11]. It is based on the following concepts:

1. *Software Agents*: active software entities representing the interface between the tuple space and the external world including any sort of device (e.g. sensors), service and application.
2. *Live Semantic Annotations (LSA)*: Tuples of data and properties whose value can change with time (e.g. temperature value injected by a sensor is updated regularly).
3. *Tuple space*: shared space (i.e. coordination media) containing all the tuples in a node. There is one shared space for each node (node could be a raspberry pi, Waspmote, etc).
4. *Eco-laws*: chemical-based coordination rules, namely: Bonding (for linking an agent with a data that he referred to, was waiting for, concerns it, etc.); Aggregation (for combining two or more LSAs value, such as keeping maximum, minimum values, averaging values, filtering values, etc.); Decay or Evaporation (regularly decreasing the pertinence of data and ultimately removing outdated data); Spreading (for propagating LSAs to neighboring nodes).

### 3.2   Reinforcement Learning

Reinforcement Learning algorithms are machine learning algorithms for decision making under uncertainty in sequential decision problems. The problems solved by RL are modeled among others through a Markov Decision Process (MDP) [28]. MDP is defined as a 4-tuple $\langle S, A, \mathcal{R}, \mathcal{T} \rangle$. It defines a set of states $S$, a set of actions $A$, a reward function $\mathcal{R}$, and a state-transition function $\mathcal{T}$.

In RL, an agent is immersed in an unknown environment. The agent is then asked to learn how to behave optimally (taking optimal actions) via a trial-and-error process. The learning process is as follows: (i) The agent is asked to select an action in a given environment state; (ii) The selected action is executed and the environment rewards the agent for taking this action using a scalar value obtained via the reward function; (iii) The environment performs a state transition using the state-transition function leading to a new environment state and a new learning step. The goal of the agent is to maximize the reward it gets from the environment by learning which action leads to the optimal reward. The policy followed by the RL agent that drives the selection of the next action is nothing more than a function that selects an action in a given environment state. Mathematically, such a policy is written $\pi(\text{state}) \rightarrow$ action. An important aspect of the RL learning process is called exploration vs. exploitation. Operating with the current best choice (i.e., exploit) can capitalize on the current optimal action, while "exploring" can discover new actions that can outperform the best choice so far [28]. The $\epsilon$-greedy and the Boltzmann exploration are popular exploration algorithms that consider those two aspects. For a more detailed survey of RL techniques and exploration algorithms, the reader can refer to [16].

Multi-Agent Reinforcement Learning (MARL) is an extension of the RL framework where multiple (in contrast with the standard RL framework) agents work in either in fully-cooperative, fully-competitive, or mixed manner [6]. In the service composition problem, agents have to cooperate (i.e., coordinate) to yield the most suitable results. The proposed approach is a simple mixed MARL algorithm as the reward is not the same for all the agent for a single query [6]. Indeed, in a non-stationary problem, such as the one tackled herein, convergence is not guaranteed as an agent's reward depends also on the action of other agents. However, we expect more sophisticated MARL algorithm (such as Win-or-Learn Fast Policy Hill Climbing [6] and its variants [9]) to increase performance of our approach. The study of such algorithms is left for future work.

### 3.3  QLearning

Herein, we decided to employ QLearning [30] as a RL algorithm. QLearning is one of the most popular model-free RL algorithm. This decision has been driven by the good performance reached by QLearning in many different fields [2,5,20] and the wide availability of libraries that propose a QLearning implementation. To learn the optimal policy, QLearning agents iteratively approximate $Q(s, a)$ (the expected reward for taking an action $a$ in state $s$). Agents update the current approximation of $Q(s, a)$ after each learning step [28] using the expected reward of the next greedy action. QLearning uses two parameters: $\alpha \in [0, 1]$ (learning rate) and $\gamma \in [0, 1]$ (discount factor). The approximation of $Q(s, a)$ is used by the agent's exploration algorithm to drive the selection of their next actions.

## 4    Coordination Model with Reinforcement Learning

Our coordination model derives from the original SAPERE coordination model. We equipped the software agents entities of the model with a Reinforcement

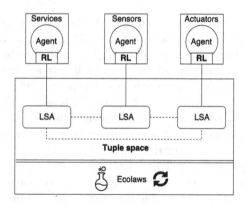

**Fig. 1.** SAPERE Coordination Model enhanced with RL

Learning (RL) module to trigger reactions with the Live semantic annotations. The coordination model with reinforcement learning is shown on Fig. 1.

Software agents are sensitive to LSAs being injected in the tuple space. Their values trigger some agent's behavior, which then starts some computation. The result of this computation can be diverse and multiple: the agent instructs some actuator to provide some effect in the environment (e.g. closing windows); the agent may inject a new tuple of data in the tuple space (e.g. the average value of temperatures); or update an LSA value (e.g. providing an updated value for noise levels). Coordination of the different agents occurs through this indirect retrieval and injection of property in the shared tuple space (some agents waiting for some properties provided by other agents to start, continue or finish their work). Such kinds of models are efficient in a dynamic open system (such as pervasive scenario), where agents can communicate asynchronously without having global knowledge about the system and its participants. Agents can join or leave the system at any moment.

In our model, everything is assimilated to services: a sensor feeding data is a service, an actuator opening/closing blinds is a service. Software agents act as wrappers, actually providing the service on behalf of these entities. They also serve to provide, at run-time, reliable self-composed services using reinforcement learning. This helps to refine the returning results and ensure a given quality of services.

As said above, agents are enhanced with a reinforcement learning module. Spontaneous service composition, as envisaged in this paper, involves many agents and is the result of their collective interactions. Thus, the learning module in each agent serves to steer the collective adaptive system towards the most meaningful or towards the correct composition of services provided by the diverse agents (among all possible combinations) and so to avoid multiple answers, some of which not pertinent for the requester.

In this paper, we decided to employ the $\epsilon$-greedy reinforcement learning algorithm [16]. This algorithm has a probability $\epsilon$ to select a random action and a probability $1 - \epsilon$ to select the action that maximizes the value of the approximation of $Q(s, a)$. $\epsilon$-greedy ensures a permanent exploration which is necessary in case of erratic environment. However, a high $\epsilon$ value will lower the QoS, whereas a small $\epsilon$ value will lower the capability of the system to adapt to changes in the spatial services. Therefore, choosing a suitable value of $\epsilon$ is critical. Agents will learn through feedback and adapt their behavior via QLearning. Each agent has two actions to take $\{react, not\_react\}$. After each composition, the requester will receive some responses and is asked to choose the right one. As it is a sequential composition, a backward is attributed to the set of agents : $\{A_i\}, \forall i \in \{1, .., n\}$ where $n$, being the number of agents that participated to that particular service composition. The agents will then take the action that maximize their reward. Our model is formed by:

- States : set of properties of agent $i$;
- Actions : $\{react, not\_react\}$;
- Exploration algorithm : $\epsilon$-greedy;
- Q function : $Q : S \times a \rightarrow \mathbb{R}$, where:

$$Q_{t+1}^i(s_t, a_t) = Q_t^i(s_t, a_t) + \alpha \times (R_{t+1}^i + \gamma \times max_a(Q_t^i(s_{t+1}, a)) - Q_t^i(s_t, a_t)))$$

$\forall i \in \{1, .., n\}$, where $n$ is the number of agents that have participated on the service composition, $t$ is the current time, $s_t$ is the state at time $t$ in which the agent took action $a_t$, and $s_{t+1}$ is the next state reached by the agent after taking action $a_t$.

Each software agent has to solve a sequential decision-making problem as each agent has to decide whether a reaction is required regarding the partial composition schema (sequence of properties to reach the requested output type). This is formalized as an MDP as follows:

$S$: The set of states is composed of all the possible combinations of composition schemas. Herein, states are modeled as sequence of interactions (see partial composition schema in Fig. 4). A state is said terminal when it contains a property that matches the output type indicated in the query.

$A$: The set of actions is composed of two actions: $\{react, not\_react\}$. For an agent, reacting (resp. not reacting) to a partial composition schema means adding (resp. not adding) its basic service information to the schema. Reacting consists in both updating its LSA and completing the schema.

$\mathcal{R}$: After completion of a query, the agent that submitted the original query is in charge of selecting among all the final schemas produced by the system the ones he wants to keep as results. The agents that have participated in at least one selected schema are rewarded with $+1$, while those that have reacted and contributed to only non selected schemas are rewarded with $-1$. A gradient reward might help to avoid long schema solutions as further partial composition schemas are less rewarded. However, sparse rewards are known to slow down learning. Thus, a continuous reward function could be an alternative. Finally, in RL, reward function are tricky to choose and depends on the problem.

$\mathcal{T}$: The state-transition function. In the present approach, the environment starts with the agent query. Whenever an agent reacts to a composition schema, it adds its basic service information to the state leading to the creation of a new state, i.e. in addition to updating its LSA with one or more values, it updates the composition schema. Reacting to composition schemas triggers reactions with LSAs. The goal of each RL agent is to participate efficiently in the right compositions in order to build the correct schemas, thus providing a reliable service with a coherent result.

## 5   Service Composition

Each agent, acting as a wrapper for a device, is represented by one LSA. An LSA specifies two sets: a set of *properties* that the agent provides (i.e. they correspond to the service provided by this agent) which we note P, and a set of other *services* (i.e. properties provided by other agents as services) to which the agent wants to be alerted to (i.e. to bond), which we note S.

Both properties P and services S are provided as a set of $< key : value >$ pairs. An LSA has the following structure:

$$LSA:: == \{P = [< key_1 : v_1 >, \ldots, < key_n : v_n >],$$
$$S = [< svc_1 : v_1 >, \ldots, < svc_m : v_m >]\}$$

It is important to note that: $key_i$ are property names the agent can provide to the system, while $svc_j$ are property names to which the agent wants to bond to, i.e. wants to be alerted to as soon as corresponding values are injected in the LSA space. Values $v_i$ can be of different nature:

- $\emptyset$: a value can be temporarily empty, due for instance to the Evaporation eco-law that removes the value. This can be the case for temperature sensor whose value is no longer valid after a certain time.
- $\{v\}$: a single value presenting the value that the agent inserts in the coordination space as the service it provides. For instance, an agent working on behalf of a temperature sensor provides the value of the temperature;
- $\{v_{i,1}, \ldots, v_{i,n}\}$: a vector that contains a list of value such as GPS coordinates.
- a matrix that contains many lists of values such as multi-dimensional coordinates.
- $*$: a special character that represents the request from the agent to bond with the corresponding property.

Depending on how the LSA is composed and when the agent injects or updates the LSA, we distinguish the following cases:

- LSA $= \{[< key_1 : v_1 >, \ldots, < key_n : v_n >]\}$: the LSA contains properties only. In this case, the agent provides only an atomic service and does not require further interaction or information with/from other agents. The agent regularly updates the values;
- LSA $= \{[< svc_1 : * >, \ldots, < svc_m : * >]\}$: the LSA contains bonding with specified services only. In this case, the agents wish to be alerted as soon as one or more of the properties corresponding to the specified services is injected in the LSA space;

- LSA $= \{[< key_1 : v_1 >, \ldots, < key_n : v_n >], [< svc_1 : * >, \ldots, < svc_m : * >]\}$: an LSA injected under this form corresponds to a request for one or more services or a self-composition of services, able to provide outputs corresponding to property names: $< svc_1 : * >, \ldots, < svc_m : * >$, and provided as the result of having injected an input corresponding to property names: $< key_1 : v_1 >, \ldots, < key_n : v_n >$. We consider this type of LSA, a *query* LSA. It corresponds to a request for a service to be provided on-demand through self-composition.

In this paper, we are concerned by the query case, once an agent injects a query for a given property, how the different other agents collectively interact by providing part of the requested service, how the whole service self-composes and the output result is finally provided to the agent that originally injected the query. Once an LSA is updated (e.g. with a new value), or a new LSA is injected in the tuple space, other LSAs present in the same tuple space will react to it, if their respective LSA specify they have to be sensitive (i.e. to bond) to the provided properties. Figure 2 shows five agents: $Agent_0$ to $Agent_4$. This example starts with $Agent_0$ injecting a query LSA, providing an input value $a$ for property $A$, and expecting an output of type $D$. Each LSA in the tuple space may then react to one or many properties. Second, LSA of $Agent_1$ provides no value for property of type $B$ at the moment, but wants to be alerted to any value injected in the system of type $A$ ($S = [< A : * >]$). Therefore, this LSA bonds with the one of $Agent_0$ (diamond arrow). $Agent_1$ is then informed of the value $a$. Upon receiving this value, $Agent_1$ after an internal computation, provides a value for $B$, say $b$. Figure 3 shows the unfolding of the different LSAs of this example. The process then continues with $Agent_2$ and $Agent_4$ both sensitive to property $B$. In turn they each update their LSAs, $Agent_2$ with a value for property $C$, let's say $c$, and $Agent_4$ for property $D$, let's say $d$. At this point, $Agent_0$ is informed through bonding of the value $d$ provided by $Agent_4$. The process continues with $Agent_3$, sensitive to property $C$, and upon the value $c$, provides the value $d'$ for property $D$. $Agent_0$ is also informed of that value since it bonds with any value for property $D$. Following this logic, services self-compose via indirect communication between LSAs, on-demand following LSAs updates. As shown by both Figs. 3 and 4, different compositions and results can arise from the collective interactions of the agents. In addition to providing several different values, some of these values may not be in relation to the original input, even though they correspond to the output property. In Fig. 5, we have generated random services and varied the number of agents. Each agent provides one service in this case. The average composition schema significantly increase in number when we increase the agents' number. This is the reason why we enhanced agents' capabilities with a RL module. Thus, they understand (semantically) when they should intervene or react to an incoming LSA (or not) even when services in LSAs matches their expected input. Indeed, collective interactions among agents do not consider the semantics of users' queries, thus leading to multiple responses. Then, we add a RL module in each agent to prune non-suitable results and to

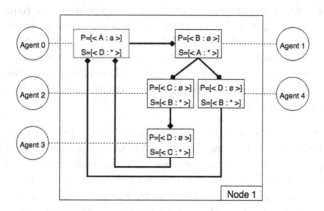

**Fig. 2.** On-demand service composition

| | t=0 | t=1 | t=2 | t=3 | t=4 |
|---|---|---|---|---|---|
| LSA$_{A0}$ | P=[<A : a >]<br>S=[< D : * >] | P=[<A : a >]<br>S=[< D : * >] | P=[<A : a >]<br>S=[< D : * >] | P=[<A : a >]<br>S=[< D : d >] | P=[<A : a >]<br>S=[< D : d,d' >] |
| LSA$_{A1}$ | P=[< B : ø >]<br>S=[< A : * >] | P=[< B : b >]<br>S=[< A : a >] | P=[< B : ø >]<br>S=[< A : * >] | P=[< B : ø >]<br>S=[< A : * >] | P=[< B : ø >]<br>S=[< A : * >] |
| LSA$_{A2}$ | P=[< C : ø >]<br>S=[< B : * >] | P=[< C : ø >]<br>S=[< B : * >] | P=[< C : c >]<br>S=[< B : b >] | P=[< C : ø >]<br>S=[< B : * >] | P=[< C : ø >]<br>S=[< B : * >] |
| LSA$_{A3}$ | P=[< D : ø >]<br>S=[< C : * >] | P=[< D : ø >]<br>S=[< C : * >] | P=[< D : ø >]<br>S=[< C : * >] | P=[< D : d' >]<br>S=[< C : c >] | P=[< D : ø >]<br>S=[< C : * >] |
| LSA$_{A4}$ | P=[< D : ø >]<br>S=[< B : * >] | P=[< D : ø >]<br>S=[< B : * >] | P=[< D : d >]<br>S=[< B : b >] | P=[< D : ø >]<br>S=[< B : * >] | P=[< D : ø >]<br>S=[< B : * >] |

**Fig. 3.** Agents behavior

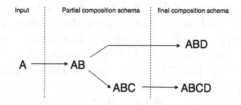

**Fig. 4.** Composition services graph

provide reliable responses. Now, our problem can be modeled as a graph of states providing different paths between graph nodes (see Fig. 4).

A *composition schema* is a concatenation of properties type, corresponding to the unfolding of the services composition. We say that a composition schema is *partial* when the input property is present but the output property is not yet reached. We say that a composition schema is *final* when it starts with the input property and ends with the output property.

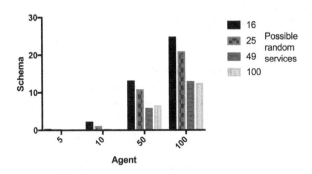

**Fig. 5.** Possible composition schemas

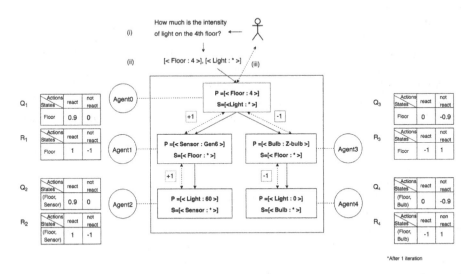

**Fig. 6.** Compose on-demand service

## 6   Scenarios

An on-demand service results from the collective interactions of a series of agents, each providing a portion of the final requested service. It arises from the self-composition of the diverse services provided by the agents at run-time. The query is first analyzed by agents which are sensitive to the input properties. One or many QLearning agents will check their approximated $Q(s, a)$ and decide to react (or not) based on their exploration algorithm. If they decide to react, they provide the corresponding LSA and update the partial composition schema. The process continues until the production of a terminal state which is a final composition schema that ends with the requested property name.

A user is a human being or another system, for which an agent works on behalf to, and that is able to provide a feedback on the provided result. Agents learn through user's feedback and adapt their behavior consequently. Once a composition is completed, the user receives one or more final composition schemas and is asked to choose the right ones. A backward reward is attributed to all agents that have participated in the service composition. To do so, the system uses the composition schemas. Figure 6 shows a basic scenario of service composition located inside a given computational node: (i) the user starts by injecting a query asking "How much is the intensity of light on the 4th floor?"; (ii) the user's query is transformed into the correct format, with a Natural Language Understanding (NLU) system, then injected into the tuple space (see Section for more details on NLU). As a result $Agent_0$ injects LSA= $\{[< Floor : 4 >], [< Light : * >]\}$; (iii) agents collectively interact, finally providing two final composition schemas, one going through $Agent_1$ and $Agent_2$ providing the information about sensor giving the level of light in the corridor at the fourth floor, and the sensor itself providing the value for light intensity ($Floor, Sensor, Light$); a second composition schema going through a service providing the information about a light bulb at the fourth floor, and the light bulb itself answering it is switched off ($Floor, Bulb, Light$); (iv) the user then evaluates the system's responses by rewarding positively the schema provided by the sensor giving the level of light, and negatively the one provided by the light bulbs; (v) the two rewards (positive and negative) propagate back to the agents following the two composition schemas.

Agents that have participated in a composition schema, update their LSA with two information. First, the partial composition schema and second a specific request for bonding with the future reward. Regarding the partial composition, $Agent_0$ injects a request to bond with the composition schema $< CompositionSchema : * >$, $Agent_1$ injects $< CompositionSchema : Floor, Sensor >$, $Agent_2$ updates it and injects $< CompositionSchema : Floor, Sensor, Light >$, while $Agent_3$ injects $< CompositionSchema : Floor, Bulb >$ and $Agent_4 < CompositionSchema : Floor, Bulb, Light >$. $Agent_0$ then bonds with both the results and the final composition schemas.

Regarding the rewards, agents injects a request for bonding. $Agent_1$ injects $< FloorSensor : * >$, $Agent_2$ injects $< FloorSensorLight : * >$, while $Agent_3$ injects $< FloorBulb : * >$ and $Agent_4 < FloorBulbLight : * >$. Once the user provides its rewards, it updates its LSA with as many partial schema as the length of the schema. In this case, it will inject the following information: $< FloorSensor : +1 >$, $< FloorSensorLight : +1 >$, and $< FloorBulb : -1 >$, $< FloorBulbLight : -1 >$. Through bonding, the respective agents will then collect their own reward and update their Q and R matrix. The right and left side of Fig. 6 show the respective agents updating their $Q^i$ and $R^i$ function based on the received reward.

# 7    Implementation, Deployment and Results

We designed and deployed a smart node equipped with the coordination platform enriched with reinforcement learning.

## 7.1    Implementation and Deployment

We attached to the node a set of basic services, as shown in Fig. 7. Our system is composed of:

- Raspberry pi 3: we used Raspberry pi to host all sensors and devices.
- SAPERE middleware enriched with reinforcement learning: we deployed our coordination model, presented above, with five agents each equipped with a RL module as discussed in the previous sections. Each agent is ready to learn when it should react or not.
- Z-wave controller Gen 5: we use the Z-wave protocol to ensure communication with sensors. It uses low-energy radio waves and has a wide communication range.
- Z-wave smart led light bulb: the bulb is used as an actuator where the light intensity can be adjusted by the bulb.
- Multi-sensor Gen 6: This provides a continuous sensing of motion, light, temperature, humidity, vibration and UV level.
- Natural Language Understanding (NLU) system: the NLU is able to extract the correct entities and intent from different questions and provides a more natural communication experience for a human user. An NLU system was implemented to transform users' questions into right query format under the form of an LSA. We used "Rasa nlu" for intent classification and entity extraction. We wrote some questions examples and then trained the system to be able to extract the same entities and intent from different questions. The entities will be considered as the input property and the intent as the output property. For instance, "How much is the intensity of light on the 4th floor?" and "What is the light's level on the floor number four?" will both lead to a query LSA of the form: $\{[< Floor : 4 >], [< Light : * >]\}$.

We implemented the scenario presented in Fig. 6 with four agents providing each a set of services. In our example, Agent$_1$ provides the corresponding sensor for a given floor. Agent$_2$ provides the light intensity of a given sensor. Agent$_3$ provides the corresponding bulb name for a given floor. Finally, Agent$_4$ provides the light intensity of a given bulb.

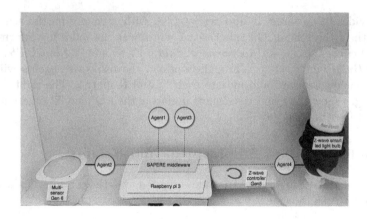

**Fig. 7.** IoT node implementing our scenario

## 7.2 Results

**Composition convergence**: Our system needs to provide reliable responses. Defining the output property's type helps agents returning an answer for the expected property. The collective interaction among the agents produces *all* the possible composition schemas, including the right solution, when the system is such that such a solution exists. Learning is then needed to select the right answer among all possible answers (see Fig. 5).

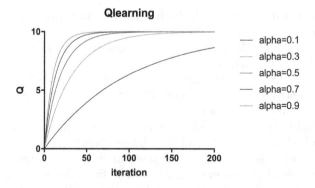

**Fig. 8.** Learning rate

**Convergence towards a correct result**: Through learning, the agents progressively update their behavior by following what they have learned based on users' feedback. The collective adaptive system will then converge towards the correct composition, i.e. the one actually expected by the user.

**Learning convergence:** It is provided through the analysis of the learning parameters. As presented above, each agent learns the right partial schema that should be returned to the user. The system should converge after few users' feedback. As shown in Fig. 8, when the learning rate $\alpha$ is close to 1, our system learns faster than when $\alpha$ is smaller. Therefore, in our implementations we chose a value of 0.9 for $\alpha$.

These preliminary results need to be confirmed and extended in large-scale scenarios under a vast variety of cases.

## 8    Conclusion

On-demand services present a new generation of services providing innovation for the software industry. Coordination models have an impact on the forthcoming IoT and Smart cities scenarios. In this paper, we show how agents collaborate to compose on-demand services using RL and a bio-inspired coordination model. This increases the quality of services in various practical applications [26]. In the future, we will investigate large-scale scenarios, first inside a single node, then on multiple nodes. This will permit to confirm or revisit our preliminary results on convergence of learning and convergence towards correct results. This will also provide a higher-level of complexity, involving other services such as Spreading, Gradient or Chemotaxis [11]. We will focus, during service composition, on guaranteeing and maintaining non-functional properties in a distributed network such as availability, reliability or performance. These aspects should be calibrated dynamically. For example, the Spreading service can adapt the distance of spreading, while the Evaporation service can adapt its evaporation frequency. Due to the stochastic aspect of our environment, parameters need to be adapted at run-time. Learning will adjust parameters related to service composition depending on the requested QoS [1], such as privacy, availability or performance.

## References

1. Algirdas, A., Laprie, J.-C., Randell, B., Landwehr, C.: Basic concepts and taxon-omy of dependable and secure computing. IEEE Computer Society (2004)
2. Banicescu, I., Ciorba, F.M., Srivastava, S.: Performance optimization of scientific applications using an autonomic computing approach. In: Scalable Computing: Theory and Practice, pp. 437–466. Wiley (2013)
3. Baresi, L., Ghezzi, C., Guinea, S.: Smart monitors for composed services. In: Proceedings of the 2nd International Conference on Service Oriented Computing, ICSOC 2004, pp. 193–202. ACM, New York (2004)
4. Beal, J., Bachrach, J.: Infrastructure for engineered emergence on sensor/actuator networks. IEEE Intell. Syst. **21**, 10–19 (2006)
5. Boulmier, A., Banicescu, I., Ciorba, F.M., Abdennadher, N.: An autonomic app-roach for the selection of robust dynamic loop scheduling techniques. In: 16th International Symposium on Parallel and Distributed Computing, ISPDC 2017, Innsbruck, Austria, 3–6 July 2017, pp. 9–17 (2017)

6. Buşoniu, L., Babuška, R., De Schutter, B.: Multi-agent reinforcement learning: an overview. In: Srinivasan, D., Jain, L.C. (eds.) Innovations in Multi-Agent Systems and Applications-1. SCI, vol. 310, pp. 183–221. Springer, Heidelbeg (2010). https:// doi.org/10.1007/978-3-642-14435-6_7

7. Canfora, G., Di Penta, M., Esposito, R., Villani, M.L.: An approach for QoS-aware service composition based on genetic algorithms. In: Proceedings of the 7th Annual Conference on Genetic and Evolutionary Computation, GECCO 2005, pp. 1069–1075. ACM, New York (2005)

8. Ciatto, G., Mariani, S., Louvel, M., Omicini, A., Zambonelli, F.: Twenty years of coordination technologies state-of-the-art and perspectives. COORDINATION 2018. LNCS, vol. 10852. Springer, Cham (2018). https://doi.org/10.1007/978-3-319-92408-3_3

9. Cook, P.R.: Limitations and extensions of the WoLF-PHC algorithm (2007)

10. Cruz Torres, M.H., Holvoet, T.: Composite service adaptation: a QoS-driven approach. In: Proceedings of the 5th International Conference on COMmunication System softWAre and MiddlewaRE (COMSWARE 2011). ACM (2011)

11. Fernandez-Marquez, J.L., Di Marzo Serugendo, G., Sara Montagna, Viroli, M., Arcos, J.L.: Description and composition of bio-inspired design patterns: a complete overview. Nat. Comput. 1–25 (2012)

12. Di Marzo Serugendo, G., De Angelis, F., Fernandez-Marquez, J.L.: Self-composition of services with chemical reactions. In: 29th Annual ACM Symposium on Applied Computing (SAC), Gyeongju, Republic of Korea, March 2014

13. De Angelis, F.L., Fernandez-Marquez, J.L., Di Marzo Serugendo, G.: Self-composition of services in pervasive systems: a chemical-inspired approach. In: Jezic, G., Kusek, M., Lovrek, I., J. Howlett, R., Jain, L.C. (eds.) Agent and Multi-Agent Systems: Technologies and Applications. AISC, vol. 296, pp. 37–46. Springer, Cham (2014). https://doi.org/10.1007/978-3-319-07650-8_5

14. Gelernter, D.: Generative communication in Linda. ACM Trans. Program. Lang. Syst. (TOPLAS) **7**, 80–112 (1985)

15. Boes, J., Nigon, J., Verstaevel, N., Gleizes, M.-P., Migeon, F.: The self-adaptive context learning pattern: overview and proposal. In: Christiansen, H., Stojanovic, I., Papadopoulos, G.A. (eds.) CONTEXT 2015. LNCS (LNAI), vol. 9405, pp. 91–104. Springer, Cham (2015). https://doi.org/10.1007/978-3-319-25591-0_7

16. Kaelbling, L.P., Littman, M.L., Moore, A.W.: Reinforcement learning: a survey. J. Artif. Intell. Res. **4**, 237–285 (1996)

17. Mamei, M., Zambonelli, F.: Programming pervasive and mobile computing applications: the TOTA approach. ACM Trans. Softw. Eng. Methodol. **18**(4), 1–56 (2009)

18. Mazac, S., Armetta, F., Hassas, S.: Bootstrapping sensori-motor patterns for a constructivist learning system in continuous environments. In: 14th International Conference on the Synthesis and Simulation of Living Systems (Alife 2014), New York, NY, USA (2014)

19. McKinley, P.K., Sadjadi, S.M., Kasten, E.P., Cheng, B.H.C.: Composing adaptive software. Computer **37**(7), 56–64 (2004)

20. Mnih, V., et al.: Human-level control through deep reinforcement learning. Nature **518**(7540), 529–533 (2015)

21. Montagna, S., Viroli, M., Pianini, D., Fernandez-Marquez, J.L.: Towards a comprehensive approach to spontaneous self-composition in pervasive ecosystems. In: De Paoli, F., Vizzari, V. (eds.) Proceedings of the 13th Workshop on Objects and Agents. CEUR-WS (2012)

22. Omicini, A., Zambonelli, F.: TuCSoN: a coordination model for mobile information agents. In: Internet Research: Electronic Networking Applications and Policy, pp. 59–79 (1999)
23. Panait, L., Luke, S.: Cooperative multi-agent learning : the state of the art. Auton. Agents Multi-Agent Syst. **11**(3), 387–434 (2005)
24. Peltz, C.: Web services orchestration and choreography. IEEE Comput. **36**, 46–52 (2003)
25. Rabanal, P., Mateo, J.A., Rodríguez, I., Díaz, G.: Data-aware automatic derivation of choreography-conforming systems of services. Comput. Stand. Interfaces **53**, 59–79 (2017)
26. Di Marzo Serugendo, G., Abdennadher, N., Mahfoudh, H.B., De Angelis, F.L., Tomaylla, R.: Spatial edge services. In: Global IoT Summit (2017)
27. Shi, W., Cao, J., Zhang, Q., Youhuizi, L., Xu, L.: Edge computing: Vision and challenges. IEEE (2016)
28. Sutton, R.S., Barto, A.G.: Reinforcement Learning: An Introduction. MIT Press, Cambridge (1998)
29. Ter Beek, M., Bucchiarone, A., Gnesi, S.: Web service composition approaches: from industrial standards to formal methods. In: Proceedings of the Second International Conference on Internet and Web Applications and Services, ICIW 2007, p. 15. IEEE Computer Society, Washington, DC (2007)
30. Watkins, C.J.C.H.: Learning from Delayed Rewards. Ph.D. thesis, King's College, Cambridge, UK, May 1989
31. Wu, Z., Ranabahu, A., Gomadam, K., Sheth, A.P., Miller, J.A.: Automatic composition of semantic web services using process and data mediation. In: Proceedings of the 9th International Conference on Enterprise Information Systems, pp. 453–461. Academic Press (2007)
32. Zambonelli, F.: Self-aware pervasive service ecosystems. Procedia Comput. Sci. **7**, 197–199 (2011)
33. Zambonelli, F., et al.: Developing pervasive multi-agent systems with nature-inspired coordination. Pervasive Mob. Comput. **17**(Part B), 236–252 (2015). 10 years of Pervasive Computing' In Honor of Chatschik Bisdikian

# Data-Driven Modelling and Simulation of Urban Transportation Systems Using CARMA

Natalia Zon[✉] and Stephen Gilmore

Laboratory for Foundations of Computer Science, School of Informatics,
University of Edinburgh, Edinburgh, Scotland
N.Zon@sms.ed.ac.uk, Stephen.Gilmore@ed.ac.uk

**Abstract.** Public transportation systems of different degrees and complexity are widely employed in cities around the world. Well-organised and efficient public transportation reduces traffic and the time spent commuting to work. In addition, more people choosing public transport rather than personal cars has a positive impact on reducing the number of vehicles on city roads: lessening their effect on climate change, improving air quality, and reducing noise pollution. Modelling and simulation of urban transportation systems is one way of analysing the influence that a variety of factors have on the overall functioning of the system. In this paper we present a Collective Adaptive Systems (CAS) model of an urban transportation system. We compare aspects of real data collected from a city bus system in the city of Edinburgh, UK, with the results of simulations of the CAS model constructed in the CARMA language. The simulations show results which are in good agreement with the real-world data, leading us to believe that the model could have useful predictive powers and thus provide an environment for experimentation with possible changes to the design of the system.

**Keywords:** Collective Adaptive Systems · Urban transportation
Stochastic modelling

## 1 Introduction

Modern urban transportation systems must be designed to have adaptive capabilities built-in because they need to respond to the unexpected events and circumstances which unfold as the delivery of the service progresses during the working day. This is particularly the case for bus services, where timetabled public transport must share the road network with private transport users who publish no timetable of their journeys and commuting plans and whose use of the road can depend on variables as diverse as the weather conditions, public holidays, and sporting events.

Set against this backdrop of hard-to-predict capacity availability of the underlying network, public transportation service providers must meet local or governmental requirements on quality-of-service as expressed through performance

© Springer Nature Switzerland AG 2018
T. Margaria and B. Steffen (Eds.): ISoLA 2018, LNCS 11246, pp. 274–287, 2018.
https://doi.org/10.1007/978-3-030-03424-5_18

metrics such as percentiles of on-time departures or arrivals, excess waiting times, buses-per-hour requirements, and other measures [1]. In order to meet quantitative targets such as these, public transport systems must have both *local* (point-of-view) and *global* (locus-of-control) adaptability, allowing system stakeholders to make both micro-scale service decisions (such as bus drivers speeding up, slowing down, or waiting at bus stops) and macro-scale decisions (such as shift operators re-routing buses, cancelling service instances, or deploying additional buses to cope with an unexpected surge in demand).

Human decision making is both in-the-loop within these systems, typically making locally autonomous micro-scale decisions, and outside-the-loop, typically making global macro-scale control decisions. Seen in this way, public transport systems can be viewed as *collective adaptive systems*, where (sometimes unexpected) behaviour emerges from the local interactions between actors in the system who are sharing resources when collaborating to meet common goals, even as they may be sometimes competing over resources in their efforts to satisfy individual priorities.

Modern smart transport systems are data-rich, making informed macro-scale decision making possible. Each vehicle in the fleet is equipped with GPS receivers and communications infrastructure to allow them to regularly report their location back to a vehicle tracking system. This *automatic vehicle location* (AVL) data provides anyone with access to the data with real-time oversight of the location of each vehicle in the fleet, making it possible to design applications which predict bus arrival times, and to compute metrics which provide statistical summaries of system performance in terms of key performance indicators which are of interest to system stakeholders.

Deeper insights into the causes of problems in service delivery can be obtained by combining data from several independent open data sources. This combination of data sets provides a different perspective on the use of the road network, allowing us to make a more detailed model which would not be possible if working from a single source of data. For the model in this paper, we have combined AVL data which was obtained from the Transport for Edinburgh company [10] with long-run average data on traffic intensity from the Tom Tom satellite navigation service [13]. These are two genuinely independent data sources, the real-time vehicle location system on the buses does not provide data to the Tom Tom network, which harvests data from their own propriety hardware installed in private vehicles.

In order to analyse a real-world example of a problem in this domain, we constructed a formal model of the system of interest in the modelling language CARMA (Collective Adaptive Resource-sharing Markovian Agents) [5,6] and studied it via simulation. In contrast to logic-based explicit state-space analysis approaches, such as probabilistic model-checking [2] with model-checkers such as Storm [3] and PRISM [4], simulation provides no absolute guarantees of correct behaviour but it scales to allow the construction of very detailed spatial models of systems such as the location-accurate bus route which we have modelled here. In contrast to blended approaches such as statistical model-checking, we have found using simulation directly with CARMA to be a more effective tool for communication of results to system stakeholders, largely because of the absence of difficult-to-understand logical characterisations of system properties, and the avoidance of the attendant formal machinery of verification-based approaches.

## 2   The CARMA Language

At its core, CARMA is a value-passing process calculus which supports both attribute-based broadcast communication and unicast communication between agents. Agents have defining *attributes* and a local store which records their current state. Agents can perform *activities* either individually, or through unicast cooperation with another agent, or through broadcast cooperation with a collective of agents which is formed dynamically at run-time via attribute-based selection. Broadcast activities are decorated with a star suffix (as in *move\**) to distinguish them from unicast activities. Agent instances can be both created and destroyed as the simulation unfolds.

CARMA builds on a long tradition of work on stochastic process calculi and incorporates ideas from the ensemble-based modelling language SCEL [7], which in turn inspired the development of the core calculus AbC [8] which focuses on a minimal set of primitives to describe attribute-based communication.

All activities in CARMA have an associated *rate* which limits how frequently they can occur as time elapses during the simulation execution. Rates can be defined by arbitrary functions which allow us to model detailed distributions of events as determined from measurement data and other sources. Probabilistic execution of activities can also be specified.

CARMA models are executed via the CARMA *Eclipse Plug-in* [9], a fully-featured development environment for CARMA which provides project structure for CARMA projects, a syntax-aware editor which is fully integrated into the Eclipse platform, efficient simulators for the language, and a reporting framework to provide plotting capabilities for results within the modelling platform itself.

In addition to these analysis tools, the CARMA Eclipse Plug-in also provides a data modelling layer on top of the CARMA process calculus. This language, CaSL, (CARMA *Specification Language*), supplements the core process calculus with data types such as integer, real and boolean, and data structures such as arrays and records. The addition of this data modelling layer on top of the core process calculus facilitates type-checking and static analysis of models which leads to detection and correction of errors in models in a way which is not possible in untyped process calculi.

The modelling advantages of having this additional expressive power in the language do not necessarily become obvious when working with smaller example models, but its benefits become clear when working with larger and more complex models, especially those which need to be maintained and updated over time. We have found this facility to be invaluable for catching modelling errors on several occasions and we believe that the added clarity which the model has through the use of data types and data structures makes it easier to explain to other stakeholders in the project, some of whom are not experts in process calculi and formal languages.

## 3   CARMA Model

### 3.1   Locations

**Coordinate System.** In our model, we use locations extracted from the real data provided to us by Transport for Edinburgh. The Transport for Edinburgh API represents a location by its geographical latitude and longitude. In order to reduce computation time when working with location datasets, we decided to translate these to the Universal Transverse Mercator (UTM) system. In this system a location is given by the tuple (easting, northing, UTM zone number, UTM zone letter). Easting and northing coordinates are equivalent to x and y coordinates on a plane, and the origins of the x and y axes depend on the UTM zone number. In our model we are considering only the city of Edinburgh. It lies in a single UTM zone (30U). This means that we do not need to take the zone number into account when performing computations. The easting and northing values give us enough information to process the data.

In the rest of this paper we refer to the easting and northing values as the x and y coordinates. (It should be noted that when applying this modelling technique to a different city one needs to take into account the possibility that the considered area lies in more than one UTM zone.)

The easting and northing coordinates are expressed in the units of metres, and so are all the distances in the presented paper, unless stated otherwise.

**Data Types.** Each location in the model is represented by the tuple (id,x,y). The id of a location is a unique identifier of a given location.

In the data from the Transport for Edinburgh API, locations are represented using latitude and longitude values from a continuous domain, as the buses move continuously and a given bus can be found using GPS at any location at the time of sampling. In our model, we represent movement as sequences of steps between discrete locations. These consist of locations of bus stops as well as any number of points on the way between two adjacent stops.

*Looking up Data Inside the Model.* The location data within the model is usually requested in the same sequence as a bus would traverse these points on its journey. For example, if a given model contains only those locations that represent a stop, each Bus entity would attempt to look them up one by one in the order in which they appear on that particular service's timetable. For this reason we map the original bus stop unique identifiers from the API sourced data into a different set of unique identifiers associated with a particular CARMA model name-space domain. In this way, we can ensure that for each service, the identifiers of locations which the bus is due to traverse, are represented by incrementing integers. This means that, conveniently, if a given bus is currently at the location with id==i, its next location has the identifier id==i+1.

Records in CARMA are indexed, and in our model the index represents the id of a given location. There are two records, x and y, for storing the x- and y-coordinate values of each location.

## 3.2  Departures

In our model, new Bus components need to be instantiated with a rate that reflects the departures of buses from the initial stop in the real data. A common pattern shared by the timetables shows buses departing less frequently in the morning and evening hours, and more frequently during the day, however the exact pattern of departures differs from service to service.

In the CARMA system, we model the departure timetables using a function which returns a transition rate for triggering an action that results in instantiating a new Bus component at a starting location. This rate should be dependent on the time of the day in a way that reflects the data in the timetables.

In order to obtain the rate of transition for the Bus component instantiation, we will use a function that returns the period of bus departure occurrences given a certain time of the day. This function is calculated from the list of departure times on a timetable (there is a timetable for every given day of the week, service and destination).

One way to calculate an approximate value of the period of bus departure events, is to look at the differences between consecutive bus departures in a certain range of time around the time for which the period is being calculated. For example, when calculating the frequency of bus departures at 12 am, we take a mean of the time differences between consecutive buses departing between 9 am and 3 pm.

Another approach is to calculate a weighted average of the differences between bus departure times, with the weight being proportional to the time difference between the considered departures and the time of sampling. For example, when calculating the frequency of bus departures at 12 am, we take into account all of the time differences between consecutive buses that can be calculated from the available data. However the closer their time is to 12 am, the higher the weight associated with their value when calculating the average. In other words, this formula is a weighted average of differences between consecutive bus departure events and the weight is the distance [in the unit of time] between the average value of the two departures whose difference we are calculating, and the point of sampling.

The comparison of the two methods described above is presented in Fig. 1. The graph is based on the timetables of two stops which are the starting locations of service number 5 to Hunter's Tryst. The early morning departures start at Brunstane, while the rest of departures start at The Jewel. The vertical lines represent actual departure times, as sampled from the timetables.

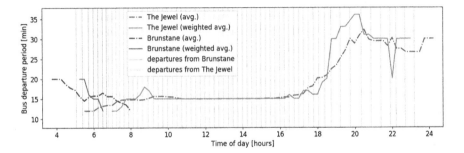

**Fig. 1.** The period of bus departures per time of day calculated using a simple average over 3 h, and using the weighted average method.

In the simulation results presented later in this paper, we used a model based on the period function generated using the weighted average method.

### 3.3    Movement

**Changing Locations.** In the presented model, a Bus is a CARMA component having two states, "ON ROAD" and "AT STOP". The state graph representing its behaviour is shown in Fig. 2.

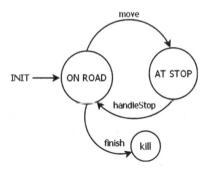

**Fig. 2.** The internal state diagram of the Bus component.

In the "ON ROAD" state, the Bus component can perform a transition which, depending on the value of the predicate expression, has two possible outcomes:

- the Bus component updates its store to reflect its new location; or
- the Bus component is removed from the system.

In the CARMA model this is represented by two actions, "move*" and "finish*". Performing either of them results in exiting the "ON ROAD" state. If the "move*" action is triggered, the bus enters the "AT STOP" state. In the other case, the bus has reached its destination, and the component is removed from the system.

In this manner, each of the Bus components traverses a number of locations on its route, until arriving at the destination. The continuous nature of movement of real-world vehicles is modelled using this step-based discrete approach.

When in the state AT STOP, the Bus component needs to perform the handleStop action in order to transition to the ON ROAD state. This action simulates the additional waiting time a bus takes when passengers are leaving and boarding. This transition's rate depends on the kind of location the bus is currently at. When in this state, the bus component can be in one of the two situations:

- the current location in the store is a stop
- the current location in the store is a point on the route but not a stop.

If the location is just a point on the route and not a bus stop, the action has a fast rate, which means its delay time can be ignored and we may assume that it is triggered instantaneously. In the other case, the rate has a constant value which reflects the waiting time.

**Speed.** The average speed at which a bus is moving is modelled by adjusting the rates of the "move*" and "handleStop*" actions of the Bus component in the CARMA system.

The rate of the "move*" action depends on the distance between the current and next location as well as the current value of traffic. The "handleStop*" action has a constant rate, but it only results in delays in locations which are stops.

### 3.4   Limitations of the CARMA Implementation

Because of the limitations that the syntax of CASL imposes on defining measures, the data obtained for the analysis couldn't be extracted directly from the CARMA simulation in the usual way. Each CARMA model for the purpose of simulation is translated to the Java programming language. This is done automatically, each time a CARMA file is saved in the Eclipse IDE.

One set of data that is not directly available through CASL, is the exact values of store variables of all components in the system, at any given time. In CASL, it is only possible to define measures that return the average, minimum or maximum from the set of sampled values. In order to obtain the complete data, sampled at each step of the simulation, the generated Java project was post-processed to save the following information, after each Bus component performs an action:

- bus identifier
- current time
- bus start time
- bus current location (x, y)

This post-processing was performed automatically using Python scripts (available for download at [12]).

# 4   Application of the Model

## 4.1   Real World Data Source

The Transport for Edinburgh company [10] has provided us with access to the REST API that can be used to obtain data gathered from their bus system. The data used for the purpose of this research is relevant to the routes, timetables and live vehicle locations of bus services provided by Lothian Buses [11], a bus operator within the Transport for Edinburgh company. The data consists of JSON-formatted text files which can be requested from the following endpoints:

- **stops** (the latest information on bus and trams stops served by Transport for Edinburgh [10], including fields such as name of the stop, available services, destinations, and its geographical location)
- **services** (the information on each available service's name, destination, routes, and stops)
- **timetables** (the full timetable information per stop, including the list of services with corresponding departure times)
- **journeys** (the list of expected stops and corresponding departure times for a given service leaving from a particular start stop at a particular time and arriving at a particular destination point)
- **stop-to-stop timetables** (timetables in the form of journeys between two stops which share a route, for a requested time)
- **service status** (up-to-the-minute information about disruptions affecting services in real time)
- **live vehicle locations** (real time information on the position of currently active vehicles)

The comprehensive documentation can be found at https://tfe-opendata.readme.io/.


**Locations and Points on Routes.** The objects ascribed location values are either bus stops or points on the route. The points on the route are included to preserve the shape of the bus route, which, when reconstructed using only stop locations may be missing important information such as road turns. In this paper the term "points on routes" is used to collectively refer to bus stops as well as other points the route whose locations are included in the Transport for Edinburgh API data. In the API data, each location is represented by its geographical latitude and longitude.


**Bus Stops.** Apart from their locations, bus stops have been additionally given a unique identifier and a name, for example "Shandwick Place".


**Services.** The `services` API endpoint provides information about all the existing services - including their names, destinations, and routes.

**Live Vehicle Locations.** The live vehicle locations endpoint of the Transport for Edinburgh Open Data API provides snapshots of the bus system at the time of request. This information includes the geographical location of all the currently active buses, as well as the next stop on their journey.

## 4.2   Traffic

The Tom Tom Traffic Flow [13] service is a service provided by the Tom Tom company, dedicated to providing traffic information in a number of large cities around the world. The service offers live traffic data as well as historic traffic data gathered from Tom Tom GPS devices in vehicles on roads.

The traffic data is available in the following three formats:

– Live Traffic Level: a measure of traffic level per time, expressed as a percentage, and described on the service website [13,14] as "Indication of the current severity of traffic congestion on monitored roads in the city area compared to the normal expected congestion level. Includes highways, major roads and minor roads."
– Live Traffic Speed: a measure of the average vehicle speed in the unit of km/h, per time. The service also provides a value of "optimal speed", that is the average speed of vehicles when no traffic is present.
– Live Traffic Reports: provides information on the causes of increased congestion, classified into three categories: roadworks, jams and closures.

In our model, we used the data from the Live Traffic Speed service, as presented in Fig. 3. To lessen the probability that an incident (roadwork, closure)

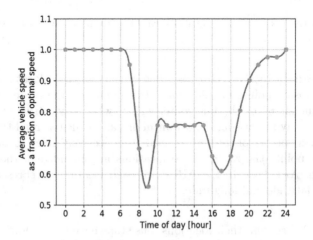

**Fig. 3.** The average speed of a vehicle in The City of Edinburgh, expressed as a fraction of the optimal speed. The data shows a congestion peak at 9 am and a smaller congestion peak at 5 pm. On that particular day, the optimal vehicle speed was equal to 25.5 mph (41 km/h), represented by 1.0 on the graph above.

not included in the simulation would affect the results, we used data from a day in which all the causes of increased congestion were categorised as "jams" in the Live Traffic Reports service.

### 4.3   Instance of the Model: Service Number 5 to Hunter's Tryst

In order to create an instance of the model, we used data collected from buses on the route of Lothian Buses' service number 5 to Hunter's Tryst, using the weekday timetables (that is, excluding Saturdays, Sundays and Bank Holidays).

This route has 124 points on routes, 58 of which are stops.

We applied the same measures to the data obtained from the Lothian Buses API and from the simulation of our CARMA model.

We compare the real-world data with the model using the number of active buses per time of day. This measure depends on two aspects of the system:

- the frequency at which new buses are introduced into the system
- the length of time a bus remains in the system.

In this case, both of these characteristics are time-dependent and at the same time independent of each other.

The results obtained from the simulation correspond well to the real-world data. The greatest disagreement can be observed in the initial stage of the system evolution (morning hours). This discrepancy may be explained by the artefacts of the real data: many vehicles that are to start their service only later in the day appear as active in the system as soon as the GPS mechanism is switched on. In the presented graphs we removed the buses that appear as active before the first departure time of the timetable, however further and more selective data cleaning needs to be performed to eliminate this inconsistency in the later morning hours.

An interesting observation can be made about the influence of the traffic on the number of active buses. In the simulation instance without traffic (i.e. the speed depends only on the distances), shown in dark blue in Fig. 4, the number of active buses is underestimated in the time ranges 9:00 am–11:30 am, 4:00 pm–9:00 pm and overestimated between 2:00 pm and 3:00 pm. In the simulation with traffic (shown in dark red), the trend seems to be reversed for the time ranges 9:00 am–11:30 am and 2:00 pm–3:00 pm. This means that if the influence of traffic was smaller by a particular amount, the simulation would fit the data with greater accuracy. The reason for the traffic to have a smaller influence on buses, than it has on other vehicles (those equipped with Tom Tom GPS devices, which are the source of the traffic information) is probably the fact that buses can travel along privileged bus lanes. If we assume that a majority of vehicles used by Tom Tom for data gathering do not travel in such lanes, this discrepancy can be explained by the lower average speed of those vehicles than that of buses.

Between 7:45 pm and 12:00 am the inclusion of traffic seems to have a negligible effect on the simulation, and the active buses count is underestimated by both simulation instances in the time range 7:30 pm–9:30 pm.

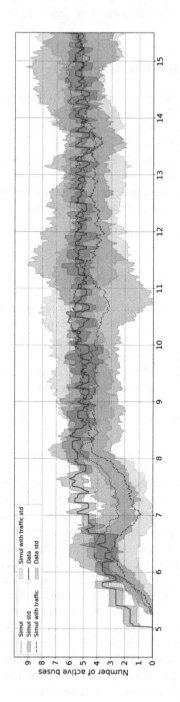
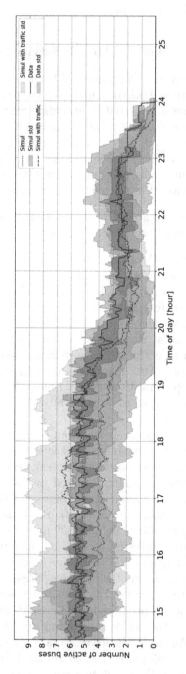

**Fig. 4.** The number of active buses versus the time of day, observed in the real data, simulation with traffic and simulation without traffic. (Color figure online)

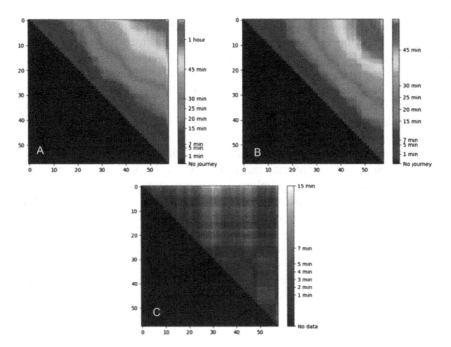

**Fig. 5.** The average journey length for each pair of bus stops on the route arriving at the destination stop between 5:30 pm and 6:30 pm. Panel (A): real data, panel (B): simulation, panel (C): absolute difference between data and simulation.

In the last time segment, both simulation instances seem to align with the real-data results very well.

An hour long snapshot of the system taken between 5:30 pm and 6:30 pm can be seen in Fig. 5. The x and y axes represent bus stops, which are indexed with integers, and sorted by the order they appear along the route. The colour of each pixel represents the average journey time from the stop designated by the x-axis value to the stop designated by the y-axis value. The striped pattern of discontinuities, which can be observed on all plots, are more pronounced in the simulation results. This is because they are the results of accumulated delayed or early departures of a bus from consecutive bus stops on the journey. In real life, when a bus arrives at the stop too early, the driver waits until the timetable departure time before continuing, minimising the overall value of headway. In this simulated model that mechanism was not represented. For this reason, we can observe that on some journeys, the duration times have been shifted for all consecutive arrival stops.

## 5    Conclusions

In this paper we applied the recently-created CARMA process calculus to model an urban transportation systems. The challenges of this technique originate from the continuous nature of the real-world data being represented in a discrete and stochastic modelling environment. The patterns one might expect to observe when viewing the system from a high-level and simplified perspective, are often distorted by numerous factors that influence the real-world data. For this reason, a stochastic model will always be an abstract interpretation of the considered system. The challenge therefore is to extract a generic paradigm that can describe a given instance with a satisfiable accuracy, while at the same time remaining applicable to a range of other instances.

The simulations based on the presented modelling approach result in patterns which are in good agreement with those observed in the real data. An interesting feature of the Transport for Edinburgh transportation system which emerged from comparing the data with simulation, is the fact that traffic influences buses to a lesser extent than other vehicles (presumably because of the existence of bus lanes).

This good agreement between simulation results produced by the model and real-world behaviour means that experiments with the model can be used to effectively evaluate potential modifications to the real-world system, or to check the accuracy of other descriptions, as in [15].

# References

1. Reijsbergen, D., Gilmore, S.: Formal punctuality analysis of frequent bus services using headway data. In: Horváth, A., Wolter, K. (eds.) EPEW 2014. LNCS, vol. 8721, pp. 164–178. Springer, Cham (2014). https://doi.org/10.1007/978-3-319-10885-8_12

2. Katoen, J.-P.: The probabilistic model checking landscape. In: Proceedings of the 31st Annual ACM/IEEE Symposium on Logic in Computer Science (LICS 2016), pp. 31–45 (2016)

3. Dehnert, C., Junges, S., Katoen, J.P., Volk, M.: A **Storm** is coming: a modern probabilistic model checker. In: Majumdar, R., Kunčak, V. (eds.) Computer Aided Verification. CAV 2017. LNCS, vol. 10427. Springer, Cham (2017). https://doi.org/10.1007/978-3-319-63390-9_31

4. Kwiatkowska, M., Norman, G., Parker, D.: PRISM 4.0: verification of probabilistic real-time systems. In: Gopalakrishnan, G., Qadeer, S. (eds.) CAV 2011. LNCS, vol. 6806, pp. 585–591. Springer, Heidelberg (2011). https://doi.org/10.1007/978-3-642-22110-1_47

5. Bortolussi, L., et al.: CARMA: collective adaptive resource-sharing Markovian agents. In: Proceedings of Thirteenth Workshop on Quantitative Aspects of Programming Languages and Systems, (QAPL 2015), vol. 194, pp. 16–31. EPTCS (2015)

6. Loreti, M., Hillston, J.: Modelling and analysis of collective adaptive systems with CARMA and its tools. In: Bernardo, M., De Nicola, R., Hillston, J. (eds.) SFM 2016. LNCS, vol. 9700, pp. 83–119. Springer, Cham (2016). https://doi.org/10.1007/978-3-319-34096-8_4

7. Nicola, R.: A formal approach to autonomic systems programming: the SCEL language. In: Lanese, I., Madelaine, E. (eds.) FACS 2014. LNCS, vol. 8997, pp. 24–28. Springer, Cham (2015). https://doi.org/10.1007/978-3-319-15317-9_2

8. Abd Alrahman, Y., De Nicola, R., Loreti, M.: On the power of attribute-based communication. In: Albert, E., Lanese, I. (eds.) FORTE 2016. LNCS, vol. 9688, pp. 1–18. Springer, Cham (2016). https://doi.org/10.1007/978-3-319-39570-8_1
9. Hillston, J., Loreti, M.: **CARMA** eclipse plug-in: a tool supporting design and analysis of collective adaptive systems. In: Agha, G., Van Houdt, B. (eds.) Quantitative Evaluation of Systems, QEST 2016. LNCS, vol. 9826. Springer, Cham (2016). https://doi.org/10.1007/978-3-319-43425-4_12
10. Transport for Edinburgh Ltd. http://transportforedinburgh.com/
11. Lothian Buses. https://lothianbuses.co.uk/
12. GitHub repository of scripts used for data handling. https://github.com/nataliazon/LothianBusesScripts/
13. Tom Tom Traffic Flow for Edinburgh. https://www.tomtom.com/en_gb/traffic-news/edinburgh-traffic/traffic-flow/
14. Tom Tom Traffic News. https://www.tomtom.com/en_gb/traffic-news/
15. Vissat, L.L., Clark, A., Gilmore, S.: Finding optimal timetables for Edinburgh bus routes. Electron. Notes Theor. Comput. Sci. **310**, 179–199 (2015)

# $\mathcal{G}o\mathcal{A}t$: Attribute-Based Interaction in Google Go

Yehia Abd Alrahman[✉], Rocco De Nicola, and Giulio Garbi

IMT School for Advanced Studies Lucca, Lucca, Italy
`yehia.abdalrahman@imtlucca.it`

**Abstract.** The attribute-based interaction paradigm has been proposed as an appropriate tool to program the interactions of Collective Adaptive Systems where a group of components can interact according to their run-time properties and the environment they operate in. It has been shown that the novel paradigm is very expressive by means of encoding other well-known interaction paradigms. However, the question on the tradeoff between its expressiveness and its efficiency, when implemented to program distributed and collective systems, is still to be answered. In a previous work, we proposed three distributed communication infrastructures to handle message exchange for the attribute-based paradigm and we proved their correctness. In this paper, we describe an actual implementation of these infrastructures in Google Go. We describe an attribute-based programming API, named $\mathcal{G}o\mathcal{A}t$, that is parametric with respect to the infrastructure that mediates the interaction between components and an Eclipse plugin for $\mathcal{G}o\mathcal{A}t$ to program in a high-level syntax which can be automatically used to generate formally verifiable Go code. Finally, we discuss the performance of the API by considering a non-trivial case study.

## 1 Introduction

*Attribute-based communication* [6] is a new interaction paradigm that has been proposed to mitigate the shortcomings with existing interaction paradigms when dealing with Collective-Adaptive Systems (CAS). The paradigm offers high level interaction primitives that are specifically designed to program the interactions of CAS at a reasonable level of abstraction. In essence, it permits a group of partners to collectively interact by considering their run-time properties. Communication takes place anonymously in an implicit multicast fashion without a prior agreement between the interacting partners. This means that rather than agreeing on a specific name or channel to interact, partners are selected according to their satisfaction of specific predicates. This anonymity of interaction allows programmers to secure scalability, dynamicity, and open-endedness more easily.

A kernel calculus, named *AbC* [2], for attribute-based communication has been proposed. The idea is to permit the construction of formally verifiable CAS systems by relying on a minimal set of interaction primitives. *AbC*'s primitives abstract from the underlying coordination infrastructure (i.e., they

© Springer Nature Switzerland AG 2018
T. Margaria and B. Steffen (Eds.): ISoLA 2018, LNCS 11246, pp. 288–303, 2018.
https://doi.org/10.1007/978-3-030-03424-5_19

are infrastructure-agnostic). In *AbC*, components anonymously interact and exchange messages based on mutual interests. Message transmission is non-blocking while reception is not. Each component has a set of attributes to represent its run-time status. Communication actions (both send and receive) are decorated with predicates over attributes that partners have to satisfy to make the interaction possible. The interaction predicates are also parametrised with local attribute values and when such values change, the interaction groups may change, and thus introducing opportunistic interactions between components.

The *AbC* calculus proved to be very powerful in terms of encoding other well-known interaction paradigms, like channel-based [12], group-based [8], and publish/subscribe-based [13]. However, the question on the trade-off between its expressiveness and its efficiency, when implemented to program distributed and collective systems, is still to be answered. Some centralised implementations have been proposed in [3,11], but any centralised solution may not scale with CAS dynamics and thus becomes a bottleneck for performance. A distributed approach is definitely preferable for large systems. However, the correctness of the overall behaviour of distributed solutions is often not obvious especially when the order of message delivery is important (which is the case for *AbC*).

One solution is to rely on existing protocols for total-order broadcast to handle message exchange. However, these protocols are mostly centralised [10] or rely on consensus [22]. Centralised solutions have always scalability and efficiency problems, while consensus approaches are not only inefficient [22] but also impossible in asynchronous systems in the presence of even a single component's failure [14]. Consensus algorithms also assume that components know each other and can agree on a specific ordering. However, this contradicts the main design principles of the *AbC* calculus where anonymity and openendedness are crucial factors. Since *AbC* components are *agnostic* to the infrastructure, they cannot participate in establishing a total ordering. Thus, we need an infrastructure that guarantees total ordering seamlessly and without involving the interacting components.

In [5], we have developed a theoretical foundation for three distributed coordination infrastructures for message exchange and proved their correctness with respect to the original semantics of *AbC* [2]. The main contribution of this paper, is the actual implementation of these infrastructures and the evaluation of their performance by means of a non-trivial case study. We implemented the three infrastructures in Google Go [1] because we believe that Go is more appropriate to deal with CAS due to its clean concurrency model. In essence, we provide an *Attribute-based API* for Go, named *GoAt* with the goal of using the *AbC* primitives to program the interaction of CAS applications directly in Go. The actual implementation of *GoAt* fully relies on the formal semantics of *AbC* and is parametric with respect to the infrastructure that mediates interactions. We provide a one-to-one correspondence between the *AbC* primitives and the programming constructs of *GoAt*. We also provide an Eclipse plugin for *GoAt* to permit programming in a high-level syntax which can be analysed via formal methods by relying on the operational semantics of *AbC*. Once the code has been analysed, the *GoAt* plugin will generate formally verifiable Go code.

The rest of this paper is structured as follows: In Sect. 2, we present the *GoAt* API and its main features. In Sects. 3 and 4, we show how to program a distributed graph colouring algorithm in *GoAt* and we briefly comment on the Eclipse plugin while in Sect. 5, we provide a performance evaluation of the infrastructures by measuring the execution time of the graph colouring algorithm. Finally, in Sect. 6 we conclude our work, discuss future directions, and briefly discuss related works.

## 2    A Go Attribute-Based Interaction API

*GoAt* is a *distributed* programming API for supporting attribute-based interaction directly in Google Go [1,19]. Go is a new programming language, developed by Google to handle the complexities of networked systems and massive computation clusters, and to make working in these environments more productive. It supports concurrency and inter-process communication through a compact set of powerful primitives and lightweight processes, called *goroutines*.

Go has an intuitive and lightweight concurrency model with a well-understood semantics. It extends the CSP model [15] with mobility by allowing channel-passing, like in $\pi$-calculus [18]. However, channel-passing in Go is possible only locally between goroutines. Go also supports buffered channels with a finite size. When the buffer size is 0, goroutines block execution and can only communicate by means of synchronisation. Otherwise, channels behave like mailboxes in Erlang which is, however, actor-based [4], and for interaction, it relies on identities rather than on channels.

The generality and the clean concurrency model of Go make it an appropriate language for programming CAS. Thus, we integrated attribute-based interaction in Go via the *distributed GoAt* API to move the mobility of Go concurrency to the next level. In what follows, we present the API syntax and describe the actual implementation of the distributed coordination infrastructure in Google Go.

### 2.1    The Programming Interface

The main programming constructs of the *GoAt* API are reported in Fig. 1. A component is the main building block of a *GoAt* system; each component contains a set of processes, defining its behaviour, and a set of attributes, defining its run-time status and contextual data. A *GoAt* system consists of a collection of *GoAt* components and is called *Herd*. Components execute in parallel and exchange messages only through message passing. In Fig. 1, Part 1, we show how to define a *GoAt* component, connect it to an infrastructure, and manipulate its attribute values. The method NewComponent(Agent, Environment) takes an infrastructure agent Agent, an attribute environment Environment and creates a *GoAt* component. Components are parametric with respect to the infrastructure that mediates their interactions and the programmer needs only to connect to an

Part 1: Initialization

```
Component := goat.NewComponent(Agent, Environment)
Agent := goat.[NewInfrastructure](Address)
Environment := map[string]interface{}
Comp(Attribute)
Set(Attribute, Value)
```

Part 2: Assign a behaviour to a Component

```
Component.Start( ... Process)
```

Part 3: Process declaration

```
func(proc *goat.Process){
  proc.Command_1
  ...
  proc.Command_n}
```

Part 4: Commands

```
Send(Tuple, Predicate)
Receive(acceptFnc func(Attributes,Tuple) bool)
SendUpd(Tuple, Predicate, updFnc)
GSendUpd(Guard, Tuple, Predicate, updFnc)
Spawn(... Process)
Call(Process)
WaitUntilTrue(Predicate)
Select(cases ...selectcase)
Case(Predicate, Action, Process)
```

Part 5: Predicates

```
Equals(_,_),  And(_,_),  Belong(_,_), Not(_), etc ...
```

**Fig. 1.** The *GoAt* API.

existing infrastructure's agent. Currently three types of infrastructures are supported, namely Cluster, Ring, and Tree. An infrastructure's agent can take three different constructors depending on the type of infrastructure in use. The agent takes as input the network address of the infrastructure being used and serves as an interface between a *GoAt* component and the communication infrastructure. For this reason, the syntax of a *GoAt* component is completely *"data-centric"* in the sense that components exchange messages only based on mutual interests and are completely unaware of the network addresses of each other. The attribute environment of a component is defined as a map from attribute identifiers to their values. The attributes of a component can be retrieved and set via the methods Comp(attribute) and Set(attribute, value) respectively. In Fig. 1, Part 2, the method Start is used to assign a behaviour to a *GoAt* component and also to start its execution. This method takes a finite number of parallel processes ... Process and execute them within the scope of the current component. Notice that the code inside the Start method represents the actual behaviour of a component.

The generic behaviour of a $\mathcal{G}o\mathcal{A}t$ process is implemented via a Go function as reported in Fig. 1, Part 3. This function takes a reference to a $\mathcal{G}o\mathcal{A}t$ process and executes its commands. Notice that beside $\mathcal{G}o\mathcal{A}t$ commands, which will be explained later, the usual loop and branching statements of Go can also be used. Furthermore, in Fig. 1, Part 4, we define the available $\mathcal{G}o\mathcal{A}t$ commands.

The main communication actions, send and receive, are implemented via Send(Tuple, Predicate) and Receive(acceptfunc(attr * Attributes, msg Tuple)bool) respectively. The send method communicates a tuple of values, Tuple, to components whose attributes satisfy the predicate Predicate. The receive method accepts a message and passes it to a boolean function that checks if it satisfies the receiving predicate of a component. We also provide two other versions of the send action: a side-effect send SendUpd and a guarded side-effect send GSendUpd. The former has immediate attribute updates once executed and the latter can also be guarded by a predicate Guard that blocks the execution until the guard is satisfied.

The Spawn method is used to dynamically create new processes and execute them in parallel with the main process at run time. The method Call(Process) implements a process call. The awareness operator, implemented via the methods WaitUntilTrue(Predicate), blocks the execution of a process until predicate Predicate is satisfied. The non-deterministic choice of several guarded processes are implemented via the method Select(cases ...selectcase). This method takes a finite number of arguments of type selectcase, each of which is composed of an action guarded by a predicate and a continuation process as shown in the syntax of a case. When the guarding predicate of one branch is satisfied, the method enables it and terminates other branches. Finally in Fig. 1, Part 5, the predicates Equals, And, Belong, and Not correspond to $=$, $\wedge$, $\in$ and $\neg$ respectively. Other standard predicates are also available.

## 2.2    A Distributed Coordination Infrastructure

The semantics of the $AbC$ calculus states that a component can interact with others by performing a one-to-many send operation. The group addressed by the message is determined by the predicates on both the sender and the receiver sides. Only components that satisfy the sending predicate and are interested in the content of the message will receive it. Otherwise they will just discard the message and stay unchanged. Send and receive operations might have immediate side effects by updating local attribute-values. The original semantics of $AbC$ assumes atomic message-exchange and a message is delivered to all parallel components in a single step. Once the message is delivered to all components running in parallel, it is the responsibility of individual components to use or discard the message. Message transmission is non-blocking, but reception is blocking. For instance, a component can still send a message even if there is no receiver (i.e., all the targeted components discard the message); a receive operation can, instead, only take place through synchronisation with an available message. The full operational semantics of $AbC$ can be found in [2]. These semantics relies on synchronisation, and abstracts from an underlying coordination infrastructure. However, any reasonable implementation need to be asynchronous.

In this section, we consider a Go implementation of three distributed coordination infrastructures for managing message exchange of the $\mathcal{G}o\mathcal{A}t$ API. We will refer to them as *cluster*, *ring*, and *tree* infrastructures. These infrastructures model faithfully the parallel composition operator of the $AbC$ calculus. Our approach consists of labelling each message with an id that is uniquely determined at the infrastructure level. Components execute asynchronously while the semantics of the parallel composition operator is preserved by relying on the unique identities of exchanged messages. In essence, if a component wants to send a message, it sends a request to the infrastructure for a fresh id. The infrastructure replies back with a fresh id and then the component sends a data message (the actual message) labeled with the received id. A component receives a message only when the difference between the incoming message's id and the id of the last received message is 1. Otherwise the message is added to the component waiting queue until the condition is satisfied.

The projection of a $\mathcal{G}o\mathcal{A}t$ system with respect to a specific component is reported in Fig. 2. It mainly consists of three parts: the component part, the agent part, and the infrastructure part. The agent provides a standard interface between a $\mathcal{G}o\mathcal{A}t$ component and the underlying coordination infrastructure and mediates message-exchange between them. Actually, the agent hides the details of the infrastructure where the component is connected and separates the behaviour of a component from that of the underlying coordination infrastructure.

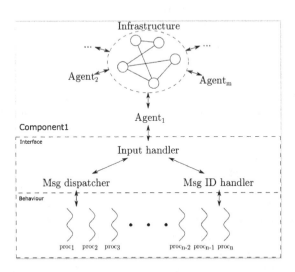

**Fig. 2.** A Component interface to a $\mathcal{G}o\mathcal{A}t$ system

In what follows, we will describe the implementation details and the dynamics of our distributed coordination infrastructures.

**The Component.** As reported in Fig. 2, a $\mathcal{G}o\mathcal{A}t$ component consists of a behavioural part represented by its running processes and an interface to deal with the infrastructure's agent connected to it. The interface consists of three entities: the Input handler, the Msg dispatcher, and the Msg ID handler. The Input handler is used to collect all incoming messages from the infrastructure's agent, forward reply messages to the Msg ID handler, and forwards the rest to the Msg dispatcher.

The Msg dispatcher stores a message until all messages with less id have been sent/delivered. Once this condition is satisfied, the Msg dispatcher forwards the message to a process. If it accepts, the message is considered to be delivered; otherwise, the Msg dispatcher forwards the message to another process. The procedure continues until either the message is accepted by some process or all processes have rejected the message. In both cases, the message is considered to be delivered and the new id is notified to the Msg ID handler. It should be noted that any changes to the attribute environment during the decision of accepting or rejecting the message can be only committed if the message is accepted, otherwise they will be rolled-back.

Furthermore, when a process wants to send a message, it requests a fresh id from the Msg ID handler. The handler forwards the request to the infrastructure's agent. While the process is waiting to send its message, it will reject any dispatched messages. Once a reply message with a fresh id is received, the Msg ID handler will forward it to the process only when all messages with less id have been sent/delivered. The process can now manipulate the attributes environment and send a new message to the Msg ID handler which will forward it to the infrastructure's agent. All attribute updates are committed and the msg dispatcher is notified about the new id.

**The Coordination Infrastructures.** These infrastructures are responsible for forwarding messages to components and also for issuing fresh message ids. Each kind of infrastructure consists of a set of server nodes that are logically connected in a specific way and collaborate to deliver sent messages to all connected components except for the sender. The implementation details of each infrastructure are reported below:

– **Cluster Infrastructure.** The cluster infrastructure consists of a registration node and a set of servers sharing a counter node and an input queue. A $\mathcal{G}o\mathcal{A}t$ component needs to register itself through its own infrastructure's agent to the cluster. The agent contacts the registration node which will forward its network address to all cluster' servers. The agent forwards its component messages to the input queue of the cluster. A cluster server gets a message from the input queue which acts as a synchronisation point. If the message is a request for a fresh id, the server asks for a fresh id from the counter node and sends a reply back to the requester; otherwise the message is forwarded to all agents connected to the cluster except for the sender. This kind of infrastructure is a straightforward generalisation of a centralised implementation where only a single server is responsible for forwarding and sequencing messages.

- **Ring Infrastructure.** The ring infrastructure consists of a registration node and a set of servers sharing a counter node. The difference here is that each server has its own input queue and is responsible for a group of agents in the infrastructure. Also the ring servers are organised in a logical ring. Upon registration, an agent is only registered to one server (a parent) in the ring. This server will be the only interface for the agent to interact with the infrastructure. The fact that agents are assigned to specific servers allows us to re-use the same TCP connection. This would avoid unnecessary delays caused by re-establishing the connection every time a message is exchanged. The agent forwards its component messages to the input queue of its parent server. A ring server gets a message from its input queue: if it is a request message, the server asks for a fresh id from the counter node and sends a reply back to the requester, otherwise the message is forwarded to all agents directly connected to this server except for the sender. The message is also forwarded to its neighbour in the ring. When a server receives a message from its neighbour, it will accept the message only when its id is greater than the id of the last message processed at this server, otherwise the message is discarded.
- **Tree Infrastructure.** The tree infrastructure consists of a registration node and a set of servers organised in a logical tree. The unique root of the tree is the only server that is responsible for generating fresh message ids. As the case with the ring, each server is responsible for a group of agents and has its own input queue. The agent forwards its component messages to the input queue of its parent server. The server gets a message from its input queue: if it is a request message and the server is the root of the tree, the server assigns it an id and sends a reply back to the requester, otherwise the server forwards the message to its own parent until the message reaches the root. Every time a request message traverses a server, it records its address in a linked list to help trace back the reply to the original requester with a minimal number of messages. If the server receives a reply message, it will forward it to the address on top of the message's linked list storing the path. Finally, if a data message is received, it will be forwarded to all connected agents and servers except for the sender.

# 3   Case Study: A Distributed Variant of Graph Colouring

In this section we show how to use the programming constructs of the *GoAt* API to program a distributed variant of the graph colouring algorithm [16] in an intuitive and easy way. We render the problem as a typical CAS scenario where a collective of agents, executing the same code, collaborate to achieve a system-level goal without any centralised control.

The problem consists of assigning a *colour* (an integer) to each vertex in a graph while avoiding that two neighbours get the same colour. The algorithm consists of a sequence of rounds of colour selection. At the end of each round at least one vertex is assigned a colour. A vertex, with identity $id$. uses messages of the form ("try", $c$, $r$, $id$) to inform its neighbours that at round $r$ it wants to select colour $c$ and messages of the form ("done", $c$, $r$, id) to communicate that colour $c$ has been definitely chosen at the end of round $r$. At the beginning of a round, each vertex selects a colour and sends a *try*-message to all of its neighbours N. A vertex also collects *try*-messages from its neighbours. The selected colour is assigned to a vertex only if it has the greatest id among those that have selected the same colour in that round. After the assignment, a *done*-message (associated with the current round) is sent to neighbours.

Each vertex can be rendered as a $\mathcal{G}o\mathcal{A}t$ component where the behaviour of a component is defined as the interleaving behavior of four co-located processes F, T, D and A. Process F forwards *try*-messages to neighbours, T handles *try*-messages, D handles *done*-messages, and A is used for assigning a final colour. The overall algorithm can be realised by running all $\mathcal{G}o\mathcal{A}t$ components (representing the vertices of the graph) in parallel.

The attribute environment of a vertex relies on the following attributes to control the behaviour of a vertex: The attribute "round" stores the current round while "used" and "constraints" are sets, registering the colours used by neighbours and possible conflicting colours respectively. The attribute "counter" counts the number of try-messages collected by a component while "send_try" is used to enable/disable forwarding of messages to neighbours. Attribute "assigned" indicates if a vertex is assigned a colour while "colour" is a colour proposal. Finally, attributes id and N are used to represent the vertex *id* and the set of *neighbours*, respectively. These attributes initially have the following values: round = 0, constraints = used = ∅, send = tt, and assigned = ff. It should be noted that new values for these attributes can only be learnt by means of message exchange among vertices.

Below, we describe the local behaviour of a single $\mathcal{G}o\mathcal{A}t$ component. To avoid verbosity, we omit all auxiliary functions, but we comment on their behaviour.

Process F, reported below, proposes a colour. If a vertex is not assigned a colour and the value of attribute send_try is true, the process sends a try message to its neighbours identifying them by the predicate Belong(goat.Comp("id"), goat.Receiver("N")). The try message contains a try label, the proposed colour, the current round, and the id of this vertex. The proposed colour is the smallest colour that has not yet been selected by neighbours (not in used). The function Evaluate(minColorNot, goat.Comp("used")) is used to propose a colour. As side effects, the attribute colour is assigned the new colour and the attribute send_try is set to false.

```
1    func processF(proc *goat.Process) {
2        for {
3            proc.GSendUpd(goat.And(goat.Equals(goat.Comp("assigned"), false),
                 goat.Equals(goat.Comp("send_try"), true)), goat.NewTuple("try", goat.Evaluate(minColorNot,
                 goat.Comp("used")), goat.Comp("round"), goat.Comp("id")), goat.Belong(goat.Comp("id"),
                 goat.Receiver("N")),
4                func(attr *goat.Attributes){
5                    attr.Set("colour", minColorNot(attr.GetValue("used")))
6                    attr.Set("send_try", false) })
7        }}
```

Process T deals with try-messages of the form ("try", y, z, tid) as mentioned before. If the current round equals the round attached in the message z then the received message has been originated by another component performing the same round of the algorithm and we have two cases (Lines 12–19). The first case is executed when the id of the vertex is greater than the id of the message tid, i.e., the sender has an id smaller than the id of the receiver. In this case, the message is ignored (there is no conflict), simply the counter of received messages is incremented. In the second case, the received colour is recorded to check the presence of conflicts. The value of y is added to constraints and the counter is incremented by 1. If z is greater than the current round, as in (Lines 21–32), then the received message has been originated by a component executing a successive round and two possible alternatives are considered (thisId > tid or thisId < tid). In both cases, round is set to z, send_try and counter are updated accordingly, and constraints is set to the value of y if thisId < tid.

```
1   func processT(proc *goat.Process) {
2       for {
3           proc.Receive(func(attr *goat.Attributes, msg goat.Tuple) bool{
4               if msg.IsLong(4) && msg.Get(0) == "try" {
5                   y := msg.Get(1)
6                   z := msg.Get(2).(int)
7                   tid := msg.Get(3).(int)
8
9                   thisRound := attr.GetValue("round").(int)
10                  thisId := attr.GetValue("id").(int)
11
12                  if thisRound == z {
13                      if thisId > tid {
14                          attr.Set("counter", attr.GetValue("counter").(int) + 1)
15                          return true
16                      } else if thisId < tid {
17                          attr.Set("counter", attr.GetValue("counter").(int) + 1)
18                          attr.Set("constraints", add(attr.GetValue("constraints"), y))
19                          return true
20                      }
21                  } else if thisRound < z {
22                      if thisId > tid {
23                          attr.Set("round", z)
24                          attr.Set("send_try", true)
25                          attr.Set("counter", 1)
26                          attr.Set("constraints", goat.NewTuple())
27                          return true
28                      } else if thisId < tid {
29                          attr.Set("round", z)
30                          attr.Set("send_try", true)
31                          attr.Set("counter", 1)
32                          attr.Set("constraints", goat.NewTuple(y))
33                          return true
34                      }
35                  }
36              }
37              return false
38          })}}
```

Process D, below, is used to receive done-messages of the form ("done", y, z, tid) where y is the assigned colour, z is the attached round, and tid is the sender id. These are sent by components that have reached a final decision about their colour. We have two cases: either the attribute round is < z or ≥ z. In both cases, the used colour is registered in used and the counter done is incremented. However, In the second case, private attributes are updated to indicate the startup of a new round (z).

```
1    func processD(proc *goat.Process) {
2        for {
3            proc.Receive(func(attr *goat.Attributes, msg goat.Tuple) bool{
4                if msg.IsLong(4) && msg.Get(0) == "done" {
5                    if attr.GetValue("round").(int) < msg.Get(2).(int) {
6                        attr.Set("round", msg.Get(2))
7                        attr.Set("constraints", goat.NewTuple())
8                        attr.Set("send_try", true)
9                        attr.Set("counter", 0)
10                   }
11                   attr.Set("done", attr.GetValue("done").(int) + 1)
12                   attr.Set("used", add(attr.GetValue("used"), msg.Get(1)))
13                   return true
14               } else {
15                   return false
16       }})}}
```

Process A, reported below, is used to assign a final colour to a vertex. It can only be executed when messages from neighbours (which are not assigned colours) have been received and no conflict has been found (i.e., the colour is neither in used nor in constraints). When the above conditions are satisfied, message ("done", colour, round + 1, id) is sent to neighbours, the attribute Assigned is set to true, and the process terminates.

```
1    func processA(proc *goat.Process) {
2        proc.GSendUpd(goat.Equals(goat.Evaluate(canAssign, goat.Comp("counter"), goat.Comp("N"),
             goat.Comp("done"), goat.Comp("colour"), goat.Comp("constraints"), goat.Comp("used")),
             true), goat.NewTuple("done", goat.Comp("colour"), goat.Evaluate(inc, goat.Comp("round")),
             goat.Comp("id")), goat.Belong(goat.Comp("id"), goat.Receiver("N")),
3        func(attr *goat.Attributes){attr.Set("assigned", true)})
4    }
```

## 4   The Eclipse Plugin for $\mathcal{GoAt}$

In this section, we would like to briefly comment on the Eclipse plugin we have developed for $\mathcal{GoAt}$. The main goal of the $\mathcal{GoAt}$ plugin is to permit programming in a high-level syntax (i.e., the syntax of the original calculus $AbC$).

This syntax can be then analysed via formal methods by relying on the operational semantics of the $AbC$ calculus. Once the code has been analysed, the $\mathcal{GoAt}$ plugin will generate formally verifiable Go code. In this paper, we focus on the implementation part and we will consider verification tools for future works.

Figure 3 shows the project explorer of a $\mathcal{GoAt}$ plugin project. The source folder src consists of two main files: the infrastructure file with .ginf extension and the system file with .goat extension. The infrastructure file is used to create an infrastructure which can be of three

**Fig. 3.** The $\mathcal{GoAt}$ plugin

types: cluster, ring, and tree. We also support local concurrency. The system file contains the actual $\mathcal{GoAt}$ specifications and a reference to the infrastructure that mediates the interaction between *GoAt* components. Once these files are saved, the *GoAt* plugin automatically generates Go code in the **src-gen** folder. We plan to integrate, in the near future, formal tools and rely on static analysis to inspect *GoAt* specifications before code generation.

Below, we show how Process F in Sect. 3 would be written using the Eclipse plugin. Clearly, the syntax is clean and less verbose which helps the modellers to focus on the problem they are trying to solve rather than worrying about complicated syntactic constructions.

```
process F {
  loop{
    if(comp.send_try && !comp.assigned)
    send{"try", minFeasibleColor(comp.used), comp.round, comp.id}@(comp.id in receiver.N)[
    comp.send_try := false,
                comp.colour := minFeasibleColor(comp.used)];
  }}
```

Other examples can be found in the WebPage[1] of *GoAt*. There, we also show how to program a complex and sophisticated variant of the well-known problem of Stable Allocation in Content Delivery Network (CDN) [17] using the *GoAt* plugin. We show that although our solution is more open and less-restrictive, the complexity of our solution is still comparable to the original one adopted by Akamai's CDN; one of the largest distributed systems available.

## 5    Performance Evaluation

In this section, we evaluate the performance of the *GoAt* coordination infrastructures by measuring the execution time of the case study introduced in Sect. 3. However, since it is very difficult, if not impossible, to perform statistical analysis on *real* distributed systems when the number of involved participants is large, like in the scenarios considered in this section, we model our infrastructures in terms of Markov processes [20] and evaluate their performance. More detailed evaluation where stress tests are used to measure how the infrastructures perform can be found in [5]. There we measure the average-message delivery time and also the throughput and we consider some simple scenarios to measure the performance at steady-state. Here the focus is on evaluating the performance when more complicated scenarios are considered.

We consider the state of a Markov process to represent possible infrastructure configurations, while the transitions (that are selected probabilistically) are associated with events on messages. We consider three types of events: a new message *sent* by a component; a message *transmitted* from a server to another in the infrastructure; a message locally *handled* by a node (i.e. removed from an input/waiting queue). Each event is associated with a *rate* that is the parameter of the *exponentially distributed* random variable governing the *event duration*. We have developed an *AbC* simulator[2] and we performed various experiments to study the performance of our infrastructures.

---

[1] The *GoAt* API:https://giulio-garbi.github.io/goat/.
[2] The simulator: https://github.com/giulio-garbi/AbCSimulator_vertex.

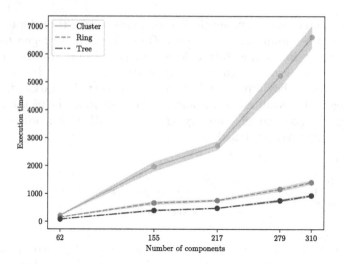

**Fig. 4.** The execution time of graph colouring.

To perform the simulation we need to fix three parameters: the *component sending rate* $\lambda_s$; the *infrastructure transmission rate* $\lambda_t$; and the *handling rate* $\lambda_h$. In all experiments, we fix the following values: $\lambda_s = 1.0$, $\lambda_t = 15.0$, and $\lambda_h = 1000.0$ and we rely on kinetic Monte Carlo simulation [21].

We consider infrastructure configurations with 31 server nodes and we consider graphs of 62, 155, 217, 279, and 310 vertices. We run the simulation which computes the average execution time needed to compute a solution of the graph colouring scenario. The simulation results of all graphs are reported in Fig. 4.

The results suggest that when the size of the graph (i.e., the number of vertices) is small, all infrastructures almost have a similar performance. However, as we increase the size of the graph, the results show drastic changes. Notice that increasing the number of vertices in a graph also implies that the number of exchanged message will increase proportionally because more vertices will participate in the colour selection. Clearly, as the size of the graph increases the cluster diverges while the ring and the tree infrastructures still have comparable performance. Of course, the tree still has less execution time and it is ($\sim 7$) times faster than the cluster and ($\sim 1.5$) times faster than the ring. So, clearly the tree infrastructure exhibits the best performance while the cluster one is the worst.

The cluster's performance degrades drastically when the number of vertices increases and this is not the case for the ring or the tree. The confidence intervals also get tighter as we go from the cluster to the ring and the tree. This indicates less variability of samples around the mean and thus more accurate results. On the other hand, the confidence intervals of the cluster are loose and show higher variability around the mean. Actually, the main reason why the cluster's performance degrades is that in the cluster all server nodes share the same input queue while in the tree and the ring each server node has its own queue. So when the number of messages increases the size of the input queue of the cluster grows proportionally while the load is distributed on different input queues in the ring and the tree. Thus, as the number of messages grows very high, the input queues of the ring and the tree will be filled with messages to be delivered concurrently while the cluster will still deliver messages in its input queue almost sequentially.

We can conclude that the cluster infrastructure can be useful for moderate-sized systems while the ring and the tree ones are more appropriate for large and geographically distributed systems.

# 6   Concluding Remarks and Related Work

We developed a programming API, named *GoAt*, to exploit the main interaction primitives of the *AbC* calculus directly in Go. The actual implementation of the API fully relies on the formal semantics of *AbC* and is parametric with respect to the coordination infrastructure that manages the interaction between components. Actually, we provided a one-to-one correspondence between the *AbC* primitives and the programming constructs of *GoAt*. We used the *GoAt* API to program a distributed variant of the graph colouring problem and commented about the simplicity of its use. We have developed three distributed coordination infrastructures to support distributed programming and we evaluated their performance by measuring the execution time of a graph colouring scenario. The simulation results showed that while the ring and the tree infrastructures have comparable performances, the cluster infrastructure does not perform well when the number of interacting components becomes large. We also developed an Eclipse plugin for *GoAt* to permit programming in a high-level syntax which is less verbose and helps programmers to focus on the problem they want to solve rather than worrying about complicated syntactic constructions.

We consider the tools that we have developed so far as a starting point for integrating formal tools that analyse the *GoAt* plugin code and ensure that it satisfies specific properties before code generation. We also plan to enhance the implementation of our infrastructures by considering fairness and reliability issues. We would like also to consider the challenging problem of verifying collective properties of *GoAt* code.

We conclude this paper by relating our work to existing approaches. For implementations of attribute-based interaction, we refer to the Java-based [3] and the Erlang-based [11] implementations. As we mentioned before, these implementations are centralised while we are aiming at distributed ones. For implementations of total order broadcast protocols, we would like to mention (1) the fixed sequencer approach [10], (2) the moving sequencer approach [7], and (3) the privilege-based approach [9]. The first approach is centralised and relies on a single sequencer of messages. We can consider our cluster infrastructure as a natural generalisation of this approach where instead of a single server, many servers collaborate to deliver messages. The second approach is similar to our ring infrastructure with the only exception that the role of the sequencer is transferred between the ring servers. This is achieved by circulating a specific token between ring servers. However, the liveness of this approach depends on the token and fairness is hard to achieve if one server has a larger number of senders than the other servers. Finally, the third approach relies on consensus between components to establish a total order. As mentioned before, consensus-based approaches are not suitable for open systems and they are hard to achieve in case of component failures.

# References

1. The Go programming language. https://golang.org/doc/. Accessed 17 Oct 2017
2. Abd Alrahman, Y., De Nicola, R., Loreti, M.: On the power of attribute-based communication. In: Albert, E., Lanese, I. (eds.) FORTE 2016. LNCS, vol. 9688, pp. 1–18. Springer, Cham (2016). https://doi.org/10.1007/978-3-319-39570-8_1
3. Abd Alrahman, Y., De Nicola, R., Loreti, M.: Programming of CAS systems by relying on attribute-based communication. In: Margaria, T., Steffen, B. (eds.) ISoLA 2016, Part I. LNCS, vol. 9952, pp. 539–553. Springer, Cham (2016). https://doi.org/10.1007/978-3-319-47166-2_38
4. Agha, G.: Actors: A Model of Concurrent Computation in Distributed Systems. MIT Press, Cambridge (1986)
5. Alrahman, Y.A., De Nicola, R., Garbi, G., Loreti, M.: A distributed coordination infrastructure for attribute-based interaction. In: Baier, C., Caires, L. (eds.) FORTE 2018. LNCS, vol. 10854, pp. 1–20. Springer, Cham (2018). https://doi.org/10.1007/978-3-319-92612-4_1
6. Alrahman, Y.A., De Nicola, R., Loreti, M., Tiezzi, F., Vigo, R.: A calculus for attribute-based communication. In: Proceedings of the 30th Annual ACM Symposium on Applied Computing, pp. 1840–1845, SAC 2015. ACM (2015). https://doi.org/10.1145/2695664.2695668
7. Chang, J.M., Maxemchuk, N.F.: Reliable broadcast protocols. ACM Trans. Comput. Syst. **2**, 251–273 (1984). https://doi.org/10.1145/989.357400
8. Chockler, G.V., Keidar, I., Vitenberg, R.: Group communication specifications: a comprehensive study. ACM Comput. (CSUR) **33**(4), 427–469 (2001)
9. Cristian, F.: Asynchronous atomic broadcast. IBM Tech. Discl. Bull. **33**(9), 115–116 (1991)
10. Cristian, F., Mishra, S.: The pinwheel asynchronous atomic broadcast protocols. In: Second International Symposium on Autonomous Decentralized Systems, 1995. Proceedings, ISADS 1995, pp. 215–221. IEEE (1995). https://doi.org/10.1109/ISADS.1995.398975
11. De Nicola, R., Duong, T., Inverso, O., Trubiani, C.: AErlang: empowering Erlang with attribute-based communication. In: Jacquet, J.-M., Massink, M. (eds.) COORDINATION 2017. LNCS, vol. 10319, pp. 21–39. Springer, Cham (2017). https://doi.org/10.1007/978-3-319-59746-1_2
12. Ene, C., Muntean, T.: A broadcast-based calculus for communicating systems. In: Parallel and Distributed Processing Symposium, International, vol. 3, p. 30149b. IEEE Computer Society (2001)
13. Eugster, P.T., Felber, P.A., Guerraoui, R., Kermarrec, A.M.: The many faces of publish/subscribe. ACM Comput. Surv. **35**(2), 114–131 (2003). https://doi.org/10.1145/857076.857078
14. Fischer, M.J., Lynch, N.A., Paterson, M.S.: Impossibility of distributed consensus with one faulty process. J. ACM **32**(2), 374–382 (1985). https://doi.org/10.1145/3149.214121

15. Hoare, C.A.R.: Communicating sequential processes. Commun. ACM **21**(8), 666–677 (1978)
16. Jensen, T.R., Toft, B.: Graph Coloring Problems, vol. 39. Wiley, New York (1995)
17. Maggs, B.M., Sitaraman, R.K.: Algorithmic nuggets in content delivery. SIGCOMM Comput. Commun. Rev. **45**(3), 52–66 (2015). https://doi.org/10.1145/2805789.2805800
18. Milner, R., Parrow, J., Walker, D.: A calculus of mobile processes, ii. Inf. Comput. **100**(1), 41–77 (1992)
19. Pike, R.: Go at Google. In: Proceedings of the 3rd Annual Conference on Systems, Programming, and Applications: Software for Humanity, pp. 5–6, SPLASH 2012. ACM, New York (2012). https://doi.org/10.1145/2384716.2384720
20. Robertson, J.B.: Continuous-time Markov Chains (W. J. Anderson). SIAM Rev. **36**(2), 316–317 (1994). https://doi.org/10.1137/1036084
21. Schulze, T.P.: Efficient kinetic Monte Carlo simulation. J. Comput. Phys. **227**(4), 2455–2462 (2008). http://www.sciencedirect.com/science/article/pii/S0021999107004755
22. Vukolić, M.: The quest for scalable blockchain fabric: Proof-of-Work vs. BFT replication. In: Camenisch, J., Kesdoğan, D. (eds.) iNetSec 2015. LNCS, vol. 9591, pp. 112–125. Springer, Cham (2016). https://doi.org/10.1007/978-3-319-39028-4_9

# Four Exercises in Programming Dynamic Reconfigurable Systems: Methodology and Solution in DR-BIP

Rim El Ballouli[✉], Saddek Bensalem, Marius Bozga[✉], and Joseph Sifakis

Univ. Grenoble Alpes, CNRS, Grenoble INP,
38000 Grenoble, France
{rim.el-ballouli,marius.bozga}@univ-grenoble-alpes.fr

**Abstract.** DR-BIP is an extension of the BIP component framework intended for programming reconfigurable systems encompassing various aspects of dynamism. A system is built from instances of types of components characterized by their interfaces. The latter consist of sets of ports through which data can be exchanged when interactions take place. DR-BIP allows the description of parametric exogenous interactions and reconfiguration operations. To naturally model self-organization and mobility of components, a system is composed of several architecture motifs, each motif consisting of a set of component instances and coordination rules. The use of motifs allows a disciplined management of dynamically changing coordination rules. The paper illustrates the basic concepts of DR-BIP through a collection of four non-trivial exercises from different application areas: fault-tolerant systems, mobile systems and autonomous systems. The presented solutions show that DR-BIP is both minimal and expressive allowing concise and natural description of non-trivial systems.

**Keywords:** Architectural motifs · Components
Reconfigurable systems

## 1 Introduction

Modern computing systems exhibit dynamic and reconfigurable behavior. They evolve in uncertain environments and have to continuously adapt to changing internal or external conditions. This is essential to efficiently use system resources e.g. reconfiguring the way resources are accessed and released in order to adapt the system behavior in case of faults or threats, and to provide the adequate functionality when the external environment changes dynamically. In particular,

Grenoble INP—Institute of Engineering Univ. Grenoble Alpes.
The research leading to these results has received funding from the European Union's Horizon 2020 research and innovation programme under grant agreement no. 700665 CITADEL (Critical Infrastructure Protection using Adaptive MILS).

T. Margaria and B. Steffen (Eds.): ISoLA 2018, LNCS 11246, pp. 304–320, 2018.
https://doi.org/10.1007/978-3-030-03424-5_20

mobile systems are becoming important in many application areas including transport, telecommunications and robotics.

There exist two complementary approaches for the expression of dynamic coordination rules. One respects a strict separation between component behavior and its coordination. Coordination is *exogenous* in the form of an architecture that describes global coordination rules between the coordinated components. This approach is adopted by numerous Architecture Description Languages (ADL) (see [8] for a survey). The other approach is based on *endogenous* coordination by explicitly using primitives in the code describing the behavior of components. Most programming models use internalized coordination mechanisms. Components usually have interfaces that specify their capabilities to coordinate with other components. Composing components boils down to composing interfaces. This approach is usually adopted with formalisms based on process calculi, such as [1, 10–12].

The obvious advantage of endogenous coordination is that programmers do not have to explicitly build a global coordination model. Consequently, the absence of such a model makes the validation of coordination mechanisms and the study of their underlying properties much harder. Exogenous coordination is advocated for enabling the study of the coordination mechanisms and their properties. It motivated the development of 100+ ADLs [16].

There exists a huge literature on architecture modeling reviewed in detailed surveys classifying the various approaches and outlining new trends and needs [8, 9, 15–17, 19, 22]. However, there is currently no clear understanding about how different aspects of architecture dynamism can be captured. We consider that the degree of dynamism of a system can be characterized as the interplay of dynamic change in three independent aspects.

- The first aspect requires the ability to describe parametric system coordination for arbitrary number of instances of component types. For example, systems with $m$ Producers and $n$ Consumers or Rings formed from $n$ identical components.
- The second aspect requires the ability to add/delete components and manage their interaction rules depending on dynamically changing conditions. This is needed for a reconfigurable ring of $n$ components e.g. removing a component which self-detects a failure and adding the removed component after recovery. So adding/deleting components implies the dynamic application of specific interaction rules.
- The third aspect is currently the most challenging. It meets in particular, the vision of "fluid architectures" or "fluid software" [22] which entails a virtual computing experience allowing services to seamlessly roam and continue their activities on any available device or computer. Applications and objects live in an environment which is conceptually an architecture motif. They can be dynamically transported from one motif to another.

Supporting migration of components allows a disciplined management of dynamically changing coordination rules. For instance, self-organizing systems may adopt different motifs to adapt their behavior to meet a global property.

The paper proposes the *Dynamic Reconfigurable* BIP (DR-BIP) framework, which encompasses all these three aspects of dynamism. DR-BIP is an extension of BIP [3,4]—a framework encompassing rigorous design captured as the interplay of behavior, interaction and priorities for static systems—and Dy-BIP [7]—a former extension for handling dynamic interactions. DR-BIP follows an exogenous approach respecting the strict separation between behavior and architecture. It directly embraces multiparty interaction [6]. It characterizes a dynamic architecture as a set of interaction rules implemented by connectors and a set of configuration rules. Although it does not allow ad hoc dynamism, it directly covers all kinds of dynamism at runtime [8]: programmed dynamism, adaptive dynamism, and self-organizing dynamism. It provides support for component/motif creation and removal at runtime. In addition, it directly supports component migration from one motif to another. It supports both programmed and triggered reconfiguration as defined in [9]. The big advantage of using motifs is that when a component joins a motif, its interactions with other components are dictated by both its behavior and the interaction rules in its new motif. So, a motif is a "world" where components live and from which they can migrate to join other "worlds" [22]. DR-BIP shares the same conceptual framework with DReAM [13], which uses an extension of interaction logic with data transfer and reconfiguration. The main difference with DR-BIP is the possibility to express coordination as a conjunction of constraints.

The paper is organized as follows. Section 2 provides a brief overview of the key DR-BIP concepts, namely architectural motifs and motifs-based systems. Section 3 presents DR-BIP models and execution results for use case systems exhibiting different degrees of dynamism. Finally, Sect. 4 presents conclusions and future work directions.

## 2    DR-BIP Overview

The DR-BIP framework is designed to cover the practical needs for the design of dynamic systems, and therefore, fulfill specific requirements for rigorous modeling and analysis. It allows to:

- specify architectural constraints/styles, i.e. define architectures as parametric operators on components guaranteeing by design specific properties,
- describe systems with evolving architectures, i.e. define system architecture that can be updated at runtime using dedicated primitives,
- support separation of concerns, i.e. keeping separate the component behavior (functionality) from the system architecture to avoid blurring the behaviors with information about their execution context and/or reconfiguration needs,
- provide sound foundation for analysis and implementation, i.e. rely on a well-defined operational semantics, leveraging on existing models for rigorous component-based design.

## 2.1   Motifs for Dynamic Architectures

In DR-BIP, a *motif* is the elementary unit used to describe dynamic architectures. A motif encapsulates (i) behavior, as a set of components, (ii) interaction rules dictating multiparty interaction between components and (iii) reconfiguration rules dictating the allowed modifications to the configuration of a motif including the creation/deletion/migration of components.

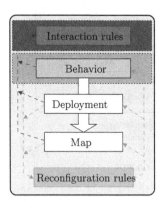

**Fig. 1.** Motif Concept

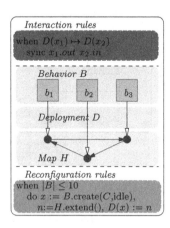

**Fig. 2.** Motif Example

Motifs are structurally organized as the deployment of component instances on a logical map as illustrated in Fig. 1. Maps are arbitrary graph-like structures consisting of interconnected positions. Deployments relate components to positions on the map. The definition of the motif is completed by two sets of rules, defining interactions and reconfiguration actions of the following generic forms:

$$
\begin{aligned}
&interaction\text{-}rule ::= \\
&\quad \textbf{sync-}rule\text{-}name(formal\text{-}args) \equiv \\
&\qquad [\ \textbf{when}\ rule\text{-}constraint\ ] \\
&\qquad \textbf{sync}\ interaction\text{-}ports \\
&\qquad [\ interaction\text{-}guard\ \rightarrow \\
&\qquad\quad interaction\text{-}action^{+}\ ]
\end{aligned}
\qquad
\begin{aligned}
&reconfiguration\text{-}rule ::= \\
&\quad \textbf{do-}rule\text{-}name(formal\text{-}args) \equiv \\
&\qquad [\ \textbf{when}\ rule\text{-}constraint\ ] \\
&\qquad \textbf{do}\ reconfiguration\text{-}action^{+}
\end{aligned}
$$

Both sets of rules are interpreted on the current motif configuration. *Formal-args* denotes (sets of) component instances and defines the scope of the rule. *Rule-constraint* defines the conditions under which the rule is applicable. Constraints are essentially boolean combinations on deployment and map constraints built from *formal-args*. An interaction rule also defines the set of interacting ports (*interaction-ports*), the interaction guard (*interaction-guard*) and the associated interaction actions (*interaction-action*). The guard and the action define respectively a triggering condition and an update of the data of components participating in the interaction. Finally, a reconfiguration rule defines reconfiguration actions (*reconfiguration-action*) to update the content of the motif. Such actions include creation/deletion of component instances, and change of their deployment on the map as well as change of the map itself, i.e. adding/removing map positions and their interconnection.

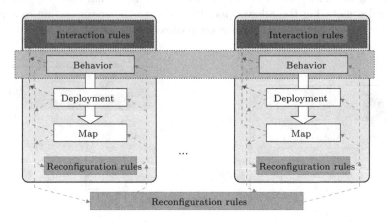

**Fig. 3.** Motif-based System Concept

Figure 2 illustrates the proposed motif concept for describing a dynamic ring architecture. Three components $b_1$, $b_2$, $b_3$ are deployed into a three-position circular map. Given the deployment function $D$, the interaction rule reads as follows: for components $x_1$, $x_2$ deployed on adjacent nodes $D(x_1) \mapsto D(x_2)$ connect their ports $x_1.out$ and $x_2.in$[1]. This rule *defines* three interactions between the components namely $\{b_1.out\ b_3.in\}$, $\{b_3.out\ b_2.in\}$, and $\{b_2.out\ b_1.in\}$. The reconfiguration rule allows to extend the ring by adding one more component. The rule is applicable as long as the number of component instances $|B|$ is less than 10. When executed, a new component $x$ is created with initial state *idle* ($x := create(C, idle)$), a new node $n$ is added to the circular map $H$ ($n := H.extend()$) and the component $x$ is deployed on the node $n$ ($D(x) := n$).

The reason for choosing maps and deployments as a mean for structuring motifs is their simplicity. On one hand, maps and deployments are common concepts, easy to understand, manipulate and formalize. On the other hand, they adequately support the definition of arbitrarily complex sets of interactions over components by relating them to connectivity properties (neighborhood, reachability, etc.). Moreover, maps and deployments are orthogonal to behavior. Therefore they can be manipulated/updated independently and they also provide a very convenient way to express various forms of reconfiguration. Both maps and deployments are implemented as dynamic collections of objects, with specific interfaces, in a similar way to standard collection libraries available for standard programming languages.

---

[1] The dot operator is used interchangeably to access a component's port/data, and to access a motif's components/deployment/map, and to apply primitives over a motif's deployment/map.

## 2.2   Motif-Based Systems

Several types of motifs may be defined separately by specifying the types of hosted components, parametric interactions and reconfiguration rules. Then, systems are described by superposing a number of motif instances of certain motif types. In this manner, the overall system architecture captures specific architectural/functional properties by design.

Systems are defined as collections of motifs sharing a set of components as depicted in Fig. 3. Each motif can evolve independently of the others, depending only on its internal structure and associated rules. Furthermore, several motifs can synchronize all together to jointly perform a reconfiguration of the system. Coordination between motifs is therefore possible either implicitly by means of shared components or explicitly by means of inter-motif reconfiguration rules.

The inter-motif reconfiguration rules allow joint reconfiguration of several motif instances. They also allow two additional types of actions, respectively creation and deletion of motif instances, and exchanging component instances between motifs.

Figure 4 provides an overall view on the structure and evolution of a motif-based system. The initial configuration (left) consists of six interacting components organized using three motifs (indicated with dashed lines). The central motif contains components $b_1$ and $b_2$ connected in a ring. The upper motif contains components $b_1$, $c_1$, $c_2$, $c_3$, with $b_1$ being con-

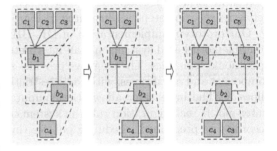

**Fig. 4.** An example: system reconfigurations

nected to all others. The lower motif contains connected components $b_2$, $c_4$. The second system configuration (in the middle) shows the evolution following a reconfiguration step. Component $c_3$ *migrated* from the upper motif to the lower motif, by disconnecting from $b_1$ and connecting to $b_2$. The central motif is not impacted by the move. The third system configuration (right) shows one more reconfiguration step. Two new components have been created $b_3$ and $c_5$. The central motif now contains one additional component $b_3$, interconnected along $b_1$ and $b_2$ forming a larger ring. Furthermore, a new motif is created containing $b_3$ and $c_5$.

## 2.3  Execution Model

The behavior of motif-based systems in DR-BIP is defined in a compositional manner. Every motif defines its own set of interactions based on its local structure. This set of interactions and the involved components remain unchanged as long as the motif does not execute a reconfiguration action. Hence in

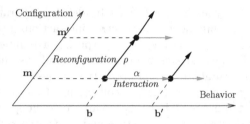

**Fig. 5.** Reconfiguration vs Interaction Steps

the absence of reconfigurations, the system keeps a fixed static architecture and behaves like an ordinary BIP system. The execution of interactions has no effect on the architecture. In contrast to interactions, system and/or motif reconfigurations rules are used to define explicit changes in the architecture. However, these changes have no impact on components, i.e. all running components preserve their state although components may be created/deleted. This independence between execution steps is illustrated in Fig. 5.

Our prototype implementation of DR-BIP includes a concrete language to describe motif-based systems and an interpreter (implemented in JAVA) for the operational semantics. The language provides syntactic constructs for describing component and motif types, with some restrictions on the maps and deployments allowed[2]. The interpreter allows the computation of enabled interactions and (inter-motif) reconfiguration rules on system configurations, and their execution according to predefined scheduling policies (interactive, random, etc.).

## 3  Four Exercises

We present hereafter four exercises for programming dynamic reconfigurable systems. We provide tentative solutions using the DR-BIP formalism and evaluate their performance at executing dynamically changing configurations.

### 3.1  Dynamic Token Ring System

A *token ring* consists of two or more identical components interconnected using uni-directional communication links according to a ring topology. A number of *tokens* are circulating within the ring. A component is *busy* when it holds a token and *idle* otherwise. A component can do specific internal actions depending on

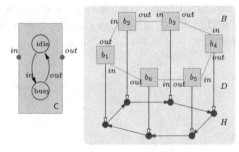

**Fig. 6.** Dynamic Token Ring

---

[2] Maps are restricted to simple graphs e.g., chain, cyclic, star.

its state, busy or idle. It can receive a token from the incoming link only its idle and send its token on the outgoing link only when its busy. A token ring is *dynamic* if idle components are allowed to leave the ring at any time leaving at least two components in the ring. and new idle components are allowed to enter the ring at any time (as long as the maximal allowed ring size is not reached). A *token ring system* consists of one or more, pairwise disjoint, token rings. A token ring system is *dynamic* if every ring is dynamic, and moreover, two rings are allowed to *merge* into a single one provided their overall size is not exceeding the maximal allowed ring size.

The behavior of component instances and the structure of the ring motif are graphically illustrated in Fig. 6. The map $H$ is a ring of locations, i.e. an instance of a circular linked list type. The deployment $D$ assigns components to locations in a bijective manner.

Interactions are defined by the rule *sync-ring-inout*$(x_1, x_2 : C)$, which connects the *out* port of a component $x_1$ to the *in* port of the component $x_2$ deployed next to it on the map. The motif reconfiguration is defined by two rules. The rule *do-ring-insert* creates a new component in the ring. The rule *do-ring-remove*$(x : C)$ removes an idle component $x$ from the ring, provided it contains more than 2 components. Finally, the inter-motif reconfiguration rule *do-ring-merge* merges two ring instances $y_1$, $y_2$ into a single ring, whenever their sets of component instances are disjoint and together do not exceed 10.

sync-ring-inout$(x_1, x_2 : C) \equiv$ <u>when</u> $D(x_1) \mapsto D(x_2)$
    sync $x_1$.out $x_2$.in
do-ring-insert$() \equiv$ <u>do</u> $x := $ B.create(C, idle), $n := $ H.extend(), $D(x) := n$
do-ring-remove$(x : C) \equiv$ <u>when</u> $|B| \geq 3 \wedge x$.idle
    <u>do</u> $n := D(x)$, B.delete($x$), H.remove($n$)
do-ring-merge$(y_1, y_2 : $ Ring$) \equiv$ <u>when</u> $y_1$.B $\cap$ $y_2$.B $= \emptyset$ and $|y_1$.B$| + |y_2$.B$| \leq 10$
    <u>do</u> B $= y_1$.B $\cup$ $y_2$.B, D $= y_1$.D $\cup$ $y_2$.D, H $=$ merge-cycle($y_1$.H, $y_2$.H),
      create(Ring, (B, H, D)), delete($y_1$), delete($y_2$)

Note that we use specific map primitives init, extend, remove, merge-cycle to respectively initialize, extend by one new location, remove one location and merge two cyclic maps. The map predicate $\cdot \mapsto \cdot$ denotes the connection relation between locations.

Figure 7 illustrates the execution of a dynamic ring system initialized with 10 ring motifs, each having 2 component instances. At each step, either an interaction or a reconfiguration (either within a motif or an inter-motif reconfiguration) is randomly executed. We remark that the number of ring motif instances decreases along the execution as idle components are removed and rings are enabled to merge into a single ring. The number of component instances varies across the execution between 6 and 20 as the *do-ring-insert* and *do-ring-remove* reconfiguration rules are executed.

Figure 8 summarizes the execution of the dynamic ring system for different initial configurations. We evaluate the performance and track the system evolution while varying the number of initial rings from 10 to 100. Each configuration is simulated for 1000 random steps. As the system grows in size and the computation of enabled interactions and reconfigurations gets more complex, the

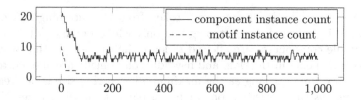

**Fig. 7.** Dynamic ring system evolution across 1,000 steps

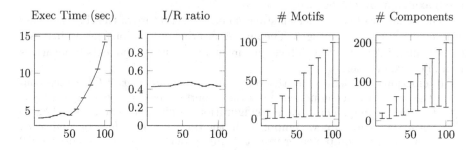

**Fig. 8.** Dynamic token ring system measurements - the $x$-axis indicates the number of rings in the initial configuration. The meaning of $y$-axis is indicated at the top

execution time increases reaching a maximum of 14 s (first plot). The average ratio of the number of executed interactions vs reconfigurations along the run is around 0.45 (second plot). Finally, the minimum and maximum number of motif and component instances are depicted in the third and fourth plots.

## 3.2 Dynamic Multicore Task System

A *multicore task system* consists of a fixed $n \times n$ grid of interconnected homogeneous cores, each executing a finite number of tasks. Every task is either running or completed; running tasks may execute on the associated cores and get eventually completed. The load of a core is defined as the number of its associated tasks, both running and completed. A multicore task system is *dynamic* if the overall number of tasks and their allocation to cores may change over

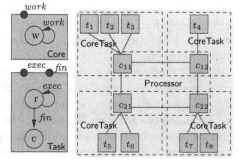

**Fig. 9.** Multicore Task System

time. More specifically, new running tasks may enter the system at the core $c_{11}$ and completed tasks may be withdrawn from the system at the core $c_{nn}$. Moreover, any task is allowed to migrate from its core to any of the neighboring cores (left, right, top or bottom) in the grid, provided the load of the receiving core is smaller than the load of the departing core minus some constant ($K$).

Figure 9 presents the overall structure of the motif-based system for four cores. We distinguish two types of atomic components, namely Task and Core. Multiple cores are interconnected together in a motif of type Processor. The interconnecting topology reflects the platform architecture (e.g., a $2 \times 2$ grid in the figure) and is enforced using a similar grid-like map and deployment. An additional CoreTask motif type is used to represent every core with its assigned tasks.

The interactions in the system are defined within the CoreTask motif. The execution of a task by the core and the task completion are represented by the rules:

sync-coretask-exec($x_1$ : Core, $x_2$ : Task) $\equiv$ <u>sync</u> $x_1$.work $x_2$.exec
sync-coretask-fin($x$ : Task) $\equiv$ <u>sync</u> $x$.fin

The migration of a task from one core to another is modeled using an inter-motif reconfiguration rule which involves three distinct motifs. A task $x_3$ migrates from motif $y_1$ (of type CoreTask) to motif $y_2$ (of type CoreTask) if the core $x_1$ of $y_1$ is connected to the core $x_2$ of $y_2$ (according to the processor motif Processor) and if the number of tasks in $y_1$ exceeds the number of tasks in $y_2$ by constant $K$:

do-migrate($y_1, y_2$ : CoreTask, $y_3$ : Processor, $x_1, x_2$ : Core, $x_3$ : Task) $\equiv$
    <u>when</u> $\langle\, y_1 : x_1 \in \mathsf{B}\, \rangle \wedge \langle\, y_2 : x_2 \in \mathsf{B}\, \rangle \wedge \langle\, y_3 : \mathsf{D}(x_1) \mapsto \mathsf{D}(x_2)\, \rangle \wedge$
        $|y_1.\mathsf{B}| > |y_2.\mathsf{B}| + \mathsf{K} \wedge x_3 \in y_1.\mathsf{B}$
    <u>do</u> $y_2$.migrate($x_3$), $y_1$.delete($x_3$)

To simplify notations in reconfiguration rules, we rely hence forth on sandwiching constraint/guard/action with angle brackets to specify the scope. For example $\langle y_1 : x_1 \in \mathsf{B} \rangle$ is a constraint stating that $x_1$ is a component instance in motif $y_1$.

Figure 10 illustrates the execution of the dynamic multicore task system with $3 \times 3$ cores for 3000 steps. Each core is initialized with a random load between 1 and 20. The constant $K$ is set to 3, hence tasks are allowed to migrate to neighboring cores (left, right, top or bottom) that differ in task load by at least 3 tasks. The cores $c_{11}$, and $c_{33}$ are used to respectively create new tasks and withdraw completed tasks. These two cores retain the maximum and minimum load. As tasks migrate, the task load of cores converges and balances along the execution having at most a difference of 3 tasks between neighboring cores. For example, in core $c_{21}$

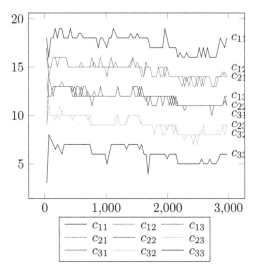

**Fig. 10.** Task load across 3000 steps

the task load increased from 6 to 14. As expected the cores ($c_{21}$, and $c_{12}$) closest to $c_{11}$ maintain a high load and as we move away from $c_{11}$ the core's load
gradually decreases. This highlights the task migration process cascading from
the top left core to the bottom right core.

Figure 11 illustrates the evolution of the dynamic multicore task system for
different initial configurations. We vary the number of cores in the processor
from 4 to 36 cores. Each core is initialized with a random load as discussed
above. The system initial size varies between 46 and 482 component instances
as depicted in the figure. Each configuration is simulated for 1000 random steps.
As the number of cores increases in size the execution time increases reaching
a maximum of 7.3 s. The motif instance count remains constant across each
configuration, however the component instance count varies as tasks are being
created and deleted once completed. Also note that the average ratio of executed
interactions vs reconfigurations is 0.7, since the task load converges to a similar
value across cores and less task migrations (i.e. reconfigurations) are required.

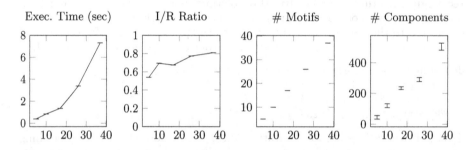

**Fig. 11.** Dynamic multicore task system measurements - the $x$-axis indicates the number of motifs in the initial configuration (i.e. $n^2 + 1$ for $n = 2, 3, 4, 5, 6$). The meaning
of $y$-axis is indicated at the top

### 3.3 Autonomous Highway Traffic System

This exercise is inspired from autonomous traffic systems for automated highways [5]. The system consists of a single-lane one-way road where an arbitrary
number of autonomous homogeneous self-driving cars are moving in the same
direction, at different cruising speeds. Cars are organized into platoons, i.e.
groups of cars cruising at the same speed and closely following a leader car.
Platoons may dynamically merge or split. A merge takes place if two platoons
are close enough, i.e. the distance between the tail car of the first platoon and
the leader car of the second is smaller than some constant $K$. After the merge,
the speed of the new platoon is set to the speed of the first platoon. A platoon
may split when an arbitrary car requests to leave the platoon e.g., in order to
perform some specific maneuver. After the split, the leading platoon will increase
its speed by 2% whereas the tail platoon will reduce its speed by 2%.

Figure 12 illustrates the motif-based system in DR-BIP. We use a component type Car to model the behavior of a car. Each car maintains its position *pos* and speed *v*. The position *pos* is updated on the *move* transition. Transitions *setSpeed* and *ack_split* are used by leader cars only to respectively define the platoon speed and acknowledge a platoon split. Similarly, transitions *getSpeed* and *split* are used by fol-

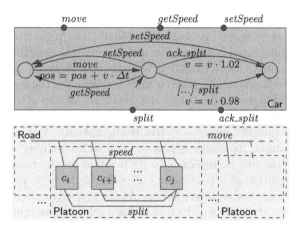

**Fig. 12.** Automated Highway Traffic System

lower cars only to respectively synchronize on the leader speed and initiate a platoon split.

The Road motif type contains all cars without additional structuring. The Platoon motif type is structured as a chain of cars. The map of the platoon motif is a (dynamic) linear graph of locations and the deployment assigns a single car to every position of the map. The Road motif defines a single interaction by the rule *sync-road-move*, which synchronizes the move ports of *all* cars and therefore performing a joint update of their positions. The Platoon motif defines several interactions by the rules *sync-platoon-speed* and *sync-platoon-split*. The first rule synchronizes the speed of the leading car with the speed of all follower cars. The second rule allows any follower car to initiate a split maneuver and become a leader in a newly created platoon.

sync-road-move($X$ : Car) ≡ when $X$=B sync $X$.move
sync-platoon-speed($x$ : Car, $X$ : Car) ≡ when $X$=B \ $x$ ∧ D($x$) = H.head
    sync $x$.setSpeed $X$.getSpeed do $X.v = x.v$
sync-platoon-split($x_1$, $x_2$ : Car) ≡ when D($x_1$) = H.head ∧ $x_1 \neq x_2$
    sync $x_1$.ack_split $x_2$.split

Two reconfiguration rules *do-platoon-merge* and *do-platoon-split* handle the merging and the splitting of platoons respectively:

do-platoon-merge($y_1$, $y_2$ : Platoon, $x_1$, $x_2$ : Car) ≡
    when ⟨$y_1$ : D($x_1$) = H.tail⟩ ∧ ⟨$y_2$ : D($x_2$) = H.head⟩ ∧ |$x_1$.pos −$x_2$.pos| < $K$
    do B := $y_1$.B ∪ $y_2$.B, H := append($y_2$.H, $y_1$.H), D := $y_1$.D ∪ $y_2$.D,
        create(P, (B, H, D)), delete($y_1$), delete($y_2$)
do-platoon-split($y$ : Platoon, $x$ : Car) ≡
    do ⟨$y$ : $H_1$ := H.sublist(0, D($x$)), $B_1$ := $D^{-1}(H_1)$, $D_1$ := D.restrict($H_1$),
        $H_2$ := H.sublist(D($x$), H.length), $B_2$ := $D^{-1}(H_2)$, $D_2$ := D.restrict($H_2$) ⟩,
        create($P$, ($B_1$, $H_1$, $D_1$)), create($P$, ($B_2$, $H_2$, $D_2$)), delete($y$)

Note that we use specific map primitives head, and tail which point to the position of the leader and tail of a platoon, namely the beginning and the end of the list.

Furthermore, we use the primitive append which appends and links two maps of type linked list together. Finally, the primitive sublist and length creates a sublist from a linked list and returns the length of the list respectively. The primitive restrict restricts a deployment keeping only the deployment mappings of components in a given map and removes the rest.

Figure 13 illustrates the evolution of the system involving 200 cars along 2000 sampled steps. Each line describes a configuration of the system. We show 13 sampled nonconsecutive configurations. A thin black rectangle represents a platoon. Its length is proportional to the number of cars contained. Its position in the line corresponds to its position on the road. For reference, we show the evolution of a particular car by highlighting it in yellow. Initially, all the cars belong to the same platoon. As the system evolves the initial platoon splits into several platoons, which then keep splitting/merging back, etc.

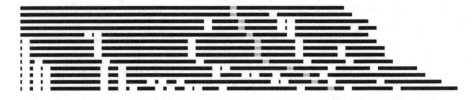

**Fig. 13.** Automated highway traffic evolution along few steps

Figure 14 summarizes the execution of several initial configurations. We evaluate the performance and track the system evolution while varying the number of cars in the initial platoon from 200 to 600 cars. Each configuration is simulated for 3000 random steps. Notice that the component instance count remains constant across each configuration as cars only rearrange within different platoons. However the motif instance count varies as platoons merge/split. Finally, execution time increases reaching a maximum of 5 min and the average ratio of executed interactions vs reconfigurations is 0.77.

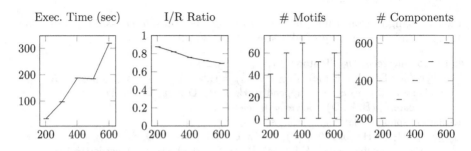

**Fig. 14.** Measurements on automated highway traffic systems

## 3.4   Self-Organizing Robot Colonies

This exercise is inspired by swarm robotics [18]. A number of identical robots are randomly deployed on a field and have a mission to locate an object (the prey) and to bring it near another object (the nest). The robots know neither the position of the nest nor the position of the prey. They have limited communication and sensing capabilities, i.e. they can display a status (by turning on/off some colored leds) and can observe each other as long as they are physically close in the field. We consider hereafter the swarm algorithm proposed in [18]. In a first phase, the robots self-organize into an exploration path starting at the nest. The first robot detecting the nest initiates the path, i.e. stops moving and displays a specific (on-path) status. Any robot that detects (robots on) the path, begins moving along the path towards its tail, explores a bit further its neighborhood and gets connected as well (i.e. becomes the new tail, stops moving and displays the on-path status). Two cases may occur, either no new robot gets connected to the path within some delay, hence the tail robot disconnects and moves randomly (away from the path), or the tail robot detects the prey and the second phase starts. The path stays in place while additional robots converge near the prey. When enough robots have converged, they start pushing the prey along the path towards the nest. The path gets consumed, and the system will stop when the prey gets close enough to the nest.

We model the first phase of the algorithm above using three different types of components and three different types of motifs as illustrated in Fig. 15. The Arena motif contains all the robots, the nest and the prey component instances. No map and deployment are used as no specific architecture is enforced by this motif. This motif defines a global tick interaction used to model the synchronous passage of time within the system. Whenever the tick interaction is triggered the robots update their positions, i.e. they move on the field.

For every robot, its Neighborhood motif is used to represent its visibility range, i.e. the set of robots physically close to it in the field. This motif uses a starlike location map. The inner robot is deployed at the center and the visible neighbors on

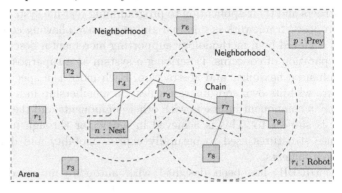

**Fig. 15.** Self-organizing robot colonies

the leaves. The motif defines a set of binary observe status interactions which are used by the inner robot to collect all the available information from its neighbors. Finally, the Chain motif represents the exploration chain linking robots to the nest. It uses a linear map to deploy the robots belonging to the chain. This motif defines a set of binary next prev interactions which are used to communicate along the chain.

For this example, reconfiguration is used to redefine the content of the Neighborhood and Chain motifs. For the former, as robots are moving in the field, they continuously enter or leave the visibility range of other robots. We use two inter-motif reconfiguration rules to update the neighborhood information:

do-neighborhood-enter($y_1$ : Neighborhood, $y_2$ : Arena, $x_1, x_2$: Robot) $\equiv$
$\quad$ <u>when</u> $\langle y_1 : \mathsf{D}(x_1) = \mathsf{H.center} \wedge x_2 \notin \mathsf{B} \rangle \wedge \langle y_2 : x_2 \in \mathsf{B} \rangle \wedge \mathsf{dist}(x_1, x_2) \leq R_{min}$
$\quad\quad$ <u>do</u> $y_1.\mathsf{migrate}(x_2)$, $\langle y_1 : n := \mathsf{H.extend}(), \mathsf{D}(x_2) := n \rangle$
do-neighborhood-leave($y_1$ : Neighborhood, $x_1, x_2$: Robot) $\equiv$
$\quad$ <u>when</u> $\langle y_1 : \mathsf{D}(x_1) = \mathsf{H.center} \wedge x_2 \in \mathsf{B} \rangle \wedge x_1 \neq x_2 \wedge \mathsf{dist}(x_1, x_2) \geq R_{max}$
$\quad\quad$ <u>do</u> $\langle y_1 : n := \mathsf{D}(x_2), \mathsf{B.delete}(x_2), \mathsf{H.remove}(n) \rangle$

The rules above describe the reconfiguration allowing any robot $x_2$ to enter (resp. leave) the neighborhood $y_1$ of any different robot $x_1$ whenever the distance between $x_1$ and $x_2$ is smaller than $R_{min}$ (resp. greater than $R_{max}$). The evolution of the chain is also described by reconfiguration. At any time, the tail can disconnect or a robot can connect if its close enough to the tail.

do-chain-connect($y_1$ : Chain, $y_2$ : Neighborhood, $x_1, x_2$ : Robot) $\equiv$
$\quad$ <u>when</u> $\langle y_1 : \mathsf{D}(x_1) = \mathsf{H.tail} \wedge x_2 \notin \mathsf{B} \rangle \wedge \langle y_2 : \mathsf{D}(x_1) = \mathsf{H.center} \wedge x_2 \in \mathsf{B} \rangle$
$\quad\quad$ <u>do</u> $y_1.\mathsf{migrate}(x_2)$, $\langle y_1 : n = \mathsf{H.extend}(), \mathsf{D}(x_2) := n \rangle$
do-chain-disconnect($y_1$ : Chain, $x_1$ : Robot) $\equiv$
$\quad$ <u>when</u> $\langle y_1 : \mathsf{D}(x_1) = \mathsf{H.tail} \rangle \wedge \langle y_1 : x_1.timeout = \mathsf{true} \rangle$
$\quad\quad$ <u>do</u> $\langle y_1 : n := \mathsf{D}(x_1), \mathsf{B.delete}(x_1), \mathsf{H.remove}(n) \rangle$

# 4 Discussion

The paper presents the DR-BIP framework as well as its basic structuring constructs and their application to programming real-life systems. We show that the proposed framework is minimal and expressive allowing concise modeling. This is achieved by a methodology supporting incremental description through strict separation of concerns. Describing a system as a superposition of motifs allows enhanced flexibility and abstraction. Each motif is a specific dynamic architecture with its own coordination rules. So membership in a motif determines the way a component interacts with other components and the reconfiguration rules it is subject to. This is achieved in particular through maps which are reference structures used to naturally express mobility and dynamically changing environments.

DR-BIP has been designed with autonomy in mind. The examples on Autonomous highway traffic system and Self-organizing robot colonies demonstrate the power of its structuring concepts. Designing systems as a superposition of motifs (architectures) with their own coordination rules tremendously simplifies the description of autonomous behavior. At the conceptual level, motifs correspond to "modes" whose behavioral content may change through component migration and can also be transformed by using higher level coordination rules.

To the best of our knowledge, there is no exogenous coordination language such as an ADL addressing all these modeling issues in such a methodologically rigorous manner. DR-BIP has some similarities with simulation and programming frameworks for autonomous mobile systems which nonetheless adopt significant domain-specific restrictions such as Buzz [20, 21].

Future work aims at showing that DR-BIP is expressive enough to directly encompass various coordination mechanisms, in particular unifying the modeling of distributed actor-based systems and thread-based shared memory systems. This can be achieved by considering threads as a special type of mobile components using maps as a shared memory structure. In addition, we aim to study parametric verification techniques for specific types of architectures (motifs) and combine them with correct-by-construction techniques based on the composition of architectures [2]. A formal definition of the DR-BIP is provided in report [14].

# References

1. Allen, R., Douence, R., Garlan, D.: Specifying and analyzing dynamic software architectures. In: Astesiano, E. (ed.) FASE 1998. LNCS, vol. 1382, pp. 21–37. Springer, Heidelberg (1998). https://doi.org/10.1007/BFb0053581
2. Attie, P., Baranov, E., Bliudze, S., Jaber, M., Sifakis, J.: A general framework for architecture composability. Form. Asp. Comput. **28**(2), 207–231 (2016)
3. Basu, A., et al.: Rigorous component-based system design using the BIP framework. IEEE Softw. **28**(3), 41–48 (2011)
4. Basu, A., Bozga, M., Sifakis, J.: Modeling heterogeneous real-time systems in BIP. In: SEFM 2006 Proceedings, pp. 3–12. IEEE Computer Society Press (2006)
5. Bergenhem, C.: Approaches for facilities layer protocols for platooning. In: 2015 IEEE 18th International Conference on Intelligent Transportation Systems (ITSC), pp. 1989–1994. IEEE (2015)
6. Bliudze, S., Sifakis, J.: The algebra of connectors - structuring interaction in BIP. IEEE Trans. Comput. **57**(10), 1315–1330 (2008)
7. Bozga, M., Jaber, M., Maris, N., Sifakis, J.: Modeling dynamic architectures using Dy-BIP. In: Gschwind, T., De Paoli, F., Gruhn, V., Book, M. (eds.) SC 2012. LNCS, vol. 7306, pp. 1–16. Springer, Heidelberg (2012). https://doi.org/10.1007/978-3-642-30564-1_1
8. Bradbury, J.: Organizing definitions and formalisms for dynamic software architectures. Technical report 2004–477, Software Technology Laboratory, School of Computing, Queen's University (2004)
9. Butting, A., Heim, R., Kautz, O., Ringert, J.O., Rumpe, B., Wortmann, A.: A classification of dynamic reconfiguration in component and connector architecture description languages. In: 4th International Workshop on Interplay of Model-Driven and Component-Based Software Engineering (ModComp 2017) (2017)
10. Canal, C., Pimentel, E., Troya, J.M.: Specification and refinement of dynamic software architectures. In: Donohoe, P. (ed.) Software Architecture. ITIFIP, vol. 12, pp. 107–125. Springer, Boston (1999). https://doi.org/10.1007/978-0-387-35563-4_7
11. Cuesta, C., de la Fuente, P., Barrio-Solárzano, M.: Dynamic coordination architecture through the use of reflection. In: Proceedings of the 2001 ACM Symposium on Applied Computing, pp. 134–140. ACM (2001)

12. De Nicola, R., Loreti, M., Pugliese, R., Tiezzi, F.: A formal approach to autonomic systems programming: the SCEL language. TAAS **9**(2), 7:1–7:29 (2014)

13. De Nicola, R., Maggi, A., Sifakis, J.: DReAM: dynamic reconfigurable architecture modeling (full paper). arXiv preprint arXiv:1805.03724 (2018)

14. El Ballouli, R., Bensalem, S., Bozga, M., Sifakis, J.: DR-BIP - programming dynamic reconfigurable systems. Technical report TR-2018-3, Verimag Research Report

15. Garlan, D.: Software architecture: a travelogue. In: Future of Software Engineering (FOSE 2014), pp. 29–39. ACM (2014)

16. Malavolta, I., Lago, P., Muccini, H., Pelliccione, P., Tang, A.: What industry needs from architectural languages: a survey. IEEE Trans. Softw. Eng. **39**(6), 869–891 (2006)

17. Medvidovic, N., Dashofy, E., Taylor, R.: Moving architectural description from under the technology lamppost. Inf. Softw. Technol. **49**(1), 12–31 (2007)

18. Nouyan, S., Gross, R., Bonani, M., Mondada, F., Dorigo, M.: Teamwork in self-organized robot colonies. IEEE Trans. Evol. Comput. **13**(4), 695–711 (2009)

19. Oreizy, P.: Issues in modeling and analyzing dynamic software architectures. In: International Workshop on the Role of Software Architecture in Testing and Analysis, pp. 54–57 (1998)

20. Pinciroli, C., Beltrame, G.: Buzz: an extensible programming language for heterogeneous swarm robotics. In: 2016 IEEE/RSJ International Conference on Intelligent Robots and Systems (IROS), pp. 3794–3800. IEEE (2016)

21. Pinciroli, C., Lee-Brown, A., Beltrame, G.: Buzz: an extensible programming language for self-organizing heterogeneous robot swarms. arXiv preprint arXiv:1507.05946 (2015)

22. Taivalsaari, A., Mikkonen, T., Systä, K.: Liquid software manifesto: the era of multiple device ownership and its implications for software architecture. In: IEEE 38th Annual Computer Software and Applications Conference (COMPSAC 2014) (2014)

# Verification and Validation of
# Distributed Systems

# ISoLA 2018 - Verification and Validation of Distributed Systems: Track Introduction

Cristina Seceleanu(✉)

Mälardalen University, Västerås, Sweden
cristina.seceleanu@mdh.se

**Abstract.** New technologies such as cloud and multi-core computing, as well as the large number of devices connected to the Internet make concurrency and distribution the main pillars that computerized systems rely on. However, developing consistent concurrent and distributed systems characterized by high performance is notoriously difficult. This in turn makes assuring the correctness of such systems challenging, due to interleavings of actions that may lead to non-deterministic concurrency faults, possible failure of components and processes, but also due to possible resource restrictions and unpredictable latencies in network communication. The track on Verification and Validation of Distributed Systems aims to discuss key challenges that need to be addressed in order to enable the efficient and scalable assurance of distributed systems, as well as present methods and tools that bear the promise to achieve the latter.

## 1 Motivation and Track Overview

Distributed systems enjoy the benefits of resource sharing, autonomy, by controlling locally stored data, and availability. The connectivity of the Internet has led to a complete merging of the virtual and physical worlds, in cyber-physical systems (CPS) and the Internet-of-Things (IoT). Features such as *concurrency*, *fault tolerance*, and *safety* are fundamental to distributed applications, hence addressing the associated challenges that such features incur when designing and analyzing modern distributed systems is critical. Most prominent design and implementation challenges come from the need of managing both concurrency and being resilient to all sorts of failures, as well as of handling unpredictable communication delays, while ensuring the system's safety and reliability. Moreover, nowadays we expect distributed systems to be more responsive to the ever-changing needs of its users, more scalable in response to constant or unexpected usage, and more automation-centric to increase manageability.

To meet the above expectations, we have to adjust the *correctness assurance* formal techniques to cope with them. At ISoLA 2018, the track on *Verification and Validation of Distributed Systems* (VVDS) consists of five contributions that focus on proposing formal analysis techniques and solutions aimed at tackling

© Springer Nature Switzerland AG 2018
T. Margaria and B. Steffen (Eds.): ISoLA 2018, LNCS 11246, pp. 323–326, 2018.
https://doi.org/10.1007/978-3-030-03424-5_21

notoriously difficult problems such as verification of parameterized fault-tolerant distributed protocols, concurrent code, timed distributed transactions, as well as ensuring reliability of IoT devices, and safety of complex CPS via testing.

Promising results have been obtained by applying *model checking* [3], *bounded model checking* [5], Hoare-style reasoning [8], as well as model-based testing [9] and theorem proving [10] to verify concurrent programs, and distributed applications and algorithms. However, more research efforts are needed to increase the efficiency and scalability of formal assurance methods, as well as make them applicable to IoT and complex CPS. In the following, we briefly describe each of the VVDS track contributions, including a short account of their respective novelty and results.

## 2    Verification of Distributed Algorithms and Concurrent Programs

The first contribution *"ByMC: Byzantine Model Checker"*, by Igor Konnov and Josef Widder [4], presents a tool, ByMC, which applies Satisfiability Modulo Theories (SMT)-based bounded model-checking to verify parameterized fault-tolerant distributed algorithms (e.g. voting algorithms). The tool is parameterized in the number of processes out of which a fraction may fail or behave Byzantine, meaning that they do not obey the protocol. In this work, the authors present the parallel extension of their sequential version of the Byzantine Model Checker, which allows the parallel execution of SMT queries in a computer cluster. Such an extension improves the scalability of verification, enabling the formal verification of complex fault-tolerant distributed algorithms, under arbitrary failure semantics. The input model of ByMC is encoded in (parametric) Promela, which can be automatically transformed in a threshold-automata model for verifying threshold-based algorithms. The authors conduct an experimental evaluation in which they compare the sequential and parallel verification techniques on various benchmarks, using both automatically generated threshold-automata models, as well as hand-coded ones. The results show that manual abstractions created by experts are verified significantly faster than the automatically-built ones.

The second contribution *"Static code verification through process models"*, by Sebastiaan Joosten and Marieke Huisman [6], introduces a novel technique of verifying concurrent programs, which combines separation logic and model checking, by introducing a specification-only variable, called ghost variable, to describe the program state and enable an intuitive way of capturing state invariants and program properties. The ghost variables are in fact event structures that can only be updated by adding events, never by removing them from the structure. The parallel program is modeled in a process-algebra-like style, with processes constraining the event structures by describing their development via class invariants that can be verified by model checking. The proposed technique enables a more intuitive verification style of concurrent programs, and the authors show three possible ways of verifying program invariants, on a semaphore lock-unlock program: by using thread permissions, via rely-guarantee mechanisms, or by thread-specific event structures.

# 3   Testing Distributed Transactions, IoT and Cyber-Physical Systems

The third contribution *"Effective Test Suite Design for Detecting Concurrency Control Faults in Distributed Transaction Systems"*, by Simin Cai, Barbara Gallina, Dag Nyström, and Cristina Seceleanu [2], proposes a mutation-based testing methodology for generating test suites that can expose lock-based concurrency control (CC) faults in distributed transaction systems. The goal is to find a manageable set of test cases able to detect unwanted interleavings that violate isolation. The inputs to the test cases are generated delays at design level, which can be then used to configure the delays at the implementation level, and the outputs are verdicts on whether unwanted interleavings have occured or not, after logs inspection. The methodology assumes high-level specifications of work units, including lock operations and inter-operations delays, as well as of the concurrency control algorithm, which are transformed into a network of timed automata checkable with UPPAAL against queries that encode required isolation properties. The transaction specification is mutated by applying selected mutation operations that describe common CC faults (e.g., remove lock, change lock type, change lock position etc.). By carrying out reachability analysis on the resulting mutated network of stopwatch timed automata, test cases are generated as clock constraints solvable by state-of-the-art SMT solvers that return solutions that kill as many mutants as possible.

The fourth contribution *"Towards automated testing of the Internet of Things: Results obtained with the TESTAR tool"*, by Mirella Martínez, Anna Isabel Esparcia-Alcázar, Tanja Vos, Pekka Aho, and Joan Fons i Cors [7], presents an extension of the TESTAR tool, used previously for automated testing of graphical interface software, to support IoT testing. The authors show the first results of applying TESTAR for testing various IoT devices used by a smart-home application. The smart home can access a set of physical devices (resources) offered on an IoT platform. TESTAR uses an extensible plugin architecture that has been extended in this work with a plugin able to test the interaction with the resources of the smart home, by executing the HTTP methods used by the RESTful API that allows one to access such resources. The plugin implements three modes of execution specific to web service behavior, and their respective oracles as regular expressions. Running TESTAR on the smart home application has revealed 4 reproducible faults, out of which one has already been corrected.

The fifth contribution *"Quantitative Safety Analysis of a Coordinated Emergency Brake Protocol for Vehicle Platoons"*, by Carl Bergenhem, Karl Meinke, and Fabian Ström [1], introduces a new methodology for estimating safety-related quantitative parameters of cooperating CPS, which uses learning-based testing implemented in the tool LBtest. In this work, LBtest has been applied to estimate the minimum safe global time headway for a vehicle platoon, under a specific coordinated emergency braking protocol, assuming perfect communication first, and then stochastic packet loss. The methodology and LBtest use active automaton learning to generate queries about a black-box system under test (SUT), which are then executed on the SUT as test cases. By observing the SUT for each test case, an automaton behavioral model of the SUT is incrementally built in polynomial time, based on the saved observations. This model (even if incomplete) can then be model checked (in NuSMV) against a requirement specified in temporal logic (propositional linear temporal logic), and test cases can be extracted from the counterexamples returned by the model checker, with false negatives being filtered out.

# References

1. Bergenhem, C., Meinke, K., Ström, F.: Quantitative safety analysis of a coordinated emergency brake protocol for vehicle platoons. In: Margaria, T., Steffen, B. (eds.) ISoLA 2018. LNCS, vol. 11246, pp. 386–404 (2018)
2. Cai, S., Gallina, B., Nyström D., Seceleanu, C.: Effective test suite design for detecting concurrency control faults in distributed transaction systems. In: Margaria, T., Steffen, B. (eds.) ISoLA 2018. LNCS, vol. 11246, pp. 355–374 (2018)
3. Nielson, H.R., Filé, G. (eds.): SAS 2007. LNCS, vol. 4634. Springer, Heidelberg (2007). https://doi.org/10.1007/978-3-540-74061-2
4. Konnov, I., Widder, J.: ByMC: Byzantine model checker. In: Margaria, T., Steffen, B. (eds.) ISoLA 2018. LNCS, vol. 11246, pp. 327–342 (2018)
5. Konnov, I., Veith, H., Widder, J.: On the completeness of bounded model checking for threshold-based distributed algorithms: reachability. Inf. Comput. **252**, 95–109 (2017)
6. Joosten, S., Huisman, M.: Static code verification through process models. In: Margaria, T., Steffen, B. (eds.) ISoLA 2018. LNCS, vol. 11246, pp. 343–354. Springer, Cham (2018)
7. Martínez, M., Esparcia-Alcázar, A.I., Vos, T.E.J., Aho, P., Fons i Cors, J.: Towards automated testing of the Internet of Things: Results obtained with the TESTAR tool. In: Margaria, T., Steffen, B. (eds.) ISoLA 2018. LNCS, vol. 11246, pp. 375–385. Springer, Cham (2018)
8. Turon, A., Dreyer, D., Birkedal, L.: Unifying refinement and hoare-style reasoning in a logic for higher-order concurrency. In: Proceedings of the 18th ACM SIGPLAN International Conference on Functional Programming (ICFP 2013), pp. 377–390. ACM (2013)
9. Vain, J., Halling, E., Kanter, G., Anier, A., Pal, D.: Model-based testing of real-time distributed systems. In: Arnicans, G., Arnicane, V., Borzovs, J., Niedrite, L. (eds.) Communications in Computer and Information Science, vol. 615, pp. 272–286. Springer, Cham (2016). https://doi.org/10.1007/978-3-319-40180-5_19
10. Wilcox, J.R., et al.: Verdi: a framework for implementing and formally verifying distributed systems. SIGPLAN Not. **50**(6), 357–368 (2015)

# ByMC: Byzantine Model Checker

Igor Konnov[1]($\boxtimes$) and Josef Widder[2]

[1] University of Lorraine, CNRS, Inria, LORIA, 54000 Nancy, France
igor.konnov@inria.fr
[2] TU Wien (Vienna University of Technology), Vienna, Austria
widder@forsyte.at

**Abstract.** In recent work [10,12], we have introduced a technique for automatic verification of *threshold-guarded distributed algorithms* that have the following features: (1) up to $t$ of processes may crash or behave Byzantine; (2) the correct processes count messages and progress when they receive sufficiently many messages, e.g., at least $t+1$; (3) the number $n$ of processes in the system is a parameter, as well as $t$; (4) and the parameters are restricted by a resilience condition, e.g., $n > 3t$.

In this paper, we present Byzantine Model Checker that implements the above-mentioned technique. It takes two kinds of inputs, namely, (i) threshold automata (the framework of our verification techniques) or (ii) Parametric Promela (which is similar to the way in which the distributed algorithms were described in the literature).

We introduce a *parallel* extension of the tool, which exploits the parallelism enabled by our technique on an MPI cluster. We compare performance of the original technique and of the extensions by verifying 10 benchmarks that model fault-tolerant distributed algorithms from the literature. For each benchmark algorithm we check two encodings: a manual encoding in threshold automata vs. a Promela encoding.

## 1 Introduction

In recent work [10–12] we applied bounded model checking to verify reachability properties of threshold-based fault-tolerant distributed algorithms (FTDA), which are parameterized in the number of processes $n$ and the fraction of faults $t$. FTDAs typically work only under arithmetic resilience conditions such as $n > 3t$. Our methods allow us to do parameterized verification of sophisticated FTDAs [3,5,6,18,20,21] that have not been automatically verified before. Our bounded model checking technique produces a number of queries to a Satisfiability Modulo Theories solver (SMT). These queries correspond to different execution patterns.

J. Widder—Supported by: the Vienna Science and Technology Fund (WWTF) grant APALACHE (ICT15-103); and the Austrian Science Fund (FWF) through the National Research Network RiSE (S11403 and S11405), and project PRAVDA (P27722). The computational results presented have been achieved [in part] using the Vienna Scientific Cluster (VSC).

© Springer Nature Switzerland AG 2018
T. Margaria and B. Steffen (Eds.): ISoLA 2018, LNCS 11246, pp. 327–342, 2018.
https://doi.org/10.1007/978-3-030-03424-5_22

```
1   // n processes follow the code:
2   input u_i ∈ {0,1};
3   send u_i to all;
4   wait until some value v_i ∈ {0,1}
5       is received ⌈(n+1)/2⌉ times;
6   decide on v_j;
```

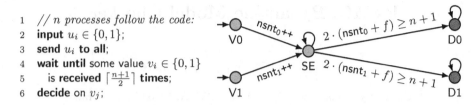

**Fig. 1.** Naïve Voting algorithm          **Fig. 2.** A threshold automaton for Naïve Voting

In [12], we conjectured that, by design, this technique allows many SMT queries to be checked in parallel. In this paper, we present a parallel extension of ByMC that executes SMT queries in a computer cluster.

The contributions of this paper are as follows:

1. We present the tool ByMC 2.4.1 that implements sequential and parallel verification [10,12]. The parallel verification is implemented with MPI (Message Passing Interface).
2. We introduce the details of the parallel extension of the technique and perform experimental evaluation, both for the sequential and parallel versions of the tool.
3. We report the experimental results both for the abstractions that are automatically constructed from Promela code (as in [10,12]) and for manual abstractions in terms of threshold automata, which we use as a direct input for the first time. Our experiments show that explicit modeling of fault-tolerant distributed algorithms with threshold automata leads to a dramatic speed up in most cases.

## 2    Distributed Algorithm Example: Naïve Voting

In order to describe what kind of distributed algorithms our tool ByMC is designed for, we start with a simple threshold-guarded algorithm. In this section, we take the point of view of an algorithm designer and apply the arguments that can be found in the distributed algorithms literature [1,16]. Consider a distributed system of $n$ processes, whose goal is to unanimously decide on a binary value $v \in \{0,1\}$. We would like to design a distributed algorithm that satisfies the following three properties[1]:

- *Agreement.* No two correct processes decide on different values (0 and 1).
- *Validity.* If a correct process decides on a value $v \in \{0,1\}$, then there is a process $i$, whose initial value $u_i$ equals $v$.
- *Termination.* All correct processes eventually decide.

Figure 1 shows a naïve attempt to solve this problem by majority voting. As usual in the distributed algorithms literature, we give a solution in pseudocode, which is supposed to work as follows. Each process starts with a binary

---

[1] Agreement, validity, and termination are typical properties of consensus [1,16].

value $u_i \in \{0,1\}$ and sends $u_i$ to all processes, including itself. When a process receives a value $v \in \{0,1\}$ from a majority of processes, it decides on $v$.

Does Naïve Voting satisfy agreement, validity, and termination? Unfortunately, the pseudo-code does not provide us with sufficient detail to answer the question: Assumptions about the process scheduler, message-delivery, possible faults, etc. are missing. For instance, if messages can be lost, a process may never receive sufficiently many messages to get over the guard in line 4. Thus we have to specify *systems assumptions*. Let us consider an asynchronous model [1,16] with crashes and Byzantine faults [19]:

- *Asynchronous computations.* Every correct process is scheduled infinitely often, and there are no assumptions on the relative processor speeds. The process steps are interleaved.
- *Reliable communication.* The processes communicate via message passing. Every message sent by a correct process is eventually delivered, although there are no timing or ordering assumptions about message delivery.
- *Faults.* A fraction $f$ of processes may fail. For instance, they can crash or behave Byzantine — the faulty processes do not follow the algorithm. There is an upper bound $t \geq f$ on the number of faults. We assume $n > 3t$ for the Byzantine faults, and $n > 2t$ for the crash faults.

*Manual proofs.* Below, we manually reason about the algorithm's correctness. Such proofs are common in the distributed algorithms literature, cf. [21,22,24].

**Validity.** We consider the Byzantine case here, which is more complicated. In order to decide on a value $v$ in line 6, a correct process has to receive $\lceil \frac{n+1}{2} \rceil$ messages carrying $v$. By the assumption on the number of faults ($n > 3t$ and $t \geq f$), we have $f < \lceil \frac{n+1}{2} \rceil$, and if a process decides on $v$ in 6, there is at least one correct process that has sent the value $v$ in line 3. Thus, the algorithm satisfies "Validity".

**Agreement.** Whether the algorithm satisfies "Agreement" depends on the considered fault model:

- *No faults or crash faults.* By line 4, a process has to receive the same value from $\lceil \frac{n+1}{2} \rceil$ distinct processes. Since $2 \cdot \lceil \frac{n+1}{2} \rceil > n$, and each process sends only one value (line 3), no two processes $i, j : 1 \leq i < j \leq n$ can reach line 6 with different values $v_i \neq v_j$. Thus, the processes cannot decide differently, and agreement is satisfied.
- *Byzantine faults.* When $f > 0$, the Byzantine processes can send value 0 to a process $i$ and value 1 to a process $j : j \neq i$. If the initial states of the correct processes are split into two equal sets, that is, $n - f = 2 \cdot |\{k \in \{1 \ldots n\}: k \text{ is correct and } u_k = 0\}|$, then the processes $i$ and $j$ reach line 6 with the values $v_i = 0$ and $v_j = 1$. As a result, agreement can be violated, and a verification tool must produce a counterexample.

**Termination.** Assume that there are no faults ($f = 0$) and the initial states are equally partitioned, that is, $n = 2 \cdot |\{k \in \{1 \ldots n\}: k \text{ is correct and } u_k = 0\}|$. No process can pass beyond line 4, as none of the initial value sets form a majority. Therefore, Naïve Voting violates liveness, namely, "Termination".

This subtle bug renders the algorithm useless! A tool should thus not only check invariants, but also find counterexamples to liveness specifications.

The manual proofs are tricky, as they combine several kinds of reasoning: temporal reasoning, local reasoning about process code, global reasoning about the number of messages, correct and faulty processes, etc. Our tool ByMC automatically proves temporal properties (or finds counterexamples) of distributed algorithms that (i) communicate by sending to all, and (ii) contain actions that are guarded by comparison of the number of received messages against a linear combination of parameter values (e.g., for a majority).

## 3   Inputs: Parametric Promela and Threshold Automata

The algorithm in Fig. 1 looks quite simple. However, as one can see from the assumptions on, e.g., faults and communication in Sect. 2, many details (that are often deemed "non-essential" by algorithm designers) are missing in the pseudo code. Our tool addresses this challenge by supporting two formal languages that are tailored for modeling of threshold-guarded distributed algorithms and the system assumptions: parametric Promela [8,9] and threshold automata [11]. Parametric Promela offers modeling that closely mimicks the behavior of the pseudo code statements, whereas threshold automata are an abstraction that allows for efficient model checking techniques [10,12]. When given code in parametric Promela, ByMC internally applies data abstraction to construct a threshold automaton, as explained in [13]. However, the automatically computed threshold automata are usually much larger than those constructed manually by a distributed algorithms expert. For this reason, the user can directly give a threshold automaton as the input to the tool.

### 3.1   Parametric Promela

Promela is the input language of the Spin model checker [7]. As it is designed to specify concurrent systems, several features are suitable for capturing distributed algorithms. However, Spin is a finite state model checker, and so Promela only allows us to specify finite state systems. We have thus extended Promela in order to have a parametric number of processes and faults, etc. In the following we will discuss some of our extensions.

Figure 3 shows a model of the Naïve Voting algorithm from Fig. 1. This example contains all the essential features of parametric PROMELA. In line 2, we declare parameters: the number of processes $n$, the number of Byzantine processes $f$, and the minimal size of a majority set, that is, $\lceil \frac{n+1}{2} \rceil$. In line 3, we declare two shared integer variables nsnt0 and nsnt1 that store the number of zeroes and ones sent by the *correct* processes. The expressions assume(...) in lines 4–5 restrict the choice of parameter values.

```
1   #define V0 0 // likewise, V1 is 1, SE is 2, D0 is 3, D1 is 4
2   symbolic int n /* nr. of correct */, f /* nr. of faulty */, majority; // majority size
3   int nsnt0, nsnt1; // counters for 0s and 1s sent by the correct processes
4   assume(n > 1 && n > 3 * f); // the resilience condition restricts faults
5   assume(n + 2 == 2 * majority || n + 1 == 2 * majority); // majority = ⌈n+1/2⌉
6   active[n − f] proctype Proc() { // run n − f correct processes
7     // control state: initialized with 0 (V0), initialized with 1 (V1),
8     // sent the value (SE), decided on 0 (D0), decided on 1 (D1)
9     byte pc = V0, next_pc = V0;
10    // counters for received 0s and 1s
11    int nrcvd0 = 0, nrcvd1 = 0, next_nrcvd0 = 0, next_nrcvd1 = 0;
12    if :: pc = V0; // non−deterministically initialize with 0 or 1
13      :: pc = V1; fi;
14    do :: atomic { // a single indivisible step
15    havoc(next_nrcvd0); havoc(next_nrcvd1); // forget variable values
16      // update message counters (up to f messages from the Byzantine processes)
17    assume(nrcvd0 <= next_nrcvd0 && next_nrcvd0 <= nsnt0 + f);
18    assume(nrcvd1 <= next_nrcvd1 && next_nrcvd1 <= nsnt1 + f);
19      // compute the new state and send messages, if needed
20    if :: pc == V0 −> next_pc = SE; nsnt0++; // send 0
21      :: pc == V1 −> next_pc = SE; nsnt1++; // send 1
22      :: pc == SE && next_nrcvd0 >= majority −> next_pc = D0; // decide on 0
23      :: pc == SE && next_nrcvd1 >= majority −> next_pc = D1; // decide on 1
24      :: pc == SE && next_nrcvd0 < majority && next_nrcvd1 < majority
25        −> next_pc = SE; // wait for more messages
26      :: pc == D0 || pc == D1 −> next_pc = pc; // self−loop
27    fi;
28      // update local variables
29    pc = next_pc; nrcvd0 = next_nrcvd0; nrcvd1 = next_nrcvd1;
30    next_pc = 0; next_nrcvd0 = 0; next_nrcvd1 = 0;
31    } od; // next step
32  }
33  // atomic propositions
34  atomic ex_D0 = some(Proc:pc == D0); atomic ex_D1 = some(Proc:pc == D1);
35  atomic all_decide = all(Proc:pc == D0 || Proc:pc == D1);
36  atomic ex_V0 = some(Proc:pc == V0); atomic ex_V1 = some(Proc:pc == V1);
37  atomic in_transit0 = some(Proc:nrcvd0 < nsnt0);
38  atomic in_transit1 = some(Proc:nrcvd1 < nsnt1);
39  // LTL formulae
40  ltl agreement { [](!ex_D0 || !ex_D1) }
41  ltl termination { (<>[](!in_transit0 && !in_transit1)) −> <>all_decide }
42  ltl validity0 { <>(ex_D0) −> ex_V0 }
43  ltl validity1 { <>(ex_D1) −> ex_V1 }
```

**Fig. 3.** Modeling Naïve Voting in Parametric Promela

The behavior of the $n - f$ correct processes is modeled in lines 6–32. To describe a process state, we introduce the following local variables:

- pc to store the algorithm's control state, that is, whether a process is initialized with values 0 and 1 (i.e., pc=V0 and pc=V1 resp.), sent a message (pc=SE), decided on values 0 and 1 (i.e., pc=D0 and pc=D1 resp.)

- nrcvd0 and nrcvd1 to store the number of zeroes and ones received from the correct *and* Byzantine processes; and
- next-state variables next_pc, next_nrcvd0, and next_nrcvd1 that are used to perform a process step.

An initial process state is chosen non-deterministically in lines 12–13.

A single process step is encoded as an atomic block in lines 14–31, which corresponds to an indivisible receive-compute-send step. In lines 15–18, a process possibly receives new messages: by invoking havoc($x$), we forget the contents of a variable $x$, and by writing assume($e$), we restrict the variable values to those that satisfy a logical expression $e$. Note that the statements havoc and assume do not belong to the standard PROMELA; they belong to parametric PROMELA and are inspired by the similar statements in Boogie [2]. Lines 20–27 encode the computations that can be found in pseudo-code in Fig. 1. Like in PROMELA, a process non-deterministically picks an option of the form ":: guard -> actions", if guard evaluates to true, and executes actions.

To specify temporal properties, we first define atomic propositions in lines 34–38. The keywords some and all correspond to existential and universal quantification over the processes; they belong to parametric PROMELA. In lines 40–43, define LTL formulas that capture the properties of consensus (cf. Sect. 2).

Promela code in Fig. 3 models the informal pseudo code of Naïve Voting. Note that the manual translation from pseudo code is straightforward, except for one thing: It may seem more honest to maintain sets of sent and received messages, instead of storing only integer message counters such as nrcvd0 and nsnt0. It has been proven that modeling with sets is equivalent (bisimilar) to modeling with message counters [14]. Obviously, modeling with message counters produces smaller transition systems (cf. [9]).

## 3.2  Threshold Automata

Our code in parametric PROMELA has several features: (i) each atomic step is encoded as an imperative sequence of statements, (ii) and the processes explicitly store the number of received messages in local variables such as nrcvd0 and nrcvd1. One can argue that this level of detail is not necessary, and it makes the verification problem harder. Threshold automata are a more abstract model for threshold-guarded fault-tolerant distributed algorithms [11], as they enable guarded transitions as soon as sufficiently many messages have been sent. Intuitively, the reception variables nrcvd0 and nrcvd1 are bypassed by such modeling. In this section, we introduce threshold automata in a way that explains how automata capture local transitions of individual processes. The semantics of threshold automata are then defined via counter systems in Sect. 4 that model runs of collections of processes, that is, distributed computations.

We model Naïve Voting with the threshold automaton shown in Fig. 2. Its code in the .ta input format of BYMC is shown in Fig. 4. We are running $n - f$ instances of the threshold automaton; each instance is modelling a correct process. The automata operate on shared variables such as $nsnt_0$ and $nsnt_1$, which

```
 1  thresholdAutomaton Proc {
 2    local pc; /* control locations:
 3                in V0 and V1, initialized with 0 and 1 resp.,
 4                in D0 and D1, decided on 0 and 1 resp., in SE, sent the initial value */
 5    shared nsnt0, nsnt1; /* the number of 0s and 1s sent by the correct processes */
 6    parameters N, T, F; /* parameter variables */
 7    assumptions (0) { N > 3 * T; T >= F; T >= 1; } /* resilience condition */
 8    locations (0) { locV0: [0]; locV1: [1]; locSE: [2]; locD0: [3]; locD1: [4];}// local states
 9    inits (0) { /* initial constraints */
10      (locV0 + locV1) == N - F; locSE == 0; locD0 == 0; locD1 == 0;
11      nsnt0 == 0; nsnt1 == 0;
12    }
13    rules (0) { /* a set of rules */
14      /* send message 0 (resp. 1) when initialized with value 1 (resp. 1) */
15      0: locV0 -> locSE when (true) do { nsnt0' == nsnt0 + 1; nsnt1' == nsnt1; };
16      1: locV1 -> locSE when (true) do { nsnt0' == nsnt0; nsnt1' == nsnt1 + 1; };
17      2: locSE -> locD0 /* decide on value 0 */
18           when (2 * (nsnt0 + F) >= N + 1) do { unchanged(nsnt0, nsnt1); };
19      3: locSE -> locD1 /* decide on value 1 */
20           when (2 * (nsnt1 + F) >= N + 1) do { unchanged(nsnt0, nsnt1); };
21      /* self loops */
22      4: locSE -> locSE when (true) do { unchanged(nsnt0, nsnt1); };
23      5: locD0 -> locD0 when (true) do { unchanged(nsnt0, nsnt1); };
24      6: locD1 -> locD1 when (true) do { unchanged(nsnt0, nsnt1); };
25    }
26    specifications (0) { /* LTL formulas */
27      agreement: [](locD0 == 0 || locD1 == 0);
28      validity0: <>(locD0 != 0) -> locV0 != 0;
29      validity1: <>(locD1 != 0) -> locV1 != 0;
30      termination:
31        <>[](locV0 == 0 && locV1 == 0 && (2 * nsnt0 < N + 1 || locSE == 0)
32                                    && (2 * nsnt1 < N + 1 || locSE == 0))
33        -> <>(locD0 != 0 || locD1 != 0);
34    }
35  } /* Proc */
```

**Fig. 4.** A threshold automaton for Naïve Voting in the `.ta` format

can be only incremented. A threshold automaton resides in a *local state* from a finite set $\mathcal{L}$, e.g., in our example, $\mathcal{L} = \{V0, V1, SE, D0, D1\}$. A *rule* (corresponding to an edge in Fig. 2) can move an automaton from one local state to another, provided that the shared variables in the current global state satisfy the rule's threshold guard, e.g., $2 \cdot (\text{nsnt}_0 + f) \geq n + 1$. If a rule is labeled with an increment of a shared variable, e.g., $\text{nsnt}_0$++, then the shared variable is updated accordingly.

# 4    Theoretical Background

## 4.1    System

We assume fixed three finite sets: the set $\mathcal{L}$ contains the *local states*, the set $\Gamma$ contains the *shared variables* that range over non-negative integers, and the set $\Pi$ contains the *parameters* that range over non-negative integers.

*Configurations $\Sigma$ and $I$.* A configuration is a vector $\sigma = (\boldsymbol{\kappa}, \mathbf{g}, \mathbf{p})$, where $\sigma.\boldsymbol{\kappa}$ is a vector of *counter values*, $\sigma.\mathbf{g}$ is a vector of *shared variable values*, and $\sigma.\mathbf{p} = \mathbf{p}$ is a vector of *parameter values*. In $\sigma.\boldsymbol{\kappa}$ we store for each local state $\ell$, how many processes are in this state. All values are non-negative integers. In every initial configuration global variables have value zero, and all "modelled" processes are in initial locations. If specifications do not limit the behavior of faulty processes (which is typically the case with Byzantine faults), we only model the correct processes explicitly, while the impact of faulty processes is modelled as non-determinism in the environment.

*Threshold Guards* are defined according to the following grammar:

$$Guard:: = Int \cdot Shared \geq LinForm \mid Int \cdot Shared < LinForm$$
$$LinForm:: = Int \mid Int \cdot Param \mid Int \cdot Param + LinForm$$
$$Shared:: = \langle \text{a variable from } \Gamma \rangle$$
$$Param:: = \langle \text{a variable from } \Pi \rangle$$
$$Int:: = \langle \text{an integer} \rangle$$

*Transition relation $R$.* A *transition* is a pair $t = (rule, factor)$ of a rule of the TA and a non-negative integer called the *acceleration factor*, or just factor for short. If the factor is always 1, this corresponds that at each step exactly one processes takes a step, that is, interleaving semantics. Having factors greater than 1 permits a specific form of acceleration where an arbitrary number of processes that are ready to execute a rule can do that at the same time.

Transition $t$ is *applicable (or enabled)* in configuration $\sigma$, if the guard of $t.rule$ evaluates to true, and $\sigma.\boldsymbol{\kappa}[t.from] \geq t.factor$. Configuration $\sigma'$ is the result of applying the enabled transition $t$ to $\sigma$, and write $\sigma' = t(\sigma)$, if

- $\sigma'.\mathbf{g} = \sigma.\mathbf{g} + t.factor \cdot t.\mathbf{u}$ and $\sigma'.\mathbf{p} = \sigma.\mathbf{p}$
- if $t.from \neq t.to$ then
    - $\sigma'.\boldsymbol{\kappa}[t.from] = \sigma.\boldsymbol{\kappa}[t.from] - t.factor$,
    - $\sigma'.\boldsymbol{\kappa}[t.to] = \sigma.\boldsymbol{\kappa}[t.to] + t.factor$, and
    - $\forall \ell \in \mathcal{L} \setminus \{t.from, t.to\}$ it holds that $\sigma'.\boldsymbol{\kappa}[\ell] = \sigma.\boldsymbol{\kappa}[\ell]$
- if $t.from = t.to$ then $\sigma'.\boldsymbol{\kappa} = \sigma.\boldsymbol{\kappa}$

Finally, the transition relation $R \subseteq \Sigma \times \Sigma$ of the counter system is defined as follows: $(\sigma, \sigma') \in R$ iff there is a rule $r \in \mathcal{R}$ and a factor $k \in \mathbb{N}_0$ such that $\sigma' = t(\sigma)$ for $t = (r, k)$.

Observe that configurations, transitions, guard, etc. can be encoded in linear integer arithmetic.

**Table 1.** The syntax of $\mathsf{ELTL_{FT}}$-formulas [10]: *pform* defines propositional formulas, and $\psi$ defines temporal formulas. We assume that $Locs \subseteq \mathcal{L}$ and $guard \in \Phi^{\mathrm{rise}} \cup \Phi^{\mathrm{fall}}$.

$$\psi ::= pform \mid \mathbf{G}\,\psi \mid \mathbf{F}\,\psi \mid \psi \wedge \psi$$

$$pform ::= cform \mid gform \vee cform$$

$$cform ::= \bigvee_{\ell \in Locs} \kappa[\ell] \neq 0 \mid \bigwedge_{\ell \in Locs} \kappa[\ell] = 0 \mid cform \wedge cform$$

$$gform ::= guard \mid \neg gform \mid gform \wedge gform$$

## 4.2 Safety and Liveness Specifications

Using counter systems, we can also easily express the temporal properties, e.g., those of Naïve Voting. To this end, for every local state $\ell \in \mathcal{L}$, we introduce a proposition "$\kappa_\ell = 0$", which tests that there are no processes in $\ell$. Since threshold automata do not explicitly track received messages, the assumption of reliable communication is modeled as a fairness assumption over local states and actions. The following formula captures the required fairness, that is, (i) eventually all processes leave their initial state V0 or V1, and (ii) if threshold guards become true, then eventually all processes fire the corresponding rules and thus evacuate the local state SE (the latter implication is written as disjunction):

$$\mathbf{F}\,\mathbf{G}\,\big(\kappa_{\mathsf{V0}} = 0 \wedge \kappa_{\mathsf{V1}} = 0$$
$$\wedge (2 \cdot \mathsf{nsnt}_0 < n+1 \vee \kappa_{\mathsf{SE}} = 0) \wedge (2 \cdot \mathsf{nsnt}_1 < n+1 \vee \kappa_{\mathsf{SE}} = 0)\big) \qquad (\mathrm{RC})$$

Agreement (A), Validity (V), and Termination (T) can be written as follows:

$$\mathbf{G}\,(\kappa_{\mathsf{D0}} = 0 \vee \kappa_{\mathsf{D1}} = 0) \qquad (\mathrm{A})$$

$$\mathbf{F}\,(\kappa_{\mathsf{D0}} \neq 0) \rightarrow \kappa_{\mathsf{V0}} \neq 0 \wedge \mathbf{F}\,(\kappa_{\mathsf{D1}} \neq 0) \rightarrow \kappa_{\mathsf{V1}} \neq 0 \qquad (\mathrm{V})$$

$$RC \rightarrow \mathbf{F}\,(\kappa_{\mathsf{V0}} = 0 \wedge \kappa_{\mathsf{V1}} = 0 \wedge \kappa_{\mathsf{SE}} = 0) \qquad (\mathrm{T})$$

In [12], we have introduced a bounded model checking technique with SMT that checks reachability in counter systems of threshold automata for all combinations of the parameters. We proved that if a configuration is reachable, then there is a short schedule that reaches this configuration. As a result, bounded model checking is a complete method for reachability checking in our case. In [10], this technique was extended to $\mathsf{ELTL_{FT}}$ — a fragment of $\mathsf{ELTL}(\mathsf{F}, \mathsf{G})$, which allows us to verify safety and liveness of counter systems of threshold automata. The syntax of $\mathsf{ELTL_{FT}}$ is given in Table 1. We use this logic to express *counterexamples*, that is, negations of the safety and liveness specifications from above.

For instance, the negation of agreement and termination in Equations (A) and (T) fit into $\mathsf{ELTL_{FT}}$, and can be written as follows:

$$\mathbf{F}\,(\kappa_{\mathsf{D0}} \neq 0 \wedge \kappa_{\mathsf{D1}} \neq 0) \qquad (\mathrm{NA})$$

$$RC \wedge \mathbf{G} \left( \kappa_{\mathsf{V0}} \neq 0 \vee \kappa_{\mathsf{V1}} \neq 0 \vee \kappa_{\mathsf{SE}} \neq 0 \right) \tag{NT}$$

Technically, the negation of the formula for validity given in Equation (V) does not belong to the fragment $\mathsf{ELTL_{FT}}$. However, it can be easily rewritten as two formulas, for the values of $i$ equal to 0 and 1:

$$\mathbf{F} \left( \kappa_{\mathsf{D}_i} \neq 0 \right) \wedge \kappa_{\mathsf{V}_i} = 0 \tag{NV$_i$}$$

## 5    Parameterized Model Checking by Schema Enumeration

Our verification technique consists of the following steps: From the $\mathsf{ELTL_{FT}}$ specifications, our tool enumerates all shapes counterexamples can have. Each of these shapes is encoded as an SMT query, and using SMT solvers, our tool checks for each shape, whether there exists a run of the system that has this shape. Such a run would then be a witness to the violation of a specification.

Consider the agreement property (A) of Naïve Voting. A counterexample is a run of the system that starts in an initial state and satisfies its negation:

$$\mathbf{F} \left( \kappa_{\mathsf{D0}} \neq 0 \wedge \kappa_{\mathsf{D1}} \neq 0 \right)$$

Each counterexample thus (i) satisfies the constraints for initial states, and (ii) is a sequence of applicable transitions, that (iii) end up in a state where $(\kappa_{\mathsf{D0}} \neq 0 \wedge \kappa_{\mathsf{D1}} \neq 0)$ holds. Indeed checking (A) boils down to checking reachability of a state that satisfies $(\kappa_{\mathsf{D0}} \neq 0 \wedge \kappa_{\mathsf{D1}} \neq 0)$. Our technique from [12] enumerates all shapes of such counterexamples.

The central notion is a *simple schema*:

$$\{pre\} r_1^*, \dots, r_k^* \{post\}$$

where $pre, post \subseteq$ are constraints that encode evaluation of guards, and constraints on the counters (e.g., $\kappa_{\mathsf{D0}} \neq 0$). Thus, the schema captures that $pre$ holds, then some transitions with rules $r_1^*, \dots, r_k^*$ are executed to reach a state where $post$ holds. We denote a simple schema by $S$. A schema is then a concatenation of simple schemas $S_1, S_2, \dots S_k$, for some $k$.

For our example, the technique from [12] would generate among others, a schema like the following

$S_1, S_2, S_3 =$

$$\{\kappa_{\mathsf{V0}} + \kappa_{\mathsf{V1}} = n\} r_1^*, \dots, r_4^*$$
$$\{2 \cdot (\mathsf{nsnt}_0 + f) \geq n + 1\} r_1^*, \dots, r_4^*$$
$$\{(2 \cdot (\mathsf{nsnt}_0 + f) \geq n + 1), (2 \cdot (\mathsf{nsnt}_1 + f) \geq n + 1)\} r_1^*, \dots, r_4^*$$
$$\{(2 \cdot (\mathsf{nsnt}_0 + f) \geq n + 1), (2 \cdot (\mathsf{nsnt}_1 + f) \geq n + 1), (\kappa_{\mathsf{D0}} \neq 0 \wedge \kappa_{\mathsf{D1}} \neq 0)\}$$

that is, initially, all of the $n$ processes are in the initial locations V0 and V1, then after application of some rules one of the threshold guards becomes true, then after another application of some rules both guards are true and finally a bad state is reached. The SMT solver now has to find whether an executions exists that has that form. This is done by replacing each Kleene star by a distinct variable that encodes how often a rule $r$ is applied.

A different schema can be obtained by changing the order in which the two threshold guards become true. In general each possible order generates a different schema. The number of different schemas to be checked is factorial in the number of guards [12]. As our benchmarks have only a small number of guards, the number of calls to the SMT solver is still practical.

## 5.1   Checking a Single Lasso Schema with SMT

In [10] we prove that for our counter systems, a counterexample to a liveness specification has lasso shape, that is:

$$S_1 \ldots S_k (S_{k+1} \ldots S_{k+m})^\omega$$

In this way we obtain a finite representation of an infinite execution, which again can be checked with an SMT solver.

Thus, our tool generates multiple schemas: for each safety or liveness specification, a different schema is obtained by changing the order in which the threshold guards become true. A detailed algorithm for constructing schemas is presented in [10, Fig. 10]. In a nutshell, the algorithm constructs a graph that represents the partial order on when propositions and threshold guards evaluate to true in an execution, e.g., the one in Fig. 5. Each linear extension of this partial order then defines a sequence on which propositions and guards become true. Two neighboring elements in the sequence are the *pre* and *post* of a simple schema; the concatenation of all these simple schemas is the schema our tool checks for satisfiability.

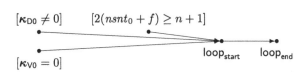

**Fig. 5.** The graph constructed from the automata guards and formula ($NV_0$)

Our tool encodes each schema in SMT and then calls a back-end solver in order to check whether the schema generates a counterexample. In [10], we explained the SMT encoding. As the schemas are independent, these checks can be done in parallel. We have implemented and exploited this feature in [15]. As [15] was concerned with synthesis, we did not discuss the effects of parallelization there. In the following we discuss and compare the sequential and the parallel approaches.

*Sequential Schema Enumeration.* In the sequential mode, the schemas are simply checked one-by-one until either a counterexample is found, or all schemas have been enumerated and no counterexample has been found. (Detailed pseudo-code of the function check_one_order can be found in Fig. 10 of [10].)

```
1    for each linear order ⪯ of graph 𝒢 {
2        if check_one_order(TA, φ, 𝒢, ⪯) = witness(SMT_model)
3            report SMT_model as a counterexample
4    }
5    report specification holds
```

*Parallel Schema Enumeration.* In the MPI mode, the tool runs as a system of $N$ processes, one per CPU; the physical arrangement of the CPUs depends on the cluster configuration. Every process is assigned a unique value *rank* from 0 to $N - 1$: The process with *rank* = 0 is the master, whereas the other processes are the workers. Every process is enumerating the schemas as in the sequential mode but checks a schema only if the schema's sequence number $i$ matches the rule: $(i \mod N) = rank$. In order to terminate quickly when one process has found a bug, the workers asynchronously communicate with the master. After leaving the loop, the workers communicate with the master to deliver a counterexample, if one was found. For presentation, we assume that the master can send to and receive messages from itself.

```
1    i := 0; found := false
2    for each linear order ⪯ of graph 𝒢 {
3        if rank = i and check_one_order(TA, φ, 𝒢, ⪯) = witness(SMT_model)
4            found := true
5            send BUG to master // notify the master
6        if received BUG from any
7            if rank = master { send BUG to all } // notify the workers
8            break
9        i := i + 1
10   }
11   results = gather found master // the workers send their 'found' flags to the master
12   if rank = master {
13       if ∃w : results[w] = true
14           send WITNESS<w> to all // pick one counterexample and declare it a witness
15           if w = master report SMT_model as a counterexample
16           else { receive CEX<model> from w; report model as a counterexample }
17       else { send WITNESS<⊥> to all; report specification holds }
18   } else {
19       receive WITNESS<w> from master
20       if w = rank { send CEX<SMT_model> to master } // I am the witness
21   } // finish and clean up stale MPI messages on exit
```

# 6  Benchmarks and Experiments

Byzantine model checker is written in OCaml. Its source code and the virtual machines are available from the tool web page [2]. For the experiments conducted in this paper, we used Z3 4.6.0 [4] as a back-end SMT solver, which was linked to ByMC via Z3 OCaml bindings.

**Table 2.** The experiments with the sequential (SEQ) and parallel (MPI) techniques on two kinds of inputs: Promela (white rows) and threshold automata (gray rows). The sequential experiments were run with GNU parallel [23] at AMD Opteron® 6272, 32 cores, 192 GB. The MPI benchmarks were run at Vienna Scientific Cluster 3 using 16 nodes × 16 cores (256 processes). The symbol "☉" indicates timeout of 24 h.

| # Input | Case | Threshold Automaton | | | | Schemas | | Time, seconds | | | Mem, GB | |
|---|---|---|---|---|---|---|---|---|---|---|---|---|
| | | | | | | | length | SEQ | MPI | | SEQ | MPI |
| FTDA | (if more than one) | $\|\mathcal{L}\|$ | $\|\mathcal{R}\|$ | $\|\Phi^{\mathrm{rise}}\|$ | $\|\Phi^{\mathrm{fall}}\|$ | number | avg | | avg | max | | avg |
| 1 frb | - | 7 | 14 | 1 | 0 | 5 | 34 | 1 | - | - | 0.1 | - |
| 2 frb | hand-coded TA | 4 | 9 | 1 | 1 | 70 | 38 | 1 | - | - | 0.1 | - |
| 3 strb | - | 7 | 21 | 3 | 0 | 18 | 72 | 1 | - | - | 0.1 | - |
| 4 strb | hand-coded TA | 4 | 8 | 2 | 0 | 38 | 22 | 1 | - | - | 0.1 | - |
| 5 nbacg | - | 24 | 64 | 4 | 0 | 90 | 243 | 6 | - | - | 0.1 | - |
| 6 nbacg | hand-coded TA | 8 | 16 | 0 | 1 | 5 | 54 | 1 | - | - | 0.1 | - |
| 7 nbacr | - | 77 | 1031 | 6 | 0 | 517 | 2489 | 523 | - | - | 0.7 | - |
| 8 nbacr | hand-coded TA | 7 | 16 | 0 | 1 | 18 | 63 | 1 | - | - | 0.1 | - |
| 9 aba | $\frac{n+t}{2} = 2t+1$ | 37 | 202 | 6 | 0 | 1172 | 850 | 659 | 12 | 13 | 1.0 | 0.2 |
| 10 aba | $\frac{n+t}{2} > 2t+1$ | 61 | 425 | 8 | 0 | 5204 | 2112 | 53992 | 1440 | 1442 | 7.2 | 0.6 |
| 11 aba | hand-coded TA | 5 | 10 | 2 | 2 | 542 | 57 | 14 | - | - | 0.1 | - |
| 12 cbc | $\lfloor \frac{n}{2} \rfloor < n-t \wedge f = 0$ | 164 | 2064 | 0 | 0 | 2 | 8168 | 1603 | 290 | 290 | 9.3 | 0.2 |
| 13 cbc | $\lfloor \frac{n}{2} \rfloor = n-t \wedge f = 0$ | 73 | 470 | 0 | 0 | 2 | 1790 | 27 | 9 | 9 | 0.6 | 0.1 |
| 14 cbc | $\lfloor \frac{n}{2} \rfloor < n-t \wedge f > 0$ | 165 | 2072 | 0 | 1 | 4 | 10213 | 10024 | 4943 | 4943 | 18.8 | 0.5 |
| 15 cbc | $\lfloor \frac{n}{2} \rfloor = n-t \wedge f > 0$ | 74 | 476 | 0 | 1 | 4 | 2258 | 273 | 47 | 47 | 1.5 | 0.1 |
| 16 cbc | hand-coded TA | 7 | 14 | 0 | 1 | 5 | 56 | 1 | - | - | 0.1 | - |
| 17 cfls | $f = 0$ | 41 | 280 | 4 | 0 | 90 | 770 | 45 | 5 | 8 | 0.2 | 0.1 |
| 18 cfls | $f = 1$ | 41 | 280 | 4 | 1 | 523 | 787 | 257 | 6 | 6 | 0.4 | 0.1 |
| 19 cfls | $f > 1$ | 68 | 696 | 6 | 1 | 3429 | 2132 | 10346 | 29 | 29 | 3.8 | 0.2 |
| 20 cfls | hand-coded TA | 9 | 26 | 3 | 3 | 13700 | 122 | 687 | 6 | 8 | 2.1 | 0.1 |
| 21 clcs | $f = 0$ | 101 | 1285 | 8 | 0 | 251 | 460 | 331 | 38 | 38 | 0.8 | 0.1 |
| 22 clcs | $f = 1$ | 70 | 650 | 6 | 1 | 448 | 303 | 239 | 11 | 11 | 0.4 | 0.1 |
| 23 clcs | $f > 1$ | 101 | 1333 | 8 | 1 | 2100 | 404 | 1865 | 89 | 89 | 1.3 | 0.4 |
| 24 clcs | hand-coded TA | 9 | 30 | 7 | 3 | $3.2 \cdot 10^6$ | $\approx 400$ | ☉ | 979 | 981 | 17.3 | 1.6 |
| 25 bosco | $\lfloor \frac{n+3t}{2} \rfloor + 1 = n-t$ | 28 | 152 | 6 | 0 | 20 | 423 | 4 | 3 | 4 | 0.1 | 0.1 |
| 26 bosco | $\lfloor \frac{n+3t}{2} \rfloor + 1 > n-t$ | 40 | 242 | 8 | 0 | 70 | 1038 | 29 | 6 | 6 | 0.2 | 0.1 |
| 27 bosco | $\lfloor \frac{n+3t}{2} \rfloor + 1 < n-t$ | 32 | 188 | 6 | 0 | 20 | 476 | 4 | 4 | 4 | 0.1 | 0.1 |
| 28 bosco | $n > 5t \wedge f = 0$ | 82 | 1372 | 12 | 0 | 3431 | 27 | 265 | 35 | 35 | 0.3 | 0.4 |
| 29 bosco | $n > 7t$ | 90 | 1744 | 12 | 0 | 3431 | 179 | 1325 | 52 | 52 | 1.0 | 0.6 |
| 30 bosco | hand-coded TA | 8 | 20 | 3 | 4 | 3429 | 43 | 82 | 4 | 4 | 0.2 | 0.1 |

---

[2] http://forsyte.at/software/bymc.

In earlier work [9], we encoded our benchmarks in Parametric Promela, using a shared variable to record the number of processes that have sent a message, and using for each process a local variable that records how many messages a process received. For this modeling we presented a data abstraction and counter abstraction in [8]. To compare later verification techniques with these initial results, we kept that encoding, although the newer techniques rest on a more abstract model of threshold automata, which have finitely many local states.

The threshold automata constructed by data abstraction are significantly larger than threshold automata constructed by a human expert. To see the influence of these modeling decisions on the verification results, we manually encoded our benchmarks as threshold automata. These benchmarks are available from our benchmark repository [3]. Table 2 compares the size of the threshold automata that are: (1) produced automatically by abstraction and (2) hand-coded. The essential features of the automata are: the number of local states $|\mathcal{L}|$, the number of rules $|\mathcal{R}|$, and the numbers of the guards $|\varPhi^{\mathrm{rise}}|$ and $|\varPhi^{\mathrm{fall}}|$, that is, the guards of the form $x \geq \ldots$ and $x < \ldots$ respectively. Moreover, due to data abstraction, we had to consider several cases that differ in the order between the thresholds. They are mentioned in the column "Case".

Table 2 shows the verification results for benchmarks in Promela as well as threshold automata. We ran the sequential schema enumeration (SEQ, [10]) and the parallel schema checking technique (MPI) that is presented in this paper. The parallel experiments were run at Vienna Scientific Cluster using 256 CPU cores. For each benchmark, we picked the most challenging specifications — many of them are liveness properties — and show experimental results for them. (Needless to say, we did not run the MPI technique on the benchmarks that could be enumerated with the sequential technique in seconds.) Two columns show the essential features of the enumerated schemas: "number" displays the total number of explored schemas, and "length avg" displays the average length of schemas. For both techniques, we report the computation times and maximal memory usage during a run. For the MPI experiments, we report the average time per CPU core (column "MPI avg") as well as the maximum time per CPU core (column "MPI max"). The deviation from the average case is negligible.

As expected, the hand-coded benchmarks are usually verified much faster. Interestingly, the manually constructed threshold automaton for one-step consensus (c1cs [3]) has more threshold guards than the abstract one: We had to more accurately encode algorithm's decisions, crash faults, and fairness. The sequential technique times out on this benchmark. The parallel technique takes about seven times longer than with the automatic abstraction.

The parallel technique benefits from running on multiple cores, though the actual gains from parallelism depend on the benchmark. As in our experiments the verification times of a single schema negligibly deviate from the average case, the uniform distribution of schemas among the nodes seems sufficient. However, one can construct threshold automata that produce schemas whose verification

---

[3]  https://github.com/konnov/fault-tolerant-benchmarks/tree/master/isola18.

times significantly vary from each other. We conjecture that an implementation with a dynamic balancer would make better use of cluster resources.

# 7 Conclusions

We presented our tool ByMC, and compared its sequential verification implementation to its parallel one. Moreover, by experimental evaluation we showed that manual abstractions give us threshold automata that can be verified significantly faster than those that result from automatic abstraction.

We observe that the sizes of the manually constructed threshold automata are not significantly larger than the (manually crafted) models of round-based distributed consensus presented in [17]. In their theory, threshold-guarded expressions also play a central role. Our gains in efficiency in this paper—due to manual encodings—show that the discrepancy was a result of automatic abstraction and not of the technique that uses threshold automata as its input.

We needed from one to three hours per benchmark to specify and debug a threshold automaton, while it usually took us less than 30 min to specify the same benchmark in Parametric Promela. The most difficult part of the encoding with threshold automata was to faithfully express fairness constraints over shared variables and process counters. In case of Parametric Promela, fairness constraints were much easier to write, as one could refer to the shared and local variables, which count the number of sent and received messages respectively.

**Acknowledgments.** We are grateful to our past and present collaborators Annu Gmeiner, Marijana Lazić, Ulrich Schmid, and Helmut Veith, who contributed to many of the described ideas that are now implemented in ByMC.

# References

1. Attiya, H., Welch, J.: Distributed Computing, 2nd edn. Wiley, Chichester (2004)
2. Barnett, M., Chang, B.-Y.E., DeLine, R., Jacobs, B., Leino, K.R.M.: Boogie: a modular reusable verifier for object-oriented programs. In: de Boer, F.S., Bonsangue, M.M., Graf, S., de Roever, W.-P. (eds.) FMCO 2005. LNCS, vol. 4111, pp. 364–387. Springer, Heidelberg (2006). https://doi.org/10.1007/11804192_17
3. Brasileiro, F., Greve, F., Mostefaoui, A., Raynal, M.: Consensus in one communication step. In: Malyshkin, V. (ed.) PaCT 2001. LNCS, vol. 2127, pp. 42–50. Springer, Heidelberg (2001). https://doi.org/10.1007/3-540-44743-1_4
4. de Moura, L., Bjørner, N.: Z3: an efficient SMT solver. In: Ramakrishnan, C.R., Rehof, J. (eds.) TACAS 2008. LNCS, vol. 4963, pp. 337–340. Springer, Heidelberg (2008). https://doi.org/10.1007/978-3-540-78800-3_24
5. Dobre, D., Suri, N.: One-step consensus with zero-degradation. In: DSN, pp. 137–146 (2006)
6. Guerraoui, R.: Non-blocking atomic commit in asynchronous distributed systems with failure detectors. Distrib. Comput. **15**(1), 17–25 (2002)
7. Holzmann, G.: The SPIN Model Checker. Addison-Wesley, Reading (2003)

8. John, A., Konnov, I., Schmid, U., Veith, H., Widder, J.: Parameterized model checking of fault-tolerant distributed algorithms by abstraction. In: FMCAD, pp. 201–209 (2013)

9. John, A., Konnov, I., Schmid, U., Veith, H., Widder, J.: Towards modeling and model checking fault-tolerant distributed algorithms. In: Bartocci, E., Ramakrishnan, C.R. (eds.) SPIN 2013. LNCS, vol. 7976, pp. 209–226. Springer, Heidelberg (2013). https://doi.org/10.1007/978-3-642-39176-7_14

10. Konnov, I., Lazić, M., Veith, H., Widder, J.: A short counterexample property for safety and liveness verification of fault-tolerant distributed algorithms. In: POPL, pp. 719–734 (2017)

11. Konnov, I., Veith, H., Widder, J.: On the completeness of bounded model checking for threshold-based distributed algorithms: reachability. In: Baldan, P., Gorla, D. (eds.) CONCUR 2014. LNCS, vol. 8704, pp. 125–140. Springer, Heidelberg (2014). https://doi.org/10.1007/978-3-662-44584-6_10

12. Konnov, I., Veith, H., Widder, J.: SMT and POR beat counter abstraction: parameterized model checking of threshold-based distributed algorithms. In: Kroening, D., Păsăreanu, C.S. (eds.) CAV 2015. LNCS, vol. 9206, pp. 85–102. Springer, Cham (2015). https://doi.org/10.1007/978-3-319-21690-4_6

13. Konnov, I., Veith, H., Widder, J.: What you always wanted to know about model checking of fault-tolerant distributed algorithms. In: Mazzara, M., Voronkov, A. (eds.) PSI 2015. LNCS, vol. 9609, pp. 6–21. Springer, Cham (2016). https://doi.org/10.1007/978-3-319-41579-6_2

14. Konnov, I., Widder, J., Spegni, F., Spalazzi, L.: Accuracy of message counting abstraction in fault-tolerant distributed algorithms. In: Bouajjani, A., Monniaux, D. (eds.) VMCAI 2017. LNCS, vol. 10145, pp. 347–366. Springer, Cham (2017). https://doi.org/10.1007/978-3-319-52234-0_19

15. Lazić, M., Konnov, I., Widder, J., Bloem, R.: Synthesis of distributed algorithms with parameterized threshold guards. In: OPODIS. LIPIcs, vol. 95, pp. 32:1–32:20 (2017)

16. Lynch, N.: Distributed Algorithms. Morgan Kaufman, Burlington (1996)

17. Marić, O., Sprenger, C., Basin, D.: Cutoff bounds for consensus algorithms. In: Majumdar, R., Kunčak, V. (eds.) CAV 2017. LNCS, vol. 10427, pp. 217–237. Springer, Cham (2017). https://doi.org/10.1007/978-3-319-63390-9_12

18. Mostéfaoui, A., Mourgaya, E., Parvédy, P.R., Raynal, M.: Evaluating the condition-based approach to solve consensus. In: DSN, pp. 541–550 (2003)

19. Pease, M., Shostak, R., Lamport, L.: Reaching agreement in the presence of faults. J. ACM 27(2), 228–234 (1980)

20. Raynal, M.: A case study of agreement problems in distributed systems: non-blocking atomic commitment. In: HASE, pp. 209–214 (1997)

21. Song, Y.J., van Renesse, R.: Bosco: one-step byzantine asynchronous consensus. In: Taubenfeld, G. (ed.) DISC 2008. LNCS, vol. 5218, pp. 438–450. Springer, Heidelberg (2008). https://doi.org/10.1007/978-3-540-87779-0_30

22. Srikanth, T., Toueg, S.: Simulating authenticated broadcasts to derive simple fault-tolerant algorithms. Distrib. Comput. 2, 80–94 (1987)

23. Tange, O., et al.: GNU parallel-the command-line power tool. USENIX Mag. 36(1), 42–47 (2011)

24. Tseng, L.: Voting in the presence of byzantine faults. In: Dependable Computing (PRDC), pp. 1–10. IEEE (2017)

# Static Code Verification Through Process Models

Sebastiaan Joosten[✉] and Marieke Huisman

University of Twente, Enschede, The Netherlands
sjcjoosten@gmail.com

**Abstract.** In this extended abstract, we combine two techniques for program verification: one is Hoare-style static verification, and the other is model checking of state transition systems. We relate the two techniques semantically through the use of a ghost variable. Actions that are performed by the program can be logged into this variable, building an event structure as its value. We require the event structure to grow incrementally by construction, giving it behavior suitable for model checking. Invariants specify a correspondence between the event structure and the program state. The combined power of model checking and static code verification with separation logic based reasoning, gives a new and intuitive way to do program verification. We describe our idea in a tool-agnostic way: we do not give implementation details, nor do we assume that the static verification tool to which our idea might apply is implemented in a particular way.

## 1 Introduction

We recognise two powerful ways of reasoning about concurrent and distributed programs: one can use concurrent separation logic and Hoare-style reasoning, or one might see the program and its environment as a state transition system and use model checking. For reasoning about concurrent and distributed systems, Hoare-style reasoning [7] has been applied successfully [5]. Using different forms of transition systems to model concurrent and distributed systems goes back a long way [9] and can often be a more intuitive method. Neither of these approaches individually is a silver bullet for reasoning about concurrent and distributed programs. Our contribution lies in presenting how to get both techniques: We present a technique to describe program behavior through an event structure, and use properties provable through model checking those descriptions to verify the program using Hoare-style reasoning. Although we do not know whether this combination actually strengthens the verification framework (in the sense of being able to prove more properties), we do believe that the combination makes the verification framework easier to use, by virtue of being able to combine the two techniques as needed.

T. Margaria and B. Steffen (Eds.): ISoLA 2018, LNCS 11246, pp. 343–354, 2018.
https://doi.org/10.1007/978-3-030-03424-5_23

As a running example, consider this pseudocode that uses a simple spinlock:

```
1    global boolean la; // true if lock is  available,  thus not locked
2    void thread(){
3        // acquire  lock
4        boolean success = false;
5        while (!success){
6           success = compare_and_swap( la,true,false );
7        }
8        assert (la == false); // we have the lock
9        // release  lock
10       la = true;
11   }
```

We will give invariants $I$ that describe that la is set and unset as a lock and unlock action is preformed. In particular, we focus on showing that the Hoare-logic statement $\{I\}$compare_and_swap( l,true,false )$\{I\}$ is valid. We will use model checking to show this.

The approach to verification of programs is as follows: we first tie the behavior of the program to an event structure, by adding ghost code that builds the event structure. For the example, this describes the lock and unlock events. This event structure is then, through an invariant, constrained to a process that describes allowed behaviors of the program. For the example, the process is one where locks and unlocks alternate arbitrarily often. To automatically prove this invariant, we use additional invariants that describe the relation of program variables to the event structure. For the example, this ties the value of the variable la to the state of the event structure. By using techniques from model checking, we can then prove both invariants. This allows us to then use the invariants in a Hoare-logic style proof.

The example is a typical concurrent program: the method of synchronisation, a compare_and_swap, assumes a single shared memory, and there are no send and receive commands as one expects in distributed code. We present concurrent code for simplicity and presentation purposes. The principle to combine reasoning about code with the use of transition systems directly generalizes to distributed systems. Typical challenges one encounters with distributed systems, like heterogeneity, faults in links or nodes, and dynamic topologies, are orthogonal to this paper. Existing solutions for dealing with faults [6] or dynamic topologies [13] use abstract models, describing them in some form of transition system. We therefore consider these challenges and solutions out of scope, but highly relevant: proving the same properties at the code level requires making a link between the abstract level and the actual code, which we demonstrate here.

This paper illustrates an idea on how to verify examples like the one mentioned above, rather than giving an implementation. We hope it is an inspiration to authors of verification tools that apply Hoare-style reasoning. Indeed, we ourselves intend to implement the ideas outlined here in Vercors [3], which is such a tool. However, the best way to implement the idea varies widely from tool to tool. We therefore consider it useful to describe the general idea in a paper separate from its implementation details.

As we are combining Hoare-style proofs and model checking, there is plenty of related work to mention. We describe the work that is most closely related to this paper: concurrent separation logic, model checking, and abstract models.

*Concurrent Separation Logic.* Hoare-style reasoning is proving a Hoare-triple $\{P\}S\{Q\}$ for the program $S$. The triple $\{P\}S\{Q\}$ states that if $\{P\}$ holds before running $S$, then $\{Q\}$ holds after the execution of $S$. Separation logic gives a default notion of how the program can be composed: The frame-rule states that if $\{P\}S\{Q\}$ is proven, then also $\{R * P\}S\{R * Q\}$ holds. Here $R *$ indicates that the environment in which $S$ is run can be extended by a disjoint set of properties $R$. In many practical examples, different threads work on different memory, and concurrent separation logic gives a convenient way to reason about such programs.

Concurrent separation logic can sometimes be adapted to new or unconventional synchronisation mechanisms as well. The thesis by Amighi nicely illustrates that some synchronisation mechanisms can fit into a separation-logic based line of reasoning [2]. A clever encoding of the synchronisation primitives allows us to reason about programs that use them. In some cases, one can even verify some of the synchronisation mechanisms themselves. In contrast to Amighi's thesis, this work presents a uniform way to verify those synchronisation mechanisms, as well as those for which verification has not been possible with techniques from concurrent separation logic.

*Model Checking.* If a program is modeled as a state machine, model checking can be used to establish which properties hold. Not all programs lend themselves to this: unbounded loops, recursion and weak-memory models pose challenges. Recent advances have made model checkers more powerful in these areas: Komuravelli et al. show how to use SMT-based model checkers for the verification of loops and recursion [8]. Model checking has been adapted to reason with weak-memory models effectively [1,15]. Calcagno et al. use model checking in a modular way, modeling the environment of a thread such that it can be used as a specification of that thread later [4]. This work aims to bring these recent improvements of model checkers to the static code verification domain.

*Abstract Models.* This paper generalizes previous work on abstract models as proposed by Oortwijn et al. [10,11]. In the work of Oortwijn, the contract for a method states which actions may or will be taken by that thread. We generalize this by storing the associated actions in a ghost variable.

An important difference between our work and the work of Oortwijn is how invariants are treated: in the work of Oortwijn et al. pre- and postconditions are specified for actions. From these conditions, some invariants follow. We start by specifying invariants, from which pre- and postconditions follow. In particular, we specify processes in the form of an invariant as well, simplifying their presentation. Simultaneously, we potentially increase the applicability of verification methods.

*Contribution.* We combine separation logic and model checking by adding a ghost variable that expresses part of an event structure of the program. A ghost variable is a specification-only variable, for the sake of static verification. It can help describe the program state, but it should not exist at runtime. As such, ghost variables aren't allowed to influence the program flow. However, ghost variables can be used to state invariants and properties of the program conveniently.

In contrast to conventional ghost variables, we introduce event structure ghost variables in a way that it gives us additional properties. An event structure is a partially ordered multiset of actions. Our event structure ghost variables can only be updated by adding events at the end of the structure: events that are added must be larger than some maximal element. This restriction means that events are never removed, the structure never shrinks, and for each event, the set of events preceding it is fixed throughout the program execution.

The power of introducing such a variable comes from its use in invariants. An invariant is a property that must be satisfied initially, and is preserved by each atomic action. Consequently, one assumes the invariant is satisfied before an atomic action. For our lock example, we could describe that our event structure must be a prefix of lock, unlock, lock, . . .. A model checker can then tell us that if we are in a state in which lock just happened, the next action will be unlock. Similarly, we can say that la is true if and only if the event structure is in the language (lock unlock)*. The combination of these invariants lets us reason about attainable values of program variables.

The contribution of this work is the description of an event structure ghost variable, as well as an indication on how one might implement them into static checkers and model checkers. By using a ghost variable, as in this work, we naturally tie into existing verification paradigms.

Section 2 describes the event structure variable we introduce. Section 3 describes how such a variable can be related to a process. In Sect. 3.3 we give ways in which to tie the variable in with a system talking about invariants. We conclude in Sect. 4.

## 2   Using an Event Structure Variable

This section introduces event structures. The purpose of event structures is to capture a program run at an abstraction level that fits reasoning about processes, which we introduce later.

In what follows, we assume that a set of actions $\mathcal{A}$ is given. The purpose of these actions is that they will correspond to program events, but this is left to the modeler: Event structures capture actions as a partially ordered multiset of actions (actions can occur multiple times). The ghost code describes how the actions are added to the event structure. We proceed by defining what an event structure is.

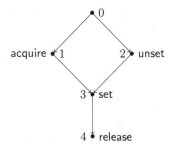

**Fig. 1.** An example event structure

Executions are modeled by an event structure $(E, l, \lesssim)$, which is a set of events $E$ and a partial order on events $\lesssim$. Events are labeled by a set of actions. The function $l : E \rightarrow 2^{\mathcal{A}}$ gives the set of labels for each event. If $E \subseteq E'$ for some event structure $(E', l, \lesssim)$, we write $l_E$ and $\lesssim_E$ for $l$ and $\lesssim$ restricted to the set $E$, such that $(E, l_E, \lesssim_E)$ is again an event structure. The idea of using an event structure for reasoning about concurrent programs was introduced by Vaughan Pratt in 1986 [12], and we incorporate it for use in a Hoare-style setting.

Figure 1 shows a possible event structure. The nodes indicate events, which are numbered so we can talk about them later. An arrow from node $e_1$ to $e_2$ indicates $e_1 \lesssim e_2$, and the set of labels $l(e)$ is written next to each node, omitting the $\{\}$ curly brackets. Arrows that follow from transitivity of $\lesssim$ are not drawn. The intuition behind an event structure is that $\lesssim$ represents the order in which events, and therefore actions, occur.

*Construction.* We construct event structures in one of three ways: Initialisation, extending an existing structure by a single subsequent action, and by combining parallel events. None of these operations removes anything from event structures, so they grow monotonically, and only through subsequent events. In other words: if $e$ takes the value of an event structure $(E', l', \lesssim')$, then at any later point $e$ holds a value $(E, l, \lesssim)$ such that $E' \subseteq E$, $l_{E'} = l'$, $\lesssim_{E'} = \lesssim'$, and for an event $i \in E, i' \in E'$ such that $i \notin E'$, we have $i' \not\lesssim i$. This monotonicity is important for reasoning about event structure variables.

*Initialisation.* Initialisation happens through declaring a variable as an event structure. The variable initializes to an event structure where the set of events is the empty set (this uniquely defines $l$ and $\lesssim$ too). We use the following syntax for this: var e = new EventStructure();.

*Extension.* If $S = \{s_1, s_2, \ldots, s_n\} \subseteq \mathcal{A}$ is a set of actions and e is a ghost variable that holds the event structure $(E, l, \lesssim)$, then e can be extended by an event with labels $S$. Let $t$ be a fresh event. We can think of $t$ as a unique timestamp, or as a counter that increases every time we use it. We ensure that $t$ is larger than any of the events in the structure to which we add it. Fresh means that for any two sets of events $E_1$ and $E_2$ appearing in our program, any common events must have been created at the same point in our program. In particular, freshness implies $t \notin E$. We define $l' : E \cup \{t\} \to 2^A$ by $l'(t) = S$ and $l'(i) = l(i)$ for $i \in E$. We define $\precsim'$ by $t \precsim' i$ for $i \in E \cup \{t\}$, and $i \precsim' j \Leftrightarrow i \precsim j$ for $i, j \in E$. Then the new value of $e$ after extending it with an event with labels $S$ is $(E \cup \{t\}, l', \precsim')$. We use v.add($s_1, s_2, \ldots, s_n$); as syntax for this.

*Parallel events.* To hand off an event structure to a forked thread, it is allowed to make a copy of a ghost variable indicating an event structure v. We write var w = v.copy(); for this. Any subsequent adding of events to v or w happens in isolation from each other as described above.

Parallelism becomes visible in the thread structure when threads are joined again, and we will use union to join the corresponding event structures. We argue that the ordinary set union suffices: Let $(E_1, l_1, \precsim_1)$ and $(E_2, l_2, \precsim_2)$ be events structures. Note that since we only added fresh events, we can define $l : E_1 \cup E_2 \to 2^A$ by $l(i) = l_1(i)$ for $i \in E_1$ and $l(i) = l_2(i)$ for $i \in E_2$, as any element $i \in E_1 \cap E_2$ must have been created with the same labels: $l_1(i) = l_2(i)$. We write $l_1 \cup l_2$ for $l$ defined this way. Similarly, $\precsim_1 \cup \precsim_2$ is again a poset by similar reasoning about freshness. Consequently $(E_1 \cup E_2, l_1 \cup l_2, \precsim_1 \cup \precsim_2)$ is again an event structure. We write v.union(w); to add the structure of w to v, after which v holds the value as described above.

*An Example Program.* We show how to combine the constructions mentioned, to create event structures through ghost code. The code below creates the event structure of Fig. 1 as the final structure for v.

```
1   var v = new EventStructure();
2   v.add();
3   var w = v.copy();
4   w.add(acquire); v.add(unset);
5   v.union(w);
6   v.add(set); v.add(release);
```

Note that despite the suggestion of parallelism in the acquire and the unset action, we did not actually use a parallel program to do so. However, changing the execution order of w.add(acquire); and v.add(unset); would create a similar event structure (equal up to isomorphism).

## 3   Relation to Processes

Our goal of using a ghost event structure variable is to constrain it by using a class invariant. We introduce processes to constrain the event structures, as a process describes the development of an event structure in an intuitive way.

For ghost variable v and a process $P$, the invariant inPrefix(v, $P$); will indicate that at any time, the event structure $e$ that is the value of v, $e \in prefix(P)$ holds. To explain what is meant by $prefix(P)$, we introduce the language in which to write $P$, in Sect. 3.1. We relate event structures to processes by defining what it means for an event structure to be valid for a process, and define the function $prefix$, in Sect. 3.2.

## 3.1  Processes

A process $P$ is defined using process variables, actions, the empty process, sequential and parallel composition, and nondeterministic choice. Process variables are written $A, B, \ldots \in \mathcal{P}$. We write $\mathsf{a}, \mathsf{acquire}, \ldots \in \mathcal{A}$ to denote actions. We write $P, Q, \ldots$ for processes. A process variable $A$ is defined by stating a declaration of the shape $A = P$, where $P$ is an expression of the shape:

$$P ::= A \mid \mathsf{a} \mid \epsilon \mid P{\cdot}Q \mid P \parallel Q \mid P + Q$$

We require all process variables to be declared exactly once[1]. The precedence of the operations is $\cdot$ over $\parallel$ over $+$, so $((P{\cdot}Q) \parallel R) + S$ does not need any parenthesis.

Here is an example of two process declarations:

$$B = (\mathsf{set} + \mathsf{unset}) \parallel B + \epsilon;$$
$$C = \mathsf{acquire}{\cdot}B{\cdot}\mathsf{release};$$

Process $B$ models any number of arbitrarily ordered setting and unsetting actions. Process $C$ models a process in which such an arbitrary set of actions happens between an acquire and a release.

## 3.2  Valid and Prefix Event Structures

We define validity to be able to relate event structures to processes. The definition will also be used to define a prefix. We inductively define what it means for an event structure to be a valid structure for a process, given a context of process variable declarations:

- If $(E, l, \lesssim)$ is a valid event structure for the process $P$, and the process variable $A \in \mathcal{P}$ is declared as $A = P$, then $(E, l, \lesssim)$ is valid for $A$.
- Let $(E, l, \lesssim)$ be an event structure with exactly one event: $\{e'\} = E$, and $l(e') = \mathsf{a}$. Then $(E, l, \lesssim)$ is valid for $\mathsf{a}$.
- An event structure $(E, l, \lesssim)$ for which $\forall e \in E . l(e) = \{\}$, is valid for $\epsilon$.
- If $(E, l, \lesssim)$ is an event structure, $E_1 \cup E_2 = E$ with $E_1$ and $E_2$ disjoint, $(E_1, l_{E_1}, \lesssim_{E_1})$ is valid for $P$ and $(E_2, l_{E_2}, \lesssim_{E_2})$ is valid for $Q$, then $(E, l, \lesssim)$ is valid for $P \parallel Q$. If additionally $\forall e_1 \in E_1, e_2 \in E_2 . e_1 \lesssim e_2$, then $(E, l, \lesssim)$ is valid for $P{\cdot}Q$.
- If $(E, l, \lesssim)$ is an event structure that is valid for $P$, then $(E, l, \lesssim)$ is valid for $P + Q$, as well as for $Q + P$.
- Nothing else is a valid event structure for a process.

---

[1] Because how validity is defined in the next section, a process defined as $A = A$ is equivalent to the process for which no event structures are valid, not even the empty one.

We could extend the language for processes (say with hiding operations), as well as the event structure (say with a conflict relation), as long as the model checker we use to reason about validity of event structures supports the added constructions.

For $l'$ and $\lesssim'$ such that $(\{0,1,2,3,4\}, l', \lesssim')$ is the event structure indicated in Fig. 1, we get: The event structure $(\{3\}, l'_{\{3\}}, \lesssim'_{\{3\}})$ is a valid event structure for $B$. Consequently, the event structure $(\{0,1,3,4\}, l'_{\{0,1,3,4\}}, \lesssim'_{\{0,1,3,4\}})$ is a valid event structure for $C$. However, $(\{0,1,2,3,4\}, l', \lesssim')$ is not a valid event structure for $C$. It is, however, a valid event structure for $B \parallel C$.

When reasoning about programs, we describe partial executions, which we also relate to processes. A prefix encompasses this idea. A prefix is an event structure that could be extended to become a valid event structure for a process $P$: Let $(E, l, \lesssim)$ be a valid event structure for $P$. Take $E' \subseteq E$ such that it is upward closed with respect to $\lesssim$, that is: if $e' \in E'$, $e \in E$ and $e \lesssim e'$, then $e \in E'$. Then $(E', l_{E'}, \lesssim_{E'})$ is a prefix event structure for $P$. The set of all such prefixes is written $prefix(P)$. Similarly, the set of all valid event structures for $P$ is written $valid(P)$.

### 3.3   Using Invariants

We use an invariant system to reason about the state of program variables in relation to a ghost variable. The invariants we consider are checked after every change to shared variables: In a valid program, all invariants hold before and after every atomic action. This fine-grained level of invariants allows us to relate processes to a program state. We illustrate this with an example of a lock.

In a program with a spinlock, a single boolean la indicates the availability of the lock. If the lock is available, a thread may atomically compare and swap la from true to false. That thread is then responsible for eventually releasing the lock by setting it back to true. We can model the lock with a very simple process:

$$L = \epsilon + \text{lock}\cdot\text{unlock}\cdot L$$

We use a global variable p to keep track of our locking process. Code for obtaining the lock could look like this (replacing lines 4 to 7):

```
1   boolean success = false;
2   while (! success){
3     success
4       = ( compare_and_swap( la,true,false )
5           /*@ atomically {
6                 if (\ result ) {e.add(lock);}
7               } *@/
8         );
9   }
```

Here the atomic compare and swap operation is executed as a single atomic action together with our ghost code. The block starting with /*@ and ending with @*/ is ghost code, and is to be ignored by a compiler, but is 'virtually' executed in symbolic analysis of the code. We put extra brackets around this single atomic action for clarity. This means no other threads can interleave between the compare and swap and the ghost code on line 6. The \ result on line 6 refers to the return value from the compare and swap operation. Note that we cannot use success yet, as the write to success does not happen until after this atomic action. A verifier checks that the expression preceding line 6 is indeed atomic, and the code in line 6 is valid ghost code in that it does not change any non-ghost parts.

Now we wish to verify that this code actually maintains $e \in prefix(L)$. That is: the event structure in the variable e is a valid prefix of the process described by $L$. For this code, that means we need to show that when e.add(lock); is virtually executed, the value of e is such that adding an event with the label lock preserves the invariant. The invariant guarantees that e is in the prefix of $L$, but that does not suffice to prove what we need to show: The event structure $(\{0,1\}, \lambda x.\text{lock}, \leq)$ where $\leq$ is the standard order on natural numbers is not in the prefix of $L$, but can be reached after e.add(lock); if the original value of e was $(\{0\}, \lambda x.\text{lock}, \leq)$, which is in the prefix of $L$. This situation should not occur, because of how la relates to e, but we have not made this explicit yet. We do so in another invariant.

The invariant $e \in valid(L) \Leftrightarrow$ la describes that la is true if and only if the value of e is an event structure in $L$. As we do the atomic compare and swap, we can prove that both invariants are maintained by case analysis: If the compare and swap fails, la is unchanged and so is e. Since the invariants holds before the compare and swap, it also does after it. For the other case, the compare and swap succeeds. This means that before the atomic action, la was true. Therefore, we must have been in an accepting state of $L$ per our second invariant. We are allowed to do the lock action from that state, which establishes $e \in prefix(L)$. Additionally, we will end up in a non-valid state of $L$ by doing this action. As la is false after the atomic action, we also established $e \in valid(L) \Leftrightarrow$ la. This shows that the two stated invariants are preserved. The reasoning required to establish this, can be stated as an isolated model checking problem.

Note that our reuse of $L$ in the invariant $e \in valid(L) \Leftrightarrow$ la is a bit of a lucky coincidence. The processes lock·unlock·$L$ and lock + lock·unlock·$L$ all have the same prefixes as $L$, so we could have used them in the first invariant. However, they differ in $valid(L)$, so they would not be suitable for the invariant that fixes la. In certain cases, one would need to write a separate process for different invariants.

## 3.4   Limitations and Extensions

We illustrate a limitation of our approach by the same example of a lock. This time, we focus on the release of the lock, rather than the acquire. We could use the same solution as for the lock, but there is a subtlety: While an acquire requires a compare and swap operation, a release can be done with the unconditional assignment la=true;. Our approach can be extended in several ways, which we will sketch now. We end this section by briefly discussing which option would be the best choice to implement in an existing tool.

The invariant we need to prove the unconditional release preserves the invariant is as follows: Only the thread or process that acquired the lock is allowed to release it. We can state this invariant in terms of permissions: every thread can do a lock action, after which it obtains permission to do an unlock action. Another way to state this invariant is in terms of a rely-guarantee invariant: all threads must guarantee to do a lock before any unlock. Finally, we could change the definition of our process to a thread-oriented version, making explicit which thread does the lock in the process.

*Using Permissions.* For using permissions, we assign permissions to actions. This ties in nicely to verification tools that already use permissions. The idea is to introduce a new permission (or resource), which we call can_unlock. In an implementation, the permission itself can be left undefined, or the write permission to an arbitrary heap location can stand in its place. We will give this permission to the thread that can perform an unlock action, which means we will need to prove that at most one thread can get that permission.

In this solution, add pre- and postconditions to e.add(lock) and e.add(unlock): As a postcondition for e, you gain the permission can_unlock. The permission can_unlock is a precondition to adding the unlock event to e. Aside from the invariants, adding a lock event to e has no preconditions, and adding the unlock has no postconditions. It follows from $e \in prefix(L)$ (by model checking $L$) that the number of outstanding can_unlock permissions is at most one. Crucially, this means that at most one thread has the can_unlock permission. This should allow us to prove that no unlock events are added to e as long as we hold can_unlock.

*Using rely-guarantee.* Using a rely-guarantee mechanism, we state that every thread, and therefore also the environment of a single thread, must do a lock before an unlock. Together with the invariant $e \in prefix(L)$, this means that the environment of some thread cannot do an unlock after our thread performed a lock. For this approach to work one needs to tie the execution of threads to that of method calls: When a thread is forked, it gets assigned a process that acts as its contract. Assigning a process to a forked thread as a method is worked out under the name 'abstract models' as currently implemented in the tool Vercors [11]. A similar principle might be usable to also state properties about the environment of a thread. Indeed, the combination of using separation logic and rely/guarantee based reasoning has been proposed by Vafeiadis et al. [14].

*Thread-Specific Event Structures.* Finally, one could add a ghost event structure variable $t(n)$ for each thread $n$. For each of these variables, we have $t(n) \in prefix(L)$. Each thread $n$ gets exclusive access to $t(n)$. Additionally, we add an invariant that states that e is an interleaving of all $t(n)$. This solution works the same way as the solution of using permissions, with the difference that having write access to a $t(n)$ that contains a lock event here takes the role of having the can_unlock permission. Again, the invariants collectively guarantee that only one thread at a time has this permission.

This solution seems to be really close to what we described in this paper so far. The main addition is to be able to express the composition of a set of thread-specific variables $t(n)$. We can use the union command, which does this for two variables. However, we need to compose an unbounded number of variables, rather than two as with union. This seemingly small detail hinders the use of model checkers at the place where we intend to use them.

*Future Directions.* In this section, we described three ways to verify correctness of the unlock. Each has its own benefits: there is a clear path for the implementation of the first solution, the second solution seems to best match existing literature, and the third solution seems to constitute the smallest change in the language of existing tools. We do not know whether the most convenient solution is among these three, or which of these would be the best for a tool user. We hope to discuss these directions with the participants of ISoLA 2018.

## 4    Conclusions and Future Work

We described the use of a new kind of ghost variable to help verify programs in an intuitive way. This gives us a way to reason about programs as if they were state machines, in a way that allows us to choose the abstraction level ourselves. Invariants allow us to tie programs into program variables, such that the reasoning also helps us to state properties about the program based on that reasoning.

We believe the ideas in this paper can be implemented by combining model checking and existing static verification tools, but have not yet worked out all necessary details on how to do so. Details on how to do this in Vercors remain future work. We hope this paper inspires readers to come up with different ways of implementing these ideas in other tools as well.

A future direction of research is to determine whether we can use this approach to verify properties that can only be stated on a process level, like the linearizability of methods. Linearizability is an important property for high performance libraries. To prove it, one would associate each method of a certain class with a single action. We would like to be able to assert that regardless of how we call these methods in instance of that class, the event structure variable registers each of those actions exactly once, sequentially. Furthermore, the sequential execution of the corresponding methods should give the same state for the instance. A proof of linearizability of a set of methods allows us to treat those methods as atomic actions themselves, giving an extra opportunity of making proofs more modular.

# References

1. Abdulla, P.A., Aronis, S., Atig, M.F., Jonsson, B., Leonardsson, C., Sagonas, K.: Stateless model checking for TSO and PSO. In: Baier, C., Tinelli, C. (eds.) TACAS 2015. LNCS, vol. 9035, pp. 353–367. Springer, Heidelberg (2015). https://doi.org/10.1007/978-3-662-46681-0_28

2. Amighi, A.: Specification and verification of synchronisation classes in Java: a practical approach. Ph.D. thesis, University of Twente (2018)

3. Blom, S., Huisman, M.: The VerCors tool for verification of concurrent programs. In: Jones, C., Pihlajasaari, P., Sun, J. (eds.) FM 2014. LNCS, vol. 8442, pp. 127–131. Springer, Cham (2014). https://doi.org/10.1007/978-3-319-06410-9_9

4. Calcagno, C., Parkinson, M., Vafeiadis, V.: Modular safety checking for fine-grained concurrency. In: Nielson, H.R., Filé, G. (eds.) SAS 2007. LNCS, vol. 4634, pp. 233–248. Springer, Heidelberg (2007). https://doi.org/10.1007/978-3-540-74061-2_15

5. Din, C.C., Dovland, J., Johnsen, E.B., Owe, O.: Observable behavior of distributed systems: component reasoning for concurrent objects. J. Logic Algebraic Program. 81(3), 227–256 (2012). https://doi.org/10.1016/j.jlap.2012.01.003, The 22nd Nordic Workshop on Programming Theory (NWPT 2010)

6. Fisman, D., Kupferman, O., Lustig, Y.: On verifying fault tolerance of distributed protocols. In: Ramakrishnan, C.R., Rehof, J. (eds.) Tools and Algorithms for the Construction and Analysis of Systems, pp. 315–331. Springer, Heidelberg (2008)

7. Hoare, C.A.R.: Communicating sequential processes. Commun. ACM 21(8), 666–677 (1978). https://doi.org/10.1145/359576.359585

8. Komuravelli, A., Gurfinkel, A., Chaki, S.: SMT-based model checking for recursive programs. CoRR abs/1405.4028 (2014). http://arxiv.org/abs/1405.4028

9. Lamport, L., Owicki, S.: Proving liveness properties of concurrent programs. ACM Trans. Program. Lang. Syst. 4(3), 455–495 (1982). https://www.microsoft.com/en-us/research/publication/proving-liveness-properties-concurrent-programs/

10. Oortwijn, W., Blom, S., Huisman, M.: Future-based static analysis of message passing programs. In: PLACES, pp. 65–72 (2016)

11. Oortwijn, W., Blom, S., Gurov, D., Huisman, M., Zaharieva-Stojanovski, M.: An abstraction technique for describing concurrent program behaviour. In: Paskevich, A., Wies, T. (eds.) VSTTE 2017. LNCS, vol. 10712, pp. 191–209. Springer, Cham (2017). https://doi.org/10.1007/978-3-319-72308-2_12

12. Pratt, V.: Modeling concurrency with partial orders. Int. J. Parallel Program. 15(1), 33–71 (1986). https://doi.org/10.1007/BF01379149

13. Sirjani, M., Movaghar, A., Shali, A., de Boer, F.S.: Modeling and verification of reactive systems using Rebeca. Fundam. Inf. 63(4), 385–410 (2004). http://dl.acm.org/citation.cfm?id=2370686.2370691

14. Vafeiadis, V., Parkinson, M.: A marriage of rely/guarantee and separation logic. In: Caires, L., Vasconcelos, V.T. (eds.) CONCUR 2007. LNCS, vol. 4703, pp. 256–271. Springer, Heidelberg (2007). https://doi.org/10.1007/978-3-540-74407-8_18

15. Vafeiadis, V.: Formal reasoning about the C11 weak memory model. In: Proceedings of the 2015 Conference on Certified Programs and Proofs, pp. 1–2. ACM (2015)

# Effective Test Suite Design for Detecting Concurrency Control Faults in Distributed Transaction Systems

Simin Cai[✉], Barbara Gallina, Dag Nyström, and Cristina Seceleanu

School of Innovation, Design and Engineering, Mälardalen University,
Västerås, Sweden
{simin.cai,barbara.gallina,dag.nystrom,cristina.seceleanu}@mdh.se

**Abstract.** Concurrency control faults may lead to unwanted interleavings, and breach data consistency in distributed transaction systems. However, due to the unpredictable delays between sites, detecting concurrency control faults in distributed transaction systems is difficult. In this paper, we propose a methodology, relying on model-based testing and mutation testing, for designing test cases in order to detect such faults. The generated test inputs are designated delays between distributed operations, while the outputs are the occurrence of unwanted interleavings that are consequences of the concurrency control faults. We mutate the distributed transaction specification with common concurrency control faults, and model them as UPPAAL timed automata, in which designated delays are encoded as stopwatches. Test cases are generated via reachability analysis using UPPAAL Model Checker, and are selected to form an effective test suite. Our methodology can reduce redundant test cases, and find the appropriate delays to detect concurrency control faults effectively.

## 1 Introduction

In many modern software systems, data are partitioned in several nodes across the network, and accessed by concurrent distributed transactions with read and write operations. Without proper control, concurrent transactions may interleave and access data arbitrarily, which may lead to inconsistent data. For instance, in a distributed automation system, whose configuration data are partitioned on different sites, a transaction may update the configuration data D1 on site S1 and data D2 on site S2, based on their current values. If another transaction modifies D2 exactly before the former's update, the configurations may end up inconsistent. To avoid this, the transaction manager often ensures the isolation property, that is, the absence of a specified set of transaction interleavings that cause data inconsistency [1].

To achieve this, lock-based Concurrency Control (CC) techniques are often applied by the transaction manager to prevent unwanted interleavings [3]. Such type of CC regulates transactions to acquire and release locks on data at specific

© Springer Nature Switzerland AG 2018
T. Margaria and B. Steffen (Eds.): ISoLA 2018, LNCS 11246, pp. 355–374, 2018.
https://doi.org/10.1007/978-3-030-03424-5_24

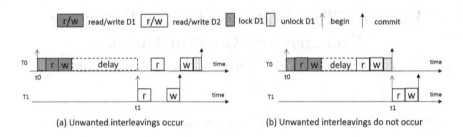

**Fig. 1.** Observation of isolation violation depending on delays

times, and resolves the conflict when two transactions request the same lock simultaneously. In the previous example, one proper way to guarantee isolation could be to lock both D1 and D2 until the modification is completed, so that no other transactions can interfere. Consequently, every transaction behaves to its caller as if it was the only one executed in the system.

In this paper, we focus on detecting CC faults in a distributed transaction system with lock-based concurrency control. CC faults are commonly found and notoriously challenging to detect in software systems [20]. Common CC faults include, for instance, misplaced locks, or erroneous time of releasing locks [14, 18]. The consequence could be the violation of the isolation requirements, that is, the occurrence of undesired interleavings of the concurrent transactions. To detect the CC faults, the implemented system are usually tested by executing the distributed transactions, and monitoring the occurrence of the undesired interleavings in the transaction logs. A fault is detected when such undesired interleavings are observed. Due to the various communication delays between different nodes, however, such undesired interleavings may not be observed, even in the presence of CC faults. In order to illustrate the impact of delays, let us consider two transactions, T0 and T1, from the previous example. T0 updates D1 and D2 by reading and write D1 on site S1, and after some delay, followed by reading and write D2 on S2. T1 reads D2 and then modifies its value. The isolation property forbids the following sequence of operations: T0 reads D2, T1 reads D2, T0 writes D2, T1 writes D2, because T1 bases its write on an intermediate value of D2. While a proper CC algorithm would be to lock both D1 and D2 during the execution of T0, we assume that the developer has made a mistake by forgetting to lock D2. However, isolation violation may not be observed with this fault. As shown in Fig. 1a, the unwanted interleavings does occur that T1 reads D2 before the final modification by T0, and can be observed by the tester. However, if the delay is shorter, as shown in Fig. 1b, the unwanted interleavings do not occur, and thus the fault is not exposed to the tester.

Traditionally, a common testing technique is to insert random delays between the operations of the transactions, and test the violation of isolation [11, 13]. However, even though a large set of various delays can be used as test inputs, it is still difficult to ensure the coverage of the unwanted interleavings. Finding a relatively small set of test cases, which is manageable yet able to expose as many unwanted interleavings as possible, remains challenging for detecting CC faults of distributed transactions.

To address this challenge, in this paper we propose a methodology for finding an effective test suite that can expose the CC faults. The inputs of the test cases are designated delays between operations at design level, which can be used to configure the delays in the implemented system in a controlled testing environment. Instead of randomly chosen delay values, we propose techniques to generate a set of values for the inserted delays as inputs, such that the CC faults can be exposed. The outputs are whether or not the predefined unwanted interleavings that violate isolation have occurred, which can be examined in the logs. The techniques central to this methodology are model-based testing [21] and mutation testing [16]. We define a set of mutation operators, each altering the transaction specification by introducing a common CC fault. For instance, one mutant operator could change the specification by removing the locking of a data. We model the transaction specification, as well as its mutants, as networks of UPPAAL Timed Automata (TA) [19], in which the delays are encoded as stopwatches [7]. Test cases including the designated delays are generated from the models via reachability analysis.

The process of applying our methodology is listed as follows. (i) We specify the work units consisting of the operations on the distributed data, the delays between these operations, as well as the lock operations, in a high-level description language. In addition, we specify the requirements of desired isolation, which are the interleavings to be prevented by CC. (ii) By extending a modeling framework for concurrent transactions in our previous work [6], we model the distributed transaction system as a network of UPPAAL TA, and formalize these isolation properties in Computational Tree Logic (CTL) [8], which can be checked rigorously by the UPPAAL Model Checker (MC) [19]. (iii) The specification in (i) is mutated by applying the mutation operators, based on which we create a series of mutant TA models that model the common CC faults. (iv) We generate diagnostic traces for each mutant model via reachability analysis and obtain test cases from the traces, which are used to form an effective test suite that can kill all the mutants with a minimal number of test cases.

The remainder of the paper is organized as follows. Section 2 recalls the background knowledge of this paper, including model-based and mutation testing, UPPAAL TA and the UPPAAL tools. Section 3 presents the details of our methodology. In Sect. 4, we apply our methodology to a case study, followed by a comparison with related work in Sect. 5. In Sect. 6, we conclude the paper and outline our future work.

## 2    Background

In this subsection, we present the background knowledge of this paper, that is, a brief overview of model-based and mutation testing in Sect. 2.1, as well as UPPAAL timed automata and the UPPAAL tools in Sect. 2.2.

## 2.1   Model-Based Testing and Mutation Testing

Model-based testing [21,27] encompasses the processes and techniques to perform testing based on behavioral or architectural models of the System Under Test (SUT). A generic process of model-based testing consists of the following major steps. (1) Create a model of the SUT. (2) Decide the test selection criteria to guide test generation. (3) Define the high-level test case specifications. (4) Generate the test cases that satisfy the test case specifications. (5) Run the generated test cases, manually or automatically.

Mutation testing [16] is a fault-based technique to provide criteria for selecting the effective test cases. Mutants, which represent common faults, are created, upon which the candidate test cases are executed. Combined with model-based testing, the mutants are also models generated from the original system model using pre-defined mutation operators. A good test case should be able to distinguish the mutated behaviors from the original behavior. An effective test suite, selected from the candidate test cases, should be able to kill as many mutants as possible, with a minimal number of test cases.

## 2.2   UPPAAL Timed Automata and the UPPAAL Tools

In this paper we use Timed Automata (TA) [2] to model the distributed transaction system. A Timed Automaton (TA) is a finite-state automaton extended with clock variables with real-type values. These clock variables progress synchronously, and are used to model the progress of time in a system. UPPAAL [19] is the state-of-art model checker for verifying TA-based models of real-time systems.

Figure 2 shows two TA, A1 and A2, in UPPAAL. A1 has two locations, $L1$ and $L2$, and has defined a clock variable $c$ to keep track of the elapsed time. An directed edge connects these two locations, meaning the it is possible to transit from $L1$ and $L2$. When a TA reaches a location, it can non-deterministically choose to delay at the same location, or take a transition to another location following an edge. An invariant, which is a propositional formula over clock variables, may be associated with a location to set an upper-bound on the delay. In Fig. 2, the invariant $c <= 10$ on $L1$ indicates that A1 may delay at $L1$ at most until $c$ equals 10 time units. A guard, which is also a predicate of variables, may be associated with an edge as the required condition to take the transition. In this example, the guard $c > 5$ ensures that the transition from $L1$ and $L2$ can be taken only if the value of $c$ is bigger than 5. During a transition, TA can take actions, as associated with the edge, to update the values of the variables.

The automaton A1 and A2 form a network of TA via parallel composition ("$||$"). The two TA can perform handshake synchronization via the channel $chan$. The "!" denotes the sender of the signal in the synchronization, and the "?" denotes receiver. In the example, A1 sends a signal via $chan$ when it transits from $L1$ to $L2$. Meanwhile, A2 receives the signal and takes the transition from location $L3$ back to $L3$.

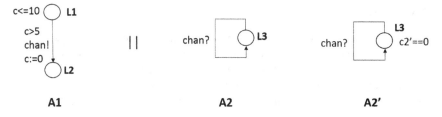

**Fig. 2.** A network of UPPAAL TA    **Fig. 3.** An UPPAAL TA with stopwatch

The requirements to be satisfied can be formalized in the UPPAAL query language, which is a decidable subset of TCTL (Timed Computational Tree Logic) [19]. These formalized requirements can then be verified exhaustively and automatically by the UPPAAL model checker. In this paper we will use the following queries:

- $A\,[\,]\,\,P$: P always holds for all possible execution paths (invariance property).
- $E\,<>\,P$: There exists a path in which P eventually holds (reachability property).

P is a logic expression that may contain clock constraints, and logical operators such as "and", "or", "not" and "imply". In case an invariance property fails, UPPAAL can provide a trace leading to the violation as a counter-example of the property. If a reachability property is satisfied, UPPAAL also returns a trace that leads to the state where P holds. Such traces contain the state transitions as well as the bounds of clock variables in each state. For more details about UPPAAL, we refer to the literature [19].

In this paper, we also use an extended version of UPPAAL TA, augmented with stopwatches [7]. Stopwatches allow clocks to be stopped at locations, so that the values of the clock variables do not progress. Figure 3 shows an UPPAAL TA with stopwatch. The invariant $c2' == 0$ assigns the rate of the clock variable $c2$ to be 0. By doing this, as long as automaton A2 stays at location $L3$, the value of $c2$ is never changed.

UPPAAL has been used for generating test cases [15]. The system under test is modeled in UPPAAL TA, in which test inputs and outputs are encoded in the model. By executing UPPAAL queries that formalize the testing goal, testers can utilize the diagnostic traces returned by UPPAAL to form test sequences, which may consist of synchronizations, discreet transitions and time delays.

## 3  A Model-Based Testing Methodology for Isolation Violation

In this section we present our proposed methodology for testing isolation violation in a distributed transaction system with lock-based CC. We first give an overview of our methodology, after which we explain the major steps and techniques in details.

## 3.1   Overview

We assume that a distributed transaction is a sequence of atomic operations that may access data located in different sites, and as a whole should satisfy data consistency requirements. Among them, the isolation requirements claim the avoidance of a particular set of interleavings of concurrency transactions. The transaction manager implements a CC algorithm with locking and unlocking mechanisms over the distributed data partitions. The delays between nodes, while their actual values unpredictable, are bounded with maximum and minimum values, which is reasonable for many distributed systems, such as automotive and factory automation systems. The maximum and minimum response times of the operations on each data item is also known a priori. While the system is tested, designated delays can be deliberately inserted between operations, and the interleavings can be examined by checking the transaction logs.

Our model-based testing methodology consists of four major steps, which are presented in Fig. 4, and listed as follows:

1. Specify the work units with bounded delays, the CC operations, as well as the isolation requirements, in a high-level description language.
2. Construct a network of UPPAAL timed automata for the work units as well as the concurrency control algorithm. Formalize the specified isolation properties in UPPAAL queries. Verify that the isolation properties are satisfied by the current design, using UPPAAL MC.
3. Mutate the transaction specification using the mutation operators presented in Sect. 3.4, and construct TA models with stopwatches for the mutants.
4. Generate an effective test suite from the mutant models.

The details of the steps are presented in the following subsections.

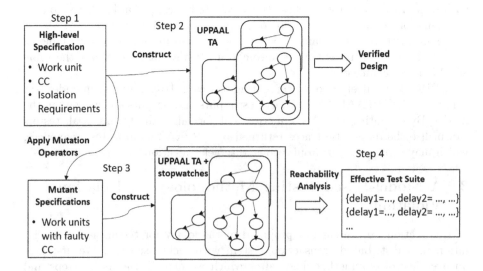

**Fig. 4.** Our proposed methodology

## 3.2    Step 1: Specification of Transactions and Isolation

Our methodology starts with the specification of the distributed transactions and the isolation properties. We assume a high level language is selected, which is able to specify the sequence of operations in the work unit of the transaction, the nodes where the data are located, the response times of the operations, as well as the lock and unlock operations. The language can also specify the delay bounds between operations, which is calculated by the designer based on the communication delays between nodes. For instance, Listing 1.1 and 1.2 specify transaction T0 and T1, respectively, in a generic exemplary high-level language. T0 updates configuration D1 and D2 on site S1 and S2, respectively. T1 reads configuration D2, and then modifies it after a calculation based on the read value. In this description language, "delay" specifies the bounded delay value between operations, with the lower and upper bounds in brackets. "Read" and "write" specify the data operations, while "calculate" specifies calculations in the client. The minimum and maximum response time of the operations are specified in the brackets as well. "On" specifies the sites. "Lock" and "unlock" specifies the CC operations. "Begin" and "commit" specify the boundary of the transaction, respectively.

The isolation property is specified as the avoidance of a set of unwanted interleavings. Such interleavings could be described as a sequence of operations, such as: T0 reads D2, T1 reads D2, T0 writes D2, T1 writes D2.

**Listing 1.1.** Specification of T0

**Listing 1.2.** Specification of T1

```
begin
delay [1, 10]
lock D1 on S1
read D1 on S1 [1, 1]
delay [1, 10]
write D1 on S1 [1, 2]
delay [1, 8]
lock D2 on S2
read D2 on S2 [1, 1]
delay [1, 8]
write D2 on S2 [1, 2]
delay [1, 6]
unlock D1 on S1
unlock D2 on S2
commit
```

```
begin
delay [1, 8]
lock D2 on S2
read D2 on S2 [1, 1]
delay [1, 8]
calculate [2, 3]
delay [1, 4]
write D2 on S2 [1, 2]
delay [1, 6]
unlock D2 on S2
commit
```

## 3.3    Step 2: Construction of TA Models for the Correct Specification

Our modeling framework for the distributed transaction system is adapted from an existing modeling framework for real-time concurrent transaction systems [6]. We extend the original model with the possibility to model distributed data partitions as well as delays between operations introduced by the distribution.

Assuming a distributed transaction system intended to achieve the isolation that avoids $k$ unwanted interleavings, we model the system as a network of UPPAAL TA, denoted as $N$, defined as follows:

$$N ::= A_0 \,||...|| \, A_{n-1} \,||\, A_{CCManager} \,||\, O_0 \,||...|| \, O_{k-1},$$

where $A_0$, ..., $A_{n-1}$ are the work units TA of transactions $T_0$, ..., $T_{n-1}$, $A_{CCManager}$ is the CCManager automaton, and $O_0$, ..., $O_{k-1}$ are the TA of IsolationOservers that observe the unwanted interleavings, respectively. A work unit automaton models the work unit, that is, the operations of a transaction, as well as the delays between them. An IsolationObserver is an automaton that monitors the occurrence of transaction executions that lead to violation of the isolation property. The CCManager automaton models the selected lock-based concurrency control algorithm.

Figure 5 shows the work unit automaton skeleton. The *begin* location represents that the transaction actually starts, while *commit_trans* represents the end of the transaction. After the start, the work unit performs a set of read, write or calculation operations, modeled by the instantiated operation patterns (Fig. 6). We extend the original pattern [6] for distributed transactions in two aspects. First, each read/write operation is performed atomically on a partition. This is modeled by a shared variable *cs[partition]* for each partition. When an operation is performed, it sets *cs[partition]* to 1, so that other operations on this partition are blocked until the current one has finished. The other extension is the modeling of delays between operations caused by the distributed communication. The time of delay for operation_k is modeled by the clock variable *Delay_k*. The operation may delay for at most $MAX\_DELAY\_k$ time units, and must delay for at least $MIN\_DELAY\_k$ time units. Each operation starts from the *start_operation* location, and moves to *operation*. Before moving to *operation_done*, it may stay at *operation* for at most $WCRT$ time units, representing its worst-case response time; and for at least $BCRT$ time units, representing its best-case response time. The work unit may also interact with the CCManager in order to acquire and release locks, which is modeled by the instantiated locking and unlocking patterns (Figs. 7 and 8). The synchronization channel *lock[ti][di]* models the locking request for data $D_j$ sent by transaction $T_i$. The channel *unlock[ti][di]* and *grant[ti][di]* represent the unlocking and granting messages, respectively. These patterns are similar to the ones in [6].

The CCManager is modeled using the CCManager skeleton proposed previously [6] (Fig. 9). It models the behavior of the concurrency control manager in managing lock requests and releases, following a selected algorithm. When a locking request is received via the *lock[ti][di]* channel, the CCManager evaluates the situation using a user-defined function *satisfyPolicy()*, and decides if it sends a grant signal, or refuses the request. When the CCManager receives a unlock signal, it picks the next transaction in the waiting queue (if any), and grants it the lock.

A violation of isolation can be seen as the occurrence of a series of inappropriate events, and is monitored by an IsolationObserver, which is modeled using the skeleton presented in Fig. 10. When the events occur in the specified order, the model eventually reaches the *isolation_violation* location.

As the violations of isolation are modeled using IsolationObservers, the verification of properties is equal to checking the *isolation_violation* locations are not reachable. This can be specified in UPPAAL query language and checked

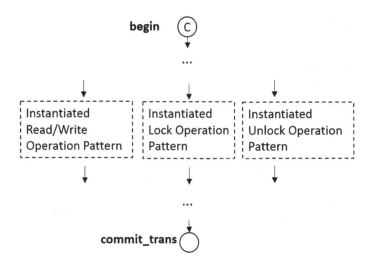

**Fig. 5.** The UPPAAL automaton skeleton of a work unit

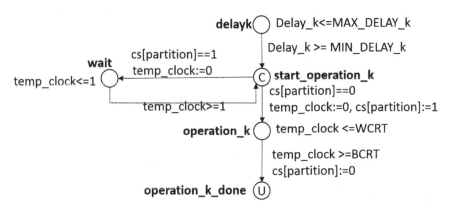

**Fig. 6.** Operation pattern extended with delay

by the UPPAAL model checker. The following query specifies that the isolation property, that is, the violations encoded by the IsolationObservers will never occur:

$A[] (not IsolationObserver1.isolation\_violation) ...$

$and (not IsolationObserverk.isolation\_violation).$

The outcome of this step is a design of distributed transactions, including the work units and the CC manager, that are proven to satisfy the specified isolation properties.

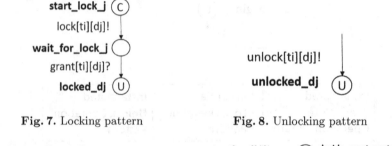

**Fig. 7.** Locking pattern                    **Fig. 8.** Unlocking pattern

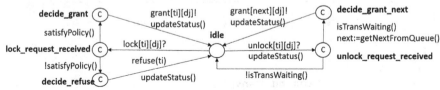

**Fig. 9.** The UPPAAL automaton skeleton of CCManager

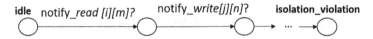

**Fig. 10.** The UPPAAL automaton skeleton of IsolationObserver

### 3.4   Step 3: Generation of Mutant Specifications and Models

Inspired by the existing work on mutation testing for concurrency bugs [5,14,18,25], which have proposed mutation operators that represent common CC faults in various implementation platforms and programming languages, we define a set of mutation operators for the high-level description language, listed in Table 1. Among them, "Remove lock", "Add lock" and "Remove unlock" models the common errors that developers may forget to lock/unlock data, or put on unnecessary locks. "Change lock type" is a useful operator for CC algorithms applying more than one type of locks. "Change lock position" and "Change unlock position" adjust the duration when the data are locked, which captures the error of erroneous length of critical sections.

As examples, Listings 1.3, 1.4 and 1.5 present three mutant specifications, respectively. Mutant 1 applies the "Remove lock" operator, as shown in Listing 1.3, which removes the lock before reading D2 in T0. Mutant 2 applies the "Change unlock position" operator, moves the unlocking of D2 in T0 to before writing D2 (Listing 1.4). We apply "Change lock position" to create mutant 3, which moves the locking of D2 in T1 to before the writing of D2, but after the calculation (Listing 1.5).

**Table 1.** Mutation operators for created specifications with CC faults

| Mutation operator | Change in the correct specification |
|---|---|
| Remove lock | Remove a line with "lock" operation for a shared data |
| Add lock | Add a line with unnecessary "lock" operation for a data |
| Remove unlock | Remove a line with necessary "unlock" operation for a locked data |
| Change lock type | Change the type of lock |
| Change lock position | Move the line with a lock operation to another position |
| Change unlock position | Move the line with an unlock operation to another position |

**Listing 1.3.** Mutant 1

```
begin
delay [1, 10]
lock D1 on S1
read D1 on S1 [1, 1]
delay [1, 10]
write D1 on S1 [1, 2]
delay [1, 8]
--Remove lock
//lock D2 on S2
read D2 on S2 [1, 1]
delay [1, 8]
write D2 on S2 [1, 2]
delay [1, 6]
unlock D1 on S1
unlock D2 on S2
commit
```

**Listing 1.4.** Mutant 2

```
begin
delay [1, 10]
lock D1 on S1
read D1 on S1 [1, 1]
delay [1, 10]
write D1 on S1 [1, 2]
delay [1, 8]
lock D2 on S2
read D2 on S2 [1, 1]
delay [1, 8]
--Change unlock position
unlock D1 on S1
write D2 on S2 [1, 2]
delay [1, 6]
--Change unlock position
//unlock D1 on S1
unlock D2 on S2
commit
```

**Listing 1.5.** Mutant 3

```
begin
delay [1, 8]
--Change lock position
//lock D2 on S2
read D2 on S2 [1, 1]
delay [1, 8]
calculate [2, 3]
delay [1, 4]
--Change lock position
lock D2 on S2
write D2 on S2 [1, 2]
delay [1, 6]
unlock D2 on S2
commit
```

The TA models of the mutant specifications are constructed using the same technique as presented in Sect. 3.3. However, in order to generate test cases with delays, the actual delay values need to be captured in the trace. We achieve this by adapting the models with stopwatches, as shown in Fig. 11. The rule is that, for each *delayk* location, only the *k*th clock is allowed to progress, while all other

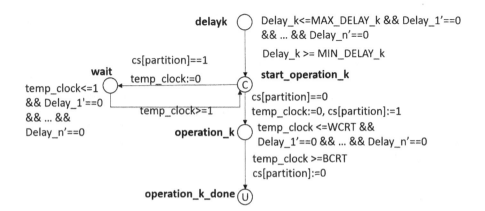

**Fig. 11.** Modified operation pattern for mutant models

clock variables $Delay\_n$ ($n \neq k$) is set to stop, which is done by $Delay\_n'==0$ in the invariants of this location. In other locations, all clocks are set to stop using stopwatches in the same way. The purpose is that, a clock variable for delay only progresses during its delay period, so that the delay values are preserved in the diagnostic trace. The output of this step is a set of mutant models, each representing a mutant specification with CC faults.

### 3.5    Step 4: Generation of Effective Test Suite

For each mutant model, we use UPPAAL tool to verify the following query:

$E <> IsolationObserver.isolation\_violation.$

UPPAAL then generates a trace that leads to the location *isolation_violation*, if this location is reachable. At the end of the trace, the clock constraints at location *isolation_violation* encode the bounds of values of the clock variables, which represent the feasible ranges of delays that can lead to the violation. Since the clock constraints are simple linear inequalities between variables and integers, it is easy to solve them using modern tools, such as Microsoft Z3 SAT solver [10].

We propose an algorithm to generate the effective test suite. If we use $CS_i$ to denote the set of clock constraints of mutant $M_i$, the delay values as the solution set of $CS_i$ are then the test inputs that can lead to the violation, therefore killing $M_i$. Ideally, the effective test suite contains only one test case, which is the set of delay values that satisfy $CS_1 \wedge ... \wedge CS_k$. Therefore, our algorithm starts with looking for one solution for $CS_1 \wedge ... \wedge CS_k$ (line 3, when $i$ equals 1). If such a solution cannot be found, we try to find a larger test suite, by dividing the constraint set into smaller groups, and finding a solution for each group. For instance, let us consider that $i$ equals 2, meaning that we try to find a solution containing two sets of delay values, one set satisfying $CS_1 \wedge ... \wedge CS_m$, the other satisfying $CS_{m+1} \wedge ... \wedge CS_k$. From line 12 to line 23, the algorithm iterates all possible two-group partitions, and tries to find a solution set for each. For each group in the partition, the algorithm tries to solve the constraints using Z3 (line 15), and records the solution (line 17). If every group in the current two-group partition is solvable, the algorithm returns the solutions as the minimum set of delays that forms the test suite (line 24, in this case the suite contains exactly two test cases). If any group is found unsolvable, the algorithm skips the current two-group partition, and tries another one (line 20). If no two-group partition is solvable, which means there does not exist a two-case test suite, the algorithm continues with a possible three-group partition (increment $i$ in line 3), trying to find a test suite that contains three test cases. Using this algorithm, the effective test suite will have at most $m$ test cases, in which each for one of the mutants; and at least 1 test case, which is able to kill all mutants.

**Algorithm 1.** Algorithm to find the effective test suite

```
1: function find_effective_suite():
2: The constraint set of m mutants CS := {CS₁, ..., CSₘ}
3: for  i ∈ [1, m] do
4:    SOLUTIONS := solve_k_partition_of_CS(i)
5:    if SOLUTIONS ≠ NULL then
6:       return SOLUTIONS
7:    end if
8: end for
9: return NULL
10:
11: function solve_k_partition_of_CS(k):
12: for each k-partition Sₖ of CS do
13:    SOLUTIONS := {}, solved := true
14:    for each constraints group Sₖⁱ in Sₖ do
15:       try solving Sₖⁱ using Z3
16:       if Sₖⁱ is solvable and solution SOLUTIONᵢ is found then
17:          SOLUTION := SOLUTION ∪ SOLUTIONᵢ
18:       else
19:          solved := false
20:          break
21:       end if
22:    end for
23:    if solved == true then
24:       return SOLUTIONS
25:    end if
26: end for
27: return NULL
```

## 4    Illustrative Example

To illustrate our proposed methodology, we present an running example, based on the aforementioned transactions in Listings 1.1 and 1.2 in an unmanned loading system on a construction site [17]. This system consists of an autonomous wheel loader, an autonomous dump truck, and a controller, each equipped with a computer, and connected by real-time industrial wireless communication. In a typical scenario, the controller configures the planned job information (paths, locations, etc.) for the truck and wheel loader, which are stored in their respective databases. The wheel loader autonomously discovers and scoops the piles in its surroundings, and dumps them into the truck. The wheel loader may also adjust its working path, in order to avoid obstacles in its working surroundings. All data are protected by CC that requires the corresponding locks in order to access the data.

In this scenario, we consider two transactions. Started by the controller, transaction T0 updates the next location of the truck (denoted as D1) in the truck's local system (denoted as S1), followed by updating the planned location and path (D2) in the wheel loader (S2). Transaction T1, started by the wheel loader, reads D2 from S2, calculates a new value, and then modifies D2. The isolation requirement demands the avoidance of the following sequence: T0 reads D2, T1 reads D2, T0 writes D2, T1 writes D2, which indicates that, the wheel loader using old data computes a new path, which overwrites the planned path. Consequently, the truck goes to the newly planned location while the wheel loader may goes to the old one and miss the truck. We apply our proposed methodology to generate a test suite for testing the CC faults that can lead to the violation of isolation.

### 4.1 Specification of Transactions and Isolation

The first step is to specify the transactions and the isolation requirement. T0 and T1 are specified in Listing 1.1 and 1.2, respectively. The isolation requirement is formulated as follows: the following sequence of operations, T0 reads D2, T1 reads D2, T0 writes D2, T1 writes D2, should never occur.

### 4.2 Construction of TA Models for the Correct Specification

We model the transactions and CC in UPPAAL timed automata. The automaton of $T_0$, as an example, is presented in Fig. 12. It is constructed by composing the instantiated operation, locking and unlocking patterns with the work unit skeletons. An IsolationObserver is created to monitor the occurrence of the unwanted interleavings, as presented in Fig. 13. Isolation is verified by UPPAAL using the following query:

$A[]\,(not\,IsolationObserver.violation)$.

The time and memory consumed by UPPAAL for the verification are 0.015 s and 28316 KB, respectively.

### 4.3 Generation of Mutant Specifications and Models

We use the mutation operators proposed in Table 1 to manually generate mutant models. In this case study, we create three mutants, which are specified as Listings 1.3, 1.4 and 1.5 in Sect. 3.4. The TA models of these mutant specifications are also constructed.

### 4.4 Generation of Effective Test Suite

We use the query in Sect. 3.5 to generate diagnostic traces for the mutant models, and obtain the constraints on the clock variables representing the delays. The time and memory consumed for the checking of each mutant, respectively, are as follows: M1 (0.014 s and 28488 KB), M2 (0.007 s and 28388 KB), M3 (0.015 s and 28492 KB). The constraint sets for mutants M1, M2 and M3 are listed in Listings 1.6, 1.7, and 1.8, respectively.

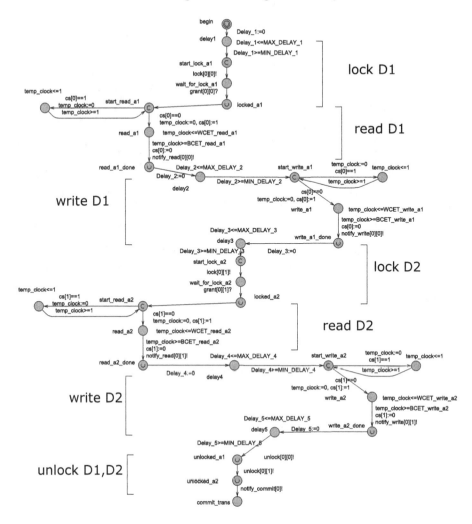

**Fig. 12.** The UPPAAL model of $T_0$

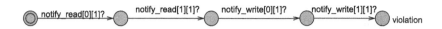

**Fig. 13.** The UPPAAL model of IsolationObserver that monitors the unwanted interleavings

**Listing 1.6.** $CS\_1$

```
3≤T0.Delay_1≤20
3≤T0.Delay_2≤15
1≤T0.Delay_3≤8
1≤T0.Delay_4≤8
1≤T0.Delay_5≤6
10≤T1.Delay_1≤20
1≤T1.Delay_2≤4
1≤T1.Delay_3≤4
1≤T1.Delay_4≤4
T0.Delay_1-T1.Delay_1≥-17
T0.Delay_1-T1.Delay_1≤0
T1.Delay_1-T0.Delay_2≥4
T1.Delay_1-T0.Delay_2≤17
T1.Delay_1-T0.Delay_3≥8
T1.Delay_1-T0.Delay_3≤19
T1.Delay_3-T0.Delay_5≥-5
T1.Delay_3-T0.Delay_5≤2
```

**Listing 1.7.** $CS\_2$

```
3≤T0.Delay_1≤20
3≤T0.Delay_2≤6
1≤T0.Delay_3≤2
1≤T0.Delay_4≤5
1≤T0.Delay_5≤6
T1.Delay_1==10
1≤T1.Delay_2≤4
1≤T1.Delay_3≤4
1≤T1.Delay_4≤4
T0.Delay_4-T1.Delay_2≥-3
T0.Delay_4-T1.Delay_2≤1
T0.Delay_5-T1.Delay_3≥-3
T0.Delay_5-T1.Delay_3≤3
```

**Listing 1.8.** $CS\_3$

```
3≤T0.Delay_1≤20
3≤T0.Delay_2≤15
1≤T0.Delay_3≤8
1≤T0.Delay_4≤8
1≤T0.Delay_5≤6
10≤T1.Delay_1≤20
1≤T1.Delay_2≤4
1≤T1.Delay_3≤4
1≤T1.Delay_4≤4
T0.Delay_1-T1.Delay_1≥-17
T0.Delay_1-T1.Delay_1≤0
T1.Delay_1-T0.Delay_2≥4
T1.Delay_1-T0.Delay_2≤17
T1.Delay_1-T0.Delay_3≥8
T1.Delay_1-T0.Delay_3≤19
T0.Delay_5-T1.Delay_3≥0
T0.Delay_5-T1.Delay_3≤3
```

Algorithm 1 is applied to find the effective test suite. The combined constraint set $CS_1 \wedge CS_2 \wedge CS_3$ is solvable using Z3, which returns the solution, which is the designated delays as inputs of one test case that kills all mutants[1]. Therefore, the effective test suite contains one test case, as shown in Table 2.

**Table 2.** Test inputs of the test case in the effective test suite

| Test input variable | Value |
|---|---|
| T0.Delay_1 | 3 |
| T0.Delay_2 | 3 |
| T0.Delay_3 | 1 |
| T0.Delay_4 | 1 |
| T0.Delay_5 | 1 |
| T1.Delay_1 | 10 |
| T1.Delay_2 | 1 |
| T1.Delay_3 | 1 |
| T1.Delay_4 | 1 |

## 4.5   Discussion

Our methodology generates a set of delays between operations, which can be utilized to create concrete test cases for a particular implementation, considering its architecture and testability characteristics. For instance, if the tested system is instrumented with configurable delayed operations on each individual site and synchronized clocks across all sites, a concrete test sequence with designated delays from the abstract test case can be achieved.

---

[1] We used the online Z3 tool provided by Microsoft (https://rise4fun.com/z3) in this running example. The time to resolve the constraints was less than one second.

Scalability is one important issue for the verification of distributed transactions, which may involve data items over many partitions. As a result, the model may include large numbers of operations, delays and synchronization signals that lead to state explosion for exact model checking. Another characteristic of distributed system is the probabilistic behavior, for which we may only know the probabilistic distribution, rather than exact bounds of the delays in the system. In both cases, we need to adapt the modeling language from UPPAAL TA to UPPAAL stochastic timed automata, in which the probability of delays can be encoded and analyzed by statistical model checking using UPPAAL SMC [9]. More scalable than exact model checking, statistical model checking can estimate the probability of the violation of isolation with a given confidence level, via stochastic simulation. Values of designated delays can be generated automatically using statistical simulation provided by UPPAAL SMC.

In this example, we manually generate UPPAAL models for the distributed transaction system specification, as well as its three mutants by applying three mutant operations directly. In practice, induced from domain knowledge in concurrency faults and distributed transaction systems, selected mutation operators can be combined and applied multiple times on a transaction. For instance, the "Change lock type" operator may be applied together with the "Change lock position" operator in one or many locking operations in a transaction. This may result in a large number of mutants and requires considerable modeling effort. Therefore, tool automation is important for the application of our methodology in practice, which should assist the testers to specify the mutated specifications easily, and generate UPPAAL models automatically. We consider it feasible to automate the generation of models by a tool, thanks to the modularization of our modeling framework. The tool should also automate the extraction of clock constraints from the diagnostic traces, as well as the resolution of the constraints with Z3, which is also possible. Tool support for our methodology is considered as our future work.

## 5   Related Work

Testing for concurrency design faults in database systems, and in software systems in general, has attracted considerable attention in recent years. Much of the effort has been dedicated in detecting the interleavings that could lead to consistency violations, and executing such interleavings in a controlled way. Deng et al. [11] have proposed techniques for testing isolation violations of concurrent transactions in database systems. They propose to use dataflow analysis techniques to identify the schedules, which are ordered operations, that can lead to violations. These schedules are then executed as test cases by the target database system. The delays between operations are neglected in this work. In our work, on the contrary, we generate not only the schedules, but also the delays between the operations, which are an important factor for isolation in a distributed transaction system. We also propose to use mutation testing to find an effective test suite. Park et al. have proposed the CTrigger method for testing atomicity violation bugs [24]. In their work, unserializable interleavings that lead to concurrency bugs are identified by a set of profiling runs of the target program. Such interleavings are ranked by their probabilities of occurrence, used as a selection metric for pruning the test suite. Similar to CTrigger, the CHESS tool proposed by Musuvathi et al. [22] also identify race conditions by a small number of runs. In the race-directed random testing (RACEFUZZER) framework proposed by Sen [26], the author has applied dynamic data race detection algorithms [23] to compute the interleavings with potential data races, and used a scheduler to execute and evaluate these interleavings at run time. Blum and Gibson [4] have proposed a stateless model checking framework called QUICKSAND to examine the interleavings at runtime. Contrary to these work, our framework proposes the identification and selection of delays, which is a common issue for testing distributed system, that can lead to unwanted interleavings. Our methodology is based on abstract models of the system, which can be automatically processed by existing model checking tools.

Mutation testing has been recognized as a promising technique for pruning test cases for concurrent systems. Deniz et al. [12] have proposed a mutation library for Multicore Communication API (MCAPI), targeting multicore embedded systems. Mutation operators are introduced for concurrent communication messages. Gligoric et al. [14] have created mutants for multithreaded code in their MutMut tool. Mutation operators have been proposed for various design and implementation languages, such as SystemC [25], C/C++ [18] and JAVA [5]. Our work shares the same objective and concepts of mutation testing with these mentioned work, and gets inspired by the existing classification of concurrency control errors. However, as we focus on the mutation at the model level, our mutation operators are more abstract, rather than concrete operations in specific programming languages as in most of the existing work.

# 6    Conclusions and Future Work

In this paper, we proposed a model-based testing methodology for designing test cases for concurrency control faults in distributed transaction systems. The test inputs are delays between distributed operations, while the outputs are the occurrence of isolation violations, which are consequences of CC faults. We model the transaction system, as well as the isolation violations, in UPPAAL TA. We create a set of mutated models that model the common CC faults, based on which we generate test cases via reachability analysis. A minimal set of test cases that can kill most mutants is generated, which forms the effective test suite.

One of our future work is to develop tool automation for our methodology, including automated mutation and model generation, and test case generation and selection. We also consider to investigate the application of statistical model checking, in order to improve the scalability and deal with probabilistic behaviors of distributed systems. The extension of the methodology for other types of concurrency bugs, such as deadlock, and other properties of distributed transactions, such as atomicity, is another interesting direction.

**Acknowledgment.** The Swedish Research Council (VR) is gratefully acknowledged for supporting this research by the project "Adequacy-based Testing of Extra-Functional Properties of Embedded Systems".

# References

1. Adya, A., Liskov, B., O'Neil, P.: Generalized isolation level definitions. In: Proceedings of the 16th ICDE, pp. 67–78 (2000)
2. Alur, R., Dill, D.L.: A theory of timed automata. Theor. Comput. Sci. **126**(2), 183–235 (1994)
3. Bernstein, P.A., Goodman, N.: Concurrency control in distributed database systems. ACM Comput. Surv. (CSUR) **13**(2), 185–221 (1981)
4. Blum, B., Gibson, G.: Stateless model checking with data-race preemption points. In: Proceedings of the 2016 ACM SIGPLAN International Conference on Object-Oriented Programming, Systems, Languages, and Applications, pp. 477–493. ACM (2016)
5. Bradbury, J.S., Cordy, J.R., Dingel, J.: Mutation operators for concurrent Java (J2SE 5.0). In: Second Workshop on Mutation Analysis, p. 11. IEEE (2006)
6. Cai, S., Gallina, B., Nyström, D., Seceleanu, C.: A formal approach for flexible modeling and analysis of transaction timeliness and isolation. In: Proceedings of the 24th International Conference on Real-Time Networks and Systems, pp. 3–12. ACM (2016)
7. Cassez, F., Larsen, K.: The impressive power of stopwatches. In: Palamidessi, C. (ed.) CONCUR 2000. LNCS, vol. 1877, pp. 138–152. Springer, Heidelberg (2000). https://doi.org/10.1007/3-540-44618-4_12
8. Clarke, E.M., Emerson, E.A., Sistla, A.P.: Automatic verification of finite-state concurrent systems using temporal logic specifications. ACM Trans. Program. Lang. Syst. (TOPLAS) **8**(2), 244–263 (1986)
9. David, A., Larsen, K.G., Legay, A., Mikučionis, M., Poulsen, D.B.: Uppaal SMC tutorial. Int. J. Softw. Tools Technol. Transf. **17**(4), 397–415 (2015)
10. De Moura, L., Bjørner, N.: Z3: an efficient SMT solver. In: Ramakrishnan, C.R., Rehof, J. (eds.) TACAS 2008. LNCS, vol. 4963, pp. 337–340. Springer, Heidelberg (2008). https://doi.org/10.1007/978-3-540-78800-3_24
11. Deng, Y., Frankl, P., Chen, Z.: Testing database transaction concurrency. In: 18th IEEE International Conference on Automated Software Engineering, Proceedings, pp. 184–193. IEEE (2003)
12. Deniz, E., Sen, A., Holt, J.: Verification coverage of embedded multicore applications. In: Design, Automation & Test in Europe Conference & Exhibition (DATE), pp. 252–255. IEEE (2012)
13. Fu, H., Wang, Z., Chen, X., Fan, X.: A systematic survey on automated concurrency bug detection, exposing, avoidance, and fixing techniques. Softw. Qual. J. **26**, 1–35 (2017)
14. Gligoric, M., Jagannath, V., Marinov, D.: MuTMuT: efficient exploration for mutation testing of multithreaded code. In: 2010 Third International Conference on Software Testing, Verification and Validation (ICST), pp. 55–64. IEEE (2010)
15. Hessel, A., Larsen, K.G., Mikucionis, M., Nielsen, B., Pettersson, P., Skou, A.: Testing real-time systems using UPPAAL. In: Hierons, R.M., Bowen, J.P., Harman, M. (eds.) Formal Methods and Testing. LNCS, vol. 4949, pp. 77–117. Springer, Heidelberg (2008). https://doi.org/10.1007/978-3-540-78917-8_3

16. Jia, Y., Harman, M.: An analysis and survey of the development of mutation testing. IEEE Trans. Softw. Eng. **37**(5), 649–678 (2011)
17. Koyachi, N., Sarata, S.: Unmanned loading operation by autonomous wheel loader. In: ICCAS-SICE, 2009, pp. 2221–2225. IEEE (2009)
18. Kusano, M., Wang, C.: CCmutator: a mutation generator for concurrency constructs in multithreaded C/C++ applications. In: Proceedings of the 28th IEEE/ACM International Conference on Automated Software Engineering, pp. 722–725. IEEE Press (2013)
19. Larsen, K.G., Pettersson, P., Wang, Y.: Uppaal in a nutshell. Int. J. Softw. Tools Technol. Transf. (STTT) **1**(1), 134–152 (1997)
20. Lu, S., Park, S., Seo, E., Zhou, Y.: Learning from mistakes: a comprehensive study on real world concurrency bug characteristics. ACM Sigplan Not. **43**, 329–339 (2008)
21. Marinescu, R., Seceleanu, C., Le Guen, H., Pettersson, P.: A research overview of tool-supported model-based testing of requirements-based designs. Adv. Comput. **98**, 89–140 (2015)
22. Musuvathi, M., Qadeer, S., Ball, T., Basler, G., Nainar, P.A., Neamtiu, I.: Finding and reproducing heisenbugs in concurrent programs. In: OSDI, vol. 8, pp. 267–280 (2008)
23. O'Callahan, R., Choi, J.D.: Hybrid dynamic data race detection. ACM Sigplan Not. **38**, 167–178 (2003)
24. Park, S., Lu, S., Zhou, Y.: CTrigger: exposing atomicity violation bugs from their hiding places. In: ACM SIGARCH Computer Architecture News, vol. 37, pp. 25–36. ACM (2009)
25. Sen, A., Abadir, M.S.: Coverage metrics for verification of concurrent SystemC designs using mutation testing. In: 2010 IEEE International High Level Design Validation and Test Workshop (HLDVT), pp. 75–81. IEEE (2010)
26. Sen, K.: Race directed random testing of concurrent programs. ACM SIGPLAN Not. **43**(6), 11–21 (2008)
27. Utting, M., Pretschner, A., Legeard, B.: A taxonomy of model-based testing approaches. Softw. Test. Verif. Reliab. **22**(5), 297–312 (2012)

# Towards Automated Testing of the Internet of Things: Results Obtained with the TESTAR Tool

Mirella Martínez[2], Anna I. Esparcia-Alcázar[2], Tanja E. J. Vos[1,2(✉)],
Pekka Aho[1], and Joan Fons i Cors[2]

[1] Open University, Heerlen, The Netherlands
{tanja.vos,pekka.aho}@ou.nl
[2] Universidad Politecnica de Valencia, Valencia, Spain
{mmartinez,aesparcia,tvos,jjfons}@pros.upv.es
http://www.testar.org

**Abstract.** As the Internet of Things (IoT) becomes a reality, the need of ensuring the security and reliability of massively interconnected devices becomes a pressing necessity. A means of satisfying this need would be automated testing of IoT devices; however, this presents many difficulties, such as the lack of standards, multitude of manufacturers, restricted capabilities (such as power), etc.

In this work we present the first results on using TESTAR tool for automating IoT testing of smart home devices. TESTAR is a tool for automated testing at the Graphical User Interface (GUI) level of an application. The tool uses the Accessibility API the obtain information about the GUI and derive actions that can be executed in test sequences. Many IoT systems use the REST API to access the resources that compose the system. Consequently, this paper looks into IoT system testing as a natural field for extending the TESTAR philosophy from GUI (Accesibility) to IoT (REST) APIs.

The results show the potential of TESTAR in this new environment.

**Keywords:** Automated testing · Internet of Things · IoT

## 1 Introduction

The number of devices connected to the Internet has experienced a tremendous growth in the recent past and it is expected to keep growing. Gartner [15] forecasts that this number will reach 26 thousand million by 2020. We are already being witnesses of this, as connected vehicles, homes, cities and health monitors have made their appearance in the past few years [6].

The popularity of the Internet of Things (IoT) stems from the fact that it has the potential to change the way we work and live. However, its uptake may be hindered by the cost of devices, as consumers see them as a non-essential expense [4]. At the same time, it is necessary to ensure the reliability of the

© Springer Nature Switzerland AG 2018
T. Margaria and B. Steffen (Eds.): ISoLA 2018, LNCS 11246, pp. 375–385, 2018.
https://doi.org/10.1007/978-3-030-03424-5_25

devices connected as a malfunction could have a very negative impact, even endangering lives.

Automated testing is already an important part of the software development cycle, but it becomes crucial in ensuring security and reliability of IoT devices, as well as reducing development costs. However, testing the IoT presents many challenges [8] stemming from the distributed functionalities and services, resource restrictions (such as limitations in memory, processing power, bandwidth and battery life), and the performance of the network communications.

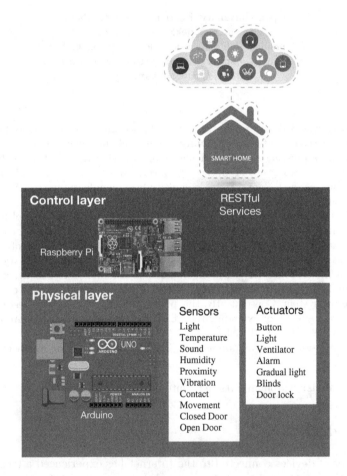

**Fig. 1.** Smart home architecture

In this paper we present the first results obtained when applying the TESTAR[1] tool [16] for automated testing of various IoT devices, in the context of a smart home. TESTAR has already been applied successfully to automate

---

[1] www.testar.org.

software testing at the graphical user interface (GUI) level in various organisations [1,3,10,12,16]. This paper will present the results of its application to an IoT system as a natural field for extending the TESTAR philosophy from GUI (Accesibility) to IoT (REST) APIs.

The rest of the paper is structured as follows. Section 2 summarises the challenges and existing work carried out in IoT testing. In Sect. 4 we describe the TESTAR tool and the modifications that were necessary in order to adapt it to support IoT testing. Section 6 describes the smart home case study, the procedure carried out for experimentation and the results obtained. Finally, in Sect. 7 we provide conclusions and outline areas for future work.

## 2   IoT Systems and Testing

Although different definitions for the term IoT can be found, they all have in common the fact that IoT tries to integrate the physical world with the virtual world of the Internet. The physical objects that you can interact with are the so-called "Things" of the IoT, or as defined in [9], the entities of interest. In order to interact with these physical objects, we need devices that can be either attached or embedded into the entities (constituting the so-called intelligent things), or installed into the environment to be monitored. Among these devices we find, for example, RFID readers, sensors, actuators, embedded computers and even mobile devices. These devices usually host resources that provide a link to the entities of interest and, for example, provide information about things (including performance capabilities).

Embedded systems have been around for a long time. However, traditionally these systems were self-contained and could work in isolation. As the IoT becomes popular, the need for connected objects "conversing" with each other to properly function is changing the considerations that need to be taken into account. As stated in [14], developers must consider ways to streamline device-to-device (D2D) and device-to-server (D2S) communication, and take into account the human interaction resulting of our everyday objects being connected to the Internet.

Therefore, testing IoT devices shares the problems encountered when testing both embedded and distributed systems. Moreover, the heterogeneity and the large scale of objects [17] increase the number of challenges when trying to ensure their security and reliability.

According to OWASP IoT Top Ten (www.owasp.org), insecure cloud interfaces need to be considered in order to greatly improve the security of any IoT product. This involves the assessment of API and cloud-based web interfaces. Testing an API requires the use of software to send calls and process the response given by the system. An overview of API testing can be found in [7,13]. In this work, we present a different approach based on automated scriptless testing. Through our approach, given a valid specification of the System Under Test (SUT), the calls made to interact with it will be automatically derived. Thereby unattended testing will be enabled.

# 3   The Smart Home

The smart home we test in this paper has a series of physical devices (things) offered on an IoT [5] platform through a set of RESTful [11] services. An overview of the architecture is illustrated in Fig. 1. The IoT platform has a microcontroller (from Arduino) to which the different electronic devices that offer capacities to perceive external situations and to act on the physical world are connected. The microcontroller is also connected to a reduced low-cost computer (Raspberry Pi) that functions as a connection gateway for the physical devices and hosts the IoT accessibility platform based on RESTful services. These services can be consumed by various customers, including laptops and smartphones, and anything else that is part of the IoT and wants to communicate with the resources available in the smart home.

The smart home tested in this paper, being a system for academic purposes [5], has a basic security mechanism through which only users with valid credentials can modify the status of resources. There are 17 available resources (10 sensors and 7 actuators), and each one of them has its own identifier (ID) and specific functionalities that determine the ways it can be interacted with. The resources and their corresponding functionalities available in the smart home and the interactions that they accept are showed in Table 1.

**Table 1.** Resources of the smart home with their interactions and functionalities

| Resources | Functionality | Interactions |
|---|---|---|
| Light sensor, Temperature sensor Sound sensor, Humidity sensor Proximity sensor | Numeric | set, read |
| Vibration sensor, Contact sensor Movement sensor, Closed door sensor Door lock, Push button Fan, Light, Alarm | Bistate | on, off toggle, read pulseOn, pulseOff |
| Blinds | Movement | open, close stop, stepOpen stepClose, movePosition moveNamePosition, up down, stepUp stepDown, read |
| Gradual light | Dimmer | set%, set0x setAng, read |

The REST API [11] that allows us to access the resources of the Smart Home, explicitly and consistently use HTTP methods. The following association is established between create, read, update and delete (CRUD) and the corresponding HTTP methods:

- POST is used to create a resource on the server
- GET allows you to obtain an available resource

– PUT is used to carry out updates of a resource
– DELETE allows you to delete an available resource

RESTful resources perform stateless communications. An application or client of a REST web service includes, between the header and the body of the HTTP request, all the necessary data to generate a response, so that each request works in isolation. This allows to improve the performance of the service and, since there is no need to synchronize session data with external applications, the design and implementation of server-side components is simpler. RESTful services are resource oriented and each has a uniform resource identifier (URI). The different URIs serve both as the name and address of a resource. In addition, they must be simple, predictable and easy to understand in a way that favors the fact that developers can predict what is being targeted and even derive related resources. The coding format of the data exchanged between an application and the service must be standard such as the extensible markup language (XML) or JavaScript Object Notation (JSON).

Since the transfer protocol is HTTP, the error codes and exceptions of HTTP must be used, we have listed them below in Table 2.

**Table 2.** HTTP response codes

| CODE | Description |
| --- | --- |
| 1xx | Informative response |
| 2xx | Correct request |
| 3xx | Redirections |
| 4xx | Client errors |
| 5xx | Server errors |

# 4  The TESTAR tool

TESTAR is a tool for automated testing at the Graphical User Interface (GUI) level [2]. We will first show the philosophy of this tool to make clear how it has been adapted to test the RESTful implementation of the Smart Home. To explain the high level logical flow of TESTAR tool, it performs the following steps (also shown in Fig. 2) to test a given System Under Test (SUT) at the GUI level:

1. Start the SUT;
2. Obtain the current *State* (when testing GUIs the *State* is represented by a widget tree that is obtained through the Operating System's Accessibility API, which has the capability to detect and expose a GUI's widgets, and their corresponding properties, such as: display position, widget size, ancestor widgets, etc.);
3. Derive a set of available actions that a user could execute in a specific state of the SUT (for example: clicks, text inputs, mouse gestures);

4. Select one of the available actions (randomly or using some search-based or other type of optimization criteria);
5. Execute the selected action;
6. Apply the available online state oracles to check (in)validness of the new GUI state. If a fault is found, stop the SUT (7) and save a re-playable sequence of the test that found the fault. If not, keep on testing if more actions are desired within the test sequence.

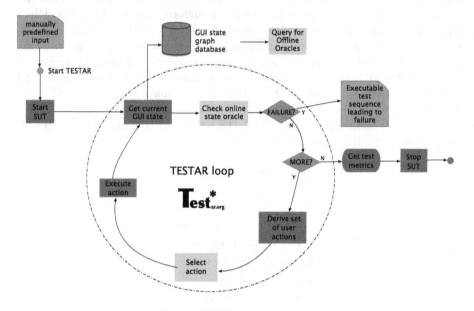

**Fig. 2.** TESTAR testing flow

The default behaviour of TESTAR includes random selection of actions and implicit oracles for the detection of the violation of general-purpose system requirements:

- the SUT should not crash,
- the SUT should not find itself in an unresponsive state (freeze), and
- the UI state should not contain any widget with suspicious titles like *error*, *problem*, *exception*, etc. The suspicious titles can be configured in TESTAR through its settings Dialog and the Suspicious titles functionality.

During testing, TESTAR stores all the information about the visited states in a Graph database. Consequently, after testing the tester can define offline oracles that query the database foe failure patterns.

TESTAR adopts the hypothesis that the majority of GUIs are conceptually very similar. The only thing that varies is the underlying technology and the look and feel. But if sufficient *State* information is available, such as: the types, positions and properties of all widgets on the screen, then testing an iPhone App is not much different from testing a Windows desktop application or a website.

TESTAR's abstraction layer and the extensible plugin architecture (see Fig. 3) makes it highly technology agnostic. The plugins deal with the process of fetching the state information and executing actions for different platforms. The abstraction layer has a uniform interface that allows to access the UI state information in a standardised way. It allows to simulate end user input in the form of clicks, drag and drop operations, swipes, pinches, audio input, etc, in order to operate the UI. The abstraction layer abstracts from different technologies, shields other components from technological details and allows testers to concentrate on strategic parts of sequence and test suite generation.

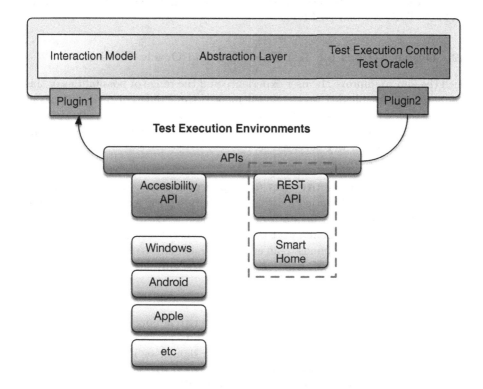

**Fig. 3.** Abstraction layer and the extensible plugin architecture of TESTAR

To implement the necessary plugins and obtain the *State* information, TESTAR needs to know which resources are available in order to interact with them. For testing at the GUI level, the Accessibility API of the Operating System provides enough information. However, when switching to IoT systems, the Accessibility API is no longer useful. In this case, we were able to use the REST API that accesses the resources in the Smart Home. Consequently, we had to develop the plugins that contained the specification how to test the interaction with the resources of a smart home to give TESTAR the information it needs for action selection, text execution and test oracles. To illustrate the plugin architecture and the work done in this paper, the new components we implemented for TESTAR are highlighted with the dotted square in Fig. 3.

## 5    TESTAR for IoT

### 5.1    Actions

TESTAR for IoT is able to execute the four HTTP methods, discussed in Sect. 1, that are associated with CRUD operations. This means, plugin1 (from Fig. 3) consist of an Action interface for TESTAR that is implemented by Java classes GET, PUT, POST and DELETE.

### 5.2    Derive Actions for Test Execution and Oracle Verdicts

With the aim to improve the user experience and the range of possibilities of this new approach, for plugin2 we have implemented three different modes of execution together with their respective oracles (in the form of regular expressions) for each one of them. These modes have been designed taking into account the intrinsic behaviour of web services.

**Positive Tests.** For positive tests (or happy path tests), all feasible actions will be derived. An authentication token will be provided when this is required for correct execution. The default oracle for these tests are based on TESTAR Suspicious Titles functionality, that checks if the received response has a HTTP response code that corresponds to an error (4xx and 5xx, as explained in Sect. 3). If there is a match, TESTAR will consider that the current sequence found is a failure.

**Negative Tests.** For negative tests, we will derive actions that try to update resources (PUT's from the REST API) in an invalid way. By doing so, we are able to check whether invalid actions will cause any danger or incorrect behaviour. For example, in a Smart House you are not supposed to open the window when the air-conditioning is on. There is a field in the Dialog of TESTAR to indicate the expected response when those kind of actions occurred. If the server response does not matches the expected expression (expected HTTP error code), TESTAR will consider that the current sequence found a failure.

**Unauthorized Tests.** Unauthorized Tests contain actions that need authentication parameters to be correctly executed. However, they will be executed without passing the required authentication token. This allows us to check whether at some point it is possible to interact with the API without the required identification. As in the Negative Tests mode, there is a field in the Dialog of TESTAR to specify the expected response when those kind of actions are executed. If the server response does not match the given expression (expected HTTP error code), TESTAR will consider that the current sequence found a failure.

# 6    Experiments and Results

## 6.1    Procedure

After having the plugins for the smart home developed, TESTAR had to be configured according to the needs of the System Under Test (SUT). First of all, we indicated which actions require authentication parameters. For the smart home, only the PUT method needs authentication so we indicated a valid token in order to give TESTAR the required credentials to execute those PUT actions.

After that, we filled the simple oracles that came with TESTAR taking into account the following information provided by domain experts:

- When executing actions without the required token, the appropriate response of the server must be 401 Unauthorized.
- For those actions derived in the Negative Tests mode we can expect either 400 Bad Request or 405 Method Not Allowed.
- For all other cases, we used the oracle that comes by default for the Positive Tests mode.

Since the Smart Home does not allow Delete nor Options actions, we needed to modify the protocol of TESTAR in order to let it know that we expect a 405 Method not Allowed as the response for those kind of actions. Another approach will be to tell the tool that it should not derive those actions, but we decided to test them in order to know if something unexpected happens when trying to execute them.

After all the configuration parameters were established, we proceeded to run TESTAR using the three different testing modes.

## 6.2    Results

After our firsts runs we already discovered a fault in which when trying to interact with the Gradual Light with a feasible action, the server response was Method Not Allowed instead of indicating that the resource had been success-fully updated. This error appeared each time a run was executed and the selected action implied the Gradual Light Resource. After communicating this to the team in charge of implementing the smart home, they discovered that an error was made when declaring the supposed functionality for that resource. After-wards, that fault was correctly solved.

Once more test were executed, we discovered a different kind of fault in which some resources were no longer available and a 404 Not Found was received when trying to interact with them.

Moreover, we noticed that after executing several actions and receiving a 404 error when trying to access a resource that was not available, the server stopped responding and a time out fault was found by TESTAR. However, the server seemed to establish itself when some time passed.

On the other hand, we noticed that in the Negative Tests mode, when trying to update the Gradual Light (which is a dimmer) with a toggle (an interaction characteristic of bistate resources), the given response was not as expected. Instead of a Method Not Allowed or a Bad Request Message we received an Internal Server Error.

Finally, we tried the Unauthorized Tests mode with two different setups: 5 sequences of 100 actions and 5 sequences of 300 actions. Therefore, a total of 2000 actions without the required authorization parameters were executed and the smart home behaved as expected through all of them.

## 7   Conclusions and Further Work

Testing IoT is an important an challenging task. In this work, we have presented the first approach of TESTAR for testing IoT devices. The tool has proved to be successful testing the communication with the resources provided by a smart home through a REST API. Once the plugin that specifies what kind of actions can be executed for a determine SUT was implemented, TESTAR offered an automated way of generating and executing tests.

To summarize the results, we have found a total of 4 reproducible faults among the firsts executions of the tool. One of them (The Gradual Light not accepting feasible actions) has already been successfully corrected after being communicated to the team in charge of the smart home. Meanwhile the other three will need further investigation.

Future work will involve different IoT devices accessed through a REST API in order to ensure that the same procedure can be applied. Moreover, we will try to extend TESTAR in order to support other communication protocols beyond REST API.

**Acknowledgement.** The authors would like to thank Vicente Pelechano, Urko Rueda and Francisco Almenar for their invaluable help that has made this work possible. This work was partly funded by the ITEA3 TESTOMAT project (16032).

## References

1. Bauersfeld, S., de Rojas, A., Vos, T.E.J.: Evaluating rogue user testing in industry: an experience report. In: IEEE Eighth International Conference on Research Challenges in Information Science (RCIS), pp. 1–10, May 2014
2. Bauersfeld, S., Vos, T.: A reinforcement learning approach to automated GUI robustness testing. In: Fast Abstracts of the 4th Symposium on Search-Based Software Engineering (SSBSE 2012), pp. 7–12. IEEE (2012)

3. Bauersfeld, S., Vos, T.E.J., Condori-Fernández, N., Bagnato, A., Brosse, E.: Evaluating the TESTAR tool in an industrial case study. In: ACM-IEEE International Symposium on Empirical Software Engineering and Measurement, ESEM 2014, Torino, Italy, 18–19 September 2014, p. 4 (2014)
4. Business. The Internet of Things: where the smart is. Economist **419**(8993), 52–53 (2016)
5. Cetina, C., Giner, P., Fons, J., Pelechano, V.: Using feature models for developing self-configuring smart homes. In: Fifth International Conference on Autonomic and Autonomous Systems, pp. 179–188 (2009)
6. Frizell, S.: The smarter home. Special report. Time Mag. **184**(1) (2014)
7. Grnbk, I.: Architecture for the internet of things (IoT): API and interconnect. In: Second International Conference on Sensor Technologies and Applications (SENSORCOMM 2008), pp. 802–807, August 2008
8. Hagar, J.: Experience report: a guide through the challenges and risks of testing the IoT. LogiGEAR Mag. **VII**(3) (2014)
9. Haller, S., Karnouskos, S., Schroth, C.: The Internet of Things in an enterprise context. In: Domingue, J., Fensel, D., Traverso, P. (eds.) FIS 2008. LNCS, vol. 5468, pp. 14–28. Springer, Heidelberg (2009). https://doi.org/10.1007/978-3-642-00985-3_2
10. Almenar, F., Esparcia-Alcázar, A.I., Martínez, M., Rueda, U.: Automated testing of web applications with TESTAR. In: Sarro, F., Deb, K. (eds.) SSBSE 2016. LNCS, vol. 9962, pp. 218–223. Springer, Cham (2016). https://doi.org/10.1007/978-3-319-47106-8_15
11. Richardson, L., Ruby, S.: RESTful Web Services (2008)
12. Rueda, U., Vos, T.E.J., Almenar, F., Martínez, M.O., Esparcia-Alcázar, A.I.: TESTAR: from academic prototype towards an industry-ready tool for automated testing at the user interface level. In: Canos, J.H., Gonzalez Harbour, M. (eds.) Actas de las XX Jornadas de Ingeniería del Software y Bases de Datos (JISBD 2015), pp. 236–245 (2015)
13. Tnjes, R., Reetz, E.S., Moessner, K., Barnaghi, P.M.: A test-driven approach for life cycle management of internet of things enabled services. In: Future Network Mobile Summit (FutureNetw 2012), pp. 1–8 (2012)
14. van der Mersch, V.: Automated testing for the Internet of Things. Nordic APIs Blog, May 2016
15. van der Meulen, R.: Gartner says 6.4 billion connected "things" will be in use in 2016, up 30 percent from 2015. Press release, November 2015
16. Vos, T.E.J., Kruse, P.M., Condori-Fernández, N., Bauersfeld, S., Wegener, J.: TESTAR: tool support for test automation at the user interface level. IJISMD **6**(3), 46–83 (2015)
17. Zhang, Z.K., Cho, M.C.Y., Wang, C.W., Hsu, C.W., Chen, C.K., Shieh, S.: IoT security: ongoing challenges and research opportunities. In: IEEE 7th International Conference on Service-Oriented Computing and Applications, pp. 230–234, November 2014

# Quantitative Safety Analysis
# of a Coordinated Emergency Brake
# Protocol for Vehicle Platoons

Carl Bergenhem[1], Karl Meinke[2(✉)], and Fabian Ström[2]

[1] Qamcom Research and Technology AB, Falkenbergsg. 3,
41285 Gothenburg, Sweden
[2] School of Electrical Engineering and Computer Science,
KTH Royal Institute of Technology, 100 44 Stockholm, Sweden
karlm@kth.se

**Abstract.** In this paper, we present a general methodology to estimate safety related parameter values of cooperative cyber-physical system-of-systems. As a case study, we consider a vehicle platoon model equipped with a novel distributed protocol for coordinated emergency braking. The estimation methodology is based on learning-based testing; which is an approach to automated requirements testing that combines machine learning with model checking.

Our methodology takes into account vehicle dynamics, control algorithm design, inter-vehicle communication protocols and environmental factors such as message packet loss rates. Empirical measurements from road testing of vehicle-to-vehicle communication in a platoon are modeled and used in our case study. We demonstrate that the minimum global time headway for our platoon model equipped with the CEBP function scales well with respect to platoon size.

**Keywords:** Vehicle platoon · Learning-based testing · Co-CPS
Safety boundaries · Quantitative analysis · Coordinated braking

## 1 Introduction

A vehicle platoon (or road train) is a collection of vehicles that coordinate and collaborate to reach goals such as traveling to a certain destination, while also improving e.g. safety, fuel economy and driver comfort. One challenge for platoon design is coordination of a platoon-wide emergency brake by means of a distributed protocol (CEBP). The overall goal is to avoid collisions within the platoon while still performing braking as efficiently (i.e. with as high deceleration) as possible. To justify the deployment of a CEBP solution it is necessary to quantitatively analyse its behaviour, especially properties that impact on safety.

In this paper, we introduce a new methodology to estimate quantitative parameters related to safety properties of cooperating cyber-physical systems (Co-CPS). Our approach is based on the method of learning-based testing (LBT)

© Springer Nature Switzerland AG 2018
T. Margaria and B. Steffen (Eds.): ISoLA 2018, LNCS 11246, pp. 386–404, 2018.
https://doi.org/10.1007/978-3-030-03424-5_26

[21]. We illustrate this methodology by estimating safety related parameters of a platoon model that includes a novel CEBP algorithm. This case study is in many ways generic. It therefore supports the claim that our parameter estimation methodology could be extended to a wider variety of cyber-physical system-of-systems through the use of simulators and virtualised environment modeling. This is one goal of the EU project *Safe Cooperating Cyber-Physical Systems using Wireless Communication (SafeCOP[1])*.

In a platoon, the lead vehicle can be manually driven and the followers (one or more) follow the leader automatically; using control algorithms for longitudinal and lateral motion. The target inter-vehicle headway is small enough (e.g. <1 s) that dependable communication is required for the platoon to be safe. A platoon capable vehicle has the technologies (e.g. communication) to lead or follow in a platoon. Issues concerning positioning, e.g. accuracy and reliability of GPS and security, are out of scope here.

A platooning system can be considered to be a cooperative cyber-physical system-of-systems (Co-CPS). This is because vehicle-to-vehicle (V2V) communication is an enabler for the technology [32]. Failures in a platoon (e.g. poor V2V communication) could potentially cause physical harm. Safety analysis for Co-CPS introduces many technical challenges. Basic problems include the system size, and the existence of black-box third-party components, which can make it technically infeasible to perform a full static analysis (see e.g. the conclusions on platooning of [17]).

For this reason, learning-based testing (LBT) [21] is an interesting contribution to safety studies of Co-CPS. LBT combines promising aspects of both testing, simulation and model based analysis. By inferring black-box abstractions of a complex system, as well as using parallel simulation to accelerate learning, we can obtain approximate but accurate results with a good degree of scalability.

LBT uses machine learning to reverse engineer multi-vehicle system-of-system (SoS) models. These SoS models can then be subject to glass box analysis techniques, such as model checking, to check violation of safety requirements. Previously in [22], we have used LBT to analyse platooning systems from the perspective of *qualitative safety properties*, such as vehicle collisions. In this paper we extend the scope of LBT to *quantitative estimation of safety related parameters*. We show how to use LBT to numerically estimate an *minimum value of an SoS parameter* such that a given system safety property is not violated. This will typically be a parameter that can be tuned to optimise a specific product for some desired performance. Thus it might be overtuned in a way that can compromise safety or is inappropriate for an environment in some (possibly rare) scenario.

A pertinent example of parameter estimation arises in our platooning case study. Here inter-vehicle distance and time gaps are typically reduced to a minimum in order to save fuel. The question arises: *what is the minimum value that could be chosen for all inter-vehicle gaps such that no crashes occur due to vehicles being too close?* This minimum value is influenced by many factors, not

---

[1] See www.safecop.eu.

only in the vehicle design itself, but also by environmental factors such as V2V communication packet loss.

Our approach to quantitative parameter estimation involves performing multiple LBT sessions to efficiently refine an estimate interval. This computationally intensive analysis becomes more feasible when simulators, models and the appropriate machine learning algorithms are executed on inexpensive multi-core hardware, which is increasingly available. We define a specific method for parameter estimation using LBT. We then illustrate it by applying it to study our distributed CEBP algorithm integrated in a platoon simulator. The CEBP algorithm is an exemplar of the Co-CPS paradigm of decentralised distributed control. An optimal design for a CEBP is influenced by many factors such as pre-existing platoon control algorithms, underlying physical dynamics models, inter-vehicle communication protocols and environmental features.

Although many safety hazards impacted by CEBP could be studied, in this paper we focus on the safety hazard due to *message packet loss* arising from radio interference. We estimate the *minimum global time headway* for different platoon sizes under both perfect communication and stochastic packet loss. This is the minimum time headway between all platoon vehicles that allows collision free motion. By extending the learning time of LBT, we can improve the reliability of this estimate to any given level.

The stochastic packet loss model we use is based on empirical data from V2V communication measurement during physical road tests with a platoon. This stochastic packet loss model, a communication protocol model and a CEBP implementation are then integrated with the platoon simulator described in [22] to model communication and vehicle dynamics performance. The main emphasis of our work however is on the analysis methodology itself, and not the problem of fully accurate platoon modeling. Since we use black-box learning methods, only platoon behavior, and not architecture or code structure are inferred. Thus our LBT approach can be transferred to more complex platoon models without difficulty.

## 1.1 Related Work

A platooning system for trucks with focus on fuel efficiency is presented in [20]. A brief survey of other vehicle platooning systems is given in [3]. Cooperative adaptive cruise control (CACC) is a similar technology to platooning, but has its focus entirely on maintaining steady-state longitudinal control. Emergency braking in a platoon is also studied in [13]. Here, a dedicated communication protocol and a novel controller (including control topology), that takes into account packet losses, is investigated. Assumptions of bounded packet losses are made to be able derive bounds of headway. In [31] different CACC strategies are evaluated regarding headway using simulation. Several different parameters associated with uncertainty are considered, including packet loss. An event-triggered control scheme and communication strategy is developed for platooning in [8].

Examples of static analysis applied to platooning problems where the collision free property is studied are [7,9]. In [17] it is shown that verifying vehicle code does not scale well to the entire system-of-systems, and a mixed top-down and bottom up verification strategy are applied.

Some (but not all) of the problems encountered in message packet loss in Sect. 6 are related to compression waves within platoon simulations. Hence they are somewhat related to the well-known phenomenon of string instability. The effects of string stability and a networked control system have been studied in [25]. Here an analytical approach of string stability is presented for a CACC application; where each vehicle is controlled by its predecessor. Quantitative results are given through an approach based on an analytical method. Communication deficiencies are described in terms of a Maximum Allowable Transmission Interval and Maximum Allowable Delay, rather than as a stochastic model of packet loss. Safety is interpreted as string stability, rather than the crash condition of zero distance between vehicles.

In [30] an analytical framework is presented which links the wireless channel characteristics with the probability of crash in a two vehicle emergency-brake scenario. The maximum tolerable delay, between the beginning of the emergency braking by the preceding vehicle and the moment the following vehicle starts braking, is found. The developed CPS analysis approach is applied to demonstrate how V2V communication packet losses and communication delays impacts safe inter-vehicular distance for specified kinematic parameters of vehicles movements.

## 1.2   Organisation of the Paper

The rest of the paper is organised as follows. Section 2 presents measurement of V2V communication in a platoon of trucks during road tests, providing the basis of our communication model. Section 3 presents our novel CEBP algorithm. Section 4 presents a methodology for quantitative safety analysis using learning-based testing. Section 5 presents the platoon simulator used for safety analysis of our CEBP algorithm. Section 6 presents the results of our quantitative analysis of the minimum global time headway under conditions of packet loss. Finally, conclusions and future work are given.

# 2   Road Testing

In this section we describe details and results of a measurement campaign[2] within the Relcommh project [18] to establish packet loss levels in different platoon driving scenarios. These measurements of V2V communication were done using a platoon of four trucks, (c.f. Fig. 1).

The motivation for this section is twofold. On the one hand, we wish to show in Sect. 6 how the reliability of quantitative safety analysis results for SoS is influenced by the accuracy of environmental modeling. On the other hand, there

---

[2] The measurements were done while the first author was employed at RISE – The Swedish Research Institute (previously SP – Technical Research Institute of Sweden).

is a need in the literature to increase understanding of the environment that a platoon is designed for. In the light of results of this section, we can point out some unrealistic assumptions made in the literature. Our measured results suggest that the low packet error rate used in [31] and assumption of no packet loss in [8] are overly optimistic.

In our measurement campaign, at each periodic message broadcast (10 Hz) from the leader truck, the perceived *packet error rate* (PER) at each of the following vehicles was measured. In Table 1, the PER is presented for three different scenarios. Messages were 500 bytes long and 5.9 GHz V2V devices according to ETSI standards [10] were used. Each truck had a left and right antenna from which it could send and receive. Therefore, two PERs are given: communication left-to-left and right-to-right. Differences between the two PERs can be motivated with differences in the immediate surrounding of either side of the vehicle. For example, on the left side of the motorway there is a metal safety barrier that separates the two traffic directions. This may impact PER. A motorway scenario and Tunnel scenarios were measured at 80 km/h vehicle speeds, with 20 m and 20–50 m inter-vehicle distance respectively. In the Parked scenario, the platoon was parked in a platoon formation with a 10 m gap between each truck. The PER between the LV and FV1 is denoted *PERbase*. First-order linear regression was used to calculate the projected average increase in PER for each vehicle hop (right most column in the table). This model was then incorporated into the platooning simulator. One result (11.14 %) could be anomalous as it falls outside the expected trend of increasing PER as the distance between communicating vehicles (LV to FV*i*) increases.

**Table 1.** Packet error rates (Upper: left-left, Lower: right-right)

|  | LV to FV1 | LV to FV2 | LV to FV3 | Average increase |
|---|---|---|---|---|
| Motorway | 3.67% | 18.03% | 40.91% | 18.62% |
|  | 2.72% | 5.93% | 22.13% | 9.70% |
| Motorway tunnel | 6.39% | 5.85% | 11.16% | 2.39% |
|  | 6.82% | 6.74% | 11.47% | 2.32% |
| Parked | 0.57% | 5.89% | 22.13% | 10.78% |
|  | 2.39% | 14.05% | 11.14% | 4.37% |

In all measured scenarios there were instances of consecutive packet loss (CPL). For the E4 motorway (left to left antenna) scenario the following was found: CPL1 = 61.53 % (single lost packet), CPL2 = 36 % (two lost packets in a row), CPL3 = 1.6 %, CPL4 = 0.8 %, CPL4..k = 0.87 %. The percentages indicate the distribution of a certain CPL, when there is a packet loss. The largest CPL (longest blackout, k) was eight packets in a row. This implies that the assumed bounds on packet loss in [13] are somewhat optimistic (at most three and five consecutive packets lost are investigated).

We note that the outcome of packet loss measurements depends on several factors such as the radio equipment, antennas, placement and environment. Further details of measurements in the road tests are found in [18].

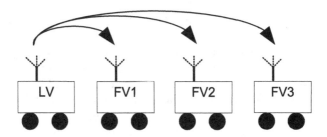

**Fig. 1.** Communication scheme in the tests. LV denotes Lead Vehicle. FV$i$ denotes Following Vehicle $i$

## 3 A Coordinated Emergency Brake Protocol

In this section, a protocol for Coordinated Emergency Brake (CEBP) is presented. The goal of the protocol is to coordinate vehicles in an emergency brake scenario to ensure safety (no crashes). An emergency brake can be initiated by any vehicle in the platoon. Here it is assumed that the platoon of $N$ vehicles is formed and no vehicles are joining or leaving. It must be ensured that the last vehicle receives the brake command and actuates first. Braking can commence at the last vehicle directly when it receives the "E-brake request" message. The braking vehicle then sends an acknowledgement (ACK) forward with an "E-brake ACK" message. Preceding vehicles can thus start to brake when the ACK from succeeding vehicles arrives. E.g. FV2 cannot brake until ACK is received from FV3 indicating that it has started to brake. This is illustrated in Fig. 2. Each vehicle also maintains a "brake-anyway"-time-out timer. When the timer expires, the vehicle will brake directly and signal this, with an "E-Brake directly" message, to the other vehicles. The value of the time-out corresponds

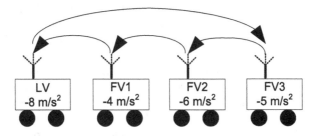

**Fig. 2.** An E-brake command from the LV. The acknowledgement then propagates back to the LV − from back to front.

to the expected latency for a returning ACK. Message sending can be done with event-triggered directed broadcast, i.e. there is a sender and an explicit receiver, but the message may be overheard by other vehicles within the platoon. In this case, a vehicle can prepare its brakes in anticipation of the ACK from succeeding vehicle.

We assume that vehicles entering the platoon cannot be sorted according to deceleration capability. Instead, other sorting goals may have priority; such as destination or aerodynamic performance. Not having a sorting procedure at vehicle join implies that a brake strategy, i.e. the description of how vehicles will brake in the event of an emergency brake, must be found in another way. A simple way is to limit braking of the platoon according to the vehicle with least deceleration capability, as is done in [24]. Alternatively, an algorithm could find cliques of vehicles in the platoon that will brake together with a lowest common brake capability. In Fig. 2 the actual deceleration capabilities are shown for an example platoon, e.g. $-8$ m/s$^2$ for the lead vehicle. As vehicles join the platoon, brake cliques will be formed, e.g. Clique 1 = (LV, FV1, $-4$ m/s$^2$), Clique 2 = (FV2, FV3, $-5$ m/s$^2$). The agreed deceleration of cliques increases towards the rear, implying that the last clique will brake the most. Note that this implies a voluntary reduction of deceleration capability in some vehicles. An algorithm for finding the brake strategy in the platoon is left for future work. CEBP assumes that a brake strategy has been decided and all vehicle will brake equally. The members and order of the platoon are known.

Our CEBP algorithm has been implemented and integrated into each vehicle in the platooning simulator of [22]. It has been studied using our quantitative safety analysis method described in Sect. 4 and the results are presented in Sect. 5.

### 3.1   Pseudo Code

Pseudo code for the CEBP is presented in Algorithm 1. Vehicles are indexed by $V_i$ where $i \equiv 0$ is the lead vehicle (first vehicle, also denoted LV) and $i \equiv 1..N-1$ are the following vehicles (also denoted FV, e.g. where FV1 implies $i = 1$). The last vehicle is $V_{N-1}$ (also denoted e.g. FV3 for $N = 4$). The algorithm, that is described in the pseudo-code, is executed in each vehicle in the platoon. The index $i$ is static in each vehicle, i.e. in each instance of the algorithm. This implies that each vehicle knows its identity and hence its position in the platoon. An E-brake command is assumed to come from an external system or to be manually initiated.

Some comments regarding the code in Algorithm 1 are appropriate: On line 11, directly receiving an "E-brake request" implies that $V_i$ is the last vehicle. This is because any vehicle that requests to E-brake will do so by sending to the last vehicle. On line 25, an ACK is sent by a vehicle that did "brake directly". This is because there could be preceding vehicles that are waiting for the ACK. If the ACK was not sent then the preceding vehicles can start to brake only after their time-out counters expire. On line 24 and 25 the messages are repeated e.g. until the algorithm is reset. On line 5 an alternative is possible. Instead of

---

**Algorithm 1.** CEBP - Loop in every vehicle

---

1: **if** Ego Vehicle $V_i$ wants to e-brake **then**
2:    send "E-brake request" to the last vehicle in the platoon $V_{N-1}$
3: **end if**
4: **if** "E-Brake directly" is received by Ego Vehicle $V_i$ **then**
5:    send "E-brake request" to the last vehicle in the platoon $V_{N-1}$
6: **end if**
7: **if** Ego Vehicle $V_i$ (has sent "E-brake request" command) **or** (overheard "E-brake request" or "E-brake ACK" from $V_j$) **then**
8:    prepare brake system
9:    Start Timer$_i$
10: **end if**
11: **if** "E-brake request" is received by Ego Vehicle $V_i$ from a preceding vehicle $V_j$, where j $\in\{0..i\text{-}1\}$ **then**
12:    Ego Vehicle Vi actuate e-brake strategy
13:    send "E-brake ACK" to the next preceding vehicle $V_{i-1}$
14: **end if**
15: **if** "E-brake ACK" is received by Ego Vehicle $V_i$ from next succeeding vehicle $V_{i+1}$ **then**
16:    Ego Vehicle $V_i$ actuate e-brake strategy
17:    Stop Timer$_i$
18:    **if** i > 0 **and** has not already sent an "E-brake ACK" to preceding **then**
19:       send "E-brake ACK" to the next preceding vehicle $V_{i-1}$
20:    **end if**
21: **end if**
22: **if** Timer$_i$ has expired **then**
23:    Ego Vehicle $V_i$ actuate e-brake strategy
24:    send "E-Brake directly" to succeeding vehicles $V_j$, where j$\in\{i+1..N\text{-}1\}$
25:    send "E-brake ACK" to the next preceding vehicle $V_{i-1}$
26: **end if**
27: **if** Timer$_i$ is started **then**
28:    decrease Timer$_i$
29: **end if**

---

EBR/ACK, a vehicle that receives "E-brake directly" could also do "E-brake directly".

# 4    An LBT Methodology for Quantitative Safety Analysis

In this section, we review some fundamental principles of learning-based testing (LBT). We then show how these methods can support a quantitative approach to safety analysis

## 4.1    Learning-Based Testing (LBT)

We begin by reviewing the fundamental principles of learning-based testing (LBT) as these have been implemented in our research tool LBTest. The earliest version of this tool (LBTest 1.x) has been described in [23]. The current tool architecture of LBTest 3.x is presented in Fig. 3. This is a concurrent software architecture designed to support LBT on multi-core hardware. Such hardware supports the parallel execution of machine learning queries in multiple threads, where each thread executes a copy $SUT_i$ of the *system under test* (SUT) (c.f. Fig. 3). This approach reduces both the simulation time and the learning time, as the learning algorithm itself can also be parallelized. Examples of computation time improvements by such parallelisation have been shown in [22]. By increasing the throughput of data, a larger data set becomes available for machine learning. This increases the accuracy or convergence of the final learned model and hence the reliability of quantitative parameter estimates. For analysing complex Co-CPS behaviors, we believe that concurrency is essential. Since the design of the architecture in Fig. 3 has been discussed in [22], we focus on the basic principles of LBT here.

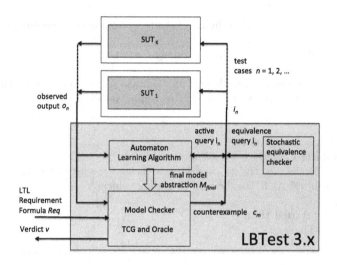

**Fig. 3.** LBTest 3.x concurrent learning architecture

LBTest uses active automaton learning aka. *regular inference* (see e.g. [14]) to generate queries about a black-box SUT. These queries are then executed on the SUT as test cases, and the SUT behaviour is observed for each test case. In an iterative and incremental process, the test cases and the SUT observations are saved and used to build up a behavioral model of the SUT in polynomial time [1]. This model is an automaton or state machine model.

For requirements testing, partial and incomplete models of the SUT can already be subjected, in the early stages of testing, to model checking against a temporal logic requirement specification. Thus, even before the learning process is complete, errors can be found in the SUT. This fact is important for large and complex SUTs such as Co-CPS, where it might not be possible to learn a complete model in any reasonable timescale, even with the use of multi-core technology. In LBTest, propositional linear temporal logic[3] (PLTL) is used as the requirements modeling language. This particular logic has the advantage that test cases can easily be extracted from the model checker, and used to filter out false negatives as we will show. LBTest makes use of a loosely integrated symbolic checker NuSMV [6]. We are also developing a more tightly integrated explicit state model checker for efficiency reasons. These two processes of learning and model checking may be interleaved, an idea first suggested in [26]. Then they incrementally build up a sequence $M_1, M_2, ...$ of models of the SUT, while generating and executing requirements test cases on each model $M_i$. However, for large and complex Co-CPS this interleaved approach is too inefficient, and model checking is then only performed on the final model. In Sect. 6 we have used model checking on the final model only. Thus no *bias* to the model from model checking and counterexample construction can exist.

To separate true negatives (genuine SUT errors) from false negatives (artifacts of an incompletely learned model) it is necessary to validate each counter-example to a requirement generated by the model checker. For this we can: (i) extract a test case representing the counter-example[4], (ii) execute it on the SUT, (iii) apply an equality test that compares the observed SUT behavior with the predicted bad behavior from the model, and (iv) automatically generate the test verdict (**pass, fail**) from step (iii).

The *soundness* of learning-based testing as an analysis method relies on the soundness of the underlying model checker, and the soundness of equality testing. The *completeness* of LBT as an analysis method relies on the completeness of the underlying model checker, as well as convergence results about the learning algorithms which are used (see [14]). However, within practical case studies of large complex systems it may not be possible for learning to be completed in any reasonable time frame (see e.g. [11]). This problem is significant for Co-CPS. Therefore, development of LBTest has focused on incremental learning algorithms that can generate incomplete approximating models of the SUT in small increments.

To measure the *test coverage* achieved by learning-based testing we currently use a *probably exactly correct* (PEC) model of learning convergence as follows. In Fig. 3, a stochastic equivalence checker is shown. This checker empirically estimates the behavioral accuracy of the final learned model $M_{final}$ for replicating the behavior of the SUT on a randomly chosen set of input sequences. For this, the input sequences are executed both on the SUT and the model. We then measure the percentage of behaviorally identical output sequences generated by both. This learning convergence model is more restrictive than the *probably approximately correct* (PAC) convergence model of [29]. There are two motivations for

---

[3] Recall that propositional LTL extends basic propositional logic with the temporal modalities $G(\phi)$ (always $\phi$), $F(\phi)$ (sometime $\phi$) and $X(\phi)$ (next $\phi$). Other derived operators and past operators may also be included. See e.g. [12] for details.

[4] Infinite counter-examples to LTL liveness formulas are truncated around the loop, and the weaker test verdict **warning** may be issued.

this: (i) our automaton learning framework does not readily support notions of approximate equivalence between data values, and (ii) for software safety analysis exact equality of data values (inputs or outputs) is often a pre-requisite to infer failed test cases.

## 4.2   Quantitative Parameter Estimation

A qualitative safety analysis of platooning using LBT was given in [22]. Here we extend this previous approach to quantitative parameter estimation. We are interested to estimate the minimum values of numerical system parameters (such as inter-vehicle distance and time headway) which lie on the boundary between safe and unsafe system behavior.

More precisely, in quantitative parameter estimation, the problem is to estimate the minimum value $v_{min}$ of some continuous SUT parameter $p$ such that an LTL safety property *prop* is not violated. The parameter $p$ could be an input variable, or a system constant that must be set to an optimal value. Now $p$ may or may not explicitly appear in the formula *prop* but it should be able to influence its truth value (see e.g. the formula 1 in Sect. 6).

If we can assume that the safety property *prop* varies monotonically with $p$, then this allows us to use a binary chop search to iteratively halve an estimate interval $v_{min} \in [v_{true}^i, v_{false}^i]$ for $i = 0, ..., n$. Here, $v_{true}^i$ is the current upper bound where *prop* is true and $v_{false}^i$ is the current lower bound where *prop* is false. The search begins from two initial endpoints $[v_{true}^0, v_{false}^0]$ that can be obtained by conservatively over-estimating and under-estimating the value of $v_{min}$.

For a binary chop search, as usual we iterate the boundary search process by refining one of the endpoints. Thus: (i) $v_{true}^{i+1} := v_{true}^i + v_{false}^i/2$ if LBT cannot find a counterexample to *prop* on the midpoint up to a given learning convergence value. Otherwise: (ii) $v_{false}^{i+1} := v_{true}^i + v_{false}^i/2$. Then we carry forward into the next iteration the other endpoint $v_{false}^{i+1} := v_{false}^i$ in case (i) and $v_{true}^{i+1} := v_{true}^i$ in case (ii) respectively. This process is iterated until a desired interval accuracy $[v_{true}^n, v_{false}^n]$ is achieved.

Refinement of the boundary $v_{true}^i$ is of course problematic here, since just because a counterexample has not been found by LBT, this does not mean that it does not exist. This is particularly true if the learned models are incomplete. Therefore, we emphasize that our methodology is a parameter estimation technique based on systematic testing, and not a verification technique. As such, our methodology provides an alternative to a traditional Monte-Carlo estimation of $v_{min}$. However, we believe there are three significant advantages to our approach compared with Monte-Carlo techniques, based on the use of machine learning.

(1)  The explicit construction of a model using machine learning gives a more powerful artifact than simply a set of execution traces (as used in Monte Carlo estimation). This model allows us to analyze complex requirements properties, including safety, fairness and liveness issues. These properties

cannot be semantically evaluated on traces alone, i.e. they are global properties of a model.

(2) Convergence estimates for the model give more insight into reliability of the estimate for $v_{min}$ than simply measuring the size and statistical significance of a randomly chosen Monte Carlo sample set. This fact is easily demonstrated, for if complete learning succeeds then a Monte Carlo approach is never aware of this and will underestimate the statistical significance of the result. A related aspect to this is the third advantage.

(3) The random query set associated with a Monte Carlo estimate contains significant redundancy when compared with a query set generated by active automaton learning. Said differently, random querying is a very inefficient way to learn the structure of an automaton.

# 5   A Platooning Simulator

The simulator implements a model for each platoon vehicle behaviour as well as a communication framework for inter-vehicle (V2V) communication modelled on the IEEE 802.11p protocol. The platooning simulator is capable of simulating an $N$-vehicle platoon travelling in one dimension along a roadway. It is an extension of the simulator presented in [22]. No steering model (i.e. lateral movement) is currently present in the simulator. This extension is part of ongoing research into more general spatio-temporal logic requirements modeling for Co-CPS, see e.g. [19].

## 5.1   The Vehicle Model

A key control algorithm in the platooning simulator is the longitudinal position controller. For this, we have implemented several published ACC algorithms which control the CACC component of each vehicle (see [28] for detailed descriptions of each). The specific ACC evaluated in Sect. 6 is Kakade's algorithm [16], which was chosen for its simplicity and a basic tendency to propagate compression waves. We were interested to know whether this effect, in combination with message packet loss, could disturb emergency braking, and whether LBTest could discover such a problem.

In the simulator there is a detailed model of vehicle braking. This includes a complete industrial model of a brake-by-wire subsystem featuring: (i) global brake torque distribution to individual wheels, (ii) ABS functionality based on slippage detection, and (iii) a friction model for tyres based on slippage rate using common physical parameter values. The simulator also includes e.g. odometry and V2V communication. The most relevant missing models are engine, powertrain and suspension models. While these models could easily be added by using an industrial simulator such as TruckMaker [15] (which is ongoing research) they would not invalidate the basic methodology of this paper.

Environment models in the simulator deal with air resistance and road friction. We assume a constant road friction value for simplicity. A message packet loss model, based on the data of Sect. 2 was used. To provide deterministic and repeatable behavior (with the exception of packet loss), the simulator is based on synchronous execution of all vehicle components. The fundamental simulation cycle is one millisecond, which provides adequate simulation accuracy for the control algorithms.

## 5.2  The Communication Model

The communication framework assumes wireless broadcast and point-to-point multi-hop communication between the vehicles in the platoon. A slotted TDMA scheme based on ideas from [5] is implemented: To avoid communication collisions, each vehicle $V_i$ is allowed to transmit only in its own TDMA slot.

As communication is broadcast-based, receiving vehicles can loose packets independently during a broadcast operation. Thus a packet can be received by one vehicle and lost by another. For example a broadcast from the LV is correctly received at FV1 and FV2, but not FV3, see Fig. 1. In a platoon of $N$ vehicles, for any sender $V_i$ and receiver $V_j$ (where $0 \le i, j \le N - 1$, $i \ne j$) let $d = |i - j|$ correspond to the distance between the sender and receiver. The probability $P$ in percent of a message being lost is $P(\text{message lost}) = PERbase + increase \cdot (d-1)$. Note that with the values from the road test, the probability of message loss (from the LV to the last vehicle) is 100% in a platoon of eight vehicles or more; hence every message is lost (unless e.g. multi-hop communication is used).

# 6  A Case Study in Quantitative Safety Analysis

In this section, we present a case study of applying our quantitative parameter estimation method. The aim was to estimate the minimum safe *global time headway* for a platoon which has two modes of behavior: high speed cruising and emergency braking.

The *local time headway* $hw_i(t)$ between two consecutive platoon vehicles $V_i$ and $V_{i+1}$ at time $t$ is the time which would be needed for $V_{i+1}$ to cross the gap which exists between $V_i$ and $V_{i+1}$ at time $t$[5]. This local dynamic parameter measures the inter-vehicle gap in terms of time rather than distance. As a runtime parameter to the CACC of $V_{i+1}$, its driver can set a desired value $HW_i$ for $hw_i(t)$, according to relevant safety and fuel economy criteria. Typical values for $HW_i$ are in the range 1.5 to 2.0 seconds [4]. This desired value $HW_i$ is then maintained by the CACC. Peturbations to $hw_i(t)$ through lead vehicle $V_0$ actions, will lead to short term deviations of $hw_i(t)$ from $HW_i$, which should be smoothed out by its CACC.

We are particularly interested to estimate system-of-system parameters. For this purpose, we assume that each platoon vehicle $V_i$ adopts the same common *global time headway* $HW$, so that $HW = HW_i$. Now we can ask: *what is the smallest value $HW_{min}$ we can choose for $HW$ which ensures safe driving for*

---

[5] Assuming $V_{i+1}$ maintains its speed at time $t$.

*all vehicles $V_i$ under all possible modes of behavior*[6]? By safe driving, we can assume as a minimum condition crash-free driving, but obviously this criterion could be strengthened. The value $HW_{min}$ we term the *minimum safe global time headway*. An estimate of $HW_{min}$ is easily obtained by LBT if communication between vehicles is perfect, as the SUT is then completely deterministic.

When communication is imperfect then message packet loss is modeled stochastically and the SUT is no longer deterministic. Although most model checkers (including NuSMV) cope well with non-determinism, currently, LBTest uses ML algorithms for deterministic automata only. To address this learning problem we inferred a set of deterministic models which support analysis of the average case behavior of the SUT. This seems pertinent, as the worst case SUT behavior involves catastrophic loss of all message packets. An alternative for future research would be to directly apply ML algorithms for non-deterministic or even probabilistic automata. (See Sect. 7.)

The integration of two control algorithms for high-speed cruising and emergency braking requires corresponding integration testing to ensure that no unwanted interactions can occur between these algorithms. In principle, high-speed cruising can bring the entire platoon to a state where emergency braking cannot be carried out safely. Such problems (if they occur) might be addressed by choosing a larger global time headway, so that unsafe states were no longer reachable. Thus one way to structure integration testing is to view it as an estimation problem for $HW_{min}$ such that platooning is safe for both cruising and emergency braking with high probability.

To conduct parameter estimation for $HW_{min}$, the following protocol was implemented in LBTest. As in [22], we focused on emulating the lead driver behavior, since all follower vehicles autonomously adapt to this. Each test case $tc$ for an $N$-vehicle platoon consisted of a sequence $tc = (r_1, r_2, ..., r_\lambda)$ of lead driver accelerator, brake or emergency brake commands $r_j$. Each such command was one of: (i) a *brake command* (-1.88 m/s$^2$), (ii) an *accelerate command* (1.25 m/s$^2$), (iii) a *neutral command* (0 m/s$^2$), or (iii) an *emergency brake command* (-2.22 m/s$^2$). The initial estimate of $HW_{min}$ was bounded between 0.5 and 2.0 seconds.

For each test case $tc = (r_1, r_2, ..., r_\lambda)$, the length $\lambda$ and torque requests $r_j$ were chosen dynamically both by the learning algorithm and the equivalence checker. For efficiency reasons, model checking was not used until after learning was concluded. Thus model checking counterexamples did not influence the analysis. The test case length $\lambda$ took an average value of 18.3. On average, random test cases amounted to 2.3% of the entire test set. This compares with 100% in the case of Monte Carlo parameter estimation. Thus 97% of test cases were generated deterministically by ML to explore the state space of the SUT. The communication wrapper loaded and executed each test case $tc$. Each torque

---

[6] Clearly $HW_{min}$ is a function of the many individual parameters of each vehicle $V_i$ such as its weight, braking power etc. Different values of $HW_{min}$ will thus be obtained if individual vehicle parameters are changed. For simplicity, we have assumed a homogeneous platoon, i.e. all vehicle parameters are the same. .

request value $r_j$ was maintained constantly for a nominal 5 seconds (5000 simulation cycles). Thus the length of the simulation corresponding to $tc$ was $5\lambda$ virtual seconds. The values chosen for $\lambda$ were sufficient to reach high cruising speeds, in excess of 120 $km/h$.

The principle SUT output recorded for the test case $tc$ was the time sequence of inter-vehicle gaps $x^i_{r,0}, \ldots, x^i_{r,\lambda}$, for each pair of vehicles $V_i$, $V_{i+1}$. Here, the time sequence term $x^i_{r,t}$, for $0 \leq t \leq \lambda$, represents the gap between the host-target pair, $V_i$ and $V_{i+1}$ measured at the end[7] of $5t$ virtual seconds (i.e. $5000t$ simulation cycles). The continuous values of each distance observation $x^i_{r,t}$ were partitioned within the communication wrapper into three discrete equivalence classes:

good, tooClose, crash,

based on host and velocity dependent distance boundaries.

To represent the physical system state of the platoon we also observed the lead vehicle velocity values $v^1_0, \ldots, v^1_\lambda$ and acceleration values $a^1_0, \ldots, a^1_\lambda$ at the same observation times. These continuous valued observations were partitioned into 1 $km/h$ and 1 $km/h^2$ equivalence classes.

During test sessions, each test case constructed by LBTest brought the entire platoon into a high speed cruising mode (using a sequence of non-random or random acceleration and braking commands). The test case would then issue the emergency brake command $e$ followed by a sequence of neutral commands $0^8$. By alternating brake and acceleration commands, each test case could establish different global dynamics in the platoon at the moment of emergency braking. For example, by choosing to evaluate the simple PID algorithm for CACC of [16], we were able to observe *compression waves* where some vehicles were decelerating while others were accelerating. When the choice of global time headway $HW$ fell below the minimum safe global headway $HW_{min}$ then at least one failed test case could be observed. Since some of these failed test cases exhibited compression waves, we concluded that compression is an important non-linear dynamic for certain CACC designs. This observation concurs with the extensive literature regarding *string stability* and ACC design, e.g. [27].

The safety requirement for collision free travel was expressed in LTL as

$$\text{always}( \bigwedge_{i=0}^{N-1} \text{Gap}_i > 0 ). \tag{1}$$

This formula expresses that a platoon of size $N$ is safe, since $\text{Gap}_i$ represents the $i$-th inter-vehicle time headway between vehicles $V_i$ and $V_{i+1}$. Notice that the time headway $t$ is not explicitly represented in this formula. Nevertheless, $t$ clearly influences Requirement 1 as too short a headway leads to crashes.

---

[7] It is also possible to use SUT observations between the output cycles by thresholding. This can yield greater accuracy, but this approach was not taken here.

[8] These terminating neutral commands 0 were redundant by the design of CEBP, but extended the test case until the platoon was stopped.

Furthermore, $t$ monotonically influences 1, since every platoon trajectory with a minimum time headway $t$ is also a legitimate trajectory for a minimum time headway of $t' \geq t$. So parameter estimation using a bisection method is valid for this problem.

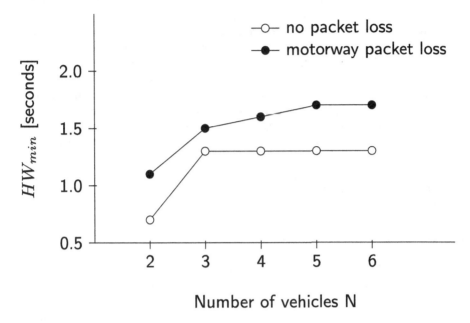

**Fig. 4.** Minimum safe global time headway $HW_{min}$ for different platoon sizes N and two packet loss rates.

The minimum safe global time headway $HW_{min}$ was estimated for two different wireless communication scenarios. In the first, perfect data transmission was assumed in order to derive a baseline time headway value. In the second, the packet loss model (c.f. Sect. 5) with parameters derived from the measurements of packet loss described in Sect. 2 was used. $PERbase$ and average increase per vehicle hop was chosen from the motorway scenario: 3.67 % and 18.6 % respectively. These values were the basis for a linear regression model to calculate the probability of a packet being lost.

The minimum safe global time headway $HW_{min}$ for these two scenarios was estimated for platoon sizes $N = 2, ..., 6$ to study its variation with platoon size. The results can be seen in Fig. 4. Significant is the observation that in both scenarios $HW_{min}$ reaches a maximum value. This can be interpreted to mean that both the CACC and CEBP algorithms are scalable to large platoon sizes.

## 7   Conclusions

In this paper we have addressed a challenge in the area of cooperative cyber-physical systems (Co-CPS) which is to quantitatively estimate safety related parameters for a system-of-systems. An inherent problem here is the significant system complexity which calls for novel analysis techniques that can even deal with the case where components may be "black box", i.e. their design and construction are not always known. Thus a black-box approach to parameter estimation based on learning-based testing (LBT) has been applied, and implemented using the tool LBtest.

To illustrate and evaluate our approach we have presented a case study in the area of vehicle platooning. This case study consisted of a platooning simulator integrated with a CEBP - a distributed protocol for coordinated emergency braking. The minimum safe global time headway for this platooning simulator was found for different platoon sizes, both with and without lossy communication.

Future research could expand this case study, for example by considering the effects of time variant communication quality, and compare schemes, such as multi-hop communication, to improve packet reception. This would increase probability of reception, but latency will scale with the number of hops. We could also study the behavior of non-homogeneous platoons.

Future research could also improve the efficiency and accuracy of the LBT algorithms used here in the case of non-deterministic SUT behavior. For such behavior, it is possible to directly implement machine learning algorithms for non-deterministic and probabilistic automata (see e.g. the survey [2]). This would avoid the need to estimate parameter values using several experiments. Furthermore, by learning probabilistic automaton models it may even be possible to estimate the statistical distribution of a parameter value by means of statistical model checkers such as PRISM [33]. Finally, our LBT approach could be empirically compared with Monte Carlo based approaches, regarding accuracy and reliability of parameter estimates.

**Acknowledgement.** The research leading to these results has been performed in the SafeCOP project, that received funding from the ECSEL Joint Undertaking under grant agreement 692529, and from Vinnova Swedish national funding. The work was partially performed in the Next Generation Electrical Architecture (NGEA) step2 project, funded by the Vinnova FFI-programme. We express special thanks for valuable comments to Magnus Jonsson and Alexey Vinel of Halmstad University.

# References

1. Angluin, D.: Learning regular sets from queries and counterexamples. Inf. Comput. **75**(2), 87–106 (1987)
2. Bennaceur, A., Meinke, K.: Machine learning for software analysis: models, methods, and applications. In: Bennaceur, A., Hähnle, R., Meinke, K. (eds.) Machine Learning for Dynamic Software Analysis: Potentials and Limits. LNCS, vol. 11026, pp. 3–49. Springer, Cham (2018). https://doi.org/10.1007/978-3-319-96562-8_1
3. Bergenhem, C., Shladover, S., Coelingh, E., Englund, C., Shladover, S., Tsugawa, S.: Overview of platooning systems. In: Proceedings of 19th ITS World Congress, Vienna, Austria, October 2012

4. van den Bleek, R.: Design of a hybrid adaptive cruise control stop-&-go system. Master's thesis, Technische Universiteit Eindhoven, Department of Mechanical Engineering (2007)
5. Bohm, A., Jonsson, M., Kunert, K., Vinel, A.: Context-aware retransmission scheme for increased reliability in platooning applications. In: Sikora A., Berbineau M., Vinel A., Jonsson M., Pirovano A., Aguado M. (eds.) Communication Technologies for Vehicles. Nets4Cars/Nets4Trains/Nets4Aircraft 2014. LNCS, vol. 8435, pp. 30–42. Springer, Cham (2014). https://doi.org/10.1007/978-3-319-06644-8_4
6. Cimatti, A., et al.: NuSMV 2: an opensource tool for symbolic model checking. In: Brinksma, E., Larsen, K.G. (eds.) CAV 2002. LNCS, vol. 2404, pp. 359–364. Springer, Heidelberg (2002). https://doi.org/10.1007/3-540-45657-0_29
7. Colin, S., Lanoix, A., Kouchnarenko, O., Souquieres, J.: Using CSPIIb components: application to a platoon of vehicles, pp. 103–118. Springer, Heidelberg (2009)
8. Dolk, V.S., Ploeg, J., Heemels, M.: Event-triggered control for string-stable vehicle platooning. IEEE Trans. Intell. Transp. Syst. 18(12), 3486–3500 (2017)
9. El-Zaher, M., Contet, J., Gruer, P., Gechter, F., Koukam, A.: Compositional verification for reactive multi-agent systems applied to platoon non collision verification. Stud. Inform. Univ. 10(3), 119–141 (2012)
10. European Telecommunications Standards Institute: Intelligent Transport Systems (ITS); Access layer specification for Intelligent Transport Systems operating in the 5 GHz frequency band. EN 302 663 V1.2.1, ETSI, July 2013
11. Feng, L., Lundmark, S., Meinke, K., Niu, F., Sindhu, M.A., Wong, P.Y.H.: Case studies in learning-based testing. In: Yenigün, H., Yilmaz, C., Ulrich, A. (eds.) ICTSS 2013. LNCS, vol. 8254, pp. 164–179. Springer, Heidelberg (2013). https://doi.org/10.1007/978-3-642-41707-8_11
12. Fisher, M.: An Introduction to Practical Formal Methods Using Temporal Logic. Wiley Publishing, Chichester (2011)
13. Giordano, G., Segata, M., Blanchini, F., Cigno, R.L.: A joint network/control design for cooperative automatic driving. In: 2017 IEEE Vehicular Networking Conference (VNC), pp. 167–174, November 2017
14. De la Higuera, C.: Grammatical Inference: Learning Automata and Grammars. Cambridge University Press, Cambridge (2010)
15. IPG Automotive: Brochure about CarMaker, TruckMaker and MotorcycleMaker (2018). https://ipg-automotive.com/pressmedia/media-library/. Accessed 11 June 2018
16. Kakade, R.S.: Automatic Cruise control system. Master's thesis, Indian Institute of Technology, Department of Systems and Control Engineering, Mumbai (2007)
17. Kamali, M., Dennis, L.A., McAree, O., Fisher, M., Veres, S.M.: Formal verification of autonomous vehicle platooning. Sci. Comput. Programm. 148, 88–106 (2017)
18. Karlsson, K., Carlsson, J., Larsson, M., Bergenhem, C.: Evaluation of the V2V channel and diversity potential for platooning trucks. In: Antennas and Propagation (EuCAP) Proceedings of the 10th European Conference, Davos, Switzerland, 11–15 April 2016 (2016)
19. Khosrowjerdi, H., Meinke, K.: Learning-based testing for autonomous systems using spatial and temporal requirements. In: Proceedings of 1st International Workshop on Machine Learning and Software Engineering in Symbiosis. IEEE (2018)
20. Liang, K.Y., Mårtensson, J., Johansson, K.H.: Heavy-duty vehicle platoon formation for fuel efficiency. IEEE Trans. Intell. Transp. Syst. 17(4), 1051–1061 (2016)
21. Meinke, K., Sindhu, M.A.: Incremental learning-based testing for reactive systems. In: Gogolla, M., Wolff, B. (eds.) TAP 2011. LNCS, vol. 6706, pp. 134–151. Springer, Heidelberg (2011). https://doi.org/10.1007/978-3-642-21768-5_11

22. Meinke, K.: Learning-based testing of cyber-physical systems-of-systems: a platooning study. In: Reinecke, P., Di Marco, A. (eds.) EPEW 2017. LNCS, vol. 10497, pp. 135–151. Springer, Cham (2017). https://doi.org/10.1007/978-3-319-66583-2_9

23. Meinke, K., Sindhu, M.A.: LBTest: a learning-based testing tool for reactive systems. In: Proceedings of the 2013 IEEE Sixth International Conference on Software Testing, Verification and Validation, ICST 2013, pp. 447–454. IEEE Computer Society (2013)

24. Murthy, D.K., Masrur, A.: Braking in close following platoons: the law of the weakest. In: 2016 Euromicro Conference on Digital System Design (DSD), pp. 613–620, August 2016

25. Oncu, S., Van de Wouw, N., Heemels, M., Nijmeijer, H.: String stability of interconnected vehicles under communication constraints. In: 2012 IEEE 51st Annual Conference on Decision and Control (CDC), pp. 2459–2464. IEEE (2012)

26. Peled, D., Vardi, M.Y., Yannakakis, M.: Black box checking. In: Wu, J., Chanson, S.T., Gao, Q. (eds.) Formal Methods for Protocol Engineering and Distributed Systems. IAICT, vol. 28, pp. 225–240. Springer, Boston, MA (1999). https://doi.org/10.1007/978-0-387-35578-8_13

27. Swaroop, D., Hedrick, J.: String stability of interconnected systems. IEEE Trans. Autom. Control **41**, 349–357 (1996)

28. Trochez, D., Tsakalos, A.: Adaptive cruise control implementation with constant range and constant time-gap policies. Master's thesis, KTH Royal Institute of Technology, EECS School (2017)

29. Valiant, L.G.: A theory of the learnable. Commun. ACM **27**(11), 1134–1142 (1984)

30. Vinel, A., Lyamin, N., Isachenkov, P.: Modeling of V2V communications for C-ITS safety applications: a CPS perspective. IEEE Commun. Lett. **PP**(99), 1 (2018)

31. van Willigen, W.H., Schut, M.C., Kester, L.J.H.M.: Evaluating adaptive cruise control strategies in worst-case scenarios. In: 2011 14th International IEEE Conference on Intelligent Transportation Systems (ITSC), pp. 1910–1915, October 2011

32. Willke, T.L., Tientrakool, P., Maxemchuk, N.F.: A survey of inter-vehicle communication protocols and their applications. Commun. Surveys Tuts. **11**(2), 3–20 (2009). https://doi.org/10.1109/SURV.2009.090202

33. Younes, H.L.S., Kwiatkowska, M.Z., Norman, G., Parker, D.: Numerical vs. statistical probabilistic model checking. STTT **8**(3), 216–228 (2006)

# Cyber-Physical Systems Engineering

# Cyber-Physical Systems Engineering: An Introduction

J. Paul Gibson[1(✉)], Peter Gorm Larsen[2], Marc Pantel[3], John Fitzgerald[4], and Jim Woodcock[5]

[1] SAMOVAR, Télécom Sud Paris, CNRS, Université Paris Saclay,
9 rue Charles Fourier, Evry Cedex, 91011 Paris, France
`paul.gibson@telecom-sudparis.eu`
[2] DIGIT, Department of Engineering, Aarhus University, Aarhus, Denmark
`pgl@eng.au.dk`
[3] Institut de Recherche en Informatique de Toulouse, Toulouse, France
`marc.pantel@enseeiht.fr`
[4] School of Computing Science, Newcastle University, Newcastle upon Tyne, UK
`John.Fitzgerald@ncl.ac.uk`
[5] Department of Computer Science, University of York, York, UK
`Jim.Woodcock@york.ac.uk`

**Abstract.** Cyber-Physical Systems (CPSs) [1] connect the real world to software systems through a network of sensors and actuators in which physical and logical components interact in complex ways. There is a diverse range of application domains [2], including health [3], energy [4], transport [5], autonomous vehicles [6] and robotics [7]; and many of these include safety critical requirements [8]. Such systems are, by definition, characterised by both discrete and continuous components. The development and verification processes must, therefore, incorporate and integrate discrete and continuous models.

The development of techniques and tools to handle the correct design of CPSs has drawn the attention of many researchers. Continuous modelling approaches are usually based on a formal mathematical expression of the problem using dense reals and differential equations to model the behaviour of the studied hybrid system. Then, models are simulated in order to check required properties. Discrete modelling approaches rely on formal methods, based on abstraction, model-checking and theorem proving. There is much ongoing research concerned with how best to combine these approaches in a more coherent and pragmatic fashion, in order to support more rigorous and automated hybrid-design verification.

It is also possible to combine different discrete-event and continuous-time models using a technique called co-simulation. This has been supported by different tools and the underlying foundation for this has been analysed. Thus, the track will also look into these areas as well as the industrial usage of this kind of technology.

This work was supported by grant ANR-17-CE25-0005 (The DISCONT Project https://fusionforge.int-evry.fr/www/discont/) from the Agence Nationale de la Recherche (ANR).

T. Margaria and B. Steffen (Eds.): ISoLA 2018, LNCS 11246, pp. 407–410, 2018.
https://doi.org/10.1007/978-3-030-03424-5_27

**Keywords:** Formal methods · Verification · Modelling · Discrete
Continuous

In this year's thematic track, we include papers that cover theoretical advances, ongoing research, industrial case-studies and tool/method development. The track will also include a session concerned with current challenges and research directions.

In *Intelligent Adaption Process in Cyber-Physical Production Systems* [9] (in this issue), the authors report on production and logistics systems, used in the manufacturing industry, and how Cyber-Physical Production System Models will help industry to improve on the key aspect of adaption—the production and logistics systems can be adapted more frequently, more precisely and more quickly when cyber-physical production systems are supporting the adaption process.

The article *Model-Based Systems Engineering for Systems Simulation* [10] (in this issue) propose a methodology for integrating simulation systems development with products systems engineering. This offers a better management and reuse of the various environment and mock-up models during system development. This general approach is independent both of the actual methods and tools used to model the system and of the simulation environment.

In *Scenario-based validation of automated driving systems* [11] (in this issue), the paper presents techniques for formalising test scenarios for automated driving systems. To assess the safety of such systems, all potentially critical situations have to be considered. The number of relevant scenarios is very large therefore testing must rely heavily on virtual, largely automatized exploration of scenario spaces. For that, classes of scenarios have to be described formally. The contribution delineates a general approach to safety assessment by virtual testing. It discusses in particular the nature and building blocks of a formal scenario language and the construction of test specifications.

In *Engineering of Cyber-Physical Systems in the automotive context: case study of a range prediction assistant* [12] (in this issue), the authors present a case study addressing the development of an assistant for estimating the range of an electric vehicle. The approach is based on the methodology and tools from the EU Horizon 2020 INTO-CPS project [13]. The paper promises an outlook on the development of similar tool chains for automotive planning. In summary, the paper shows that flexible and integrated tool-chains that rely on open standards for data exchange are key to efficient development of CPSs in the automotive domain.

The article *Testing Avionics Software: Is FMI up to the Task?* [14] (in this issue) compares the FMI and RT-Tester test engine architectures in the context of safety-critical avionics software. To do this, it uses one principal case study: a version of an aircraft controller application, synthesised from an existing system requirement.

The article *Co-simulation: the Past, Future, and Open Challenges* [15] (in this issue) provides an interesting historical overview of co-simulation, together with a couple of recent example of co-simulation technology, and some selected discussion points on directions in which the technology might evolve in future.

In *Lessons Learned Using FMI Co-Simulation for Model-based Design of Cyber Physical Systems* [16] (in this issue), the authors provide a critical analysis of the pros and cons of using FMI for model integration when co-simulation CPSs. The case study - a building Heating, Ventilation and Air Conditioning (HVAC) system – illustrates very well the advantages and disadvantages of the approach based on FMI.

# References

1. Rajkumar, R.R., Lee, I., Sha, L., Stankovic, J.: Cyber-physical systems: the next computing revolution. In: Proceedings of the 47th Design Automation Conference, pp. 731–736. ACM (2010)
2. Shi, J., Wan, J., Yan, H., Suo, H.: A survey of cyber-physical systems. In: 2011 International Conference on Wireless Communications and Signal Processing (WCSP), pp. 1–6. IEEE (2011)
3. Haque, S.A., Aziz, S.M., Rahman, M.: Review of cyber-physical system in healthcare. Int. J. Distrib. Sens. Netw. **10**(4), 217415 (2014)
4. Ilic, M.D., Xie, L., Khan, U.A., Moura, J.M.: Modeling of future cyber-physical energy systems for distributed sensing and control. IEEE Trans. Syst. Man Cybern.-Part A: Syst. Hum. **40**(4), 825–838 (2010)
5. Sampigethaya, K., Poovendran, R.: Aviation cyber-physical systems: foundations for future aircraft and air transport. Proc. IEEE **101**(8), 1834–1855 (2013)
6. Kim, J., Kim, H., Lakshmanan, K., Rajkumar, R.R.: Parallel scheduling for cyber-physical systems: analysis and case study on a self-driving car. In: Proceedings of the ACM/IEEE 4th International Conference on Cyber-Physical Systems, pp. 31–40. ACM (2013)
7. Fink, J., Ribeiro, A., Kumar, V.: Robust control for mobility and wireless communication in cyber-physical systems with application to robot teams. Proc. IEEE **100**(1), 164–178 (2012)
8. Banerjee, A., Venkatasubramanian, K.K., Mukherjee, T., Gupta, S.K.: Ensuring safety, security, and sustainability of mission-critical cyber-physical systems. Proc. IEEE **100**(1), 283–299 (2012)
9. Muller, D., Schumacher, C., Zeidler, F.: Intelligent adaption process in cyber-physical production systems. In: Margaria, T., Steffen, B. (eds.), ISoLA 2018, LNCS 11246, pp. 411–428, 2018. Springer, Heidelberg (2018)
10. Leroux, R., Pantel, M., Ober, I., Bruel, J.M.: Model-based systems engineering for systems simulation. In: Margaria, T., Steffen, B. (eds.), ISoLA 2018, LNCS 11246, pp. 429–448, 2018. Springer, Heidelberg (2018)
11. Hungar, H.: Scenario-based validation of automated driving systems. In: Margaria, T., Steffen, B. (eds.), ISoLA 2018, LNCS 11246, pp. 449–460, 2018. Springer, Heidelberg (2018)
12. Konig, C.F.J., Meisl, G., Balcu, N., Vosseler, B., Hormann, H., Holl, J., Fäßler, V.: Engineering of Cyber-Physical Systems in the automotive context: case study of a range prediction assistant. In: Margaria, T., Steffen, B. (eds.), ISoLA 2018, LNCS 11246, pp. 461–476, 2018. Springer, Heidelberg (2018)

13. Larsen, P.G., Fitzgerald, J., Woodcock, J., Gamble, C., Payne, R., Pierce, K.: Features of integrated model-based co-modelling and co-simulation technology. In: Cerone, A., Roveri, M. (eds.) SEFM 2017. LNCS, vol. 10729, pp. 377–390. Springer, Cham (2018). https://doi.org/10.1007/978-3-319-74781-1_26
14. Brauer, J., Moller, O., Peleska, J.: Testing Avionics Software: Is FMI up to the Task? In: Margaria, T., Steffen, B. (eds.), ISoLA 2018, LNCS 11246, pp. 477–487, 2018. Springer, Heidelberg (2018)
15. Gomes, C., Thule, C., Deantoni, J., Larsen, P.G., Vangheluwe, H.: Co-simulation: the past, future, and open challenges. In: Margaria, T., Steffen, B. (eds.), ISoLA 2018, LNCS 11246, pp. 504–520, 2018. Springer, Heidelberg (2018)
16. Couto, L.D., et al.: Lessons learned using FMI co-simulation for model-based design of cyber physical systems. In: Margaria, T., Steffen, B. (eds.), ISoLA 2018, LNCS 11246, pp. 488–503, 2018. Springer, Heidelberg (2018)

# Intelligent Adaption Process in Cyber-Physical Production Systems

Daniel Müller[1]([⊠]), Christin Schumacher[2], and Felix Zeidler[3]

[1] Chair of Enterprise Logistics, TU Dortmund University,
Leonhard-Euler-Straße 5, 44221 Dortmund, Germany
mueller@lfo.tu-dortmund.de
[2] Chair of Modeling and Simulation, TU Dortmund University,
Otto-Hahn-Str. 16, 44221 Dortmund, Germany
christin.schumacher@tu-dortmund.de
[3] Chair of Materials Handling and Warehousing, TU Dortmund University,
Joseph-Von-Fraunhofer-Straße 2-4, 44227 Dortmund, Germany
felix.zeidler@tu-dortmund.de

**Abstract.** Current developments towards the buyer's market and related trends such as more diversified production programs, shorter product life cycles and more volatile fluctuations in demand are leading to an increasingly dynamic and complex business environment. For this reason, productions and logistics systems face even more frequent adaptions. In order to react to these challenges in a structured manner, a sequential adaption process with six individual phases was developed. This paper points out, that production and logistics systems can be adapted more frequently, more precisely and quicker when cyber-physical production systems (CPPS) are supporting the adaption process. In particular, the availability of real-time feedback data from production and logistics processes in CPPS has proven to be advantageous for a more intelligent adaption process. In addition, the requirements for an intelligent adaption process are formulated based on these new technological possibilities. The paper especially focuses on the logistics and production technical aspects of the adaption process and the adaption object. On the one hand, possible applications of CPPS technologies are presented for each of the six phases, on the other hand, this paper analyzes the overall impact on the whole adaption process when individual CPPS technologies are used.

**Keywords:** Adaption process · Adaption intelligence
Cyber-physical production system · Flexibility · Transformability
Logistics · Production

## 1 Introduction

Today, actors in the manufacturing industry are challenged to satisfy consumers' requirements of more individualized products, which leads to a higher variety of products for the companies. This development towards "lot size one" production is a good example of an external influence factor that is currently crucial for the manufacturing market and can force a production to change completely. Other instances of

© Springer Nature Switzerland AG 2018
T. Margaria and B. Steffen (Eds.): ISoLA 2018, LNCS 11246, pp. 411–428, 2018.
https://doi.org/10.1007/978-3-030-03424-5_28

factors that companies should react to are order fluctuations, technical progress, legislative amendment, or changes in the own business strategy [1, 2].

A study by Staufen AG reports an example of successful adaption in the German industrial market. The study shows that one fifth of the industrial companies are already able to produce products in lot size one with the cost level of serial production [3]. This example indicates that companies must react flexibly and quickly to their environment to remain competitive under changed external conditions. That means, that they must adjust their production and logistics processes permanently [2]. Due to this continuous adaption needs, the concept of flexibility and transformability has been established in literature. Besides, in literature a structured adaption procedure with six steps is defined to determine a process for effective modifications [4].

The current technological developments towards an increasing digitization of production processes called Industry 4.0 or Internet of Things (IoT) have major potential for helping companies to observe and adapt their production systems in the manufacturing industry [5, 6]. An essential element of Industry 4.0 are cyber-physical systems (CPS). CPS contain embedded systems as well as electro technical and mechanical components. They use sensors to record physical data in real time and can also influence physical processes [5]. Using global digital networks, the CPSs are connected with each other and can use data and services worldwide [5]. CPS in production are defined as cyber-physical production systems (CPPS) and include, for example, intelligent work equipment or smart warehouse systems that are networked via information and communication technologies. This new level of quality and quantity of response data enables dynamic and self-organized supply chains, which can be optimized in a real-time by adapting various factors [5]. For instance, actors in manufacturing industry establish the more frequent use of smart and decentralized production and logistics systems, which can be also used in a more intelligent adaption process.

In Delbrügger et al. [4], we have already introduced preconditions for providing a fast and precise adaption with the six-step adaption process in all areas of a manufacturing system under the influence of a dynamic and complex environment. We especially elaborated, which requirements shall be fulfilled by the adaption team, the adaption process and the adaption object to be adaption intelligent. Based on this previous publication and due to the gradually spread of CPPS in the manufacturing industry, it is now interesting to determine the potential of CPPS for supporting the adaption process in terms of adapting a production and logistics system more frequently, more precisely and quicker. Therefore, the purpose of this work is to analyze the adaption process in its individual six phases regarding the possible use of the upcoming CPPS technologies in each step. In addition to possible applications of these modern technologies in each step, we will analyze the overall impact on the whole adaption process when CPPS technologies are used. Whereas our previous paper provided a general overview, including a wide range of disciplines and discussing the adaption object, the adaption process and the adaption team, the current study focuses in detail on the logistics and production technical point of view. In addition, the paper concentrates on CPPS technologies for the adaption process and the adaption object.

After the introduction in section one, including the current challenges in the manufacturing industry, the paper presents the adaption process underlying this work and an overview of terms and concepts for flexibility and transformability in the second section. Section three constitutes the main part of the paper, which is divided into six subsections according to the six steps of the adaption process. It begins with the first phase of observation. Then the analysis and evaluation phase are examined in more detail. Especially the conjunction between the observation phase and the analysis and evaluation phase will be discussed, which in the future may change with the gradual implementation of CPPS in factories. Afterwards, CPPS tools for planning and decision support are discussed in the sections on planning and decision. In the two final phases "Implementation" and "Impact", the CPPS instruments supporting the realization and control of adaption measures are discussed, before summarizing the findings of this approach and giving a future research perspective in the last section.

## 2    Flexibility, Transformability and Adaption Process

The stronger the influence factors which have been described in the previous section and the more factors repeatedly disturb the market balance, the more dynamic and complex is the company's environment [7]. These factors, which can have an influence on a production and can force a company to an adaption, are described in the literature as drivers of change. Drivers of change can be subdivided into internal and external, whereas the external drivers of change can further be classified into company-specific and those caused by the company's environment. As illustrated in Fig. 1, to these three categories, drivers of change which are repeatedly mentioned in the literature can be assigned [8, 9].

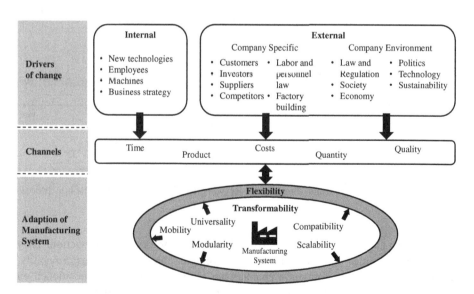

**Fig. 1.** Concept of flexibility and transformability in response to adaption requirements through internal and external drivers of change [acc. to 9, 40–42]

Although there are many different drivers of change, they only affect manufacturing systems via specific channels (see Fig. 1). Drivers of change have an impact on the company through the five channels of time, product, cost, quantity and quality. Through these channels, a company reacts with flexibility and transformability with the help of transformation enablers [8]. If a factory system can be adapted without any major expenditure of time or money to counteract drivers of change, the literature uses the term flexibility. Flexibility measures represent reversible changes in the system configuration within existing flexibility corridors [10] (Figs. 1 and 2). In contrast, transformability is always connected with investments of additional time and costs and includes irreversible adaption measures that surpass existing flexibility corridors. A factory system is classified as highly changeable if it offers the potential to act beyond previously conceived organizational and technical structures using its process, structural and behavioral variability and while requiring as few additional investments as possible [10]. From the system theory point of view, the reaction to drivers of change with flexibility represents a structural linkage, so that only the relations between the system elements are changing. An example is a change in material flow due to a change in the order flow. In contrast, adaption measures in the context of transformability not only change the element relations, but also their properties and functions in such a way that new structures and systems are created. One example is a change in the form of production when switching from shop floor production to line production [10].

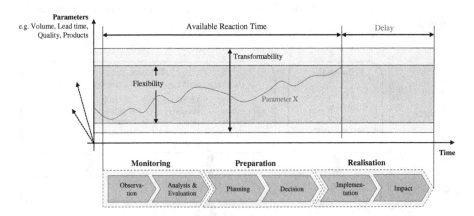

**Fig. 2.** Flexibility corridors and transformability with the six phases of the adaption process [acc. to 16, 43, 44]

Transformation enablers form the basis for adaption processes in production. They provide opportunities to react quicker to drivers of change with transformability. Simple examples of transformation enablers are shelving units that are positioned on rolls and thus enable a quick change of the production layout. Another example are flexible work time models with which different workloads can be handled [12].

In order to evaluate the influences of drivers of change on a factory system and to identify adaption needs, besides the internal and external drivers of change, the systemrelevant parameters of an enterprise must be analyzed. These internal key performance indicators (KPIs) are all related to different so-called types of flexibility. Each type of flexibility is described by at least one parameter or a qualitative factor. If a quantitative description of the flexibility type is possible, upper and lower flexibility limits can be assigned to the KPIs that describe the flexibility type. Figure 2 shows an illustration of a flexibility corridor. The different types of flexibility interact with each other. An extensive itemization of flexibility types was listed by Luft [13].

For both drivers of change and flexibility types, limits can be set for warning and intervention. There is a need for adaption if at least one of the KPIs of the internal or external company's environment exceeds the predefined limits or if a flexibility corridor limit is reached in the case of the flexibility types. Another possibility is to react to potential changes in the environment before they arise by forecasting of the parameters. However, this way involves a higher risk because it is not certain whether the progress of the KPIs will fulfil the prediction [14, 15].

In order to be able to react to drivers of change, i.e. to the development of KPIs, a structured procedure was developed according to Fig. 2. The procedure to initiate adaptions is divided into six phases which together represent the adaption process, which is based on works of Morales, Dormayer and Hopfmann [16–18]. The six phases included are of iterative nature and are not necessarily run through completely each time, since an adaption only needs to be initiated in the event of a critical change in the parameters that are relevant to the system. Further details to this iterative nature can be found in Delbrügger et al. [4]. The six steps of the adaption process described in Fig. 2 are explained in more detail in the following Sect. 3. For each of the steps, CPPS technologies will be identified that support and accelerate the transformation enablers. The theoretical findings are illustrated by practical examples.

Other authors also analyzed the combination of transformability and technologies of the industry 4.0. For example, Zäh et al. [19] found that elements of the digital factory which are already implemented in the factories are suitable for supporting changes and with that also the traditional concept of flexibility and transformability which was also presented in this section. Furthermore, Schel [20] for instance notes that IT particularly support transformability of productions when they are adaptable themselves through a modular, expandable and standardized structure. But to the best of our knowledge, there is no approach which highlights how CPPS technologies can support each of the six steps of the introduced adaption process.

## 3   Adaption Process in Cyber-Physical Production Systems

This section presents the potentials of CPS for the adaption process sequentially along the six phases (see Fig. 2), in order to adapt a production and logistics system more frequently, more precisely and quickler [4].

## 3.1    Observation

The aim of the classical phase of monitoring of the factory adaption process (see Fig. 2) is to systematically assess the drivers of change causing a need for adaption and to analyze and evaluate their effects on all systemrelevant parameters [4]. It is necessary to use suitable models to characterize the significance of the influencing factors of the factory system and to reduce the perception time by using suitable instruments for monitoring and evaluation. The central task of the observation phase, which initiates the adaption process, is to acquire all operating conditions of the production and logistics system in the form of feedback data. The generated data pool represents the basis for a subsequent evaluation within the phases of analysis and evaluation of adaption requirements. The quality and quantity of the feedback data are of fundamental importance for the perception of changes in the production and logistics system and can decisively support this.

A joint study by leading german production engineering institutes [21] has examined the current state for the collection of feedback data in the industrial environment. The key finding of this study is that all sizes of companies, especially small and medium-sized enterprises, have deficits in automated acquisition and use of feedback data [9]. It has been shown that at least Enterprise Resource Planning (ERP) systems are currently used as the central instrument for managing enterprise data in most industrial companies (94%) [21]. The enterprise data managed by the ERP system can basically be divided into relatively static master data and much more dynamic transactional data, whereby both types of data are kept up-to-date by status feedback from the production [21].

In contrast to managing the data by ERP systems, the study has revealed regarding data collection, that production data and machine data acquisition systems (PDA-/MDA-systems) with spreads of 52% and 37% are the most established methods for generating feedback data on the process control level [21]. Thereby in industrial practice, these two systems are mainly used to link machines and systems with IT. Machine data acquisition is the collection of technical feedback data, which is carried out directly at the sensors or controls of the production plants. In the course of production data acquisition, the collection of order and personnel data as well as the primary processing of the collected data is realized in addition to MDA-systems [22]. Typical feedback data is the start and end of a manufacturing process (including time stamps), interruptions and runtime of a machine, manufacturing or assembly orders, resource utilization and the number of pieces produced [22].

The collection of feedback data is carried out at least partly manually by 80% of the companies surveyed, whereby mostly (with 71% of the manual feedback) PDA systems are used. 43% of the participating companies fear to invest in automated data acquisition solutions and prefer to collect the feedback data manually. Almost half of the companies (49%) collect feedback data automatically, depending on the process, at least in some areas. A complete substitution of manual data acquisition systems with solutions for fully automated feedback data acquisition such as Radio Frequency Identification (RFID) technology is not yet widespread (8%) in the industrial environment and is only used by selected large companies [21].

The current technological advancement towards interconnected, CPPS enables the automated provision, acquisition and evaluation of relevant feedback data of the production and logistics processes in real time [23]. For the successive integration of an existing machine park into the company-internal data network, retrofitting measures enable the demand-oriented retrofitting of corresponding sensors and actuators. A central prerequisite for networking a factory system is the interoperability of the data interfaces of the various production plants and logistical objects [23].

This innovative form of data diversity and quality generates a significantly increased transparency along the entire value chain. The aim of an intelligent monitoring phase is the advantageous use of this increased data diversity in order to derive adaption needs on the one hand more well-founded and on the other hand directly, without performance-reducing latencies (see Fig. 2). In the context of automated data acquisition, the observation phase and the analysis and evaluation phase largely merge with each other because of the automatic possibilities for processing data. Hence, the "production factor" data is of great importance in general, which will continue to increase in the future against the background of the current industrial digitization efforts. The targeted use of data is already a significant competitive factor.

### 3.2 Analysis and Evaluation

The analysis and evaluation phase processes the data and prepares it for the planning phase. For this purpose, real-time data availability in CPPS enables to create a digital shadow, which is a complete digital image of the physical processes based on the collected feedback data [24]. The digital shadow provides the data basis for integral analysis and evaluation processes. Through target-group-specific visual and statistical data aggregation, for example in the form of KPI, the digital shadow empowers enhanced decision-making competence [24–26]. Especially controlling as well as production planning and control benefit from this databased support.

According to Humm and Wietek [27] and Fasel and Maier [28] the analysis of large amounts of data and its conversion into profitable information and knowledge is often subsumed under the terms Business Analytics, Business Intelligence or Big Data Analytics. These collective terms characterize all data evaluation methods, which aim to recognize relationships, correlations and patterns, to develop forecasts and to define action measures based on an existing data framework. Evans [29] classifies Big Data Analytics in the consecutive phases Descriptive Analytics, Diagnostic Analytics, Predictive Analytics and Prescriptive Analytics (see Fig. 3).

Descriptive Analytics still addresses the phase of observation, which was described in the last subsection. Descriptive Analytics therefore focuses on data collection using the digital shadow to increase process transparency. The objective is to identify and quantify relevant drivers of change and also to collect and preprocess the feedback data from the production and logistics system. For the operationalization of qualitative influencing variables, the fuzzy logic represents a potential solution [29].

Diagnostic analytics (or: Inquisitive Analytics [30]) describes recognition of patterns and correlations within data to identify cause-effect relationships and thus it can be explicitly assigned to the phase of analysis and evaluation described in this section. In this context, an intelligent adaption process models the relationship between relevant

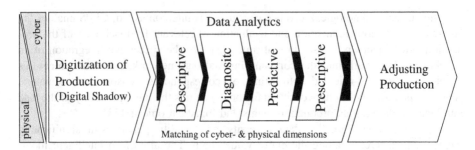

**Fig. 3.** Data analytics as enabler for the recognition of adaption requirements in CPPS [acc. to 21]

drivers of change, channels and parameters considered in order to derive interdependencies within the factory system. Diagnostic Analytics thus provides an important contribution to the causal analysis in the phase of monitoring. Furthermore, the use of tools of diagnostic analytics like neural networks offers application potential for weighting the significance of individual drivers of change on a factory system. These depict the system's behavior under the influence of various drivers of change. The informative value of this tool increases with growing data volume due to the ability of self-learning [29].

The third step, Predictive Analytics, aims to forecast future developments both within the production and within logistics system based on patterns and correlations identified and the relevant drivers of change of the business environment. The forecast of the influencing factors allows to monitor the development of system-relevant parameters permanently, and to evaluate them proactively based on the systems' performance and flexibility. On the basis of past data, it could be predicted, for example, whether strong fluctuations in the workloads are a merely seasonal phenomena or whether they imply a sustainable need for adaption of capacities. Thus, methods of predictive analytics are mainly used in the analysis and evaluation phase and partly in the planning phase. The forecasting of future developments serves as a basis for planning, particularly when scheduling adaption measures.

Prescriptive Analytics uses the forecasts of predictive analytics as a basis for deriving measures during the planning phase. In this way, operational, tactical and strategic management is also supported in the form of an assistance system when deciding on the implementation of adaption measures [25]. But first of all, this section continues with the phase of analysis and evaluation of the adaption process.

Obtaining and applying knowledge about the structural interdependencies of production and logistics systems are relevant throughout the entire adaption process and are key characteristics of an intelligent adaption process. Without an understanding of the complex and dynamic interdependencies between drivers of change and the individual system elements as well as individual elements among each other, it is not possible to derive adaption requirements in a targeted manner or to plan countermeasures precisely. For further view on the structural relationships and the effects of drivers of change on factory systems, have a look at the current works by Bertsch [31], Schmitt and Gloeckner [9], Klemke [32], Luebkemann [33] and Besenfelder [34].

In addition, the factory structure also has a significant influence on the dynamic behavior of a factory system, as it determines the material flows in production decisively. The achievement of a high logistical efficiency and thus the resulting manufacturing costs when operating an existing factory structure are essentially determined by the production control. The production control is challenged to implement increasingly volatile specifications of the production planning on the shop floor. Due to different configurations, the production control has a certain flexibility in order to adapt the production to changed requirements according to the best possible target achievement. As already indicated, the use of CPPS enables the practical implementation of a significantly increased flexibility and short-cycle adaptability of production control through real-time data availability and direct feedback. A specific feature of this flexibility are defined performance bounds that limit the compensation of changes in production requirements by the control system.

Schuh et al. [35] has shown that these performance bounds are strongly dependent on the factory structure. This means that the factory structure has a significant influence on the inherent flexibility potential of a production and logistics system. In this context an intelligent adaption process always strives to exploit the full flexibility potential of a system using various configurations of control parameters before economically intensive adaption measures in the field of transformability become necessary to change the factory structure or resource configuration. Therefore, the entire flexibility potential of the system and the interactions between the flexibility types must be fully known.

Adaption requirements cannot be completely identified by deviations between target and actual values of the four classical logistical target values. Instead, it requires an extended view of the system status by evaluating other characteristic parameters, such as process and transition time and transport intensity, i.e. the material flow in real-time. To enable an intelligent adaption process to identify adaption needs semi-automated, an assistance system consisting of an objective evaluation system for drivers of change is required. Gille and Zwißler [36] provide an initial approach of an evaluation system.

When analyzing and assessing adaption needs, it is necessary to consider both the level of individual resources and the level of related resources (resource pool). In this context, the adjective "related" describes resources, which are used jointly in a defined factory area and have identical processing capabilities. The following example is descended from production logistics and illustrates the connection or difference between individual resources and the resource pool: An Automated Guided Vehicle (AGV), which is used in the area of assembly for material supply, represents a single resource. If several vehicles with identical transport capabilities are used for material supply in the above-mentioned assembly area, they form a resource pool, which in this context can be referred to as a material supply system. Such a material supply system needs to be identified in the phase of analysis and evaluation. With the help of CPPS it becomes much easier to display and then recognize these relations.

Depending on the type of flexibility or the related corridor model to be analyzed, it is important to choose a reasonable resource level. To clarify this statement, the introduced example from above is used: Within the material supply system, the situation may arise that the limits of the capacitive flexibility corridors of single vehicles are exceeded or not reached, while the aggregate capacitive flexibility corridor of the resource pool has no exceeding of the corridor boundaries. Seebacher [37] defines the capacitive flexibility of an object as its quantitative performance capability. The described effect of a temporary transgression or shortfall might derive from the static linkage of AGVs with workstations. Increasing volatile material demands at the workstations can lead to over- or underload conditions of individual transport vehicles. In the case of this example, the analysis of both resource levels reveals an unbalanced use of flexibility potentials. Instead of initiating adaption measures and expanding the resource pool with additional transport vehicles, the objective of the analysis and evaluation phase is to demonstrate that it might be advantageous to implement an intelligent use of existing capacitive flexibility potentials.

### 3.3  Planning

If predictive analytics methods during the analysis and evaluation phase show that the course of a relevant parameter in the future will be outside the corresponding flexibility corridor at resource pool level, which means there is no longer sufficient flexibility potential available, it is important to immediately plan appropriate adaption measures. By realizing adaption measures, the flexibility corridor can be shifted, or its size can be modified.

The planning phase includes identification, concretization and evaluation of potential adaption measures. The objective of identification is to derive adaption measures which influence the flexibility corridor in the way that the corridor boundaries encompass the predicted development of parameters. To deliberately modify the flexibility corridor, it is possible to use both individual measures and a bundle of measures, which means the use of various individual measures at the same time. Unless it is made an explicit distinction, an adaption measure includes the possibility to be a bundle of measures in the further course. The concretization step extends the identified adaption measures by time and cost information, which means the required time and costs to implement an adaption measure. The subsequent evaluation quantifies the efficiency of an adaption measure using the cost-benefit analysis in consideration of the impact on other corridor models.

As already indicated, when planning adaption measures it should be considered that due to complex interdependencies within the factory structure, the implementation of a measure usually does not only affect one type of flexibility but also several types of flexibility or rather their corridor boundaries (see Fig. 4).

For example, if a need for adaption has been identified in the area of capacitive flexibility of a particular resource pool, the initiation of an adaption measure for optimizing the capacitive flexibility corridor boundaries may also lead to a shift of the corridor boundaries of other types of flexibility, such as the expansion flexibility [38].

As already described during the monitoring phase, the cross-system interaction mechanisms within a factory structure are usually very complex and dynamic. Therefore, the connections between an adaption measure and the resulting impacts on different flexibility corridors can neither be "manually" overviewed nor analytically described. However, an adaptive-intelligent system has an assistance system connected with the CPS which provides case-specific options for action as part of the measure planning. A focus here is on emphasizing the interdependencies of the impact of

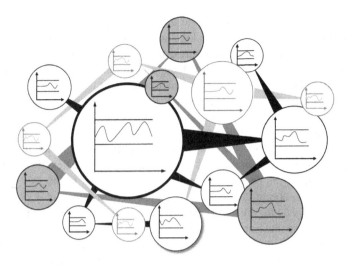

**Fig. 4.** Schematic representation of the interdependencies between different flexibility corridors

measures which arise in case of bundles of measures. The planning must therefore not be limited to measures for eliminating the identified difference between existing and future performance respectively cost profile but has to take into account all system elements and their connections of the considered system.

Based on the transfer of a real production process into the virtual world in the form of the digital shadow, a digital twin can also be created as the basis for the described assistance system. A digital twin is a simulation-enabled and real-time data driven process model of the structures and operations of the real factory environment which can generate additional or future data [24]. In contrast to the digital shadow, a digital twin can already be designed before the physical systems and includes not only performance descriptions but also future orders and system loads [39]. The simulation capability of the digital twin enables the automated recognition of (future) deviations from target settings. Furthermore, it serves as "virtual testbed" by simulating the implementation of various individual measures or bundles of measures and evaluating their impacts on changes in corridor boundaries, or by examining the influence of control measures. Thus, the digital twin is the basis for a decision support system, so that a precise adaption planning in complex logistical structures becomes reality [45].

Due to the complex and dynamic structural connections between the factory subsystems, the multi-criteria evaluation of adaption measures represents the most challenging step of the planning phase. The evaluation is based on a company-specific weighting of the time and cost information determined in the concretization step as well as the four logistical target values. The data basis for evaluation of the logistical target values comes from an experimental examination within the digital twin. In the first step of the experimental examination, the adaption measure, which needs to be evaluated, is integrated into the virtual factory model. In the second step, the system behavior is simulated by taking into account the adaption measure, in order to be able to quantify the four logistical target values in the subsequent third step. All identified and specified adaption measures must run through the described procedure model. The adaption-measure-specific quantifications of the logistical target values (results of the procedure model) as well as the time and cost information resulting from the concretization step are subjected to a joint multi-criteria evaluation in the last step of the planning phase.

For the sake of completeness, a supplement must be made which further increases the complexity of the evaluation mechanism. For simplification, the above-mentioned explanations on the evaluation of adaption measures assume that the parameter courses of a corridor model are not influenced by the measures taken, which means they are considered to be independent of those. However, reality shows that the implementation of adaption measures has an impact not only on the shape of the flexibility corridors but also on the course of the parameters considered. In addition to the shift of flexibility corridor boundaries, abrupt changes in the course of parameters may occur when an adaption measure is taking effect. These changes in the course of parameters may in turn require adaption measures elsewhere in the system. When evaluating adaption measures, it is important to consider these dependencies in the simulation environment. The generated evaluation results represent the output of the planning phase as well as the input for the subsequent decision phase.

### 3.4 Decision

In the decision phase, an adaption measure or a bundle of adaption measures has to be selected. The multi-criteria-evaluated adaption measures of the planning phase form the basis for the decision. Depending on the generated evaluation results an appropriate decision level is defined. Adaption measures, which have comparatively little impact on the factory system or rather on the logistical target values and which furthermore can be implemented cost-effectively and rapidly, are likely to be assigned to a system autonomous decision level. In this context, system autonomous means that the decision regarding the implementation of an adaption measure is made independently by the affected subsystems of the factory and thus without any human intervention. Cost-intensive decisions which have a corresponding impact on the factory system will still require human intervention.

As a general rule, the decision to implement an adaption measure should be made as early as necessary, but as late as possible. This basic rule minimizes the risk of wrong decisions and thus also of bad investments. The digital twin is used to implement this basic rule. Due to the experimental simulation properties, the adaption measures can be projected scenario-based into the future within the digital twin. This procedure allows the identification of an optimal decision point at which a timely implementation of the adaption measure can still be ensured and the uncertainty concerning the future course of parameters can be minimized.

Autonomous decisions of a system regarding the implementation of adaption measures require a corresponding infrastructure. The following example gives an insight on how such an infrastructure could be designed, but it makes no claim to completeness: An infrastructure suitable for making system autonomous decisions should include that the factory subsystems, which are affected by the adaption, are able to directly contact the machine suppliers in order to independently retrieve the adaption measures developed during the planning phase (e.g. adding a single device or an entire process module). In order to reduce the delivery times of the technical units which are required to implement an adaption measure, business models based on the principle of a consignment warehouse are conceivable. In doing so, machine suppliers would stock certain, previously defined technical equipment units inside the customer's factory, which can autonomously be retrieved and used by the corresponding subsystems of the factory if required. Expenses are only charged to the customer if the equipment units held in the consignment warehouse are actually used. The procedure described above is about the outsourcing of technical flexibility to machine suppliers and thus about a "consignment warehouse of technical flexibility" for the customer. The consideration of change enablers in the design of technical equipment (e.g. modularity) supports the implementation of the described concept. The speed of provisioning can be integrated into the machine price with an appropriate bonus. On the side of machine suppliers, again, industry 4.0 technologies such as forecasts can be used to estimate requirements and thus provide parts as far as possible in line with the demand and in the appropriate quantities.

### 3.5    Implementation

During the implementation phase, the selected adaption measure or the selected bundle of measures has to be implemented. The digital twin can also be used to support in this phase. For example, it can be used to carry out a virtual commissioning before the real implementation of the measures take place. The virtual commissioning can generate time and cost savings during the subsequent real implementation of the adaption measure.

Another possibility to increase the efficiency of the implementation phase is the use of an automated initial master data management. In this case, the initial master data of the process which is influenced by the implementation of the measures is determined in advance by simulation. If the adaption measure to be implemented is e.g. the development, implementation and commissioning of an additional production facility, the initial master data of the facility can already be determined by simulation before its real commissioning and be stored on the corresponding facility computing unit. As soon as the real commissioning is completed and the facility can be integrated into the existing production network, the initial master data is automatically sent to the corresponding information receiver, e.g. to the ERP system.

The availability of an always up-to-date factory image can generate additional benefits. Thus, the non-productive times of the real commissioning can be reduced because for example media supply points in the digital image are directly visible or are even actively highlighted in a context-specific view. The given example shows that in the context of the real implementation of measures, wasting processes such as search processes can be reduced or in the best case completely eliminated by using the digital factory image. In order to ensure real-time availability of the current status with regard to the implementation of the measures, the responsible commissioning engineer can for example be equipped with a smart device (e.g. Tablet PC). The commissioning engineer's input combined with the technical functions of the device offer amongst others the seamless utilization of the following modules:

- Project management: always up-to-date overview of time and cost trend (always up-to-date project status)
- Digital factory image: influences on the digital image caused by the implementation of the adaption measure (e.g. layout changes) are automatically transferred into the virtual model (always up-to-date virtual factory image)
- Fault management: if complications occur during the implementation of the measures, the digital image can be used to examine solution alternatives on short notice. If, for example, a technical facility cannot be built at the planned location for a variety of reasons, alternative installation locations as well as the associated impacts on surrounding trades can directly be examined and evaluated.

### 3.6 Impact

If the implementation of an adaption measure or a bundle of measures can be completed, a corresponding impact will occur in the processes influenced by the measure. Via various data collection points, the impact of an adaption measure is recorded and automatically sent to the digital twin. Within the simulation image, the impact leads to changes in the course of flexibility corridor boundaries and parameters. By means of quantitative validation, it can be checked whether the impact that has occurred reflects the target state defined in the planning phase. The validation results are integrated into the knowledge management of the adaption process in the form of empirical values and can be taken into account in future planning phases.

Depending on the type of the implemented adaption measure, the number of data points, which need to be considered for the up-to-dateness of the digital twin, changes (e.g. new production facility, technical expansion module) or remains constant (e.g. replacement of an existing with a more powerful facility module). With the integration of the new data collection points and the impact of an adaption measure, the circle of adaption intelligence is closed and the new or changed data is recorded in the observation phase again.

## 4 Conclusion and Outlook

The paper investigated that adaption in CPPS can be done more frequently, quicker and more precisely than in classical systems. There is a growing need for this development to an intelligent adaption process considering the increasingly dynamic and complex business environment. For this reason, first, the corridor model and the six-step adaption process was presented as a fundamental concept for dealing with a dynamic and complex environment within the company. On this basis the paper demonstrated how the current technological developments in the context of industry 4.0 can help to address these challenges along every step of the six-step process of adaption. It has been shown that the potential of real-time data availability of cyber-physical systems is a key component for increased adaptability. A data-driven digital image of the factory system supports the adaption process in every phase. In particular, the monitoring phase is massively supported by feedback data from production when it comes to perceiving changes and deciding on adaption requirements. This is particularly reflected in the significantly increased speed and precision of demand detection. The higher precision achieved by the data-supported derivation of adaption needs is also due to an improved utilization of inherent flexibility potentials through production planning and control. Furthermore, it was shown that future adaption needs can also be predicted based on methods of predictive analytics. Since the structural interdependencies of production and logistics systems are very complicated and the effects of adaption measures therefore cannot be viewed holistically by humans, the adaption process is supported in the planning and decision phase by an assistance system based on a digital twin of the production and logistics system. This enables to investigate the various effects of adaption measures on different types of flexibility and the course of the parameters considered by means of simulation. In addition, the implementation phase can be supported in CPPS by virtual commissioning, initial master data management and context-specific factory views. All these described capabilities characterize an intelligent adaption process of a production and logistics system against the background of current technological and market developments.

This article is very visionary and forward-looking. In the future, it will be necessary to establish the remarks mentioned in practice by first demonstrating the applicability and cost-effectiveness in a first step with the help of use cases. However, there are numerous hurdles in companies that have to be overcome. For the use of the above-mentioned statements, appropriate preconditions and structures for the applicability in companies must first be created in future research.

**Acknowledgment.** The authors gratefully acknowledge the financial support of the Deutsche Forschungsgemeinschaft (DFG, German Research Foundation) within the Research Training Group GRK-2193 "Adaption Intelligence of Factories in a Dynamic and Complex Environment".

# References

1. Westkämper, E., Zahn, E.: Wandlungsfähige Produktionsunternehmen: Das Stuttgarter Unternehmensmodell (engl.: Transformable production companies: The Stuttgart business model). Springer, Heidelberg (2009). https://doi.org/10.1007/978-3-540-68890-7
2. Karl, F., Reinhart, G.: Reconfigurations on manufacturing resources: identification of needs and planning. Prod. Eng. Res. Devel. **9**(3), 393–404 (2015)
3. Staufen Digital Neonex GmbH und Staufen AG (2017): Deutscher Industrie 4.0 Index. (engl.: German Industry 4.0 Index) http://www.staufen.ag/fileadmin/HQ/02-Company/05-Media/2-Studies/STAUFEN.-studie-deutscher-industrie-4.0-index-2017-de_DE.pdf. Accessed 20 Mar 2018
4. Delbrügger, T., et al.: Anpassungsintelligenz von Fabriken im dynamischen und komplexen Umfeld (engl.: Adaption intelligence of factories in a dynamic and complex environment). ZWF Zeitschrift für wirtschaftlichen Fabrikbetrieb **112**(6), 364–368 (2017)
5. acatech (ed.): Cyber-Physical Systems. Driving force for innovation in mobility, health, energy and production (acatech POSITION PAPER). Springer, Heidelberg (2011). https://doi.org/10.1007/978-3-642-29090-9
6. Klötzer, C.; Pflaum, A.: Toward the development of a maturity model for digitalization within the manufacturing industry's supply chain. In: Hawaii International Conference on System Sciences 2017 (HICSS-50) (2017)

7. Barrows, E., Neely, A.: Managing Performance in Turbulent Times. Wiley, Hoboken (2012)
8. Gossmann, D., Wagner, C., Klemke, T., Nyhuis, P.: Change-beneficial process architectures and the human as a change enabler. In: ElMaraghy, H.A. (eds.) Enabling Manufacturing Competitiveness and Economic Sustainability. Proceedings of the 4th International Conference on Changeable, Agile, Reconfigurable and Virtual production (CARV 2011), Montreal, Canada, 2–5 October 2011, Springer, Heidelberg, pp. 370–375 (2012). https://doi.org/10.1007/978-3-642-23860-4_61
9. Schmitt, R., Glöckner, H.: Identifikation von Wandlungsbedarf: Eine Kernaufgabe des unternehmerischen Qualitätsmanagements (engl.: Identification of the need for change: a core task of corporate quality management). wt Werkstattstechnik online 102(11/12), 801–806 (2012)
10. Wiendahl, H., Reichardt, J., Nyhuis, P.: Handbook Factory Planning and Design, 2nd edn. Hanser, München (2014)
11. ElMaraghy, H., Wiendahl, H.P.: Changeable manufacturing. In: Laperrière, L., Reinhart, G. (eds.) The International Academy for Production Engineering, CIRP Encyclopedia of Production Engineering. Springer, Heidelberg (2014). https://doi.org/10.1007/978-3-642-35950-7
12. Nyhuis, P., Heinen, T., Brieke, M.: Adequate and economic factory transformability and the effects on logistical performance. Int. J. Flex. Manuf. Syst. 19(3), 286–307 (2007)
13. Luft, N.: Aufgabenbasierte Flexibilitätsbewertung von Produktionssystemen (engl.: Task-based flexibility assessment of production systems). Dissertation. Technische Universität Dortmund, Verlag Praxiswissen, Dortmund (2013)
14. Albrecht, F., Kleine, O., Abele, E.: Planning and optimization of changeable production systems by applying an integrated system dynamic and discrete event simulation approach. Procedia CIRP 17, 386–391 (2014)
15. Stricker, N., Lanza, G.: The concept of robustness in production systems and its correlation to disturbances. Procedia CIRP 19, 87–92 (2014)
16. Hernandez Morales, R.: Systematik der Wandlungsfähigkeit in der Fabrikplanung (engl.: Systematics of transformability in factory planning). VDI-Verlag, Düsseldorf (2003)
17. Dormayer, H.-J.: Konjunkturelle Früherkennung und Flexibilität im Produktionsbereich (engl.: Early economic detection and flexibility in production). München: Ifo-Institut für Wirtschaftsforschung, Ifo-Beiträge zur quantitativen Wirtschaftsforschung (1986)
18. Hopfmann, L.: Flexibilität im Produktionsbereich - Ein dynamisches Modell zur Analyse und Bewertung von Flexibilitätspotentialen (engl.: Flexibility in production - A dynamic model for the analysis and evaluation of flexibility potentials.). Dissertation. Verlag Peter Lang (1989)
19. Zäh, M. F., Moeller, N., Vogl, W.: Symbiosis of Changeable and Virtual Production. The Emperor's New Clothes or Key Factor for Future Success? In: Reinhart, G., Zäh, M. F. (eds.): Proccedings of the 1st International Conference on Changeable, Agile, Reconfigurable and Virtual Production (CARV 2005), pp. 3–10. Utz, München (2005)
20. Schel, D., Henkel, C., Stock, D., Meyer, O., Rauhöft, G., Einberger, P., et al.: Manufacturing service bus: an implementation. Procedia CIRP 67, 179–184 (2018)
21. Schuh, G., et al.: Produktionsdaten als Enabler für Industrie 4.0 - Gemeinsame Studie der produktionstechnischen Institute IFA, IPMT, Fraunhofer IWU und WZL (engl.: Production data as enabler for industry 4.0 - Joint study by the production technology institutes IFA, IPMT, Fraunhofer IWU and WZL). Werkstattstechnik online 105(4), Springer, Düsseldorf, pp. 200–203 (2015)
22. Hornyák, O., Erdélyi, F.: Manufacturing execution systems for advanced shop floor control. In: The Eleventh International Conference on Machine Design and Production, Antalya (2004)

23. Kagermann, H.: Umsetzungsempfehlungen für das Zukunftsprojekt Industrie 4.0: Abschlussbericht des Arbeitskreises Industrie 4.0. acatech – Deutsche Akademie der Technikwissenschaften e.V. (engl.: Implementation recommendations for the future project Industry 4.0: Final report of the working group Industry 4.0. acatech - Deutsche Akademie der Technik-wissenschaften e.V.), München (2013)

24. Bauernhansl, T., Krüger, J., Reinhart, G., Schuh, G.: WGP-Standpunkt Industrie 4.0 (engl.: WGP Position Industry 4.0). Wissenschaftliche Gesellschaft für Produktionstechnik WGP e. V., Darmstadt (2016)

25. Schuh, G., et al.: Cyber physical production control. In: Jeschke, S., Brecher, C., Song, H., Rawat, D. B. (eds.): Industrial Internet of Things, Springer, Wiesbaden, pp. 540–559 (2017). https://doi.org/10.1007/978-3-319-42559-7_21

26. Wegener, D.: Industrie 4.0 – Chancen und Herausforderungen für einen Global Player (engl.: Industry 4.0 - Opportunities and challenges for a global player). In: Bauernhansl, T., ten Hompel, M., Vogel-Heuser, B. (eds.): Industrie 4.0 in Produktion, Automatisierung und Logistik: Anwendung, Technologien, Migration, Springer Vieweg, Wiesbaden, pp. 342–358 (2014)

27. Humm, B.; Wietek, F.: Architektur von Data Warehouses und Business Intelligence Systemen (engl.: Architecture of data warehouses and business intelligence systems.). Informatik-Spektrum 28(1), 3–14 (2005)

28. Fasel, D., Mcier, A.: Big Data. Grundlagen, Systeme und Nutzungspotenziale (engl.: Big Data. Basics, systems and potential uses), Springer Vieweg (Edition HMD), Wiesbaden (2016)

29. Evans, J.R.: Business analytics. Methods, Models, and Decisions, 1st edn. Pearson, Boston (2013)

30. Sivarajah, U., Kamal, M.M., Irani, Z., Weekakkody, V.: Critical analysis of big data challenges and analytical methods. J. Bus. Res. 70(January 2017), 263–286 (2016)

31. Bertsch, S.: Logistic changeability-application of a methodological framework for designing logistic changeability. World Acad. Sci., Eng. Technol., Int. J. Mech., Aerosp., Ind., Mechatron. Manuf. Eng. 7(10), 2068–2073 (2013)

32. Klemke, T.: Planung der systemischen Wandlungsfähigkeit von Fabriken (engl.: Planning the systemic transformability of factories). Dissertation Leibniz Universität Hannover, Garbsen: Berichte aus dem IFA, Garbsen (2014)

33. Lübkemann, J.: Ermittlung des Restrukturierungsbedarfs von Fabriken (engl.: Determination of the restructuring needs of factories). Dissertation Leibniz Universität Hannover, Garbsen: Berichte aus dem IFA, Garbsen (2016)

34. Besenfelder, C.: Fertigungsstrukturwandel – organisatorische Gestaltungsfelder der Produktionslogistik (engl.: Production structure change - organisational design fields of production logistics), Tagungsband „Produktion und Arbeitswelt 4.0 - Aktuelle Konzepte für die Praxis?", 15. Tage des Betriebs- und Systemingenieurs (TBI 2014), Wissenschaftliche Schriftenreihe des Institutes für Betriebswissenschaften und Fabriksysteme, Sonderheft 20 (2014)

35. Schuh, G., Potente, T., Thomas, C., Nuyken, T., Hausberg, C.: Approach to Assess and Compare the Performances of Production Structures. In. Advanced Materials Research, vol. 1018, pp. 469–476 (2014)

36. Gille, C., Zwißler, F.: Bewertung von Wandlungstreibern: Voraussetzung einer wandlungsfähigen Unternehmensausrichtung (engl.: Evaluation of change drivers: prerequisite for a changeable corporate orientation). ZWF Zeitschrift für wirtschaftlichen Fabrikbetrieb 106 (5), pp. 310–313 (2011)

37. Seebacher, G., Winkler, H.: Evaluating flexibility in discrete manufacturing based on performance and efficiency. Int. J. Prod. Econ. 153, 340–351 (2014)

38. Seebacher, G.: Approaches to assessing production flexibility. Dissertation Alpen-Adria Universität Klagenfurt, Logos-Verlag, Berlin (2013)
39. Besenfelder, C., et al.: Whitepaper: Paradigmenwechsel der Planung und Steuerung von Wertschöpfungsnetzen (engl.: Paradigm shift in the planning and control of supply chains). In: ten Hompel, M., Henke, M., Clausen, U. (eds.): Future Challenges in Logistics and Supply Chain Management, Fraunhofer IML, Dortmund (2017)
40. Gudehus, T.: Dynamische Märkte: Grundlagen und Anwendungen der analytischen Ökonomie (engl.: Dynamic markets: Fundamentals and applications of the analytical economy). Springer Gabler, Berlin (2015)
41. Cisek, R., Habicht, C., Neise, P.: Gestaltung wandlungsfähiger Produktionssysteme (engl.: Design of transformable production systems). ZWF Zeitschrift für wirtschaftlichen Fabrikbetrieb **97**(9), 441–445 (2002)
42. Heinen, T., Rimpau, C., Wörn, A.: Wandlungsfähigkeit als Ziel der Produktionssystemgestaltung (engl.: Transformability as a goal of production system design). In: Nyhuis, P., Reinhart, G., Abele, E. (eds.) Wandlungsfähige Produktionssysteme. Heute die Industrie von morgen gestalten, pp. 19–32. GITO-Verl. (Schriftenreihe der Hochschulgruppe für Arbeits- und Betriebsorganisation e.V. (HAB)), Berlin (2010)
43. Kaluza, B.: Flexibilität der Industrieunternehmen (engl.: Flexibility of industrial companies). Diskussionsbeiträge des Fachbereichs Wirtschaftswissenschaften der Gerhard-Mercator-Universität Gesamthochschule Duisburg, Nr. 208, Duisburg (1995)
44. Reinhart, G., Kerbs, P., Schellmann, H.: Flexibilität und Wandlungsfähigkeit – das richtige Maß finden (engl.: Flexibility and transformability - finding the right balance). In: Hoffmann, H., Reinhart, R., Zäh, M. F. (eds.) Münchener Kolloquium. Innovationen für die Produktion. Produktionskongress, 9. Oktober 2008, München, pp. 45–55 (2008)
45. Qi, Q., Tao, F.: Digital twin and big data towards smart manufacturing and industry 4.0. 360 degree comparison. IEEE Access **6**, 3585–3593 (2018)

# Model-Based Systems Engineering for Systems Simulation

Renan Leroux[1,2,3], Marc Pantel[1,2](✉), Ileana Ober[1,2], and Jean-Michel Bruel[1,2]

[1] Institute Technology (IRT) Antoine de Saint-Exupéry, Toulouse, France
[2] University of Toulouse/Institute for Research in Informatics of Toulouse,
Toulouse, France
{renan.leroux,marc.pantel,ileana.ober,jean-michel.bruel}@irit.fr
[3] ALTRAN, Toulouse, France
Renan.Leroux@altran.com

**Abstract.** Model-Based Systems Engineering and early simulation based Validation & Verification are now key enablers for managing the complexity in the development of modern complex systems like Cyber-Physical Systems. Models provide a formal account of system requirements and design decisions. Model simulation enables both design exploration and design versus requirements correctness assessment. Model simulation activities rely on Simulation Systems (i.e. systems that execute the model simulation). System execution environment models play a key role during these activities. Appropriate models must be developed for each kind of analysis conducted during Validation & Verification. More and more often, complex Systems Engineering is conducted in Extended Enterprises and the simulation activities are performed using partial models that must be completed with mock-up models for missing parts of the system. The development of Simulation Systems is thus costly and error prone and would benefit from the same Systems Engineering principles that are applied to the product. We propose a methodology for a seamless integration of the Simulation Systems development in the Products Systems Engineering. This method imports the available elements from the models of the system and its environment, from the Systems Engineering for Product space to a dedicated Systems Engineering for Simulation space. The required mock-up models are then defined in the Systems Engineering for Simulation space. As a result, we target a better management and reuse of the various environment and mock-up models in the various simulation activities during the development of the same product. This proposal is independent both of the actual methods and tools used to model the system and of the simulation environment.

## 1 Introduction

The use of MBSE (Model-Based Systems Engineering) and early simulation-based V&V (Validation & Verification) offers effective means to handle the complexity of real-life industrial development projects. Regularly, such projects need to combine several engineering fields in the context of EE (Extended Enterprise)

© Springer Nature Switzerland AG 2018
T. Margaria and B. Steffen (Eds.): ISoLA 2018, LNCS 11246, pp. 429–448, 2018.
https://doi.org/10.1007/978-3-030-03424-5_29

where many stakeholders are involved such as *Cyber Physical Systems* (CPS). In this context, the simulation activities are often performed in an ad-hoc manner depending on the project, the involved partners, etc. To our knowledge and understanding, there exists no common reference methodology helping the various engineers involved in the product development in making the best choices seamlessly and efficiently for the simulation activities. Our work aims at filling this gap by proposing a methodology that specifically addresses the simulation and its needs. This paper provides a first draft of this methodology illustrated through a realistic case study.

This paper first provides insights on approaches that achieve early simulation-based V&V in the context of MBSE in common industrial settings, in particular within the MOISE (MOdels and Information Sharing for System engineering in Extended enterprise) project of the IRT-SE (Institut de Recherche Technologique Saint Exupéry – Institute of Technology Saint Exupéry), where our work takes place. One key aspect is that these activities are nowadays mostly conducted in EEs where many stakeholders target an efficient cooperation while protecting their know-how (usually named wrongly IP (Intellectual Property) which is a legal term that may only cover partly the stakeholder purpose). Thus, the various parts of the systems models are built in a concurrent engineering manner and simulation activities are conducted on partial models that must be completed with mock-up models for missing parts of the system. These models must also be completed with environment models whose content depends on the kind of validation and verification activities that are conducted relying on simulation. The building of these *Simulation Systems* (SS) is thus, in itself, costly and error prone and would benefit from the same SE (Systems Engineering) principles that are applied to the product.

Our contribution advocates the use of a rigorous methodology to build SSs tailored for its specific needs. We introduce such a methodology, by adapting to SSs development, many principles specific to SE. In this context, a particular attention is given to the representation of the environment that plays a key role in the simulation. Particularly, for needs that are specific to simulation activities, its representation must be carefully handled and shall be included to a certain degree in the modelling. Our approach is generic and potentially compatible with various actual system development and simulation technologies.

The rest of this paper is organized as follows: in Sect. 2, we present existing efforts for simulation-based early V&V in the industry, in particular in the MOISE project, as well as our running example: the AIDA inspection drone that will be used throughout the rest of the paper. Section 3 overviews the principles of our generic methodology for performing simulation in the context of MBSE, which is detailed in Sect. 4 with illustrations from the AIDA case study. Section 5 presents the expected benefits for the use of a rigorous methodology for SSs development and gives some directions for future work.

## 2  Context Presentation

### 2.1  Industrial Concerns

MBSE and early V&V are now key enablers for the development of complex CPSs in many application domains like transportation [1–3]. Model simulation is an effective approach for early V&V, allowing design decisions to be assessed earlier in the product life cycle. The duration and costs of the system development can thereby be reduced [4–6].

According to [7], simulation-based design is a *"process in which simulation is the primary means of design evaluation and verification"*. Given the increasing complexity of the systems and in order to manage the structural complexity of the systems simulations, [8] proposes a MBSE [9] method to integrate simulation activities in the development process of complex systems. This approach seems all the more relevant in the concurrent design of systems involving multiple engineering domains such as: mechanical, hydraulic, electrical, etc. parts. Depending on the point of view to be assessed, different simulation activities allow to estimate, and/or to refine the different interactions between components [7,8].

While aiming at time and development costs reductions, [2] focuses on issues related to the integration, verification, validation and qualification of the simulation models. To reduce the potential ambiguities between system engineers and domain experts in charge of simulation model development, [2] adds a new actor in the process called *"Model Architect"* that coordinates the various MBSE activities. This new actor should have a multidisciplinary vision of the product whose architecture is under design and some knowledge in simulation technologies used for modeling the various parts of the architecture.

In [2], the authors propose an ontological DSL (Domain Specific Language), MIC (Model Identity Card), that covers the needs of various application domains, including the specification of interfaces and the building of simulation models. This DSL targets all the actors of the models, unfortunately it does not integrate a precise account of the behavior of simulation models. To overcome this, [10,11] use the concept of MoI (Model of Intention), defined as a model based approach to request and specify model(s) or simulation(s) for a specific scenario.

The combination of MIC and of MoI proposed by [10,12] allows to fill the gap existing between the requirements for the simulation performed by the system architect and the implementation of all the required simulation models, therefore reducing the problems related to their integration.

The importance of the simulation for early V&V of requirements and design while protecting IP in EEs is highlighted by the presence of a standard dedicated to the implementation of such SSs - the FMI (Functional Mock-up Interface) standard [13]. The co-simulation part of this standard (FMI 2.0), allows to implement multi-simulations [14] or heterogeneous simulations [15] (see Fig. 1-a), while preserving the IP in simulation models [14]. This IP protection only allows the supplier to visualize the content of its own models and not the one of the others (see Fig. 1-b).

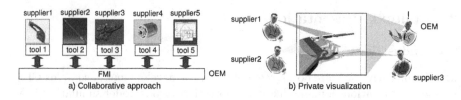

**Fig. 1.** Collaborative and private aspects of the FMI 2.0 standard (from [13]).

Furthermore, in order to build distributed simulations, [15] creates a bridge between FMI and the HLA (High-level architecture) standards [16,17]. In the same purpose, [18] extends the FMI 2.0 standard and supplies a tool (independent of HLA) to implement the simulations on distributed and multi-core architectures.

However, as far as we know, there is no common reference process offering a global and structured vision that allows to implement co-simulation platforms for systems models.

To address this, we advocate that the use of MBSE is meaningful not only for the development of the products, but also for the development of the SSs used during the development of the products. The current contribution illustrates how MBSE can be used for the development of the simulation tools and what are the expected associated models specific to the simulation.

The proposed method for the development of executable simulation models is generic with respect to product and SS development Methods and Tools. This is achieved by clearly separating concerns related to the (i) Systems Engineering for the Product under development, (ii) Systems Engineering for the Product Model Simulations, and (iii) simulation execution and results analysis. This separation can be expressed, for example, in this way: SEPS (Systems Engineering for Product Space) could rely on the MBSE method CESAM for developing the product, while SESS (Systems Engineering for Simulation Space) could rely on the ARCADIA method for developing the SS required for the simulation activities during the product development. Modelica [19], C, C++, Java languages, for example, could be used for implemented the various mock-ups, in the simulation execution space.

The core ideas, of this proposal, are that (i) each model simulation can be a project in itself, with its own constraints and costs; (ii) MBSE can also be applied to these simulation projects; and (iii) commonalities and building blocks can be reused for the different models involved in the development of the same product. Indeed, the development of a product using MBSE involves many different models that may be assessed using simulation. This results in a family of related, yet distinct, models that are conjointly developed and assessed as they are all involved in the development of the same product. Their assessment is done through various simulations which subsequently may require specific simulation models and tools. In this particular context, building blocks developed for the various simulation projects could be reused in the same manner as reuse occurs in SE.

## 2.2    The MOISE Project

The approach presented in this paper takes part in the MOISE project within the IRT-SE in Toulouse (France), with industrial partners, consulting companies, tools vendors and public research institutes (e.g., ISAE, IRIT, LAAS-CNRS, S/C ONERA).

MOISE develops a collaborative MBSE in EEs with the aim to both improve the development activities and reduce their costs. For this, in MOISE we consider requirement validation and design verification, for embedded systems, to enable seamless co-engineering between industrial partners and to manage requirements waterfall with agility and continuity. Furthermore, in MBSE, designers must ensure that the models that they have built are a correct expression of the design they had in mind. This is a specific kind of model validation that occurs each time a formal language is used to express human ideas. This is similar to requirement validation as the ideas a designer has in mind when he is building a model are similar to the informal requirements given by the user at the beginning of a project.

One of the key goals of the project is to reduce V&V costs by using early model simulation activities. The purpose of our proposal is to ease the development of SSs using MBSE and reduce the associated costs by improving reuse both in the transfer of models from product to simulation space [20] and in between the SSs built for the various models involved in the development of the same system.

## 2.3    The AIDA Inspection Drone Case Study

To illustrate our method, we apply it on a use case targeting an inspection drone that moves around a plane on the runway before take off (see Fig. 2). Its purpose is to support the pilot in the mandatory inspection of the aircraft before each flight. This drone should (i) quicken the pilot inspection task and (ii) improve its precision, by scrutinizing not-visually-accessible parts of the plane (e.g., the top of the wings, fuselage, . . . ), in order to detect irregularities, such as forgotten caps on sensors, ill closed trap doors, or mechanical defects such as thunderclaps or impacts of hail.

This drone should be manually controlled following predefined paths (drone flight plans), with enhanced automated safety capacities to avoid hurting ground staff. For this purpose, the drone is aware of the cartography of the plane and of the location of the points of interest to be scrutinized. The drone is equipped with various sensors: vision system, GPS locator, and a radar, for a greater precision, to ensure a sufficient safe distance with respect to the plane and the ground staff.

To enable the diagnostic in case of malfunction, the flight data are saved locally and transferred in real-time to the ground. Moreover, the operator can watch live images taken by the drone, to make sure that control points do not present any irregularities, and adapt the drone flight plan if needed.

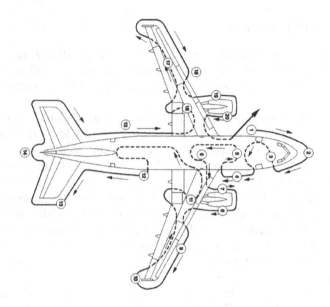

**Fig. 2.** External Walk around a plane.

# 3    The V Cycle and Simulation Activities

## 3.1    Overview

The main purpose of our work is to ease the simulation-based early V&V activities in MBSE. Let's recall the distinction between Validation and Verification: According to Boehm, Validation targets building the right product (i.e. the product that fits the user needs – the implicit requirements that are the source for writing the product specification) and Verification targets building the product right (i.e. the product that satisfies its explicit requirements – the product specification). Thus, if the product is correct (i.e. has been verified), Validation mainly targets detecting an erroneous translation from the implicit requirements in the user mind to the explicit requirements – the product specification. This analysis must involve the user. A first assessment may be conducted without the user in the loop: checking that the explicit requirements are complete and consistent. When the development process involves several phases that each have explicit requirements and expected results, these definitions needs to be adapted to be applied to each phase: Phase Verification assesses the compliance of the results with respect to the requirements; and Phase Validation assesses the requirements (completeness and consistency). When all phases have been conducted, Verification is complete whereas final Validation activities are still needed for the user to accept the product. The IEEE Standard Glossary of Software Engineering Terminology states that Verification is *"The process of evaluating a system or component to determine whether the products of a given development phase satisfy the conditions imposed at the start of that phase"* and that Validation is

*"The process of evaluating a system or component during or at the end of the development process to determine whether it satisfies specified requirements"*. This user part of the validation can be extended to any human activities conducted in a development that require translating the implicit human ideas to explicit documents. In MBSE, these documents are expressed as models. Thus, Model Validation assesses that the model is a correct rendering of the ideas the developer had in mind, whereas Model Verification checks that the resulting model satisfies the explicit requirements, that are most of the time also expressed as models resulting from the previous phases. This can even be extended to documents that have no formal semantics (e.g. natural language, drawing, etc.) used as requirements. Formal Model Validation assesses that a formal model is a correct rendering of an informal document, whereas Formal Model Verification assesses that a formal model satisfies explicit requirements available as formal models.

One of the oldest and most common life-cycle model for system development processes is the *V-Model*. This is a theoretical model that was never applied as it was defined. It consists of sequential process phases, where each phase must be completed before the next one begins. The *V-Model* is rather common in the manufacturing industry such as aviation, automobile, and many others where there exists usually three main phases: product, systems and equipments. A product combines several systems that integrates various equipments. Each phase consists of sequential process steps defined in the development method used. For example, ARCADIA experimented in MOISE relies on the Requirement, Function, Logical and Physical steps.

On the theoretical side, which has almost never been applied as is, the left side of the V corresponds to the development of the product and the right side of the V corresponds to the various V&V activities.

Before the introduction of MBSE, the left hand side of the *V-Model* roughly corresponded to the product development with very little efficient V&V activities conducted. Indeed, only proofreading could be conducted as the results of each steps where semi-formal graphical or textual documents targeting human readers. The right hand side of the model covered test-based V&V of the equipments; then equipments integration and test-based V&V of the systems; systems integration and, in the end, test-based V&V of the product.

Its use could raise problems of diverse natures as most of the efficient V&V activities were only conducted quite late when the various equipments needed for a product had been implemented. It often resulted in the late discovery of Requirement, Functional, Logical or Physical issues during the integration of the various validated and verified equipments. For minor issues, minor changes in the requirements, design and implementation may be possible, while staying efficient and cost effective. However, in some situations, issues discovered during late V&V activities will require major architecture changes or local patches to circumvent and prevent the problem. In all cases, this leads to increased costs and delays in delivery, additional maintenance difficulties, and potentially the addition of new weaknesses.

Furthermore, architecture exploration suffered from the same issues. Either, it was conducted early in the development by humans based on document reading. It was usually far from optimal for complex systems. Or, it was conducted later using tests based on the implemented equipments. But, this led to very high costs as all the equipments required by all the variants of the architecture had to be developed and all the variants of the architecture also had to be implemented.

Last, design document proofreading is not well adapted to IP protection in EE. Indeed, in order to conduct a V&V activity using proofreading, the designer needs to have access to all documents related to the system he designed including the ones built in other enterprises.

To prevent this, the introduction of MBSE and early V&V was shown to be of precious help and is currently being deployed in most manufacturing industries. MBSE enforces the writing of formal models in each step of each phases instead of semi-formal documents, and the assessment of these models using simulation-based testing. These assessments allow the early validation of requirements and verification of design steps. Furthermore, it allows validating the models written by the designers to assess that they are a correct rendering of the ideas he had in mind. The early V&V can take various forms, such as model exploration and structural analysis. That would allow to check for instance that there is no isolated communication port and that the direction of communication paths is unambiguous, thus detecting issues in the architecture that would only be detected in the integration V&V activities.

The actual interpretation of the V cycle depends on the abstraction level at which we consider the system. Figure 3 provides the product, system and equipment views that correspond to the main engineering phases.

At the highest level of abstraction – the one covered by the upper left part of the *V-Model* – the customer needs are expressed and coarse models of the environment of the future product are required to validate the expression of these needs. An exploratory phase is usually conducted to assess the appropriate use of new technologies (see Fig. 3, phase 1) with respect to previous similar products.

The exploratory phase must respond to questions like: (i) what kind of material should be used for its physical parts: steel, aluminum, carbon, composite fiber? (ii) what is the worse case of winds the drone will be submitted to? (iii) can the AIDA drone be protected from radio or EMC interference? To answer these questions, material models or environment models (atmospheric, radio, EMC (Electromagnetic compatibility)) should be simulated with more or less precise description of known and already identified interactions with the system to be studied.

This phase handles the expression of customer needs. For example, in AIDA (see Sect. 2.3), the drone shall conduct an inspection around the plane to detect irregularities.

In this exploratory phase, simulation can be used to illustrate high-level behaviour, under the form of textual requirements using customer vocabulary, or sequence, activity, or state diagrams: operational scenarios that will be executed in front of the user that can accept or not the simulated behaviour. For instance, the procedure of drone intervention around the plane needs to interact with the pilot, the meteorological data provider, and eventually the control tower. These diagrams allow to precisely define the order of interaction with different stakeholders, and simulation can be used to validate it.

In this exploratory phase, the environment models must have the appropriate accuracy to assess that models, within this phase, reflects really its intended semantics and behavior. The environment models, in the simulation, could be later refined to better capture reality.

The second phase of the *V-Model* (see Fig. 3, phase 2) is the *system phase* that takes into account higher-level requirements stemming from the previous phase in order to express operational requirements associated with the various systems to be designed in order to build the final product. This is an essential part, that represents the core of our work, although our proposal is generic enough to be applied to the other phases. Models and activities involved in this phase will be provided in the following sections of this contribution.

The *equipment* phase (see Fig. 3, phase 3) focuses on the underlying hardware platform and the associated deployed software. It is developed on the basis of the requirements produced at the system phase (phase 2). In the context of simulation, at this stage we target particularly accurate simulations. That could cover the simulation of a processor whose behaviour is described at the clock cycle level of accuracy, the simulation of a communication protocol taking into account the physical layers of the OSI standard, etc.

This last kind of simulation is not addressed in this paper, but our proposal could be easily adapted to handle such constraints, usually involving HIL (Hardware In the Loop).

### 3.2   MBSE-RFLP Method

The MBSE approach, used for the AIDA use case, relies on the RFLP (Requirement, Functional, Logical, Physical) general methodology that drives many industrial methods and tools, like the ARCADIA methodology [21] and the associated CAPELLA toolset. With this toolset, during the development of the

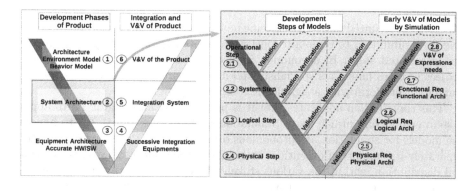

**Fig. 3.** Global V cycle and focus on system development layer.

system models, it is possible to build several kind of architecture corresponding to each layer (see Fig. 3, phases 2.1 to 2.4). These models, in each layer,
can be assessed through simulation, both to check that models reflect the system designer intention (validation) and that models satisfy the requirements
expressed in the previous layer (verification).

The first step of the System phase, Operational Analysis, analyzes the operational requirements issued from the Product phase and builds corresponding
models that will drive the following steps of the System phase. These models
can be validated using simulation.

To meet the operational requirements expressed in these first models, the next
step is the "System Architecture design" that mostly consists in refining models
from the previous phase. The obtained architecture shall meet the requirements
of the operational layer, which can be assessed through V&V. Newly defined
functions and their communications interfaces (see Fig. 3, phase 2.2) adds new
requirements to be met by the next steps.

When this functional architecture is complete and mature enough, it may
be significant to group similar elements into common and specific functions,
providing logical components (as it is the case with the *Allocation functions*
from Figs. 8, 9 and 10). This results in an intermediate architecture layer (the
*Logical layer* in Fig. 3, phase 2.3) situated between the functional layer expressed
above and the physical layer to which these logical functions will be allocated.
This logical layer can ease the deployment and the assignment of components
(more precisely, their inner functions) to the equipments in the physical layer.

Finally, the *physical layer* specifies the physical architecture of the equipment,
as well as deployment and inter-dependency links. Additional requirements are
added to this layer to specify/constrain component deployment, communication
means and interfaces between them (see Fig. 3, phase 2.4).

The principles of the MBSE method used previously are quite similar to other
approaches like CESAM [22]. Therefore, the MOISE approach can be adapted
to other methods.

## 4   Proposed Approach

Building the required tools for a specific model simulation activity can be expensive. It is submitted to temporal constraints related to the development process
and associated steps. In a common industrial frame, this kind of simulation
project involves numerous specialists and may require the building of a specific
simulation platform with a significant computing power.

This contribution advocates that it is possible and meaningful: (i) to apply
system engineering principles to Simulation Systems (see Fig. 4), (ii) to handle
the models for simulation as autonomous objects, and (iii) to take into account
separately its support of execution, including the computing power and its spa-
cial distribution, within the various stakeholders in the EE, that participate in
the development of the product whose models must be simulated (see Fig. 6).

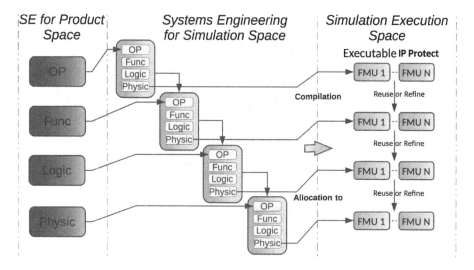

**Fig. 4.** Global View of the methodology, without processing platform allocation.

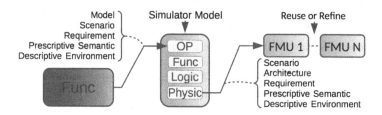

**Fig. 5.** Data transfer from ES product space to ES simulation space. (Color figure online)

### 4.1 Model-Based Systems Engineering for Simulation

MBSE helps the system engineer in assessing the relevance of the system architecture and the compliance with the desired system properties. The same results can be expected from its application to Simulation Systems. Our proposal has the particularity that both methodologies (e.g., CESAM [22], ARCADIA [21], ...) are independent: the one used for the development of the simulation system can be different from the one used for the design of the product.

The clear separation between the Systems Engineering for the Product and the Systems Engineering for the Simulation offers numerous advantages. The main benefit of our approach is that it offers flexibility and adaptability. Diligent to the (cultural) context of the companies involved, it allows to comply to the methods and the working habits of the involved people and facilitates the collaboration of the various actors involved in the development and simulation.

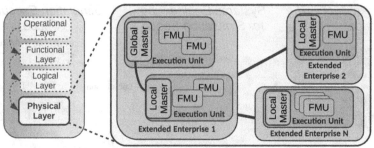

Simulation Physical Layer detailed representation, for allocating
FMU models on Execution Units, in the Extended Enterprise models

**Fig. 6.** Content of the simulation physical layer.

### 4.2   Systems Engineering Product Space

The SEP (Systems Engineering for Product) space is the entry point of our method. It relies on models to represent the various aspects involved in the system design phase of the product. To illustrate our point, we use the MBSE-RFLP design method, as explained in Subsect. 3.2. The system engineer in charge of the product plays the role of the *System Architect*. By acting on the four layers, he will be able to use simulation, throughout the design cycle to assess that the obtained models correctly capture his purpose, and are conforming to the models from the previous phases: operational architecture for the requirements, functional architecture of the provided services, components in the logical architecture and allocation of these logical components in the physical architecture.

### 4.3   Simulator Systems Engineering Space

Each simulation project for each simulation V&V activity in the SEP space will be developed in the SES (Systems Engineering for Simulation) space. The system engineer in charge of the simulation project is called the SA (Simulation Architect). SA has the choice of the most appropriate method of conception. To illustrate more easily our proposal, we have chosen the same design method as the one from the SEP: the MBSE-RFLP method. It is also in this space that the SA specifies the inputs/outputs of simulation models and shares them for execution on the simulation platform of each stakeholder (see Fig. 6).

### 4.4   Models Simulation Execution Space

This space is dedicated to the management, integration and execution of executable simulation models. These activities can be facilitated by the use of co-simulation standards like FMI. Due to space limitations, we do not address the specifics of this space in this contribution.

## 4.5   Simulation Architect

The SA should have some particular skills, such as: (a) have a wide knowledge of the various domains being simulated, and (b) be open minded and endowed with communication skills [2]. Indeed, typically the simulation involves different actors that are each expert in their field of activity. The SA is the interface between the System Architect and these experts involved in the implementation of the simulation models. The SA performs in the SES space and the models simulation execution space and thus will also communicate with people in charge of the infrastructure of the simulation, in the various companies. Let us mention, for example, the people in charge of the implementation of computers and OS, of the security of the internal and external networks, of the management of physical access rights to the hardware and software.

## 4.6   Simulation: From Its Request to Its Execution

The description of the process proposal is generic, regardless of the system design method used, and of the selected layer in the SEP space: Operational (OP), Functional (Fun), Logical (Logic) or Physical (Physic) as illustrated in Fig. 4: Product Space.

The starting point is the System Architect needs to assess properties of the product's architecture. Therefore, he transmits all the information needed to the SES space. Figure 5 illustrates the information flow between the functional layer of the product and the operational layer of the SES space.

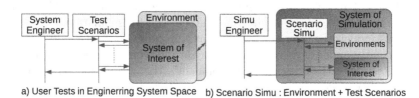

a) User Tests in Enginerring System Space   b) Scenario Simu : Environment + Test Scenarios

**Fig. 7.** Evolution between Product Space & Simulation Space.

Our approach is illustrated using the AIDA drone use case introduced in Sect. 2.3. With respect to Fig. 7-a, the drone is the *System of Interest* whose architecture is currently being designed and must be assessed using simulation. The System Architect is currently assessing the behavior of the "Move" function (see Fig. 8, Product Model) present in the System of Interest at the "Func" layer of the SEP space (see "Func" layer in Figs. 4 and 5). The "Move" function shall control correctly the position and the speed of the drone.

To perform a simulation, the System Architect provides some information to the SA:

- *the system architecture model.* With respect to our case study, it includes the "Move" function and all the directly related functions ("Compute Actual Position and Speed", "Inertial Central", "Compute Next Position and Speed", "Receiver GPS")
- *test scenarios models* describing the interactions between the "System Engineer" actor and the System of Interest during the simulation
- *requirements for traceability*
- a *prescriptive semantic model* of the function to be simulated. In our case, this corresponds to a model of the execution semantics of the "Move" function, as an UML activity or state diagram, or as a Modelica or Simulink model, or even as software code, etc.
- *environment models requirements.* In our case (see Fig. 8-Product Model), the System Engineer asks to include in the simulation, the "Provide Signal from GPS Environment" and "Create Lift force from Atmosphere Environment" models.

The System Architect transfers all these information to the SES space, as one can see in Figs. 4 and 5).

The SA handles these data as requirements, and places them in the dedicated operational layer for simulation (see Fig. 5).

From these elements, he begins to build the simulation system functional architecture whose purpose is the simulation of the "Move" function (see Fig. 5: OP → Func). This layer imports functions from the "Product Model", provides functions to describe environments and the scenario for simulation.

The SA models the internal environment (turquoise blue) as a family of functions, currently under development, directly or indirectly connected to the function of interest. In this "Internal Environment", the output and input of functions, directly connected to function of interest, describes the expected behaviour of the function of interest and are thus considered as correct by construction. For the AIDA use case, functions placed in "Internal Environment" are "Inertial Central", Compute Actual Position & Speed".

For instance, the "Compute Next Position & Speed" function is not part of the "Internal environment" because, this function has already been designed and the associated validated and verified models are already available.

The external environment model describes the environment of the System of Interest at an appropriate level of detail to ensure the expected quality of the analysis. These models can be reused, with eventual refinements, from previous simulation (see Fig. 5).

In the SEP space, the GPS satellite sends signals to the GPS receiver. However, for simulation purposes, we do not need to provide details of the relations between GPS signal and the GPS receiver. Thus, in our example, the path "Provide signal" and "Receiver GPS" from SEP are modeled in SES space by the simpler "Position & Speed" function of the "GPS Environment".

The System of Interest of the simulation is the "Move" function which is identified in dotted red line in Fig. 8. All the other simulated functions are drawn with full red or green line.

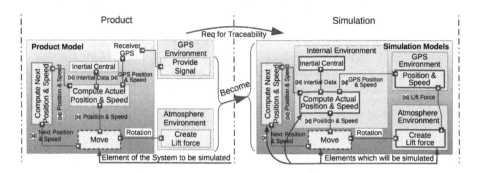

**Fig. 8.** From product SE Space to Simulator SE. (Color figure online)

When the successive refinements of the functions reach a precise enough description in functional layer for the assessment under way, these functions (see Fig. 9) are assigned to the components of the logical layer (see Fig. 10).

However, before actually assigning them to a logical layer, the refinement of Fig. 9 can be interpreted in two ways: (i) It may be a refinement provided by the system architect. In this case, the SA must rely on this refinement instead of the container "Move" function. If needed, the System Architect must provide the Prescriptive Semantic Model for the refined function (the intended behaviour), (ii) It may also be a Model of Intention represented by the functions: "Regulation Pos&Speed", "Compute Motor Speed", "Regulation i^th Motor Speed" and "Create Rotation i^th Motor". The SA keeps the "Move" function unchanged, retrieves the Prescriptive Semantic Model from the System Architect, and forwards it to the experts in the Simulation Execution space.

In our case study, we consider that it is a simple refinement. The logical layer groups related functions as "logical components". The relation used for the grouping depends on the purpose of the model designer. For example, in

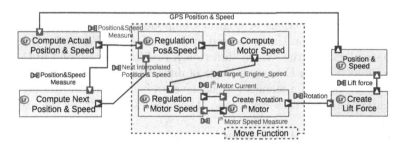

**Fig. 9.** Detail of "Move" function, in simulation SE Space. Env Functions in Turquoise Blue. (Color figure online)

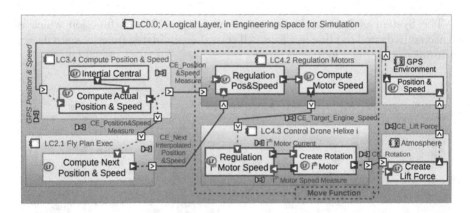

**Fig. 10.** Allocation of functions to logical components. Internal&External Env in Turquoise Blue. (Color figure online)

the SES, the notion of component is preserved, to which is added the notion of business domain (mechanical, electrical, etc.). The component becomes a logical and specialized container for a particular business domain.

In the Fig. 10, we can see functions grouped in logical components from our example: Functions "Inertial Central" and "Compute Actual Position & Speed" are grouped in the logical component "LC3.4 Compute Position & Speed", "Compute Next Position & Speed" in "LC2.1 Fly Plan Exec(ution)" for example.

The physical layer (see Fig. 6) allows expressing the EEs elements: the entities (companies), the physical execution supports (Execution Unit, down to possibly, Processors and associated Threads), the communication means (Networks), and the simulation models. In this layer, the SA will deploy the inner functions of Logical Components using, for example, FMU (Functional Mock-up Unit) on the execution platform. These FMU are placed in companies, on their simulation platforms. As evoked in the state of the art, FMUs have a standardized communication interface, and the model comes in the form of an executable binary.

At this point, the SA engineer has taken into account the model from the space of SE, set up the necessary environments of simulation, refined the functions, created Logical Components, defined the hardware structure of simulation and assigned inner functions of Logical Components to Physical Components FMU-type on Execution Units, located in companies (see Fig. 11 for the AIDA use case simulation of the "Move" function.). Red lines correspond to Communication Links between Execution Units of different Extended Enterprises. The Global Master algorithm manages exchange data between Local Master, placed on Execution Units of each Enterprise. The Local Master drives the execution of its attached FMU.

It remains for the SA to transform scenarios of the requested tests, as simulation scenarios that will drive the execution. The purpose is to integrate the environments of simulation, to specify the order of execution, in order to provide

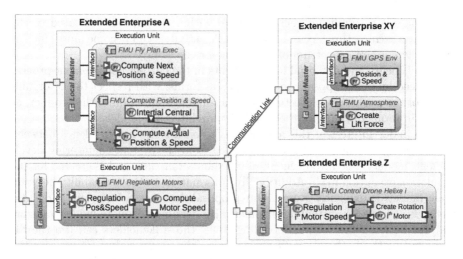

**Fig. 11.** Allocation of inner functions of LComponents to FMU, in Physical Layer.

the necessary data for the "Move" functions of the product model (see Fig. 4). For instance, a requirement for the environment could be: "a wind of Northwest sector and speed of 5 knots", or "a fog with visibility of 20 m".

This diversity of approaches leaves to the experts the choice of the most appropriate model, still respecting the inputs/outputs of the FMI interface.

Besides the aforementioned files, he will forward to each company involved in the co-simulation, the data regarding the configuration of the appropriate algorithm (global/local master) that are provided in the physical layer and the simulation scenario. These data provide useful information to enable companies to schedule their own simulations. These local algorithms executed in each company must allow to send and receive all the intermediate data of the simulation toward the algorithm controlling the simulation from a global point of view (global master). At the end, the SA distributes the appropriate resulting simulation data towards the concerned companies.

## 5   Conclusion and Future Work

This contribution proposes an approach to improve the integration of early simulation in the model based systems engineering development life-cycle in the context of extended enterprises. The proposed approach is generic, thus independent of any particular system development methods or tools. We illustrate and discuss our approach using the AIDA drone case-study for plane inspection.

The major benefit of this approach is to put the simulation at the core of the development process, by carefully defining its own development steps and positioning it against the overall product development. Moreover, our approach contributes to a better organization of the development, by making explicit links between simulation models and other models built during development.

Also, there is a significant reuse potential within the models dedicated to the simulation architecture. As a result the V&V activities can become more efficient and explore a large spectrum of situations for the same cost.

The benefits and potential improvements in the current development process introduced by our proposal come in different forms: with respect to the organization of the work, to architecture exploration and simulation of the product, as well as in terms of re-use of the simulation architecture models.

The major interest of this approach is to ensure the independence between various categories of models: models issued from the system engineering development, models issued from the SE of the simulation, and models created for the simulation execution itself. Additionally, information on the traceability between these models is explicitly stored. Our proposal does not enforce any particular methods or tools for system development. By defining adequate model transformations between the various modeling tools, the stakeholders can use the SE tools and methods that best fit their needs. The same analysis stands for the company responsible for the design and the integration of the simulation. This approach also allows to clearly separate the responsibilities between the design of the product and the design of the simulations in a *"don't be both judge and jury"* spirit (independence between specification, implementation and verification usually required by certification bodies).

Another advantage of our proposal is to be able to successively reuse (partial) models and results of the previous simulations for similar systems. That would be the case for instance for models of functions, components, hardware equipment, or simulation architecture. Similarly, it is possible to reuse or refine executable mock-ups or FMU. This approach facilitates the set up of exploratory simulations for architectures, and allows to conduct partial simulations of the product that may be later refined.

The clear separation between the product and simulation spaces will provide a high flexibility in the construction of the simulation platform: knowing partners interested in the design, it is possible to model and then create gradually, the simulation platform, inside and between partners, in accordance with the available budget.

Environment models are key elements for simulation. We intend to explore and to specify attributes needed to give a precise account of their nature.

**Acknowledgements.** The authors would like to thank the MOISE project members for their contributions as well as the IRT-SE and the French *Commissariat Général à l'Investissements* and the *Agence Nationale de la Recherche* for their financial support in the frame of the *Programme d'Investissement d'Avenir*.

# References

1. Leroux, R., Ober, I., Pantel, M., Bruel, J.-M.: Modeling co-simulation: a first experiment. In: Proceedings of MODELS-2017, Satellite Event: Workshops, September 2017. http://ceur-ws.org/Vol-2019/gemoc_3.pdf
2. Sirin, G., Paredis, C., Yannou, B., Coatanéa, E., Landel, E.: A model identity card to support simulation model development process in a collaborative multidisciplinary design environment. IEEE Syst. J. **9**(4), 1–12 (2015)
3. Capasso, C., Hammadi, M., Patalano, S., Renaud, R., Veneri, O.: A multi-domain modelling and verification procedure within MBSE approach to design propulsion systems for road electric vehicles. In: Mechanics & Industry, vol. 18, p. 107. AFM, EDP Sciences 2016, January 2017. www.mechanics-industry.org
4. Fiorese, S.: Découvrir et comprendre l'Ingénierie Système. AFIS - Cepaduès, March 2012
5. BKCASE, SEBoK: guide to the engineering body of knowledge. http://sebokwiki. org/wiki/Guide_to_the_Systems_Engineering_Body_of_Knowledge_(SEBoK)
6. Topper, J.S., Horner, N.C.: Model-based systems engineering in support of complex systems development. Johns Hopkins APL Tech. Digest **32**(1), 419–432 (2013)
7. Shephard, M.S., Beall, M.W., O'Bara, R.M., Webster, B.E.: Toward simulation-based design. Finite Elem. Anal. Des. **40**(12), 1575–1598 (2004). https://doi.org/ 10.1016/j.finel.2003.11.004
8. Graignic, P., Vosgien, T., Jankovic, M., Tuloup, V., Berquet, J., Troussier, N.: Complex system simulation: proposition of a MBSE framework for design-analysis integration. Procedia Comput. Sci. **16**, 59–68 (2013)
9. INCOSE, Systems Engineering Handbook, A Guide for System Life Cycle Processes and Activities, 4th edn. Wiley, New York (2015). https://sepnobrasil. yolasite.com/resources/INCOSESystemsEngineeringHandbook4e2015.pdf
10. Retho, F., Smaoui, H., Vannier, J.-C., Dessante, P.: Model of intention: a concept to support models building in a complex system design project. In: ERTS, pp. 115–126 (2014)
11. Retho, F., Smaoui, H., Vannier, J.-C., Dessante, P.: A model-based method to support complex system design via systems interactions analysis. In: Proceedings of the Posters Workshop at CSD&M (2013)
12. Sirin, G., Retho, F., Yannou, B., Callot, M., Dessante, P., Landel, E.: Multidisciplinary simulation model development: early inconsistency detection during the design stage. In: Advances in Engineering Software (2017). https://hal.archives-ouvertes.fr/hal-01673538
13. FMI: Functional Mockup Interface. http://fmi-standard.org/
14. Galtier, V., Vialle, S., Dad, C., Tavella, J.-P., Lam-Yee-Mui, J.-P., Plessis, G.: FMI-based distributed multi-simulation with DACCOSIM. In: Proceedings of the Symposium on Theory of Modeling and Simulation: DEVS Integrative Symposium, ser. DEVS 2015, San Diego, CA, USA: Society for Computer Simulation International 2015, pp. 39–46 (2015). http://dl.acm.org/citation.cfm?id=2872965. 2872971
15. Neema, H., et al.: Model-based integration platform for FMI co-simulation and heterogeneous simulations of cyber-physical systems. In: Proceedings of the 10th International Modelica Conference, 10–12 March 2014, Lund, Sweden, vol. 96. Linköping University Electronic Press; Linköpings universitet, pp. 235–245 (2014)
16. Dahmann, J.S., Fujimoto, R.M., Weatherly, R.M.: The department of defense high level architecture. In: Winter Simulation Conference (1997)

17. Dahmann, J.S., Fujimoto, R.M., Weatherly, R.M.: The DoDHigh Level Architecture: an update. In: Winter Simulation Conference (1998)
18. DACCOSIM: Distributed architecture for controlled co-simulation. https://sourcesup.renater.fr/daccosim/index.html
19. The Modelica Association: Modelica. https://www.modelica.org/
20. Bossa, B., Boulbene, B., Dubé, S., Pantel, M.: Towards a co-simulation based model assessment process for system architecture. In: Proceedings of the 2nd Workshop on the Formal CoSimulation of Cyber Physical Systems, Satellite Event of the Software Engineering and Formal Methods Conference (2018)
21. Voirin, J.-L.: Model-Based System and Architecture Engineering with the Arcadia Method. ISTE Press - Elsevier, London (2017)
22. CESAM-Community, CESAM: Cesames systems architecting method, January 2017. http://cesam.community/wp-content/uploads/2017/09/CESAM-guide_-_V12092017.pdf

# Scenario-Based Validation of Automated Driving Systems

Hardi Hungar[(⊠)]

German Aerospace Center (DLR), Institute of Transportation Systems,
38108 Brunswick, Germany
hardi.hungar@dlr.de

**Abstract.** To assess the safety of automated driving systems (ADS), all potentially critical situations have to be considered. One way to do so is to test the function performance in *scenarios* which lead to these situations. A scenario is a description of an evolution of traffic situations, consisting of snapshots capturing important intermediate states and operators specifying what happens between these states.

The number of relevant scenarios is very large, even if the ADS is supposed to operate in a restricted domain. Therefore, testing must rely heavily on virtual, largely automatized exploration of scenario spaces. For that, classes of scenarios have to be described formally, to enable the dynamic generation of test cases.

The contribution delineates a general approach to safety assessment by virtual testing. It discusses in particular the nature and building blocks of a formal scenario language and the construction of test specifications.

**Keywords:** Safety assessment · Testing of automated driving functions
Formal test specification

## 1 Introduction

To assess the safety of an *automated driving system* (ADS), its behavior has to be checked in all potentially critical situations. There are very many such situations, even for systems with a restricted *operational driving domain* (ODD). This makes it impossible to use standard, manual procedures of safety assessment. Most of it will have to be automated, so that classes of events are explored without human interaction.

1. The ongoing research project PEGASUS ("**P**roject for the **E**stablishment of **G**enerally **A**ccepted quality criteria, tools and methods as well as **S**cenarios and **Sit**uations for the release of highly-automated driving functions") studies how to establish the safety of an ADS on the example of a function called "highway pilot".

This research was partially funded by the German Federal Ministry for Economic Affairs and Energy, Grant No. 19A15012F (PEGASUS), based on a decision by the Parliament of the Federal Republic of Germany. The responsibility for the content lies with the author.
A previous version of this article (in German) was presented at the AAET 2018 (Automatisiertes und vernetztes Fahren), Brunswick, Germany, 2018.

T. Margaria and B. Steffen (Eds.): ISoLA 2018, LNCS 11246, pp. 449–460, 2018.
https://doi.org/10.1007/978-3-030-03424-5_30

The highway pilot shall be able to drive automatically on a highway, if conditions are in the ordinary range, i.e., not too challenging (weather. traffic density, etc.). It is thus a function of SAE level 3 (conditional driving automation) [1]

In PEGASUS, such classes of events are described by so-called *logical scenarios*. A scenario [2] in general resembles a movie storyboard. It describes a traffic event by a number of snapshots, Each snapshot captures velocities and positions of traffic participants, the road and its furniture, and external conditions like weather. Additionally, information of how one snapshot develops into the next is given. The notion of a scenario according to [2] covers a wide range from highly abstract, imprecise, to very detailed, concrete descriptions of a single evolution in traffic.

A logical scenario shall formally describe a class of scenarios. It consists of

- A "storyboard" fixing the sequence of discrete events.
- Discrete and numerical parameters with associated distributions of the probabilities of their occurrence.

In this way, a logical scenario captures a whole class of concrete traffic evolutions.

At least in principle, it is possible to compute the cumulated risk which results from an active ADS in that class of traffic evolutions. And if the ODD is fully covered by logical scenarios, this enables the desired risk assessment.

However, there is yet no agreed precise definition of a logical scenario. It is not clear how they should be formalized. There are several difficulties to be overcome. One is, that a test scenario must be open to the actions of the system under test. Therefore, its parameters cannot be fixed. Further, the trajectories of other traffic participants should also be somewhat flexible, to adjust to the test object's behavior.

This paper contains an approach to tackle this and other problems. It sketches the constituents and the operators of a language for expressing logical scenarios. And it discusses aspects of structuring of the set of logical scenarios to cover the full ODD of an automation like the highway pilot. Furthermore, it delineates what results might be expected from an exploration of the scenario space by simulation, and how these results could contribute to a safety assessment of the AVS.

Though this paper refers to the project PEGASUS and draws on its developments, what is laid out here does not constitute results of the project itself, nor does it constitute an agreed position. Instead, the concept of introducing a precise layer specifying test cases is taken up, and a proposal is made how this might be realized in a hopefully useful way. Different as well as somewhat similar approaches are considered in the project.

## 2   Definitions

The paper [2] gives an overview over approaches, concepts and terms for describing traffic evolutions, and proposes a set of definitions which shall form a basis for a unified taxonomy. These definitions are not yet fully precise. So the need for a language to formally capture relevant classes of traffic evolutions remains.

The following section recalls the proposal from [2], and extends this with some elaborations of that coming from the PEGASUS project.

## 2.1   Basic Definitions

**Scene.** A *scene* describes a snapshot of the traffic and environment constellation. This includes both dynamic and static elements.

**Situation.** A *situation* is a scene from the perspective of one traffic participant, i.e., a subjective scene.

The elements which make up a scene or situation can be assigned to four categories (after [3]).

### Description Levels

- L1: Street level (permanent): Geometry, topology, composition, street furniture
- L2: Street level (temporary modifications): construction sites etc.
- L3: Dynamic objects: traffic participants (mostly), types, dynamics
- L4: Environment: Weather, lighting

This classification goes well with many practical purposes. L1 comprises the content of (digital) maps. L2 also concern the traffic space, but will usually not be represented in maps. L3 makes up the traffic which deploys itself on the static space from L1 and L2. The last level, L4, is also dynamic in nature and comprises all other factors having an impact on the traffic evolution. Together, by specifying a scene or situation on all four levels, the scene or situation can be described.

Descriptions of traffic evolutions result by conjoining scenes. These are then *scenarios*, which will get the most attention in this paper.

**Scenario.** *Scenarios* represent traffic evolutions. They are defined by linking scenes. The linking need not be linear, it may also be branching.

The semantics of a scenario is a set of time series. Each time series represents a traffic evolution.

For scenarios that are to be used to specify or test the behavior of an ADS, it is necessary to identify an ego vehicle in the scenarios. A test scenario would for instance bring some situation with potential for criticality to pass, which the ego vehicle shall resolve.

Figure 1 shows the main scenes (snapshots) of a cut-in scenario. The ego vehicle (red, **E**) follows a leading vehicle (green, **F**). It is overtaken by another (blue, **C**) in Scene 1. After that, **C** changes to the lane of the ego vehicle (Scene 2 and 3).

Scenarios, and also scenes and situations, need not always be specified in all detail. Indeed, it is very useful to start with imprecise specifications to get an idea how to structure the possible traffic events in which the ADS is supposed to operate. A scenario might be rather open to different behaviors of ego vehicle. Thus, one scenario may represent a large number of evolutions in real traffic. This is elaborated in the following section.

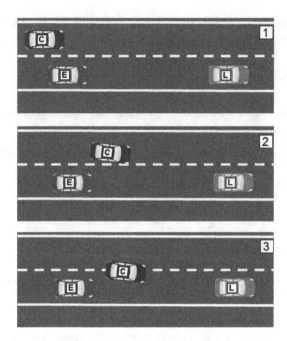

**Fig. 1.** Illustration of a cut-in scenario (Color figure online)

## 2.2    An Abstraction Hierarchy of Scenario Notions

In the PEGASUS project, a hierarchy of three levels of scenarios of different degrees of abstraction is used. The following definitions of *functional, logical* and *concrete* scenarios constitute one of the proposals which are being considered. These definitions are based on [2].

**Functional Scenario.** A *functional scenario* is an abstract, imprecise description of a type of traffic evolutions. It defines the main maneuvers and events of one evolution.

For instance, the functional scenario "cut-in" captures evolutions in which a vehicle enters the lane of the ego vehicle in front of it.

Functional scenarios are mainly used to derive more precise scenario specifications. For the PEGASUS use case "highway pilot", a number in the order twenty functional scenarios is considered.

**Concrete Scenario.** A *concrete scenario* fixes a start scene, and provides as many details for the evolutions following it as possible.

This definition is not yet precise. "As many details as possible" leaves room for different interpretations. This is motivated by the fact that concrete scenarios are intended to be used for different purposes.

In PEGASUS, two variants of concrete scenarios are being employed. One is the representation of measured data, real world or simulation. Then, a concrete scenario captures a unique sequence of events. But not all parameters might be known, or known exactly. It may even occur that vehicles appear in the middle of a concrete scenario, or vanish. The other variant of concrete scenarios are test cases. Then, the parameters of the ego vehicle are not fixed (they may be bounded, though), and the other vehicles might react to it. Such a test case may even capture different sequences of events. For instance, if the ego vehicle may choose between braking or changing lanes to resolve some situation, the test case can contain different continuations. With the help of functions measuring criticality (e.g. accident probability and severity), the result of a test run can be evaluated and enter a computation estimating the risk level of an ADS. This will be explained in more detail in Sect. 3.

*Logical scenarios* are more abstract than concrete scenarios and more concrete and precise than functional scenarios.

**Logical Scenario.** A *logical scenario* defines precisely a class of concrete scenarios. It begins with a start scene. The permitted concrete instantiations of the elements of the four description levels are given in the form of parameter spaces. The occurrence frequency of instantiations (start scene and evolution) may be given in the form of probability distributions.

In PEGASUS, logical scenarios are mainly used to precisely specify tests. A functional scenario will be covered by a number of logical scenarios. Also, more general than tests, logical scenarios can also precisely capture requirements. By providing occurrence probabilities, the requirements can be made quantitative, detailing a risk level to be achieved.

The project uses an extension of OpenSCENARIO [4] in combination with OpenDRIVE [5] to denote logical scenarios. Details are not yet completely fixed. This paper is concerned with the denotation of the third level of scenarios (L3), the dynamic objects. Compatible with considerations in PEGASUS, maneuver macros are proposed as important language features for that purpose. Before these macros are presented in detail, the subsequent chapter gives a short overview of test goals and procedures to motivate the way tests are going to be defined.

## 3 Testing to Determine the Safety Level (of Automated Driving)

### 3.1 Test Goal

Testing is usually employed to check that a set of requirements is satisfied by an implementation. That is true of testing to determine the safety level of AVS, as well. But the first difficulty here is the absence of a detailed specification. The AVS shall be rather safe, at the very least it shall not cause more accidents (fatalities, injured persons) than a human performing comparable driving tasks. Each OEM will have some operational rules for the driving function to guide the development. But that the implementation of the rules will achieve a certain safety level cannot be guaranteed beforehand.

The approach which is followed is to determine the safety level afterwards, without considering the "rules", which might constitute an inconsistent set, anyhow. Also, the

ADS will not be compared to the human driver on a case-by-case basis. Currently, not enough data about human behavior in safety-relevant situations are available. Also, systematic and legal difficulties would have to be solved to do that (defining an acceptable "human reference" would require a consensus among many stakeholders). Instead, the risk incurred by the automation is determined, or, more to the point, estimated by systematic testing.

The underlying notion of risk is similar to that employed by insurance companies. It is, roughly said, the product of accident probability and accident severity. Severity is measured in terms of injuries and fatalities. The probability is related to the exposure to critical situations and the ability to handle them.

The general risk level of human driving is more or less known from accident statistics. So there is a reference for the global level, even though single cases cannot be reliably assessed. The technical goal for the test campaign is to estimate the cumulated risk over all situations which might be encountered. A more detailed goal might be set, e.g. by categorizing the situations into a number of classes. This does not change the general approach, which can be characterized as the computation of the risk integral over a large class of traffic evolutions.

### 3.2    Test Procedure

Figure 2 illustrates how such a risk integral might be computed approximatively. On the left, an exemplary function is depicted. This function has two parameters, distance and velocity difference. Its values represent the risk, which combines accident probability, severity and occurrence probability. The cumulative risk is the volume below the function graph. This volume is to be approximately measured by tests.

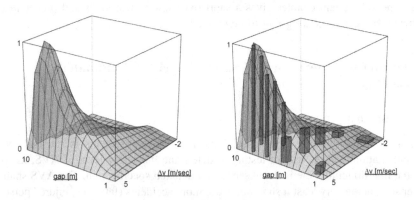

**Fig. 2.**  Illustration of a risk computation (Color figure online)

The red columns in the graphics on the right represent tests. Each test determines a risk value for a particular set of parameter values. This is taken as approximation of the risk for a small range of parameter values, which gives the base area of the column. From that and the measured risk, the volume of the column is computed. By adding up these volumes, an estimate of the cumulated is computed. This resembles the Riemann definition of the integral of a function. The estimate gets more precise, if more tests are run and the base areas of the columns are reduced. In areas with low or zero risk, which will make up most of space, the parameter spacing can be enlarged to make the computation more efficient.

To realize this concept of risk computation in a practically useful procedure, several difficulties have to be overcome. One is, that a very large number of tests have to be performed. In reality, there are many more than two parameters to a test scenario. The space to be covered is thus very large, and no critical situation should be overlooked. Also, the system under test acts in a socio-physical environment. This entails, that the test specification is not easy to derive-it is not per se digital and discrete in nature.

Since the number of tests to be performed is large, simulation plays a key role in testing. For that, the driving automation control is embedded into a computer simulation of traffic environment. Today, one cannot rely on simulation alone, as its results are of limited validity. The validity aspect will not be treated in this paper. Instead, the problem of how to denote and derive tests will be considered. To handle the large number of tests, automation is needed in generating them, while there is no simple, computer usable form available capturing the environment evolution which make up the stimuli for the test cases. The proposed solution to the test specification problem relies on a notion of logical scenarios.

## 4 Formalizing Test Specifications

### 4.1 Requirements

We consider by which means the traffic dynamics (L3 according to the definition of description levels) may be represented. As we want to specify tests, there is always a distinguished ego vehicle representing the system under test. This has a specific role in a scenario, as its actions must not be restricted, while the other vehicles adapt their behavior to that of the ego car. Examples will be taken from highway traffic, but this is no general restriction.

A logical scenario stands for a set of concrete scenarios. These concrete instantiations should be rather realistic in the form and mode in which the traffic participants do act. Longitudinal and lateral control should follow real behavior patterns. And the collection of logical scenarios shall cover the full set of relevant traffic evolutions. Thus, it must include complex ones like the scenario from Fig. 3.

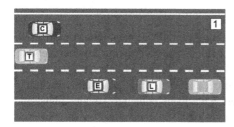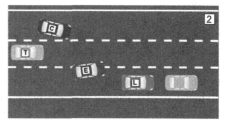

**Fig. 3.** Conflicting lane changes (Color figure online)

The scenario starts in a stable situation where **E** (red, ego vehicle) follows **L** (green) at a constant velocity. **T** (yellow) on the middle lane is going at the same velocity, with a distance which would permit **E** to change to the middle lane. The vehicle **C** (blue) on the left lane is much faster, but in the beginning far behind **T**.

The situation gets interesting when L decelerates. In reality, this might be due to a slower vehicle in front of **L** on the right lane (indicated by the other, unnamed, yellow vehicle). The reason for **L** getting slower is not important for the test scenario-the vehicle in front of **L** would usually not be visible to **E**. As a reaction to that, the automated vehicle **E** might be provoked to change lanes to be able to keep the desired speed. Then, **C** comes into play. Unnoticeable to **E**, it overtakes **T** at a high speed and starts to change to the middle lane form the left. Now a potentially dangerous situation has arisen, and an emergency reaction from **E** is required. It might not be easy to return to the right lane, as L might have a much lower velocity now.

Of course, **E** could, instead of changing to the middle lane, stay on the right lane and brake. This would be a safe decision. But even automated vehicles will strive to keep up a desired velocity. So the outcome cannot be predicted without very detailed knowledge about the internal decision procedures, or, to be on the safe side, without testing.

This scenario is far more complex than the simple cut-in scenario from Fig. 1, but there will be even more involved scenarios to be tested. To enact such action sequences without of course having control of the system under test, the environment vehicles must be precisely regulated.

Summarizing the considerations above, the means to define test have to satisfy the following three requirements

- **Completeness:** There are means to produce every situation which may be encountered by the ADS
- **Realism:** The test sequences must be realistic to produce valid data for a risk assessment
- **Reactivity:** The traffic environment must adapt to the ego vehicle behavior to be able to produce complex sequences

## 4.2   Approach

Reactivity entails that a scenario description includes features of a control program. This work elaborates particularly on this aspect. Basic building blocks of a scenario description are *maneuver macros* controlling elementary actions of the environment vehicles.

There are many approaches to describe traffic sequences. Very often, the catalogue of driving maneuvers from [6] is taken as a starting point. This catalogue comprises 17 maneuvers. These include following a lead vehicle and overtaking another vehicle. Each car trip can be divided into sections where each section is characterized by one maneuver. This approach is descriptive in nature, it does not aim at actually producing the behavior. To achieve that, the maneuvers have to be split into smaller units, and these must be made more precise, defining trajectories depending on discrete and numeric parameter values.

Using such macros, a scenario is described by

- A start scene which defines the initial setting, including a start macro for each vehicle
- Conditions which control the changing between macro controlling the current behavior of a car
- Exit and completion conditions which define when to abort or finish a test run

Such a scenario is essentially a program which controls the execution of a test run. Predefined maneuver macros will help to give those "programs" a clear structure and ease their implementation in test tools.

## 4.3  Building Blocks of Formal Scenario Specifications

A macro is given by a name, which characterizes the maneuver type, and a set of execution parameters. In that, it resembles a method or procedure. On call, it produces a vehicle trajectory.

Parameters are

- A geometry type of the trajectory (discrete). Examples are straight or sinusoidal. These may be numerically modified, e.g. by specifying deviations from the trajectory shape.
- Timing/control of the longitudinal and lateral movements (numeric). Examples are the time to complete a maneuver like a lane change, or the distance to other vehicles. Complex macros will permit a detailed control of the execution, or might even include complex controllers like an adaptive cruise control
- Exit conditions in the form of a list of conditions. For instance, the lane change of vehicle $C$ in an extension of the scenario of Fig. 3 might be broken off, depending on the relative position to the ego vehicle.

Such macros should be defined to be able to express all (relevant) regular and irregular maneuvers. It is useful to have simple macros even for behaviors which is subsumed by more complex ones. This helps in making test specifications comprehensible and traceable.

## 4.4  Scenario Specification Operators

In a logical scenario, the global course of action is described by calling and arranging maneuver macros. It has a set of global parameters which can be used within the logical scenario. The global parameters have defined range. Range boundaries may depend on other bounds, provided the dependency graphs is acyclic.

For the start scene, all vehicles are initialized by defining position and velocities. Each vehicle but the ego vehicle is assigned a maneuver macro. Positions, velocities and macro parameters may of course be derived from global scenario parameters.

Each time a maneuver macro is terminated, a new one is assigned to the respective vehicle. This is done in a global control loop, which observes termination and exits of macros. The assignment of a new macro may depend on the global traffic state as well as on the termination/exit condition of the previous macro. Again, global scenario parameters may be used.

Additionally, on the global level, conditions for terminating or breaking off a test run are specified. These may coincide with respective conditions of macros, but may also depend directly on the traffic state. One particular termination condition identifies accidents.

## 4.5 Constructing Test Scenarios: An Example

Considering the conflicting lane change example from Fig. 3, most of the macros needed to define the scenario are rather simple. Vehicle **T** (yellow) and **L** (green) start with following their respective lane at a constant velocity. **T** keeps this behavior throughout the scenario. **L**, on the other hand, initiates the build-up of the critical situation by decelerating. This also is rather easy to specify. The most challenging task in specifying the scenario is to get the right velocity and timing for **C** to get to the conflict in case **E** will be provoked to change lanes. The best way to do this will most likely be an intelligent control of the speed of **C** which takes the viewpoint of E into account.

It is obvious that it will not be possible to construct the scenario without some testing or, for adherents of formal methods, some other means of studying the semantics of the logical scenario. In other words: A logical scenario describing a complex evolution is like a program, and few nontrivial programs are correct without being tested.

## 4.6 Frequencies

To complete a test specification, information about the occurrence probabilities should be added to logical scenarios. These are in general multi-variate probability distributions over the parameters of a scenario. The semantics of the probabilities will be in "occurrence per travel distance". Together with an occurrence probability of the set of scenarios represented by the logical scenario, this would permit a quantitative interpretation of test results as indicated in Sect. 3.2.

For the numeric parameters, a multivariate Gaussian distribution should cover most relevant cases. This would be specified by expectation values and a covariance matrix. In practice, for most cases the data basis necessary to define reasonably precise values is lacking today. Expert estimations may replace data, but their validity will of course be questionable. In other words, it will be very difficult to even come up with a valid specification of the test specification necessary to start the computation of Sect. 3.2. N.B., that even in cases where good frequency estimations are available, to represent probabilities by multivariate Gaussian distributions requires the logical scenario to have a rather smooth variance over the parameter space. Disruptions from different discrete decisions within the scenario would almost surely lead to more complex occurrence distributions. Thus, logical scenarios should either have a "simple" structure, or one would have to resort to other distributions and representations. These might take the form of discretized "bin" distributions.

# 5 Test Definitions

## 5.1 Formal Representation of Test Cases

The instantiations of the logical scenario result from assigning concrete values to the global parameters.

To be able to execute one of the tests specified by the logical scenario, the activation conditions of the automation must be taken into account. If the automation can be activated under conditions which are true in each instance of the start scene, one can use the instantiation directly as a test case. If not, an initiation sequence which leads to the start scene has to be added. This, again, should be done in the style of a logical scenario. In other words, a general test specification like e.g. one for the highway pilot in PEGASUS, will often have to be adapted to the specifics of the system under test. This may be necessary even within a particular development, where the test specification is composed at a stage where not all details of the system are fixed (or get modified in a later stage).

Given logical scenarios adapted to the system under test, each set of parameter values gives rise to a concrete test case. The outcome of a test run is, other than in simpler settings, not a pass or fail. Instead, we get one of the following

1. A regular <u>termination</u>, with or without dangerous situations having occurred
2. An break of the execution resulting from an <u>exit condition</u> becoming true
3. An <u>accident</u> leading also to a break of the execution

As these results contribute differently to the overall risk integral, they form the implicit evaluation criteria of the test cases. The accident evaluation is another ingredient for practical testing which is difficult to provide. There are estimation functions for potential injuries and fatalities, but their prediction accuracy is limited.

## 5.2 Generating Test Cases

Despite the problems of coming up with a perfect test specification, tests can be run once the ranges of the parameter values of logical scenarios are fixed. However, the number of parameters, even for simple scenarios, makes the test space very large. A scenario like the cut-in from Fig. 1 might be formalized with, e.g., ten numeric parameters. Therefore, to cover the parameter space with a reasonably close mesh will result in billions of test cases. To avoid to have to run all these, the generation of test cases must be done in a clever way.

The generation should be done dynamically, taking the results of performed simulations into account. I.e., as long as all risk indicators report zero risk, a large spacing between parameter sets is chosen. Fortunately, by far, the critical regions will be small, and the most parameter sets will result in uncritical evolutions. But when the criticality indicators shows a rise, the spacing is reduced, and bulges of the criticality function are measured precisely.

Thus, test case generation will be done by an intricate algorithm in close cooperation with the simulation itself. If simulations of different degree of precision are available, also the choice of the simulation variant will go into the integrated procedure.

## 6  Summary and Outlook

This paper discussed methods and means to construct test specifications for automated driving systems. It is proposed to use logical scenarios in the formal specification. A logical scenario stands for a large number of concrete test cases, which can be derived by systematic variations of the free parameters. Internally, a logical scenario has a program-like structure, with control elements and maneuver macros as basic building blocks.

These test specifications are used first in comprehensive simulations, covering the ODD of the ADS by a large number of virtual tests. In later stages of testing, the simulation itself, respectively, its results will have to be validated. For that, the logical scenarios will have to be turned into a form suitable for guiding an execution on a proving ground. This aspect has not been considered, here. Also, several aspects of scenarios like environmental influences have not been addressed. This will have to be done in future work. Even the level of dynamic traffic elements, which was the focus of this work, certainly needs further elaboration. To be able to express all relevant traffic evolutions, a comprehensive catalogue of maneuver macros will have to be defined.

Other topics in the field of test specifications are questions of systematic derivations of the specification, the test process itself and, last but not least, the assessment of test results.

## References

1. International, SAE: Surface Vehicle Recommended Practice: Taxonomy and Definitions for Terms Related to Driving Automation Systems for On_Road Motor Vehicles J3016-Jun2018 (2018)
2. Ulbrich, S., et al.: Defining and substantiating the terms scene, situation and scenario for automated driving. In: IEEE International Annual Conference on Intelligent Transportation Systems (ITSC) (2015)
3. Schuldt, F., et al.: Effiziente systematische Testgenerierung für Fahrerassistenzsysteme in virtuellen Umgebungen. In: AAET, pp. 114–134 (2013)
4. VIRES Simulationstechnologie GmbH: OpenSCENARIO (2017). http://openscenario.org/. Zitat vom: 31 Jan 2018
5. VIRES Simulationstechnologie GmbH: OpenDRIVE (2015).http://www.opendrive.org/. Zitat vom: 31 Jan 2018
6. Nagel, Hans-Hellmut: A vision of 'vision and language' comprises action: an example from road traffic. Artif. Intell. Rev. **8**, 189–214 (1994)

# Engineering of Cyber-Physical Systems in the Automotive Context: Case Study of a Range Prediction Assistant

Christian F. J. König[✉], Gerd Meisl, Natalia Balcu, Benjamin Vosseler,
Henrik Hörmann, Jos Höll, and Victor Fäßler

TWT GmbH Science & Innovation, Stuttgart, Germany
christian.koenig@twt-gmbh.de

**Abstract.** Cyber-Physical Systems (CPS) are complex systems that combine features from different domains, such as control engineering, mechanical engineering or software engineering. Development of such CPS requires methods and tools from various disciplines, using different formalisms. Furthermore, for efficient development of these CPS, the engineering tools ideally support the whole development cycle and the life cycle of the CPS. This calls for a Systems Engineering approach to tackle the complexity of the engineering task under the constraints of short time-to-market. This paper presents a case study on the development of a CPS in the automotive context, where an assistant for estimating the range of an electric vehicle is developed. This case study illustrates the benefits of a modern tool-chain that is based on the Systems Engineering approach. In addition, an outlook is given on the development of similar tool-chains for the domain of automotive production planning. The benefits from applying open tool-chains in the engineering of CPS in the automotive domain is discussed.

## 1 Introduction

Cyber-Physical Systems (CPS) can be described as complex systems that comprise controllers and their logic, as well as the surrounding physical elements, such as sensors or actuators, and also additional data sources, such as data from cloud services. Due to their complexity, design of these systems requires knowledge and tools from various disciplines. While it might be possible to develop such systems in a single framework or methodology, it is not very likely to happen in industrial practice. This is because many systems use legacy parts, such as models or code, and developers tend to prefer the languages and formalisms they have experience in. Therefore, it is important to enable interoperability of tools and workflows to increase efficiency of the development process. Tool-chains which integrate various specialized tools are becoming more and more important in industries that develop complex systems [12].

One major industry where CPS play an important role is the automotive industry, which is investing significant resources into smarter products and

© Springer Nature Switzerland AG 2018
T. Margaria and B. Steffen (Eds.): ISoLA 2018, LNCS 11246, pp. 461–476, 2018.
https://doi.org/10.1007/978-3-030-03424-5_31

production systems. In the vehicles themselves, subsystems are increasingly connected among each other, vehicles are connected with other vehicles, infrastructure or a backend. In automotive production, constantly increasing requirements on flexibility of plants, due to more product variants add to the goals of lower cost of the production planning and production itself. Therefore, both areas for CPS development within the automotive industry are discussed in this paper.

The first part of this paper presents a case study of a CPS development from the automotive domain, which was developed in the INTO-CPS project [5]. The case study develops a system for route planning, in particular for electric vehicles. While electric vehicles are beginning to gain significant market shares, one of the main concerns is the lack of range, and the currently scarce density of re-charging stations, combined with the rather long duration of a battery re-charge. The goal of this case study is to develop a system that is able to realistically predict the energy consumption of a given route, and consequently indicate to the driver if the remaining range is sufficient or not. This case study is developed as part of the INTO-CPS project. In this project, a tool-chain is created for the model-based design of CPS. The tools are using the Functional Mock-up Interface (FMI) standard in its version 2.0 [1].

In the remainder of this paper, an approach to design of CPS in the context of automotive production is given. This approach is being developed in the ENTOC project, which is briefly summarized below. Together, both application areas demonstrate the common requirements, and some of the differences, for tool-chains that enable engineers to efficiently develop CPS.

## 2   Case Study: Electric Vehicle Range Assistant

This paper presents mainly a case study that develops functions for vehicles, in particular electric vehicles. Its goal is to create an assistant system for estimating the range of an electric vehicle, based on a vehicle model and real data from the environment, such as route topology or weather. Furthermore, the range estimation is dynamic, as it takes changes in the initial assumptions into account, and influences the vehicle behavior accordingly. However, the focus of this work is on the development methodology, and less on the actual accuracy of the results. While the model for the longitudinal dynamics has been validated previously, a complete validation is out of the scope of this work.

The case study can be considered a Cyber-Physical System because it contains local intelligence and autonomy in the vehicle. This is assisted by information about its environment typically derived from a cloud context (here, information on weather and traffic/route) and the logic depends upon the physical dynamics of the electric vehicle. A part of the system is transferred seamlessly from a simulation model to real hardware (here, as Raspberry Pi) and simulated with the remainder of the system.

Since the case study was developed as part of the INTO-CPS project [5], one aim was to evaluate the INTO-CPS tools and methods. Here this is in particular the Co-simulation Orchestration Engine (COE), which is a FMI 2.0

compliant master algorithm that allows coupling of continuous-time (CT) and discrete-event (DE) models in a Co-simulation setup [5,6]. Furthermore, the system was modeled in SysML, using the CPS-extension of the Modelio tools [11]. The models themselves were created using Matlab[1], 20-sim[2], C++ and Overture[3] [2].

## 2.1 Scenarios

The overall case study of automotive range prediction was developed in two main scenarios. In the first scenario, the start and end point are determined once, and the calculation of the vehicle dynamics is performed for this static route, returning the remaining battery charge at the end of the trip. Therefore this scenario is labeled "offline", since it does not take any changes during the actual trip into account.

The second scenario is more dynamic, as it takes unforeseen changes in the actual trip into account, by monitoring some relevant parameters. Consequently, this scenario is labeled "online". Furthermore, it closes the feedback loop, by allowing to modify the driving style in an attempt to drive more economically, if the calculation shows that the remaining range is too low. Development of strategies for more economic driving is however out of the scope of this paper. Finally, a part of the system is executed on real hardware and coupled to the Co-simulation.

**Offline Scenario.** The goal of this scenario is to create a realistic simulation of the energy consumption of a trip with a pre-determined route, taking weather data into account. Weather data, such as temperature is particularly relevant for Air Conditioning and the heating system of the vehicle, which is a consumer of energy that should not be neglected.

The overall system structure of this scenario is depicted as a SysML connections diagram in the following Fig. 1. It shows three SysML blocks that constitute the system, the Route calculation, the Longitudinal dynamics and the Weather data, and the signal flows between these blocks.

The calculation of the vehicle dynamics is performed by the longitudinal dynamics model, which is implemented in Matlab. The longitudinal dynamics of the vehicle is modeled with the total vehicle force $F_{vehicle}$ opposed by the aerodynamic drag $F_{air}$, the rolling resistance $F_{roll}$ and the downhill force $F_{incline}$. The total force needed to overcome the resistance forces to reach a desired velocity profile $v_{vehicle}$ is transformed into torque $T_{out}$ and speed $\omega_{out}$ demand. This is modeled by the differential equation 1, which is a form of Newton's second law of motion, such that the acceleration (dv over dt) of the vehicle with mass m is equal to the sum of forces acting on the vehicle. The force that is generated

---

[1] See https://www.mathworks.com/products/matlab.html.
[2] See http://www.20sim.com.
[3] See http://overturetool.org.

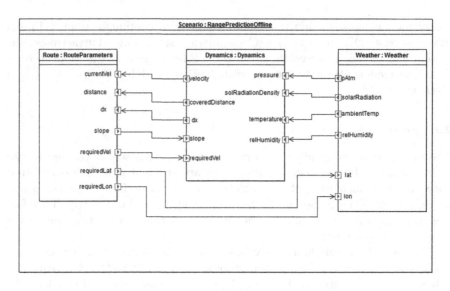

**Fig. 1.** SysML connections diagram for the "offline" scenario.

by the engine ($F_{vehicle}$) is positive, while aerodynamic drag $F_{air}$, the rolling resistance $F_{roll}$ and the downhill force $F_{incline}$ have a negative sign.

$$m\frac{dv}{dt} = F_{vehicle} - F_{air} - F_{roll} - F_{incline} \tag{1}$$

The total force needed to overcome the resistance forces to reach a desired velocity profile $v_{vehicle}$ is transformed into torque $T_{out}$ and speed $\omega_{out}$ demands as per

$$T_{out} = F_{vehicle} r_{dyn} \tag{2}$$

with the wheel radius $r_{dyn}$ and

$$\omega_{out} = \frac{v_{vehicle}}{r_{dyn}}. \tag{3}$$

The electrical motor is modeled as a permanent magnet AC E-motor. In the E-motor component the mechanical power requirements

$$P_{mot,mech} = T_{mot}\omega_{mot} \tag{4}$$

are converted into an electrical performance requirement $P_{in,el}$ model by a look-up table, which also includes the energy losses.

The motor power requirements $P_{in,el}$ along with the power requirement coming from the auxiliary components are passed to the battery module.

The battery is modeled as a resistance capacitance model (RC) as described in [4]. The variation in the state of charge of the battery $\Delta SOC$ was estimated using the widely used Coulomb counting method [9]. This approach takes the discharging current of a battery $I(t)$ and integrates it over time $\Delta t$ as

$$\Delta SOC = \frac{I(t)}{Q_n} \Delta t \tag{5}$$

where the nominal capacity $Q_n$ represents the maximum amount of charge that can be stored in the battery. While the Coulomb counting method is known to have some shortcomings (e.g. losses or parasitic reactions need to be taken into account, regular re-calibration is necessary, since it is only a cumulative method, not an absolute measure for the SoC), it is considered to be a sufficient approach for SoC modelling in the context of this work.

The route model generates a velocity and altitude profile for a given start and end point of a route. The start and end destination are obtained from a request to the Google Maps REST API and coupled to the Co-simulation via Matlab, and can therefore be characterized as a CT model. Google provides a list of alternative routes consisting of multiple road segments characterised by parameters like distance, estimated duration and GPS coordinates. For each of the road segments a velocity profile is then generated. The velocity profile is estimated by ramps and constant functions under the constraint that the segment's distance is traveled in the given time. The slopes of the ramp functions are restrained by the characteristic acceleration curve of the electrical vehicle that will travel along the given route. Further, the altitude profile is calculated based on the GPS coordinates.

To provide realistic conditions for the A/C control, the most relevant environmental parameters (ambient temperature, air pressure, air humidity and cloudiness) are generated for a given route by the weather module. Latitude and longitude coordinates previously generated by the route planning (see previous section) are taken as input and forwarded to the OpenWeatherMap API, and the resulting data is processed with Matlab, and can therefore be considered a CT model. The weather information along the route is then estimated based on the data gathered from the weather station nearest to the coordinate points. The solar radiance $Q$ is then calculated as a function of the solar zenith angle $\theta_s$ for given time and location and the air mass $M_{air}$.

The solar zenith angle $\theta_s$ can be calculated as described in [10] and the air mass as

$$M_{air} = \frac{-r_{Earth}\cos(\theta_s) + \sqrt{(r_{Earth} + h)^2 - r_{Earth}^2 \sin(\theta_s)^2}}{h} \tag{6}$$

with the radius of the Earth $r_{Earth}$ and the atmospheric height $h$. The solar radiation can be then calculated as

$$Q = S_o \frac{\cos(\theta_s)}{M_{air}} \tag{7}$$

with the solar constant $S_0$. When the cloudiness parameter is taken into account, the solar radiation becomes

$$Q_{cloudiness} = Q(1 - 0.75 \, cloudiness^{3.4}) \tag{8}$$

To demonstrate the plausibility of the simulation, a route in the vicinity of Stuttgart (Germany) was chosen for a simulation. The route on the map section, the velocity profile and the altitude profile calculated for this route is shown in Fig. 2. The Co-simulation was performed using the INTO-CPS application[4] and the COE.

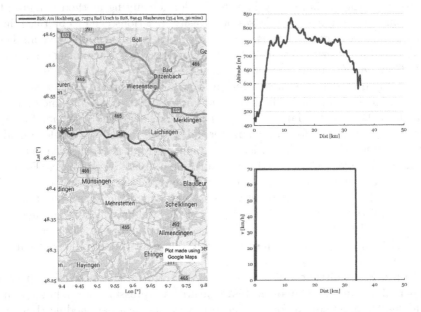

**Fig. 2.** Velocity and altitude profile for a route of 35 Km in the vicinity of Stuttgart. The route consists here of a country road only, and thus the velocity is stable at 70 km/h, while the altitude varies between 450 m and 850 m above sea level.

The simulation results for the vehicle state are plotted below in Fig. 3. Initially, the vehicle speed is around 25 km/h, since the route is on an inner city road. After the first kilometer, the route leads onto a country road for the remainder of the trip. The figure also shows that the vehicle is able to follow the set velocity closely, despite the slope of the road shown in the previous Fig. 2. As there is no gearbox considered in this electric vehicle, the motor speed follows exactly the vehicle speed. The battery voltage starts at around 330 V and drops finally to around 310 V. Along the trip, the voltage oscillates within a range of about 10 V, due to the acceleration and recuperation that is required by the profile of the road. As expected, the battery SoC (State of Charge) drops from initially 100% to approximately 70% at the end of the trip.

The temperatures that are calculated from the air conditioning module are displayed in Fig. 4. Initially, the temperature of the air inside the vehicle is 20 °C, while the temperature outside is 5 °C (e.g. when the vehicle was parked in a

---

[4] See https://github.com/INTO-CPS-Association/into-cps-application.

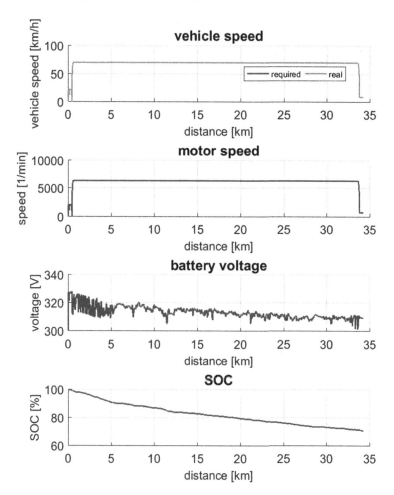

**Fig. 3.** Simulation results for vehicle speed, motor speed, battery voltage and SoC.

garage in winter). The setpoint for the temperature controller is 23 °C. While the temperature of the air inside the vehicle quickly rises, the fixtures (e.g. the seats) only heat up slowly. At the same time, the temperature at the windows and at the vehicle case drops quickly and reaches a steady state at 7 °C.

**Online Scenario.** To allow more flexibility, the online scenario extends the offline scenario with more functionality, to allow dynamic adaptation of the vehicle's behaviour. Here, this consists of two additional parts: an "alarm system" to monitor the vehicle's state, and a module to alter the gas pedal curve to influence the acceleration, and hence the energy consumption.

The SysML connections diagram of the online scenario is shown below in Fig. 5. Here, deviations from the predicted route and scenario are monitored

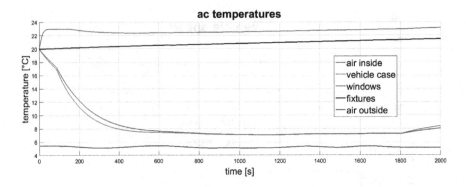

**Fig. 4.** Simulation results for temperatures inside and outside the vehicle.

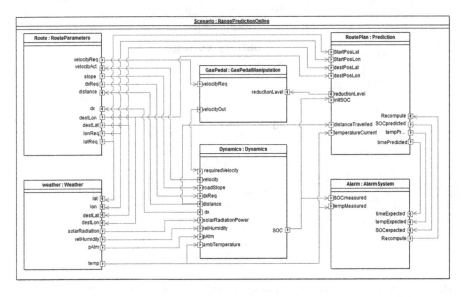

**Fig. 5.** SysML Connections Diagram for the "online" scenario.

by the Alarm system. The Prediction module is able to re-initialize the Co-simulation once the Alarm System has triggered a new calculation after a deviation was detected. In addition, one part of the system, the gas pedal controller, was first developed as a model (in 20-sim), and later transferred to hardware (a RaspberryPi 3) and connected to the Co-simulation by using 20-sim4C[5].

The purpose of the Alarm System is to monitor the state of the vehicle, in terms that are relevant for the route assistant that is developed in this case study. It consists of four functions which monitor the state of the battery (i.e. the SoC), the traffic, the weather and the route. If any of these changes, the simulation is reset, to take the changed conditions into account. The state diagram of this

---

[5] See http://www.20sim4c.com.

alarm system is displayed in Fig. 6. The Alarm-System is implemented in VDM-RT, using the Overture tool. The model is exported as stand-alone Functional Mock-up Unit (FMU), using the Overture FMI extension[6].

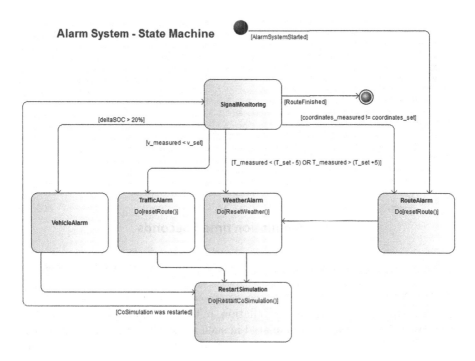

**Fig. 6.** State diagram of the alarm system.

The default state is *SignalMonitoring*, in which the alarm system continuously checks the vehicle parameters. If any of these is out of its boundaries, the Co-simulation is re-started. If the driver decides to take a different route than the proposed one, the route needs to be calculated before these values then are handed over to the weather module, for delivering the weather values to the Co-simulation. A sudden change in weather conditions also triggers the restart of the weather module, and in consequence of the Co-simulation. If the measured velocity of the vehicle is on average significantly lower than the planned velocity, a traffic jam is assumed, which requires a re-start of the Co-simulation as well. Finally, if certain vehicle parameters (such as the battery SoC) suddenly change, the new values need to be taken into account.

In a first step, this scenario was implemented to evaluate the correct function of the Alarm System and a newly developed "COE wrapper", that shall restart the route prediction after the detection of an event by the Alarm System. This is shown in the Fig. 7 below. Here, the predicted SoC and the "real" SoC

---

[6] See https://github.com/overturetool/overture-fmu.

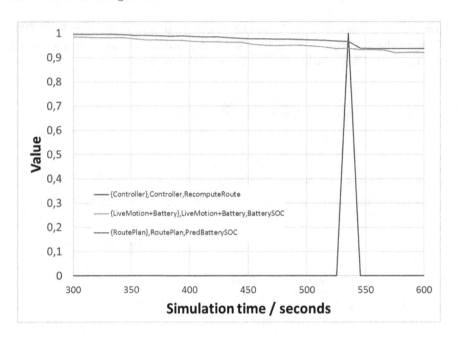

**Fig. 7.** Selected results for a nested simulation run, using the COE wrapper.

(although this also comes from a simulation, in this stage) are plotted over simulation time. The system is manipulated in such a way that the vehicle uses more energy than is predicted, by using a negative reduction factor for the gas pedal, in effect increasing speed, and thereby energy consumption. The Alarm System monitors the difference between the predicted SoC and the "real" SoC. At $t = 535$ s, the difference becomes greater than 3%, and triggers an alarm. This alarm generates the `RecomputeRoute` signal, which re-initializes the range prediction with the current values. Therefore, at the next time step, the predicted SoC is the same as the measured SoC in the previous step. This demonstrates the correct functioning of the Alarm System, and the subsequent triggering of a new simulation run by the COE wrapper.

Another example of the Alarm System in conjunction with the nested Co-simulation is shown in Fig. 8 below. Here, the longitudinal and lateral position of the vehicle is plotted, both for the predicted route (red diamonds) and the simulated position (blue line). The simulation starts at the position in the middle of the figure, indicated with "Start". However, the driver chooses an alternative route and the vehicle moves in the opposite direction of the predicted route, towards the lower left side of the figure. It should be noted that the vehicle position is here also simulated, but in principle this position can be either set in a driving simulator, or measured in a real vehicle.

Once the deviation between predicted and simulated position is reaching a threshold, which corresponds here to approximately 500 m, an alarm is triggered,

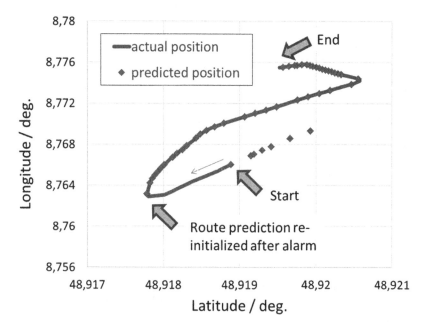

**Fig. 8.** Vehicle position (predicted and simulated) with a deviation detected by the Alarm System and subsequent re-initialisation of the Co-simulation. (Color figure online)

and the Co-simulation is re-initialized with the current position of the vehicle as a new start position. This is indicated in Fig. 8 with the arrow in the lower-left corner. In the subsequent steps, the simulated values correspond to the predicted values. Towards the end of this trip, the velocity decreases, as indicated by the lower distance between the points (at constant simulation step size). It should be noted, that the threshold of 500 m is used here merely for illustration, and can be easily adapted.

The model for the gas pedal adaptation was first modeled in 20-sim and evaluated in a Co-simulation. Then, the model was transferred to a Raspberry Pi, which is running a real-time operating system (Xenomai Linux, see https://xenomai.org/). The model for the gas-pedal adaptation is running on the hardware, and receiving its inputs from 20-sim4C, which in turn communicates with the COE.

This scenario therefore demonstrates how the INTO-CPS tool-chain can be used to develop embedded systems (here, for the adaptation of the gas-pedal curve) in multiple steps, with very little effort to change the tools, models or methods.

Using the 20-sim4C extension, the model for adapting the gas pedal curve was deployed onto a Raspberry Pi 3. The following Fig. 9 shows a simple scenario, where the acceleration is constantly increased until $t = 80s$. At $t = 50s$, the parameter "ReductionLevel" is increased from 5 to 10. This is shown on the

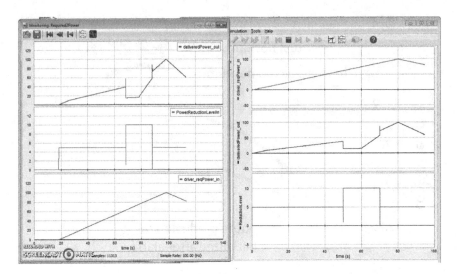

**Fig. 9.** Screenshot of the HiL simulation. On the left hand side the signals that are calculated on the Raspberry Pi are shown, on the right hand side the simulated signals are shown.

right-hand side. The left-hand side of the figure shows the corresponding signals as they are calculated on the Raspberry Pi, where the "deliveredPower_out" is reduced correspondingly at $t = 70\,s$. Note that the input from the simulation is only started approximately 20 s after the Raspberry is initialized, which is leading to the delay in time between the right and the left plot.

This demonstrates that a model that was developed in a purely virtual setting (also described as "Model-in-the-Loop") can be easily transferred to a Hardware-in-the-Loop setting, using 20-sim4C and the INTO-CPS tool-chain.

To summarize, in the online scenario new components were added to the system, which allowed more flexibility in the simulation, and close a feedback loop between calculated range and vehicle behavior. Furthermore, a part of the system was transferred to a hardware platform and coupled to the simulation. For these tasks, the INTO-CPS tool-chain was used and integrated seamlessly into the existing work-flow and the models from the offline scenario.

## 2.2   Evaluation of the Model-Based Co-simulation Approach

In the case study that was described above, several aspects of model-based engineering of Cyber-Physical Systems were evaluated. It should be noted that the focus of this study was on the evaluation of the method and less on the accuracy of the modeling itself. For example, the battery model that was chosen here is fairly simple and does not account for effects such as battery aging.

The design begins with high-level design of the system in SysML. Here, the CPS extension of Modelio allowed a smooth transition between the SysML connections diagrams, and the modeling and simulation tools. The connections diagram, which describes the signal flow between the single models, was imported into the INTO-CPS application, and the FMI ModelDescription.xml files were imported into respectively Overture or 20-sim. This seamless connection of the different tools makes the iterative development very efficient. Legacy models, or those models that are implemented in a different tool (here in Matlab) can be easily integrated into the workflow through the use of the FMI standard.

Furthermore, development in teams is facilitated by the Co-simulation approach in general, and by the INTO-CPS tool suite in particular. Each model can be developed, tested and refined individually without disturbing the overall development process. Since the INTO-CPS tool suite supports versioning systems, such as SVN or Git, this is facilitated even more. Similar observations were made in other case studies using the INTO-CPS technologies [7,8].

In summary, the INTO-CPS tool suite is well suited for the development of systems such as the one shown in this case study.

## 3    Automotive Production

Another related field with strong focus on CPS development is the engineering of automotive production lines, and here in particular virtual engineering and virtual commissioning of production plants. One major goal here is the increase of virtual development, to minimize downtime of the actual production facility by maximizing the outcome of the virtual planning. Furthermore, the whole process chain, from gathering the requirements to the production line and its components, through engineering and commissioning, to operation and maintenance, shall be integrated more closely to take advantage of the data that is generated, such as requirements, models or measurements.

In the context of automotive production, the CPS as a whole is the controller and the different machines and robots in a given production cell that are coordinated by this controller. Most of the components are standard parts from suppliers, and the task of the production planner is integration of these physical or logical components into a larger system, and designing the control logic for that system.

Regarding the engineering tool-chain, the requirements and constraints of an (automotive) production environment differ from the development of automotive functions and the products themselves. Most parts of a production plant, such as robots, motors or other moving parts, are commercial off-the-shelf components which are bought from suppliers. Thus the engineering is not concerned about detailed development of parts, but rather focuses on geometric placement of the parts inside a production line and the control programs for the controllers running the stations. To avoid collisions of moving parts and decrease the need for adjustments during ramp-up of a new model, the geometry of each station as well as its control need to be designed as detailed as possible. The processes for design of production lines are typically more standardized than for the development of automotive functions. Therefore, tool-chains for CPS development in the field of automotive production are more focussed on CAD layout tools and the whole engineering process, compared to tool-chains for automotive functions.

### 3.1   ENTOC Approach

The ITEA project "ENTOC" (Engineering tool-chain for Efficient and Iterative Development of Smart Factories)[7] aims at offering solutions for the issues that were outlined in the previous paragraph. Similar to the INTO-CPS project, the main goal of ENTOC is integration of the engineering tool-chain for development of complex systems, such as production plants [3].

In particular the technical goals of ENTOC are:

- formalization of requirements for automated test generation
- developing ways to package mechatronic components in standardized formats and distribute them
- enabling of simulation of standardized component models
- continuous use and update of engineering data throughout the lifecycle of commissioning, operation and maintenance

Some aspects of ENTOC are very similar to the INTO-CPS project. This is in particular the integration of simulation tools to couple simulation models of components (such as motors or controllers), using the FMI standard as a common data and interface format. Another important aspect of INTO-CPS is traceability, which aims at linking engineering artifacts, such as requirements, to others, such as models, simulation results or test runs. While INTO-CPS relies on the tools to communicate with each other for exchanging the relevant data, ENTOC integrates the links between requirements, models or simulation results already in the packaging format that contains models, requirements and geometry. In contrast to INTO-CPS however, ENTOC does not rely on a model-based approach, which focusses on SysML, but rather on a common packaging format, which contains all the relevant engineering data. Furthermore, the distribution of component models requires a new business model, which is rarely the focus of technically oriented research. The feedback of changes during operation and maintenance is also a special feature of the ENTOC approach, which particularly has the engineering process and the lifecycle of production plants in mind. Both approaches can also work at different ends of the same application spectrum. Single components can be developed in the model-based fashion in the INTO-CPS approach. When a validated model of the overall system is created (as an FMU), it can in principle be enriched with AutomationML data, and then distributed via the ENTOC distribution store, using the format that is being developed in ENTOC.

## 4   Conclusions

This paper presents the challenges in development of CPSs in the automotive domain, and presents attempts for solutions, given at the example of a case study. This case study develops a system for route planning, which represents

---

[7] See http://entoc.eu/.

a CPS, using tools and methods from the INTO-CPS project. This shows that CPS development benefits from integrated and flexible approaches, as they are realized in the INTO-CPS tool chain. In this case, this integration is demonstrated by usage of standards as interface between different tools, such as the Functional Mock-Up Interface 2.0 standard. Flexibility is incorporated into the tool-chain by allowing a number of different tools, thereby supporting the use of legacy models. Different scenarios are derived from the same set of initial models. The possibility to run a part of the system on hardware (the Hardware-in-the-Loop approach), and its support through the INTO-CPS tool-chain, is also demonstrated in the framework of this case study. The core parts of the INTO-CPS technology are now further developed and maintained by the non-for-profit INTO-CPS Association (see www.into-cps.org).

Beyond the case study, an outlook on CPS development in the domain of automotive production is given by the example of the ENTOC project. There, similar requirements exist for the tool-chains that are used to develop controllers of production cells. Due to domain-specific differences however, the project has a different approach and focus. These differences are not so much on a fundamental technical level, but rather on the process level. Therefore, tools and technologies can be used in various domains.

In summary, flexible and integrated tool-chains that rely on open standards for data exchange are key to efficiently develop Cyber-Physical Systems in the automotive domain.

**Acknowledgments.** This work is partially supported by the INTO-CPS project (Horizon 2020, 664047) and the ENTOC project (ITEA, 15015). We would like to thank all the participants of those projects for their efforts making this a reality.

# References

1. Blochwitz, T., et al.: The functional mockup interface 2.0: the standard for tool independent exchange of simulation models. In: Proceedings of the 9th International Modelica Conference, Munich, Germany, September 2012
2. Couto, L.D., Larsen, P.G., Hasanagic, M., Kanakis, G., Lausdahl, K., Tran-Jørgensen, P.W.V.: Towards enabling overture as a platform for formal notation IDEs. In: 2nd Workshop on Formal-IDE (F-IDE), Oslo, Norway, June 2015
3. Höll, Jos, König, C., Ritter, Y., Auris, F., Bär, T., Süß, S., Paul, M.: Seamless simulation toolchain for virtual engineering and virtual commissioning of smart factories. 18. Internationales Stuttgarter Symposium. P, pp. 797–811. Springer, Wiesbaden (2018). https://doi.org/10.1007/978-3-658-21194-3_61
4. Johnson, V.: Battery performance models in advisor. J. Power Sources **110**, 321–329 (2002)
5. Larsen, P.G., et al.: Integrated tool chain for model-based design of cyber-physical systems: the INTO-CPS project. In: 2016 2nd International Workshop on Modelling, Analysis, and Control of Complex CPS (CPS Data). IEEE, Vienna, Austria, April 2016. http://ieeexplore.ieee.org/document/7496424/

6. Larsen, P.G., et al.: Integrated tool chain for model-based design of cyber-physical systems. In: Larsen, P.G., Plat, N., Battle, N. (eds.) The 14th Overture Workshop: Towards Analytical Tool Chains, pp. 63–78. Department of Engineering, Aarhus University, Cyprus, November 2016. ECE-TR-28

7. Neghina, M., Zamrescu, C.B., Larsen, P.G., Lausdahl, K., Pierce, K.: Multi-paradigm discrete-event modelling and co-simulation of cyber-physical systems. Stud. Inform. Control **27**(1), 33–42 (2018)

8. Pedersen, N., Lausdahl, K., Sanchez, E.V., Larsen, P.G., Madsen, J.: Distributed co-simulation of embedded control software with exhaust gas recirculation water handling system using INTO-CPS. In: Proceedings of the 7th International Conference on Simulation and Modeling Methodologies, Technologies and Applications (SIMULTECH 2017), pp. 73–82. Madrid, Spain, July 2017. ISBN 978-989-758-265-3

9. Piller, S., Perrin, M., Jossen, A.: Methods for state-of-charge determination and their applications. J. Power Sources **96**(1), 113–120 (2001)

10. Reda, I., Andreas, A.: Solar position algorithm for solar radiation applications. Sol. Energy **76**, 577–589 (2004)

11. Sadovykh, A., et al.: SysML as a common integration platform for co-simulations: example of a cyber physical system design methodology in green heating ventilation and air conditioning systems. In: Proceedings of the 12th Central and Eastern European Software Engineering Conference in Russia, CEE-SECR 2016, pp. 1:1–1:5. ACM, New York (2016). https://doi.org/10.1145/3022211.3022212

12. Sztipanovits, J., Bapty, T., Neema, S., Koutsoukos, X., Jackson, E.: Design tool chain for cyber-physical systems: lessons learned. In: Proceedings of the 52nd Annual Design Automation Conference, DAC 2015, pp. 81:1–81:6. ACM, New York (2015). https://doi.org/10.1145/2744769.2747922

# Testing Avionics Software: Is FMI up to the Task?

Jörg Brauer[1,2](✉), Oliver Möller[1,2], and Jan Peleska[1,2]

[1] Verified Systems International GmbH, Bremen, Germany
{brauer,moller,peleska}@verified.de
[2] Department of Mathematics and Computer Science,
University of Bremen, Bremen, Germany
jp@informatik.uni-bremen.de

**Abstract.** This paper compares two test engine architectures, one based on the RT-Tester test system, and one based on FMI, and analyzes how these different approaches satisfy the needs for verification and validation of safety-critical avionics software. The study is based on an aircraft controller application, which motivates the requirements to the test engine designs.

## 1 Introduction

For almost two decades, Verified Systems has developed and produced real-time test engines dedicated to hardware-in-the-loop (HIL) testing of aircraft controllers. The design of these test engines, and of course also the design of competing products, has always addressed the problem of testing a cyber-physical system in a co-simulating environment, long before terms such as co-simulation [5] have been adopted by industry and academia. Aircraft controllers frequently embed numerous different applications on a single device and are connected to different hardware interfaces. Devices such as cabin controllers manufactured by Airbus for contemporary Aircraft, for example, include more than 50 different applications, and are connected to the aircraft via CAN bus, discrete I/O, AFDX, and special-purpose buses such as topline or middleline. They are connected to hundreds of separate devices, which are installed somewhere in the aircraft, and contain safety-critical as well as not so safety-critical functionality.

Such controllers are inherently cyber-physical by definition. Clearly, to test and verify such controllers in HIL tests, it is necessary to simulate the interaction of the controller with hardware devices, and exercise the interaction of the controllers with external devices in certain scenarios. For example, a set of smoke detector devices could be connected to an aircraft controller via CAN bus, and a natural test would be to exercise the behavior of the system if startup of one of the smoke detectors is delayed, for whatever reason. The interaction of these controllers with external devices that implement some logic on their own has always posed the need for co-simulating these devices in parallel to the test

T. Margaria and B. Steffen (Eds.): ISoLA 2018, LNCS 11246, pp. 477–487, 2018.
https://doi.org/10.1007/978-3-030-03424-5_32

execution; otherwise, meaningful tests of the aircraft controller would hardly be possible.

FMI [2] has become an established standard for co-simulation of systems composed from a set of components, which provides notions for encapsulating the behavior of the components—components are merely visible via their external interfaces—and controlling the timing of the interactions between the components. Co-simulation standards promise improved collaboration through the entire supply chain, and enable frequent integration of devices while the system or certain subsystems are still under development. From our own perspective as a vendor for special-purpose test systems and simulations, FMI and comparable industrial standards are highly relevant, which raises the question whether FMI could serve as the basis for a HIL testing architecture for aircraft controllers, which necessitates support for parallel, real-time discrete event techniques [4]. This is the topic of this paper.

The contribution of this paper is a comparison of our traditional test system architecture with one based on FMI. It discusses some of the core challenges that we are facing when testing aircraft controllers, how our test engines address these challenges, and how they fit into the FMI approach. The presentation is based on a fictitious application, which is nevertheless strongly inspired by a system that can be found in many contemporary aircraft families.

The remainder of this paper is structured as follows. First, Sect. 2 introduces our case study application and the system architecture, followed by a set of requirements for tailored HIL test engines in Sect. 3. The key contribution of this paper, namely the comparison of our established test engine architecture and one based on FMI is located in Sect. 4. This section also discusses to what extent the requirements sketched in Sect. 3 can be satisfied using either approach. Finally, the paper concludes with an overview of related work in Sect. 5 and a discussion in Sect. 6.

## 2    Worked Example

Let us start this discussion with an example application that is inspired by a system used in contemporary aircrafts. Suppose one of the purposes of an aircraft controller is to control and monitor the interaction between heating controllers and at least one human-machine interface (HMI), and the aircraft controller is connected to these devices via CAN bus and AFDX (ARINC 664), respectively. The purpose of such a system is to avoid icing in cargo compartments during flight. Each heating controller is directly connected to a set of up to 32 heaters. Further, an electrical load supervisor unit is connected to the aircraft controller via AFDX bus. This unit has the ability to autonomously switch all heating devices into a power-save mode. The overall architecture of the system is depicted in Fig. 1. For the example, we focus on a small subset of the functionality of this system:

- Each HMI displays the current temperature of each heater and allows to control the target temperature. To do so, it sends AFDX commands to the aircraft controller sporadically, and cyclically receives AFDX status messages from the aircraft controller.
- Each heater sporadically receives a target temperature from the aircraft controller via CAN bus (corresponding to the selection on the HMI device), and cyclically returns the selected target temperature and the current temperature to the aircraft controller via CAN bus, and whether the heater is in power-save mode. Each heater controls its physical heating behavior depending on these two values.
- Each heating unit monitors the health status of the directly connected heaters and cyclically sends status data to the aircraft controller via CAN.
- The electrical load supervisor sporadically sends a power-save command to the aircraft controller via AFDX, which forwards the command to the HMI via AFDX and to all heating panels via CAN.

This is an extremely simplified subset of the functionality, yet involves sufficient components and dependencies to be considered complex already. An additional challenge stems from the fact that the layout of the device connections is

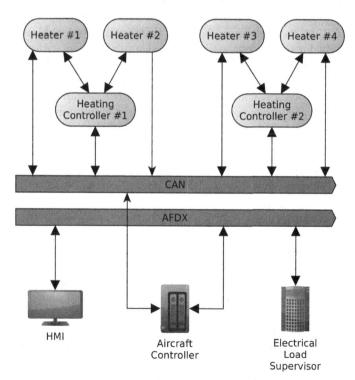

**Fig. 1.** Architecture of the system under test including external devices

configurable. For instance, one aircraft may have six heating controllers installed, each of which is connected to 16 heaters, whereas another aircraft may have only two heating controllers with a differing number of heating panels.

A typical test cases for this application would then, for example, cover the following scenario:

- The aircraft controller boots successfully and detects all connected heating devices.
- On the HMI, the target temperature for each heater is manually increased to the maximum value and then decreased to the minimum value. It is expected that the heating devices receive the correct temperature selection. During this step, the temperature changes of the heating devices are simulated, and it is expected that the HMI displays the correct values.
- A power outage is simulated and all heaters are turned off. The HMI shows a warning message and indicates that all heaters are turned off.

## 3   Test System Requirements

Both, the application to be tested and the domain of the application, impose certain requirements on feasible test engines. First of all, it must provide hard real-time guarantees in order to enable predictable and reproducible tests. From the application domain, it is necessary that the overall test system is qualifiable, which means that it must be possible to show—with reasonable effort—that the system is fit for use in certification-related verification activities for avionics software. The applicable avionics development standards RTCA DO-178B and RTCA DO-178C prescribe certain guidelines for when a test system is fit for use in development processes. For example, one of the core requirements is that the test system—just like other development software—is deterministic, which may provide an unsurmountable gap for application of off-the-shelf FMI solutions in practice.

**REQ-REALTIME.** The test engine must support hard real-time.
**REQ-QUALIFIED.** The test engine must be qualifiable according to RTCA DO-178B [7] and/or RTCA DO-178C [8].
**REQ-AUTOMATED.** All tests have to be executed automatically.

Additional requirements emerge from the system under test, its components and its hardware interfaces. During tests, the different heating devices, the HMI and the electrical load supervisor shall be simulated by the test engine, but proper hardware buses shall be used to connect to the system under test, that is, the aircraft controller. Much computational power is required to serve interfaces such as AFDX, which necessitates network of computational nodes within the test engine; otherwise, it would not be possible to fulfill all tasks in real-time.

**REQ-CAN.** The test engine must be connected to a CAN bus and serve the CAN bus in real-time.

**REQ-AFDX.** The test engine must be connected to an AFDX bus and serve the AFDX bus in real-time.

**REQ-DISCRETES.** The test engine must be connected to a discrete I/O interface.[1]

**REQ-SIM.** The test engine must support simulation of (virtually) arbitrary external hardware devices.[2]

**REQ-DISTRIBUTED.** Due to the heavy computation load involved in serving AFDX buses etc. it must be possible to spread the hardware connections for AFDX and CAN to different computations in the test engine.

**REQ-CONFIG.** It must be straightforward to configure the simulations and hardware connections for a specific test.[3]

**REQ-SCHEDULING.** The different components of a test (such as heating controller simulations or the HMI simulation) need to executed in predictable order using adaptable scheduling policies.[4]

# 4 Test Engine Architectures: Comparison

So far, we have discussed the structure of the SUT and domain-specific requirements to a suitable test engine. However, how the test engines can be designed differs significantly depending on the underlying technology. This section discusses two different approaches to test engine architectures.

## 4.1 RT-Tester Test Engines

The RT-Tester test engines developed by Verified Systems can be seen as a cluster of standard desktop computers (called cluster nodes), each of which runs a modified Linux kernel in order to provide real-time guarantees. The cluster nodes are connected via InfiniBand, which is a serial low-latency bus that can reach transfer rates of up to 2,5 GBit/s. Each cluster node runs an RT-Tester installation, which is a test software specifically developed for these test engines. There are two noteworthy peculiarities of RT-Tester, which are important to the overall test engine design.

---

[1] Handling of discrete I/O is necessary to start or reset the aircraft controller. Without discrete I/O, automated testing is thus not possible.

[2] Controlling external devices is essential to reach the test goals, for instance, verify the stability of the SUT with respect to unexpected timings of incoming CAN messages.

[3] The devices connected to the aircraft controller are configured via software parameters, and different tests may have to exercise different parameter settings. The parameter settings include, for example, the number of heating controllers and the association of heaters to heating controllers. It must therefore be possible to straightforwardly adapt the set of simulations, as well as simulation parameters and the order in which these simulations are executed, for each single test.

[4] A predictable order is necessary since the different simulations and checkers running on the test engine may depend on one another.

– RT-Tester provides signals and channels as a communication mechanism both between test components running on a single cluster node as well as test components running on different cluster nodes. The advantage of this approach is that tests and simulations do not differ depending on the layout of the test engine, but only the test configuration file has to be adapted.
– RT-Tester provides its own process and thread handling functionality as follows: A *lightweight process* (LWP) is the RT-Tester counterpart to a typical process. However, an LWP consists of a fixed number of abstract machines (AMs), which are essentially threads. The threads are predictably scheduled using a round-robin strategy and the scheduler is configurable with respect to timings.

A typical structure for one of the RT-Tester based test engines is given in Fig. 2. The test engine consists of four cluster nodes. The first one is solely responsible for serving the AFDX interface. It runs an LWP which consumes the incoming signals from other cluster nodes and provides the connection to the AFDX bus. Likewise, the second cluster node handles the CAN bus and the discrete I/O interface. The remaining two nodes run the simulations and the test driver, which stimulates the SUT. All cluster nodes are connected via InfiniBand and communicate via the built-in communication channels and signals.

A test configuration then merely consists of a test driver implementation (the stimulations of the inputs of the SUT and checks for the outputs) and a configuration file, which specifies which cluster node executes which LWPs. The LWP configuration can simply be adapted in order to enable additional heater simulations, for example, or disable the HMI simulation. Similar architectures are used for the verification of a variety of aircrafts, including the Airbus A350XWB or the Airbus A380, and have proven both powerful and flexible.

However, one of the drawbacks of the architecture is that it is cumbersome to exchange components. For instance, if one would replace the simulation of heaters by real heater devices, this would amount to significant effort.

### 4.2  FMI-Based Architecture

By way of comparison, a test engine architecture based on FMI promises interesting benefits. For example, the encapsulation of devices (or simulations thereof) allows to easily replace simulations against real hardware devices. An FMI master algorithm could handle the distribution of signal values, and access to the entire hardware interface of the aircraft controller could be encapsulated within a functional mockup unit (FMU), which thereby provides a unified interface to the functionality of the aircraft controller. A potential test engine architecture based on FMI is depicted in Fig. 3. As opposed to the architecture sketched before, there is no direct connection between the simulation nodes (cluster nodes #2 and #3) and the hardware interfaces (cluster nodes #1 and #2). Data exchange between the simulations and the hardware interface is established via the *Aircraft*

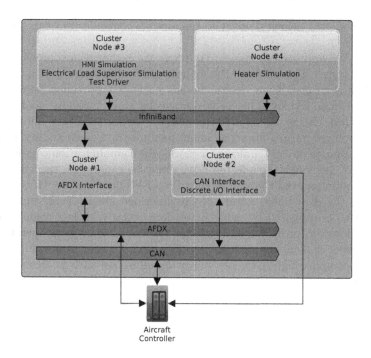

**Fig. 2.** Test engine architecture using RT-Tester

*Interface FMU*, which provides an interface to the aircraft controller interfaces[5]. For example, if a heater simulation FMU sends a status message to the aircraft controller via CAN, then this status message becomes visible at the interface of the heater FMU and is transmitted to the Aircraft Interface FMU via the FMI master. Observe that there is intentionally no connection between cluster nodes #1 and #2 and the InfiniBand bus. The exchange of data between the Aircraft Interface FMU and these two cluster nodes is internal to the FMU, and thus independent of how the different FMUs interact with each other via the FMI Master. Of course, this could be implemented via InfiniBand.

Let us discuss a possible example of how data flows through the architecture in Fig. 3. Assume that the test driver stimulates the HMI so that a temperature for a heater is selected. This stimulation is sent from cluster node #3 to the FMI engine running on the *FMI Master Node*, which returns the stimulation to the HMI simulation running on cluster node #3. The HMI simulation then generates an AFDX signal, which is sent to the FMI engine and forwarded to the *Aircraft Interface FMU*. This FMU then internally communicates the signal

---

[5] Please note that this is one possibility for defining the interface to the actual aircraft controller. It would likewise be possible to summarize the interfaces to a specific hardware device in one FMU, or to structure the interfaces based on applications. This decision, however, does not influence the principled architecture.

to cluster node #1, which sends it to the aircraft controller through the AFDX interface.

Overall, the approach promises to improve the exchange of components while a system is tested. For instance, the manufacturer of a heater device could provide FMUs generated from design models or FMUs providing access to the actual hardware devices. This is advantageous since virtually no knowledge about the test engine is required to integrate external FMUs into the test engine, thereby promising improved maintainability and extendability. However, the above example already indicates a significant communication overhead since all signals, even though the affected FMUs may be running on the same cluster node, are communicated through a centralized FMI master node. Of course, this stems from the distributed nature of the described architecture, and could to some extent be mitigated by using many-core nodes with less communication overhead. However, providing real-time guarantees on many-core operating systems kernels is challenging, and such nodes will still suffer from computational overload if complex high-frequency hardware interfaces such as AFDX need to be handled.

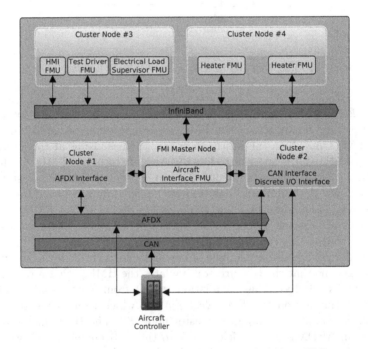

**Fig. 3.** Possible test engine architecture based on FMI

### 4.3   Analysis

Two core requirements, namely **REQ-REALTIME** and **REQ-QUALIFIED**, stem directly from the targeted application domain. While it is certainly possible to implement or generate FMUs that provide real-time guarantees, we are not aware of any such FMI master implementation. Indeed, if hard real-time requirements are define for an FMI master, then these are not dissimilar to requirements for a real-time operating system kernel[6]. It is certainly possible to replace the logical notion of time prescribed by the FMI standard by a physical one, with the use of appropriate synchronization mechanism. However, timeliness of serving the *Aircraft Interface FMU*, which is connect to the hardware device drivers, is critical. Further, to the best of our knowledge, none of the existing commercial or non-commercial FMI master implementations come with a tool qualification (or tool qualification kit) for the applicable avionics standards.

These are major obstacles that prevent the application of FMI to certification-related verification activities in the avionics domain. Tool qualification for an FMI master is time-consuming, but not considered risky. The situation differs for **REQ-REALTIME**. As argued before, the process architecture in RT-Tester consists of a form of processes and threads, which are scheduled using a round-robin strategy, so as to guarantee predictability of test execution. There is no principled need for sequential execution of threads within a process, but one that stems from the complexity of the target system. Contemporary aircraft controllers frequently define hundreds of thousands of signals, and if each thread were to filter the relevant signals from all signals, significantly higher computing power would be required. A practical solution is to filter the signals once, and then make the filtered results available to all threads, thereby drastically reducing the runtime. It is not obvious how this approach fits into schemes such as the one proposed by FMI.

From a business perspective, significant research efforts and development investments are required to satisfy the requirements **REQ-REALTIME** and **REQ-QUALIFIED**. An overview of how the different architectures satisfy the requirements is given in Table 1.

## 5   Related Work

There has been significant research interest in taking the co-simulation framework from plain model-in-the-loop scenarios further to software-in-the-loop and hardware-in-the-loop problems. The latter one, applying FMI [2] to domains with strict real-time requirements, can still be considered an open problem. An excellent overview of the state-of-the-art in co-simulation and FMI is given in [5]. Co-simulation has, of course, been applied to problems with strict timing requirements. To name just one example, special-purpose solutions have been applied to the ISS [3]. As argued in the introduction, the technique of co-simulation has

---

[6] Observe that this requirement is strongly related to predictable scheduling and a suitable scheduling policy, as specified by requirement **REQ-SCHEDULING**.

**Table 1.** Satisfaction of test engine requirements by each architecture

| Requirement | RT-Tester | FMI |
|---|---|---|
| **REQ-REALTIME** | Yes | No |
| **REQ-QUALIFIED** | Yes | No |
| **REQ-AUTOMATED** | Yes | Yes |
| **REQ-CAN** | Yes | Yes |
| **REQ-AFDX** | Yes | Yes |
| **REQ-DISCRETES** | Yes | Yes |
| **REQ-SIM** | Yes | Yes |
| **REQ-DISTRIBUTED** | Yes | Yes |
| **REQ-CONFIG** | Yes | Yes |
| **REQ-SCHEDULING** | Yes | No |

to some extend been applied in industry before the term was coined, but to the best of our knowledge always based on dedicated solutions. The RT-Tester based test engine discussed in this paper is one such instance.

Real-time capability of co-simulation is a problem on two somewhat separate levels. Each FMU has to satisfy hard real-time requirements, which can be achieved by simply embedding a real-time capable process within an FMU. A related problem is that of determining or estimating the worst-case execution time of FMUs, as discussed in [9].

As an ongoing research effort, the ACOSAR project [1] shall be mentioned. The expressed goal of this project is to define a so-called *Advanced Co-Simulation Interface*, which shall both ease the configuration workload for co-simulation setups and support the real-time domain. As a related project, INTO-CPS [6] has focussed on the integration of different development phases—such as modeling, design space exploration, and testing—into a tool-chain based on FMI. Real-time testing, however, has not been addressed during the course of the project.

## 6    Concluding Discussion

FMI has been developed as a standard for model-in-the-loop or software-in-the-loop simulations and tests and has received high visibility in both academia and industry. By way of contrast, this paper addresses the issue of applying FMI to the problem of hardware-in-the-loop testing and simulation for hard real-time systems, namely avionics system. In this domain, the application of dedicated solutions, developed with the specifics of the application domain in mind, still are the defacto standard. FMI and competing solutions are compelling, yet contain some gaps for which no definite solution was found. It will be interesting to observe the impact of current research projects on the state-of-the-art used in industry, and how it will impact the industrial practice in the future, especially with respect to real-time guarantees and the integration of scheduling policies into co-simulation frameworks. A timeliness guarantee for one FMU is one issue that has been addressed, but the more compelling and challenging one is from our perspective the timeliness of the entire test system, built from a collection of FMUs. In test engines based on RT-Tester, structuring the tests using lightweight processes and abstract machines combined with scheduling strategie has proven powerful. Integrating such mechanisms in order to control the co-simulation and provide hierarchies of FMUs appears promising.

# References

1. ACOSAR: Advanced Co-Simulation Open System Architecture. http://www.acosar.eu
2. Blochwitz, T.: Functional Mock-up Interface for Model Exchange and Co-Simulation, July 2014. https://www.fmi-standard.org/downloads
3. Formaggio, L., Fummi, F., Pravadelli, G.: A timing-accurate HW/SW co-simulation of an ISS with systemc. In: Proceedings of the 2nd IEEE/ACM/IFIP International Conference on Hardware/Software Codesign and System Synthesis, pp. 152–157. CODES+ISSS 2004. ACM, New York (2004)
4. Fujimoto, R.M.: Parallel discrete event simulation. Commun. ACM **33**(10), 30–53 (1990)
5. Gomes, C., Thule, C., Broman, D., Larsen, P.G., Vangheluwe, H.: Co-simulation: state of the art. CoRR abs/1702.00686 (2017). http://arxiv.org/abs/1702.00686
6. Larsen, P.G., et al.: Integrated tool chain for model-based design of cyber-physical systems: the INTO-CPS project. In: 2016 2nd International Workshop on Modelling, Analysis, and Control of Complex CPS, CPS Data 2016, Vienna, Austria, 11 April 2016, pp. 1–6. IEEE (2016)
7. RTCA SC-167/EUROCAE WG-12: Software Considerations in Airborne Systems and Equipment Certification. Technical report RTCA/DO-178B, RTCA Inc., 1140 Connecticut Avenue, N.W., Suite 1020, Washington, D.C. 20036, December 1992
8. RTCA SC-205/EUROCAE WG-71: Software Considerations in Airborne Systems and Equipment Certification. Technical report RTCA/DO-178C, RTCA Inc., 1140 Connecticut Avenue, N.W., Suite 1020, Washington, D.C. 20036, December 2011
9. Saidi, S.E., Pernet, N., Sorel, Y., Khaled, A.B.: Acceleration of FMU co-simulation on multi-core architectures. In: The First Japanese Modelica Conferences, May 23–24, Tokyo, Japan. pp. 106–112. No. 124 in Linköping Electronic Conference Proceedings, Linköping University Electronic Press, Linköpings Universitet (2016)

# Lessons Learned Using FMI Co-simulation for Model-Based Design of Cyber Physical Systems

Luís Diogo Couto[1], Stylianos Basagiannis[1(✉)], El Hassan Ridouane[1],
Erica Zavaglio[1], Pasquale Antonante[2], Hajer Saada[1],
and Sara Falleni[3]

[1] United Technologies Research Center, Cork, Ireland
{CoutoLD,BasagiS,RidouaE,ZavaglE,SaadaH}@utrc.utc.com
[2] Area17, Inc., Oakland, CA, USA
pantonante@a17.ai
[3] ECE Department, Northeastern University, Boston, USA
falleni.s@husky.neu.edu

**Abstract.** Model-Based Design is an effective way to carry out Cyber-Physical Systems (CPS) development. One of the main sets of challenges in CPS projects is dealing with the highly heterogeneous nature of the development teams. These challenges can be brought to the forefront by focusing on model integration through standards, such as the Functional Mockup Interface (FMI). We report on a case study of the application of an FMI-based workflow to the development of a Heat Ventilation and Air Conditioning (HVAC) system of a building. We report on ten challenges and lessons learned when using the FMI standard, focusing on collaborative aspects and model integration. As a conclusion we provide recommendations and examples for dealing with the CPS development challenges assessing to that end the importance of the FMI standard.

## 1 Introduction

One of the main challenges of Cyber-Physical System (CPS) development is dealing with the highly heterogeneous nature of the development teams – in terms of technical background, discipline, tools, and work methodology [14]. The use of Model-Based Design (MBD) and simulation tools is an important part of CPS development, common to most disciplines. However, for an efficient development process, it is import to integrate the work of these disciplines early and frequently. In this context, standards for coupling together models and simulations such as the Functional Mockup Interface (FMI) [2] become an important part of CPS development [1,6,7].

FMI is appealing to industry [15] due to the simple interface and the growing number of tools that support it.[1] For organizations such as UTC, that have a significant knowledge and technical information captured in models, understanding

---

[1] FMI-compatible tools can be found at http://fmi-standard.org/tools/.

© Springer Nature Switzerland AG 2018
T. Margaria and B. Steffen (Eds.): ISoLA 2018, LNCS 11246, pp. 488–503, 2018.
https://doi.org/10.1007/978-3-030-03424-5_33

the capabilities of the FMI and its role in CPS development becomes essential. To this end, in order to assess the potential of the FMI, we have carried out a large case study for the development of a building Heating, Ventilation and Air Conditioning (HVAC) system.

The case study was developed as part of the EU H2020 INTO-CPS Project[2] [12]. It was built with the INTO-CPS FMI-based tool chain, so that model integration through co-simulation is a first class citizen in the development process.

The main contribution of this paper is an evaluation of the FMI for CPS development in the form of a series of issues encountered, lessons learned, and guidelines and recommendations for dealing with them.

In the remainder of this paper, we provide background information on FMI and the associated INTO-CPS tool chain in Sect. 2. We describe the building HVAC system under development in Sect. 3. Section 4 presents the core contribution of the paper – experiences with the FMI standard. Finally, we conclude in Sect. 5.

## 2    Background

A CPS can be defined as an integration of computation with physical processes. It consists of networked embedded systems and devices that monitor and control physical process, based on feedback loops, where physical phenomena affect and are affected by computations [5].

One of the approaches to CPS development is based on co-simulation frameworks with standards such as the FMI. The FMI is a tool-independent standard to support both model exchange and co-simulation of dynamic models using a combination of XML-files and compiled C-code [2]. Under the FMI co-simulation, models are exported as Functional Mockup Units (FMUs) – standalone components with descriptions that specify the inputs and outputs of the model. Co-simulations are executed with a master algorithm that coordinates the exchange of data between FMUs and the progress of the overall co-simulation time. In the INTO-CPS project, the implementation of the master algorithm and the execution of co-simulations are handled by a tool called the Co-Simulation Orchestration Engine (COE).

The INTO-CPS project backbone is based upon the FMI standard. As shown in Fig. 1, the INTO-CPS workflow offers a combination of CPS analysis features spanning from requirements traceability through to co-simulation results and generated source code. The entry point for the workflow is through the development of a SysML model of the system and its requirements – in this case using Modelio[3]– in order to for the CPS to be decomposed into tractable blocks. The INTO-CPS SysML profile defines architecture and internal block diagrams that will support the engineer in describing the connections between the CPS. From

---

[2] https://into-cps.github.io/.
[3]  http://www.modelio.org/.

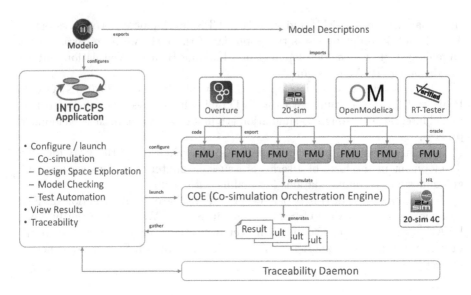

**Fig. 1.** INTO-CPS Workflow from requirements through to co-simulation results and generated source code

the SysML artefacts, the engineer automatically generates the system's multi-model which describes the system in terms of FMUs and connections between them. Additionally, FMI model descriptions are generated to be imported into the various modelling tools that will elaborate the constituent models of the system. Legacy FMUs can also be accommodated by importing the associated model descriptions into the SysML description. Thus, it is possible to compose system models from a mix of new and pre-existing CPS elements. The reader can refer to [8] for additional information related to the INTO-CPS workflow.

As already mentioned, the multi-model is analyzed primarily through co-simulation purpose, but a series of additional features complement the analysis of the CPS. These include model-based testing, code generation that powers Software-in-the-Loop (SIL) and Hardware-in-the-Loop (HIL) co-simulations (e.g. using 20-sim 4C). The engineer is able to configure these analyses through the INTO-CPS application depending on system-level requirements. Starting from the traceability feature, the workflow allows the engineer to track, log and validate each constituent model of the system and its requirements, by providing all necessary information back to the engineer. In cases where multiple, automated co-simulation executions are needed e.g. for parameter tuning, then the engineer can use the Design Space Exploration (DSE) technique [10]. At the same time, test automation and model checking are also employed in the INTO-CPS workflow for obtaining coverage and verification results from the CPS elements. After building a system using the INTO-CPS SysML profile, the engineer is able to launch model-based testing activities that generate evidence of system correctness. Co-simulations can be re-executed based on generated test traces (wrapped as FMUs) and monitored using Liner Temporal Logic (LTL) formulas to ensure that user-defined constraints are respected. Finally, bounded model checking of the system is also enabled via state-chart representations of the constituent models DE and abstracted CT models, giving also the opportunity for the generation of verification results of certain CPS properties.

## 3 Case Study

As a reference for the application of a FMI-based workflow, we focused on a building case study. This case study is based on the modelling and the thermal analysis of a building and its HVAC system which accounts for the control of the indoor temperature. The system is illustrated in Fig. 2. The implemented HVAC model describes a $1052\,m^2$ office building supplied by a hydronic system in cooling mode. As shown in Fig. 2, the building consists of 3 rooms, one of them larger and composed by two zones. The HVAC system has 3 main components:

- Fan Coil Units (FCUs), responsible for controlling the temperature of each room by using the fan to direct air through the coil to cool the air, and then flowing it back into the room.
- a chiller, responsible for providing cold water to the FCUs in the occupied spaces,
- an Air Handling Unit (AHU), responsible for providing and circulating air to the system and maintaining indoor fresh air requirements.

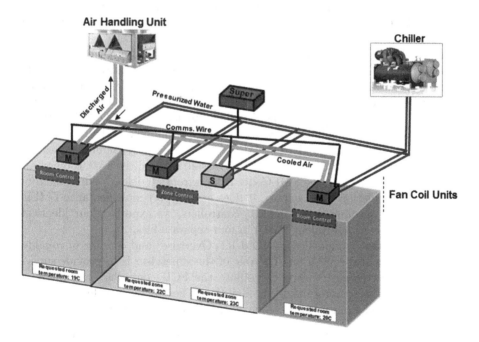

**Fig. 2.** Detailed schematic of building HVAC case study

For each room, the FCU works off a user-defined set point and drives the temperature of the room towards the desired set point. To represent the entire system, we developed several models using different tools and later exported as FMUs to be coupled together in a co-simulation environment. Further details about the various models described in this section can be found in [13]. The main models and FMUs are listed and described below:

- Plant modeled in Dymola
- FCU controller modeled in Simulink
- Supervisor modeled in VDM-RT/Overture
- System Decomposition and connections in SysML (omitted from this paper)

The *Plant* model represents an actual building site in Montluel, France. It is composed by the building envelope, the air volumes and by various HVAC components (Chiller, AHU, FCUs and water and air pipes). It accounts for all the relevant fluid flows and heat transfer phenomena, and thus it shows a quite high level of complexity especially the HVAC devices such as the Chiller. The model of the building is a simplified representation of the actual building in which the 71 FCUs are grouped into 4 groups - one per zone. Each indoor space is modelled as single air volume and supplied by one large FCU equivalent to the sum of the FCUs in the corresponding zone. This model was created in Dymola 2016, which is a commercial tool based on Modelica language and supports FMI 2.0 standard. It is composed by 11278 unknowns and equations and based on proprietary Modelica libraries that accounts for years of UTC experience in thermal modeling, dealing with building HVAC systems. The calibration and validation of the model were then performed using actual data from the existing building.

The *FCU controller* model was created in Simulink and used to control the respective FCU. It is a standard Proportional-Integral (PI) controller that acts both on the water valve position, thus allowing less/more cold water to supply the FCU, and on the speed of the fan responsible for the air circulation inside the unit. The controller was calibrated taking into account specific requirements on temperature control in buildings. The choice of Simulink as the tool used to model the controller is a standard practice in UTC. Currently, Simulink does not support the FMI standard natively, for this reason, we used the FMI Toolbox for MATLAB/Simulink with the FMI Coder Addon from Modelon.[4] While the tool supports co-simulation FMU export, it does not support multi-instance FMUs. As the system is composed of 4 FMU controllers, we exported four identical FMUs (one for each equivalent FMU) in four separate files.

The *Supervisor* is modelled in VDM-RT/Overture[5] and consists of roughly 540 lines of formal specification. The role of the supervisor is to provide supervisory control strategies, i.e. to coordinate the FCU controllers to achieve a better temperature control inside the building. These actions include: defining an FCU as master (and possibly redefine it, if faults are detected), distributing

---

[4] http://www.modelon.com/products/fmi-tools/fmi-toolbox-for-matlabsimulink/.
[5] http://overturetool.org/.

set points from masters to slaves, and ensuring that any set point in the FCUs is within certain maximum and minimum bounds. The supervisor also performs fault detection action by monitoring the difference in room temperatures and set points. Communication between the FCUs and the supervisor is also modelled within the VDM-RT model.

All models are exported according to the FMI standard and used for co-simulation based on a dedicated master algorithm – the INTO-CPS COE – according to the INTO-CPS workflow. To evaluate the performance and behaviour of the models when integrated together, we performed a set of co-simulations, using the INTO-CPS platform. We investigated a range of different conditions through several scenarios representing a variety of boundary conditions and situations where the system may operate, i.e. a wide variation in the external temperature or a different building occupancy profile.

We defined a *baseline scenario*, thus considering standard conditions, as the reference for further analysis, and then, to evaluate the co-simulation results, we consider 2 main metrics: the total energy consumption associated with the operation of the HVAC systems and the thermal discomfort inside the building. We also evaluated the behaviour of the control strategy in the presence of a fault in one of the FCU controller. The Supervisor was able to detect the fault and act accordingly to mitigate the impact on the temperature inside the corresponding zone. A more detailed discussion about the co-simulation results can be found in [13].

Among all the defined scenarios, we used the baseline scenario to explore HIL co-simulation capabilities. The 4 FCUs controllers were deployed to the Zynq-7000 System-on-Chip using Simulink functionalities to generate the code from the model. We also used the 20-Sim 4C[6] tool to import an FMU with source code, to cross-compile it for a Raspberry-Pi 3 and to deploy it to the board. With both solutions, we were able to directly communicate with the INTO-CPS COE in real-time.

## 4   Experiences

In this section, we discuss and reflect our conclusions and experiences of working with FMI-based tool chains for the design and development of CPSs. We group our experiences into several challenges and include practical recommendations on how to address each. The section focuses on methodological, process and occasional tool challenges that we have experienced in the course of developing our case study.

### 4.1   Design Erosion

In the INTO-CPS approach, one begins CPS design by modelling the system architecture at a high level using SysML. This design is then distributed to the

---

[6] http://www.20sim.com/products/20sim4c.html.

various developers who will work on the constituent models that make up the CPS design. In the INTO-CPS tool chain, FMI model description files can be exported from the SysML design. The configuration of FMI co-simulations an also be derived from this design. However, neither step is mandatory – it is possible to develop constituent models without the model description, and it is also possible to configure co-simulations without the SysML design.

Because FMI model descriptions detach the SysML design from the constituent models, there is a threat that individual constituent model developers are unaware or simply do not care about the SysML design. This can particularly affect larger heterogeneous teams where individual members are only responsible for a single constituent model. As a result, the project can be affected by design erosion due to the constituent models violating the SysML design. These violations can range from minor errors such as different FMI variable names to more serious ones such as different sets of FMI inputs and outputs.

**Recommendation 1:** It is important for a project to have a common CPS design description that is central and shared by all project members. This design should evolve over time, but these evolutions should be visible and agreed upon by all members. Ideally, this design should be enforced through distribution and adherence to constituent model specifications through FMI model descriptions. Where the tools do not mandate this, it should be a project policy to do so nonetheless. Tools that do not support importing of FMI model descriptions should be avoided if at all possible. The primary design artefact shared across the team is the connections diagram for the case study, shown in Fig. 3.

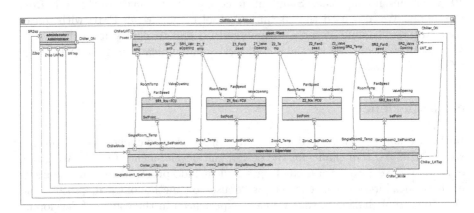

**Fig. 3.** FMU Connections in the building case study, realised as a SysML INTO-CPS Connections diagram.

## 4.2  Undocumented Assumptions

FMI co-simulations rely heavily on the exchange of numerical values between the FMUs wrapping each constituent model. These values are represented as C types

– for example, an FMI real is a C double. However, in the models these numeric values may have restrictions on them – for example, there may be a minimum limit that must be respected, or the value must be within a certain range.

While the FMI standard enables setting a minimum and maximum limit on a value, these are for information purposes – to signal warnings during a co-simulation. Constituent models may have no way of knowing what restrictions will be placed on their output variables when they are received. While some kinds of restrictions may be documented in the FMI model description, we have thus far not encountered tools that enable us to place these restrictions in place when designing the system. Likewise, the modelling tools for each constituent model do not take this information into account when importing a model description nor do they statically check for it when generating FMUs. Though, it must be said that this last point cannot always be checked statically. Another issue lies with the units of the exchanged variables. Internally, different tools or constituent models may use different units. When values are exchanged between FMUs, it is important that they are converted. Once again, the FMI standard has a feature for defining the units of exchanged variables. However, thus far we have observed that the tools we are using do not employ this feature and simply exchange generic Reals or Integers. Therefore, we have found that FMI-based CPS development is particularly vulnerable to these kinds of undocumented assertions. This is aggravated by the fact that CPS teams are highly heterogeneous and the "default" units and values may not be the same for all disciplines which leads to a higher likelihood of incompatible undocumented assumptions on multiple sides.

**Recommendation 2:** To combat undocumented assumptions slipping through the FMI tool chain, all restrictions, units and other kinds of assumptions must be properly documented. Ideally, this should be done in the main design document or SysML model. If this is not possible, an independent document containing the assumption should be created. This document must be shared and accessible by all partners. From a tooling perspective, such assumptions should be encoded in the constituent models and the FMI interface. Ideally, these assumptions would be statically checked before generating FMUs. In addition, when such assumptions are violated, warnings should be issued in a co-simulation so that unexpected results may more easily be diagnosed. An example of mismatched assumptions occurred in our project due to temperature unit mismatches. We were building a heating scenario, but the temperature was dropping away from the set point throughout the simulation. This was because the plant model was outputting temperatures in Kelvin and the FCU controller model was considering set points in Celsius – in this case $281.85\,K/18.7\,C$. Therefore, the temperature continuously lowers as the FCU is working towards a much lower set point than it should be.

### 4.3   FMU Coordination

In FMI-based CPS design projects of significant size, the project will be carried out by a heterogeneous team whose members have expertise in different fields. As such, it is unlikely that there will be any single team member that has detailed knowledge or understanding of every constituent model and its associated notation and tools. Indeed, this is one of the purposes of FMI – to provide an abstraction layer for interacting with other models. Therefore, for many team members, other constituent models will be treated as blackboxes and interactions with the model will be done exclusively using its generated FMUs. However, when doing CPS development, individual constituent models will have to change quite frequently. These changes may affect other models and even the system level connections. Nevertheless, the changes may be "hidden" inside the FMU blackbox. Thus, it is not easy for the developer of one constituent model to understand what has changed in a given FMU and if he should "upgrade" to the new version of the FMU or not.

Thus, it is important that the FMUs used in a project be properly documented and versioned in order to avoid coordination issues. We have experienced many variations of the following question: "Which version of the FMU am I supposed to use?" This issue can be further complicated if FMUs are copied locally, and each project member has their own workspace. On the other hand, a shared workspace is very vulnerable to changes in one FMU introducing errors in the co-simulation due to unexpected or poorly understood changes.

**Recommendation 3:** To combat coordination and synchronisation issues with FMU files, a project should have a central archive of FMUs. FMUs in this archive should be properly documented and versioned. Members can download and submit FMUs to this archive. For complex project teams, a service of some sort may be deployed. For smaller projects, it can be something as simple as a local version control repository. For our case study, FMUs were initially stored in a structured shared folder with README.txt files providing relevant information. Having a common shared folder was helpful in synchronization, but version control on the FMU was missed.

### 4.4  Constituent Model Validation

When using FMI-based CPS design and development, the complete behaviour of the system will only emerge at the co-simulation level. This also holds for some constituent models that are so dependent on their inputs and outputs that their standalone behaviour is either meaningless or cannot be simulated. This makes it quite challenging to ensure that the constituent model is being developed correctly and evolving without regressions. If one needs to perform FMI co-simulations to validate every change to the model, two issues arise. First, it will significantly increase the validation loop since it will involve generation of an FMU and execution of a co-simulation. Second, and perhaps worse, the constituent model becomes dependent on other models in order to evolve. This removes the ability to effectively develop multiple constituents models in parallel which is one of the significant advantages of FMI.

**Recommendation 4:** There must be a validation strategy in place for each constituent model in the CPS design. This strategy needs to enable standalone and independent validation of each constituent model in the context of its tool. This validation strategy should also be such that it is easily reproducible by any other project member to assist in diagnosing co-simulation for FMU issues. It is difficult to provide generic recommendations for validation strategies since the strategy will depend on the features and capabilities of each modelling tool. However, in our experience, we have found that most validation strategies employ test doubles such as Mocks or Stubs to represent the parts of the system that are being modeled in other constituent models. As an example of validation strategy, we show an excerpt of VDM-RT test classes in Listing 1.1, where the environment behaviour which is provided by the plant FCU is replaced by a simplistic MockEnv class. While this environment is too simple to properly evaluate controller performance, it does enable executing basic unit tests to provide initial validation and error detection for the VDM model.

```
class MockEnv
instance variables
--FCU1
fanSpeed1 : RealPort :=new RealPort(0.0);
tempLvl1 : RealPort :=new RealPort(0.0);
valveOpening1 : RealPort :=new RealPort(0.0);
operations
reactFcu1: real ==> ()
reactFcu1 (c) == (
if c > 0 then
tempLvl1.setValue(tempLvl1.getValue()+1)
elseif c < 0
then tempLvl1.setValue(tempLvl1.getValue()-1);
);
-- ...
end MockEnv
```

**Listing 1.1:** Exceprt from mock environment class.

## 4.5  FMU Integration

In an FMI-driven workflow, integration of models is an integral part of the project. Indeed, it is one of the main objectives of a project. This is desirable, as we want to catch problems in the interactions between the modelled systems as soon as possible. However, integration brings its own set of challenges that must be addressed. Many of them are minor technical issues (such as an incorrectly working exporter), others are larger and related to one of the challenges highlighted in this article.

All integration issues can be handled, but it takes time and effort, and if not addressed in an efficient and timely manner, they will add up over time and compromise the project. It is worth highlighting that certain domain experts come from disciplines where integration is not a significant concern so that they may be particularly vulnerable to integration pitfalls.

**Recommendation 5:** Consider model FMUs integration from the beginning of a project. Attempt to integrate models as early as possible, even if they are not fully working and results are not yet correct. On the other hand, even if the underlying models are working correctly, plan for significant troubleshooting activities while integrating FMUs. Ideally, use an automation server to automatically generate FMUs and co-simulate them whenever changes are checked in to models. If this is not possible, a good fall back is to check in modified FMUs and automate the co-simulation only. Manual execution is also possible, but requires significant discipline. In our case study, the INTO-CPS workflow helped ensure alignment of FMI signals from the beginning, so integration was a matter of continuously communicating and updating signals and ports across the team, using a simple iterative process illustrated in Fig. 4. On the other hand, we sometimes faced issues with models that would not export correctly (due to usage of unsupported language constructs).

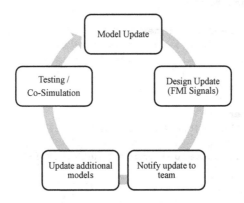

**Fig. 4.** FMI update and integration process.

## 4.6    Model FMI Maturity

It can sometimes occur that we are working on models that are poorly suited to be exported as FMUs. This can happen because important parameters or signals are not exported, or model variable names are incomprehensible or one of the other challenges highlighted in this paper. Exporting variables can be particularly challenging since certain signals or parameters may be located quite "deep" in the model and require significant effort to expose via FMI. Having a well-defined architecture, as suggested in Sect. 4.1 can help mitigate this, but in highly iterative settings (where the architecture changes) or when working with legacy models, this challenge cannot sometimes be avoided. We have found that domain experts from certain disciplines are not used to these concerns and are particularly liable to be affected or cause this issue.

**Recommendation 6:** Develop a notion for model maturity/quality for FMI export. It should account for aspects such as naming conventions, signal and parameter accessibility, absence of "magic" constants, and so forth. Ideally, the notion of maturity should be formalised and mechanised so that it can be statically checked by tools. If that is not possible, a check-list can provide a reasonable alternative, but it can become tedious to go through it very frequently in highly iterative processes. For our case study, we used the Jenkins[7] automation server to run jobs that tested the VDM-RT model and generated the associated FMU. The trend showing build results and durations for this job is shown in Fig. 5.

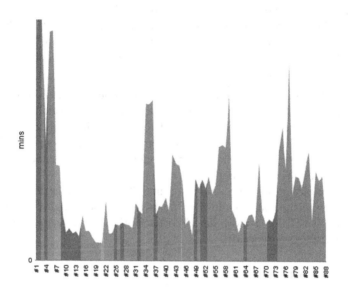

**Fig. 5.** Jenkins build results for VDM FMU job.

### 4.7 Naming Conventions

The FMI supports annotation of model variables through the definition of units, types[8] and textual descriptions. However, we have found limited support for these features across tools. Therefore, we often found ourselves having to connect variables using only their names and base types. In this case, the name of the variable becomes an important source of information. However, variable names were often inconsistent and following conventions from different disciplines which were not always known to the whole project team.

**Recommendation 7:** Have a standard set of rules and conventions for naming FMI variables, across the organization and specialized for projects as necessary. These conventions must be communicated and acknowledged by the entire team. The naming convention should strike a balance between providing useful information and being clean and concise. The central design document is a natural place to document naming conventions.

---

[7] https://jenkins.io/.
[8] Type definitions can only specialize existing types.

As an example, one of the naming conventions for the building case study are that all signals have the same name on both ports (except for the FCUs) and that Signal names should be: `[AreaName]_[ValueExchanged](_Unit)`.

## 4.8   Modelling Communication

Communication modelling across multiple FMUs is in general challenging, due to the nature of the FMI protocol and its general unsuitability for modelling (DE)-intensive phenomena and high-level abstractions such as messages or API calls. While there are various approaches to handle it, each has their drawbacks. Approaches that extend the standard can be an effective way to address the issue, but broad tool support would be key. They should become part of the standard.

**Recommendation 8:** If communication is a significant part of the project, a pure FMI solution may not be well-suited. Consider other modelling options, or a coordination environment with native network modelling capabilities. If this is not possible and it is necessary to model communication through the FMI, we recommend developing a strategy before diving into the models and investigating the various trade-offs beforehand.

As an example, in our case study, we modelled communications across FMI using a set of multiple inter-connected ports to represent highly abstract communication – see [4] for a more detailed description of this aspect of the communications aspects case study.

## 4.9   FMI Exporting

The FMU export feature is in general robust, but the exporting of models as FMUs can be a challenge under certain conditions. Firstly, we are naturally bound by the availability and coverage of the export tools. While coverage is broad, we occasionally had to work around a missing exporter or feature coverage.

Certain tools (such as Dymola or Simulink) posses the ability to link models with native code (sometimes in the form of a DLL). Exporting these kinds of models into working FMUs can be a large challenge, due to lack of clarity in documentation and poor co-simulation error messages (often core dumps). These issues can be dealt with, but they are a large source of frustration and often outside the typical skillset of many disciplines involved in the projects.

Another potential issue is handling 32 and 64-bit FMUs, but this can be handled by a good coordination environment. There is also a wide variety of exporter options (such as solver selection) that can impact co-simulation results, so it is important to be aware of them and have someone on the team with knowledge of these options. As an example, see the FMI export options for Dymola in Fig. 6.

**Recommendation 9:** Be aware that FMU exports may not work out of the box. Check exporter availability and coverage of the project models. Be particularly wary of legacy models, or models that use native code.

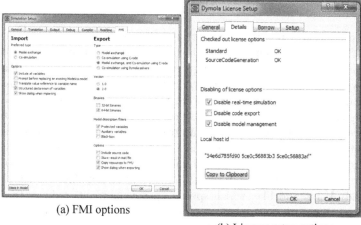

(a) FMI options

(b) License setup options

**Fig. 6.** Dymola options menus.

## 4.10    Co-simulation Project Versioning

In co-simulation projects, there are many kinds of sources and generated arte-facts such as models, simulation, and co-simulation results, FMUs, and configu-ration files. Tracking and synchronising versions of all these artefacts can be a big challenge, particularly since sets of versions are interconnected around work-ing co-simulations. It is often necessary to quickly return to a prior version of a model in order to modify or correct it for the purposes of a co-simulation. An FMU repository (suggested in Sect. 4.3) can help mitigate some of these prob-lems, but version control across the project sources is essential. However, the heterogeneous nature of the team means that different members have different practices and habits when it comes to version control, so it is not guaranteed that the team will adopt consistent version control practices without explicit guidance.

**Recommendation 10:** All models and relevant source files should be tracked using a version control system. To ensure smooth coordination, a single repos-itory housing all models and sources in a structured layout is preferable. This means the chosen version control system should feature excellent branching and collaboration features.

In our project, we struggled to stabilize version control across the project due to existing repositories for some models and differing practices across the team. Towards the end project, we started to adopt Git [3].

## 5    Conclusion

We have presented a report on industrial experiences with FMI co-simulation drawn from the development of a building HVAC system. These experiences have been synthesized as a series of challenges and associated recommendations when working with co-simulation. Overall, we have found co-simulation helps significantly with CPS development. One of the main challenges in CPS development is ensuring early integration of systems and through co-simulation it is to carry out integration form the beginning of a project and use MBD techniques. Being able to integrate a wide amount of tools is also very valuable, particularly for organizations such as ours that have significant existing IP in certain notations. The broad tool support also allows all the different stakeholders to use the tools they already know and like, which speeds up development, reduces the barrier to entry and allows more people to contribute effectively to a CPS development.

On the other hand, the handling of DE phenomena such as communication is limited. While it is possible to work around these limitations, it introduces challenges. For projects where DE analysis such as communication is key, FMI should be complemented with extensions or additional tools as part of a larger tool kit. Several possibilities exist [11], but we must be careful not to rely on extensions that lockout significant tools.

Finally, it is worth noting that while FMI co-simulation helps bring integration activities to the forefront, integration brings its own set of challenges of a project. Some of these challenges are compounded by the multi-disciplinary nature of CPS teams. However, there are several approaches to handle this, such as continuous integration [9], that can be adopted to CPS development.

**Acknowledgments.** This work is supported by the INTO-CPS H2020 project: *Integrated Tool Chain for Model-based Design of Cyber-Physical Systems*. Funded by the European Commission-H2020, Project Number:664047.

## References

1. Bertsch, C., Ahle, E., Schulmeister, U.: The functional mockup interface-seen from an industrial perspective. In: Proceedings of the 10th International Modelica Conference, 10–12 March 2014, Lund, Sweden, pp. 27–33, No. 096 (2014)
2. Blochwitz, T.: Functional mock-up interface for model exchange and co-simulation, July 2014. https://www.fmi-standard.org/downloads
3. Chacon, S., Straub, B.: Pro git. Apress (2014)
4. Couto, L.D., Pierce, K.: Modelling network connections in FMI with an explicit network model. In: The 15th Overture Workshop, September 2017
5. Derler, P., Lee, E.A., Sangiovanni-Vincentelli, A.: Modeling cyber-physical systems. Proc. IEEE **100**(1), 13–28 (2012). (special issue on CPS)
6. Feo-Arenis, S., Verhoef, M., Larsen, P.G.: The mars-rover case study modelled using INTO-CPS. In: The 15th Overture Workshop, September 2017
7. Fitzgerald, J., Gamble, C., Payne, R., Larsen, P.G., Basagiannis, S., Mady, A.E.D.: Collaborative model-based systems engineering for cyber-physical systems - a case study in building automation. In: INCOSE 2016, July 2016

8. Fitzgerald, J., Gamble, C., Payne, R., Pierce, K.: Methods Progress Report 3. Technical report, INTO-CPS Public Deliverable, D3.3b, December 2017

9. Fowler, M., Foemmel, M.: Continuous Integration. Thought-Works, vol. 122 (2006). http://www.thoughtworks.com/ContinuousIntegration.pdf

10. Gamble, C.: DSE in the INTO-CPS Platform. Technical report, INTO-CPS Deliverable, D5.3e, December 2017

11. Gomes, C., Thule, C., Broman, D., Larsen, P.G., Vangheluwe, H.: Co-simulation: a survey. ACM Comput. Surv. **51**(3), 49:1–49:33 (2018)

12. Larsen, P.G., et al.: Integrated tool chain for model-based design of cyber-physical systems: the INTO-CPS project. In: CPS Data Workshop, April 2016

13. Ouy, J., et al.: Case Studies 3, Public Version. Technical report, INTO-CPS Public Deliverable, D1.3a, December 2017

14. Törngren, M., et al.: CPS: State of the Art. Project Deliverable D5.1, EU Framework 7 Project: Cyber-Physical European Roadmap & Strategy (CyPhERS), March 2014

15. Wetter, M., van Treeck, C.: IEA EBC Annex 60: New Generation Computing Tools for Building and Community Energy Systems, September 2017

# Co-simulation: The Past, Future, and Open Challenges

Cláudio Gomes[1,4(✉)], Casper Thule[2], Julien Deantoni[5,6], Peter Gorm Larsen[2], and Hans Vangheluwe[1,3,4]

[1] University of Antwerp, Antwerp, Belgium
{claudio.gomes,hans.vangheluwe}@uantwerp.be
[2] Aarhus University, Aarhus, Denmark
{casper.thule,pgl}@eng.au.dk
[3] McGill University, Montreal, Canada
[4] Flanders Make, Lommel, Belgium
[5] University Cote d'Azur, I3S, Sophia Antipolis, France
julien.deantoni@polytech.unice.fr
[6] INRIA Kairos, Sophia Antipolis, France

**Abstract.** In the engineering of heterogeneous systems, there have always been challenges related to ensuring a common understanding of the interfaces between the constituent systems.

In these systems, the systematic analysis of the relevant artefacts is governed by different kinds of models based on different kinds of formalisms (e.g., state machine models for software-based controllers, and differential equations for physical sub-systems). In such a hybrid setting, it makes sense to examine how to combine different kinds of models in ways that enable a well-founded analysis of the interaction between these.

Co-simulation has been proposed as a way forward by different stakeholders in different disciplines. It is a technique to couple multiple simulation tools, so that the interactions with, and within, a coupled system can be simulated through the cooperation of these tools.

In this paper, we: provide an historical overview of the different facets of co-simulation; describe examples of industrial applications; identify the emerging trend and the challenges (both theoretical and practical) for the future use of this technology.

**Keywords:** Co-simulation · Complexity · System engineering

---

This work was executed under the framework of the COST Action IC1404 – Multi-Paradigm Modelling for Cyber-Physical Systems (MPM4CPS), and partially supported by: Flanders Make vzw, the strategic research centre for the manufacturing industry; the INTO-CPS project funded by the European Commission's Horizon 2020 programme under grant agreement number 664047; and PhD fellowship grants from the Agency for Innovation by Science and Technology in Flanders (IWT, dossier 151067).

T. Margaria and B. Steffen (Eds.): ISoLA 2018, LNCS 11246, pp. 504–520, 2018.
https://doi.org/10.1007/978-3-030-03424-5_34

# 1   Introduction

Integration—the interconnection of the components that comprise a system—
is identified as a major source of problems in the concurrent development of
complex engineered systems [62]. This is because each component is developed
with assumptions and/or incomplete knowledge about other components of the
system, which later turn out to be wrong [63].

To tackle these challenges, there is a need for improved development cycles,
with better tools, techniques, and methodologies [65]. While modeling and simulation has been successfully applied to reduce development costs, it falls short
in fostering more integrated development processes [7]. To see why, note that
a model of the complete system is required for simulation, and consider the
following obstacles:

- Accurately simulating a complete system model might be difficult. For example, the transient simulation of digital circuits is difficult because there are
  sub-circuits whose dynamics change significantly faster than others [49], forc-
  ing the simulation to be run at a prohibitively high level of detail.
- Heterogeneous systems are best modelled with a mix of formalisms [66] or
  example, consider a power window system [56], present in the majority of the
  vehicles produced today. It includes both software elements (best modelled
  with a Statechart like formalism), and physical elements (best modelled with
  differential equations based formalism).
- Subsystem models might be costly. In systems that encompass subsystems
  produced by external suppliers, the licensing costs required to get access to
  models might be too high, due to the Intellectual Property. For example,
  consider the exhaust gas recirculation water handling system, reported in
  [55], where the dirty water is pumped to a water treatment center (externally
  developed) to be purified and reused. As claimed by the authors, having
  higher fidelity models of each of the subsystems would allow the engineers to
  design better control strategies.
- Models of subsystems might be black boxes. At later stages in the development process, prototypes for subsystems may be coupled to models of the
  remaining subsystems, to enable global validation of the system. For example,
  the validation of the power window controller might be done by simulating
  the controller in a computer, and connecting it to a real motorized window
  [18], which is considered a black box from the point of view of the controller.
  Other black boxes include inductive models of subsystems, produced from
  extensive physical experimentation. For example, an anti-lock braking system controller might be validated against black box wear and tear models of
  the braking pads, to evaluate its performance when the effectiveness of these
  subsystems decreases [21].

A prospective concept to address the above challenges, and unleash the full
potential of simulation, is collaborative simulation, also known as co-simulation
[40]. This concept concerns coupling of models created in different formalisms
and makes it possible to simulate the entire system by simulating its constituents

and exchanging data between them. Thus, the behavior of a coupled system is computed by the communication of multiple simulation tools, each responsible for computing the behavior of a constituent subsystem [30,44,51]. Each simulator is broadly defined as a *black box* capable of exhibiting behaviour, consuming inputs and producing outputs. Examples of simulators include dynamical systems being integrated by numerical solvers [12], software and its execution platform [16], dedicated real-time hardware simulators (e.g., [34]), physical test stands (e.g., [69, Fig. 3]), or human operators (e.g., [13, Fig. 24], [53, Fig. 6]).

Co-simulation foments a more integrated development process by allowing different teams to observe how their subsystem behaves when coupled to the rest of the system (full system analysis), while reusing the work made by the other teams. Furthermore, it improves the relationship between external suppliers and system integrators, where the system integrators can use virtual surrogates of the subsystems produced by the suppliers, to test their adequacy. With the appropriate Intellectual Property protections, these virtual surrogates can even be provided by the supplier, for increased validity.

In order to run a co-simulation, all that is required is that the participating simulation tools expose the outputs and consume the inputs, of the allocated subsystem over simulated time. The same loose requirements that make co-simulation great to integrate many different simulation tools, also raise difficult challenges.

In the following sections, we explore those challenges by first providing an historical overview of co-simulation, then examples of industrial case studies, and finally the emerging trend.

## 2     The Facets of Co-simulation: Historical Overview

Co-simulation is not a new concept. Instead, it is the aggregation of multiple research trends that were sparked by the advances in computer simulation techniques, and the increased demands on this field. In the following paragraphs, we summarize some of the main milestones that lead to the facets of co-simulation. Figure 1 situates these in time.

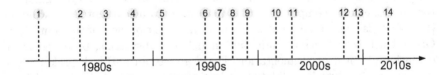

**Fig. 1.** Timeline of co-simulation milestones. From 1970s up to 2015.

## 2.1 Late 70s and 80s

(1) To the best of our knowledge, the first discrete event synchronization algorithms were published in the late seventies [39], around the same time that Lamport [42] published his seminal paper regarding the ordering of events in distributed process networks. Discrete event simulators compute the behavior of a system by isolating the most important events and computing the state evolution of the system from one event to the next [23]. The state evolution evolves discontinuously, with each discontinuity being caused by an event. In this paradigm, a coupled system can be broken down into subsystems that exchange events, which then are simulated in parallel, each in a separate process. Since processes run in parallel, and react to incoming events by updating their state, and potentially sending events, it is important to ensure the correct *synchronization* of the subsystems, so that no event happening at time $t_i$ is processed by a subsystem which is at time $t > t_i$.

Around the same time, in the continuous simulation domain, new challenges were being uncovered. The main difference between the continuous and discrete event simulation domain lies in the fact that the state of a continuous system evolves continuously over time. Simulators of continuous systems that run in digital computers cannot compute every point of its state. Instead, they rely in the smoothness of these systems (coming from physical laws), to approximate the state evolution at countable points in time [12]. The fundamental tradeoff is: the closer one wants the time points to be, the more accurate the approximation is, but the higher the performance cost.

(2) In the late seventies and early eighties, as electrical circuits increased in size, their simulation algorithms were becoming a bottleneck in the development process because of the long simulation times. Practitioners noticed that, for sufficiently large circuits, only a small fraction of the subsystems had actively changing voltage levels, at any point in time. This led to the development of simulation techniques that, in a similar way to their discrete event based counterparts, only computed a new state of each subsystem when its outputs had changed significantly [49]. Additionally, to exploit parallelism and reduce numerical instabilities, the waveform relaxation techniques were introduced. In these, during a computation interval $t \rightarrow t + H$, each subsystem was assigned to a simulator which approximated its solution in that interval, using whatever simulation step size was required to keep the approximation error of that subsystem within tolerance. Then the simulators exchanged the solution trajectories, and were asked to re-compute the same interval, using the updated input trajectories.

These techniques made possible the simulation of large scale circuits because they exploited parallel computers, and naturally supported subsystems with different dynamics: systems which changed slowly where more quickly driven to convergence, and with larger simulation step sizes. Additionally, these techniques were subject to extensive numerical analysis [47], highlighting their interesting theoretical properties.

③ In the late eighties, the release of the Time Warp Operating System represented the optimistic facet in parallel discrete event simulation. It acknowledged that the performance of a parallel discrete event simulation could be increased by allowing the different processes to simulate as fast as they could, and correcting causality violations. The corrections are made by rolling back the processes to a state that is consistent with the time of the event that caused the violation.

④ The performance of optimistic discrete event synchronization algorithms was such that it sparked the research into large scale simulations with humans interacting in realistic environments created by collaborating simulators. Developed during the 80s, SIMNET was dedicated to military trainings involving thousands of simulators representing, for instances tanks or helicopters [48]. It encompasses an architecture and protocol to implement the optimistic synchronization of simulators in a distributed environment, with real-time constraints. In order to keep a reasonable level of accuracy and realism, one of the innovations is the concept of dead-reckoning models. A dead-reckoning model is a computationally lightweight version of some other model, whose purpose is to be used by interested simulators when there is a failure of communication, or when the synchronization times are far apart.

## 2.2    90s

⑤ In the early nineties, coordination languages emerged (*e.g.*, Linda [6], Manifold [4]). These focused on the specification of the interaction between different parts of the system. According to [25], *"Coordination is the process of building programs by gluing together active pieces"*. A system designer defines one or more coordination model(s) to specify how the system models interact with each other.

During the same period, the *software architecture* research field proposed languages to abstract, structure, and reason about complex systems. One example is the Architecture Description Languages (ADL) [24]. An ADL description usually specifies a system in terms of components and interactions among those components. Such languages helped (1) to clarify structural and semantics difference between components and interactions, (2) to reuse and compose architectural elements, (3) to identify/enforce commonly used patterns (*e.g.*, architectural styles).

Coordination languages and ADLs have common objectives [52]. They build/understand/analyse a system based on "components" possibly written in different languages and connectors (which include the specification of the interaction/coordination).

In 1990, United Airlines ordered 34 Boeing 777s, the first aircraft to be developed with concurrent engineering [37,38]. The design was communicated fully in digital form, later aptly named a DMU (Digital Mockup Unit [3]), using CAD tools to showcase the different views of the system. This central repository of information served many purposes: (i) every team could consult the specifications of the subsystems made by any other team; (ii) simulations could be carried out periodically, to detect problems in the design; (iii) both the assembly and maintenance phases of the system could affect the design phase, by running simulations of repairs and assembly.

This milestone represented an increase in the information that is taken into account for the design of the product. It now did not come only from requirements, but also from other stages of the life-cycle of the system: manufacturing, assembly and maintenance. The milestone also highlights the many different purposes for which models of systems have to be available, and new kinds of simulations.

(6) As digital circuits became more complex, they comprised microprocessors running software. This field spawned the need for hardware/software co-simulation [57], highlighting the heterogeneity facet. Before using co-simulation, software developers had to develope their code with little information about the underlying hardware, leading to painful integration efforts later on. Thanks to the coupling of circuit emulators and the software execution, they were able to quickly identify miscommunication errors before building hardware prototypes.

In the field of physical system simulation, researchers realized that there should be a standardized way of representing physical system models, so that there could be easily coupled to form complex systems [50]. This was called the DSBlock (Dynamical System Block) standard [50]. This proposal later inspired a widely adopted standard for co-simulation: the Functional Mockup Interface standard. (7) While the composition of DSBlocks still needed a solver, and is therefore not strictly considered co-simulation, this was a milestone in highlighting the need for standardization for continuous system co-simulation, which was also identified as a research priority [67]. (8) SIMNET evolved into the DIS (Distributed Interactive Simulation) standard [35], for discrete event based co-simulations.

As embedded systems were enhanced with communication capabilities, researchers noticed that the simulation of these distributed systems should not always be run at the same level of detail. Instead, the designers should be able to choose the level of detail they wanted for each embedded system: from the highest level of detail (circuit simulation), to the lowest (software simulation). This highlights the facet of multi-abstraction co-simulation, and identified the main issues in coupling simulators that were in different levels of abstraction.

## 2.3  2000s

⑨ The early 2000s was marked by multiple reported applications of co-simulation being used in industrial case studies [5,43]. These had in common one facet: two simulators were coupled, each specialized in one domain, in a feedback loop. ⑩ For example, in [5] the authors reports on the study of the interaction between the pantograph (a mechanical structure on top of a train, connecting it to the electric grid), and a catenary (over hanging cable that transmits electricity to the train). A flexible body simulator was used to compute the behavior of the catenary, and a multi-body simulator was used for the pantograph. ⑫ In the meantime, the DIS standard, and its protocols, were generalized to non-real time applications, in what became the HLA (High Level Architecture) standard [1].

⑪ In order to ensure the correctness of coordinated heterogeneous model simulations, the Ptolemy and the Modhel'x projects proposed to expose some information about the behavioral semantics of languages (named Model of Computation) [9,20]. Then, they defined adaptations so that they could be co-simulated.

⑬ In 2008, the MODELISAR project published the FMI (Functional Mockup Interface) standard [7], whose essential contribution to co-simulation was the concept of Intellectual Property protection. It was an evolution of the DSBlock proposal, but recognizing that each subsystem might need its own simulator. This standard is widely adopted in industry[1] [58], where the simulation of externally supplied components can be costly due to high licensing costs.

Although there was some research about the coordination of black-box physical system simulators before the FMI Standard was published (*e.g.*, [5,31,41], and other references in [29]), it does not standardize the synchronization protocol between simulators. The main reason is that, as in continuous system simulation, there is no one-fits-all simulation algorithm. This is in contrast to discrete event simulation, where the implementations of the DIS and HLA standards provide everything to run the co-simulation.

## 2.4  2010s

The current decade is marked by several applications of co-simulation across many domains (see, *e.g.*, [29,59]), the Digital Twin [26] concept, and an effort to systematically study co-simulation, with the publication of surveys [30,32].

⑭ The Digital Twin extends the DMU concept not just to the design and assembly phases of the system, but also to the maintenance. The essential idea is to use high fidelity models of the system, calibrated from sensory information collected during its operation, to affect how the system should operate, predict failures, schedule maintenance, etc.

---

[1] http://fmi-standard.org/.

# 3   Applications

## 3.1   Exhaust Gas Recirculation (MAN Diesel and Turbo)

MAN Diesel & Turbo (MDT) is one of the largest producers of two-stroke com-
bustion engines with distributed embedded control system. Due to new emis-
sions legislation on $NO_x$, the systems that reduce the emission of this gas need
to be improved. Since the development is split between different departments,
using different tools, with limited sharing of models, co-simulation was applied
to maximize reuse of models [55].

The work in [55] describes an exhaust gas recirculation system, and a water
handling system. The purpose is to clean and recirculate exhaust gas to a ship
engine intake manifold. The exhaust gas is cleaned by spraying water into it,
and allowing the mixture to cool down and flow into a receiving tank. Then, the
(dirty) water is pumped to a water treatment center (externally developed) to
be purified and reused.

The initial approach consisted of developing the control system in an in-
house application framework, that simulated both the control system and the
physical models of the ship engine. While the traditional setup allows for simulation, the physical models are often implemented at a lower level of detail than
e.g. Matlab/Simulink® models. The co-simulation approach, based on the FMI
standard, coupled the in-house application to MATLAB, so that higher fidelity
physical models could be used. They believe that, had this approach been used
from the start, then a water tank overflow problem could have been discovered
before running the software on an expensive engine test bench.

## 3.2   Driverless Lawn Mower (Agro Intelligence)

Another application of co-simulation is the development of a steering controller of
an industrial size driverless lawn mower [22]. Besides aiding in the development of
the control and navigation system of the lawn mover, co-simulation was applied
to investigate alternative designs that would otherwise be both costly and time-
consuming to test with physical prototypes.

The co-simulation scenario consisted of three parts: a simulator representing
the vehicle dynamics, a simulator representing the control algorithm and a simulator to convert values between the two. Additionally, each alternative design
was projected in a 3D animation based on the game engine Unity, that it could
be visually inspected by designers and clients.

To make sure the co-simulation results were valid and accurate, an initial prototype was conceived and tested. Afterwards, multiple designs were evaluated with co-simulation, to find the optimal look-ahead distance and velocity. The simulation results for multiple look-ahead distances, and fixed velocity, are shown in Fig. 2.

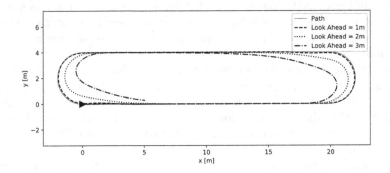

**Fig. 2.** Simulated trajectories for look-ahead distance with velocity 1 m/s [54]

## 4    Emerging Trend and Challenges

### 4.1    Towards Full Virtualization

Throughout the history of co-simulation, a common trend emerges: a gradual shift towards the virtualization of not just the design of the system, but also assembly, operation, and maintenance.

The virtualization of the design of the system has been one of the primary uses of co-simulation, backup by concurrent engineering processes.

The virtualization of the assembly reflects an increased demand in the information that should be taken into account at the design phase, with concepts like the Digital Mockup Unit.

Complex systems that need interaction with human operators require training interfaces. Marked by military training simulators, the virtualization of operation refers to the creation of complex training environments at almost no cost by leveraging the same co-simulation scenarios used in the design phase. As an example towards this future, we highlight the design of a motion compensated crane [14], by ControlLab, where the crane operators are trained using a virtual reality environment (see Fig. 3).

**Fig. 3.** 3D real-time simulation of a motion compensated crane. Taken from [14].

Finally, extending the lifespan of systems, and reducing their downtime through the virtualization of their maintenance, is becoming a priority. This means that co-simulation can be combined with advanced sensors to create smart monitors (Digital Twins) that predict failures.

## 4.2   Challenges

The historical overview, and main trend identified, can be used to highlight some of the challenges that researchers and industry will need to overcome in the upcoming years.

We divide these challenges into four categories: Design Space Exploration (DSE), X-in-the-Loop Co-simulation, Incremental Testing/Certification (IT/C), and Education.

**Design Space Exploration** consists of the systematic analysis and evaluation of different designs over a parameter space. When the evaluation involves running a co-simulation, then ensuring that co-simulations can be run quickly, accurately, and respecting the physical constraints of the system.

Since the results of these simulations are typically not inspected by experts, it is crucial that these can be trusted. To this end, we highlight the need to ensure that each configuration of the system is valid, and the need for the co-simulation to preserve any properties that the configuration of the system satisfies.

Validity refers to whether the composition of subsystem models (induced by the co-simulation scenario) reflects a physically meaningful coupled system [17,70]. This property is important because physical system models have many implicit assumptions, and their combination may violate those assumptions, purging their predictive value. For example, in [60] the authors ran a questionnaire through several experts in various domains of physics, asking them to identify the implicit assumptions in a simple model of a particle moving in a viscous medium. No expert was able to identify all the 29 assumptions, identified by their combined expertise.

The evolution of many engineered systems can be summarized by their evolution from one equilibrium to another [19], and it is important that their corresponding co-simulations reflect this property. While analyses have been developed that enable the automated verification of this property for continuous co-simulations (see [30, Sect. 4.3] and references thereof), there are many open challenges with the co-simulation of hybrid systems [27], and adaptive co-simulations [28].

**X-in-The-Loop** refers to co-simulations that are restricted in time and computing resources, due to the presence of human operators, animation requirements, or physical subsystems. In this context, there is a need for simulators which can provide contracts with timing guarantees on their computation time, based on the inputs and parameterization.

**IT/C** consists of the co-simulation activities that are applied as part of concurrent engineering activities, where the models of each subsystem are refined over time and integrated frequently. We highlight the need for co-simulations that provide formal guarantees on the accuracy of the behavior that is computed. Since the definition of correct co-simulation is elusive and depends on the domain of application, each simulator should provide some form of contract. It should be possible to obtain an abstraction of each simulation units that is appropriate to the kind of contracts defined. Existing research could be used as a starting point [8,11,36,46].

Once each simulator provides formal guarantees, then the orchestration algorithm should ensure that the composition of those contracts, and other formal properties, can be satisfied. As highlighted by works on heterogeneous simulations and more recently in [45], the way to orchestrate the different simulators can lead to incorrect results. This is especially true when discrete models (with frequent and natural discontinuities) are in the loop since a minor change in timings can result in different behavior (let consider for instance a double click versus two consecutive clicks).

To illustrate, consider a simulator that guarantees that there are no more than one discontinuity every 10 s. Then, depending on similar contracts satisfied by other simulators, a similar kind of contract could be satisfied by the co-simulation.

**Education** refers to those challenges that are of non-technical nature, but are nonetheless crucial to attain the full virtualization vision.

In order for companies to adopt co-simulation there are several concerns that hinder the theoretical possibilities from being employed in practical setting. One of these is the protection of intellectual property, which limits the information that is available for a given simulation unit. It is not an issue in itself, but it is an issue when considering other desirable properties of co-simulation, e.g. performance. For example, [61] describes two master algorithms, one that allows parallel computation but is limited in its applicability, and another that is less limited in applicability but requires a sequential execution. However, the information required to choose the optimal master algorithm in this case is not available. Similarly, [64] concerns precompiling a master algorithm optimised for a given scenario, but this also requires information, that is not available in a black box implementation.

Another challenge is related to the current co-simulation standards. This is described in [10], which puts forth several requirements for hybrid co-simulation, such as superdense time, and relates them to the FMI standard. In general, time representation is a very important aspect of co-simulation, and [15] presents several extensions to FMI. One of these is that in theory several theorems uses real numbers, which has infinite precision. However, these are often represented as numbers with finite precision.

Finally, proper integration with existing development processes. Co-simulations are initiated by different users with different backgrounds. This is not just about pushing a button and getting results: there is a need to integrate robust co-simulation frameworks into existing tools, such that each different kind of user can use the most comfortable tool as a front end to run the co-simulations, and that user understand what he is doing. To this end, education and technology transfer are crucial steps.

## 5  Conclusion

Co-Simulation holds the promise to unleash the full potential of simulation. However, it is not a new concept. In this paper we present the historical events that resulted in what is today known as co-simulation. These highlight a trend towards the virtualization of every interaction with complex systems. Based on this trend, we identify several exciting challenges that lie ahead.

## References

1. IEEE. IEEE Standard for Modeling and Simulation (M&S) High Level Architecture (HLA) - Federate Interface Specification. IEEE Standard 1516-2010 (2010). https://standards.ieee.org/findstds/standard/1516-2010.html
2. Åström, K.J., Elmqvist, H., Mattsson, S.E.: Evolution of continuous-time modeling and simulation. In: ESM, pp. 9–18 (1998)

3. Andert Jr., E.P., Morgan, D.: Collaborative virtual prototyping and test. Naval Eng. J. **110**(6), 17–23 (1998). http://www.ingentaconnect.com/content/asne/nej/1998/00000110/00000006/art00007

4. Arbab, F., Herman, I., Spilling, P.: An overview of manifold and its implementation. Concurrency Pract. Exper. **5**(1), 23–70 (1993). https://doi.org/10.1002/cpe.4330050103

5. Arnold, M., Günther, M.: Preconditioned dynamic iteration for coupled differential-algebraic systems. BIT Numer. Math. **41**(1), 1–25 (2001)

6. Bjornson, R., Carriero, N., Gelernter, D., Mattson, T., Kaminsky, D., Sherman, A.: Experience with linda. Yale University Computer Science Department, Technical report RR-866 (1991)

7. Blochwitz, T., et al.: The functional mockup interface for tool independent exchange of simulation models. In: 8th International Modelica Conference, pp. 105–114. Linköping University Electronic Press, Linköpings universitet, Dresden, Germany, June 2011

8. Bouissou, O., Chapoutot, A., Djoudi, A.: Enclosing temporal evolution of dynamical systems using numerical methods. In: Brat, G., Rungta, N., Venet, A. (eds.) NFM 2013. LNCS, vol. 7871, pp. 108–123. Springer, Heidelberg (2013). https://doi.org/10.1007/978-3-642-38088-4_8

9. Boulanger, F., Hardebolle, C.: Simulation of multi-formalism models with Mod-Hel'X. In: Proceedings of ICST 2008, pp. 318–327. IEEE Computer Society (2008)

10. Broman, D., Greenberg, L., Lee, E.A., Masin, M., Tripakis, S., Wetter, M.: Requirements for Hybrid Cosimulation. Technical report (2014)

11. Carter, R., Navarro-López, E.M.: Dynamically-driven timed automaton abstractions for proving liveness of continuous systems. In: Jurdziński, M., Ničković, D. (eds.) FORMATS 2012. LNCS, vol. 7595, pp. 59–74. Springer, Heidelberg (2012). https://doi.org/10.1007/978-3-642-33365-1_6

12. Cellier, F.E., Kofman, E.: Continuous System Simulation. Springer, New York (2006). https://doi.org/10.1007/0-387-30260-3

13. Chen, B.C., Peng, H.: Differential-braking-based rollover prevention for sport utility vehicles with human-in-the-loop evaluations. Vehicle Syst. Dyn. **36**(4–5), 359–389 (2001)

14. Controllab Products: Design of a Compensated Motion Crane using INTO-CPS. Technical report, Press Release EU, Enschede, Netherlands (2018)

15. Cremona, F., Lohstroh, M., Broman, D., Lee, E.A., Masin, M., Tripakis, S.: Hybrid co-simulation: it's about time. Softw. Syst. Model. (2017)

16. Denil, J., De Meulenaere, P., Demeyer, S., Vangheluwe, H.: DEVS for AUTOSAR-based system deployment modeling and simulation. Simulation **93**(6), 489–513 (2017). http://journals.sagepub.com/doi/10.1177/0037549716684552

17. Denil, J., Klikovits, S., Mosterman, P.J., Vallecillo, A., Vangheluwe, H.: The experiment model and validity frame in M&S. In: Proceedings of the Symposium on Theory of Modeling and Simulation, vol. 49 (2017)

18. Denil, J., Meyers, B., De Meulenaere, P., Vangheluwe, H.: Explicit semantic adaptation of hybrid formalisms for FMI co-simulation. In: Barros, F., Wang, M.H., Prähofer, H., Hu, X. (eds.) Symposium on Theory of Modeling and Simulation: DEVS Integrative M&S Symposium, pp. 99–106. Society for Computer Simulation International San Diego, CA, USA, Alexandria, Virginia, April 2015

19. Distefano, J.: Feedback and Control Systems (2013)

20. Eker, J., et al.: Taming heterogeneity - the Ptolemy approach. Proc. IEEE **91**(1), 127–144 (2003)

21. El-Garhy, A.M., El-Sheikh, G.A., El-Saify, M.H.: Fuzzy life-extending control of anti-lock braking system. Ain Shams Eng. J. **4**(4), 735–751 (2013). https://doi.org/10.1016/j.asej.2012.12.003
22. Foldager, F., Larsen, P.G., Green, O.: Development of a driverless lawn mower using co-simulation. In: 1st Workshop on Formal Co-Simulation of Cyber-Physical Systems, Trento, Italy, September 2017
23. Fujimoto, R.M.: Parallel discrete event simulation. Commun. ACM **33**(10), 30–53 (1990)
24. Garlan, D., Shaw, M.: An introduction to software architecture. Technical report, Pittsburgh, PA, USA (1994)
25. Gelernter, D., Carriero, N.: Coordination languages and their significance. Commun. ACM **35**(2), 96 (1992). https://doi.org/10.1145/129630.376083
26. Glaessgen, E., Stargel, D.: The digital twin paradigm for future NASA and U.S. air force vehicles. In: Structures, Structural Dynamics, and Materials Conference: Special Session on the Digital Twin, pp. 1–14. American Institute of Aeronautics and Astronautics, Reston, Virigina, April 2012. https://doi.org/10.2514/6.2012-1818
27. Gomes, C., Karalis, P., Navarro-López, E.M., Vangheluwe, H.: Approximated stability analysis of bi-modal hybrid co-simulation scenarios. In: Cerone, A., Roveri, M. (eds.) SEFM 2017. LNCS, vol. 10729, pp. 345–360. Springer, Cham (2018). https://doi.org/10.1007/978-3-319-74781-1_24
28. Gomes, C., Legat, B., Jungers, R.M., Vangheluwe, H.: Stable adaptive co-simulation: a switched systems approach. In: IUTAM Symposium on Co-Simulation and Solver Coupling, Darmstadt, Germany (2017). To appear
29. Gomes, C., Thule, C., Broman, D., Larsen, P.G., Vangheluwe, H.: Co-simulation: State of the art. Technical report, February 2017. http://arxiv.org/abs/1702.00686
30. Gomes, C., Thule, C., Broman, D., Larsen, P.G., Vangheluwe, H.: Co-simulation: a survey. ACM Comput. Surv. **51**(3) (2018). Article 49
31. Gu, B., Asada, H.H.: Co-simulation of algebraically coupled dynamic subsystems. In: American Control Conference, vol. 3, pp. 2273–2278. IEEE, Arlington (2001)
32. Hafner, I., Popper, N.: On the terminology and structuring of co-simulation methods. In: Proceedings of the 8th International Workshop on Equation-Based Object-Oriented Modeling Languages and Tools, pp. 67–76. ACM Press, New York (2017). http://dl.acm.org/citation.cfm?doid=3158191.3158203
33. Hairer, E., Wanner, G.: Solving Ordinary Differential Equations II: Stiff and Differential-Algebraic Problems (1996)
34. Himmler, A.: Hardware-in-the-loop technology enabling flexible testing processes. In: 51st AIAA Aerospace Sciences Meeting Including the New Horizons Forum and Aerospace Exposition, pp. 1–8. American Institute of Aeronautics and Astronautics, Grapevine (Dallas/Ft. Worth Region), Texas, January 2013. https://doi.org/10.2514/6.2013-816
35. IEEE: IEEE Standard for Distributed Interactive Simulation-Application Protocols (2012). Publication Title: IEEE Std 1278.1-2012 (Revision of IEEE Std 1278.1-1995)
36. Immler, F.: Formally verified computation of enclosures of solutions of ordinary differential equations. In: Badger, J.M., Rozier, K.Y. (eds.) NFM 2014. LNCS, vol. 8430, pp. 113–127. Springer, Cham (2014). https://doi.org/10.1007/978-3-319-06200-6_9
37. Jo, H.H., Parsaei, H.R., Sullivan, W.G.: Principles of concurrent engineering. In: Parsaei, H.R., Sullivan, W.G. (eds) Concurrent Engineering, pp. 3–23. Springer, Boston (1993). https://doi.org/10.1007/978-1-4615-3062-6_1

38. Jørgensen, N.: The Boeing 777: development life cycle follows artifact. In: World Conference on Integrated Design and Process Technology (IDPT), pp. 25–30. Citeseer (2006)
39. Kent Peacock, J., Wong, J., Manning, E.G.: Distributed simulation using a network of processors. Comput. Netw. (1976) **3**(1), 44–56 (1979). http://linkinghub.elsevier.com/retrieve/pii/0376507579900539
40. Kübler, R., Schiehlen, W.: Modular simulation in multibody system dynamics. Multibody Syst. Dyn. **4**(2–3), 107–127 (2000)
41. Kübler, R., Schiehlen, W.: Two methods of simulator coupling. Math. Comput. Model. Dyn. Syst. **6**(2), 93–113 (2000)
42. Lamport, L.: Time, clocks, and the ordering of events in a distributed system. Commun. ACM **21**(7), 558–565 (1978)
43. Le Marrec, P., Valderrama, C.A., Hessel, F., Jerraya, A.A., Attia, M., Cayrol, O.: Hardware, software and mechanical cosimulation for automotive applications. In: 9th International Workshop on Rapid System Prototyping, pp. 202–206 (1998)
44. Li, W., Zhang, X., Li, H.: Co-simulation platforms for co-design of networked control systems: an overview. Control Eng. Pract. **23**, 44–56 (2014)
45. Liboni, G., Deantoni, J., Portaluri, A., Quaglia, D., De Simone, R.: Beyond time-triggered co-simulation of cyber-physical systems for performance and accuracy improvements. In: 10th Workshop on Rapid Simulation and Performance Evaluation: Methods and Tools, Manchester, United Kingdom, January 2018. https://hal.inria.fr/hal-01675396
46. Maler, O., Batt, G.: Approximating continuous systems by timed automata. In: Fisher, J. (ed.) FMSB 2008. LNCS, vol. 5054, pp. 77–89. Springer, Heidelberg (2008). https://doi.org/10.1007/978-3-540-68413-8_6
47. McCalla, W.J.: Fundamentals of Computer-Aided Circuit Simulation, vol. 37. Springer, New York (1987). https://doi.org/10.1007/978-1-4613-2011-1
48. Miller, D., Thorpe, J.: SIMNET: the advent of simulator networking. Proc. IEEE **83**(8), 1114–1123 (1995). http://ieeexplore.ieee.org/document/400452/
49. Newton, A.R., Sangiovanni-Vincentelli, A.L.: Relaxation-based electrical simulation. SIAM J. Sci. Stat. Comput. **4**(3), 485–524 (1983)
50. Otter, M., Elmqvist, H.: The DSblock model interface for exchanging model components. In: Proceedings of the Eurosim 1995, Simulation Congress, pp. 505–510 (1995)
51. Palensky, P., Van Der Meer, A.A., Lopez, C.D., Joseph, A., Pan, K.: Cosimulation of intelligent power systems: fundamentals, software architecture, numerics, and coupling. IEEE Indus. Electr. Mag. **11**(1), 34–50 (2017)
52. Papadopoulos, G.A., Arbab, F.: Coordination models and languages. Technical report, CWI (Centre for Mathematics and Computer Science), Amsterdam, The Netherlands (1998)
53. Pedersen, N., Bojsen, T., Madsen, J.: Co-simulation of cyber physical systems with HMI for human in the loop investigations. In: Symposium on Theory of Modeling and Simulation, Society for Computer Simulation International, Virginia Beach, TMS/DEVS 2017, Virginia, USA, pp. 1:1–1:12 (2017). http://dl.acm.org/citation.cfm?id=3108905.3108906
54. Pedersen, N., Lausdahl, K., Sanchez, E.V., Thule, C., Larsen, P.G., Madsen, J.: Distributed co-simulation of embedded control software using INTO-CPS. In: International Conference on Simulation and Modeling Methodologies, Technologies and Applications, Madrid, Spain, July 2017. To appear

55. Pedersen, N., Lausdahl, K., Vidal Sanchez, E., Larsen, P.G., Madsen, J.: Distributed co-simulation of embedded control software with exhaust gas recirculation water handling system using INTO-CPS. In: 7th International Conference on Simulation and Modeling Methodologies, Technologies and Applications, pp. 73–82. SCITEPRESS - Science and Technology Publications (2017). https://doi.org/10.5220/0006412700730082

56. Prabhu, S.M., Mosterman, P.J.: Model-based design of a power window system: modeling, simulation and validation. In: Proceedings of IMAC-XXII: a Conference on Structural Dynamics, Society for Experimental Mechanics Inc, Dearborn, MI (2004)

57. Rowson, J.A.: Hardware/Software co-simulation. In: 31st Conference on Design Automation, pp. 439–440 (1994)

58. Schweiger, G., Engel, G., Schoeggl, J., Hafner, I., Gomes, C., Nouidui, T.: Co-simulation – an empirical survey: applications, recent developments and future challenges. In: MATHMOD 2018 Extended Abstract Volume, pp. 125–126. ARGESIM Publisher Vienna, Vienna, Austria (2018). https://www.argesim.org/publications/a55286

59. Schweiger, G., Gomes, C., Hafner, I., Engel, G., Nouidui, T.S., Popper, N., Schoggl, J.P.: Co-simulation: leveraging the potential of urban energy system simulation. EuroHeat Power 15(I–II), 13–16 (2018)

60. Spiegel, M., Reynolds, P., Brogan, D.: A case study of model context for simulation composability and reusability. In: Proceedings of the Winter Simulation Conference, vol. 2005, pp. 437–444. IEEE (2005). http://ieeexplore.ieee.org/document/1574279/

61. Thule, C., Gomes, C., Deantoni, J., Larsen, P.G., Brauer, J., Vangheluwe, H.: Towards the Verification of Hybrid Co-simulation Algorithms. Submitted to CoSim-CPS (2018)

62. Tomiyama, T., D'Amelio, V., Urbanic, J., ElMaraghy, W.: Complexity of multidisciplinary design. CIRP Ann. Manufact. Technol. 56(1), 185–188 (2007)

63. Uchitel, S., Yankelevich, D.: Enhancing architectural mismatch detection with assumptions. In: 2000 Seventh IEEE International Conference and Workshop on the Engineering of Computer Based Systems, (ECBS 2000) Proceedings, pp. 138–146 (2000)

64. Van Acker, B., Denil, J., Meulenaere, P.D., Vangheluwe, H.: Generation of an optimised master algorithm for FMI co-simulation. In: Barros, F., Wang, M.H., Prähofer, H., Hu, X. (eds.) Symposium on Theory of Modeling and Simulation-DEVS Integrative, pp. 946–953. Society for Computer Simulation International San Diego, CA, USA, Alexandria, Virginia, USA, April 2015

65. Van der Auweraer, H., Anthonis, J., De Bruyne, S., Leuridan, J.: Virtual engineering at work: the challenges for designing mechatronic products. Eng. Comput. 29(3), 389–408 (2013)

66. Vangheluwe, H., De Lara, J., Mosterman, P.J.: An introduction to multi-paradigm modelling and simulation. In: AI, Simulation and Planning in High Autonomy Systems, pp. 9–20. SCS (2002)

67. Vangheluwe, H.L., Vansteenkiste, G.C., Kerckhoffs, E.J.: Simulation for the future: progress of the esprit basic research Working Group 8467. In: Proceedings of the 1996 European Simulation Symposium, pp. XXIX–XXXIV. Society for Computer Simulation International, Genoa (1996)

68. Wanner, G., Hairer, E.: Solving Ordinary Differential Equations I: Nonstiff Problems, vol. 1. Springer, Heidelberg (1991). https://doi.org/10.1007/978-3-540-78862-1. Springer s edn.
69. Wu, M.C., Shih, M.C.: Simulated and experimental study of hydraulic anti-lock braking system using sliding-mode PWM control. Mechatronics **13**(4), 331–351 (2003)
70. Zeigler, B.P.: Theory of Modelling and Simulation. Wiley, New York (1976)

# Author Index